What Jane Knew

What Jane Knew

Anishinaabe Stories and American Imperialism, 1815–1845

MAUREEN KONKLE

The University of North Carolina Press
Chapel Hill

© 2024 The University of North Carolina Press
All rights reserved

Set in Minion Pro by Westchester Publishing Services
Manufactured in the United States of America

Library of Congress Cataloging-in-Publication Data
Names: Konkle, Maureen, author.
Title: What Jane knew : Anishinaabe stories and American imperialism, 1815–1845 / Maureen Konkle.
Description: Chapel Hill : University of North Carolina Press, [2024] | Includes bibliographical references and index.
Identifiers: LCCN 2023047028 | ISBN 9781469675381 (cloth ; alk. paper) | ISBN 9781469678436 (paperback ; alk. paper) | ISBN 9781469675398 (epub) | ISBN 9798890887368 (pdf)
Subjects: LCSH: Schoolcraft, Jane Johnston, 1800–1842—Criticism and interpretation. | Schoolcraft, Henry Rowe, 1793–1864. | American literature—Indian authors—History and criticism. | Ojibwa literature—Michigan—History—19th century. | Ojibwa literature—Political aspects. | Ojibwa literature—Social aspects. | White people—Relations with Indians—History—19th century. | BISAC: SOCIAL SCIENCE / Ethnic Studies / American / Native American Studies | BIOGRAPHY & AUTOBIOGRAPHY / Literary Figures
Classification: LCC PS2789.S73 Z76 2024 | DDC 810.9/897—dc23/eng/20231115
LC record available at https://lccn.loc.gov/2023047028

Cover art: *Top*, Jane Johnston Schoolcraft (ca. 1825), courtesy of the Bentley Historical Library, University of Michigan; *bottom*, drawing of Sault Ste. Marie (ca. 1837) by Anna Brownell Jameson, courtesy of the Toronto Public Library.

This book will be made open access within three years of publication thanks to Path to Open, a program developed in partnership between JSTOR, the American Council of Learned Societies (ACLS), the University of Michigan Press, and the University of North Carolina Press to bring about equitable access and impact for the entire scholarly community, including authors, researchers, libraries, and university presses around the world. Learn more at https://about.jstor.org/path-to-open/.

Contents

List of Illustrations and Map, vii

Prologue, 1

PART I

Chapter 1 This Vain and Transitory World, 23

Chapter 2 Belles Lettres, 54

Chapter 3 Of Mrs. Schoolcraft, You Have Heard, 75

Chapter 4 A Precious Wild Flower, 101

Chapter 5 A New Creation, 124

PART II

Story of Manahbosho, 153

Chapter 6 Leech Lake, 164

O Mr. C!, 189

Chapter 7 Treaty of Washington, 191

Paup-Puk-Keewiss, 216

Chapter 8 Mercenary and Stupid White Man, 225

Six Indians Visit to the Sun and Moon, 252

Chapter 9 Wauchusco and the Spirits, 260

Mukakee Mindemoea; or, The Toad-Woman, 281

Chapter 10 At the Depot, 284

PART III

A Narrative of Wabwindigo, 317

Epilogue, 319

Acknowledgments, 343
Notes, 345
Bibliography, 399
Index, 421

Illustrations and Map

Illustrations

John Johnston, artist unknown (oil portrait, ca. 1790), 26

Ozhaawshkodewikwe by Charles Bird King after James Otto Lewis (oil portrait, ca. 1825), 30

Sault Ste. Marie from Waishky's Lodge/The Falls of St. Mary's by Anna Brownell Jameson, *Voyage to America Portfolio* (drawing, 1837), 32

Shingabawossin by Henry Inman (oil portrait, ca. 1831–34), 55

Jane Johnston Schoolcraft, artist unknown (ca. 1825, daguerreotype of a miniature [?]), 78

The canoe on Lake Huron by Anna Brownell Jameson, *Voyage to America Portfolio* (drawing, 1837), 128

Island of Mackinac, Lake Huron, by Anna Brownell Jameson, *Voyage to America Portfolio* (drawing, 1837), 171

Charlotte McMurray Johnston, artist unknown (photograph, ca. 1860), 239

Anna Jameson by David Octavius Hill and Robert Adamson (salted paper print, ca. 1844), 241

The beach at Mackinac by Anna Brownell Jameson, *Voyage to America Portfolio* (drawing, 1837), 243

Voyage with Mrs. Schoolcraft by Anna Brownell Jameson, *Voyage to America Portfolio* (drawing, 1837), 245

Wayish-ky's Lodge by Anna Brownell Jameson, *Voyage to America Portfolio* (drawing, 1837), 246

Jane Susan Ann Schoolcraft, artist unknown (oil portrait, ca. 1837), 289

John Johnston Schoolcraft, artist unknown (oil portrait, ca. 1837), 290

Elizabeth Oakes Smith by John Wesley Paradise (oil portrait, ca. 1845), 308

William Johnston, artist unknown (carte de visite, ca. 1850), 320

Anna Maria Johnston, artist unknown (carte de visite, ca. 1850), 327

George Johnston and son Samuel Abbott, artist unknown (daguerreotype, ca. 1850), 336

Mary Rice Johnston and daughter Eliza Jane, artist unknown (daguerreotype, ca. 1850), 337

Map

Anishinaabe villages, ca. 1830, xii

What Jane Knew

The Weendigoes

Saginaw, from Algic Researches, *translated by William Johnston (1839); Michilimackinac, Winter 1836–1837*[1]

Once there lived in a lonely forest, a man and his wife, who had a son. The father went out every day, according to the custom of the Indians, to hunt for food, to support his family. One day while he was absent, his wife, on going out of the lodge, looked toward the lake that was near, and saw a very large man walking on the water, and coming fast toward the lodge. He had already advanced so near that flight was useless. She thought to herself, what shall I say to the monster that will please him. As he came near, she ran in, and taking the hand of her son, a boy of three or four years old, led him out. Speaking very loud, "See, my son," said she, "your grandfather," and then added in a conciliatory tone, "he will have pity on us." The giant advanced, and said sneeringly, "Yes, my son." And then addressing the woman asked, "Have you anything to eat?" Fortunately the lodge was filled with meat of various kinds. The woman thought to please him by handing him some cooked meat, but he pushed it away in a dissatisfied manner, and took up the raw carcass of a deer, which he *glutted* up, sucking the bones, and drinking the blood.

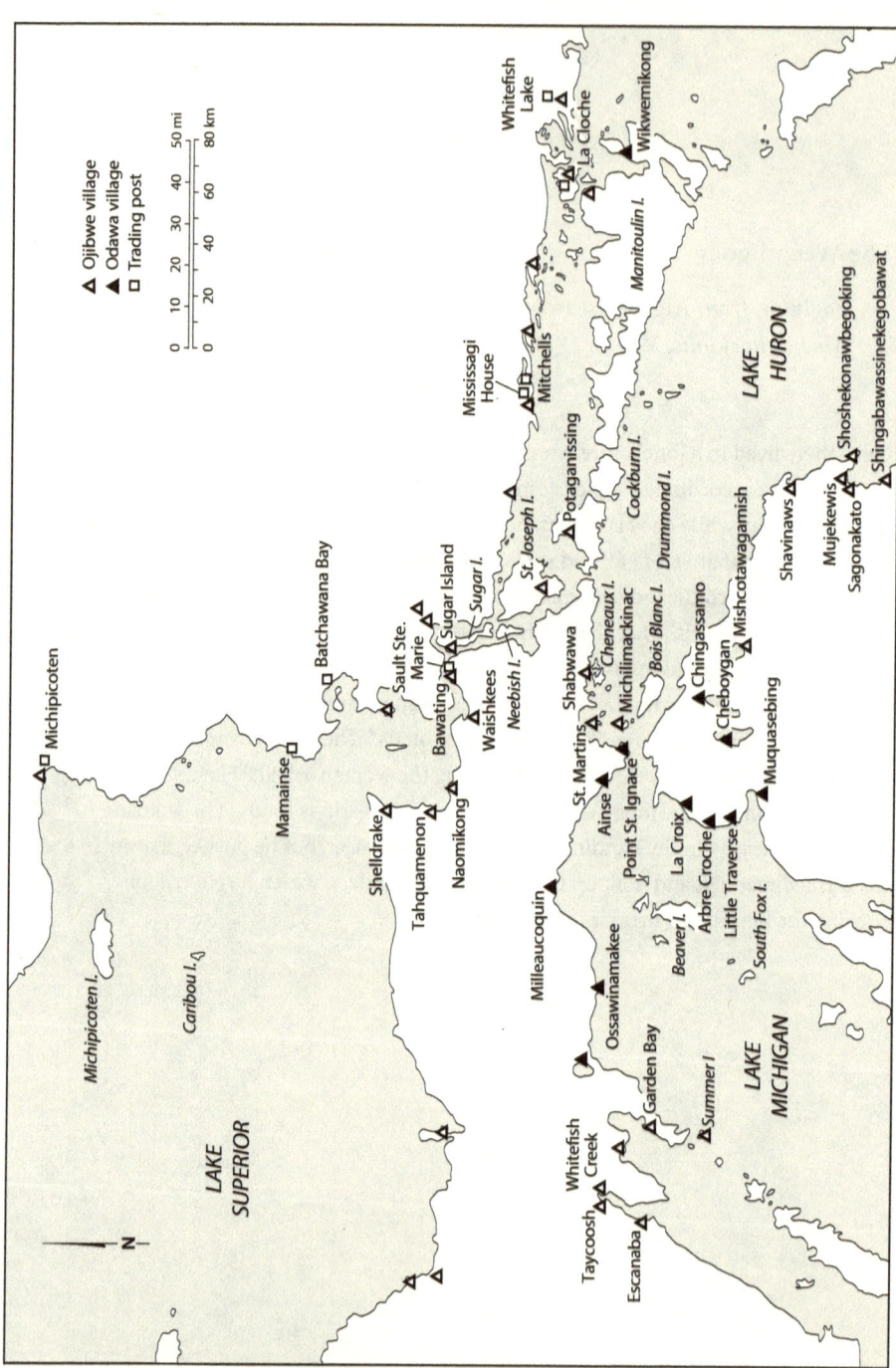

Anishinaabe villages (ca. 1830).

Prologue

He'd been pestering her about the story for weeks. It was the winter of 1838, and Henry Schoolcraft was at the agency in Detroit while Jane, his wife, was at home on Mackinac Island, worn down by illness and managing a fractious household. "Try to finish & transmit me, in its rough state, the tale you have in hand," he wrote. "I will see to it, that your reputation shall suffer, in the phraseology."[1]

His anxiety about her writing had only grown over time. This latest story was unusual among those she and her brother and sister had been writing down, lacking what she called "majic" and even somewhat Christian, on the origin of corn. "Once upon a time," she began, also unusually, for the Anishinaabe stories they'd been writing generally didn't begin that way. Once upon a time there was a poor Indian living in the forest with his wife and children, not especially accomplished at anything, but he had a son who wanted to help "his poor fellow creatures."

"'*There must be a Great Spirit* who has made all things and takes care of all!'" said the youth; "'I must try and find out who it is.'" One day a beautiful stranger appeared to him dressed in shades of green with waving yellow plumes on his head who challenged him to wrestle over three days. At the end of three days the stranger was defeated and buried and became corn. "'It is my friend and the friend of all mankind,'" the youth said, and "'none need ever depend *alone* upon hunting and fishing, as long as there is *Mondaumin* to live and grow from the ground.'"[2]

Schoolcraft read the story to advocate agriculture over hunting; that was why he wanted it. "Correct whatever you find amiss," she wrote. As far as she was concerned, he was neglecting her and their two children, this time making treaties with the smaller Ojibwe bands his primary excuse to be in Detroit. "*Public* duties bring their own fame & reward, when discharged faithfully," she added, "but the unobtrusive duties of domestic life are not *even* thought upon with all its cares & troubles & *incessant* appeals to forbearance, patience, nor is a word spoken in praise or encouragement to the devoted person who sacrifices health & *ease* in the fulfillment of these *oft* neglected duties, & yet human nature is the same in *Man* and *Woman*—perhaps the latter needs more encouragement."[3]

The story was "very pretty," he wrote back, ignoring her irritation. "No people are more prone to ascribe their gifts to providence, and the invention of the present story, is a sufficient proof, were there none recorded, of their possession of intellect & fancy."[4] He took out most of the psychological detail and made the youth's vision of the spirit merely a fantasy, then added Indian names, which he was fond of making up.

In the spring of 1822 Schoolcraft had arrived with the US Army at Sault Ste. Marie to oversee the federal government's relations with the Indigenous tribes from that place across the western Great Lakes region to the upper Mississippi. This included villages at L'Anse at the Keweenaw Peninsula on Lake Superior, La Pointe and Fond du Lac at the western end of the lake, Lac du Flambeau, Lac Vieux Desert, and Lac Courte Oreilles in present-day northern Wisconsin, and Leech Lake and Red Lake in present-day Minnesota. In 1824, he estimated the Indigenous population of his agency at 7,324 living in twenty-five independent bands, the most distant of which at Pembina was over a thousand miles away.[5] There were relatively few white settlers, mainly workers in the fur trade married into Indigenous communities; the trade was centered on Mackinac Island, south of Sault Ste. Marie. In a departure from the normal course of affairs for government officials, the territorial governor and superintendent of Indian affairs Lewis Cass additionally charged Schoolcraft with collecting information on the Indigenous inhabitants, including especially their language. Cass had got it into his head that he could prove the inferiority of those he viewed as savages once and for all, but he needed facts to back himself up. He was writing a book about it.

That the Indian agent wanted Ojibwemowin, the language, must have been quite a surprise and even a little thrilling for Jane. An American who seemed to care about the language that she loved so much and who even wrote poetry, as did she, would not have been common in those postwar years. He set up his office in one of her father's outbuildings and moved in with the family. They lived in a log house that backed onto the rapids of the St. Mary's River, surrounded by the storehouses of a fur trade that hadn't recovered from the Americans plundering and burning the family business in 1814 and never would. Her parents were Ozhaawshkodewikwe, a daughter of Waabojiig, a powerful hereditary leader of the Adik or Caribou doodem (clan or totem) at Shagwaamikong at the western end of Lake Superior, and John Johnston, a Protestant Irishman with literary habits and a sometimes romantic view of the world into which he had married. They believed it prudent to accommodate the Americans because Johnston had fought for the British in the last war and had no intention of either becoming an American or moving across the river.

It was mainly Jane, aged twenty-two, to whom Schoolcraft turned to fulfill his duties. Within two months of his arrival they had formed an attachment; they were married in October of the next year.

She might have missed becoming an explainer of her relatives to outsiders had her uncle not died. When she was nine years old her father decided that his favorite child should be turned over to his sister and her naval officer husband in Wexford, Ireland, for proper finishing and better prospects. Ozhaawshkodewikwe's feelings about this proposal are unrecorded. Her namesake aunt was eager to take up what had been Jane's recently deceased grandmother's plan; to commemorate the new start, the family cut Jane's hair short in the style for children of the day and had her miniature painted in Dublin on a visit to her uncle, the bishop of Dromore. All along she cried for her mother and home. Then her uncle died of apoplexy and her aunt was too grief-stricken to care for a child. According to family lore, when his cousin, the attorney general of Ireland, offered Johnston a position and a chance to stay, he declined, saying, "I have married the daughter of a king in America and I shall return to comfort her & educate my children."[6] Before six months had passed, Jane and her father began their journey home. One night in November 1810 Ozhaawshkodewikwe dreamed that they were camped on an island in the St. Mary's River, unable to get any farther in the night; she sent out boatmen, who found them and brought them home. The next day the river froze for the season.[7]

After this episode Jane became subject to gentle contention between her parents. Her father made her a Christian on his own model, a reader of the bluestocking Hannah More and a writer of devotional verse. Her mother taught her so well the practices and beliefs of Ojibwe people and especially Ojibwemowin that her father by his own account couldn't succeed in his business without her. He relied on her "perfect knowledge" of Ojibwemowin, so much so that when he raised up a troop of his workers to help defend Mackinac against the Americans in 1814, he took Jane along to interpret.[8]

Ozhaawshkodewikwe's father had forced her to marry Johnston because he traded with their band. By her own account she was terrified. He was twice her age; they spoke to one another in French, of which he had only a rudimentary knowledge at the time. After her father's death and the birth of two sons, she still wasn't sure of the marriage, so she returned to her mother for a period of time to think it over.[9] Eventually she went back to the Sault, which was overlaid on a place called Bow-e-ting, significant to the Anishinaabe people (the collective name for culturally and politically related tribes, including Ojibwe, Odawa, Potawatomi, Saulteax, and Algonquin) from time immemorial, the site of medicine society ceremonies and the home place of the

Crane band of Ojibwes. Many of Ozhaawshkodewikwe's family members lived in the village or in the vicinity, including two of her brothers, Waishkey and Keewyzi, and a sister, whose daughter Ogeewyahnoquotokwa was a member of the Midewiwin, the medicine society, and performed the shaking tent ceremony to divine the future.[10] Two of Waabojiig's sisters lived in the village. One, named Obemauunoqua, was married to another Irish trader, John Sayers.[11]

Ozhaawshkodewikwe had eight children with John Johnston: Lewis, George, Jane, Eliza, Charlotte, Anna Maria, William, and John. All of them received Ojibwe names, which were given by an elder, who would have received the name from the spirits and maintained a relationship with the child.[12] Ozhaawshkodewikwe followed her relatives' traditional round of activities: sugar-making in the late winter, fishing at the rapids in late summer. She was said to have produced 3,000 pounds of sugar in a typical season.[13] She always attended the annual distribution of presents from the British Crown reaffirming its relationship with Indigenous nations, first at Drummond Island at the mouth of the St. Mary's River, then, after the United States and the British changed their border in 1828, at Penetanguishene, at the eastern end of Georgian Bay. She raised a number of Indigenous children not her own, including a girl named Nancy whose father died in a duel, a boy named Tom Shaw, and another named Colin. Despite her husband's piety, she remained uninterested in Christianity until after he died, when Ojibwe Methodist exhorters came to the Sault in the 1830s.

Like many Indigenous people whose lives are recorded in archives, she understood English but refused to speak it; her husband learned to speak Ojibwemowin. She inculcated in her children an attentiveness to the aesthetics of Ojibwemowin, and like her father she was said to have been a skilled storyteller, although she seems not to have been responsible for the principal story cycle of the culture hero Manabozho.[14] Her children seem not to have known it until William came back from Leech Lake in the spring of 1834 with an almost complete version from a teller whose name is unknown.

Peculiarly for a fur trader, Johnston had a fascination for the stories told by Ojibwe people from the moment he first heard them through an interpreter at Shagwaamikong. In Ireland he'd read James Macpherson's translations of Ossian, the ancient Scottish bard whose Highlanders must have seemed the figure of the Ojibwe warriors he encountered, Waabojiig not least of all. The Highlanders lived "free and independent" lives, Macpherson wrote, their language and customs "pure"; they were "fond of military fame, and remarkably attached to the memory of their ancestors."[15] Johnston heard living bards tell stories about heroes and their adventures, and inspired, he began to write them down. Unfortunately he soon discovered that his French-Canadian interpreters had been playing tricks on him; he threw his manuscripts into the fire.[16]

His family were seventeenth-century Scottish settlers in Ireland rewarded with a grant of land near the Giant's Causeway for their loyalty to the English king, but in straitened circumstances after his father's death when he was a boy.[17] He sought his fortune in Canada in the 1790s with no idea what he would do; he ended up in the fur trade as a last resort. John Johnston was still a gentleman, however, for whom writing poetry was a social grace, who valued literature for its "beauties" and its moral instruction. A practiced writer of occasional verse and odes on writers he admired, like Samuel Johnson, and, before emigrating, on ladies who caught his eye, he kept a large library, if the account left by a British surveyor who dined with the Johnstons in the mid-1820s is anywhere near accurate.[18] It included the full range of seventeenth- and eighteenth-century English literature (Shakespeare, Milton, Pope, Johnson, Goldsmith); numerous works of Protestant theology, including particularly the sermons of Hugh Blair; English history, popular poetry (Robert Burns was a favorite); moral works for children; and a selection of French literature. According to Schoolcraft, among contemporary writers John Johnston read Walter Scott, Washington Irving, and, interestingly, James Fenimore Cooper, as well as the poets Robert Southey, Thomas More, Thomas Campbell, and Lord Byron.[19] The house would have been packed with books. He taught the children to read and write until Jane could take his place. Like other fur traders, he sent his sons to Montreal to study with, in his case, the available Protestant ministers (John was sent to New York after his father's death). While Jane received no formal education after the aborted trip to Ireland, Eliza and Charlotte briefly attended school in Upper Canada after the war, and Anna Maria was later sent to a school in Massachusetts for a few years.

His children acquired his enthusiasm for literary play. George and Charlotte kept commonplace books; George rearranged famous poems to make new ones. Jane made up her own collection of poetry copied from the family library. After the war Jane, George, and their father made up two anthologies of Ojibwe literature, one of stories and the other of songs.[20] The stories included Jane's versions of mythological traditions or *aadizookaanag*, and examples of *dibaajimowinan*, or stories about human beings or historical events—these were told to Johnston by his friend Gitche Gauzinee. Jane and George wrote down *nagamonan*, or songs in both Ojibwemowin and English.[21] The collections also included Jane's inventions based on Ojibwe songs and stories, something no other Indigenous person seems to have written down before she did. From this play Jane and her brother learned that the beauties of Ojibwemowin could be conveyed both in writing and in English.

Under Cass's mentorship, Schoolcraft pursued a career as an Indian expert parallel to his duties as agent. He published accounts of his official travels in the West, newspaper articles on the prospects for missionizing the Indians, and long reviews of books he couldn't have read because they were written in French. (Jane was fluent in French.) After Jane showed him the family's writing, to further ingratiate himself with Cass he included stories from that collection as well as new ones in a manuscript newspaper that circulated in Sault Ste. Marie, Detroit, and possibly New York in the later 1820s. When Cass eventually abandoned his research for more straightforward political propaganda, Schoolcraft became fixated on producing a dictionary and grammar of Ojibwemowin, an endeavor for which he was entirely dependent on Jane, who worked on it, off and on, for the duration of their marriage. By the early 1830s he was conducting interviews and soliciting translations and various reports from Jane and her family, anticipating writing his own books on Indians.

He seems not to have understood how important the stories his wife and family had been writing down were until William returned from a winter trading at Leech Lake with a number of stories and other narratives, including a long account that he titled "Story of Manahbosho." Schoolcraft couldn't deny what "Story of Manahbosho" looked like: it was an epic, the story of a culture hero.[22] The category may have had no meaning for Anishinaabe people, but to Schoolcraft it meant that Indigenous people were much more sophisticated than he had been prepared to accept. He tasked Jane, William, Charlotte, and later George with gathering what eventually became dozens of Ojibwe and Odawa mythological and historical stories. The family gave him the stories in English, always—despite his claims to expertise, he never learned to speak Ojibwemowin. He copied the stories over repeatedly, obsessively, and edited, taking out the obvious sexual and scatological references, inserting what were to his ear more pleasing names. After several years of collecting he published *Algic Researches: Comprising Inquiries Respecting the Mental Characteristics of the North American Indians* (New York: 1839), listing Jane and her family as informants and giving the impression that he'd written everything himself.[23] This was not true. Though he added notes, comments, prefatory remarks, afterwords, and sometimes his own poems—those mainly to stories written by Jane—he didn't change the substance of the stories that were handed to him, or much of the writer's original language. Despite his literary affectations, Schoolcraft thought himself primarily a scientist with an obligation to fact, and the stories as written were fact.

The facts were disturbing, if you were Henry Schoolcraft. The stories revealed that Indians were ruled by a "doctrine of metamorphosis," he wrote in the book's "Preliminary Observations." Indians lived surrounded by "thousands" of spirits—their Great Spirit was no supreme being, but one spirit among many. Spirits could take any shape.[24] They infused the landscape, in places and natural things, and they "[presided] over daily affairs and over the destinies of men."[25] Even animals were "endowed with reasoning powers and faculties.... They endow birds, and bears, and all other animals with souls, which ... will be encountered in other shapes in another state of existence."[26] These were "the actual opinions of the natives," he wrote, and furthermore although they weren't limited to this function, the stories were also the means of educating children in the Indians' "moral, mechanical, and religious" knowledge.[27] Jane told him that, certainly. Another reality coexisted with the United States itself, heretofore unknown. Ultimately no matter how charming the stories might appear to be, they demonstrated that Indians were sunk in "demonology, witchcraft, and necromancy."[28] Something had to be done about it.

He was both greedy for the authority that he imagined this knowledge gave him and worried about what he thought it meant. He hoped that once the stories' horrors had been widely perceived by the American public, the Protestant missionaries who seemed to be abandoning their posts in the Upper Northwest would recover their resolve and return to stamp them out.[29] Close to the publication of *Algic Researches* he had another idea. A few weeks after receiving "Corn Story," he wrote to tell Jane about how important his book would be to the development of American literature. "I am of opinion," wrote he, feeling quite impressed with his new plan, "that American literature must be based on the mythology of the Indians. That of Greece & Rome is exhausted.... All our poetic associations—all our ideas of poetic justice must be directed to the Indian tribes, who once occupied the continent. They will become to us what the Celts & Britons are to England. And as we have no architectural ruins in our landscape, we must take the Indian Character for our fallen columns and our encrusted medals."[30]

He wished to destroy the stories as practiced, as living things ensuring the future of Anishinaabe people, and to incorporate them into American literature as Americans incorporated Indigenous land into the United States. For this he needed them written down. He would publish more books, "traditions & history, language, superstitions & antiquities," he continued in his letter to Jane. It was her responsibility to see this work through. "I ... trust that all the literary leisure you can command, or further, which providence gives you, from a shattered and weakened constitution, will be devoted to enrich and encrease [sic] my stock of materials & my means of correct judgment upon this all," he wrote.[31] What Jane knew was like the supply of copper in the ground or whitefish in the rapids, endless. But the stories stopped when she died in May 1842; none of the others wrote stories for him after that.

Nothing else like the collection of stories written by the Johnstons exists for the period or by early Indigenous writers in North America. In addition to the family anthologies after 1815, the manuscript newspaper in the 1820s, then *Algic Researches* in 1839, several more stories appeared in a short-lived periodical Schoolcraft published in the 1840s (the periodical was later published as a book). He reprinted a few stories in his multivolume government-sponsored compendium *Historical and Statistical Information on the Indian Tribes of the United States* in the 1850s. Much to Schoolcraft's delight, Henry Wadsworth Longfellow raided *Algic Researches* for his narrative poem *Hiawatha* (1855), taking numerous stories (many of them written by William) and even the central character from it, although he found "Manabozho" insufficiently sonorous and went with the name of the Haudenosaunee culture hero instead. The stories then circulated, individually and collectively, in numerous revisions, rewritings, and reprintings, beginning with Schoolcraft's *The Myth of Hiawatha* (1856) (a revision of *Algic Researches*) and his friend Cornelius Mathews's *The Indian Fairy Book: From the Original Legends* (1856) (a more "Indian" rewriting of the same). The stories appeared in works of folklore and children's literature through the early twentieth century and beyond.[32]

The collection includes thirty-three stories by identifiable writers and sixteen so far unattributed. William wrote thirteen stories, Jane twelve, George four, Charlotte two, and Mary Holiday and Eleanor Bailly, friends of the family who were also the children of Indigenous mothers (respectively, Ojibwe and Odawa) and fur trader fathers, wrote one each. They wrote during a time of upheaval for Indigenous people in the Lake Superior region as the fur trade declined and the Americans began asserting themselves. For the Ojibwes and Odawas in northern Michigan and the eastern Upper Peninsula, that trauma was compounded by the 1836 Treaty of Washington, orchestrated by Schoolcraft for Cass, then secretary of war, through which the United States acquired land in exchange for annuities and hunting and fishing rights. Although they were eventually successful at resisting it (and lost much of their land in the effort), the threat of expulsion from their land hung over all of the bands in the region.[33] In the midst of these ongoing struggles, people agreed to let their relatives write down their stories. While their reasons for doing so were not recorded, the fact that the Johnstons were also related to the Indian agent and that, by the 1830s, the request for the story was ultimately coming from the agent himself could not have been far from anyone's mind.

It was uncommon for Indigenous writers to write down traditional narratives before the end of the nineteenth century. From the late eighteenth century to the mid-nineteenth, Indigenous writers like Samson Occom (Mohegan), William Apess (Pequot), and Elias Boudinot (Cherokee) produced religious, political, and historical works arguing for equality and sovereignty against the United States' drive to expel tribal nations west of the Mississippi. One exception was David Cusick, a Tuscarora writer who published *Sketches of Ancient History of the Six Nations* in 1827. Cusick organized traditional narratives of the Haudenosaunee Confederacy (Mohawk, Oneida, Onondaga, Cayuga, Seneca, and Tuscarora) into a three-part history that in form echoed Americans' own histories: first a creation story, then a history of the Indigenous settlement of North America, then a history of the Haudenosaunee Confederacy's formation. All of this happened hundreds of years before Columbus, Cusick repeatedly pointed out, in the process making the same argument for tribal sovereignty as other Indigenous writers at a time when land speculators were running rampant in western New York in the wake of the Erie Canal. He reprinted his book with his own woodcuts in 1828—it was sold to tourists at Niagara Falls—and it's possible that the Johnston family's writers read it themselves.[34]

The Johnstons wrote the stories as literature rather than history, probably reflecting both parents' influence and their own prior writing. While Schoolcraft was only trying to humor Jane in the moment that they wanted the same things, she and her family actually were trying to convey the "intellect and fancy" of Anishinaabe narrative, and Anishinaabe people, in their writing, even if it was in English. They had learned from their father that literature had aesthetic and moral dimensions through which they could show the humanity of Indigenous people. Their initial model was short fiction of the type found in periodicals and anthologies at the time; Jane especially sought out suitable forms in which to represent the stories, including allegory, origin story, and moral fairy tale. After receiving the Manabozho story, William wrote what can be read as adventure stories, including a number told by Wauchusco, an Odawa healer and Presbyterian convert living at Mackinac, who told William both mythological and historical stories.

While after her death Schoolcraft reported that Jane wrote her earlier stories from memory, it appears that especially in the case of the stories written down in the 1830s and early 1840s, all of the writers took down stories from tellers who knew what the Johnstons and Schoolcraft were doing. A pencil draft of one of Jane's late stories shows her writing quickly, in partial sentences, as if listening to someone talk.³⁵ Charlotte asked a man named Little Salt to tell two stories in particular, which he did in a setting where he spoke, Charlotte translated, and her husband wrote the story down.³⁶ Wauchusco told William multiple stories that are so long and complex, it is difficult to believe that he could have produced an account without at least having taken notes. It seems likely that the tellers would have thought about what stories could be made accessible to outsiders and balanced the desire to protect traditional knowledge against a desire to tell white people who they were, if white people were so interested. They had good stories to tell.

Not everyone at the time may have agreed with the tellers' decisions to speak. Protecting knowledge has been a concern for Indigenous people throughout the history of colonization and settlement to the present day.³⁷ They could choose not to speak or to manage what information they did give in order to protect it. In *The Lenape and Their Legends* (1885), the ethnologist Daniel Garrison Brinton (a late protégé of Schoolcraft's) lamented that Shawnees living on the Quapaw Reservation in Indian Territory refused to allow him to hear and write down "a long, probably mythical and historical, chant" that they recited annually because, they told him, "[repeating] it to a white man would bring disasters on their nation."³⁸ Some Ojibwe tribal leaders refused to acknowledge that pictographs even existed when Schoolcraft started soliciting information on them in the later 1840s.³⁹ The teller of "Story of Manahbosho" (or William, or both of them) reversed a key sequence in the narrative (it differs from subsequent narrators' versions collected by anthropologists) and denied any knowledge of Manabozho's life before the point where their version of the story began.⁴⁰ It's also possible that tellers or writers or both wished to preserve the stories for future Anishinaabe readers—another concern on the part of Indigenous tellers and writers that emerges in the nineteenth century.⁴¹

Understanding Schoolcraft to have been the writer, scholars have in the past dismissed the stories as they were published in *Algic Researches* as inauthentic because of their literary qualities.⁴² But compared with versions taken down by Canadian, US, and Indigenous anthropologists, folklorists, and historians, all of the writers represented the common plots, figures, and relationships in the stories they wrote.⁴³ Like David Cusick, the Johnston writers chose suitable forms through which to represent traditional narratives to a white audience that could be presumed to be skeptical of if not hostile to the idea of Indigenous humanity. The written narratives are a representation of traditional knowledge, taken out of its dynamic community setting; their content was interpretable by Anishinaabe readers who knew what they were looking at, but something entirely unknown to white readers. The Johnston writers didn't explain to those readers who the figures in the stories were or what the stories meant to Anishinaabe people, or even apparently to Schoolcraft himself. Revealing secret knowledge was not the point. For the white readers of the Johnstons' stories, their form and the literary style in which they were written made the content not necessarily interpretable but recognizable. The stories were beautiful or charming or fantastic, like stories told by other people, including white people.

In light of how Indigenous people were represented, that made the stories subversive just by having been written down. Indians, according to Schoolcraft in *Algic Researches* and the vast majority of westerners at the time, "existed so completely in the hunter state as to have no relish for any other kind of labour, looking with an inward and deep contempt on the arts of husbandry and mechanics." Their rejection of regular labor meant that they had "little knowledge of numbers, and none of letters," and they therefore "failed in comprehensive views, deep reaching foresight, and powers of generalization."[44] Indians were incapable of reason, acting only on the basis of "manners and customs"; they could have no history, no political society, no art. They merely roamed over the landscape, entirely unattached to it.

These ideas about Indians—about savages—were necessary to Western capitalist societies. Capitalism's power came from its continuous incorporation of frontiers and their resources, and in order to justify taking those frontiers, Raj Patel and Jason W. Moore write, capitalists posited as an "organizing principle" a conceptual dichotomy between Nature and Society (that dichotomy wasn't new, they point out, but the fact that it had become an organizing principle was). Capitalists imagined Nature as an empty space of resources waiting to be exploited and themselves as the only Society fit to do that exploiting. Everyone other than themselves was on the Nature side of the divide, little more than animals, like machines, unthinking potential resources, naturally without political status and rightfully exploitable.[45] Capitalists emptied the natural world of its owners, its stories, its histories, and its consciousnesses, the other-than-human persons integral to Indigenous life. They claimed all the consciousness for themselves—only they thought, or loved, or had free will.

The Johnstons' stories represented proliferating consciousnesses in the form of the spirits in a radically different but contemporaneous reality, where the natural and the supernatural were "interwoven," as Blackfeet scholar Roslyn LaPier writes.[46] The relation of human beings to the natural and spirit world was also recognizable to white readers even if the story and the figures in it were unfamiliar. Schoolcraft readily perceived that Anishinaabe spirits violated Christian notions of bodily integrity and the superiority of human beings to the rest of creation. The spirits and the stories that they inhabited were also a problem for a capitalist society whether or not Schoolcraft was fully conscious of that to which he was reacting. They were evidence of Indigenous identification with the land, their knowledge about it, and their claim on it. Schoolcraft also understood because Jane told him that the stories were the lifeblood of the people, the means of their continuity as Anishinaabe. The connection between the people and the land had to be broken—hence Schoolcraft's desire for missionaries to destroy the stories on the one hand and for American literature to incorporate them on the other.

The Johnston writers made recognizable to white readers the humanity of Anishinaabe people in the art and morality of Anishinaabe narrative but also in the depiction of the different reality that the people inhabited, which was as beautiful and compelling as the Anishinaabe language itself. Schoolcraft so fully depended on what Jane and his relatives told him and was so used to writing down the facts they reported to him or copying over what they had given him that he persistently recorded their ideas in his published work. Just as persistently he would backtrack and try to deny the point in the same piece, as if he'd belatedly realized what he'd done to validate it. Sometimes he observed that the stories recalled Ovid's *Metamorphoses* (a disreputable book in the period for its transformations of humans to animals, but classical nonetheless), and often they recalled *The Arabian Nights* (also largely disreputable in the period for its magic and subject to the same kind of ethnographic cleansing to which Schoolcraft subjected Indigenous stories but still widely popular).[47] Sometimes the stories and what Jane and the family had to say about them left him—and others—carried away, and they struggled to recover themselves.

Americans had one story about Indians that they told, over and over again. The story was that a fight to the death raged between savagery and civilization, in the present moment and all around, in every way. It was a conflict in which civilization must and would prevail, even if it was ever ongoing.[48] An expression of the Nature/Society split, the story became a prominent feature of US discourse by the late eighteenth century. In part it adapted Scottish Enlightenment historiography that posited four stages through which human societies progressed (or didn't): hunting and gathering; pastoral or nomadic; agricultural; and, finally, mercantile, from the most primitive to the most advanced.[49] The story's adaptation of that history read the existence of Indigenous people in North America as a usurping of that order that had to be righted, where the beginning and the end were locked in a battle for the future. By the time Schoolcraft turned up at Sault Ste. Marie to study the locals the better to manage their demise, the story of savagery and civilization permeated US society; it was the frame through which he and most other Americans understood themselves and the world in which they lived.

The story was about who was virtuous and who wasn't, who owned land and who could have no claim to it, who was a human being and who was not. The story may be understood as a founding myth of white supremacy in the United States: it wasn't only Indigenous people who were savages. Robert Parkinson, a historian, has recently documented American revolutionary leaders' conscious and widespread deployment of the story, featuring Indigenous people but also enslaved African Americans and Hessian foreigners, as a means of maintaining support for their rebellion after 1775.[50] The story is enshrined in the climax of the Declaration of Independence's litany of George III's crimes against civilized society: "he has ... endeavoured to bring on the inhabitants of our frontiers, the merciless Indian Savages, whose known rule of warfare, is an undistinguished destruction of all ages, sexes and conditions."[51] You had to kill the savage before he killed you.

The story had evolved by the early nineteenth century, picking up important details along the way. In sixteenth- and seventeenth-century Ireland—a test ground for the expansion of capitalist markets and further English imperial ventures—English colonists at first followed international law and either leased land from Irish owners or claimed it through military conquest; when the Irish landowners resisted their encroachment, in addition to introducing more violent means of control the English began to justify their dispossession of Indigenous inhabitants by arguing that the Irish were savages who didn't use the land properly.[52] Although the idea that unoccupied land could be taken if it wasn't being used properly was not unheard of at the time, the innovation that English capitalists introduced was to argue that any land, occupied or not, that wasn't being "improved" in the sense of being used to participate in the market and produce a profit, was "waste" and could be taken by someone who would make it profitable. In this way, these early capitalists argued, they weren't taking land from people but rather giving something back to the community by making the land productive.[53]

The argument about improvement denied other ways of claiming land, by commoners in the English countryside, the Irish in Ireland, and North American Indigenous people.[54] While the customary land use rights of English commoners are not equivalent to Anshinaabe stories, they do perform a similar function with respect to establishing history on and claims to land. The idea that savages didn't "improve" the land—as Schoolcraft wrote in 1839, Indians "existed so completely in the hunter state as to have no relish for any other kind of labour"—was essential to the process of redefining property rights in favor of capitalist expansion in North America as in Ireland.[55] The process was given an early theoretical treatment in John Locke's *Second Treatise of Government* (1690), which explicitly brought Indigenous North Americans into capitalism's effort to redefine property rights by using them as the model for savages in the state of nature.[56] Locke was well versed in colonial affairs as secretary to Lord Shaftesbury and the lords proprietor of the Carolina colony, in which capacity he'd written the Fundamental Constitutions of Carolina in 1669. He amassed a collection of books on the topics of America and colonization, regularly questioned English settlers about their experiences, and wrote on the theory and administration of the North American colonies.[57] In his theory of property he defined the savage state as that which preceded both the ownership of land and the existence of government, establishing that savages could have no claim on the land by definition.

In the beginning, Locke famously wrote, "all the world was America," a state of nature unimproved by "regular labor" and thus an empty "waste." "The wild Indian" lived the state of nature, where the products of "the spontaneous hand of Nature"—a phrase associated forever afterward with Indigenous people in North America—were possessed in common by all. Natural man had a property in whatever he could take from the spontaneous hand of Nature in order to subsist; natural law held that he could take as long as "there is enough, and as good left in common for others."[58] Once proto-civilized man decided to cultivate the soil through regular labor to produce a surplus for market, he needed to protect the land he worked through positive laws that established ownership. This required government to administer laws, which were formed when property owners consented to be governed. Consent for enclosure of commonly held land was not required, Locke reasoned, first, because God "commanded [man] to subdue the Earth, i.e., improve it for the benefit of Life," and, second, because "there was still enough, and as good left." Those who protested his reasoning disputed God's will.[59]

Locke told a story about capitalists acting in everyone's best interests. He insisted that natural men would not be adversely affected by the taking of their land because if they had been affected, he would have had to find some means of incorporating their consent into his theory.[60] Luckily, theoretical Indians didn't desire to engage in commercial agriculture, they didn't own land, and they didn't form governments. The spontaneous productions of Nature were all that theoretical Indians wanted or needed; they chased animals through the woods or ate whatever fell off the trees and knocked them on the head, perfectly satisfied.

Locke's theory didn't have much practical effect in North America for about a hundred years. In the seventeenth and eighteenth centuries, English settlers bought land from Indigenous people or claimed it as a result of war. They made treaties with Indian nations to secure land but more often to establish political and diplomatic relations during a time of ongoing power struggles within and between colonies and among European and Indigenous nations.⁶¹ At the conclusion of the Seven Years War, Britain attempted to control American settlers' encroachment on Indigenous land through the Royal Proclamation of 1763, which established the Crown as the sole authority for treating with Indigenous nations, outlawed land speculation, and set a boundary between the colonies and the Indigenous nations of the West that colonists were not to cross. It became one of the precipitators of the revolution.⁶² Immediately after the revolution Americans tried to assert their authority over Indigenous nations by claiming that the British surrender had automatically transferred title to Indigenous land to the US government. This initial belligerence didn't work, mainly because the United States had neither the money nor the military power to enforce their claims, and so a new policy was instituted, based on the recognition of Indigenous ownership and sovereignty in both previously made treaties (the United States claimed authority as successor to Britain) and newly made treaties with Indigenous nations.

The fact that the legitimacy of the US government itself was at stake in the early years of its existence reinforced the significance of the treaties. Secretary of War Henry Knox outlined the issue in his report to the first Congress, in 1789, in which he argued that Indians' land could not "be taken from them unless by their free consent, or by the right of conquest in the case of a just war." Any other means of dispossessing them of their land (through subterfuge, for example) "would be a gross violation of the fundamental law of nature, and of that distributive justice which is the glory of a nation." While Knox conceded that the United States didn't have the capacity to advance a conquest of Indigenous nations, he argued that it wouldn't engage in aggressive empire-building anyway because "the blood and injustice" of a "system of coercion and oppression ... would stain the character of the nation ... beyond all pecuniary calculation." Thomas Jefferson, Benjamin Franklin, and George Washington, all of whom speculated in Indigenous land, made the same argument.⁶³ The United States bought Indian land through treaties to which Indians freely consented, they said, because of its high moral and political ideals, which stood in heroic contrast to British tyranny. "The obligations of policy, humanity, and justice, together with that respect every nation sacredly owes its own reputation, united in requiring a noble, liberal, and disinterested administration of Indian affairs," Knox concluded with a flourish.⁶⁴

Treaties complicated capitalist expansion in the United States. They are contracts, and contracts with inferiors aren't valid, and thus Indians couldn't be inferiors; since contracts required the free will of the parties involved, Indians exercised free will.⁶⁵ If consent was required for a treaty to be legitimate, refusal to consent was implied. Locke dispensed with the consent of theoretical Indians by claiming that they would be unaffected by losing their land, but the Americans hung their legitimacy on that consent because they had no other good option at the time. To put this in terms of the Nature/Society split, treaties conceded that Indigenous people lived in the same Society (and at the same time) as property-owning capitalists; Americans needed to send them back to Nature—and the past—in order to erase their political status and claim supremacy over the land for themselves. The threat to Americans was that Indigenous nations would adapt to the US presence while maintaining their political autonomy and control of land. In response to the threat, Americans simultaneously claimed superior moral virtue for themselves, did everything they could to undermine Indigenous consent, and insisted on the inherent savagery of Indians.

Continually protesting their own beneficent intentions, US officials worked hard to break down Indigenous polities in order to coerce Indigenous people into selling land—they thought about it, tried different strategies, and gave each other advice on the topic.[66] Their methods included entrapping Indigenous people in debt to fur-trading houses so that they would sell land to pay it off and redefining legal relations with Indian nations in state and federal courts.[67] Americans applied the threat of violence, if not violence itself, whenever they had the means and opportunity.[68] And they told, in every conceivable setting, ad infinitum, the heroic story of civilization's conflict with savagery, which by the end of the eighteenth century incorporated the Lockean conceptions of property and the origin of government that denied the existence of Indigenous political society in the first instance. The story told Americans that what they were doing—anything they did—was natural and right.

That the savage story exemplifies the Nature/Society split, defining Indigenous people as animals and the land as a resource rightfully owned and exploited by white men, can be seen in the writing of a man named Hugh Henry Brackenridge, a Presbyterian minister who served as George Washington's chaplain during the revolution. Brackenridge brought Locke's theorizing to the late eighteenth-century North American frontier, reprinting one article setting out his argument against the "Indian right of the soil" over thirty years as a newspaper publisher, lawyer, and judge. He even wrote a poem about it. Indians were animals, he wrote in "Thoughts on Indian Treaties," comparing them to foxes, ducks, geese, cows, raccoons, otters, and dogs. Talk of their rights was absurd. He denounced "philosophers . . . ignorant as bears" who "talk like girls that read romances . . . about the goodness of a savage / And how 'tis us excite to ravage" and "eastern block-heads" who "talk of simple human nature / And think a savage a good creature." General Knox should leave off Indians and "only stick to war." "Were it with me to manage these [Indians]," Brackenridge wrote,

> Instead of ever making peace,
> Would kill them every mother's son
> Because the work is then well done
> And there's an end of blood and burning,
> And parents for their offspring mourning,
> The devils gone where they should dwell,
> In some very hottest place of hell.[69]

Brackenridge made his case one last time in his book *Law Miscellanies: An Introduction to the Study of Law* (Philadelphia, 1815).[70] It was plain that man was superior to the animals, Brackenridge began, because he had "the *power to subdue them*, and this evidence is sufficient for *power* gives dominion, and is the *ultima ratio* of it."[71] Superior men naturally dominated inferior ones, and superior men were obviously "such as cultivate the earth; because it is ameliorated or made more productive by the skill and labour of such." After all, God commanded man to "be fruitful and multiply and replenish the earth, and subdue it," and in this He could only have meant regular labor in commercial agriculture, since that was the most efficient way of being fruitful and multiplying.[72] Savages refused regular labor; without regular labor "the powers of genius are inactive, the arts and sciences remain unknown, and man continues to be an animal differing in nothing but in shape from the beasts of prey that roam upon the mountain." Savages were therefore "not human; for it is abhorrent from the way of life which God and nature points out as the life of man."[73]

Savages impeded white men from doing what God commanded. They were immoral. All of the preceding being the case, the entire continent of North America "may ... on the first discovery of the coast, by any civilized European nation, be considered as, the greater part of it, a vacant country and liable to become the property of those who should take the trouble to possess it."[74]

For most of his life (he died in 1816) Brackenridge was an enraged westerner shouting at other enraged westerners, but as the years went by a wider range of people accepted the ideas he espoused because Americans' desire for land was unceasing and Indigenous people kept resisting. By 1823, when the US Supreme Court ruled in *Johnson v. McIntosh* that Europeans had full title to and ownership of all of North America from the moment they laid eyes on it because they were Christians and Indians were not, arguments of the type Brackenridge employed had done their work of normalizing what had once been absurd.[75] By the 1830s many politicians and intellectuals represented treaties as mainly proof of Americans' disinterested benevolence: they bought the land because they cared about the poor savages crippled by their inability to live in the modern world. Even the chief justice of the Supreme Court was known to drop a tear or two. Americans didn't have the ability to subdue all the Indigenous people that they wanted to in the early nineteenth century, but what they did have in their own minds was the authority to do whatever they needed to do to get what they wanted because morally the land was already theirs. Their job was to wrest it away from usurping savages.

The story of savagery and civilization taught Americans how to think about Indigenous people but also about themselves. It was personal. If every Indian was the embodiment of savagery, every white person was the embodiment of civilization and furthermore doing God's work. Indians who resisted, who behaved as if they were sovereign, not only disobeyed God's commands; they were a grievous insult to Americans' own moral virtue. Americans were deeply fearful of Indians. Fear of tomahawks and scalping knives hid a more profound fear. As the Declaration of Independence had it, savages wanted to violate your women and murder your children; they wanted to destroy your future, which was the future of civilization itself. It's no wonder that fear of savages left some Americans unhinged; the story they told about themselves promised an epic battle between good and evil, a potential resolution of which would always be their own annihilation.[76]

When the Americans arrived in the Lake Superior region like their European predecessors, they wanted to know whether or not Manabozho was Christian (not especially) and where the copper was (most people weren't saying). The extent of what Indigenous people knew and thought about was shocking to those who inquired. Early in his study of Ojibwemowin, Schoolcraft breathlessly wrote to Cass that these Indians might have as many as a thousand words.[77] The stories were a complete surprise. The Americans sought to alienate that knowledge from Indigenous humanity because capitalism required them to take possession of the land by emptying it of Indigenous meaning. It required them to dehumanize Indigenous people and turn them into savages. This was Schoolcraft's job, even his purpose in life as he saw it. Publishing books and making treaties were of a piece. Eventually he decided that Jane and her family were savages too.

Anishinaabe scholars have turned to stories about the cannibal monster Windigo to think about how communities are confronted with and manage both internal and external threats.[78] Traditionally a Windigo was a giant, male or female, emaciated, decaying, and always hungry, that ripped its victims to pieces as it devoured them. The more it ate, the hungrier it got.[79] "Windigos literally and figuratively suck the life out of people to satisfy their own appetites," Anishinaabe legal scholar John Borrows writes. In the present, they "might even consume entire environments through their greed, lust, and desire for money, power, or prestige."[80] Eating up Indigenous land required eating up Indigenous knowledge. Schoolcraft wanted to snatch the thoughts right out of Indigenous skulls. He acted like a Windigo, never satisfied, always wanting more, taking everything he could get.

The children of Ozhaawshkodewikwe and John Johnston didn't know what they faced at the beginning. When Schoolcraft appeared Jane and her family treated him like any of the other white people who wanted them to explain their relatives; they humored him and gave him charming stories. After some time it seemed that their charming stories might convince Americans that their relatives were human beings, not savages, and they wrote more. Then Schoolcraft began to insist that the stories were evil and that God willed that the savages must die. He was difficult to manage, to say the least. They ignored him when possible, manipulated him when they saw an opening, placated him when necessary. They kept writing. The stories got more strange, more full of "majic." They kept on saying what he didn't want to hear and writing what he didn't want to know. In the end they weren't writing for him at all.

PART I

Chapter 1

This Vain and Transitory World

In the summer of 1814, after having surrendered Mackinac Island two years previously, the Americans returned, although they at first went looking for the British fur trade depot in Georgian Bay, several hundred miles to the east. This gave Lt. Col. Robert McDouall, the commander at Mackinac, time to call for help, and for the second time John Johnston armed a party of his workers. He, Jane, and the rest made their way down the St. Mary's River, luckily by a seldom-used route, because by the time they left, the Americans had returned from Georgian Bay and sent their men to the Sault to attack the trade outposts on both sides of the river.[1] Ozhaawshkodewikwe and the children, and everyone else in the village except for George and John Holiday, the Johnstons' clerk, fled to the woods, warned by Ojibwes who'd escaped the Americans. They took George and Holiday prisoner and plundered the family home and storehouses, taking even the women's and children's clothes that they found, then trashed the villagers' gardens, killed their horses and cattle, and burned what was left.[2] When the expedition returned to Mackinac on 26 July, the Americans had five ships, ten gunboats, 400 sailors, and about a thousand troops, both regular and militia, to begin their assault. About ninety British soldiers, fifty militia, and fifty Indigenous warriors waited on the island in two forts, one on a cliff overlooking the village harbor on the south side of the island where McDouall put Johnston in charge, and a second one at the island's height that McDouall had just had built.[3] The Americans then sat, in bad weather and unable to decide how to attack, until 4 August.[4]

The only plausible reason for Jane's presence at Mackinac, aged fourteen, would have been to serve as an interpreter.[5] Securing competent interpreters seems to have been a persistent concern during the war. Warriors might arrive but decide not to participate in an engagement, do things in battle over which British commanders had little control, or leave when they decided they were finished with an engagement, regardless of British plans.[6] After the first battle of Mackinac in 1812, John Askin Jr., a Scottish-Ojibwe fur trader at Mackinac, wrote to his father that "in spite of all my exertions & [those of] six or seven interpretors & volunteers," he could barely keep the warriors from immediately attacking the Americans, so eager were they to fight.⁷ Jane's services would have been necessary wherever there was information to be passed between the British military and their Indigenous allies.

After attempting a bombardment of the old fort that didn't last long because they couldn't angle their cannons high enough to hit anything of consequence, the Americans decided to attack as the British had in 1812, from the north, where they would have to fight through dense woods to get to both forts.⁸ The second battle for Mackinac was brief. The warriors "gallantly repulsed" the enemy, John Johnston later wrote to George, turning the tide of the battle.⁹ They quickly picked off the man who had terrorized the Sault, Maj. Andrew Holmes of Virginia (a friend of Thomas Jefferson's), because, the story was, he refused when warned by a local to change out of his fine officer's uniform of blue wool jacket, red cuffs, silver lace, and light-colored breeches.¹⁰ Some said it was an Indigenous boy only ten years old who killed him; others believed that two Menominee chiefs, L'Espagnol and Yellow Dog, shot him simultaneously. Fleeing panic-stricken down a slope back to their ships, the Americans left the deceased major behind; the next day they asked for his body back, which was given, and they sailed their ships back to Detroit, leaving two of them to blockade the island. Within a month McDouall's men snuck up on and took first one ship and then the other, boarding them both without a fight and sending their captives to prison in Canada.¹¹

After the battle Jane and Josette Laframboise, the daughter of the Odawa fur trader Madame Magdelaine Laframboise, sewed shirts for two wounded Americans left behind by their compatriots, one of whom died before they could be handed back. Jane didn't write anything down about her experiences at Mackinac, but she did tell Anna Jameson, an English critic who visited the Schoolcrafts in the summer of 1837, about a woman warrior who was there. Mrs. Jameson put this story into her book, *Winter Studies and Summer Rambles in Canada* (1838), one of several books by travelers in which Jane featured over the years. The woman warrior had taken her husband's place after he'd been killed previous to the battle at Mackinac. When she came to the old fort after the battle, everyone gathered around to see. She was "slight and delicate in figure" and "covered with rich ornament, silver armlets, with the scalping-knife, pouch, medals, tomahawk—all the insignia ... of an Indian warrior, except the war-paint and feathers," Jane told Mrs. Jameson. In front of a large mirror in the officers' quarters, the woman warrior admired herself, "turning round and round before it, and laughing triumphantly." The officers invited her to dine, "perhaps as a joke," wrote Mrs. Jameson, "but she conducted herself with such intuitive propriety and decorum, that she was dismissed with all honour and respect, and with handsome presents."[12] Of course there is no other record of this woman in anything else written about Mackinac.[13]

Circumstances kept intruding on John Johnston's plan for his precocious daughter to grow up in a cocoon of polite Christianity, protected from a "base and wicked world." "The improvement of your mind is dearer to me, than every other accomplishment," he wrote to Jane from Montreal the year previous to the battle at Mackinac. He must have had regrets about his failed Irish plan, but as was his habit he made the best of the situation. It was "a blessing from providence" that she was "sequestered from the world" at Sault Ste. Marie, with "the time and means of storing your mind with good and religious ideas."[14] He taught her to write poetry, if not directly then by example. "First to my god, my heart and thoughts I'll raise," she wrote, aged fifteen, "Then to my earthly father counsel take / From him I'll learn to sing my Saviour's praise / Who bids me from the sleep of death awake."[15]

John Johnston was his children's first teacher in everything because he never could get a Protestant missionary to come to the Sault, and even if the war hadn't intervened, he wouldn't send Jane or her younger sisters to Montreal to be educated by nuns like other girls whose fathers were fur traders. (In 1810 he arranged for an English missionary to be sent to the Sault, but the missionary was so shocked by the state of society on landing in the New World that he refused to go any further, presumably returning to Europe on the next available ship.)[16] For religious instruction he led morning and evening prayers for the family, and on Sundays he read psalms or a sermon, concluding with his own remarks. For entertainment, especially in winter, he or one of the children—Lewis or George, or when she was old enough, Jane—read from the library, history or literature or more sermons. This was what he had done when he was a boy, in Ireland, with his widowed mother and spinster aunt, and afterward they all discussed the particularly fine passages and the lessons to be drawn from the reading.[17] There were also stories from their mother or her relatives from near and far away. Everyone spoke Ojibwemowin, even Johnston by then. The girls listened while sewing or doing quillwork, or making birchbark containers for sugar.[18]

When he wrote about his life in North America, Johnston depicted it as a Rousseauian state of nature, free from the corruption of civilized society. He was in the habit of contrasting it with that of the "fashionables" of cosmopolitan cities. This seems an odd concept for a fur trader to find useful. At the time Johnston was writing, "fashionables" referred to the titled, wealthy,

John Johnston, artist unknown (ca. 1790). Chippewa County Historical Society, Sault Ste. Marie, Michigan.

and very public elite of London who by the late eighteenth century were popularly associated with aristocratic immorality and fecklessness.[19] He was in this habit at the same time that, although late in life his moral failure bore down on him, like all the other fur traders he sold liquor to Indigenous people just to stay competitive, knowing full well the destruction and despair it unleashed in Indigenous communities.[20] When he thought about his children, and especially Jane, however, he compartmentalized. Despite the trade that after his losses in the war he couldn't escape, he would bring them up in a world of order, moderation, and politeness.[21] He seems to have willed himself to it. Schoolcraft described him as "at once pious and cheerful," an assessment that Johnston's correspondence bears out.[22]

Under her father's guidance Jane studied Hannah More, a friend of Samuel Johnston's who began her career writing plays for David Garrick in the 1770s but later became better known as a writer of tracts encouraging the poor to piety and acceptance of their lot in life.[23] More fused Christianity and polite sensibility in a way that father and daughter found quite amenable. "To exclude reason from religion . . . is not the way to attract its truth," wrote More; "to exclude elegance from its exhibition, is not the probable method to invite men of taste to speculate on its beauty."²⁴ She recommended "leisure with dignity" for spiritual development, combining "repose, elegance and literature."²⁵ Above all More counseled faith in the divine order in a supremely disordered world. "There is no way of disentangling the confusion but by seeing God in every thing," she wrote in *Christian Morals*, a book that inspired Jane to write a poem commemorating its influence on herself.²⁶ "The most oppressive and destructive agents are [God's] mysterious ministers; they are carrying on, though unconsciously, his universal plan—a plan, which though complicated is consistent; though apparently disorderly will be found finally harmonious."²⁷ Christians must submit to God's sometimes painful teaching but not become abject; they should continue to do good and oppose evil, however it manifested itself. "If it be his will to permit sin," More wrote, "it is an opposition to his will when we do not labour to counteract it."²⁸

Hannah More wrote extensively about the importance of women's charity, which was probably on Jane's mind when Ozhaawshkodewikwe once told her that they were going to visit with a mother who'd lost a child to a Windigo somewhere north of Lake Superior. Windigo is both the name of a cannibal monster spirit and the name for a psychological condition in which a person believes he or she wants to eat human flesh—an incipient Windigo didn't necessarily have to have committed cannibalism already but rather to feel compulsively that it would if it were not stopped.²⁹ It's not clear whether the child—more than likely a son—was a victim of a Windigo or had become a Windigo himself. Although Schoolcraft in copying over this poem wrote that the family was French, it was more than likely given the population of the Sault and the fact that Ozhaawshkodewikwe was involved that they were Ojibwe and French and that the mother of the lost child was Ojibwe.³⁰ Jane wrote the poem before leaving on the visit:

> Language divine! Thy aid impart
> To breathe the feelings of the heart
> That burns with sympathetic woe
> For those whose tears incessant flow
> Those, to whom fortune now doth prove
> A tyrant stern, to him they love.
> Sweet charity, now points the way
> And I the summons must obey
> Quickly thy magic flowers impart,
> To soothe the broke and bleeding heart
> To lull dispair into a calm
> And make my every word a balm

> To cheer the agonized breast
> And point to heaven—a place of rest.
>
> Then, shall I ne'er the time repent,
> In service of my neighbour spent.[31]

As a Hannah More–reading Christian, Jane would have known that nothing is the result of mere fortune; the Christian God is in control even when someone was turned into or eaten by a Windigo. "Many seem to ascribe to chance the common circumstances of life, as if they thought it would be an affront to the Almighty to refer them to him," More wrote in *Christian Morals*, "but the gracious Father of the universal family thinks it no dishonour to watch over the concerns, to supply the wants, and dispose the lot of creatures who owe their existence to his power, and their redemption to his mercy."[32] The purpose of Jane's "sweet charity" was to "point to heaven"—to speak to the bereaved family of Christ, to convert them.

Numerous writers have left accounts of the psychosis, which was believed to have been caused by starvation or by a spirit angry that ceremonies had not been properly observed.[33] George Nelson, a British fur trader in Wisconsin and Saskatchewan in the early nineteenth century, wrote down what he could find out about Ojibwe beliefs. Windigos lived "somewhere about the *North Pole*," and while they often appeared only to frighten human beings, sometimes they "delegate their Power to the indians [*sic*] . . . and *this* occasions that cannibalism which is Produced, or proceeds rather from a sort of distemper much resembling *maniaism*."[34] The eyes of these Windigos glistened, Nelson wrote; their illness was evident in their being "sullen, thoughtful . . . and perfectly mute" one minute, convulsive and jabbering in "incoherent and extravagant language" the next. He was surprised that such behavior was rare. Food could often be scarce for weeks or months, "during all which time the men are out from star-light to star-light and have never anything more to *eat* than some bit of leather, moss, bark and such like."[35]

It was more common for the people to try to cure the condition than to kill the person afflicted—and that when the afflicted person often pleaded to be killed, as did one of Nelson's best hunters. Nelson remembered a local girl recently married, "small and diminutive," who was "seized with this phrenzy" during the winter. "The men durst not leave the tent for any length of time, being obliged to assist the women in holding and preventing her from biting or eating any of the children, and perhaps herself." Afterward, the girl remembered nothing: "I thought I was always on the tops of the Trees," she said.[36] In another instance, at Lake Winnipeg, one day in December a man "began staring at his daughter with extraordinary intenseness: 'My daughter! I am fond of thee! I love thee extremely.'" The daughter, who lived with her father and husband, replied, "I know thou dost." But the father continued. He loved her so much, he said, "I think I could eat a piece of thee." At night the father, fearful of what he would do, got up "stark-naked and uttering a strong tremulous noise, and his teeth chattering in his head as if thro' cold, rose up and walked out of the Tent and laid himself curled as a dog in a heap" on a wood pile, remaining there all night. He continued to sleep out on the wood pile, naked, for the next month. He ate nothing but raw meat and then only occasionally. "In the day time he was more composed," Nelson writes, "but his face &c, [had] the appearance of one possessed of the Devil. He recovered and became as usual, composed, and good natured."[37]

Her mother likely wanted Jane to go on this visit to show her what her duties to her relatives were and, possibly, to remind her about the world beyond her father's fantasies. It could have been that the mother of the dead son was a Christian and Jane could help, knowing the right words to say. It could also have been that Ozhaawshkodewikwe was a healer, and those words would have been a terrible violation at the worst moment. Hannah More would say that it was God's will and there was nothing more to say or do than to convert to Christianity. Ojibwe spirituality is concerned with living well in this world, or *bimaadiziwin*. This requires proper relations with other-than-human persons, who give what anthropologist Mary Black Rogers calls the "power to live" to human beings, while human beings in turn owe them "'offerings' and 'respectful behavior.'"[38] Ozhaawshkodewikwe's visit would have had at least in part to do with restoring that order in the community. There's a very good chance that Jane would have kept quiet.

Only a few letters from her father, and only one from her to him, have survived, and those because Schoolcraft copied them to include in a biography he wrote after Johnston's death. "We only want you again with us, to live as happy as this vain, transitory world can make us," he wrote Jane in 1817. She was at the new British fort on Drummond Island, probably visiting Lewis, who was stationed there with the British Indian Department, and her half-sister Marguerite, who was born after John Johnston's first visit to Mackinac in 1791. (Her mother was Indigenous, and she had recently married William Solomon, a former trader who was an interpreter at Drummond. His father was Ezekiel Solomon, a Jewish fur trader from Berlin, and his mother was Okimabinesikwe, or Louise Dubois, a Catholic Ojibwe.)[39] Jane had planted a rose garden at the Sault and, he wrote, her sisters were tending it in her absence. The roses "seem to await your arrival to bloom forth with all their beauty and fragrance." This called for a lesson. "What, my beloved child, is all the pomps and vanities of the sublunary senses, but

Ozhaawshkodewikwe by Charles Bird King after James Otto Lewis (ca. 1825). Buffalo History Museum, Buffalo, New York.

the fugitive blow of a flower?" he asked. "One thing alone, we are sure of, that truth, purity of mind, love and submission to God our Saviour, can never fade, but will bloom and bear the sweetest fruit to eternity! Oh that my most fervent petitions merited to be heard at the throne of infinite grace and love, and you should long remain the brightest patterns of every virtue here, and when translated, should become one of the loveliest and most welcome guests at the supper of the Lamb."[40]

"My Mama and the rest of the family (thank God) have enjoyed pretty good health since you left us, and we only want you again with us to be happy in our situation, as this vain and transitory world can make us," Jane wrote to her father July 1818, when he was away at Mackinac. "Believe me, my dear Papa, the greater my knowledge of the World, the more my heart is raised in gratitude to the Great giver of all good, for my immanent situation where I can contemplate & reflect on the pleasures of the fashionable crowd, without one stifled sigh or wish to partake of their ideal happiness." She reported on the state of the crops grown for sale or distribution (potatoes, oats, peas, timothy, clover) to her father's workers. The family's garden (peas, beans, cucumbers, melons) fared not so well. Her rose garden, however, was quite fine.

> These two days I have taken in fifty of the most luxurious roses I ever saw, besides the ones that are still blooming on the bushes. The poor queen of flowers, has very few subjects, this season, of its own species, but is numerously attended by the different tribes of humming birds. I do not recollect ever having seen so many, as there are at present. One of the smallest kind was near being caught by its own blindness, but happily from the swiftness of its motion, it escaped unhurt. Charlotte having a shawl "of many colours" in her hand, it foolishly imagined that it was the desired object of its searches, she had just stretched out her hand to take the little creature captive, when it found its error, flew out of sight in a moment, the circumstance gave a good moral lesson, which you may be assured I quickly imparted to my sisters.[41]

Eliza's life stands in contrast to Jane's. Eliza was two years younger than Jane and differed from her brothers and sisters in her marked lack of interest in wishing to have anything to do with American society beyond the household. Unlike everyone else, she is not recorded to have translated or interpreted anything, even church services; also unlike everyone else, she is not recorded to have acted as a kind of docent to Americans or other outsiders who wished to have something Indian explained to them. Eliza didn't go along when Jane and Charlotte visited Drummond and Mackinac with their father after the war, to see their brothers and half-sister as well as their recently married friend Josette Laframboise. The two sisters attended a "grand ball" at the garrison, where they were all very well received, according to their father.[42] Jane and Charlotte remained at home while Eliza went to the sugar bush with her mother in the spring, an expedition lasting several weeks.[43] In 1826, the visiting commissioner of Indian affairs Thomas McKenney couldn't persuade Eliza to speak English, although her sisters and parents were the picture of solicitous hospitality. He thought her nevertheless to be a "fine young lady, and of excellent disposition"; her complexion, he observed, was rather dark, like her mother's.[44] She never married. Despite the presence of Protestant missionaries at the Sault by the mid-1820s and her own father's inclinations as well as those of her sisters, she didn't formally embrace Christianity until after her father died, when both she and her mother were converted by the Ojibwe Methodist missionary John Sunday, in 1832. She was twelve when the Americans

Sault Ste. Marie from Waishky's Lodge/The Falls of St. Mary's, drawing by Anna Brownell Jameson, *Voyage to America Portfolio* (1837). Baldwin Collection of Canadiana, Special Collections and Rare Books, Toronto Public Library, Toronto, Ontario, Canada.

burned down the Sault and plundered the family homestead. It's possible that traumatic event had something to do with her aversion to Americans and to English itself, even though she received the same education as did her brothers and sisters.

In the fall of 1815 his father sent George to trade at Drummond Island under McDouall's supervision. For the moment he thought that keeping his son out of the Americans' way was the best plan. The previous June, at about the time McDouall handed over Fort Mackinac, a US general and his party appeared at the Sault looking for a suitable place to build a fort and to see Lake Superior, the future of commerce in the interior. They arrived at the time of the Midewiwin ceremonies and set up their marquee next to the burying ground. This was provocative. Some of the people there planned an attack, but an Ojibwe woman told one of the traders what was going on, and he told John Johnston. Johnston invited the Americans to tea, gave them guns, and sent George and Holiday to guard them through the night. Nothing happened, and the next day the Americans sailed away.[45] Despite his cordiality the Americans accused Johnston and other British traders of not paying proper duties, threatening to confiscate their goods, Johnston complained to his son, and the governor of Canada was doing nothing.[46]

He sent candles, currycombs, horseshoe nails, and a man who needed to work off the twelve dollars; his mother sent George moccasins. George was also to keep an eye on Lewis, who was supervising the construction of the fort and its dependencies. Lewis was drinking or gambling or both.[47] Some or possibly all of his distress may have had to do with his relationship with Janette Piquette Cadotte, or Sangemanqua, who lived in the next house over at the Sault and was married to Jean-Baptiste Cadotte Jr.[48] Sangemanqua's first child with Lewis, Sophie, was born in 1812, when Lewis was about nineteen and Sangemanqua in her thirties. His parents didn't approve and "encouraged" Lewis joined the British navy; he did and was badly wounded in the Battle of Lake Erie and taken captive for a time. In 1815 Jean-Baptiste, who'd been dismissed from the North West Company for drinking some years before, was at Drummond with Lewis, working as an interpreter for the British Indian Department.[49] It was a hard winter; scurvy broke out in the garrison, and the surgeon David Mitchell, who was married to the Odawa fur trader Elizabeth Mitchell, desperately sought vinegar, lemons, and vegetables to fight it off.[50]

McDouall transferred out that summer. Before leaving he informed his superiors that "a strong confederacy" of tribes on the Mississippi had formed to resist the building of US forts in the region, one that expected British support because they "comprehended clearly, that by an article in the Late Treaty of Peace their *lands rights and priviledges* were secured to them by the King their Father as in 1812." "It is inconceivable the horror they entertain at the idea of the English & *their Traders* being prohibited from going amongst them," he wrote. "The Little Corbeau, who frequently distinguished himself in our cause during the Late War, and who from his abilities, takes a lead in Indian Politics, told me this evening with much sensibility, that he considered this measure as sealing the ruin of the Indian nations and arriving at their final extinction."[51] In a last council with the Dakota, Ho-Chunk, Menominees, and Odawas, the Ho-Chunk chief Karahmannie said, "When the Master of Life or Great Spirit put us on this Land, it was for the purpose of enjoying the use of the Animals and Fishes, but certain it never was intended that we should sell it, or any part thereof which gives us Wood, Grass and everything. The fish fowls and wild animals were made for us and for the Support of our Men Women & Children, and we will not part with that Land, which supply us with them."[52] McDouall pledged to fight for their cause at Montreal.[53] He went there with John Johnston and made his arguments for several months, but his superiors remained unmoved and eventually he left for home.[54]

George returned to Drummond in the fall of 1816, bringing with him a thick blank book that he kept for the rest of his life.⁵⁵ He inscribed the first few pages as follows:

> George Johnston
> St. Mary's Falls, 4th Septr. 1816
> Be but my friend. I ask no dearer name.
> Memorandum Book.

followed on the next page by

> Let not your sorrow die Though I am Dead,
> * * * *
>
> Lend me thy hand and I will give thee mine
> * * * *

Then

> No fly me, fly me, far as pole from pole;
> Rise alps between us and whole oceans roll!
> Ah! Come not, write not, think not once of me.
> Methinks we wandering go
> Through dreary wastes and weep each other's woe,
> Where round some mould'ring tower pale Ivy creeps,
> And low-browed rocks hang nodding o'er the deeps.⁵⁶
>
> Eloisa.

He was about nineteen. The first quotation is from William Shenstone, a well-connected late eighteenth-century poet better known today for his interest in gardening; it's spoken by a fallen woman begging the father of her child to at least be her friend, now that her virtue was gone. Of course, says the man, Henry; he "wasn't born of savage race."⁵⁷ This is not much comfort, or not for long, since the girl (Jessy) drowns. The last quotation is taken from two different passages in Alexander Pope's "Eloisa to Abelard," in which Eloisa first pleads with Abelard to appear before her but then tells him to stay away.

The two lines in the middle come from Shakespeare's *Titus Andronicus*, both lines referencing spectacular violence driven by an unrepentant "barbarous Moor" named Aaron. Set in the last days of the Roman empire, the play concerns Titus Andronicus, a Roman general, who is engaged in a cycle of revenge with Tamora, Queen of the Goths and wife of the emperor Saturnius. Aaron is Tamora's lover. The two lines George quotes are again out of order. The first, "Let not your sorrow die, though I am dead," is from Aaron's speech to Lucius in Act V of the play. Lucius is the son of Titus Andronicus, who has captured Aaron, and Aaron, to save his and Tamora's child, confesses all of his nefarious deeds, for which he has no regrets.

> Even now I curse the day (and yet, I think
> Few come within the compass of my curse,)
> Wherein I did not some notorious ill;
> As kill a man, or else devise his death;
> Ravish a maid, or plot the way to do it;
> Accuse some innocent, and forswear myself;
> Set deadly enmity between two friends;
> Make poor men's cattle break their necks,
> Set fire on barns and hay-stacks in the night,
> And bid the owners quench them with their tears.
> Oft have I digg'd up dead men from their graves,
> And set them upright at their dear friends' doors,
> Even when their sorrow almost was forgot;
> And on their skins, as on the bark of trees,
> Have with my knife carved in Roman letters,
> Let not your sorrow die, though I am dead.
> Tut, I have done a thousand dreadful things,
> As willingly as one would kill a fly:
> And nothing grieves me heartily indeed,
> But that I cannot do ten thousand more.[58]

The second line that George quoted (from Act III, Scene 1) is spoken by Titus Andronicus at the moment when Aaron has convinced him to chop off his own hand. The context of the line is convoluted. As revenge for Titus's defeating the Goths and killing Tamora's eldest son, Aaron persuades Tamora's surviving sons to rape Titus's daughter Lavinia and kill her betrothed. He frames Lavinia's brothers Martius and Quintus for the murder. Afterward Aaron goes to Titus and persuades him that Saturnius will spare his sons for what they supposedly did if any one of Titus, his brother Marcus, or his son Lucius cuts off his hand and sends it to Saturnius. Titus says, "Come hither, Aaron; I deceive them both; / Lend me thy hand, and I will give thee mine." And then Aaron chops off Titus's hand.[59] George's reversal of the two quotations allows Aaron his revenge.

The play was considered so barbarous in the eighteenth century that Samuel Johnson wasn't entirely ready to concede that Shakespeare had written it.[60] In the many compilations of Shakespearean and other quotations in circulation in the eighteenth and early nineteenth centuries, the play was not often cited, and when it was, Aaron seldom if ever figured. John Johnston would have found him an inapt character for quotation.

Contemporary critics have remarked on the complexity of Aaron's position in the play. Though he and Tamora are "barbarous" and "beastly" and their child is "'a joyless, dismal, black, and sorrowful' thing," it was the arbitrary violence of Rome—the killing of Tamora's older son—that set events in motion.[61] Aaron is an educated barbarian who uses myth and classical poetry to revenge himself on a society that claims to be civilized but that Shakespeare represents as anything but.[62] That is shown in the play's climax, where in revenge for the death of his sons and his daughter's rape and mutilation (her tongue cut out and her hands chopped off), Titus Andronicus captures Tamora's sons Chiron and Demetrius, beheads them, grinds them up, and feeds them to their mother at a banquet. Titus appears at the banquet wearing a cook's outfit, quite pleased with himself. He kills Lavinia for the shame of having been raped, then kills Tamora, but not before letting her know that she's just eaten a pie filled with her own sons. Saturnius, Tamora's cuckolded husband, kills Titus, which prompts Titus's son Lucius to kill Saturnius, after which Lucius is proclaimed the new emperor. Buried chest deep and left to starve, Aaron remains extravagantly defiant to the end: "I am no baby, I, that with base prayers / I should repent the evils I have done," he says. "If one good deed in all my life I did / I do repent it from my very soul."[63]

Say that George Johnston identified with the character Aaron as a young man. He was educated in the classics and beyond, yet in some circles, primarily but not exclusively American ones, he was considered a savage for his Indigenous blood. Visitors to the region were unnerved by the close proximity of savages and had plenty to say about it. When the British boundary surveyor Jeremiah Bigsby visited David Mitchell at Drummond, he remonstrated to the old man (he was almost seventy at the time) about the men and women continually interrupting their dinner, wandering in and out of the house. "Down they squatted in the corners, putting their abominable weed-smoke in our faces, and joining freely in the conversation," he wrote in his book *The Shoe and Canoe* (1850).[64] Mitchell pointed out that that was the custom and they were "all respectable people," and besides, "if I denied them, my trade would stop; and I might soon have in my ribs a knife-thrust, sharp and sufficient."[65] (Whether a trader would be murdered for not being sociable when there were always more traders available seems at least somewhat questionable.) Mitchell had come to New York City from Scotland as a common sailor, joined the British army during the revolution, served as a surgeon's mate, and ended up at Mackinac, married and unwilling to leave when his regiment did. He joined his wife in her lucrative trade with her relatives. He was the paragon of social order and authority and was always addressed as "doctor." Like John Johnston, he had a large library and sent his sons to Montreal but his daughters to Europe to be educated. It was he who served as priest whenever anyone needed a wedding at Drummond, including those of his daughter and granddaughter. He was the one who knew how to treat scurvy.[66] Yet he associated with dirty savages, which gave outsiders pause, and like Bigsby they were often quite willing to express their surprise and dismay.

These were George's relatives, too, and those attitudes can't have escaped his notice. He had been the Americans' captive at the Sault and helpless while they plundered the village in 1814. The record is conspicuously silent on what else may have gone on at the Sault in 1814, just a few oblique asides referencing transgressions that could only be imagined, which suggests sexual violence against women that couldn't be spoken in historical accounts.[67] George knew warriors like the Odawa Assiginack, who had a blue silk flag from the British in appreciation for his heroism on the Niagara frontier. He worked at Drummond as an interpreter for the Indian Department alongside Jean-Baptiste Cadotte and William Solomon. In the first years after the war Assiginack was lost. He was in his forties, he knew as McDouall knew that the British government had abandoned their former allies, and he did not know what would come next or what to do. The story was that when he was drinking he was so physically powerful and unpredictable that his friends habitually got him drunk enough to pass out as quickly as possible in order to limit the damage.[68] When George was on the island Assiginack was several years away from the transformation that would eventually make him a respected leader at Manitoulin for over forty years (he died aged about ninety-eight, in 1866).[69] In the fall of 1816 the general outlook at Drummond was bleak.

There were limits to his father's doctrine of Christian forbearance in the face of adversity when one was recognized as an Indian or a "half-breed." The two epigraphs from *Titus Andronicus* were easily misconstrued as sentimental platitudes; George kept his anger disguised. The rest of the excerpts in the commonplace book were all religious and likely to have met with his father's approval. These included acts of contrition, "A Prayer for Penitence," a hymn from the *Book of Common Prayer*. He prayed to "love my neighbour and to dispise the world"; to subdue "lust by mortification, covetousness by liberality, anger by mildness, and lukewarmness by zeal and fervency." He prayed for prudence, courage, patience, and to be directed in all things by God's grace.[70] The entries quickly fall off, but George did copy an entire essay by Hugh Blair, a mentor and defender of James Macpherson, titled "On the Importance of Order in Conduct." Blair was the young man's Hannah More. "Order, method, and regularity" were essential to religious faith, wrote Blair. Since disorder "coincides with vice, so the preservation of [order] must assist virtue."[71] Order was the answer to all of life's questions: order "in the distribution of your time"; in "the management of your fortune"; "in your amusements"; and "in the arrangement of your society."[72] The disordered, warned Blair, were infected with a contagious disease: "The spots of death are upon them. Let every one who would escape the pestilential contagion, fly with haste from their company."[73]

This must have seemed pertinent to George when his older brother was living such a disordered life. Lewis's second daughter with Sangemanqua, Polly, was born in early 1817. The Johnstons seem to have known nothing about the situation until the last moment. To John Johnston, Sangemanqua was "that abandoned woman"; he wrote to George that Lewis's "unblushing falsehood" about the relationship "makes me feel he has lost all sense of shame and honor."[74] His father warned George to avoid "any species . . . of misconduct, let alone the least appearance of vice," either in himself or in the men he hired to trade. "What is to come of us in the future—God alone knows. I fear there is no other alternative, but to become American citizens or to abandon trade and country, which without proper knowledge of any other business and what is worse, without capital is next to an impossibility. May the Almighty counsel and direct us."[75] With McDouall gone from Drummond, he sent George to trade on the south shore of Lake Superior in the summer of 1817. Lewis took an interpreting job temporarily but then returned to the Indian Department within the year, transferring south to Amherstburg—along with Jean-Baptiste Cadotte.[76]

A year later George had returned to the Sault, and a more persistent US general appeared. In a reminiscence that appeared in a Detroit newspaper in the 1850s, George wrote that, like his predecessors, Alexander Macomb wanted to see the entrance to Lake Superior, so his father assembled the boatmen and Ozhaawshkodewikwe filled up a basket with food and wine. "The gentlemen walked up leisurely on the Portage Road, observing the falls and adjoining scenery," George wrote, and Johnston saw them off at the portage. The boatmen "[struck] up the voyageur song," and "away went the canoe, skimming the water as lightly and gracefully as a water-fowl," trailing a US flag. They landed at a large encampment at Pointe aux Pins, along the river on the Canadian side, before the entrance to the lake. By the time the guide, Le Clair, jumped out to secure the canoe, "the warwhoop reached and assaulted their ears and simultaneously was seen infatuated and intoxicated Indians emerging from their lodges with guns and war clubs in hands." As he wrestled a gun out of one man's hands, Le Clair "informed the general it would be improper at this time to proceed to the entrance of Lake Superior, for while they would be absent the Indians would become sober and on their return be better prepared to do him and 'les messieurs' serious if not fatal injury." The Americans turned around. "We saw the canoe coming down the rapids in gallant style, men singing and in full chorus, and soon landing the general and his party on our dock," wrote George.[77] Unlike the previous generals, Macomb was undeterred; he reported to Secretary of War John C. Calhoun that a garrison at Sault Ste. Marie "would have an excellent effect both as it regards our Indian relations & the revenue laws."[78]

After the war and before the Americans arrived at Sault Ste. Marie, Jane and George, along with their father, wrote translations of songs and stories from Ojibwemowin.[79] Schoolcraft published some of the material in his book *Travels in the Central Portions of the Mississippi Valley* (1825), writing that they were taken from a "manuscript collection of traditionary songs" and a collection of "tales . . . taken from the oral relations of the Chippewa" that the Johnstons had produced some years prior to the time of his writing.[80] He was always cagey in print about where his information came from and in what form it was; it's likely that some of Jane's and her father's other early writing that Schoolcraft published elsewhere was part of either or both of the collections.[81] It's also likely that there was more in the anthologies than Schoolcraft published but that it was subsequently lost.

Taken together the material suggests the kind of literary anthologies with which John Johnston would have been familiar from childhood. Beginning in the late seventeenth century, anthologies or miscellanies of literary works began to appear in England, a product of loosening restrictions on publication, an abundance of things to publish (including pirated things), and advances in printing, advertising, and distributing books. These books had titles like *A Collection of Scarce, Curious, and Valuable Pieces, Both in Verse and Prose; Chiefly Selected from the Fugitive Productions of the Most Eminent Wits of the Present Age* (Edinburgh, 1785) and *Poetic Amusement, Consisting of a Sample of Sonnets, Epistolary Poems, Moral Tales, and Miscellaneous Pieces* (London 1809). They included brief prose forms like anecdotes or tales, established genres like the pastoral or georgic, and new poetic forms the genesis of which the anthology itself encouraged, including, literary critic Barbara Benedict writes, "the printed ballad . . . the ode, the occasional poem, the extemporaneous rhyme, the epitaph, the epigraph, the fragment, and meditative verse." Most of the material was written in a more informal mode than had been the case in the previous century.[82] From the late seventeenth to the early nineteenth century the anthology as genre helped define standards of taste; it also became a means of establishing the idea of a national tradition in English literature.[83] The Johnstons may have had this idea of a national tradition in mind when they put their anthology or anthologies together.

They wrote at the moment when Americans' steadily increasing encroachment on their lives was on everyone's mind. Once established at Mackinac in 1815, the Americans began a campaign of harassing islanders deemed disloyal, trashing gardens, and throwing stones from the cliffs at passing canoes; soldiers attacked and stole goods from families returning from the British distribution of presents at Drummond Island. William Puthuff, the new Indian agent at Mackinac, prohibited Elizabeth Mitchell and her son George, a British naval officer, from even talking to their relatives who came to the island. While it was true that Elizabeth's service to the Crown in recruiting her relatives to fight for it was so appreciated that the British granted her an annuity, the pointed harassment she received after the war was over enraged her husband and Robert McDouall. She'd had to flee the island in the middle of the night by canoe.[84]

In keeping with their father's literary sensibilities and more than likely their mother's thinking as well, Jane and George treated Ojibwemowin as a poetic language and Anishinaabe narrative as a source of moral instruction. They followed an aesthetic code that was widespread in Britain by the eighteenth century. Early in the century British criticism valued a work's "design," by which was meant the author's intention and the work's plot and other formal structures.[85] By the middle of the century, critics as well as readers (and particularly readers of anthologies) began to value as well passages that made for especially pleasurable reading—what were called the work's "beauties."[86] One can imagine that George and Jane wrote these poems and stories purely for the pleasure of writing down Ojibwemowin on the page and translating it (there was no standard orthography), of choosing the right form for the story and carrying it out, and more than likely of pleasing their father, who wished to do this very thing almost from the moment he arrived at La Pointe. But one can also imagine that, like George, Jane had been exposed to white people with opinions about savages—at Mackinac, for example, at a ball, among the US soldiers.

That Indigenous languages could be used to write poetry or that Indigenous people might produce anything appreciable for its moral sentiment and beauty was unthinkable to Europeans. According to William Robertson, a Scottish historian and an authority on Indians from the late eighteenth to the mid-nineteenth century, in the savage state, man's "reason is but little exercised, and his desires move within a very narrow sphere," such that his intellectual powers are "extremely limited. . . . Like a mere animal, what is before his eyes interests and affects him; what is out of sight, or at a distance, makes little impression."[87] Indians couldn't engage in "speculative reasoning or research," let alone write poetry.[88] The figure of the eloquent savage giving elaborate metaphorical speeches might seem to contradict this. That savage arose out of actual translated treaty speech (often European treaties with the Haudenosaunee Confederacy) that became widely available through printed treaties and periodicals in the seventeenth and eighteenth centuries.[89] By the time the eloquent savage speech became a genre of its own in the later eighteenth century, eloquent savages mainly gave speeches telling white men what they wanted to hear (that Indians were naturally dying out), and British intellectuals had decided that the use of metaphor marked an inferiority of intellect regardless of how elaborate or clever it might be.[90]

The songs that George and Jane wrote down were sung by men, and though they are about war, they are also beautiful. Writing songs as poetry in Ojibwemowin was an assertion that the language was beautiful both in written form and translated into English. It also announced the skill of the translator, because most of the meaning in Ojibwe songs (except for love songs and Midewiwin songs) was not in the often repetitive words but in the music, so part of the pleasure to be had by readers of the collection who knew the material was in how George or Jane translated the music into words and arranged the words on the page.[91] George translated a war song sung by Tsheetsheegwyung, who was from La Pointe, that is unlike any poetry in English of its time. It begins,

> I sing—I sing, under the centre of the sky,
> Under the centre of the sky;
> Under the centre of the sky, I sing, I sing,
> Under the centre of the sky, &c.

Jane translated a song that her mother remembered, sung by Waabojiig on leaving with a war party against the Outagamies and Sioux. There are three stanzas in the Ojibwemowin but only two in English (there's no explanation given for the discrepancy):[92]

> Do not—do not weep for me
> Loved woman, should I die,—
> For yourselves alone, should you weep.
> Poor are ye all, and to be pitied,
> Ye women! ye are to be pitied!

Over the course of her writing, Jane often wrote about the emotional and domestic lives of Indigenous men, conscious of the stereotypical bloodthirsty savage who had no real attachment to his family because he wasn't capable of it. "To despise and to degrade the female sex, is the characteristic of the savage state in every part of the globe," wrote William Robertson, who got his information from the best-informed travelers. Indians, "perhaps from that coldness and insensibility which has been considered as peculiar to their constitution, add neglect and harshness to contempt" for their women.[93] The readers of this family collection would have been aware of that stereotype, too.

Jane's choice of form for the two mythological stories in the collection, "Peboan and Seegwun" and "Origin of the Robin," brought Ojibwe tradition into relation with the mythological and literary traditions of the West.[94] She wrote the first story (both of them were told by Ozhaawshkodewikwe) as an allegory featuring personified seasons, a trope stretching back to antiquity. An old man sits alone in his lodge in a frozen landscape, listening to the storm outside, when one day a young man carrying a sweetgrass wreath and flowers arrives. They smoke a pipe and tell each other about themselves:

> "I shake my locks," retorted the old man, "and snow covers the land. The leaves fall from the trees at my command & my breath blows them away. The birds get up from the water, & fly to a distant land. The animals hide themselves from my breath, and the very ground becomes as hard as flint."
>
> "I shake my ringlets," rejoined the young man, "and warm showers of soft rain fall upon the earth. The plants lift up their heads out of the earth, like the eyes of children first opening in the morning. My voice recalls the birds. The warmth of my breath unlocks the stream. Music fills the groves, where I walk, and all nature rejoices."

As the sun rose, Peboan melted away, and "nothing remained on the place of his lodge but the miscodeed a small white flower, with a pink border, which is one of the earliest species in a northern Spring."[95] The story exemplifies the kind of literary beauties valued in writing of the period.

"Origin of the Robin" similarly juxtaposes Indigenous and Western form and theme. Robins, and specifically robin redbreast, were common features of English popular poetry and to a lesser extent prose in the eighteenth and early nineteenth centuries, so much so that there was at least one anthology, *Tales of the Robin* (1815), dedicated to that figure alone. In English folklore, robins were said to be attached to human beings and to care for the unburied dead by covering them with flowers and moss. One nineteenth-century critic called the robin "half sacred"[96] The legend of robin redbreast—its origin story—was that the bird lighted on Christ's crown of thorns when he was on the cross and pricked itself so that it bled on its breast.[97]

In Jane's story an old man pushed his only son to seek a vision to fulfill his (the father's) own desire for fame, insisting that he should fast for eleven days, longer than anyone else. On the ninth day of the fast, the son tells the father his dreams "are ominous of evil!" and begs to break his fast, but the father refuses.[98] Two days later, the boy asks again and his father refuses again; two days after that, at the allotted end of the fast, his father goes to the lodge and hears his son talking to himself. "He stooped to listen," Jane writes, "and looking through a small aperture, was more astonished when he beheld his son painted with vermillion on his breast, and in the act of finishing his work by laying on the paint as far as his hand could reach on his shoulders, saying at the same time: 'My father has ruined me, as a man; he would not listen to my request; he will now be the loser. I shall be forever happy in my new state, for I have been obedient to my parent; he alone will be the sufferer; for the Spirit is a just one, though not propitious to me. He has shown me pity, and now I must go.'"[99] The father bursts into the lodge, "exclaiming, 'My son! my son! do not leave me!'" But his son was changed into a robin. He looks on his father "with pity beaming in his eyes," saying that "he should always love to be near men's dwellings, that he should always be seen happy and contented by the constant cheerfulness and pleasure he would display, that he would still cheer his father by his songs, which would be some consolation to him for the loss of the glory he had expected; and that, although no longer a man, he should ever be the harbinger of peace and joy to the human race."[100]

"Pity" is a meaningful term in Anishinaabe discourse. It doesn't signify virtuous feeling for an abject person as it often does in English, but invoking it is an appeal to establish right relations between the less powerful and the more powerful. In speeches given to the US government and its agents, Anishinaabe leaders often demanded that the United States show pity, meaning that its responsibility as the more powerful entity was to give aid to the less powerful.[101] In Jane's story the "Spirit" was the spirit from whom the youth would have received power during his fast. But the youth loses that connection because of the father's greed. Instead, the spirit shows pity on the youth and transforms him into a robin, and in turn the youth has pity for his father because he is now the one in the position to show it, promising to return as a "harbinger of peace and joy to the human race." In Jane's story the robin ultimately has the same relationship with human beings as in the English story, only in her telling it's an Anishinaabe relationship. She seems to have been working out a puzzle, how to make Anishinaabe and Western thought converge in literary form.

Despite his enthusiasm for the project, John Johnston couldn't quite equal his children's skill in translation or their understanding of Ojibwe thought. His rendition of Waabojiig's "War Song" (he was in the habit of giving copies of this to interested travelers) thumps along in quasi-ballad style, and the stories told by his friend Gitche Gauzinee that Johnston wrote down treat Gitche Gauzinee's experiences in the land of the dead as a fantasy.[102] The stories, published as "Gitche Gauzinee" and "The Funeral Fire," were *dibaajimowin*, or stories about human beings or historical events, rather than mythological *aadizookaan*. In both Gitche Gauzine seems to die, during which time he learns what the dead desire. In both cases, the story has to do with making travel to the land of the dead easier for others, in the first case by not burying so many things with the deceased (who then had to carry them to the land of the dead) and in the second by keeping a fire lit on the gravesite for four days to light the way. That Johnston didn't write mythological stories raises the question whether it would have been considered proper for him as a non-Indigenous person to write them down.

Jane invents more freely in the last two pieces, a poem and a story that appear to be based on Ojibwe traditions but that are more embellished than the other works in the collection. The poem "Oh how can I sing the praise of my love!" is not obviously based on a traditional song (although it may well have been), but it describes an explicitly Ojibwe scene, of a woman lamenting her dead lover and calling on his *jiibay* to come to her. Ojibwe theology posits the existence of two souls, the *jiibay*, situated in the mind and able to leave the body during sleep or trances, and the *ojichaag*, which is situated in the heart and stays with the body until death, after which it immediately passes on to the afterworld where it waits to be rejoined by the *jiibay*.[103] The poem is written in the voice of a woman who is enticing her lover's *jiibay* away from its journey because she can't bear to let him go.

> Oh how can I sing the praise of my love! His spirit still lingers around me. The grass that is growing over his bed of earth is yet too low; its sighs cannot be heard upon the wind.
>
> > Oh he was beautiful!
> > Oh he was brave!
>
> I must not break the silence of this still retreat; nor waste the time in song, when his spirit still whispers to mine. I hear it in the sounds of the newly budded leaves. It tells me that he yet lingers near me, and that he loves me the same in death, though the yellow sand lies over him.
>
> > Whisper spirit,
> > Whisper to me.
>
> I shall sing when the grass will answer to my plaint; when its sighs will respond to my moan. Then my voice shall be heard in his praise.
>
> > Linger, lover! Linger,
> > Stay, spirit! stay.

The spirit of my love will soon leave me. He goes to the land of joyful repose, to prepare my bridal bower. Sorrowing I must wait, until he comes to conduct me there.

Hasten, lover; hasten!
Come, spirit; come![104]

The speaker succeeds in getting what she wants, the *jiibay*'s presence, through the power of her voice. Though at the end the speaker is waiting for death to reunite with her lover, this is not a poem about an expiring Indian maiden of the type her future husband and other Americans would become so enamored. For one thing, she's not necessarily dying, and for another, she has a voice so powerful that she can bring her lover back from the dead.

That the stanzas are in prose could mark this poem as a translation or an imitation of a translation. Jane was writing in this poem and the story "The Two Ghosts; Or, Hospitality Rewarded" in a way that North American Indigenous writers didn't write again until well into the twentieth century, freely and consciously combining Indigenous and Western elements to make something that spoke to her experience. This is more clear in "The Two Ghosts," which appears to be based on an Ojibwe narrative but incorporates the gothic, treaty language, a critique of imperialism, Christian sentiment, and the concept of *bimaadiziwin*.[105]

The model for this story and for several of Jane's subsequent stories is what scholars call the moral fairy tale. While late seventeenth- and early eighteenth-century fairy tales, most famously those by Charles Perrault and other French writers, were intended for adult readers, over the course of the eighteenth century fairy tales became associated with children, especially in Britain. By the later eighteenth century, concern for children's moral improvement led to a great deal of criticism of fairy tales, not least because of their supernatural content. Writers and publishers of fairy tales adapted to the times and began to produce moral fairy tales, according to M. O. Grenby, "works [that] fused the didactic aims of the moral tale with the themes, language, and style of the fairy tale."[106] Writers like Ann Laetitia Barbauld (whose poetry Jane included in the anthology of poems she copied from the family library) could incorporate fairy tale elements into stories about the importance of good behavior, or fairy tales could be rewritten to conform to the didactic requirements of the moral tale.[107]

"The Two Ghosts or Hospitality Rewarded" begins with a hunter and his wife living contentedly in the woods on the shore of Lake Superior. "Game was then very abundant," Jane writes, evoking a time before the present of about 1815, when game in the vicinity of the Sault was depleted as a result of overhunting. It was the time before the "white man" made his appearance, before blankets and clothes of cloth, before cutting down trees, before guns, and before the "wrathful phials of liquid [that poured] fire upon the Indian nations."[108] In American writing of the period, lamenting the lost worlds of the Indians carried with it the idea that there was nothing to be done because they were savages and would die because God willed it. In Indigenous discourse, the recitation of the ill effects of Europeans establishes that Europeans consciously sought to destroy Indigenous people, with the corollary (implied or stated outright) that they should stop doing that and could if they wanted to.[109]

The hunter and his wife are a picture of comfortable domesticity. Every evening the hunter returns to a "cleanly-swept lodge" where "he entertained his wife in conversation, or in occasionally relating those tales, or enforcing those precepts, which every good Indian esteems necessary, for the instruction of his wife and his children."[110] He never offends the Great Spirit and wants only "to support his family, with a sufficiency of food and clothing by his own unaided exertions, and to share their happiness around his cheerful evening fire." He's "happy in his ignorance, but still happier in his simplicity, and his full reliance upon the superintending care of an overruling Great Spirit."[111] Jane was a good Christian and believed, like her father, that her relatives needed to be converted, but her use of "ignorance" is not an assessment of her relatives' moral worth, only of their not yet having been informed about Christianity.

The approach of the ghosts to the family's lodge has a noticeably gothic sensibility. "Darkness had already veiled the face of nature," Jane writes of the evening on which the two ghosts appear; the man's wife "listened attentively to catch the sound of coming footsteps, but nothing could be heard but the wind mournfully whistling around the sides of their slender lodge." The wife is in a "state of suspense," when "suddenly [she] . . . heard the sound of approaching footsteps, upon the frozen surface of creaking snow."[112] She invites the two ghosts in, but they hide their faces in their clothes and refuse to go near the fire. "They seemed shy and taciturn," Jane writes, "and when a glimpse could be had of their faces, they were pale, even to a deathly hue; their eyes were vivid but sunken; their cheek bones quite prominent, and their whole persons, as far as could be judged, slender and emaciated."[113] When the hunter comes home with a deer, the women rouse themselves, exclaiming, "Behold! what a fine and fat animal!" and race to "[pull] off pieces of the whitest fat, which they ate with avidity." Both the hunter and his wife are taken aback by the women's frenzy but "forbore to accuse [the women] of rudeness."[114]

As time goes on, the strange women continue to take the best part of the meat and more than their share, every day. The hunter, "a just and prudent man," remains calm, however, thinking that they might be "persons of distinguished rank" visiting in disguise.[115] As time passes the women begin to look healthier and stronger, and eventually they "threw off some of that cold reserve, and forbidding austerity" that had prevented the hunter from getting a sense of their "true character."[116] Things seem to be going well until one day, when the women tear at the meat as was their habit, the wife "suffered the thought to pass hastily in her mind, 'This conduct is certainly most extraordinary! How can I bear with it any longer!'" This causes the two ghosts to burst into tears, at which the hunter finally asks, "Ye women, who appear to be not of this world, what is it that causes you pain of mind, and makes you utter these unceasing sighs?"[117]

"We are weeping for the fate of mortals," say the women, "whom death awaits at every stage of existence. Proud mortals! whom disease attacks in youth and in age. Vain men! whom hunger pinches, cold numbs, and poverty emaciates. Weak beings! who are born in tears, who are nurtured in tears, who die in tears, and whose whole course is marked upon the thirsty sands of life in a broad line of tears. It is for these we weep!"[118] They had been sent from the Great Spirit to test the man and his wife; if they had been treated hospitably for the three months allowed for the test, they would have been permitted to return to the land of the dead. The trial isn't even half over when the hunter's wife has her incriminating thought.

After explaining what has happened and why, the two ghosts provide a moral for the story in a form commonly used for treaty speech:

> Brother—It is proper that one man should die to make room for another, who is born in his place. Otherwise the world would be filled to overflowing. It is just that goods, gathered by one, should be left to be divided among others; for in the land of the spirits there is no want. There, there is neither sorrow nor hunger, death nor pain. Pleasant fields spread before the eye, filled with game, and with birds of handsome shapes. Every stream has good fish in it, and every hill is crowned with groves of fruit-trees, sweet and pleasant to taste. All kinds of games have been invented to amuse, and instruments to play upon. It is not here, brother, but *there*, that men begin truly to live. It is . . . for you that are left behind, that we weep.[119]

The emphasis on fulfillment in the afterlife makes this a Christian sentiment, but the description of the afterlife is decidedly Ojibwe; the admonition to leave possessions behind when going to the afterlife is the same as that made by Gitche Gauzinee.

Even though the test technically failed, no one seems to suffer (the wife isn't mentioned). The ghosts promise the hunter that "thy luck shall still be good in the case; and a bright sky prevail over thy lodge" and tell him, "Mourn not for us, for no corn will spring up from tears; but join our lamentations for the fate of mankind." Their message conveyed, the women disappear into a "blue vapour," sobbing. The conclusion also bespeaks the Ojibwe context. The hunter becomes "celebrated" and "never wanted for anything necessary to his ease. He became the father of many children, all of whom grew to manhood: and health, peace, and long life, were the rewards of his hospitality."[120] He lived well on this earth, in keeping with *bimaadiziwin*.

His father's next plan for George was to send him to Montreal over the winter of 1818–19, to sell the previous seasons' furs. A new law banned foreign traders in US-claimed territory; as a noncitizen, Johnston could only trade within the confines of his post at the Sault.[121] He still had no intention of becoming a US citizen, he wrote to George, and "therefore to this Post shall I restrict myself until the Almighty in mercy enables me to quit their Territories for ever."[122] It fell on George then to become a US citizen. His father sent George off to Montreal with spiritual advice. "Let me beseech you neither to permit pleasure or business to estrange you from your duty to that Almighty and Most Merciful God who has hitherto guided and protected you, for if we forget him he will most assuredly call us off and then we are in a worse state than the beasts that perish."[123] By the time his father wrote, however, George had left Montreal—in January—to return home.

He would have traveled for weeks by snowshoe. He'd sent a letter telling of his plans to Ramsay Crooks, a Scottish-born fur trader who had long been John Jacob Astor's partner in the American Fur Company at Mackinac who spent the winters tending to business in New York City.[124] George was to have visited Crooks in New York; he had nothing to say about why he was leaving Montreal. "I suppose you have found Lower Canada, with *all* the luxuries and refinements incident to what those who know no better call a *highly polished* state of society; still far inferior to the substantial comforts, and positive happiness, you can command at St. Mary's," Crooks wrote, reaching for an explanation. "If my opinion is correct, I shall not blame your flying from a *forced* state of existence, we observe in every large town.... Was it optional with me, New York enticing as she is, could not detain me another day."[125] He wrote in the same vein to John Johnston. "I suppose he ... discovered that happiness intruded but seldom into the circles of modern refinement, saw wealth and ostentation however profoundly ignorant, caressed, flattered, yet almost adored, while worth and merit if unassisted by fortune, were left to depend for existence on the food of the Camelia."[126]

It may have been that George felt out of place and even ostracized, in comparison to his father, because he was a "half-breed." It could just as well have been romantic longing. George's fondness for Pope's "Eloise and Abelard" seems to have had a subtext. Although there is no trace of her in George's papers, he married Wassidjeewunoqua or Louisa Raimond (or Raymond) in October of 1822; their first child, also Louisa, was born in September of the following year.[127] "I should not wonder did he not stop short of the inmost recesses of our forests," Ramsay Crooks continued to Johnston, "and certainly cannot be blamed for undertaking a toilsome and tedious journey to regain comforts and friends, whose *real* value he would perhaps never have known, had he never left St. Mary's."[128]

George made it back to the Sault, but his father sent him to Montreal again the next winter, and that time he stayed.[129] In the spring of 1820 Johnston went to Montreal himself from which he left for Ireland and England to settle his financial affairs there (he sold land he inherited from his mother to his sister and her husband). In fact, half the family would have left Sault Ste. Marie with him, as he deposited Eliza and Charlotte, aged seventeen and thirteen, then William, aged eight, at school, Charlotte and Eliza at a boarding school in Sandwich, Lower Canada, and William with a minister in Cornwall, south of Montreal.[130] They would have traveled by canoe from the Sault to Detroit, then across Lakes Erie and Ontario to the St. Lawrence River. Left at home were Ozhaawshkodewikwe, Jane, Anna Maria (aged six), and John McDouall (aged about three).

Also in that fall of 1819, Lewis Cass outlined his plans for Calhoun, the secretary of war. They'd just concluded a treaty for most of the southern part of present-day Michigan in September. Indians' continued attachment to Britain perplexed him. Despite American threats, they continued to receive annual presents from the British at Malden, across the Detroit River from the city, and Drummond Island. Considering the goodwill Americans had shown, this was frustrating if not enraging to Cass. "The dignity of the Government, the interest of the Nation, the permanent welfare of the Indians, and above all a wise and provident regard for the future, founded upon a retrospective view of the past, imperiously call for a speedy & effectual exclusion of this foreign interference in our Indian relations & properly speaking in our domestick policy," he wrote. He had been thinking. The agents should give speeches telling the Indians they were not permitted to go into Canada. They should cultivate "faithful Indians" to spy on their relatives and "faithful Interpreters" to patrol the rivers, persuading anyone they happened upon mid-crossing to turn around and go back. At the moment, however, British agents continued to prevail by appealing "directly to the love of property" in the tribes, which was "one of the strongest & most active passions, which influence and guide the Indians."[131] Cass read political and economic relations as savages' love for shiny things.

He proposed an expedition along the southern shore of Lake Superior to the source (he hoped) of the Mississippi River and finally down to Fort Dearborn to show the flag and impress the Indians with the might of the United States, then negotiate yet another treaty. He imagined a fact-finding mission combined with a charge to extinguish Indian title to land in the three trade centers of Sault Ste. Marie, Prairie du Chien, and Green Bay as well as the routes between them, for future settlement. He also wanted to visit an enormous copper boulder on the south shore of Lake Superior at the Ontonagon River.[132] Calhoun rejected the proposed land cessions except for that to establish a garrison at Sault Ste. Marie. Congress thought it prudent not to extinguish Indian title so quickly, he wrote in April 1820. The Indians might get "dissatisfied" and resist giving up more in the future, although the actual issues would seem to have been too much land, too many Indigenous people, and not enough white settlers.[133]

Along with eight gentlemen associates, including Schoolcraft as geologist, ten soldiers, a dozen voyageurs, an interpreter, a guide, and ten Indigenous men to row, Cass left Grosse Point in May 1820. At the Sault they transferred themselves to four large canoes and acquired an additional detachment of twenty soldiers, led by Lt. John Pierce, brother of the future president, in its own barge.[134] Once again the Americans arrived when the people were gathered for the Midewiwin ceremonies. George wrote an account of this episode, in 1843. Both sides of the river, he wrote, were "dotted ... with ... wigwams, and the probable assemblage of Indians at this time could not have been less than fifteen hundred men capable of bearing arms."[135] His father was in Europe, so George once again invited the officers over to the house for tea. Cass then invited George to attend the council he had called, and the next day George and John Holiday were seated on either side of Cass under his marquee—rather a different position than they had been in just a few years before. The chiefs arrived and sat on the ground in a semicircle in front of Cass, but Sassaba, brother to Shingabawossin, leader of the Crane band at the Sault, stood at the back wearing a full British uniform, with a scarlet general's frockcoat, epaulettes, and sword given him by Robert McDouall.

Cass demanded that the Ojibwes hand over all the territory at the site of the old French fort on a rise above the rapids by virtue of the 1795 Treaty of Greenville, which he said had transferred European land acquired by treaty from Indian nations to the United States after the revolution. This was a ridiculous claim, and the chiefs rejected it out of hand. In apparent disdain for their resistance, the interpreter threw "an armful of plug tobacco" on the ground in front of them. "At this time," George wrote, "one of the head men observed, and casting his eye on the pile of tobacco before him, 'I presume,' said he, 'that this tobacco is designed for our smoking,' and, drawing one of the plugs towards him with his long pipe stem and taking it in his hand, drew his scalping knife from his belt and commenced cutting the tobacco." This did not please Sassaba. As the man picked up the tobacco, Sassaba stepped into the tent, "shoved the tobacco lying on the ground with his foot, and addressing himself to the head man who was cutting the tobacco, with a frown, said to him: 'How dare you accept of tobacco thrown on the ground as bones to dogs?'" Sassaba stalked off to his lodge, where to the amazement of everyone in attendance he hoisted the British colors.[136] Pierce and his men "sprung to their arms," and the council broke up in general chaos as an enraged Cass grabbed his interpreter and strode away to confront Sassaba. "The jingling of the ramrods in the muskets soon reached the ears of the women and children at the village, and the affrighted began to fly to their canoes lying on the beach," George wrote. The dogs barked and howled in the confusion.

The story of Lewis Cass's heroic confrontation with Sassaba has often been told, first by Henry Schoolcraft, whose 1821 account of Cass's heroism was certainly meant to flatter the man and improve his own prospects. Schoolcraft got his information from the interpreter, Cass himself being too modest a man to have said anything, of course. According to Schoolcraft, the assembled chiefs were cowed by Cass's manly decisiveness. Cass entered Sassaba's lodge and informed him that raising the British flag

> was an indignity they were not permitted to offer upon American territories,—that we were their natural guardians and friends, and were always studious to render them strict justice, and to promote their peace and happiness; but the flag was the distinguishing token of national power, connected with our honour and independence,—that two national standards could not fly in peace in the same territory, and that they were forbid to raise any but our own, and if they should again presume to attempt it, the United States would set a strong foot upon their necks, and crush them to the earth.[137]

A historian has expressed surprise that, surrounded by Ojibwe warriors and with only a comparatively few men himself, Cass would do such a thing.[138] It's entirely plausible, though, that something like the language that Schoolcraft wrote actually came out of Cass's mouth in the moment, since these were common enough sentiments in Cass's correspondence with Calhoun. Given that history, it seems that stark rage drove Cass, that the people whom he considered so inferior—recalcitrant children as far as he was concerned, improvident, and too attached to property—would simultaneously refuse their natural subordination and reject the benevolence so generously offered to them by the United States.

George returned home to find his mother "much agitated." "For God's sake, George," she said, according to him, "send instantly for the elder chiefs, for that foolish young chief, Sassaba, will bring ruin to the tribe, and get them assembled here." Ozhaawshkodewikwe's role in the story has also been much mythologized, again mainly by Schoolcraft himself, who ignored her in his first version but eventually praised her "Pocahontean" aid to Cass.[139] In a scrap of a journal from 1822 that seems to have survived intact, Schoolcraft remembered that she sent for the chiefs, telling them, "My relatives, it is too late for you to assert your rights. The country has been given up by treaty, & if you contend for it, the English government will not sustain you. It is better that you should receive the Americans, with friendship."[140] This account is muddied too; it was only Americans who asserted that the land was already theirs, not the Ojibwes whose land it was. In this account, Ozhaawshkodewikwe recognizes that the Americans were good people whose word could be trusted. One aspect of the story does ring true, and that is that Ozhaawshkodewikwe would have known, possibly better than the chiefs themselves owing to Robert McDouall's friendship with the family, that the British had entirely abandoned the Ojibwes, and thus Sassaba's defiance was a dead end. Her response to the Americans was strategic, not a recognition of their superior moral qualities.

George first offered tobacco and apologized for addressing the chiefs when he was so young, but then he told them that the British would not come to their aid in any conflict. "The firing of one gun will bring ruin to your tribe and to the Chippewas," he said, "so that a dog will not be left to howl at your villages." Then Ozhaawshkodewikwe appeared, and "with authority commanded the assembled chiefs to be quick, and suppress the follies of Sassaba."[141] Shingabawossin selected Shingwaukonse to head a party to confront Sassaba, whom they met on the portage road out of his British uniform and into war paint, leading his own party and determined to attack Cass and the soldiers. When Shingwaukonse told Sassaba that he had to stop, Sassaba reminded him that they had fought for the British in the late war and that Shingwaukonse was the leader of a war party in which Americans had killed Sassaba's brother. "How dare you come to put a stop to my proceedings," said Sassaba, striking Shingwaukonse with his war club. Shingwaukonse was "undismayed," George wrote, "and still kept up his oration and with his eloquence and the power vested in him by the chiefs, he prevailed on the party to return quietly to their respective lodges."

Probably under instructions from his mother, George told the chiefs that after apologizing to Cass, they should "listen to what he had to say to them, and if they found anything adverse to their principles, it was their time to reject in a proper manner the propositions he should make to them," to which they assented.[142] After meeting in council for a day, the chiefs agreed to meet with Cass. Still rejecting the idea that the Americans already owned the land by virtue of the Treaty of Greenville, they sold four square miles of land to the Americans on which they would build their fort, receiving goods in exchange and retaining hunting and fishing rights on the land as well as the right to camp on the banks of the river.[143]

Cass felt restored to his rightful place. "I did not require the Indians to cede to us a larger tract, because more would be useless for the objects, which the Government have in view, and because it is important to our character and influence among them, that our first demand should be distinctly marked with moderation," he wrote to Calhoun, representing the agreement the chiefs struck as his own idea all along. That benevolence would win the Indians over and away from the British, Cass was certain: "After the establishment of a post here, & after they shall be enabled to appreciate those principles, which regulate our intercourse with them, there will be no difficulty in procuring such cessions, as subsequent events may render it important for us to procure," he wrote.[144] In official discourse the Americans seldom broke from the story they decided to tell, that they were merely benevolently offering the savages a chance to better themselves.

In a draft of a poem signed "Rosa" and dated 1820, Jane sits "lonely in my Father's hall," when despite the tranquility of the natural world around her, she hears the falls "like the murmur of far distant voices / or like warriors waving their banners, / With sounds of defyance rending the air; / Warning all those who approach to beware." But she tries to push aside that potential trouble, to make herself think "pure thoughts." "Reflecting on God's works," she turns her attention instead to God's love:

> Oh! how much more will He hear when we mourn,
> And heal the heart that by anguish is torn;
> When he sees the Soul to his will resign'd
> Patiently Waiting his love [which] to the end [will shine.][145]

Like George, Jane tried to follow her father's model when it came to adversity in the form of Americans, although while George leaned heavily on the codes of honor and polite behavior, Jane had faith in God's will. Still, her anguished heart gives some indication of how the Americans were received at the Sault when it became clear that they had come to stay.

Chapter 2

Belles Lettres

Schoolcraft didn't have much to do after he arrived to stay in the spring of 1822 besides issue licenses to traders and make pronouncements: the Great Father had only the most benevolent intentions toward his Indian children, whom he warned against intemperance and visiting British posts. Within two weeks he was living with the Johnston family. In June, Jane's cousin Ogeewyahnoquotokwa's husband, Songageezhig or the Strong Sky, was murdered one night while drinking with several other men; Schoolcraft had a coffin built, attended the funeral, and issued provisions to his widow and their three small children.[1] Few of the tribal leaders visited his makeshift office. He wondered whether fear of the soldiers put some of them off, but since there were comparatively few soldiers and they were all engaged in building the palisaded fort, it seems unlikely that fear was the issue. He was impressed with the Ojibwes' looks. They had "very bright hazel eyes & jet black coarse hair," which they bound up with headbands ornamented with falcon's feathers, he wrote in his journal. They were all very picturesque, with moccasins and leggings, calico shirts and bright togas, and wild face paint.[2] And red colored, he noted; the half-breeds were more olive complected.

In the course of clearing a road behind their fort in order to secure the wood to build it, the soldiers soon destroyed a sacred place, a blown-down tree from which people had heard the voices of spirits and where they had left offerings that the soldiers threw aside. In September, Sassaba and another man, along with their wives and children, were capsized above the rapids while trying to cross the river in a canoe. The two men had been drinking, and while Sassaba and everyone else drowned, the other man, Odabit, washed up on the bank, still alive.[3]

Shingabawassin came to Schoolcraft's office a few days after his brother's death. He'd been gone for several weeks deliberating on the best course of action with regard to the Americans; he told Schoolcraft he was now prepared to "take the Americans firmly by the hand." He was one of twenty children of Maidosage, who had had four wives. Shingabawassin had one wife and eight living children. He'd fought both the Dakotas and the Americans, joining Tecumseh in 1813. He was tall, well proportioned, dignified, and with "an open commanding countenance," Schoolcraft observed. "The removal of the hair from his forehead & temples, according to the Indian custom, give the idea

Shingabawossin by Henry Inman (ca. 1831–34). High Museum of Art, Atlanta, Georgia.

of greater cerebral expansion that would ordinarily appear," he wrote, phrenologically; he "has an acqualine [sic] nose & lips expressively parted. These traits, with a dark & rather deep set eye, & prominent cheek bones, serve to make his face more than usually impressive, so that he is easily remembered by his features." He found Shingabawossin's "mode of oratory is less gesticulatory & violent than is usual with the Indians." Shingabawossin was the picture of the noble savage. Schoolcraft was certain that he could convince him that Americans were his friends.[4]

In January 1822 Cass had sent John Johnston an elaborate questionnaire on the Indians that he was circulating widely among men he thought knowledgeable on the subject, in government and out. He wanted to know about their traditions, their histories, their governments, their laws, their habits of war, their funeral customs, their treatment of children, their marriage practices, their medicine, their astronomy and mathematics, their music and poetry, and their religion but particularly their language. Is the language guttural? he asked, to start with; do their nouns and pronouns decline? The questionnaire went on for over sixty-four pages.[5] "I am exceedingly anxious, that Mr. Johnston and his family should furnish full and detailed answers to my queries," he wrote to Schoolcraft in September 1822, "more particularly upon all subjects connected with the language, and, if I may so speak, the polite literature of the Chippewas." He was in the perfect situation, as far as Cass was concerned. "There is no quarter, from which I can expect such full information upon these topics, as from them.... I pray you in the spring to let me have the fruits of their exertions."[6]

Cass's reference to "polite literature" indicates that he may have known something about the family's writing before Schoolcraft did. Jane and her father were in the habit of either reciting or giving copies of some of their pieces to inquiring visitors—especially "Peboan and Seegwun" and Johnston's rendition of Waabojiig's war song. While he later claimed to have "detected fanciful traditionary stories among the Chippewa" himself in the fall of 1822, Schoolcraft wasn't especially interested in them at first, preferring to report to Cass on his progress in the language.[7] A month after receiving Cass's letter, he sent the first 150 words, grouping them in categories of natural history and topography. He was already learning that, as he put it, "some ears [were] much nicer in the discrimination of verbal sounds than others"; his official interpreter, for instance, had an inferior knowledge of the language. He didn't mention how he came to this conclusion. He also edited the transcription, dropping syllables and vowels as he thought necessary "to rid the language of that barbarous appearance, to the eye, which Indian words usually present" as well as to make them shorter and therefore, he thought, more accurate. Manipulating the Johnstons' transcriptions of Ojibwemowin in this way became a lifelong habit. As to pronunciation and orthography, everything he sent had the "full sanction" of "Miss Jane and her mother," he wrote at first, but then on consideration he crossed it out and wrote "the Johnstons." It was a noble and agreeable task, to devote oneself to rescuing the language "from that oblivion, to which the tribe itself, is rapidly hastening," particularly during the long winter already commenced. "I am led to think that there may be *one thousand words* in common use by this tribe."[8]

By the time Schoolcraft wrote this letter in October 1822, he and Jane had declared their feelings for one another. She wrote him playful notes in the third person—"Miss Johnston presents her compliments to Mr. Schoolcraft"—as he worked away in his office across the yard. "I read your kind note last night at a *time* and *place*, when I always think of you, and indeed, you are never absent from my mind," he wrote to her; "I will only say in reply how happy you make me by such tender and beautiful expressions respecting me. To merit them, is to meet what I most *ardently desire*."[9] She was frequently ill, but that only added to the romance. Away from the Sault in January, he wrote to say, "How sincerely I am afflicted by all that affects you, & to express that affectionate regard which I must ever cherish for your amiable qualities, sweet disposition, and improved understanding."[10] He wrote her poems:

> Still, still the same, a too romantic maid,
> Why ever sad, secluded or dismay'd?
> Why lost to mirth, too fond enthusiastically, tell!
> Say, dost thou hope too much; or love too well,
> Or is it fame, philosophy or pride,
> That makes thee dead to all the world beside
> Or are thy hopes—thoughts—passions—wishes—love,
> Etherish all, and fixed on heaven above?[11]

It went on for several more stanzas. She wrote back:

> An answer, to a remonstrance on my being melancholy, by a Gentleman, who,
> *sometimes* had a *little pleasing* touch of melancholy himself
> Still—Still! the same—my friend you cry!
> Still—Still! the same—until I die—
> Unless *your* friend, and *mine*, soft maid—
> I chase away the darksome shade.
> With her, too sure, would *there* repair,
> The joys that make, dull life, more fair.
> Should I awhile her presence shun,
> And join in frolic, laughter, fun—
> Yet would my heart, unconquer'd fly,
> And woo her back, with many a sigh,
> Or with her walk the haunted groves,
> Where lovely sorceress, Fancy roves,
> Such silent joy in her there lies,
> 'Tis but to taste them once—and prize.
>
> Since then such bliss you'd have me lose,
> Teach me to gain thy pleasing muse.
> Enchanted then I'll sing my lays!
> And cheerful spend my happy days.[12]

That there was a difference in the quality of their writing neither of them could have failed to perceive.

He seems to have always wanted an intellectual, and a polite, life, as he understood it. Despite his family's lack of interest, as a boy and young man Schoolcraft wrote a manuscript newspaper and collected a library of, as his biographer Richard Bremer put it, "popular plays, cheap novels, and volumes of light verse together with the obligatory Shakespeare."[13] He drew and painted watercolors; when he told his family he wanted to be apprenticed to a painter in New York City, they offered him house-painting instead. He began to study for college, but in 1811, when he was fifteen, his father fired the overseer of one of his glass factories in upstate New York and put Henry in charge of it.[14] After that business failed with the postwar return of cheap British imports, he went prospecting for lead in the Ozarks, in the course of which he discovered that the federal government had an interest in facts and that could work to his benefit. His 1819 book about the lead mines of Missouri gained the attention of Secretary of War Calhoun, with whom Schoolcraft succeeded in ingratiating himself. Schoolcraft fancied himself US secretary of mines, but Calhoun offered him a job as agent at Sault Ste. Marie, and Cass set him on his path of studying the savage for the benefit of government policy and science.[15]

John Johnston and Schoolcraft were both broadly concerned with politeness, but they imagined the idea very differently. John Johnston's politeness was centered on the Enlightenment ideals of conversation and harmony; Henry Schoolcraft was concerned with rising up in the world by establishing himself as the right sort of person.[16] Throughout his life his writing shows an unceasing need to acquire a veneer of knowledge in order to demonstrate his social and moral superiority. The more he thought of himself as an author, Bremer writes, the more he "resorted to the use of literary allusions, apt or otherwise; the scattering of names and phrases in foreign languages with varying degrees of accuracy; and a certain tedious pomposity" in his writing.[17] He was apparently unchurched. While he could parrot the sentiments, he was unable to recognize the provenance of well-known Bible passages, and his casual reference to Jane's devotional poetry as "etherish" would not have gone over well with John Johnston. By his own account in his *Personal Memoirs*, he began to concern himself with his spiritual life only after his marriage, in conversations with the Presbyterian missionary who performed it, Robert McMurtrie Laird.[18] Those conversations were not so extensive; Laird remarked at the time that Schoolcraft was "at least, a well wisher to Christianity."[19]

He was charmed by Jane and her family—their refinement, their intellectual pursuits, and the romance of their, or mainly her, Indianness. Later Schoolcraft would tell Jane that as a young man he had written epic poetry but burned it, knowing its inferiority.[20] At Sault Ste. Marie, he lost his literary inhibitions. Inspired by the scenery, by Jane, by the significance of his new position, Schoolcraft unleashed a torrent of poetry that abated only when he could no longer pick up a pen, several decades later. Most of it, from beginning to end, involved the dead and dying Indians that Americans found so romantic:

> St. Mary's falls are swift & strong
>   And race as on they go,

> The waves from shore to shore prolong
>   A hollow sound of woe.
>
> That sound upon [minion's] ear doth write,
>   The note of my tribe's decay
> That, like a murmuring stream by night,
>   Is rapidly passing away.
> The storm that o'er it hangs in black
>   And that gathering still apace,
> And on its cold unforgiving track,
>   Shall sweep away my race.[21]

He would make use of Indian personae for the rest of his life. Jane answered this with "Invocation to My Maternal Grandfather on Hearing His Descent from Chippewa Ancestors Misrepresented." Her grandfather Ma Mongazida had first married a Dakota woman and had two children with her; eventually, because of the conflict between Ojibwes and Dakotas, she returned with them to her relatives. Ma Mongazida subsequently married an Ojibwe woman who was the mother of Waabojiig, Jane's grandfather. That Dakota ancestry would be considered a slur of the kind that would destroy Waabojiig's authority or memory seems to have been Jane's romantic invention. The poem protests Waabojiig's valor, and the speaker positions herself as the one who will continue to proclaim Waabojiig's bravery and fidelity: "Rest thou, noblest chief! in thy dark house of clay, / Thy needs and thy name, / Thy child's child shall proclaim."[22]

At that time the daughters of white fur traders and Indigenous mothers at Sault Ste. Marie and Mackinac typically married men in the British or US military, fur traders, or employees of the British Indian Department, many of whom at that time were the sons of fur traders and Indigenous women themselves.[23] The daughters of David and Elizabeth Mitchell married within that group.[24] In the spring of 1816 at Mackinac, Josette Laframboise had married the US artillery captain Benjamin K. Pierce, another brother of the future president Franklin Pierce, but it doesn't appear that her mother approved of the marriage, which occurred when she was away at her trading post at Grand River, in southwest Michigan.[25] Madame Laframboise insisted on a second, Catholic ceremony when she returned, at which she and her sister Thérèse Schindler (Thérèse was also a fur trader) appeared, according to Thérèse's granddaughter, in "full Indian costume."[26] In the 1830s missionaries needing expertise in Indigenous languages sought fur traders' mission-educated Indigenous daughters for wives, including Charlotte Johnston and Hester Crooks, the daughter of Ramsay Crooks and Abanokue, an Odawa woman.[27] John Holiday had married Omuckackeence, the daughter of Gitche Iauba, headman at L'Ance Kewaywenon on the south shore of Lake Superior; their daughters Mary and Nancy would both marry surgeons posted at Fort Brady.[28]

Few if any of the available men when Jane Johnston was a young woman would likely have shared her passions for poetry and Ojibwemowin. It would have seemed like fate that a man like Schoolcraft appeared when he did. She pledged him her undying love, copying out Portia's speech to Bassanio in *The Merchant of Venice*:

> The full sum of me,
> Is sum of something; which to term in gross,
> Is an unlesson'd girl, unschool'd, unpractis'd:
> Happy in this, she is not yet so old
> But she may learn; and happier than this,
> She is not bred so dull but she can learn;
> Happiest of all, is that her gentle spirit
> Commits itself to yours to be directed
> As from her lord, her governour, her king.[29]

There are different ways to read this passage. She could have been utterly sincere in the moment she copied it down and showed him, knowing that he would be pleased. But she may well have thought it was a good idea to reassure him that he was the teacher, the one in charge. Johnston built a wing onto the house for their use and promised Schoolcraft Jane's inheritance from his not-yet-deceased sister, $10,000.[30] Their son, William Henry, was born eight months after their marriage, in June 1824. He was blond and perfect; they called him Penaysee, or little bird, as was the practice in Ojibwe families.

Petitioning Calhoun for an agent at Detroit in 1821, Cass had complained of being saddled with the duties of the job, enduring "the visits and applications of an importunate, hungry, wretched, and generally, drunken people," who came not only from Michigan Territory but from all points "by business, interest, or poverty." Indians never quit: "Day after day, month after month, and year after year, to hear their demands, their complaints of partialities, and to divide and satisfy, require a greater share of patience than is usually found."[31] Cass was about forty years old, having been territorial governor for almost ten years, and lived with his family on a large farm on the outskirts of Detroit. He rose from the Ohio militia to brigadier general in the regular army during the war; a fever contracted during it caused all of his hair to fall out, and as he aged he increased in girth. The Indigenous people reportedly called him "Big Belly." He accessorized this with an auburn wig that curled at the temple.[32] "We must think for them," he wrote to Calhoun. "We must frequently promote their interest against their inclination, and no plan for the improvement of their condition will ever be practicable or efficacious, to the promotion of which their consent must in the first instance be obtained."[33] This was the same kind of consent that Americans sought with respect to treaties. The impetus behind Cass's pursuit of knowledge about Indians, first as surveillance, then as a general study, was to learn about Indigenous people in order to bend them to his will and produce their consent.

His questionnaire on the manners, customs, and language of the savages was another order of things entirely from the kinds of inquiries that had preceded it.[34] There were hundreds of questions. Even as its first part roughly followed the standard taxonomies for Indian "manners and customs," the questionnaire was both inordinately detailed and idiosyncratic in that it seemed to reflect personal experience with Indigenous people. "What is their opinion respecting the planetary system?" he asked; "what do they think of the size, shape, &c. of the earth?" Are their musical instruments wind instruments, and "are they used exclusively, as is said, by the young men in love?" He wanted to know whether they visited one another, whether they had parties, how they behaved on returning home after a long absences. Do the Indians have beards or hair on their bodies, he wondered; and "if they have hair, is it thinner than upon the whites?" "Are they in the practice of telling stories?" he asked.[35]

The second part of the questionnaire, on language, was even more remarkable for its time. In the eighteenth century, North American writers, Thomas Jefferson among them, gathered vocabularies of Indigenous languages both to compare them against each other and European languages and to facilitate trade.[36] Cass's effort was part of a rising interest among American intellectuals in a more systematic study of Indigenous languages.[37] He wanted not only words but also grammar, orthography, and pages and pages of sentences translated into Indigenous languages:

> Indians are better than white people.
> But the Indians are not as good as they were.
> Their fathers were better.
> Before the white people came,
> We had plenty of game,
> But now we have none.
> If the game does not increase, we shall starve
> If it does increase, you will not starve.[38]

He seems to have had in mind what Indigenous people had said to him and he to them. He was especially concerned about their capacity for abstract thought. "I suppose it will be difficult to make the Indian understand the meaning of abstract terms," he wrote in the questionnaire's instructions.

"They can readily perceive that such a man may be a coward but the passion of fear, abstracted from its operation upon any person, may be beyond their comprehension." He needed to be sure, though, whether they possessed abstract thought. "An examination . . . of this subject, is not merely an inquiry into the language of the Indians," he wrote, "but it is also an examination into the state of their knowledge respecting the mind."[39]

The trigger for Cass's sudden shift from a strategic interest in the surveillance of Indians to an obsession with general knowledge about their culture and language was the 1819 publication of a volume of the *Transactions* of the venerable (for the United States) American Philosophical Society featuring the work of two men who became Cass's nemeses: John Heckewelder, a retired Moravian missionary, and Peter S. Du Ponceau, a lawyer with an interest in philology, both of them members of the society. While the bulk of the volume was taken up with Heckewelder's *Account of the History, Manners, and Customs of the Indian Natives Who Once Inhabited Pennsylvania and the Neighbouring States*, Du Ponceau contributed a general assessment of numerous vocabularies, dictionaries, and grammars of Indigenous languages held by the society, including those contributed by Heckewelder, and participated with Heckewelder in an epistolary dialogue on the subject of American Indian languages. These works shocked American intellectuals because they found that Indigenous people had orderly and happy societies, a low opinion of white people, and languages as sophisticated as ancient Greek.

Heckewelder became an assistant missionary to Christian Delawares in western Pennsylvania in 1762, when he was nineteen. During the revolution the British charged Heckewelder with treason for providing information to the Americans despite the Moravians' official neutrality; he escaped when a Delaware war chief, Captain Pipe, refused to testify against him and his fellow missionary David Zeisberger. While the two missionaries were held in Detroit, Americans attacked Gnadenhutten, a settlement that Heckewelder had helped to found, and slaughtered almost a hundred Delaware Moravian converts. After the revolution he continued his duties as a missionary; he was called upon a number of times to aid in treaty negotiations for land in the Ohio Valley. After his retirement in 1810 he devoted himself to writing and his studies of the Delaware language.[40]

Heckewelder's account at first glance seems to reiterate the usual ideas about Indigenous people. They didn't have governments, were awash in superstition, tended to be vengeful, and were overly fond of metaphors, which as far as Heckewelder was concerned were tasteless, as they occluded the truth.[41] It was in the details that Heckewelder departed from both his contemporaries and those who preceded him. While the Indians didn't have written laws, he noted, their societies were orderly, their chiefs supported by "experienced counsellors, men who study the welfare of the nation, and are equally interested with themselves in its prosperity."[42] Children were educated through example, such that "a strong attachment to ancient customs, respect for age, and the love of virtue are indelibly impressed upon the minds of youth."[43] Indians were physically strong and their medicines were on the whole successful, the result of their physicians' persistent efforts to hone their knowledge. Heckewelder himself had benefited from their medicines and sweat lodges, the last for "a stubborn rheumatism," and the wives of white missionaries had often "experienced good results" from the efforts of women physicians "for the cure of complaints peculiar to their sex."[44] Indians had compassion for the old and the ill, including the mentally ill; they took care of one another.[45] Though the marriages lasted only as long as both partners were willing, they were happy when they did, with each partner recognizing his or her duties. As for the common idea that there was little romantic love shown by Indians, Heckewelder himself had "known a man to go forty or fifty miles for a mess of cranberries to satisfy his wife's longing." Such demonstrations only increased a man's status in the community.[46] "It is a striking fact," Heckewelder observed, "that the Indians, in their uncivilized state, should so behave towards each other as though they were a civilized people!"[47]

Heckewelder found Indians to be generous, hospitable, kindhearted, and quite witty.[48] He was fond of their dances, and their songs were "not unpleasing."[49] He listened to their creation and other stories, and though he found them to be "ridiculous," he knew that Indians' "belief in them is not to be shaken."[50] The stories led him to wonder about "the curious connexion which appears to subsist in the mind of an Indian between man and the brute creation." While he struggled to understand this, he could at least say that they thought themselves "only the first among equals, the hereditary sovereigns of the whole animated race, of which they are themselves a constituent part." This relationship was reflected in their language: "Those inflections of their nouns which we call genders, are not, as with us, descriptive of the masculine and feminine species, but of the animate and inanimate kinds." They even "go so far as to include trees and plants within the first of these descriptions. All animated nature, in whatever degree, is in their eyes a great whole, from which they have not yet ventured to separate themselves. They do not exclude other animals from their world of spirits, the place to which they expect to go after death."[51]

Indians' desire for vengeance was not as dominant as was supposed and entirely understandable given their experiences with white people. They expected to be treated with "perfect equality," a point on which Americans typically foundered, occasionally to their great misfortune. Those who cursed Indians within their hearing and thought they could get away with it because they had spoken English were soon surprised by how much Indians knew. "Many white men have been ... put to death, who had brought their fate on themselves by their own imprudence," Heckewelder wrote.[52] Delawares considered whites deceitful as a race. They learned quickly that "kind speeches and even acts of apparent friendship do not always proceed from friendly motives, but that the bad spirit will sometimes lurk under the appearance of the good."[53]

They found inquisitive whites annoying and rude, never waiting for them to answer one question before jumping to the next. Because of this and especially when they were being asked about their "usages," many Delaware people were inclined to not exactly lie but to stretch the truth. "Nothing is further from their character" than lying, Heckewelder wrote; "but they are fond of the marvelous, and when they find a white man inclined to listen to their tales of wonder or credulous enough to believe their superstitious notions, there are always some among them ready to entertain him with tales of that description, as it gives them an opportunity of diverting themselves in their leisure hours, by relating such fabulous stories, while they laugh at the same time at their being able to deceive a people who think themselves so superior to them in wisdom and knowledge." Perhaps Heckewelder gained this knowledge from hard experience. He advised anyone who went into the Indian country and didn't know the language to feign indifference when anything involving "superstitions" came up so that the potential trickster would not easily spot his opportunity and, presumably, face would be saved.[54]

The conclusions most astonishing to American intellectuals were those made about Indigenous languages. Heckewelder's historical account touched on the issue, but Du Ponceau's report and the epistolary exchange between the two went into detail. Du Ponceau drew several conclusions from the material under review. Indigenous languages were "rich in words and grammatical forms" and "in their complicated construction, the greatest order, method, and regularity prevail." The languages were "polysynthetic," meaning speakers formed new words by compounding words and syllables. Finally, despite many years of speculation on the similarity of Indigenous languages to Hebrew (supposedly proving the idea that Indians were the descendants of a lost tribe of Israel), the languages "[differed] essentially" from "ancient and modern languages of the old hemisphere."[55] Heckewelder's examples from the Delaware "would rather appear to have been formed by philosophers in their closets, than by savages in the wilderness." How this could possibly be true of savages, he had no idea. "I have been ordered to collect and ascertain facts, not build theories," he wrote; "there remains a great deal yet to be ascertained, before we can venture to search into remote causes."[56]

The correspondence began in April 1816, when Heckewelder forwarded David Zeisberger's Delaware grammar to Du Ponceau in Philadelphia, and it continued until October of that year as Heckewelder finished his account of his missionary work and Du Ponceau wrote his report. While Du Ponceau quickly became impressed with the complexity he found in the languages (a complexity that only Americans could perceive, because Europeans were hopelessly prejudiced), it took several months for him to truly understand what he was looking at.[57] In July, Heckewelder wrote that Du Ponceau had not yet grasped the "copiousness of the Indian languages, which possess an immense number of comprehensive words, expressive of almost every possible combination of ideas."[58] In Delaware and other Indigenous languages with which he was acquainted, the compounding of words or parts of words could be "multiplied without end, and hence the peculiar richness of the American languages."[59] "Horse" is *nanayunges* in Delaware, formed from *awesis*, a beast, and *nayundam*, to carry a burden on the back or shoulders (as distinct from in the hands or arms). "The word which signifies 'horse' ... literally means, 'the beast which carries on its back,' or in other words a 'beast of burden,'" Heckewelder wrote. "Were asses or camels known to the Indians, distinctive appellations for them would soon and easily be formed."[60] Indigenous people could always account for new things in their own languages.

It was the verb, "truly the *word* by way of excellence," that finally opened Du Ponceau's eyes. "It combines itself with the pronoun, with the adjective, with the adverb; in short almost every part of speech," he wrote; "there are forms both positive and negative which include the two pronouns, the governing and the governed; *ktahoatell*, 'I love thee'; *ktahoalowi*, 'I do not love thee.' The adverb 'not,' is comprised both actively and passively in the negative forms, *n'dahoalawi*, 'I do not love'; *n'dahoallgussiwi*, "I am not loved'; and other adverbs are combined in a similar manner."[61] "Every verb has a long series of participles," he wrote, "which when necessary can be declined and used as adjectives":

Wulamalessohaluwed, he who makes happy
Wulamalessohalid, he who makes me happy
Wulamalessohalquon, he who makes thee happy

Wulamalessohalat, he who makes him happy

Wulamalessohalquenk, he who makes us happy
Wulamalessohalqueek, he who makes you happy
Wulamalessohalquichtit, he who makes them happy.[62]

"Now comes another participial-pronominal-vocative form; which may in the same manner be conjugated through all the objective persons. Wulamalessohalian! THOU WHO MAKEST ME HAPPY!"[63]

"It is with the greatest difficulty that I can guard myself against enthusiastic feelings," wrote Du Ponceau; "what would Tibullus or Sappho have given to have had at their command a word at once so tender and expressive?"[64] "How delighted would be Moore, the poet of loves and graces, if his language, instead of five or six tedious words slowly following in the rear of each other, had furnished him with an expression like this, in this which the love, the object beloved, and the delicious sentiment which their mutual passion inspires, are blended, are fused together in one comprehensive appellative term?"[65] The beauty of the language was in its capacity "to raise at once in the mind by a few magic sounds, whole masses of thoughts which strike by a kind of instantaneous intuition." "Such in its effects must be the medium by which immortal spirits communicate with each other," he wrote, "such, I should think were I disposed to indulge in fanciful theories, must have been the language first taught to mankind by the great author of all perfection."[66] The sad thing was that, once it had been established that the American Indian languages operated on the same synthetic principles as Latin and Greek, "philosophers" had decided that "the beautiful organisation of those languages" should be "[ascribed] . . . to stupidity and barbarism," and rather than "to acknowledge our ignorance. . . . Philosophers have therefore set themselves to work in order to prove that those admirable combinations of ideas in the form of words, which in the ancient languages of Europe used to be considered as some of the greatest efforts of the human mind, proceed in the savage idioms from the absence or weakness of mental powers in those who originally framed them."[67] Du Ponceau had to have known that this was how his and Heckewelder's findings would be received.

A response came immediately, in the form of two articles in the *North American Review* written by John Pickering, another philologist-lawyer, this time in Boston. Pickering was a member of the American Academy of Arts and Sciences who'd written on the state of the English language in the United States and on the pronunciation of Greek; he was soon to become recognized as an authority on American Indian languages. He considered the history in one article and the correspondence in another. After expressing skepticism about the accounts the Delawares gave of their origins and a long excerpt on their first meeting with Henry Hudson (their origin in English consciousness), Pickering considered their general disdain for white people. "It is undeniable that the settlement of the Europeans in this country has produced a ruin and almost total extinction of the ancient people," Pickering began, but that was their own fault. They had every right to sell their land, and when they did, if Americans made out much better for the purchase, it certainly wasn't because of any dishonesty on Americans' part. It was a free exchange, conducted in an entirely unexceptional manner, and the difference in outcomes was because of Americans' superior moral character. "It is the certain consequence of industry, enterprise and skill, to prevail over indolence and ignorance," he wrote.[68] Americans' acquisition of Indigenous land was natural, and it was also natural that Indians would "regard the settlement of the Europeans in this country, and the establishment of an empire, rich in industry, knowledge and virtue, on the ruins of their nation, as the greatest of human calamities." They were jealous. Their situation was not anyone's fault but their own, however; "their decay and ruin are to be ascribed to their own mode of life, and not to injustice and rapacity in those who knew better than they how to improve the bounties of providence."[69]

Pickering then observed that Heckewelder's account "abounds in facts and anecdotes," both entertaining and revealing, "in the most authentic and satisfactory manner, the character and condition of this people." Pickering's compartmentalizing is impressive. "There is no work upon the North American Indians which can bear any comparison with it for the means of correct information possessed by the author, or for the copiousness of its details," he observed.[70] Only after he contained Heckewelder within the overarching narrative of civilization's triumph over savagery could Pickering turn his attention to what Heckewelder said, which he could assimilate as discrete facts unfortunately distorted by Heckewelder's obvious prejudices.

The implications of Heckewelder's and Du Ponceau's findings on Indigenous languages were more difficult to contain. Of those findings, Pickering could only say that he was "astonished," although, because he was a regional chauvinist, he pointed out that Roger Williams and other early New England writers had come to similar conclusions years previously, even if those conclusions had been ignored in Europe.[71] He continued worrying the problem in an 1820 review of Samuel Farmer Jarvis's *Discourse on the Religion of the Indian Tribes of North America*, noting Jarvis's conclusions about the complexity of the Cherokee language as well as the unlikelihood that it was in any way connected to Hebrew, thus undermining the lost tribes theory and reinforcing Heckewelder and Du Ponceau. "This extraordinary profusion of grammatical forms in the languages of the Indian, is indeed a most curious and interesting subject of investigation for philologists," wrote Pickering, "nor is it less a subject of surprise with those persons, who have been accustomed to consider the Indian languages as so poor and barren that they do but just answer the most necessary purposes of life, to be informed of the great number of words which they use to express the same action when applied to different objects."[72] He couldn't deny what he saw.

At the time, what's been called the "political conception" of language dominated Western thought. In this, language was the expression of the nation—to understand the language was to understand the character of the people who spoke it. A "mechanical conception" of language that theorized the possibility of a universal grammar was gaining adherents however. These scholars were uninterested in the society and the beliefs of a language's speakers but rather focused on the forms of the language itself.[73] "If we wish to study human speech as a science, just as we do other sciences," Pickering wrote in his review of Jarvis, "by ascertaining all the facts or phenomena, and then proceeding to generalize and class those facts for the purpose of advancing human knowledge; in short, if what is called philosophical grammar is of any use whatever, then it is indispensable to the philologist of comprehensive views, to possess a knowledge of as many facts or phenomena of language as possible; and these neglected dialects of our own continent certainly do offer to the philosophical inquirer some of the most curious and interesting facts with which we are acquainted."[74] Pickering rescued himself from Indigenous humanity by positioning their languages as strings of facts related to other facts in support of a theory that didn't have to do with them in particular. After this review Wilhelm von Humbolt, an adherent of the new approach to philology, wrote to Pickering about their mutual interests, and then Du Ponceau, drawn to the idea of a universal grammar, joined them in pursuit of the new theory, putting an end to his previous enthusiasms.[75]

The demonstration of a language's sophistication for Pickering and for Du Ponceau was its literature, but as far as Pickering was concerned there was no point in even investigating the subject, because savages couldn't have one. (Despite expostulating on the aesthetic potential in the Delaware language, Du Ponceau didn't have anything to say about the existence of a literary tradition.) "What use is it to examine the structure of languages in which there is no literature to compensate us for our labour?"[76] Pickering asked. But both he and Du Ponceau would certainly have known that investigation into oral traditions of both ancient and "primitive" people was a well-established pursuit in Britain by the late eighteenth century. Alexander Pope translated the *Iliad* and the *Odyssey* at the beginning of the eighteenth century and William Cowper at the end; English ballad collections began to appear by midcentury. Theorists held that songs, poetry, and narratives could reveal both the history of literature and the history of the societies in which that literature was produced.

James Macpherson's work on Ossian began in the late 1750s, when a group of Edinburgh intellectuals, most prominent among them Hugh Blair, soon to be professor of rhetoric and belles lettres at the University of Edinburgh, "virtually commissioned" Macpherson to produce a translation of the ancient Scottish stories written down in medieval manuscripts and still told in some communities. Macpherson was a poet and native speaker of Gaelic; he'd known local *seanchaidhean* or storytellers as a child and grown up conscious of the threat of encroaching Anglicization, especially its threat to the survival of the Gaelic language.[77] He published *Fragments of Ancient Poetry* in 1760, followed by *Fingal, an Ancient Epic Poem in Six Books, together with Several Other Poems composed by Ossian, the Son of Fingal, translated from the Gaelic Language* in 1761, and *Temora* in 1763, all of which were collected as *The Works of Ossian* in 1765.[78] Though Samuel Johnson denounced the Ossian poems as inauthentic, they became immediately popular in Scotland, Germany, France, and Scandinavia and continued to be popular through the late eighteenth century and into the nineteenth. Irish intellectuals, both Catholic and Protestant, dismissed Macpherson's claim that the poems were of Scottish origin, arguing (rightly) that the traditions were in fact Irish, part of the Fenian cycle of pre-Christian oral traditions that Irish emigrants brought to the Scottish Highlands. Despite the controversy, by the 1780s, writes one scholar, "Ossian . . . could no longer be ignored or dismissed."[79]

Poetry arose from primitive societies rather than from civilized ones, according to Hugh Blair. Men of those societies spoke in a manner "picturesque and figurative" and were capable of producing "some of the highest beauties of poetical writing." "The powers of imagination are most vigorous and predominant in youth; those of understanding ripen more slowly, and often attain not their maturity, till the imagination begin to flag," he wrote; "poetry, which is the child of imagination, is frequently most glowing and animated in the first stages of society." Therefore "we may expect to find poems among the antiquities of all nations, even among Indians," who were often compared to Highlanders in the eighteenth century. "An American chief, at this day, harangues at the head of his tribe, in a more bold metaphorical style, than a modern European would adventure to use in an Epic poem," Blair observed.[80] It should have been a fairly obvious scientific thing to do then, once the capacities of Indigenous languages became clear, to, possibly, send someone like James Macpherson to write down the songs and stories in those languages and then translate them, to see what they offered, no matter how primitive they supposedly were.

Instead, in the early nineteenth-century United States, "Indian poetry" referred to stereotypical eloquent speech, particularly when the white writer sought to mock it. "Indian story" was seldom if ever used, and "Indian tradition" referred to the accounts that Indigenous people gave of their historical origins, the origins of place names or beliefs about places, and accounts of historical curiosities. Heckewelder published an account of a rattlesnake monster told by a Delaware man that circulated in newspapers and other books in the late eighteenth and early nineteenth centuries.[81] These stories were usually very brief and presented not for the story itself but the fact about primitive Indians that it illuminated. Indian "tales" or "legends" that proliferated in magazines and newspapers were invariably stories by Americans about Indians that retold the story of Indians' inevitable and natural demise or demonstrated how much they needed to be converted to Christianity before meeting said natural demise.[82]

"Are they in the practice of telling stories?" Lewis Cass asked in his questionnaire. The fact that he asked the question in the first place probably indicates that, in addition to the Johnstons' writing, he knew that an oral narrative tradition did exist because he had heard evidence of it. If so, he also likely perceived that Pickering's dismissal of Du Ponceau and Heckewelder's conclusions about the sophistication of Indigenous languages on the supposed absence of a literary tradition potentially had a serious weakness. No one had actually looked for it. Cass considered himself an intellectual man. He was a graduate of Phillips Academy in Massachusetts; when he traveled by canoe on his many treaty-making trips, he carried a "well selected, through necessarily small library," from which one of his acolytes read aloud as the voyageurs paddled along.[83] His pursuit of Indigenous knowledge was like his pursuit of Sassaba into the Ojibwe village. He would not allow himself to believe that those people were possessed of an intellectual life, and the evidence that they were so possessed enraged him. He sought stories because their potential existence threatened to demonstrate that he was wrong about Indians' savagery, and he had to satisfy himself that that was not the case. But then he started receiving the stories, and he was drawn in and charmed by what stories do, make you want to know what happens, make you want to hear another.

"I wish the young ladies would employ all their leisure hours in providing me with specimens of aboriginal belles lettres," he wrote on receipt of Schoolcraft's first installment of stories in May 1823. He thanked Schoolcraft for his "able and satisfactory" analysis of the language (neither of them had any philological training of which to speak), but he was more interested in the stories. "Those which I have received have rendered me anxious for more, and I should esteem the favour beyond all others which could be rendered to me."[84] Since neither Eliza nor Charlotte was interested in writing and Schoolcraft habitually hid the extent of Jane's work for him in his collections, it was likely the case that it was only Jane's writing that Cass had seen. There's a manic quality to his correspondence with Schoolcraft at this time that's absent from his official and other personal correspondence. He always wanted more but complained about what he got; the more information he got, the more overwhelmed he became. "My Indian materials have so increased upon my hands, that I am frightened of their bulk," he wrote to Schoolcraft, "and yet I am greedy to add to them as a miser to increase his riches."⁸⁵ This state of mind couldn't have been helped when Schoolcraft sent Jane's translation into Ojibwemowin of an extensive list of sentences designed to show the nonexistence of Indigenous abstract thought ("We conquered our country by our bravery, and we will defend it with our strength"). It turned out that Ojibwes did perfectly well on the test.⁸⁶

Cass's agitated accumulation of information about Indians had a larger context. In February 1823, the Supreme Court handed down its decision on *Johnson v. McIntosh*, a decision Cass knew in detail, as it established the United States' claim to ownership of Indigenous land on assertions about the kind of people Indigenous people were, exactly the topic of Cass's researches.⁸⁷ Chief Justice John Marshall's rewriting of the "discovery" of the Western Hemisphere is at the center of the decision. First, he argued, European nations maintained from the beginning that they had absolute title to the land only temporarily occupied by Indigenous nations because Indians' "character and religion . . . afforded an apology for considering them as a people over whom the superior genius of Europe might claim an ascendancy." Furthermore, European nations had made "ample compensation" to Indian nations for all that land "by bestowing on them civilization and Christianity."⁸⁸ According to Marshall, Europeans—who like the Americans after them benevolently didn't "entirely disregard" the rights of Indigenous people—owned all that land from the moment they saw it from their ships offshore.⁸⁹

He didn't invoke the usual story about purchasing Indian land fairly through treaties, and he explicitly rejected the Lockean argument that commercial agriculture established property in land. Instead, he talked about conquest, which had the advantage of sounding decisive while being vague. "Conquest gives a title which the courts of the conqueror cannot deny, whatever the private and speculative opinions of individuals may be, respecting the original justice of the claim which has been successfully asserted," he declared.⁹⁰ The United States didn't even have control of its claimed territory east of the Mississippi in 1823; how could merely getting a bead on a shadow of land in the distance translate to ownership? The only conquest Marshall could have had in mind is the imaginary conquest of civilized over savage. "The tribes of Indians inhabiting this country were fierce savages, whose occupation was war, and whose subsistence was drawn chiefly from the forest," he continued. "To leave them in possession of their country, was to leave the country a wilderness; to govern them as a distinct people, was impossible, because they were as brave and as high-spirited as they were fierce, and were ready to repel by arms every attempt on their independence."⁹¹ The Europeans could "relinquish their pompous claims" to the land or stand and fight the savage menace. But at the same time that

Indians were fiercely defending their land and menacing benevolent whites, resisting the inevitable, they also naturally "receded," following the animals on which they entirely depended farther west "into thicker and more unbroken forests."[92] The contradiction didn't matter, because the point was savages were going to die in the face of civilization, one way or another, and good white Christians owned that land regardless of whether or not they had possession of it.

It did not escape Cass that *Johnson* made the savage the legal as well as moral justification for American ownership of land.[93] From the moment he started collecting, his object was to demonstrate that that savage was real because he wanted it to be and now, with this case, he needed it to be. But then the questionnaires, however haphazardly answered, started coming in; the information was too much, and much of what it did convey was similar to if not the same as what Heckewelder had said himself. Cass tried collecting his own information to counterbalance what he'd received, for example, asking that a shaking tent ceremony be performed for him. He gave this information to Henry Whiting, a US Army captain in Detroit, to publish in the notes for his narrative poem on doomed seventeenth-century Erie lovers, *Ontwa: The Son of the Forest* (New York, 1822). The ceremony was used for divination and occurred in public. In it, a healer constructed a lodge of saplings covered with skins, drawn tight to form a pyramid shape, the saplings a particular number and each a different kind of wood. Then, covered in cloth and bound up tightly, the healer was placed in the lodge and the spirits would answer questions and speak to him or her.[94] "Immediately ... the poles were violently agitated," Cass wrote, "and he began a monotonous recitation, which I understood to be an invocation to the evil spirit to make his appearance." (All spirits were evil spirits according to Cass and other American writers, including Schoolcraft.) It was announced "that the evil spirit was about to appear," and then the spectators heard a voice from the lodge. The healer "changed as much as possible the tone of his voice, and spoke at one time close to the ground, and at another, at the greatest height he could attain," but "the deception was so gross, and the whole ceremony so tedious and uninteresting, that I retired without waiting for the termination."[95]

After this failed attempt at field work, Cass petitioned Calhoun for a researcher, which permission was given. Cass appointed Charles Christopher Trowbridge and sent him to Indiana to research the Indians there over the winter of 1823–24; he returned the subsequent winter.[96] Like Cass and Schoolcraft the son of a revolutionary veteran, Trowbridge was born at Albany in 1800; after his father died when he was young, he was indentured to a merchant. He arrived in Detroit to make his fortune on the first steamboat to cross Lake Erie, in 1819. Cass discovered him while he was working for the US

Marshal in Detroit and added him to his 1820 expedition as assistant topographer, the beginning of several years spent as Cass's protégé. When the expedition returned to Detroit, Cass appointed him an interpreter (he spoke no Indigenous languages, having been in the West a little over a year) as well as assistant secretary and accountant to himself.[97] He sent Trowbridge to Green Bay, Saginaw, and New York City on Indian business, among other things, and then off to Indiana.[98]

The stories Trowbridge sent to Cass have not survived. None of them would have survived if Trowbridge hadn't found copies of eleven of them while rummaging in his office in 1874. By then he was a rich man, having gone into banking in 1825 and railroads after that, although he still lived in the house he had built for his new wife in 1826, after he left Cass's service.[99] He feared, he wrote Lyman Draper, the head of the Wisconsin Historical Society to whom he sent the stories for safekeeping, that no one would appreciate them. Some might question the authenticity of similar tales published by Schoolcraft because "they flow so smoothly, and some of them have so much plot, that it would not be surprising if the readers of Schoolcraft thought his pen had been used to give grace or point." But that was how the stories were told in his presence, through the aid of "an honest and intelligent Interpreter."[100]

In "The Gambler or The Man without Eyes," a blind man who hunted guided by "three small birds fastened to each arm" defeated a gambler in a series of hunting contests, then freed the people the gambler had enslaved.[101] In "The Red Head," the main character, a beautiful young man, impregnated Itchwoman, who was ugly until he killed her and she returned to life—twice—as she pursued him with their son. Eventually she was turned into a shell and he, finally regretting what he'd done, became a blue jay.[102] The one story Trowbridge wrote down that can be attributed to a particular tribe is "The Star Woman," a Shawnee story about a hunter named Waupee M'skwoalonyaa or White Hawk, who falls in love with the youngest of twelve sisters, the Alark Oakwaakee or Star Women, who descend from the sky world to play ball on the prairie. After much tribulation he goes to the sky world with her to live, where they and their son are transformed into white hawks.[103] Cass himself helped to transcribe—badly—a story about an old man who lived on lichen and who chased a group of twelve young women out of their home and into the trees, where they transformed themselves into ducks, who then "flew away, leaving the old fellow to run along the bank in the form of a wolf, howling and crying bitterly at his disaster."[104]

These stories were the last thing Cass expected out of the savages he so reviled. There wasn't much to which they could be compared in the early nineteenth century. The fairy tales of the seventeenth- and eighteenth-century French writers were literary inventions; the German folk tales that the Grimm brothers were beginning to publish (the first edition appeared in 1812) weren't translated into English until 1821, and the book was rarely noticed in the United States before the 1840s. None of these kinds of stories featured the proliferation of spirits and the transformation of humans to the degree that Indigenous stories did. Cass was in possession of Jane's early stories and possibly other stories written by her and now lost before he sent Trowbridge on his mission. Her object when they were written was to demonstrate the literariness of Ojibwemowin and Anishinaabe narrative in English because it pleased her to do so. Cass's anxiety about "belles lettres" was the result. His use of the term might have been mockery in whole or in part, but it also exposed the problem. From the beginning of his researches, Indians were more than what he wanted or indeed needed them to be. They were too human, and he didn't know what to do about it.

Chapter 3

Of Mrs. Schoolcraft, You Have Heard

In the spring of 1824 a man named Kewaynokwut or Passing Cloud was so ill that he vowed if he survived he would lead a war party against the Dakotas. When he did survive, in early summer he and twenty-eight men made their way from their village on the Ontonagan River near the present border between Wisconsin and Michigan, down the Flambeau and Chippewa Rivers to Lake Pepin on the Mississippi, heading into Dakota territory. When they arrived at the lake there were signs of an encampment. Kewaynokwut sent a few men in to investigate under cover of darkness and fog; they found four white traders, an American named Finley and three French Canadians, one of whom spoke Ojibwemowin. Once the white men recovered themselves, Kewaynokwut said there was no cause for alarm; they only wanted to know if there were any Dakota warriors in the vicinity. There were—about thirty, headed east toward Prairie du Chien. Kewaynokwut decided that thirty Dakotas were too many and called off the expedition. But his men wanted to fight. They stripped the traders of their meager food supplies (half a bag of flour, half a bag of corn, a few biscuits) and then, disappointed in that haul, their clothes. Cacabichin (Screech Owl), Ocwaygan (the Track), Kawawbandebay (the White head), and Waymitiggoashance (Little Frenchman) wanted to kill the traders; Sagetoo (The Man Who Makes Fearful) said, according to George Johnston, who got the story from some of its participants, "Why have we come here? Is it not to kill?" The agitators opened fire, dispatching three of the traders. The fourth, who'd been trying to retrieve papers from the plundered goods, threw himself into the lake up to his neck. Little Thunder killed him with a second shot, then cut off his head so that he could scalp it. The party took its four scalps and "danced & sang and recited their brave actions" from Green Bay to the south shore of Lake Superior for several weeks.[1] When they reached L'Ance Keewaywenon, John Holiday took exception and informed Schoolcraft of what had happened.[2]

Holiday arrived at the Sault at the end of August 1824 bearing a black box with just one scalp inside. Schoolcraft forwarded the "scalp-coffin" to Cass with an embroidered tale of its history. He made the war party bigger by a dozen and gave the traders a full load of goods; he turned all of the traders into Americans and gave them a flag planted in their encampment, outrageously violated; and finally he had the Indians sneak up on the unsuspecting traders in the night in order to kill them in their beds.[3]

The Schoolcrafts, Anna Maria (aged ten), and a nursemaid who may have been Lewis's daughter Sophia spent the winter of 1824–25 in New York City. Schoolcraft had picked fights with two consecutive commanders at Fort Brady, and Cass thought he should get out of the village for a season.[4] He was also eager to see them when they stopped to visit him and his family along the way. "I am anxious you should bring with you when you come down, your collection of Indian tales &c. I shall be happy to see them," he'd written to Schoolcraft in May, warning him to "not let them go out of your hands." "You know how easily such things get abroad," he added, "and their originality in fact constitutes half their value."[5]

Cass lived close by the Detroit River, near an old fort and along a road crossing several ancient mounds that regularly gave up their bones, by erosion or pillage. The house had been built by Detroit's founder, the fur trader Antoine de la Mothe Cadillac, over a hundred years since and was later occupied by a Huron chief. Its walls were clapboarded cedar logs; it had dormer windows and a front porch made from a former gazebo but several imposing rooms, including an entry saloon housing Cass's museum. This included portraits of Indian chiefs on the walls and pipes, snowshoes, bows and arrows, and medals, presumably British and French, scattered about.[6] What kind of pleasure he derived from the portraits staring down at him can only be surmised.

He must have liked what they brought. He wrote to Schoolcraft in December with more plans and advice, his spirits even more frenetic than usual because his youngest child had died after the Schoolcrafts left Detroit and he was trying to occupy himself in his grief. Instead of producing a government report with his collections, he decided to make his "entre upon the literary stage" by using his "immense labyrinth of material" to produce an account of the history, conditions, and prospects of the Indians of the Great Lakes and northern Mississippi. This would be relatively brief "in order to feel the publick pulse" and include only two chapters on languages because the study of languages was "so laborious, and will require so much time." More to the public taste, he hoped, would be the inclusion of several tales and a "consideration of [Indians'] progress in belles lettres." "What think you of Indian belles lettres?" he asked, again. Trowbridge had forwarded a "rich mine" of Shawnee stories. Some of the stories "rival the exuberance of eastern imaginations," he added, and he thought the stories "reflect great light upon their traditions, mythological opinions, and . . . manners and customs."[7]

Cass was beginning to get a fix on how to think about the stories, one that became common over the next few years. These newly discovered Indian stories were like the stories in *The Arabian Nights*, he and many others thought. First translated into French by the orientalist scholar Antoine Galland in the early eighteenth century and translated into English soon thereafter, *The Arabian Nights Entertainments* became wildly popular and remained so through the eighteenth and nineteenth centuries. By the beginning of the nineteenth century, eighteen English editions had been published, and the stories "Ali Baba and the Forty Thieves," "Aladdin, or the Wonderful Lamp," and "Sinbad the Sailor" were often separately printed for children in Britain and the United States.[8] Contemporary scholars have wondered why, in the midst of the Enlightenment and during a period in which the moral education of children was of great concern in Britain and the United States, a book like *The Arabian Nights* was so popular.[9] Galland himself expected it to be read for what he construed as its revelation of the manners and customs of the East.[10] But the reading public valued the stories for their "magic," Marina Warner writes, despite the grumblings of some critics about the dangers of the supernatural.[11] The stories featured powerful spirits, human transformation, and talking animals—this seems to have been the connection to Anishinaabe stories. If Anishinaabe stories didn't involve the luxury and eroticism of *The Arabian Nights*, they did offer a similar escape from rationality and a vision of a fantasy world. Later the problem would be that the spirits were real and the Anishinaabe world was no fantasy and furthermore that world was close by if not right there, but as an initial account of what the Johnston stories looked like, *The Arabian Nights* almost always sprang to mind.

Cass warned Schoolcraft again to keep his stories close: "I am anxious you should not suffer yours to go out of your hands, because first impressions are everything."[12] It's one of the many disappointments of the archives to not know what Jane Schoolcraft thought about Cass and his fixation. She would have known to be suspicious of a man whose enthusiasm for gobbling up information didn't in any way obscure his disdain for the people from whom that information came. But her husband admired that "truly great and excellent man."[13] Cass in turn felt the responsibility of training Schoolcraft up, given his lack of education. He advised Schoolcraft not to risk his "high reputation . . . upon ill digested materials or careless works."[14] As he pumped Schoolcraft for more and more information, Cass encouraged Schoolcraft's ambitions. Schoolcraft ought to look into the possibility of going to Europe. "You might easily perceive some reason to execute your studies. . . . I think there would be no difficulty in procuring permission from the Government. I see incalculable advantage which would result to you from it, and you would go under very favourable auspices and with a rich harvest of literary fame."[15]

Jane Johnston Schoolcraft, artist unknown (ca. 1825). Box 1, Johnston Family Papers, 1822–1936, Bentley Historical Library, University of Michigan, Ann Arbor, Michigan.

In New York it was Jane who was known. Previous to their arrival, the Reverend Laird had written about Jane in the evangelical newspapers, noting that she was "a half breed and wife to the Indian agent" who'd translated the Lord's Prayer into "the Chippawa dialect" and planned on translating scripture too.[16] This information seems to have circulated in New York City ahead of the Schoolcrafts' arrival because, as Schoolcraft recounted it in his *Personal Memoirs* (1855), there was a great deal of interest in Jane herself, as "a person of Indian descent, and of refined manner and education . . . with an infant son of more than ordinary beauty of lineament and mental promise." People they didn't know came to their boarding house to visit. "There was something like a sensation in every circle and often persons, whose curiosity was superior to their moral capacity of appreciation, looked intensely to see the northern Pocahontas."[17]

After a lecture on silver deposits in the Lake Ontario region at the New-York Lyceum of Natural History, Schoolcraft met Samuel Conant, a lawyer and newspaper editor who wanted to save the "noble but persecuted race" of

Indians.[18] Conant invited Jane to stay with him and his wife at their house on the Bloomingdale Road in what was then the northern outskirts of the city while Schoolcraft went down to Washington. Conant and his wife were devotees of "nature untrammelled with fashion & unsophisticated with arts," and they thought they had a "true heart" in common with Jane. They called William Henry the "little American Eagle."[19] Conant was planning his own Indian-themed periodical and wanted both Schoolcraft and Jane to contribute, which indicates that Jane was known as—or spoke of herself as—a writer, not just as a translator of scripture.[20] In the meantime Cass kept writing to Schoolcraft, wanting more books: Hakluyt, Colden, Bartram, several writers on Florida despite what he'd said his topic was; the chief justice's history of the United States, and French books from Montreal.[21]

Schoolcraft narrated his trip as if Jane were a captured Indian chief on tour, illustrating the power and might of the United States as he made his way south to the capital. From New York he traveled to Perth Amboy, New Brunswick, Princeton, Trenton, the Delaware River, Bristol, and eventually Renshaw's Mansion House, Philadelphia, in fourteen hours. "I have given you a rapid sketch of my route, & the principal places past; which I hope may not be altogether useless in fixing in your mind the principal features & divisions of our very extensive & diversified country." He went on, the next day, by coach to Chester, Wilmington, and Newport and on to Elkton and Havre de Grace at the head of Chesapeake Bay, traveling 110 miles in twenty-seven hours. Then on to Baltimore and Barnum's Mansion House, which, he noted, was "kept by the *father* a certain officer at the *Sault*." "Can you forgive all this dry detail?" he asked. He couldn't help himself. Surveying the nation's power had him ruminating on fatherhood as well. Sometimes the "feelings, pleasures and anxieties" of it overwhelmed him. "We can never be sufficiently thankful to God for the gift of so fine a child," he wrote; "how ardently do I hope that our sweet, interesting little boy will be permitted to grow up to man's estate, and answer my prayers that he shall become virtuous and possess understanding."[22]

He visited members of Congress and dined "en famielle [sic]" with Calhoun, lobbying him for a house at Sault Ste. Marie with which to impress the Indians.[23] Jane wrote to say she'd accepted the Conants' offer knowing that he would have wanted her to, despite "how loath I am to leave my *den*, but for your sake I did." "I am sure you will be pleased to hear from me so soon after your safe journey and a welcome to the metropolis of your country," she added. It wasn't until she'd received all of his letters and he was almost on his way home that she realized her mistake. "I feel grateful to you for your kind solicitude about my health, & at the same time that you have not lost sight of what may tend to improve me," she wrote then. "I mean the geography of the country; for tho' I cannot boast of having seen with my own eyes, that interesting portion you have passed, yet I can form a pretty good idea of its richness, beauty & situation from your having so kindly described your route, & I hope you will be pleased to find that your instruction is not quite thrown away." She didn't say anything about whose country they were talking about. Regardless of her husband's less-than-interesting habit, she waited anxiously for his return. "Your absence is almost insupportable to me & my lonely hours are spent in sighs & the unbidden tear steals frequently down my cheek, even when I wish most to suppress or smother my feelings," she wrote, like a heroine in a sentimental novel. "Such a sense of unprotected loneliness creeps over my mind that it is impossible to withstand or control them, especially when I hear our lonely, helpless infant calling on his far distant *absent* Father."

Jane would use the children to remind Schoolcraft of his obligation to his family, including herself, throughout their marriage, often depicting them calling on him or crying for his presence. Willie was not even a year old at the time. At the beginning her fear seems to have been that, like many of the white fur traders who married into Indigenous families, Schoolcraft would leave her and her children whenever he decided that he was finished with that part of his life.[24] But her anxiety was entirely misplaced; she was increasingly necessary to his plans for himself, most of which centered on his claimed expertise in Indian languages. In *Travels in the Central Portions of the Mississippi Valley*, an account of Cass's 1820 tour for which he found a publisher in New York that winter, he set out the idea to which he stuck for the rest of his life that languages were "the only standards which can be depended on" for an account of Indian history, Indians themselves being unable to narrate it.[25] Hypothetically this approach established authority over Indigenous languages without dealing too closely, if at all, with what Indigenous people had to say in those languages, similarly to the philologists' interest in discovering a universal grammar. And fortunately for himself, Jane gave Schoolcraft the advantage over everyone else who might put themselves forward as an expert. Every plan he had for his own authority and success depended on her; whatever he said to her, he couldn't imagine a future without her.

He was in the habit of reminding Jane of her subordination to himself. Occasionally he embedded his own stories in a collection of the Johnstons' without identifying it as his own; inevitably the stories were directed at Jane. In the midst of the excerpts from the Johnstons' postwar anthologies in *Travels in the Central Portions of the Mississippi Valley*, he included his story, "Love and War," about the chief Wawanosh, his daughter, and her poverty-stricken suitor. Wawanosh (he took the name from a tribal leader in Sarnia, Upper Canada, and would use it as a persona over the years) was "tall and commanding," and had "dazzling qualities of great personal strength, courage, and activity"; he was a great hunter but also a great sage, and everyone sought his counsel.[26] His beautiful daughter "had now lived to witness the budding of the leaves for the eighteenth spring," he wrote, "Indian"-style. She was much celebrated for "her gentle virtues, her slender form, her beaming eyes, and her dark and flowing hair."

"Where is there a warrior who does not wish he may some day be equal in bravery to Wawanosh?" asked Wawanosh of the young man; "have you not also heard that my fathers came from the far east, decked with plumes and clothed with authority?" He commanded the suitor to "go . . . and earn a name for yourself" before he would allow his daughter to marry, and so the young man got his reluctant friends together to go off on an expedition against an unnamed enemy. This gave Schoolcraft an opening to demonstrate his expertise in manners and customs, as he describes their arrows ("tipped with flint or jasper"), their pemmican, their dance, and their song: "The eagles scream on high, / They whet their forked beaks; / Raise—Raise the battle cry, / 'Tis fame our leader seeks."[27] The suitor—Schoolcraft didn't give him or the daughter names—told the daughter that the worst part of her father's denunciations was his "imputations of effeminacy and cowardice" and that whatever happened he would always love her.[28] While he "distinguished himself by the most heroic bravery," being an Indian he of course died, and on hearing this the daughter "[flew] to a sequestered spot in the woods, where she would sit under a shady tree, and sing her mournful laments for whole hours together." This was Jane's poem "Oh how can I sing the praise of my love."[29] Then she died.

Schoolcraft's Indian stories always followed the American model. Indian chiefs were brave and noble savages, except when they were savage savages; Indian maidens were beautiful and meek; and at the end of the story everybody died—no one ever got turned into stars or wolves or hawks. Jane was the bereft and dead Indian maiden in the story, he told her later, although she probably didn't need to be told.[30] Because the very things that made him an expert, gaining him authority if not directly money, were undeniably hers, he represented her back to herself as incapacitated to the point of death by his potential absence. For the succeeding years of their marriage, they remained at an impasse. She remained fearful that he didn't love her and their children and he remained fearful of her knowledge, she using his neglect of herself and the children as a rebuke, betraying increasing anger at her situation, and he using the threat of withdrawing his love as leverage for her compliance with his wishes, whatever they happened to be.

Travels received an early notice from the *New York Review and Atheneum Magazine*. The writer was generally supportive of Schoolcraft's mineralogical observations and promised to take up the matter of the Ojibwe materials at a later date, but made what would become the usual complaints about Schoolcraft's style for the duration of his career. He moralized; he had a "curious habit... of taking sudden and startling leaps, from politics to poetry, from rhyme to mineralogy, from trilobytes to trochees, and so back again, by way of stanzas and statistics." Schoolcraft should "forget his Shenstone, his Goldsmith, and his Pope; his Damaetas, his Anon, his MSS, and his Old Play."[31] The list is a trace of the Johnston library. By the time this review appeared in July, the family had returned to the Sault after first stopping to visit Schoolcraft's family near Albany, New York. They brought Schoolcraft's younger brother and sister, James and Maria, with them, leaving Maria Schoolcraft in Detroit to pass the coming winter with friends before coming up in the next spring.

Lewis had died at Amherstberg before they returned. He last wrote Jane in February, a letter she may not have received before she left New York. There is very little of Lewis in the surviving family papers, and what does exist indicates more than anything else constant concern about what had happened to him or what he was doing. He wrote to Jane, with the enthusiasm of those desperate to lift themselves out of a bad situation, that he had taken four months' leave of absence and hadn't had a drink in three weeks. Their father had written in the fall, wishing to leave the Sault owing to harassment by the commandant at Fort Brady, Major Cutler; Lewis was hopeful about a grant of land "which the Indians have given me on the river St. Clair." He needed it sanctioned by the British government. "I shall try if possible to prevail on them to settle it, the situation is beautiful and there is already 40 acres cleared on it, & I really think it would please our Dear Mother. The Natives pass and repass throughout the year, the river abounds with fish, and the woods with deer and various other kinds of game." He would have the thirty dollars he owed Henry on their return but wished him to buy a book on farming.[32] Ozhaawshkodewikwe was inconsolable when he died, but the silence of everyone else—so prone to writing poetry to ease their minds—suggests that his death was too upsetting to even commemorate.

That summer the United States called a council at Prairie du Chien to establish boundaries and make peace among the Dakota, Anishinaabe, Iowa, Menominee, Sac and Fox, and Ho-Chunk nations. Appointed US commissioner in his capacity of superintendent of Indian affairs for Michigan territory, Lewis Cass went first to Indiana, where he participated in writing down the Shawnee story, negotiated with a group of Senecas there for their deportation farther west, then proceeded with Trowbridge, who was on his last assignment for Cass, to the council by way of Detroit, Mackinac, and Green Bay, mainly by canoe.[33] The other US commissioner at the treaty was William Clark, who came up from St. Louis. Cass wrote Schoolcraft that he should go to the Prairie by way of the Chippewa River in order to explore it, and that once they met, he had "at least a thousand things... to say." One thing couldn't wait: at the treaty he would insist on the surrender of the Lake Pepin war party, because "the apprehension of the Chippewa murderers is essential to the presentation of our character [and] influence among the Indians."[34]

That the boundaries established at Prairie du Chien would be of future use in the acquisition of Indigenous land was not part of the official rationale. At the time, the Monroe administration had begun to advance the idea of expelling Indigenous nations, particularly the southeastern nations that were currently battling occupation by the citizens of Georgia and other states. In January 1825 Monroe requested a removal bill from Congress, prefacing it with a story of the United States' benevolent concern for the welfare of the Indians that echoed similar sentiments from Chief Justice Marshall in *Johnson v. McIntosh*. It was a sad fact, he wrote, that "in their present state, it is impossible to incorporate them, in such masses, in any form whatever, into our system," and therefore those tribes must be "removed" in a manner that would be "satisfactory, and honorable to the United States."[35]

Monroe's sentiments were certainly on Cass's mind as he made his way to Prairie du Chien. He would also have been satisfied when he heard that several of the members of the Lake Pepin war party had handed themselves over at Sault Ste. Marie in June.[36] Schoolcraft charged five men—but not Kewaynokwut, whom he didn't think was guilty—with murder.[37] This may have been the reason for Kewaynokwut attempting to stab one man and threatening to kill more of the Americans in the aftermath of the arrest.[38] Major Cutler, enraged that Schoolcraft didn't charge the leader of the war party (and enraged generally at Schoolcraft himself), threw Kewaynokwut in the guardhouse at Fort Brady after Schoolcraft left for Prairie du Chien, in part, he said, to force two other men to surrender.[39] The warriors were taken to jail at Mackinac to wait for their trial; they may already have been there when Cass passed through.

At home Willie, just over a year old, said "Papa" and "garden," where he walked while holding on to his mother's finger; Schoolcraft and Jane were expecting their second child in the fall. "I shall often 'backwards turn my view' to the sweet domestic circle at the 'Hall,' & put up my petitions to the giver of these things, that he may vouchsafe health and happiness to you all," Schoolcraft wrote, leaving Jane to supervise his brother in reading and writing for as long he could be made to sit still.[40] Jane wrote back with news of Kewaynokwut, whose actions made her suspect that he may have been more involved in the attack on the traders than her husband had thought. She advised him to be "well provided with instruments for self defence, there is no knowing what might happen in a voyage such as yours, in the present state of excitement among the unrestrained, vengeful feelings of the Indians, and I trust you will find a good, intrepid, faithful Interpreter who will be of essential service to you. I hope you will see the necessity of being 'as cunning as a Serpent' & at the same time 'as harmless as a Dove.'" She caught herself in the act of dispensing advice. "But I need not thus preach to you my beloved Husband!," she added, reminding him that he was no longer his own person as before they were married, but now "you are *mine*, yes; *mine for Life*! & We are both our darling Childs.'"[41]

From Green Bay, Schoolcraft marveled at Cass's erudition and reminded Jane that his absences were necessary for his future prospects.[42] On his arrival at Prairie du Chien, waiting for the council to begin, he continued in the same vein. "That delicacy of sentiment, modest deportment, equanimity of temper, benevolence of disposition, engaging simplicity, correct taste, and good understanding which did so much to captivate the father, will certainly suggest the best mode of directing the son," he wrote. But Jane hadn't written about managing their son; she wrote again about her longing that her husband remain at home. "I know you will rule the one, as you have contrived to rule the other," he wrote, "by . . . force of love, more powerful than the authority of custom, or the power of law."[43] He wanted her to stop complaining.

He waited for Clark and various tribal parties to arrive, working on a seal for the Sault Ste. Marie agency, a peace pipe with a bow and arrow with the motto, "Choose. But choose wisely" or "Onaidun," which he translated as "Make up your mind." He took a few notes on Ojibwemowin.[44] By the time the council was winding down, he'd recovered from his petulance. He reminded her of "Love and War," and "that devoted girl whose noble sentiment I . . . attempted to present . . . and whose noblest sentiments I have ever thought you to possess in the fullest, methinks I hear you repeat into my ears—'Hasten! Lover hasten! Come, spirit come!'"

> I could not know the strength of those ties that bind me to you, before this separation. . . . I feel as if it was doing injustice to you—to act, or feel, or think, under any circumstances where you are not present to share the pleasure, or to appreciate the pain. In company, or out of company, the thoughts of you, and of our dear William Henry, are ever quick to work upon my mind, & they seldom come without a train of hopes & fears, of recollections & anticipations which none but a husband can feel, and none but a wife can appreciate.[45]

Instead of exploring the Chippewa River on his way home, he returned the way he came, up the Wisconsin, then the Fox River to Green Bay, across Sturgeon Bay and into Lake Michigan. He kept a journal of the trip for her. After some travelogue and remarks on the character of the Menominees passing by on the river, he wrote poetry that he admitted was bad: "Oh Jane, Jane, Jane! / When shall I see thee again / To smile or to speak, to rejoice or complain."⁴⁶ He tried another poem but observed that "it does not jingle smoothly, and I cannot tolerate the business of rhyming, when it requires me to stop & consider what is to come next."⁴⁷ "My thoughts were employed upon home & upon you" and "our dear little pledge. If you knew what an image of perfection my mind had formed you to be, you would probably give me credit for."⁴⁸ He remembered what she had said to him in New York when he returned from Washington. "With a tender and affectionate manner you said—'you must never never leave me again so long alone.'" He knew he had disobeyed her "injunction," but "imperious necessity" had imposed, as usual.⁴⁹

Jane delivered a stillborn girl in early November. This song is undated in the Schoolcraft papers, but it's one of the few in Jane's hand:

Naw! nin daun, nin dau niss ance,
Naw! nin daun, nin dau niss ance;
Nin zhick á no goom nin di a,
Waus suh noon goom ke de zhau
Waus suh noon goom ke di zhau
Nin zhick á dush noon goom nin di au

Ne gush kain dum ne zhick a,
Ne gush kain dum ne zhick a;
Nin zhick e ea, can ge ga,
Cau be ge zhick mow é me non;
Can be ge zhick mow é me non,
Ne gush kain dum, ne zhick a.

Shaw wain dan me tow é shin,
Shaw wain dan me two é shin;
Nosa gezhick ong a be yun
Caw now wain im, in dau niss
Caw now wain im, in dau niss,
Shaw wain dau me tow é shin.

1.
Oh my daughter—my little daughter—oh my daughter my little daughter! Alone now am I—far far you are gone, and alone now am I.

2.
Sorrowful and lone am I—sorrowful and lone am I. Always alone—all day alone, my tears are shed for you. Sorrowful and lone am I.

3.
Have pity on me—have pity on me, My Father abiding above—Take care of my daughter—my little daughter—Have pity on my love.⁵⁰

Despite invoking God "abiding above" as a Christian would do, Jane imagines her daughter traveling to the afterworld, like an Ojibwe. Rather than meekly submitting to God's mysterious plan for her and her child, she demands that God show pity, do something to address her sorrow and loss. "Between sickness and grief, [she] was brought to the verge of the grave," her father wrote to George, who had gone to Lac du Flambeau to trade in the winter of 1826–27, and although she eventually recovered physically, as George knew, her father wrote, her health was never very good.[51] Conant, who hadn't heard, wrote from New York, hoping Schoolcraft would not "fail to prosecute your Indian inquiries this winter—getting out of them all the stories and all the Indian you can." "You and Mrs. S will doubtless feel some new delights at your own fireside, as well as new cares," he added; "that is the way to live for married people, as most congenial with domestic happiness."[52]

The Lake Pepin prisoners had broken out of the jail at Mackinac in October. A few weeks later Little Thunder and the White Head went to see George at Lac du Flambeau and told him what happened. Both the jailer and their fellow prisoners (all French) told them that they were in worse trouble than they thought—the implication being that the Americans were going to kill them. So they cut a hole in the logs, waited a day, and escaped at night by canoe. They then made their way back to their own villages. Little Frenchman, Sageto, Cacabichin, and Kewaynokwut were at Lac Vieux Desert, to the northeast of Lac du Flambeau. The White Head wanted to know about American fortifications to the west, at St. Peters—and George told them that the fort there was as strong as the one at Quebec and there were "more Americans there than in any other fort." Nevertheless it was a long way off at the confluence of the Minnesota and Mississippi Rivers and the only substantial military outpost in the region west of Mackinac. Little Thunder and the White Head left the next day to join their relatives.[53]

In March 1826 George found out from Pierre Duvernay, a Canadian fur trader, that after the men were taken prisoner that summer both Little Thunder's nephew and the White Head's stepson had tried to kill him when they heard he was on his way to Lac du Flambeau.[54] Monsoketick, Little Thunder's nephew, was prevented from killing George, George wrote in his journal, by "the Old Tabac pure [who said] to him '"Bad dog are we not miserable enough, that you should render us more so by committing such an action?"' Monsoketick then tried to kill one of the men transporting George's supplies at a portage, but the people he was with took his gun away.[55] Awbota-ki-chick, the White Head's stepson, also thought he would kill George as soon as the Canadians left the post, but he also was prevented from doing so.[56] Duvernay reported, as George put it, "All the Indians of Old Desert village . . . in general say that I am the cause of their being persecuted by government, and that I came to this place, not for the purpose of trade, but to watch their conduct, and that I was so appointed by government, as being connected with the Indian agent at the Sault [and] I am the cause of their being persecuted."[57]

That the White Head and Little Thunder traveled to see George so soon after escaping was perhaps partly meant to call off their relatives. That past summer the people were anxious, "constantly [wishing] to know what would become of their friends and relatives" who'd been imprisoned, Duvernay reported. When the escapees appeared they were defiant. Little Thunder returned to his village and "struck the post before an assembly of Indians, consisting of about one hundred, saying that he had killed Americans on the Mississippi."[58] When Ocwaygan returned to his band, they were preparing to move after having heard a rumor that the Americans were coming up the Chippewa River, the same river that Cass urged Schoolcraft to explore because the Americans knew nothing about it. Duvernay asked Ocwaygan, George wrote, "why he wanted to desert the camp, & that the earth was not large enough to hide him?" Ocwaygan "replied that he had no intentions of going away, that he was not afraid of such trifling objects as Americans, & furthermore he was fully determined, or disposed, to receive them."[59]

While George wasn't the cause of their troubles, the people were right that he was watching them. As far as Cass was concerned, George was in a position to become the kind of agent/interpreter/informant that he had envisioned in 1815—knowledgeable about Indigenous people and loyal to the United States. It was a logical step for someone who had connections to the Americans by marriage and who had become a citizen in the first place in order to protect his father's business to make himself useful to that government in hopes of getting a living out of it. He had no interest in going elsewhere than the Lake Superior region, and by the time he was at Lac du Flambeau he had a family to support. His and Wassidjeewunoqua's daughter Louisa had been born at La Pointe in 1823; their son Henry William was born in 1825 at Lac du Flambeau; their son John George followed in 1827 at Sault Ste. Marie. There was another aspect to George's connection to the US government. He believed the Americans when they said they wanted what was best for Indians, that they felt benevolently and paternalistically toward them. What they said was entirely consistent with the ideals his father instilled in him through the likes of Hugh Blair—honor, order, Christian morality. This inclination caused George a great deal of conflict over the years.

In January 1826 Schoolcraft sent George instructions to call a council at Lac du Flambeau and read a "parole," a pre-written talk from Schoolcraft on behalf of the Great Father, demanding the apprehension of the escaped murderers and the surrender of those who had not been jailed the first time around.⁶⁰ The government's objective, Schoolcraft wrote to George, was to "increase the power of the chiefs, that they may exercise it over their followers."⁶¹ He had several copies made for individual chiefs in the region; George was to send Gitche Iauba's parole to Holiday, who was to return Gitche Iauba's answer to George, then George was to forward it with his own report to Schoolcraft.

Schoolcraft began the parole to Gitche Iauba by saying that he would not mention the escape, because of course Gitche Iauba would know of it immediately, he being always informed as to what was going on. As usual the talk employed the stilted "Indian" speech that US officials used with Indigenous leaders. The nefarious murderers "cannot go so far but their Great Father can reach them, his hands are strong, he can reach over the whole Chippewa country," wrote Schoolcraft. The Great Father "has Forts on every great stream," and he would not stand for "the insults which Kewaynokwut & his followers have put upon him, first by killing his people, & next by breaking out of his hands." The Great Father also knew that Gitche Iauba's "words have great influence in your Village & throughout the neighbouring villages on the Ontonagon." Gitche Iauba was "a wise man, and worthy chief," the proof being his cooperation at Prairie du Chien and his sending "the murderers to the Sault the first time." Indeed, Schoolcraft wrote that he had "reported your good conduct to your Great Father who looks to you as the principal man in authority on the Lake shore."

Now the Great Father wanted Gitche Iauba to send a messenger to Kewaynokwut telling him that he had to turn himself and all of the murderers in, so that the Great Father in his benevolence could sort out who was guilty and who was not. "They will be treated kindly, while they are kept as prisoners ... [and] those who are not guilty will be suffered to return." But "*they must atone for their guilty deeds.*" Then Schoolcraft produced his only real threat: if Gitche Iauba and the other chiefs didn't get the murderers to turn themselves in voluntarily, the Great Father would take away their traders. "They are allowed to visit you by his permission, and they are obliged to do what he commands," Schoolcraft wrote.⁶²

George wrote to Schoolcraft on receipt of his instructions that the Ojibwes who had been at his post had been "keeping secret smoking councils, the tenor of which I am not fully acquainted with yet." Though the general attitude toward the escapees was hostile, George thought they'd be given up only if forced.⁶³ When he had his council in April 1826, the chiefs at Lac du Flambeau listened and brushed aside his demands. "You must consider that we Indians, have not the same authority over our young men as you have," said Moozobodo, rejecting the government's attempt to redefine Indigenous leadership; "our fathers & chiefs are all no more, and we have no one to give us instruction, and it's now a long time we do not get good council."⁶⁴ They weren't confessing weakness but putting off George and the government. Though there was real anxiety about Americans among the people, the leaders appear to have concluded that the threat to take away their traders didn't amount to much. They knew those traders intimately—many of them were family members—and they bet on the traders and not the United States prevailing in any contest.

That that was the case seems to be confirmed when two days after Moozobodo gave his speech Duck Wing, another man from Lac du Flambeau, told George that Gitche Iauba had sent the village at Lac Vieux Desert a messenger who told them that while Holiday "had something to say to them last year," at this time "he had not any thing to say to them." Specifically, Holiday had received letters from the United States, about which he "had nothing to say."⁶⁵ That stood as Gitche Iauba's response to the government's parole. In his journal George noted that Gitche Iauba and his band "considered the parole delivered by the chief of Lac du Flambeau as sufficient, and that they have nothing to say further." George felt betrayed, not least because Holiday had got the entire episode underway by showing up at the Sault with his scalp-coffin in the summer of 1824. He found out later that Holiday had prevented anyone from taking the government speech to other villages, saying to a man named Two Hearts, "You must leave them alone, they are Indians that give me occasionally beaver skins, and if Government wanted the murderers out they ought to come for them, themselves, and in fact, if you go you cannot prevail on them to go to St. Maries, and its far better to leave them alone." Furthermore, George wrote in his journal, Holiday either told the people directly or gave them the message that "they need not fear, their lands would remain quiet, and he would see [that] they were so." Now, observed George, "the Indians of Lac Flambeau all think [that what] I have said to them is mere composition of mine, and that I am the cause of their being persecuted."⁶⁶

By late 1825 and more than likely in relation to the Monroe administration's efforts around securing a removal bill, Cass was beginning to change his mind about the usefulness of his researches into the nature of Indians.⁶⁷ Instead of publishing a book, he wrote a long essay in the *North American Review* for January 1826, the ostensible subjects of which were John Dunn Hunter's *Manners and Customs of Several Indian Tribes* (Philadelphia, 1823) and John Halkett's *Historical Notes, Respecting the Indians of North America* (London, 1825).⁶⁸ The essay begins with Cass's general account of Indians, which summarizes the prevailing thought at the time as well as what he expected to find when he began his project:

These people were in the rudest condition of society, wandering from place to place, without sciences and without arts, (for we cannot dignify with the name of arts the making of bows and arrows, and the dressing of skins,) without metallic instruments, without domestic animals; raising a little corn by the labor of their women, with a clamshell or the scapular of a buffalo, devouring it with true savage improvidence, and subsisting, during the remainder of the year, upon the precarious supplies furnished by the chase, and by fishing. They were thinly scattered over an immense extent of country, fixing their summer residence upon some little spot of fertile land, and roaming, with their families, and their mat or skin houses, during the winter, through the forests, in pursuit of the animals necessary for food and clothing.[69]

He devoted most of the essay to a denunciation of the recently deceased Heckewelder's history, Du Ponceau's philological writing, and the *London Quarterly Review*'s endorsement of Heckewelder and blaming Americans for Indians' suffering. To the extent that there is an argument in the essay, it is that all of these were outrageously wrong both in their criticism of the United States' relations with Indians and in the appreciative things they had to say about Indian character, because Indians were really savages and that's all there was to it.

He used his research to present himself as an expert with firsthand experience, but his account of that experience didn't quite paint the Indians as the savages he said they were. "We have ourselves [he used the royal 'we' throughout], in the depth and solitude of our primeval forest, and among some of the wildest and most remote of our Indian tribes, gazing with ardent curiosity, and perhaps with some slight emotion of awe, upon the *Jongleur*, who with impudent dexterity performed feats, which probably it is wiser to witness than to relate," he wrote, unable to explain away what he'd seen. He insisted that Indians had no governments but then marveled at the fact that "their lives and property are protected, and their political relations among themselves, and with other tribes, are duly preserved."[70] He admitted that not much was known about "the moral character and feelings of the Indians, of their mental discipline, of their peculiar opinions, mythological and religious, and of all that is most valuable to man in the history of man." But that admission did not stop him from opining that Indians were "jealous and suspicious, unwilling to associate with strangers, and slow to give them their confidence."[71] He noted with disdain that the Ojibwes had an expression: "As stupid as a white man."[72]

Heckewelder was naive and credulous. The polysynthetic nature of the Delaware language was a sign of its poverty, not its complexity.[73] Furthermore, if what Heckewelder said about Indian character was true, "it would unhinge all our knowledge upon these subjects."[74] His writing had already dangerously "furnished materials for the writers of periodical works, and even of *history*," including that "beautiful [delineation] of American scenery, incidents, and manners," James Fenimore Cooper's recently published *Last of the Mohicans*.[75] What Cass seems to have been getting at is that Heckewelder's account of the humanity of Indian people as expressed in Cooper's invoking the missionary directly and in his depiction of the character Chingachgook would ultimately have a negative effect on the United States' geographic expansion and political power if left unchecked. Cass recognized that telling stories about savages was more effective for what he wanted to do than gathering facts that never really fit the story he wanted to tell anyway.

He gave up his research. Most of the material he collected disappeared, likely by his own frustrated hand. From January 1825 forward, his writing about Indians always told the savage story, from the longest essay to the shortest squib. He wasn't the only US official who participated in this effort—it seems to have been widespread if not endemic among US officials. William Clark opined in the newspapers about how the western Indians were in such an abject state that they killed their children because they were unable to feed them at the same time that they were supposedly a terror to the frontier.[76] Thomas McKenney, the commissioner of Indian affairs, contributed an entire book. *Sketches of a Tour to the Lakes* (Baltimore 1827) was about the next of the ostensible boundary-line treaties, the Treaty of Fond du Lac of 1826.[77] This book also made the Johnston family known to American readers for their charming and romantic forest life and presented Jane to that public as a writer of poetry and Indian stories.

At the outset of his account McKenney found a way to incorporate Secretary of War James Barbour's recent argument that it was necessary to expel Indigenous nations west of the Mississippi by putting it into the mouths of acquaintances. On a barge in the Erie Canal, McKenney told the story of the Oneida chief Skenandoah, a Christian convert, to a party of Quakers—conveniently enough, a denomination associated with the defense of Indigenous treaty rights from the time of William Penn. (McKenney himself was a Quaker.) "I am an aged hemlock," said the chief on his deathbed; "the winds of an hundred winters have whistled through my branches.... When I am dead, I wish to be buried by the side of my minister and friend, (the Rev. Mr. Kirkland.) Pray to my Jesus that I may go up with him at the great resurrection."[78] One of the Quakers, a woman, asked, "Why is it ... that beings capable of such feelings, and of such views should be so neglected?" Why indeed, responded McKenney. It was true that the Indians had suffered "a most inexcusable neglect ... from the beginning; but I hope the remnant of the race will be saved." The Quaker woman hoped so as well, "but if they should not be, when our experience has shewn that *it is practicable* to save them, our nation cannot look for the smiles and blessings of Providence whose watchful care extends over all; and who sees that the lands we live on, and all this wide and beautiful country, were once theirs." Here her husband interrupted her, adding that Providence "sees also... that it is owing, wholly, as James Barbour has truly said, at least in substance, *to our avarice*."[79]

A few months before McKenney's trip, Barbour had transmitted another request for a "removal" bill, this time to the House Committee on Indian Affairs, writing that such a bill was necessary because Americans couldn't control their desire for land even when—especially when—under the influence of missionaries Indians became sedentary farmers and householders.[80] Though this would seem to have been the idea, it would not do, according to Barbour, because whites' relentless natural drive for more land was not going to let up and eventually the Indians would just have to go. And then the Indians would be indignant and believe that the Americans' sole purpose was to get them off their land, an unfair but not unpredictable response given the circumstances. "They see that our professions are insincere," wrote Barbour, "that our promises have been broken; that the happiness of the Indian is a cheap sacrifice to the acquisition of new lands: and when attempted to be soothed by the assurance that the country to which we propose to send them is desirable, they emphatically ask us, what new pledges can you give us that we shall not again be exiled when it is your wish to possess these lands?"[81]

It's remarkable the extent to which, early in the process of arguing for expulsion, US officials were so open about why they wanted to do what they did, even to the point of contradicting their own assertions about the nature of Indians as Barbour did in conceding that "civilized" Indians were doing pretty well for themselves and wanted to keep it that way. McKenney praised Oneida farmers in New York, Odawa Catholics at Drummond, an Ojibwe family who gave his party fish on the way out to Fond du Lac.[82] Ultimately their adaptation to new circumstances didn't matter when the issue was white Americans and their unstoppable desire for more land. After expulsion, Barbour wrote, the United States ought to work toward the "extinction of tribes, and their amalgamation into one mass, and a distribution of property among individuals."[83] It was the only way to save them.

The soldiers paraded and the Indians danced at the council at Fond du Lac. McKenney ministered to a paralyzed young woman, feeding her broth from the first spoon that had ever been in her mouth, he noted, lamenting dirt and ignorance along the way. "Nothing can exceed the poverty and wretchedness of these people!" he exclaimed.[84] Despite his confidence in his cause,

McKenney's own record shows the people pushing back against the Americans. He accepted the offer of witnessing a shaking tent ceremony, but the "ceremony" was an elaborate joke on him by people who knew what Americans thought. Before any questions could be asked of the healer, the lodge started shaking and the people outside heard "a tremulous crying kind of voice" and loud thuds, fifteen times, which the interpreter said were "the lighting down of the devils sent him by the Great Spirit." And then the question was asked: what was the Great Father at Washington doing at this time? "The answer was presently announced, preceded by another shake. It was this—'He is doing nothing; but is sitting quietly thinking about this treaty: but has people all around him with white papers before them.'"[85] After a few questions that McKenney unfortunately didn't record, it was announced that "the devils were thirsty, and wanted something to drink," that is, a little whiskey. Which they got, "well diluted," as well as some tobacco.[86] McKenney recovered himself from this embarrassment by insisting that of course Indians were superstitious and the healer was a fraud. Furthermore, he and everyone gathered to see him "doubtless" believed "that this treaty is the greatest thing that is now going on upon the face of the earth; and that as such, it is that which engrosses the attention of the President to such a degree, as to make it impossible for him to think of anything else."[87]

Besides boundaries and a promise to recapture the "Chippewa murderers," Cass wanted copper from the Ojibwes, telling them at the council that copper "does you no good, and it would be useful to us to make into kettles, buttons, bells, and a great many other things."[88] He and the Missouri senator Thomas Hart Benton were in pursuit of a 3,000-pound copper boulder on the Keewenaw Peninsula.[89] Scholars are not entirely sure what copper signified to Ojibwe people in the 1820s, but they are clear that it did have important spiritual significance. It was used in Midewiwin ceremonies and for amulets to aid in hunting or war. They didn't like to talk to outsiders about copper, however, and even less about Mishipeshu, the underwater spirit, usually described today as a lynx or panther, who controlled it.[90] In response to Cass, several speakers at the treaty council denied knowing that there was copper anywhere. One man from Ontonagon said that the copper boulder came from the Great Spirit and thus could belong to no one; he remembered when the Americans had last tried to get it out and that before them the British lost three men in an effort to do the same.[91]

But Shingabawossin told the Ojibwes that they ought to sell whatever copper they had—here it seems he was referring to granting the right to explore for minerals. "It is of no advantage to us," he said, according to McKenney.[92] Shingabawossin wanted land grants for his relatives who lived at Sault Ste. Marie and nearby villages. There isn't much discussion of this in the journal of the treaty that McKenney appended to his narrative, but in a collection of Indian portraits published in the late 1830s and early 1840s (assembled by himself for the War Department) McKenney wrote that Shingabawossin saw the large gardens cultivated by the Johnstons and the soldiers at the Sault and wanted the people who received the land grants to do the same and then to share with their relatives when they were in need.[93] The treaty ultimately provided for land grants of one section each in Sault Ste. Marie and various islands in the St. Mary's River, running in strips back from the riverbank in the French style, to a list of "half-breeds and Chippewas by descent." The first grantees on the list were the children and grandchildren of Ozhaawshkodewikwe; the second grantees were the widow and children of Jean-Baptiste Cadotte, including Sangemanqua's two children with Lewis Johnston. Also on the list was George's wife Wassidjeewunoqua and their children, who were each allotted one section.

The final version of the treaty offered a school, to be located on the St. Mary's River and with a $1,000 yearly stipend attached, and a $2,000 annuity payment, in addition to the land grants. Of the school Shingabawossin remarked, "I am willing—it may be a good thing for those who wish to send their children."[94] Thinking ahead, the Americans inserted an article into the treaty that more or less invited the Senate to disregard the articles benefiting the Ojibwes, which it eventually did, keeping only the school and its stipend. After the council concluded, the Americans sent a detachment to get the copper rock. Traveling upriver through deep ravines, thick underbrush, and bogs, they finally reached it, thirty-five miles south of the lake on the west bank of the river. They tried digging under it, pushing it into the river, and lighting a fire under it, to no avail.[95] McKenney reported himself "mortified" by the failure.[96]

He spent most of his time while at the Sault on his way to and from Fond du Lac with the Johnstons and Schoolcrafts. John Johnston immediately became "my old friend." He described his host as "feeble and decrepid" though possessed of "genuine Irish hospitality" and fond of "strikingly graphic" language.[97] Mrs. Johnston was a "genuine Chippeway . . . tall and large, but uncommonly active and cheerful." "She has fine teeth," he observed; "indeed, her face, taken together, (with her high cheek-bones, and compressed forehead, and jutting brows), denotes a vigorous intellect and great firmness of character, and needs only to be seen, to satisfy even a tyro like myself in physiognomy, that she required only the advantages of education and society, to have placed her upon a level with the most distinguished of her sex."[98] Proof of Mrs. Johnston's intelligence was in her aid to General Cass. It was her "luminous exposition of [the Ojibwes'] own weakness, and the power of the United States," as well as her "assurances of the friendly disposition of the government towards them, and their own mistaken views of the entire object of the commissioner" that saved the day.⁹⁹

Ozhaawshkodewikwe's supposed submission to the Americans protected the family from too close an association with their relatives. McKenney marveled at the sophistication of the dinner the Johnstons prepared for the commissioners and other officials, praising "the variety, the cooking, and the exquisite preparation of the *beaver's tail*, that nice morsel which could not be dispensed with even in Lent."¹⁰⁰ Ozhaawshkodewikwe and her daughters were better than all the "professed cooks in Washington."¹⁰¹ When McKenney and the commissioners left to return to the East, the Johnstons threw a party, where to McKenney's great surprise, Mrs. Johnston danced in the English style.¹⁰²

"Of Mrs. Schoolcraft, you have heard," he wrote to his unnamed correspondent (this was an epistolary account). She was tall and thin, and spoke slowly and distinctly with a "feeble, and tremulous voice." McKenney commented phrenologically on her high cheekbones and broad jaw, which bespoke her Ojibwe blood, as well as her "dark and fine eye." "Mildness of expression, and softness, and in all respect in manners, as well as of voice, characterize her," he continued. "She dresses with great taste, and in all respects in the costume of our fashionables, but wore leggins of black silk, drawn and ruffled around the ankles, resembling those worn by our little girls. I think them ornamental." These were neither Ojibwe, where the leggings would be of a dark cloth, ungathered, and embellished at the bottom and outside seams with beading or quillwork, nor American, where the pantalettes would be white, gathered at the bottom, and not made to be seen after childhood. They were a bit eccentric. Mrs. Schoolcraft owed her considerable accomplishments to her father, observed McKenney, who gave the Irish Johnstons a higher pedigree than they in fact had. One wouldn't believe her mother was an Indian, "except on her own confession, upon some equally responsible testimony, were you to hear her converse, or see her beautiful, and some of them highly finished compositions, in both prose and poetry."¹⁰³

He asked about stories, and Ozhaawshkodewikwe told him "Peboan and Seegwun," "in Chippeway with great spirit," while Charlotte and her father translated.¹⁰⁴ The family let him copy from the postwar anthologies or other manuscripts so that he could include the stories he was told in his book. John Johnston told Gitche Gauzinee's stories about his experiences, including the story published as "The Funeral Fire," and a second one, in which Gitche Gauzinee refuses to cannibalize defeated enemies as others were doing (no copy of this survives). They were "queer stories, but go for a great deal among the Indians," McKenney wrote, not as enthused as Cass.¹⁰⁵

Though Eliza refused to speak to him in English, the family kept him entertained, especially Charlotte, whom he thought the most beautiful of the sisters.[106] Charlotte sang an Ojibwe song called "The Ojibway Maid" that Jane wrote, perhaps thinking of herself and Schoolcraft. She supplied the translation:

> Why? What's the matter with the young American?
> He crosses the river with tears in his eyes!
> He sees the young Ojibway girl preparing to leave the place:
> He sobs for his sweetheart, because she is going away!
> But he will not sigh long for her, for as soon as he is out of her sight
> He will soon forget her.[107]

McKenney didn't understand the mockery in the song; he just wanted to hear it over and over again because Charlotte was singing it. He included in his book a version of the song by one of the Fort Brady officers that made the girl melancholy rather than mocking. "New loves will make you pleased to weep," sang the improved girl; "Nor e'er again, remember me!"[108]

A month after McKenney left Sault Ste. Marie, soldiers snuck into the Ojibwe burial ground next to their fort, broke into two recent graves, and stole one woman's body and another woman's head. They then carried their spoils to the post's hospital in the night, boiled off the flesh, and sold the two skulls to one of the post's two surgeons, Dr. Lyman Foot, a graduate of Yale College's medical school. Abraham Paul, who'd been invited to join the graverobbers but refused, reported that he saw Robert McKain carrying one of the heads in a handkerchief to the hospital, then giving it to a soldier who took it to the roothouse. There was another accomplice in the burying ground. McKain was long in the habit of disinterring Indians for money, and Dr. Foot was a repeat customer. Their previous exploits either had not involved the Ojibwe burying ground or had not been discovered. Soldiers who'd been on guard duty had seen lights in the post hospital that night—those who investigated further saw kettles on the fire and complained about "a most abominable stench."[109]

Phrenology promised to reveal the secrets of mind through the geography of skulls. Franz Joseph Gall, a Viennese physician credited with introducing phrenology to Europe in the 1790s, collected the skulls of persons with whom he was familiar, including friends, in order to test out his theories. His collection consisted of a general, a couple of poets, and a number of "ideots."[110] Gall's protégé Johann Gaspar Spurzheim, a great evangelist for phrenology, converted an Edinburgh lawyer named George Combe, who, once he founded the Edinburgh Society for Phrenology in 1820, began to influence Americans, including the man who made phrenology a legitimate pursuit in the United States, Charles Caldwell, a well-regarded physician at Transylvania University in Lexington, Kentucky. Caldwell's *Elements of Phrenology* appeared in 1824.[111] By the mid-1820s, most major cities—New York, Philadelphia, and Boston but also Cincinnati—had their own phrenological societies. They met weekly or bimonthly, heard lectures from learned physicians, and kept libraries of books and collections of skulls. Unlike Dr. Gall with his collection of friends, American phrenologists, following their Scottish and English compatriots, were much more interested in crania of the "less developed" peoples—Indians, South Sea Islanders, Africans, Irish, criminals, the insane. Of Indians, phrenology promised a surer way into their character than observation of their behavior or actually talking to them, since they were so cunning and secretive.[112]

It was entirely of the moment that Dr. Foot handed over cash for the skulls of Ojibwe women buried so tantalizingly close to the fort's pickets. The Ojibwes were enraged, and Dr. Foot beat it out of the Sault in fear for his life. Schoolcraft wrote the post commander that he expected all efforts would be made to bring the culprits to justice as well as reinter the bones "to allay the present excitement among the Indians."[113] "[The Indians] are now beating their drums & uttering their lamentations, mixed with execrations upon the perpetrators of this atrocious crime," he wrote to Cass. Before the graves were opened that morning, "the chiefs commenced, by addressing the spirits of their relations, and asking their forgiveness for the act they were about to commit.... They found the coffin of the first grave split open, and the body taken therefrom. The lid of the other grave examined by them, was cut off, about 14 inches from the top, and the head only, taken. This separation, as is reported, was effected by a sharpened spade, and the loathsome trophy conveyed away.[114] Schoolcraft insisted that Zina Pitcher, the second post surgeon, had nothing to do with this outrageous act. Dr. Foot deserved to be "severely *fined*[,] the only thing that ever can touch his sensibilities."[115] Foot was one of Schoolcraft's many enemies, who not only took the military's side in Schoolcraft's numerous conflicts with them but also, according to Schoolcraft, overcharged him for medical services before Dr. Pitcher arrived at the Sault in 1825.[116]

Shingabawossin and other members of the Crane band demanded a hearing with Schoolcraft. Schoolcraft copied over speeches given on 8 September 1826 by Shingabawossin and another chief, Naugichigomie, expressing the band's displeasure. George was the likely translator and writer. He'd attended the Fond du Lac treaty as Schoolcraft's "confidential interpreter" and went back to the Sault, then returned west to become subagent at La Pointe.[117] His job as before was to surveil and report on both Indians and American traders, Cass told Schoolcraft, who passed the letter on to George, as well as on any activities on the part of the British and their traders.[118] "Great reliance is placed upon your intimate knowledge of the language spoken in that quarter, your acquaintance with the geographical features of the country, and with the wants & feelings of the Indians, as connected with the former & present course of trade which our citizens are permitted to carry on, with them," Schoolcraft wrote.

George didn't leave for La Pointe until mid-September at the earliest, and so he was more than likely present on 8 September when Shingabawossin and Naugichigomie, along with the rest of the band, came to the agency. Shingabawossin said,[119]

> My Father: I speak to you in the name of all whom you see present. We come here on a friendly visit. We have something in our hearts, that we wish to open to you. It is painful to mention it: but while we do so, you must believe that our hearts are right, and feel with you. What I utter, is the voice of my nation. You know my way of life, and the path in which I tread. Why should I speak of it?
>
> What I have to say relates to those living inside the pickets. They have disturbed our graves. They have taken away the bones from our hill. How could we miss knowing it? We do not live in a confined place: we live at large, and see what is done. We may sometimes act foolishly; but when the graves of our dead are opened, our hearts find their right places, and we feel great pain of mind (gushkain' dum).[120] You have heard our drums. Not in joy are they sounded—not in anger. . . . But in grief. We have shut up our feasting lodges.
>
> My Father: The Americans asked us for the land those pickets are set in. We gave it. I was one of the first who consented to it. My mark is upon the paper. You know it. They have also asked us on other occasions for lands. We gave them. It is only the other day that they requested us to give lands, and that which is upon the lands. We gave it. We hoped, at least, that the bones of our dead would be allowed to lie in quiet upon the lands. Why should I say more of the graves being opened at night—secretly—the coffins split open, and the bodies carried off? You know it. You also know my sentiments & feelings. I say again, we have been friendly to you, and to the Americans, from the moment of your first arrival here, when the great chief of Detroit, first landed here.
>
> Ask Oshaucoushcodaywayqua whether I did not raise my voice against the foolish and headstrong men who wished to oppose your coming. Who stopped the murder that was about to be committed on

the night after the treaty of St. Mary's was signed? She can tell! She now sees the hard treatment we receive, and she approves the public visit of my band. It is the Crane—the Crane whose bones have been taken.

My Father: We impute no blame to you. We have received nothing but kindness and charity from you. But tell me the reason why the bones were taken? What are they so treated for? We know that they are gone. We have opened the graves, and find the bodies gone. We know it was nobody outside the pickets. If you had known it, you would have stopped it. Pity us—pity us—we expect it from you. We expect you to see right done towards us.

The bones ought to be given up. Why should those who carry lances (Shesmau' gunish) meddle with the *dead*? I am an old man now. You see my eyesight is failing. But I have been where battles were fought, and know what belongs to a *warrior*. I would rather my heart's blood should flow out upon this hill of our fathers, than fight a coward (Shaugsda' aih).

Naugichigomie, Center of the Great Lake, said,

My Father: I cannot speak a different language from my chief. I assent to what he has said. He has uttered my feelings. He has spoken truth. The Americans are blameable for this act. They have carried off our bones, and our flesh. It is a most bad act. But we knew before they came here, that they would disturb our dead. On their first arrival I knew not where to go, and fix my lodge. I went about from place to place. But at last, I came back, to sit by the fire our American fathers had kindled; and to look at those little fishes (alluding to the whitefish) that the Good Spirit has placed in the rapids. It is here that my totem belongs.

My Father: When the French were in power here, we always had peace and presents. They came and kissed us. They never molested our dead. Just—very just, were they ever towards us. At last, the British (Sauganosh) came. They told us "I will treat you as the French have treated you," and they annually gave us presents. The Americans have now set themselves down here. This chief (pointing to Shingabawossin) speaks truly: they have spoiled our ground: they have taken the dead out of it. This, we know, is not done by you, or with your knowledge. It was done by the soldiers. Had you known it, we know you feel like a parent towards us, and would have forbidden it.

My Father: I implore you to try your utmost to keep our grounds quiet. Take pity on our weakness: correct us if we do wrong; and give us your counsel in our affairs. You sit in the chair of our great father (Gitshee Koasinaun). What you speak is from him. We want to hear the sound of his voice across the lakes.

Shingabawossin and Naugichigomie pointed out that Schoolcraft had it in his power to address the "great pain" that the people had suffered and it was his responsibility to do that.[121] The only thing Schoolcraft did, however, was to send the speeches as well as two affidavits and some other papers on to Cass. Though Cass told Schoolcraft he had forwarded everything to the War Department, none of that material is in any of the relevant archives.[122] This is not surprising. Shingabawossin made it clear that it wasn't Cass who saved the day at the Sault in 1820 but himself, and that Ozhaawshkodewikwe wasn't the subservient handmaiden she was supposed to have been but an authority in her own right.

The speeches are in Schoolcraft's hand; it looks like he was thinking about publishing them. He made some minor edits and added a few explanatory notes. The only significant changes he made were to delete the description of the desecrated bodies and to change the sense of Shingabawossin's last line, so that he would be called a coward himself rather than refuse to fight one. It was a speech by an eloquent savage about Indian graves, an ever-popular subject; even better for Schoolcraft, it made the military look bad. But in the end he didn't publish the speeches, likely because he was unable to obscure what they were really about.

Dr. Foot landed at Fort Washington, outside that city, and went on to a distinguished career, more than likely collecting skulls along the way, until he was killed in the Mexican War.[123] The skulls and body at the Sault never were recovered; the Chippewa murderers never were handed over.[124]

Chapter 4

A Precious Wild Flower

Before Schoolcraft and Cass, Jane wrote down stories to entertain herself and her family, free to invent and unconcerned about whether she was exposing anything that shouldn't have been exposed to outsiders. After, though, her husband started soliciting stories told by Indians, not by her. It's possible that Schoolcraft had Jane write down stories between 1822 and 1826 explicitly (but not exclusively) for Cass and that those stories were lost, particularly after he abandoned his researches and apparently his papers. Schoolcraft probably didn't know that Cass had lost interest in stories when in the fall of 1826 he started a manuscript newspaper in which he published new stories by Jane and also by William, who was about sixteen and working for his father as a clerk after George left for La Pointe. He called it *The Muzzeniegun* or *Literary Voyager* (the contemporary spelling is *mazina'igan* and it means book, document, or paper), and although at the beginning it was meant mainly for the perusal of select villagers and officers at Fort Brady, eventually and inevitably, considering Schoolcraft's ambitions, it circulated at Detroit and New York. Thirteen of sixteen issues survive in Schoolcraft's papers.[1]

The new stories show Jane working out how to represent the source material to a white audience. In "Origin of the Robin" and "Peeboan and Seegwun" she wrote stories that in context read like exercises in translating Ojibwe narrative to eighteenth-century form, and "The Two Ghosts" reads as gothic in its embellishments. Those were for her own pleasure and her family's entertainment. The new stories were written in the wake of Cass's obsession with Indian "belles lettres" and his obvious disdain for Indigenous intellect, which, considering his habits, he could well have expressed to Jane personally. For Cass as for the philologists Du Ponceau and Pickering, literature was beyond the capacity of savages because savages could have no understanding of what was beautiful or moral. Cass's use of "belles lettres" was always mocking even if it also conveyed his initial astonishment and later frustration. The category "literature" for these men referred to works that could be judged by the same aesthetic as that espoused by eighteenth-century British readers of anthologies—the work must have its design and its beauties. From her earliest writing, for Jane the representation of Anishinaabe narrative and song in English demonstrated those qualities, and the new stories rejected Cass's bloviations in the same way that she produced sentences in Ojibwemowin that refuted Cass's insistence that Indigenous people had no capacity for abstract thought.

She was ambitious. She translated the rolling head legend, a long narrative common among Algonquian nations that may have been a favorite of the family, or popular in the region, as both George and William translated versions in the 1830s.[2] It's the only story that the Johnstons translated more than once. The legend begins with a wife's infidelity to her husband, which leads him to kill her, sending their sons fleeing as their dead mother's head rolls along in pursuit. The father gives the children several objects (an awl, a flint, punk) to throw in her way to slow her down; these objects create mountains and other natural features. When they come to a river, the children cross on the back of a bird to escape their mother; when she demands that the bird take her across, too, she falls into the water, breaks apart, and is turned into fish that provides sustenance for the people. The boys then encounter a magician in a lake who kidnaps the elder brother, leaving the younger behind. The magician controls objects (such as his canoe), and despite the fact that he marries the kidnapped youth to one or both of his daughters, he seeks to kill off the youth in a series of contests. In the meantime, the neglected younger brother turns into a wolf. The youth finally kills off the magician once he realizes his own powers.[3]

In versions of the legend written down by both George and William, the wronged hunter is a thunderbird who returns to the sky world after killing his wife. In William's version of a Saginaw teller's story, a Windigo kills the wife and the hunter's younger son, who becomes a spirit before the hunter leaves for the sky world where, William writes, he "placed his abode as directed by the Great Moneto towards the North, and he has his name to the present day, which is the Thunder often heard in the fall of the year, commencing at the North & going South, and generally the last in that season that is heard; and Indians say of them, they are falloing or halloing home."[4] In the version George took down from a man named Nabunway or Nabinoi at Sault Ste. Marie in 1838, both the hunter and his wife are thunderbirds, and the story tells the origin of the Crane band as the two brothers decide to stop their traveling and live at Bow-e-ting.[5]

Manabozho created the thunderbirds to "counteract the influence of the Underwater Manito," Christopher Vecsey writes, which he describes as a combination of two beings, the underwater panther Mishipeshu and the horned serpent Mishiginebig. They appeared above ground only in warm seasons and controlled game animals on land and in the water. Thunderbirds are powerful guardians who control birds, the game animals of the air.[6] In Jane's stories thunderbirds are nowhere to be found. Each of the stories uses one of the forms she used in the postwar anthology, and each begins with a different set of transgressive family members. "Origin of the Whitefish" is an origin story that follows the central narrative of the rolling head legend; "Forsaken Brother" is a moral tale about siblings who abandon their younger brother, who is turned into a wolf; "Mishosha" is a moral fairy tale that features two irresponsible parents, both of whom abandon the children, the elder of whom is kidnapped by a magician (rather than one murdering the other, although the mother does think about it). Unlike most English and American moral tales of the era where children transgress and must be instructed in good behavior, and like the father in "Origin of the Robin," in all three parts of Jane's rolling head stories the older person has abandoned responsibilities to the younger, who need the help of animals and the spirit world.[7]

Jane appears to be demonstrating what anthropologist Mary Black Rogers described as the "power-control belief system" in Ojibwe society, in which human beings depend on and receive the "power to live" from other-than-human persons, and in turn owe other-than-human persons "'offerings' and 'respectful behavior.'"[8] Other-than-human persons included "large animals, small animals, insects, birds, fish, some plants, and spirits," and the spirits included "the culture hero, thunderbirds both male and female, the master of the fish, the mermaid, some forest spirits and some lake spirits, and the sun, moon, stars, winds, and shells and stones, among others."[9] Individuals sought to be "in control" of themselves, or "*not . . . controlled* by [their] environment—'environment' including other people as well as other natural beings or forces that could affect one's outcomes and render one helpless."[10] Maintaining these relationships required "listening, watching, and learning of proper ritual relations," anthropologist Michael McNally writes.[11]

"Origin of the Whitefish" begins with a woman "receiving clandestine visits" from another man while her husband is away hunting, and when her two sons warn her to stop "she rebuked them sharply, and finally, on their intimation of disclosing the secret, threatened to kill them if they made any disclosure."[12] The sons tell their father anyway, after which he "took up a war club at a moment when he was not perceived, and with a single blow despatched the object of his jealousy." He buries his wife, takes down his lodge, and moves away. After her death the mother "harassed [her sons'] imaginations wherever they went, so that their life was a life of perpetual terrors." They leave home to escape her, but when they stop at the rapids at Bow-e-ting, they turn to see their mother's skull "rolling along the beach after them."[13] Petrified, they call out to a large crane sitting on a rock "in a state of stupor, in the midst of the most violent eddies of the foaming water" of the rapids, pleading to be taken across the river to escape the skull. "With great deliberation," Jane writes, the crane "stretched forth his neck . . . then rising himself on his wings flew across to their assistance." "Be careful . . . that you do not touch the back part of my head," the crane says; "it is sore, and should you press against it, I shall not be able to avoid throwing you both into the rapids." They fly to the opposite shore where the crane deposits the boys; then he returns to his rock.[14]

"I have lost my children, and am sorely distressed," the skull cries out, imploring the crane to be taken across the river to her sons. The crane tells the skull the same thing he'd said to her sons and proceeds to take her over. But the skull wants to know "how so aged a bird could have acquired such a bad wound," and when they are halfway over the rapids she touches it. He immediately drops the skull into the rapids, where it "floated down from rock to rock, striking violently against their hard edges, until it was battered to fragments." As the skull shatters, "the brains of the woman . . . fell into the water, in the form of small white roes, which soon assumed the shape of a novel kind of fish, possessing a whiteness of color peculiar to itself; and these rapids have ever since been well stocked with this new and delicious species of fish."[15]

The two brothers survive because the Crane helped them in their distress. In "The Forsaken Brother," the abandoned younger son teaches his siblings a lesson about what they owe to their relations. The story begins with a deathbed scene that wouldn't have been out of place in a literary periodical. "The door of the lodge was thrown open to admit the refreshing breeze of the lake, on the banks of which it stood," Jane writes, "and as the cool air fanned the head of the poor man, he thus addressed his weeping family. 'I leave you—thou, who has been my partner in life, but you will not stay long to suffer in this world. But oh! my children, my poor children! you have just commenced life, and mark me, unkindness, and ingratitude, and every wickedness is in the scene before you.'" To save his children from just such miseries, he'd "left my kindred and my tribe" and kept his children "[separate] from the haunts of men." No longer able to watch over his children, he begged them "to cherish each other, and on no account . . . forsake your youngest brother."[16] With his dying breath, the man takes the hands of his older children: "'My daughter! never forsake your little brother. My son, never forsake your little brother.' 'Never, never!' they both exclaim. 'Never—never!' repeated the father and expired."[17] But of course that's exactly what they do after the death of their mother some months later.

Many of the stories the Johnstons wrote down and several of those Trowbridge wrote down begin with a person or family living alone and then going out to find other human beings, out of curiosity or loneliness. Jane uses that feature of Anishinaabe narrative to illustrate the moral failure of the two siblings. First the elder brother becomes restless. "Are we always to live as if there were no other human beings in the world?" he demands of his sister; "must I deprive myself of the pleasure of associating with my own kind?"[18] His sister could only remind him that they were to "cherish each other" and "do nothing independent of each other—that neither pleasure nor pain ought ever to separate us, particularly from our helpless brother."[19] But the elder son takes his bow and arrows and leaves. Soon his sister begins to lose her resolve; "Years, which added to her strength and capability of directing the affairs of the household, also brought with them the desire of society, and made her solitude irksome."[20] She puts her younger brother in the lodge with provisions and wood, telling him to stay there while she goes to find their other brother. Then she travels to a village, where she "was so much taken up with the pleasures and amusements of society, that all affection for her brother was obliterated."[21] She marries and "never more thought of the helpless relative she had abandoned."[22]

The boy eats all the food while he waits for his sister, then picks berries and digs up roots around the lodge. Out of food and desperate by winter, he goes off into the woods and lives among wolves. "He became so fearless of these animals, that he would sit close to them whilst they devoured their prey," Jane writes, "and the animals themselves seemed to pity his condition, and would always leave something."[23] When the ice breaks up in spring, he follows the wolves back to the lakeshore. There his brother is fishing in the lake. His brother hears a child's cry, and then, listening more closely, a song:

Neesya, neesya, shyegwuh gushuh!
Ween ne myeengunish!
    ne myeengunish!

My brother, my brother,
I am now turning into a Wolf!—
I am turning into a Wolf.

When the elder brother sees the younger, the younger howls like a wolf.

> [The elder brother] . . . leapt on shore and strove to catch him in his arms, and soothingly said—"My brother, my brother, come to me." But the boy eluded his grasp, and fled, still singing as he fled—"I am turning into a Wolf—I am turning into a wolf," and howling in the intervals.
>
> The elder brother, conscience struck, and feeling his brotherly affection returning with redoubled force, exclaimed in great anguish, "My brother, my brother, come to me." But the nearer he approached the child, the more rapidly his transformation went on, until he changed into a perfect wolf,—still singing and howling, and naming his brother and

sister alternately in his song, as he fled into the woods, until his change was complete. At last he said, "I am a wolf," and bounded out of sight.[24]

For the rest of their days, the brother and sister "felt the bitterness of remorse." "The sister, when she heard of the fate of the little boy whom she had so cruelly left, and whom both she and her brother had solemnly promised to foster and protect, wept bitterly," Jane writes, "and never ceased to mourn until she died."[25]

With its evil magician and separated brothers, "Mishosha, or The Magician and His Daughters," the last of the three rolling head stories, reads more like a fairy tale than not. But the substance of the story is about how Panigwun, the elder of the two brothers, must learn to use the power he received from the spirit who comes to his aid in his fast. The story opens by repeating parts of the legend that appeared in "Origin of the Whitefish," although in this case both parents are derelict. A family lives "in isolation" in the woods, happily, until the husband "discovered a wanton disposition in his wife, who had become infatuated with a beautiful young man.[26] Thinking that he will kill her if he finds out, she plans on killing her husband first, but before that can happen, the husband follows her and, hidden behind a tree, watches as "a tall, handsome man" leads his wife away. He decides to leave her with their children, "thinking that her own conscience would in the end, punish her sufficiently."[27] When the woman returns to the lodge and sees that her husband is gone, she leaves her sons behind and goes away with her paramour. Before leaving, she tells them that she's "going a short distance, and would return."[28]

Soon after their mother disappears, the two boys become lost in the woods.

> At last they saw an opening through the woods, and were shortly after delighted to find themselves on the borders of a broad lake. Here the elder boy busied himself in picking the seed pods of the wild rose. In the meanwhile the younger, amused himself by shooting some arrows into the sand, one of which, happened to fall into the lake. The elder brother, not willing to lose his time in making another, waded into the water to get it. Just as he was about the grasp the arrow, a canoe passed by him with the rapidity of lightning. An old man, sitting in the centre, seized the affrighted youth, and placed him in the canoe. In vain the boy addressed him. "My grandfather" (a term of respect for old people) "pray take my little brother also. Alone, I cannot go with you; he will starve if I leave him." The old magician (for such was his real character) laughed at him. Then giving his canoe a slap, and commanding it to go, it glided through the water with inconceivable swiftness. In a few minutes they reached the habitation of Mishosha, standing on an island in the centre

of the lake. There he lived, with his two daughters, the terror of all the surrounding country.²⁹

Though Mishosha announces to his elder daughter that he's brought home a young man for her to marry, neither she nor her sister believes him. "'There again!' she said; 'our father has brought another victim, under the pretense of giving me a husband. When will his enmity to the human race cease; or when shall we be spared witnessing such scenes of vice and wickedness, as we are daily compelled to behold.'"³⁰

Mishosha makes four attempts on Panigwun's life. In the first two attempts, he leaves Panigwun on an island and commands first gulls and then the king of the fishes to eat him. Panigwun threatens them with his knife and reminds them that the Great Spirit had given them to man to eat, not the other way around. Each time his intended killers take Panigwun back to Mishosha's island and his daughters express their surprise at his escape. Mishosha's third trick is to take Panigwun to an island full of eagles ostensibly to capture young ones so that Mishosha could tame them. He tells Panigwun to climb a tall tree where the eagles nest; as Panigwun reaches the summit of the tree, Mishosha commands the tree to "stretch yourself up, and be very tall." The tree does so and Mishosha tells it that he's giving it a gift, "this boy who has the presumption to molest your young. Stretch forth your claws, and seize him."³¹ Panigwun beheads the first eagle to attack and challenges the others: "What right have you, ye ravenous birds, to eat living flesh? He is an old woman. . . . Respect my bravery, and carry me back to the lodge of the old man, that I may show you how I shall treat him."³² Impressed with Panigwun's "spirit"—that is, his personal spirit, acquired when he fasted for a vision as a youth—the eagles carry him to the island on their backs. As the eagles fly over Mishosha sleeping in his canoe, the let him know whose side they are on by "[treating] him with great indignity."³³

In his last effort to kill Panigwun, Mishosha throws one of Panigwun's leggings and one of his moccasins into the fire while he sleeps. "I believe this is the moon in which fire attracts," he offers innocently in the morning, "and I fear they have been drawn in."³⁴ Panigwun remains silent. "Drawing his blanket over his head," Jane writes, Panigwun "communed with himself. 'I have full faith in my spirit, who has preserved me thus far, and I do not fear that he will now forsake me. Great is the power of my Manito; and he shall prevail against this wicked old enemy of mankind.'"³⁵ He puts his one moccasin and one legging on, and invoking his personal spirit, blackens his other leg with coal and ventures out, protected from the cold. This gave Panigwun the courage to "try his own powers" rather than merely react to the magician; and having agreed with the sisters that "the life

A Precious Wild Flower 107

the old man led was detestable, and that whoever would rid the world of him, would entitle himself to the thanks of the human race," he decided to take action.[36]

Panigwun invites Mishosha to hunt and this time, while Mishosha is asleep, Panigwun throws the magician's legging and moccasin into the fire, having learned "by some secret means, that the foot and leg were the only assailable parts of the magician's body; which could not be guarded by the spirits who served him."[37] Panigwun calls on his spirit to produce snow, cold, and sleet, and in the morning when Mishosha discovers what had happened says, "I believe, my grandfather . . . that this is the moon in which fire attracts, and I fear your clothes have been drawn in."[38] He encourages Mishosha to hunt, all the while "leading him around about ways; to let the frost take complete effect." Soon Mishosha's legs stiffen and he becomes "fixed to the spot, but he still kept stretching out his arms and swinging his body to and fro. Every moment he found the numbness creeping higher he felt his legs growing downwards like roots, the feathers on his head turned to leaves, and in a few seconds he stood a tall and stiff sycamore, leaning towards the water."[39] Panigwun climbs into the magician's canoe and returns to the sisters, who "agreed to put on mortal shapes, become wives to the young men, and forever quit the enchanted island." They went over to the mainland, the story concludes, "where they lived in happiness and Peace."[40]

There was much more that Jane could have included in this story. While it begins differently, William's Saginaw version incorporates all of the parts of the rolling head legend but adds an interesting twist at the end. After the defeat of the magician and the escape by canoe, Panigwun, his wife, and her sister hear his brother singing—"Half turned I am into a wolf, half turned I am into a wolf"—from across the lake. The boy runs off when they approach, but the sister-in-law digs a hole and baits it with meat to capture him, which she soon does. The sister-in-law was "somewhat a Maujeekequawis," William writes. (Maudjee-kawiss is the eldest brother of Manabozho [the name means "beginning son"]; Basil Johnston, an Anishinaabe elder and scholar, writes that the name and its feminine form illustrate the responsibility elder brothers and sisters have for their younger siblings.[41]) Unfortunately, even after his brother returned him to his former shape with medicines and charms, the younger brother remained "very soured" and "gloomy." He also doesn't return Maujeekequawis's amorous attentions, so she decides to trap him again, by digging another hole into which he promptly fell. "Ha, ha, cried Maujeekequawis," William writes; "you are mine I have caught you at last," at which "a smile came over the young man's face, and [he] said, So be it, I will be yours, and from that moment they lived happy as man and wife."

Eventually the brothers announce their desire to visit a high mountain far away and "see the country which lay beyond it." They wanted to join their father in the sky world. Their wives don't want them to go, but they do, knowing that their wants will be taken care of by the elder brother's son. They leave on a dark, still night when "not a breath of air could be felt." At first they hear "the rumbling noise of the rolling Thunder . . . advancing from the north," then "suddenly the quietness of the night gave place, to one of the most terrible tempests ever witnessed," William writes. "The dark air was lit up with flashes of vivid and forked lightning, and the roar of that ear-stopping thunder was incessant, and the suddenly rushing south wind laid many a stately forest level with the earth." Along with their father they unleashed "just vengeance on all Weendigo & Magicians; for it appears that after [the father] was fixed in his ethereal abode, he beheld the bad actions of the Weendigoes & other wicked men. And he thought it best to destroy them, and rid the earth of such monsters, and also to take just vengeance for what he suffered."[42]

One of the reasons why Jane avoided more explicit references to Anishinaabe spirits and other figures might have been that, even at the very outset of his career, Schoolcraft was ready to represent traditional narratives as not only exotic but in need of a quasi-scholarly apparatus to properly frame—and contain—them for a white audience. William seems to have contributed "Papuckewis," which unlike Jane's stories isn't signed, is described as a "myth" in the prefatory material, and concerns two important figures from Anishinaabe narrative, Papuckewis and his younger brother Manabozho. Basil Johnston describes Pukawiss (the contemporary spelling) as a wanderer, a dancer, and an actor, someone who disappointed his father because he was uninterested in the usual pursuits of men and couldn't compare to his warrior older brother, Maudjee-kawiss. His father rejected him; his name signifies "cutoff, disowned, unwanted." "Pukawiss was a wanderer with only his clothing and bundle in which he carried all his worldly possessions," Johnston writes. "As much as he would have liked to linger for a few days in one village, he could not; he had to go on, drawn forward by his people or urged, pressed onward, by some force or instinct within himself that he could not resist."[43] Pukawiss also liked to provoke "those who took life and themselves too seriously and who could not take a joke."[44] This group included Manabozho especially.

The preface notes that there were usually two winter storms in March or April, about which people would say "'Ah! Papuckewis is now gathering his harvest,' and this immediately puts the whole circle into the best humor, although perhaps the moment before, they were suffering from cold and hunger." The story itself takes place "in old times, during a long and severe winter" when Papuckewis and his family are starving; there are no more fish in the lake and the caribou are gone to the interior. Papuckewis travels along the shore of Lake

Superior where the wind had piled the ice "into high pinnacles resembling castles," to seek the pity of the "spirits of Cabebonoca," the North Wind. The spirits tell him to fill his sacks with ice and snow, go back toward his lodge, and without looking back drop his sacks at a certain place and return home, and in the morning he would find fish. The spirits caution him "that he must by no means look back, altho' he would hear a great many voices crying out 'Thief! Thief!' as he went along, for it was nothing but the wind sighing among the branches of the trees."[45]

Papuckewis does as he was told. When he brings the fish home, Manabozho—"who is often the subject of ridicule"—stops at his lodge, and so Papuckewis invites him to a feast. Papuckewis tells Manabozho his secret, and Manabozho goes off to get his own sacks of fish. This "brought upon him the displeasure of the spirits of Cabebonoca," and "as he ran along with his sacks of ice and snow, he continually heard 'Thief! Thief!' vociferated in his ears. 'He has stolen fish from Cabebonoca' cried one. 'Catch him! Catch him!' cried another. 'Muckumick! muckumick! muckumick!' cried a third. In fine, his ears were so assailed by these continued cries, that he could not avoid turning his head to see who it was, that uttered these opprobrious epithets."[46] The next morning Manabozho finds his sacks full of ice and snow. And because of his disobedience, the spirits "condemned him every year, during the month of March to run about over the hills with his bags of ice and snow upon his back, the cries of thief! thief! stop him! stop him! Muckumick! muckumick! still following him."[47]

William would always write about the spirits good and bad, but at this early moment in her career as a writer of Indigenous narratives Jane remained cautious, recognizing that the more specific she was about the nature of the spirits and their powers, the more exotic the stories would seem, making it easier for white readers to dismiss the idea that Indigenous people were like themselves. At the same time, however, while she emphasized moral behavior and wrote the stories as charmingly as she could, she also conveyed Anishinaabe beliefs about, in the case of the rolling head stories, relations between human beings and the spirit world and the responsibility of family members to each other. That was one way to answer Cass's ignorant questions.

Over the course of the *Muzzeniegun* Schoolcraft tried to assert himself over Jane and everyone else in her family. He began, in the first issue, by ventriloquizing the powerful people around Jane—her mother and Shingabawossin. He attributes "Character of Aboriginal Historical Tradition" to Ozhaawshkodewikwe as the daughter of Waabojiig. The narrator declares herself a "poor Orphan" who is relating her "own humble thoughts" to readers where previously they had only been "breathed out to the moaning of the winds through our dark forests." She promises to supply "a more correct opinion of the ideas peculiar to the Ojibways" and relates how well her parents got along with "the whites," how her father, a great leader, felt "himself bound by [his peace medal] to observe a strict attention to the duties of friendship" with the United States. The whites "knew the truth," instructed her father, because they wrote things down and were thus able "to relate . . . the great and noble actions of your forefathers, without variation," a decidedly Western sentiment. The promise of Christianity brought "tears of gratitude" to her eyes: "When the man in black comes to teach us poor young ignorant people the right way, I shall know better; and when I can write, I shall not forget to send you all the pretty songs and stories my mother used to tell me—to be put in your paper." (Ozhaawshkodewikwe showed no interest in Christianity at the time.) Shingabawossin appears as the narrator of "Friendly Speech of Shingabowossin to His Band," a fantasy in which the old chief (he would die in 1828) tells his people that they ought to sell their land to the Americans because Americans always paid for it, the proof of which was that all the tribes that had sold land were presently rolling in money.[48] Besides that, writes Schoolcraft as Shingabawossin, "your American father" sent you an "Agent to see to your wants, to feed you when you are hungry; to clothe you when you are naked, and to give you drink when you are thirsty." "Is this not evidence of his kind big heart?" wrote Schoolcraft about himself.[49]

Possibly this was attempted wit. Elsewhere in the same issue, he told an anecdote about ostentatiously offering and then dumping out ceremonial whiskey at a treaty, at either Prairie du Chien or Fond du Lac, observing that "the Indian is not a man of moral sensibilities." In another issue he included a "Chippewa Fable," "Weasel and Wolf," plainly written by himself, as it includes a sheep; in passing he told a story about his dog, Ponti, named for the great chief Pontiac. He touted his knowledge of the "Meda Society," relating how Shingwaukonse willingly revealed his "necromatic tricks" in Schoolcraft's own office.[50] Among several long poems is one called "Algonac, a Chippewa Lament on Hearing the Revellie [sic] at the Post of St. Mary's." This is about a depressed Chippewa warrior alternately pleading with white men to "teach me! ye wise men" and lamenting lost "arts, manners, customs," asking, "can they tell me, where joy shall abide, / without, national costumes, or national pride!"[51] He closed off one issue with "Conundrums": "When did a wagon crush the western Indians? Ans. When Gen. Wayne drove over them at Maumee."[52]

He devoted a good deal of attention to Jane, in various guises. He published her Ojibwe narratives under the pseudonym "Leelinau" and her melancholic poems under "Rosa" and juxtaposed the two throughout the *Muzzeniegun*'s run. The second issue includes an account of the "irreproachable" character of Catherine Brown, a famous Cherokee convert who, like good Indian maidens everywhere, died young. "She had a beautiful hand & conversed in a spirited style," Schoolcraft wrote, which described Jane but not necessarily Catherine Brown. "No heady denunciation proceeded from her lips, but she was ever, a produced example of truth, she taught to others," he added. This account includes yet another of Schoolcraft's poems: "And of the pious step shall go / To seek the spot where Catherine lies / And hopes, from her example, show / To lend her people to the skies."[53] In "The Vine and Oak," he produced an allegory on his relationship with Jane that seems particularly telling. "'I wish to grow *independently*,' said the vine [to the oak], 'why cannot you twine around me, and let me grow up straight, and not be a mere dependent upon *you*.' 'Nature,' answered the oak, 'did not *so* design it. It is impossible that you should grow to any height *alone*, and if you try it, the winds and rain, if not your own weight, will bring you to the ground. Neither is it proper for you to run your arms hither and yon, among the trees.'" Then the oak told the vine that if she went off to be tangled among the other trees, not only would the trees reject her but "nobody will *then* admire thee, or pity thee." And nobody, certainly not the vine, wanted that to happen, so "she twined herself around the oak, and they both grew and flourished happily together."[54]

Cass had made it clear to his protégé that he had the opportunity to make his mark in the world as an Indian expert, but Schoolcraft knew who and what the source of his authority actually was. One of the ways he beat back his unease was by continually invoking dead Indian maidens who could be associated with Jane in his writing. The third issue of the *Muzzeniegun* began with his faux Indian story featuring Olla, "the pride of her village, modest kind and respectful, [who] became an example and pattern for the village maidens." After a poetic interlude, she dies and becomes a rainbow.[55] In a later issue, he rewrote Jane's song "The Chippewa Maid" in his own "free version" so that instead of the girl mocking the departing soldier, she dies. "Alas what grief—what pain of mind / I felt when I was left behind," he writes, as the girl; "The kiss he gave—oh grief may kill, Brave youth! but I shall love thee still."[56] In the same issue he included Jane's poem "Lines Written under Severe Pain and Sickness," which ends in a similar fashion. Supplicating the Almighty, Jane writes, "Teach me each duty always to fulfill, / And grant me resignation to Thy will, / And when Thy goodness will that I should die, / This dream of life I'll leave without a sigh."[57] But this is a Christian sentiment, not the last words of a doomed Indian maiden.

It's true that for American writers at that time and for long afterward, even to the present, every Indian is a dead Indian, and it's also true that Schoolcraft was fond of literary cliché. The parade of dying and dead Indian maidens in his writing is striking because the connection to Jane is so obvious. He doesn't appear to have consciously wished his wife dead. But like his invented Indians who praised the virtue and beneficence of white men exactly as he and other Americans imagined they ought, Schoolcraft's dead Indian maidens embodied what he wished his wife to be—"modest, kind and respectful" (of himself) and completely inert without him, like the vine without the oak, a nonentity. The fact that he returned to dead Indian maidens again and again over the course of their marriage bespeaks Jane's noncompliance. She knew too much, questioned what he had to say, had opinions.

He seems to have taken the fourth new story from Jane before she was finished with it, more than likely because the theme appealed to him. "Moowis" is a story about a coquette who gets her comeuppance from a man made of excrement, which is what the word *moowis* means.[58] Schoolcraft would have found the plot attractive, as it is a story about a young woman who violated the codes of female behavior and was punished for it. The fact that in the text "excrement" is translated as "dirt" and the term "moowis" appears only as the name of the "dirt-image" raises the question whether or not he understood what exactly the story was about when he first read it. He understood later. Though the story isn't included in *Algic Researches*, after Jane died, in 1844, he sanitized it for *The Columbian Lady's and Gentleman's Magazine* and then a year later reprinted it in his own short-lived magazine, *Oneota*, with a preface noting its usefulness for teaching girls the dangers of flirtation. In those versions he noted in a preface that "the term Moowis is one of the most derogative and offensive possible. It is derived from the Ojibwa substantive, mo, filth, or excrement."[59]

The story may give some insight into how Jane went about producing a version for public consumption that she didn't write from memory, probably by first writing as the teller told it, then modifying it for a public setting. "There was a village full of Indians, and a noted belle or *muh-muh daw go qua* was living there," the 1827 version of the story begins, and "a noted beau or *muh muh daw go minnie* was there also. He and another young man went to court this young woman, and laid down beside her, when she scratched the face of the handsome beau. He went home and would not rise till the family prepared to depart, and he would not then arise. They then left him, as he felt ashamed to be seen by even his own relations."[60] The oddness of the diction—"noted beau"—and the unexplained actions ("laid down beside her") make this look like a rough transcription made as Jane listened to someone tell the story in Ojibwemowin. Repetition in the narrative also suggests an oral account. "It was winter, and the young man, his rival, who was his cousin, tried all he could to persuade him to go with the family, for it was now winter, but to no purpose, till the whole village had decamped and had gone away."[61]

The beau "gathered all the bits of clothing, and ornaments of beads and other things, that had been left," then "made a coat and leggins of the same, nicely trimmed with the beads, and the suit was fine and complete. After making a pair of moccasins, nicely trimmed, he also made a bow and arrows. He then collected the dirt of the village, and filled the garment he had made, so as to appear as a man, and put the bow and arrows in its hands, and it came to life."[62] Once having created his well-dressed man of excrement, the beau with the dirt-image rejoins his relatives, who think he's died. The dirt image is self-conscious of his effects. He asks one of the children to sit between himself and the fire, so that he wouldn't stink, but it doesn't help much. "All smelt the dirt. Some said, 'some one has trod on, and brought in dirt.' The master of the family said to the child sitting in front of the guest, 'get away from before our guest, you keep the heat from him.' The boy answered saying, 'he told me to sit between him and the fire.'"[63]

According to plan the belle immediately falls in love with the dirt-image, and the beau moves things along by directing the dirt-image to her lodge, where "towards morning, the image said to the young woman (as he had succeeded) 'I must now go away.'"[64] It's now the belle's turn to be desperate for lost love. She insists on going with the dirt image, although he warned her off. As for the beau, "the young man thought it a pity" that the belle had got herself in this position by treating *him* badly; he thinks to himself "how sadly she would be punished."[65] Then the dirt-image goes on his way while the belle follows behind, trying to keep up.

> When the sun rose high, she found one of his mittens and picked it up, but to her astonishment, found it full of dirt. She, however, took it and wiped it, and going on further, she found the other mitten in the same condition. She thought, "fie!! why does he do so," thinking he dirtied in them. She kept finding different articles of his dress, on the way all day, in the same condition. He kept ahead of her till toward evening, when the snow was like water, having melted by the heat of the day. No signs of her husband appearing, after having collected all the cloths [sic] that held him together, she began to cry, not knowing where to go, as their track was lost, on account of the snow's melting. She kept crying *Moowis* has led me astray, and she kept singing and crying Moowis nin ge won e win ig, ne won e win ig.[66]

The story in English is poignant rather than moralizing and vindictive as Schoolcraft wished to read it, perhaps another connection to its source. Considering the meaning of *moowis*, however, the story in Ojibwemowin could just be a joke. Its existence also raises other questions. Given her choice of stories up to that point, why was Jane writing down a story so obviously about sex? It may point to other stories she wrote that she didn't give or want to give to Schoolcraft, stories told by women, for example, which she would write down later in her career.

Who would say that the Indian is not a man of moral sensibilities to Ozhaawshkodewikwe or John Johnston, who contributed pieces to the *Voyager* and so presumably read it, let alone to Jane herself? A possible explanation might be that anyone Schoolcraft counted as an intimate must believe what he believed. And, being intimates, they would always be the exception to the rule. Or, possibly, he ran roughshod over everyone else's sensibilities because, consciously or unconsciously, he felt the need to defend himself. The people with whom he was most intimate were not always and in some cases not often intelligible to him. Ojibwemowin was the main language spoken in the village even after the Americans arrived. English was the third language of the village, after French, which Schoolcraft also didn't speak. The Johnston household ran in Ojibwemowin, but so also did his own. John Johnston knew the language well enough to converse at length and translate songs as they were being sung—so he knew the language well by the time Jane was grown. Jane spoke Ojibwemowin to Willie; so did her mother. Everyone in the house spoke it but Schoolcraft. He was dependent on interpreters for all his official transactions down to the most mundane. Every waking moment he was in danger of not knowing what they were saying, all around him.

He began to work out a system for asserting his mastery of the language and of the minds of the people who spoke it. But for two small innovations, everything he thought was common enough at the time. His first step—his contribution to intellectual and scientific history—was to give Ojibwemowin another name. "Algic" was his neologism for "Algonquin," a word that originated with the seventeenth-century French Jesuits in Canada to refer to a particular tribe; the Jesuits also asserted that the tribe's language was shared by many other tribes, including the Anishinaabe people, a range of tribes from the northeastern woodlands (Abenaki, Massachuset, Mahican), and the Delawares (Lenni Lenape), among others. The different tribal languages were construed as dialects of Algonquin. The category remains today, as "Algonquian languages." "Algic" appears to have been one of Schoolcraft's aestheticizing efforts, like his inserting random syllables into the transcribed Ojibwemowin Jane provided him. It was his word, different enough from the source for him to claim an original contribution. He also decided that it wasn't the Algonquins who spoke the essential form of the language but, conveniently for him, the Ojibwes.[67]

The language was "very copious," he wrote, in the third issue of *Literary Voyager*, having "many open vowel sounds," on account of which the language was at the same time "pompous" (he seems to have meant this as a positive quality, closer to "dignified") and "rather pleasing and agreeable."[68] It could not have originated with the people who currently spoke it—this was his second innovation. "Neither the state of society in which they live, or have ever lived, so far as history extends, nor their physical wants or moral habits, seem to demand a language so varied in its pronominal range & combinations, and so complex in its syntax," he opined.[69] The origin of the language must have been "Asiatic," then, although that was impossible to trace in the language because that history was "literally buried under the grammatical rubbish of accumulativeness." In this (and in contrast to Heckewelder and Du Ponceau) he simultaneously invoked Americans' favored theory of the origin of Indigenous people in the Americas, that they were one of the lost tribes of Israel who had wandered over the Bering Strait land bridge, and exempted himself from having to prove his assertion. He was focused on the future. What the language needed to raise it up out of the "barbaric wastes" of contemporary Ojibwe life was to be "reformed, & reduced to regular rules of science"; it needed "polish proportions, & chiseling." It needed a dictionary and a grammar.

Despite the "backwardness" of the people who actually spoke the language, it was still "capable of bold and energetic combinations through which philosophy might pour the richness of thought, and genius breathe the enchantments of poesy and eloquence." In conceding the language's complexity and aesthetic qualities, he could only have been repeating what the members of the family had already told him, Jane chief among them, as always. As far as he was concerned, though, it was only he who could do the necessary reducing the language to rules, "unravelling . . . its grammatical involutions and [comprehending] its recondite principles."[70]

He returned to the question of who could really know the language in subsequent numbers of the magazine. In response to "our correspondent 'A native'" on the topic of the purity of Ojibwemowin—this was probably William Johnston—Schoolcraft observed that the language was pure in relation to "the degree of refinement of living and manners of the people," meaning that it was not very pure at all. Despite this, he continued, "the chief orators pride themselves on using the best language; they never violate the class of nouns; and their example becomes a standard to the young, while those families, in which there is a mixture of European blood, pique themselves on their superior knowledge of both the vocabulary and grammar."[71] The Johnstons could make no claims about the correctness of their Ojibwemowin, even less than the chief orators, who being savages were incapable of having a true knowledge of that which the language was capable. That left (again) the American scholar, himself, as the only one who could sort things out and truly know.

His opinions about the debased nature of Ojibwes extended to other conclusions about their moral and mental condition. At the end of his long poem "The Yellow Isle," which features a dialogue between the "red-man" and the "white-man," the white-man exclaims to the red-man that his own people "[will] them aught but good" through education and the religion that "seeks by truth's prophetic rod, / Aught, but to bring them back to God."[72] This brief reference to bringing Indians "back" stemmed from Schoolcraft's idiosyncratic gloss on the lost tribes story. According to Schoolcraft, it wasn't that the Indians descended from one of the tribes that had been expelled from Israel; it was that they left of their own accord, and in doing so, in refusing what Schoolcraft saw as proto-Christianity, they also willfully refused Christianity itself. Everyone knew Indians were "impoverished, feeble, and erratic," Schoolcraft wrote in "The Unchangeable Character of the Indian Mind," a summary account of his nascent theory. They were a "moral problem" because they refused to change, despite the "manners and opinions urged upon them by precept and example of centuries," courtesy of Europeans.[73] The Indian of 1827 and the Indian of 1534 possessed the same mental characteristics. "Both exhibit the same patient endurance of human suffering, the same stoical indifference to pain and hunger, the same passion for warlike achievement and love of a wild forest independence, which have cost them so many battles, so many defeats, and so profuse a loss of numerical force, and territorial sovereignty," he wrote.[74]

To explain their mystifyingly unchangeable nature, there must be some "principle in the Indian mind" that resisted not only "intellectual culture" but also "agriculture and the mechanic arts."[75] Along with other American writers, Schoolcraft was looking for some way to say that Indians would never change because they were incapable of it—that they were inherently different from whites and permanently inferior. In the eighteenth century, environmentalism held that the environment ultimately produced differences among human beings, and it had a built-in weakness in that, according to its logic, if people could be taken out of their environment, they could change. By the early nineteenth century, that potential for change had to be denied if anyone was going to be able to justify the Indigenous dispossession and African American slavery that were essential to the political and economic order. How could you justify slavery if that slave could become a poet, like Phillis Wheatley?[76] How could you justify expelling Indigenous people if they successfully adapted to change but still insisted on their political sovereignty, like the Cherokees?

As Schoolcraft and other Americans struggled to say what they wanted to think, the meaning of the phrases they used to describe Indigenous people's minds and dispositions began to shift. "Indian character," a common phrase, still described a set of qualities, but those qualities were increasingly posited as permanent and, the implication was, inherent. "Indian mind" was an offshoot of Indian character representing the intellectual lives of Indigenous people, given all those qualities. It had to do with Cass's question, whether or not Indians were capable of abstract thought. The answer was no. That was the primary characteristic of Indian mind. Only civilized white men were capable of abstract thought. It would be a few years before skin color became a signifier of inherent difference, and several more after that before the idea of inherent difference became a matter for scientific theorizing. In the meantime Schoolcraft and many others fixated on how strangely, how maddeningly impossible it was for Indians to change.

Indians were doomed, wrote Schoolcraft, "doomed to extinguishment by some inscrutable fiat... like the primitive inhabitants of Canaan, falling before their invaders like grain beneath the scythe, and leaving their rich inheritance 'to men of other minds.'"[77] It was the responsibility of those "men of other minds" to study those whom they had replaced, to "improve every opportunity for acquiring fresh information, and eliciting new and authentic traits of their character and history."[78] This was common argument for collecting information about Indians at the time, information that would then be used to justify the dispossession of Indigenous people. But Schoolcraft was talking about his wife and in-laws. Four and a half years after Schoolcraft arrived at the Sault, not quite three and a half years after marrying into the Johnston family, he had decided that the family was "impure" and had no claim to real knowledge about their own language; that Indians, despite everything Jane and others had told him, didn't have abstract thought or much of any other kind of thought; and that their refusal to submit themselves to his and US authority (one and the same, according to himself) was a moral outrage.

William had little patience with Schoolcraft's bullying claims to expertise about all things Indigenous, an attitude he maintained for the rest of his life even when he was on superficially good terms with his brother-in-law. He submitted two pieces under the pseudonym "R. A. Native," the same "A Native" to whom Schoolcraft responded on the purity of the Ojibwe language.[79] The first, "Native Comity," is a letter to the editor. "I am an Indian," wrote R. A., "and although I do not pretend to the knowledge of politeness, I mean that sort which regards domestic manners, yet I believe there is a native politeness existing, in some measure, in every human breast; and that an Indian feels it, and exercises it, as well as the most refined and civilized of the whites." No Indian, he continued, "would ever think of snatching anything out of another's hand, unless he were angry" and "we take care, at social meetings and feasts, &c. never to appear angry, even if we feel so." Of course the editor would find "such conduct vulgarity and rudeness," but R. A. wants to be sure: "I beg you will give me your opinion, and tell me if I am right or wrong."[80] R. A.'s need to protest Indian civility would seem to have arisen from personal experience. He may also have contributed the acrostic,

> Cunning, active, full of bravery,
> Hating av'rice, toil, and slavery,
> Iron-hearted in their daring,
> Prizing valor, and way-faring,
> Prone to give, in cot or waste,
> Ever happy to the feast,
> Who shall say, they lack the merit,
> All may seek—but few inherit.

Schoolcraft answered this plea for a reassurance of equality among human beings with musings on Lewis Cass's "repose of character" and an acrostic "to his excellency": "L.over of letters—mild and able, / E.ver zealous, prompt and stable" and so on.

William also contributed a love story where mixed-race people are pure Indians, Indian men have emotional lives, and everyone lives happily ever after, narrating the story in the guise of a white gentleman traveler not unlike his brother-in-law, although better informed. "Some years back I was brought to notice some of the characteristic traits, of the natives of our forests and the rarity of such circumstances," he began. "Even in polished societies, as that to which I was an eye witness induces me to state the particular. The occurrence which I shall relate, took place at what may be called the farthest, at least it was then so considered, and which few of the enterprising Eastern adventurers had as yet reached at that period." This alludes to Schoolcraft's own writing which more than a few reviewers, Cass among them, noted for its lapses into tedious travelogue.[81]

Morning Star and Waving Plume were Indians even though "they may have had some of the blood of the white-man," writes William.[82] Morning Star "was nature's pure child, and the impulses of her bosom had always flamed in the same channel, up to the present time, and they were such as what the whiteman would call very moral, although unacquainted with the standard by which civilized moralists are guided."

> Free from flattery and deceit, she belonged to a class whose manner of life differed essentially from refined society. Pure in mind & simple in appearance, she was exempt from evil, and feelings which she had formed in early life were lasting. . . . As to her appearance she was tall

A Precious Wild Flower 119

and very fair, remarkably so for one who could or would claim but little of the white man's blood, her head was covered in black flowing hair, which fell over her shoulders, and which was kept smooth by a head comb, over the edge of her high forehead she wore a black ribbon, which showed that to advantage.

Her teeth were white as pearl, her features were exact, her appearance at first sight was engaging and modest, and in all her movements very graceful, she was adept in all the simple accomplishments of her sex, she looked handsome in her garnished mockesins, & her neat plain blue mantle, which induced others to copy her neatness. There was a peculiar pleasantness in her looks, and her dark beaming eyes gave a finish to the whole.[83]

Morning Star is pure, yet mixed; fair, yet Indian; virtuous, yet unrefined. The story has echoes of Jane's stories in its crossing up of Ojibwe and sentimental themes and even of his father's romantic idealizing of North American life, but it was also a direct challenge to Schoolcraft, incorporating as it does his favorite figure of the pining Indian maiden—only in William's telling, she pointedly doesn't die.

Waving Plume requests the narrator to come along as he says goodbye to his betrothed, as he had to go "to the Mississippi" for a year. They "found her seated on a rock, listening to the passing bubbling stream, and gazing on the smooth surface of the river, as it glided along a short distance below, and which the declining rays of the sun, gave a golden appearance, and those rays cast their mellow shades over the beautiful scenery around."[84] Morning Star's pleasure at seeing Waving Plume soon gives way to despair. "She gazed at him with a look of vacancy, and extended her arms, and said, 'will you thus leave me,' and both clasped each other in their arms," William writes, and "when she was again seated, I used all the encouraging language I could to relieve their feelings. I told them to hope for future happiness, and brighter prospects. I then took the young man by the arm, and led him away from the painful scene. The young woman cast a wild look after us, and then dropped her head on her bosom, and we turned an angle of the road or path, and she and all the village was lost to our view."[85] Waving Plume spends the entire time "sad and melancholy," lamenting his "fears and hopes" to his traveler friend, while Morning Star is so distressed for days she can't even cry.[86] She loves to walk in the forest and "pour out her feelings in that low plaintive and melancholy strain which is so peculiar to Indian women, and which only those who understand it, can appreciate."[87]

Finally Waving Plume returns. Before his canoe lands "they clasped each other in their arms." "I never witnessed a more affecting meeting," says the narrator. "They are indeed ornaments to their sexes and a blessing to a man, and may all such realize the joys which this world can give. I witnessed the ceremony which connected their hearts for life, & they were happy in the circle of their friends. A pleasant period after I bid adieu to them and the interesting scenes of the West."[88] In the ironic guise of this traveling white man, William maintains that to say something intelligent about Indigenous people you had to know the language, as it was the key to everything, and to have experience living with the people. He was pointedly talking to his brother-in-law, who may or may not have understood what he was saying because as far as Schoolcraft was concerned, he did consider himself as living among Indigenous people and having an expert knowledge of the language.

Jane pushed back too. There are strong signs that she was very consciously parodying her husband's favorite Indian maiden tropes in "Origin of the Miscodeed, or, The Maid of Taquimenon," which appeared late in the series, in issue eleven. The story is about Miscodeed, the daughter of Ma Mongazida, who lived with her parents in the valley of the Tahquamenon River. Ma Mongazida was Jane's great-grandfather, the father of Waabojiig, and the Tahquamenon River was across Whitefish Bay from the Sault. "Beauty sat upon her lips," she writes of Miscodeed, "and life and animation marked all her motions." She is fourteen years old, possessing "happy simplicity," wishing only to "[revel] amid the wild flowers of her native valley." When she fasts to obtain a guardian spirit, she receives a "little angel . . . in the shape of a small white bird, of purest plumage."

> Happy were her slumbers in this delightful visitation, and happy her awakening, as she hasted back, with fawn-like fleetness, to her parents lodge, with one more charm—one more pleasing recollection—one more tie to bind her fancy and her heart to the sweet valley of the Taquimenon. Beautiful valley of soft repose! there, she had first learned how to know the sweet face of nature, and see the river leap & laugh in foam, from the rocks, and then pursue its sylvan course through the green leafed forest. Sweet enthusiast of nature! wild gazer of the woods! There, too, were the sacred graves of her forefathers, and there, she hoped, when the Great Spirit should summon her to depart, her friends would lay her simply bark-encased body, under the shady foliage in a spot she loved.[89]

As a beautiful Indian maiden, it probably didn't hurt to plan ahead.

As springtime bursts forth around Miscodeed, her father worries about the Outagamies. "He lay on his couch," and dreams that he was "the leader of a hostile band, who broke from the ambush, at the earliest dawn, and carried death and desolation to a slumbering village." Remembering that "birds of ill omen had crossed his path, the day before," he says to his wife,

> Had it been my *enemies*, the Dacotahs . . . I should have feared no evil, but to dream of raising the war club against the Outagamies, my own blood kindred, and with whom we have long been in peace, bodes me more disaster. Some hostile foot is, even now, on the track. Some evil bird has flown over my lodge. I will no longer abide here. Had I sons to stand by my side, most freely would I meet the foe; but, single-handed, with no one but thee, to bury me, if I am slain, and my tender Miscodeed to witness my fall, and become their prey, it were madness to abide. And this day, even before the sun is at its zenith, will I quit the peaceful valley I love—the sweet valley of the Tacquimenon.[90]

The family hurriedly eats breakfast and "made their preparations to leave a scene, so loved and cherished, but loved and cherished by none, more than the gentle and enthusiastic Miscodeed," Jane writes, adding that "she was indeed a precious wild flower."

It may be sometimes difficult to tell what is mocking and what is not in the distance of time when it's not possible to know the entire context of a piece of writing, but when the enthusiastic Miscodeed (and "enthusiasm" in US writing at the time was popularly used to mock romantic sentiments), the precious wild flower, is compared to the son lamenting his father's folly in "Origin of the Robin," or the bereft coquette at the end of "Moowis," or the strange spirits of "The Two Ghosts," the character appears purposefully overblown. Moreover, she and her father from the first are preparing to die. Which they soon did. Suddenly, the family is "alerted by the instinctive sagacity of the Red Hunter, the household dog" (shades of Schoolcraft's dog Ponti), which begins barking and "flew out the door." It was not the Outagamies attacking but the Mendawakantons or Dacotahs. "A volley of arrows followed, piercing the thin barks, which hung, like tapestry, around the lodge, and sealing in death at the same instant, the lips of both father and mother," Jane writes. "'Oh, bird of my dreams,' cries Miscodeed, 'my beautiful white wing!—my angel of promise! save me from the hands of my cruel enemies.' So saying, she sunk, lifeless to the ground."[91]

In comes the eldest son of a warrior who's been killed by the Chippewas, with red-painted brows and "spear poised," seeking his revenge. But Ma Mongazida and his wife are already dead, and as "the eye of the savage leader rolled in disappointment around," he sees only a white bird fly from the lodge. "The knife and the tomahawk were cheated of their prey," writes Jane, using one of the most stereotypical phrases associated with Indigenous people in the nineteenth century (along with the typical savage's "rolling" eyes when on the attack); "[Miscodeed's] guardian angel had saved her from being the slave of her enemy."[92] Better to die than to live. The warrior takes the scalps and leaves; when friends come to the lodge, "all they saw on the ground where the maid of Tacquimenon had fallen, was a modest little white flower, bordered with a pink border which was at once destined to be her emblem."[93]

Despite the fact that he published everything of Jane's he could get his hands on after her death when he was desperate to make money in New York in the 1840s and when he was churning out the Indian history in Washington in the 1850s, Schoolcraft never republished this story. Despite its suitability for a ladies' magazine readership—no editing was necessary—and despite the fact that he was not above inserting his own inventions into his collections of Indian stories, he ignored it. He even shunned it. The next edition of the *Voyager* contained only a page-long excerpt of an old travel account of his, and the thirteenth, more miscellany, beginning with "Lament for the Race," spoken by yet another defeated Indian warrior at the falls of St. Mary's, comments on the fur trade, geographical discovery in Michigan, a character sketch praising Gitche Iauba for his loyalty to the United States, more old travel, and two poems on Waabojiig: his own, and Jane's old "Invocation to My Maternal Grandfather." After "Miscodeed" everyone seems to have lost interest in his little magazine.

Chapter 5

A New Creation

In the middle of March 1827 Willie had a cold, and the next day he was dead of the croup. Jane took to her bed, subsumed by overwhelming grief. Weeks later Zina Pitcher was still in daily attendance on her. "It has pleased the almighty to take to himself my beloved and *ever to be lamented* Son William Henry," she wrote from her bed to George by the last winter express, enclosing a ribbon of black crepe for his hat, "& it is a consoling thought to me that my *Sweet Willy* is rejoicing with exceeding joy before the throne of his Heavenly Father, where he will never know pain or sickness more."[1] After Willie died, she and Schoolcraft left their rented house on the village green and returned to their old quarters in the Johnston homestead to await the completion of the new agency house. She wrote and rewrote a poem in English eulogizing Willie; given her habits, it seems there would have been one in Ojibwemowin, but if it did exist it hasn't been found. She was pregnant with their third child at the time.

Schoolcraft struggled with the meaning of Willie's death. When he wrote about his son in the penultimate, memorial, number of the *Voyager*, published two weeks afterward, he described his son as having "a face of the purest Caucassian [*sic*] whiteness," and "eyes with the brilliancy of a polished diamond, auburn hair, and features of the sweetest amenity of regularity." The baby was so beautiful that in New York people stopped on the street to marvel, and when they found out that "his mother was another Pocahontas, Chippewa blood by the maternal line, and a sire from the coasts of Dalraida in the north of Ireland, where [his mother] was educated," they were amazed, and many came to call on mother and child in their boardinghouse just to get a closer look. Willie was "precocious in every thing," he wrote in a passage that shows how closely he paid attention to his son, which was not his habit with anyone or even anything else. "He chased his shadow on the wall, as a phenomenon; he talked to his little dog, as if possessed of reason, and he, manfully got out of his little carriage, on any little account, offering to aid in repairing the mechanical interruption. The completion of the garrison saw mill, became a new and very exciting object of his notice. The roaring of the water, and above all, the action of the surf arrested his deepest attention." Ozhaawshkodewikwe spoke to him in Ojibwemowin, calling him "by [the] native infantile exhibition for boys, of penaysee or little Bird, a term of manly endearment, birds being symbolically, referred to as figures of speech in war." She made him a pillow of swan's down "plucked from the game brought in by aboriginal friends."² Willie was more intimately tied to Ojibwemowin than Schoolcraft himself was. Willie was effortlessly intelligent, unlike his father, who strained and when necessary, faked it.

"God saw that we had erected an idol in our hearts," Schoolcraft wrote to Samuel Conant. Christianity taught that earthly existence was full of "trial and affliction, in which no true happiness is permitted, and that we must look forward to a future state for that 'peace, which passeth all understanding.'"³ Conant agreed. When love of God became the "'master passion,' when the Saviour is preferred 'above our chief joy,'" Conant wrote, "then shall we see that it is truly a *benevolent* [God] which cuts off our idols, shows us our weakness, & schools us for Heaven." Conant's health was declining and he'd withdrawn to his home; he'd be dead in a few years. He had four sons and a wife. "I cannot bear to think of your calamity," he wrote, but still: "It is often the case, when a series of afflictions are adopted as the means of creating moral improvements, that the hand of God is laid on heavier & heavier, until the sufferer is brought to submission, sometimes in the last extremity, & then he is released & made an heir of eternal life." Willie's death gave Schoolcraft another chance. "Is not this benevolence from God?" Conant asked.⁴

Schoolcraft found in evangelicalism an answer to God's rebuke. In the early nineteenth century, evangelicalism was an approach to Protestant spirituality whose believers could belong to established or upstart denominations—Presbyterians, Baptists, Methodists, even Episcopalians. It downplayed doctrine in favor of an emphasis on a profound conversion experience, a sincere connection to God, and a charge to convert the unconverted. A good Christian was required to live by the precepts adherents saw in the Bible—temperance, chastity, honesty, industry, obedience. That self-discipline was the only means of gaining true freedom in Christ, and its practice was often construed as an individual's moral character. Because evangelicals believed that God was in control of everything, they also believed that any material benefit they gained was the result of God rewarding them for that moral character. Evangelicals had no interest in political or economic systems as such; they knew that providence and good Christians of moral character such as themselves would prevail.

While evangelicalism made some adherents abolitionists—"God is no respecter of persons" was their refrain, from Acts of the Apostles—others were slavers for whom evangelical precepts became a justification for and defense of their own greed and viciousness. Slave labor gave the godless Africans self-discipline, they maintained, and someday, maybe, they would achieve enough self-discipline to be free. In the meantime the planter and overseer were doing God's work, the proof of which was in the vast wealth they had accumulated. According to these Christians, the more money a man had, the more moral character.[5] This aspect of evangelicalism as practiced especially appealed to Schoolcraft.

Evangelicals "knew that no earthly source of judgment was superior to their own," writes historian John Patrick Daly in his book *When Slavery Was Called Freedom* (2002).[6] Evangelicalism's logic was so powerful and so attractive that it became pervasive in US antebellum society, so that you didn't need to be an evangelical believer to have absorbed its precepts in reduced form: self-discipline produces moral character, which God would reward here and now.[7] This infusion of evangelical thought put a finer point on American thinking about Indigenous people, making the insistence on benevolence somewhat less belabored if only because US officials could make more shameless moral claims. As they moved into the 1830s, Americans weren't just offering civilization to the Indians; they were, they said, offering Indians self-discipline, true freedom, and God's grace when they took Indigenous land, along with the few implements and lackadaisical agency farmers the Great Father sent for their transformation into Lockean agriculturalists. Under the influence of evangelicalism the existing national story of the conflict between savagery and civilization became, as Daly observes of evangelicalism proper, both "rigidly didactic and almost miraculously exuberant" with regard to the fortunes and destiny of the United States.[8] As for the white American man at the center of this, evangelicalism offered a more precise conception of him on whom civilization's triumph over savagery depended. He was not just a property-owning white man, but a white man of supreme moral character, doing as God commanded, world history at his back.

That man would be Henry Schoolcraft, who took all of this into himself. The pieces didn't fall into place immediately after Willie's death, but by the time he had his conversion experience in the fall of 1830 his transformation was complete. He had unshakable belief in his own moral rectitude, and that moral rectitude required everyone, Jane especially, to recognize it and fall in line with his desires. Everything that he did in relation to Indigenous people, every treaty he struck, was done, he said, for their benefit, moral and otherwise. What Jane thought about this she didn't keep to herself. But after the deaths of two children and the evangelical fervor that swept through the Sault in the next few years, she became less confident in her Christianity and more inclined to anxiety over the state of her soul, a feeling of which Schoolcraft took advantage, consciously or not.

Jane's depression remained as her pregnancy advanced. In the summer as a distraction she'd gone by steamboat with Schoolcraft as far as Green Bay when he had to attend yet another treaty about boundaries, this time at Butte des Morts. Afterward he told her to remember that whatever had happened to them, other people had it worse. And if they were not as happy as they thought they should be, "it is to be imputed in a great measure to our own imperfections and the state of worldly trial in which it has pleased a wise creator to place us." Jane needed to stop pining and work on her imperfections.[9] By the time she received this advice, she was at Mackinac in bed at the home of George Boyd, the agent there, having almost miscarried at five or six months. McKenney had been with her in the steamboat and went on to the Sault to bring George, Eliza, and Charlotte down to take Jane home when she was able. "I can yet declare the goodness of God my Saviour, who tho' he has chastened me, yet hath not given me over to death," she wrote to Schoolcraft. She wrote something odd, though. "Everything depended on my keeping as still & quiet as possible, & with the blessing of God I have received no farther injury, but shall have to be very careful of myself," she wrote, and in parentheses, "Oh that *you* my dearest dearest Husband was near enough to see that I did take that care, & precaution which will be necessary for the preservation of not only *my life* but that of———."[10] She felt it necessary to reassure him that she was taking care of herself and her unborn child. She'd been so distraught after Willie's death and a year and a half before that the stillbirth of her daughter that she didn't want another baby, and she didn't want to live. Schoolcraft praised God when he found out that despite their "weakness and wickedness," she had been spared. "You could give me no more flattering proof of your love & respect, than by cherishing a constant & tender regard for your physical well-being. . . . You know not how light an exertion may tend to frustrate *our hopes*."[11] Jane's father came from Drummond, and in a few days Charlotte, Eliza, and Jane traveled home with Indigenous men who worked for Thomas Anderson, the British Indian agent at Drummond, which incensed Schoolcraft.[12]

Jane Susan Ann Schoolcraft—her middle names were her Ojibwe grandmother's English names—was born in October, and later that month the family moved into the agency house Schoolcraft had fought to have built for several years through numerous reprimands from McKenney and Cass about cost overruns.[13] It had a white clapboarded two-story central building with an attic connected to a kitchen on one side and an office on the other by breezeways. Inside there were heavy arched wooden doors to close off the main rooms in winter; the windows were double-paned. A builder of townhouses from Detroit oversaw its construction so that instead of a symmetrical house with a center hall, the door was on the left side, as a townhouse's would be. Schoolcraft sited his manor house across the river from the imposing stone

The canoe on Lake Huron, drawing by Anna Brownell Jameson, *Voyage to America Portfolio* (1837). Baldwin Collection of Canadiana, Special Collections and Rare Books, Toronto Public Library, Toronto, Ontario, Canada.

house only recently vacated by the fur trader Charles Oakes Ermatinger and his Ojibwe wife Mananowe, who had moved to Montreal with their numerous children. There was a perfect view of Elmwood across the river from its windows.[14]

As a further sign of his importance, Schoolcraft was elected to the territorial legislature in November 1827 for the first of four years. As his status increased, his trips away from home became longer and more frequent. So also did his desire to know what Jane was doing in his absence—what she thought about, whom she talked to, what she wrote. For the rest of their marriage she wrote diaries at his request when he was away at the legislature and later, at the agency office in Detroit or at Washington during the winter, mailing sections of it to him at intervals. Only one of these has survived intact, from Schoolcraft's first winter away at Detroit. It began in April 1828 and lasted into May, while Jane was supervising Elmwood's landscaping and first garden. "How can I better employ the stillness of my lonely evenings, after my lovely, *precious* Babe has peacefully sunk to repose," she began, "than by committing the little occurrences of each succeeding day during my dearest Husband's absences, to writing?"[15]

Eliza and Charlotte visited daily, by canoe; the household included Lewis's daughter Sophie and Anna Maria, whom Jane was tutoring in penmanship, and Tom Shaw, an Ojibwe man who had grown up in the Johnston

128   Chapter 5

household and whose wife had just had a baby. He baked bread when Jane sprained her wrist. One evening Anna Maria "read aloud two very interesting Tales" while the baby slept (she doesn't say what kind of tales these were). Lieutenant Morton visited with Charlotte and Eliza several days to work on his Ojibwe vocabulary. He "knows just enough of the Ojibwa to perceive he knows nothing about it," he told her. He presented Jane with a map of London when he was transferred out, giving some indication of what they may have talked about, as Jane would have remembered London from childhood. Francis Audrain, the subagent, made periodic and occasionally mystifying appearances along with the interpreter Henri Leveque. Whiteheaded Woman brought a makak of sugar and others, waiting to see the subagent, brought more sugar for the "Chief's little son," making Jane sad.[16]

Over the weeks the men, including Francis Deshome, another agency employee, sodded the bank and cleared the garden and lawn plots, pausing to chase away locals who insisted, Jane wrote, on making "the garden & front of the house their highway." They planted elm trees along the riverbank in front of the house, apple trees along the fence between plum trees and sweet briar, cherry trees in boxes on the piazza under the dining room windows. Charlotte brought two lilac bushes; Captain Anderson sent Lombardy poplars and golden willows from Drummond. The garden was planted with celery, cabbage, carrots, beets, beans, turnips, radishes, lettuce, bell peppers, cucumbers, and chives. Despite the best efforts of Kautshedaus, another young man who sometimes worked for Jane, the asparagus bed continued to disappoint. She laid out her flower garden and had the potato lot seeded after Audrain "[ordered] a family away . . . composed of two of the *worst women* of the place, one of them was the mother of the girl that was ravished last fall. Soldiers were seen at their lodge every night since they landed."

She showed the baby pining for her father multiple times over the course of the diary. Little Janée "has cryed [sic] 'Papa!' Papa!' very often during the day & evinced a strong desire to go to the study which I have more than once gratified," she wrote on the second day of her diary; "I need not say how much I felt for her, as well as for myself." Janée was about seven months old. Complaints crept in. Jane discovered that Schoolcraft hadn't arranged to get fish for the household, so she had Leveque contract with Akeewainzea to supply it. She started salting fish to fill a barrel to send him. She wrote another poem lamenting his absence but also complained about being left alone to supervise the men working on the house and grounds, some of whom were in the habit of wandering off. Audrain tried to blame her for his own decision to revoke Isaac Butterfield's trading license (he was trading liquor) after having asked her opinion what he ought to do. She assured Schoolcraft she kept copies of what were essentially thank you notes to Captain Anderson for sending trees and Mrs. Pitcher for giving her apples and oranges "to shew my Henry on his return." This seems to have been something he expected.

Jane dreamed about Willie, anguished that her own sinfulness would keep him from her in the afterlife. She declared her love for Schoolcraft—"O! My Husband you *little know* how much my heart is *yours*! & how much of my *happiness in this World* depends upon you. I hope that our *hearts*, as well as our *lives* are *forever* united"—and on the next day compared him to the sun. But she soon tired of writing. She felt it a "duty" to "render a faithful account of every thing that occurs *in* or *about* the house to my dear Husband, & I never wish to violate a *known* duty." She pointed out that while she'd never missed an opportunity to write to him, he hadn't done the same. Still, she hoped he would be pleased with her writing. If he was, "I shall be amply compensated for the loss of an hour or two of sleep every night, as it is only at night that I can think of writing." She hoped Schoolcraft would forgive its imperfections, she wrote several days later. She didn't write to please, but to tell the truth. "Perhaps I give vent to too many opinions, in matters my Henry may think concerns me not, but as I am resigned in relating faithfully whatever affects him or myself, I think I ought to do it without disguise, I love candor, and I wish to be candid myself in all things."

She finally gave up the journal, claiming exhaustion and describing one last trip with Janée to the study to cry for "Papa" after horrific news relating to William Holiday, John Holiday's son. Schoolcraft's sister Maria, by then married to the Fort Brady sutler John Hulbert, told Jane the details. Mrs. Pitcher was at the house as well, visiting in order to avoid "the painful and disagreeable sight" of a soldier being drummed out of camp. It had only just then emerged that two summers previously William and three other young men, all of them white except for William, had raped and murdered an Indigenous girl at Mackinac. One of his accomplices was a son of George Boyd, the agent at Mackinac, one was a son of Maj. William Whistler, an at the time former commandant at Fort Mackinac, and the other was the brother of a man named Baily, possibly the fur trader Joseph Bailly, who lived at Mackinac.[17] At the time William Holiday was nineteen and a student at the mission school at Mackinac, as were his younger sisters Mary and Nancy.[18] George Boyd and Baily, wrote Jane, "are striving to hush up the business and the latter, it is said, knew all about it, whilst he was a magistrate at the time it happened; but concluded it *like a traitor*." "The outrage committed on the poor unfortunate girl, is almost unparalleled, for atrocity and villainy, the brutality of these diabolical young men, deserves the execution of the law without mercy. The blood of the slaughter'd victim crys [sic] to *Justice (if it is to be found)* for vengeance on the heads of the horrid perpetrators . . . an example is much wanted, in the country to show that the laws of *both God and man* can be put in force, which might deter, many a daring, hardened wretch from the commission of crimes."[19]

Her anxiety about this news, compounded by the fact that William Holiday was at large in the vicinity, probably motivated a third-person reproach of her husband in the same entry. "I trust his health and spirits continue good," she wrote, referring to Schoolcraft.

> But I must not be too sanguine, neither ought I to be so selfish as to engage any of that time which he laudably employs for the good of the public, yet I cannot help feeling an anxious solicitude about him at times, and I very foolishly apprehended at intervals his disapprobation of my management at home and often fear the declension of his attachment towards me, tho' I console myself by thinking he will never change unless I provokingly deserve it, and that idea encourages me to strive to act in a manner that may ensure his good opinion of me, by which I may hope to secure his affections.[20]

This wasn't the first time in the journal that Jane openly wondered whether her husband loved her, but that these sentiments are couched in reproach for his not being at home to protect her and for his leaving her without enough money for food suggests that his simultaneous emotional detachment and moralizing surveillance were exhausting.

He remained oblivious—on paper, at least. He wrote what Jane perceived as perfunctory letters that thanked her profusely for her "*journal domestique.*"[21] The diary had him waxing poetic; the house (which he'd lived in for about six months) was the scene of the "happiest" times of their marriage. As "the wild winds of winter have whistled around our dwelling . . . it is there, that we have been more truly at any other time . . . *united in heart*, and have thought, & felt, & wished as *one*," he wrote. Perusal of her "*more than affectionate journal*" inspired him to write a poem about "our dear, lovely, promising, lamented Willy!"[22] He reflected on the state of his soul. Only those capable of choosing good over evil, "who have strength enough to resist, & to hold out to the last . . . have any well-grounded hopes, of their condition & prospects hereafter." How one must choose was clearly set out in the Bible, following the tenets of which ("purity, uprightness, charity") would "as much advance a man's standing *here*, as they will *hereafter.*" As it developed, Schoolcraft's spirituality was in his own mind never separable from the authority and status to which he aspired. "Nothing that renders a man more acceptable to his *fellow beings* (I speak alone of *Christian* society) but what will at the same time, render him more acceptable to God."[23]

John Johnston's death in the summer of 1828 elevated Schoolcraft to the position of family patriarch. Johnston had gone to New York that summer to sell his furs to John Jacob Astor, and he wanted to go home as soon as he arrived, he wrote to Schoolcraft; "one smile of affection from those I love is worth all the rest of the world."²⁴ On his return in September he fell ill, then the ship was stuck in fog on Lake Huron for days. He was carried off it when he finally returned to the Sault in mid-September and died, Schoolcraft wrote to the husband of Johnston's sister Jane. Despite his recent impairments, the death was a shock that "has overwhelmed his affectionate family & inconsolable widow."²⁵ This was true. Years later a visiting missionary walking in the graveyard one day came upon Oshaawshkodewikwe prostrate on her husband's grave, her face in her hands, sighing and weeping.²⁶

Schoolcraft began prohibiting Jane from going to or staying at her mother's house after her father's death. When he again attended the legislative council in the fall of 1829, he refused to allow her to close up Elmwood and stay with her mother while she waited for the birth of their son Johnston. "I cannot help feeling as tho' I had been cast off by *you* & *yours* in the approaching terrors of—of perhaps dissolution," she wrote to him in September 1829, a month before Johnston was born. Considering how common it was for women and their babies to die in childbirth, and how it was a month before her daughter's stillbirth that she realized her baby wasn't alive, this anxiety wasn't the product of an overactive imagination. She was angry at him for abandoning her. "I hope you are enjoying your health & spirits & that the pleasing attention of your friends may tend to dissipate any uneasy thought that may sometimes obtrude themselves in behalf of those you have left at home," she wrote. "Sister Charlotte is staying with me & every attention that affection can suggest on the part of my dear Mother & Sisters I receive, but Oh! how much better I should feel to hear from your *own lips* one expression of kindness, under the present circumstances." She was also resentful of his dictates keeping her from her mother, who was suffering from rheumatism. Ozhaawshkodewikwe and her sisters wanted her with them, "as it would be more convenient & less painful for mamma to attend me, but as you seem'd to have set your face against my going when I asked you, I have steadily declined to be persuaded & *now* every succeeding hour makes me feel a trembling anxiety so little strength is left me that I cannot go, had I ever so great an inclination."²⁷

In Detroit Schoolcraft wrote up a memorandum on "aboriginal names, so far as they are suitable, or can be *Anglicized*" as place-names for the impending state of Michigan. He wrote "Lines to My Pen," which pen he addressed as "my dearest friend": "Teach erring man . . . that no state is free from want & pain, / That love and fame are but a fleeting breath / And the true object of our living, death!"²⁸ He wrote to the editor of the *North American Review*, Jared Sparks, letting him know that he had been thinking of writing on "the relation of the white man to the Indian" for the *Review*, but that Cass had just finished his own essay, which Sparks would receive soon (this would be published in the January 1830 number of the journal). In Cass's essay "the great question of the removal of the Indians" was "put to rest," Schoolcraft wrote. "Time and circumstances have decided it against them.... The Indian is weak and vacillating, a desponding and suffering being, which he is painted in this review wasting his time in sensual quiescence, occasionally roused to active exertion, by war or hunger, but soon sinking back to a state of mental lassitude, in which he neither governs those around him, or is capable of being governed."[29]

The legislative council adjourned in early November, and Schoolcraft left, not knowing whether either mother or child lived or died. But on his arrival, there was his son, and in this case the boy's enlistment papers for the 1st Regiment, Company K, Veterans Reserve Corps thirty-five years later tell the story:

Hair:	Black
Eyes:	Hazel
Complexion:	Dark[30]

God sent him an Indian. Perhaps that's why, when he returned to Detroit the following spring, he took Jane and the children along and had the children baptized in the Episcopal Church on the fourth of July.[31]

He gave a lecture to the Historical Society of Michigan (he was one of its recent founders) while they were in the city, reiterating his theory that the only means of establishing a history of Indians in North America was through the study of their languages, along with thoughts on Indian character, reiterating the usual points. "They neither desire our knowledge, nor our religion," he declared; "they are not in a situation to appreciate our customs or institutions. They distrust our power, decry our refinements, and condemn our laborious industry." Their prospects are "gloomy," and the sooner their "political power [is] ... destroyed, the better for their own sakes."[32] There's a good chance that Jane would have read this address. She certainly would have read the collection of poems that someone, possibly Henry Whiting, the literary US Army captain, took to New York to be published as *Indian Melodies* (1830).[33] Inevitably, Jane featured in the collection. Schoolcraft rewrote her song on her stillborn daughter, changing the subject to a son; he rewrote her melancholy poem written in the voice of an Ojibwe woman calling for her lover's ghost so as to be almost unrecognizable ("Oh Zhayba, give me back my heart").[34] In "To Leelinau" he wrote,

> She—who in my bark-built tent,
> Smiling sits with sweet content

> Sweeps with bough my mossy seat,
> And prepares my mountain-meat.
> Blow, ye winds! 'tis nature's changeless law,
> But spare, oh spare, my smiling Leelinau.

But of course she wasn't spared:

> Gloomy storms will cease to howl,
> And fair skies succeed to foul;
> Wants will cease, and snows will melt,
> And reviving spring be felt;
> But, ah! while here on earth our breath we draw,
> What can restore life to my Leelinau?[35]

Schoolcraft seems confident in his path forward at this point in his life. He could think of himself as an increasingly important man, a public man, despite some personal burdens that he perhaps couldn't even say aloud, like his son's appearance and, according to his logic, the inevitable features of his character (Johnston would grow up to become difficult and rebellious according to his father). The issue of where his knowledge came from remained, however. John Johnston's death and Schoolcraft's increasing sense of himself as a Christian made Jane's subordination to him even more imperative in his mind. He doesn't seem to have ever let up.

After the publication of McKenney's book, travelers to the lakes began to seek out the charming Mrs. Schoolcraft. On a steamboat returning to the Sault from the family's trip to Niagara Falls, a former Presbyterian missionary named Calvin Colton (he'd lost his voice after his wife died a few years earlier and took to the road as a result) encountered Jane and wrote about it in a book about his travels. When their steamboat met a "gallant Indian canoe, propelled by eight men, in such display of their grotesque and glittering paraphernalia, shooting over the tops of the waves, and scarcely touching them," Colton wrote that Jane responded as if she were a child "at the sudden appearance of a loved object, that had been too long out of sight for his happiness."[36] Colton has her tell him, "I am glad. This is home. That canoe was launched from before my mother's door this morning. I know what it is—and who they are. That has been the delight of my youth—the familiar object of my childhood—it was the wonder of my infancy—and I shall be where it came from to-night."[37] When another canoe drew up to the steamboat, she began a conversation with the people on it, which Colton dissected linguistically despite never having heard Ojibwemowin before. Jane bent "over the side of the vessel, to welcome and receive the welcomes of this simple and untaught people—and *they*, manifesting the most evident satisfaction, on her return among them . . . they seemed delighted, and overjoyed to hear the sound of her voice."[38]

It's difficult to separate Colton's sentimental religiosity from whatever it was that he may have been seeing and what Jane said, particularly since American writers were in the habit of applying extra Indianness wherever they thought it necessary. Colton's account of Jane being received by the people in their canoes as an "idol" does seem a stretch. But this much can be taken from it: it's highly unlikely that she would have had a second thought about being taken home by Captain Anderson's men. Or that she would have agreed with her husband's high opinion of Lewis Cass, or his thoughts about the nature and prospects of Indians.

As Schoolcraft related it to Jane, his conversion experience was mainly about her. It happened at Mackinac on 22 November 1830 between ten and eleven at night. He was on his way, again, to Detroit to attend the territorial council, where he would remain until the following April. He was at the house of William Ferry, the Presbyterian missionary at Mackinac, engaged in religious conversation with Ferry and Robert Stuart, an American Fur Company official and leader almost twenty years previous of a doomed attempt to establish a post in Oregon (Indigenous people killed the traders while Stuart was away). "We all knelt, & Mr. F. made a most fervent prayer, in my behalf, reciting the vow, from that moment to lead a christian life, according to the 'spirit & truth,'" Schoolcraft wrote to Jane. Then he went to his room and read in *Rise and Progress of Religion in the Soul*, by the eighteenth-century English nonconformist Philip Doddridge. Afterward he wrote Jane a letter over several days about what his newfound religious feeling meant for her. He began with Ezekiel 11:23: "The prophet is speaking of Lyria & Jerusalem, under the symbol of the sisters, who have grossly departed from virtue, & turned their hearts to strange things. The 'Assyrians'—'captains & rulers'—horsemen riding horses &c are the vanities, passions, weaknesses, and idolatries of the inhabitants of these cities." It was a message for themselves. "Have not *we* also partaken of these weaknesses. Have we in all things done what we ought to have done & left undone nothing that we ought to have done? . . . Our religious transgressions have been manifold, and every day that we suffer to pass, without Christ in the world, is augmenting the fearful sum of human errors." In effect, though, he was talking about Jane.

The next day he continued the letter. He exhorted Jane to examine her heart and "see whether there is no thing there adverse to Christian principles—whether there are not opinions which are improper, weaknesses which ought to be strengthened, & hopes which ought to be abandoned." She didn't have to answer. We know, he wrote, "that such must be the case." She must change her ways, and strictly adhere to "Bible doctrine" in her conduct. "It is the domestic conduct of a female that is most continually liable to errors, both of judgment & feeling," he continued; "nothing is more clearly scriptural, than that a woman should forsake her 'father & mother' & cleave to her husband, & that she would look up to him with a full confidence as, next to God, her 'guide philosopher & friend.'" This too was nothing new, he admitted. "Often have I *felt*, often have I *said* that this should be the case, but never more sincerely than at this moment."

She needed to direct all of her attention to him and to his desires. "You are surrounded by many persons, who will express, & *some* who may feel a real friendship, but you have nobody, this side of the grave, who, next to God, is so near & dear to you as myself." Conversion intensified his need to surveil her. His next thought was that, since she was at present "placed in that authority, as head of a family, which a husband is invested within his own house," she particularly needed to "act & feel & see & hear, with wisdom & judgment." He was tired of her reproaches when he was gone. "Pray to God that he will strengthen you in the exercise of these duties—that he will fortify your heart—give you [a] just & humbling conception of yourself & lead you in all things, to forsake the wrong & pursue the right. . . . May you see & feel how kindly God has provided you with every comfort & enabled you to say, in sincerity, Lord how foolish have I been to murmur in the midst of these blessings." Piety gave Schoolcraft a means to transform his complaints about his wife into religious instruction and to construe her compliance as a matter of life and death. "Life is, itself, uncertain," he wrote, "& should it please providence to remove you by death, you will then truly see the force of this remark."

And then he told his version of her life.

> Brought up in a remote place, without any thing which deserves the name of a regular education, without the salutary influence of society to form your mind, without a mother, in many things, to direct & with an over-kind father, who saw every thing in the fairest light, & made even your sisters & brothers & all about you to bow to you as their superior in every mental & worldly thing, you must indeed have possessed a strength of intellect above the common order, not to have taken up some maxims & opinions & feelings, as false & foolish, as flattery & self deceit can be.

Deep thoughts always tangled Schoolcraft's syntax. What he meant was, his wife was so damaged from an inadequate upbringing that she didn't have the moral or intellectual fortitude to resist being led astray and therefore especially required his instruction. "What these things are, let your subsequent knowledge of the world decide," he wrote, "& when you have detected any thing of the kind, implore the father of light, that he will enable you to expunge it from your bosom."

He was well practiced in this kind of emotional abuse. "Let me entreat you, not to expect too much from *others*, from whom you have, in reality, no right to expect it," he wrote; "let it be impressed upon your mind that kindness and conciliation & gentleness are more potent than swords." She must have had sharp words for some of these thoughts in the past. "My dear Jane, whom I have taken 'for better or for worse,' & who is mine whatever may betide," he concluded, "Oh my dear friend, who are a part of myself—Kind mother of my children, turn your thoughts frequently & trustfully to me—Turn them seriously & solemnly to God, and remember, that while breath is mine, I am, & shall be, faithfully, your husband."[39]

By the time Jane received this letter, she had written three times to him, telling him that the father of their servant Harriet's baby had been discovered (Harriet herself wouldn't say), that the children (aged two and one) were both sick, and that his brother James was in jail at Mackinac, having drunkenly stabbed a man at a dance who was thankfully still clinging to life. When she did respond to its contents, she congratulated him on joining her as a dedicated Christian. "Tho' you have *probed deeply*, yet I thank you, because I know it was intended for my good," she wrote, unconvinced by what he wrote. She admitted that she had "indeed imbibed 'false & foolish feelings as much as flattery & self deceit could make me." "But alas who has not!" she added, deflecting his cruelty. "*But that is nothing to me*, neither shall it, *without the blessing of heaven* prevent me from striving to become 'a new creation' in sincerity & truth." And that was all she had to say about it, except for a casual mention of her mother's sleeping at the house every night.[40]

The letters unleash a torrent of annoyance. The ten-year-old girl she'd got to help with the children while Schoolcraft was gone decided to leave on the day she arrived. Jane had had to put her in clean clothes, after which Jane and her sisters saw her "standing at the end of the Office with her bundle of *old clothes* watching a canoe that was about to cross the river." She sent for the girl's parents the next morning. She was disappointed "at not receiving a line, a *pencil line* from you" by the express, and the children wondering innocently when Papa would come home make their appearance.[41] George and Audrain had "*broken loose, as it were*" a week after Schoolcraft had left. "George in particular carries on with a high hand in the name of '*Subagent and Interpreter for the United States*,'" she wrote; "I shall not enter in to particulars, suffice it to say, *all is not as it should be* in the Ind. Dept. & every one talks loudly of their conduct."[42] Before James, her problem was Harriet. "I shall now give you an extract of my diary without making any comments on the subject myself, but leave it to your *serious* consideration," she wrote in her first letter. (This diary has not survived.) "16th Nov.: a few hours after the departure of my dear Husband, Mrs. Audrain came to see me & informed me that her *black-man* had slept *two nights* in this house, (*unknown to us!*) & that he had owned himself the father of Harriet's unborn child." "Heaven preserve *me* & *my little ones* from the inmates of my own house!" she wrote, adding, "It pains me as much to write thus, as it will be for you to peruse it, but *you ought to know such doings* either at home or abroad."[43]

Harriet Gardiner was an African American woman from Western Massachusetts who seems to have replaced Lewis's daughter Sophia in the household after Sophia ran away with Henri Leveque (she eventually returned). She hid her pregnancy as long as she could; Schoolcraft thought that she should be let go in the spring. She could stay, he wrote initially, "but she should be made to know that a continuance of the intercourse, is not only highly criminal but totally inadmissible"—for or to what, he doesn't say. She was at the time about eight months pregnant. There might be "difficulties in the way of a legal marriage between her & the man," Schoolcraft thought. Joseph Bowen, the man in question, seems to have been a slave.[44]

Slavery was legal in Michigan Territory until statehood in 1837, and the fact that Francis Audrain was involved may explain why Harriet kept silent. Audrain was the youngest child of Peter, born in France, who came to Detroit via Pittsburgh and always made his living as an official (justice of the peace, commissioner of land claims, register of deeds) wherever he lived.[45] In 1812 Francis Audrain's older brother James married a woman from Kentucky whose father, Gen. Samuel Wells, sent the newlyweds an enslaved woman named Kate, for whose services they were to pay Wells. Instead, James hired Kate out in St. Louis and went to sell whiskey with Francis at Fort Osage on the Missouri River. A few years later James and his wife returned to Kentucky, leaving Francis to settle James's debts. To do so, Francis sold Kate to a Rufus Easton (before 1818 she was sold again to another man, James Irwin). General Wells filed suit against both Audrains.[46] The fact that Francis Audrain was the kind of man who would sell a person he didn't own to settle his debts—that would have been something that people, not least enslaved people, would have been interested to know. And for Harriet, isolated at the Sault in winter, what could she have thought—that Audrain would snatch her baby away, regardless of the fact that she was free? Considering that Audrain had proven himself not one to let the law get in his way, it was certainly possible.

"She has promised to marry her seducer," Jane wrote subsequently to Schoolcraft, "& *he* is only waiting to get a coat made for the occasion." She was still in high dudgeon. She kept house as Schoolcraft insisted, she wrote, "but to tell the honest truth, I should far rather have taken shelter with my mother [as] both a place of security, as well as to escape the disgrace of attending Harriet, which *will take place in a short time*, but you know the motives that induced me to keep house during your absence & those sentiments sustain me still, notwithstanding the ignominy of keeping *such a character in the house*."[47] On the eve of the wedding on 7 December, Jane had changed her mind about Harriet. "She is an excellent servant & I believe her morals are not absolutely depraved. I keep giving her good books to read when she has leisure, which may do *silent* tho' *effectual* good."[48] The sudden about-face suggests that, as when she wrote about the children pining for their father, she was ginning up moral outrage about Harriet and her "black-man" because it would be something to which Schoolcraft might respond. Harriet's baby was born on Christmas Day with the help of Jane, her mother, Mrs. Audrain, and Mrs. Deshome. They built a lodge away from the house for the birth, as if she were an Ojibwe woman.[49] Harriet stayed in bed with her baby upstairs, and Jane got another girl to help with the children, this one sent to Ozhaawshkodewikwe by White-headed Woman, her grandmother, who wished her to learn "the *White's Religion*."[50] Although Harriet's husband caused "some things to vex & perplex me" in mid-January, that situation was at least settled. When she was able, Harriet was to continue working at least through the fall.

Schoolcraft sent along Jonathan Edwards's plan for moral improvement to Jane, as well as medical advice on "the misery you endure from eating."[51] She found neither useful. Her news in late January that she was again pregnant (she later miscarried) was tempered by James's ongoing problems. In mid-February Edwin James, the post surgeon at Fort Brady, testified that the stabbed man had recovered, so someone was sent from the Sault to bring James back. He'd already escaped, though, evidently before the wounded man recovered, and soon turned up at Elmwood with his "natural *vivacity & gaiety*" intact, Jane reported. Some of that gaiety was attributable to an attachment he had formed with sixteen-year-old Anna Maria, who'd written to him in jail that despite what everyone else said about the hopelessness of his reforming himself, "I will never change my *opinion* of you, tho' friends & foes may unite to banish you from me."[52] Jane perceived what was going on, but, she wrote, "my ambition is *not only*, to *civilize* him (if I may be allowed that expression, which is not out of the way after all, as he has despised the forms & restraints of *refined* society) but my ardent wish is to *Christianize* him in every sense of the word."[53] The day after Jane wrote that letter, two men came to the village to arrest James and return him to Mackinac. He panicked and threatened suicide, but Jane told him to go across the river in order to save himself. Deshome and Baptiste rowed him over, and he stayed with Angus Bethune, the Hudson's Bay factor. The next day James wanted newspapers, which Jane sent, without having had the chance to read them herself. It was depressing, she wrote, "the impudent conduct of the obstinate, self-willed James."[54]

In early February Schoolcraft was accepted for membership in the Presbyterian Church, which he attended as often as possible, keeping track of who was "serious" about their souls.[55] He had thoughts on prayer. More Christians ought to pray regularly to avoid "spiritual deficiency," he wrote to Jane. "We say that if men do not ask for favours, it would be unreasonable for them to expect favours," he wrote, "yet we act, as if it were reasonable to expect God would give what he is not asked to give." This was folly. "I also believe that private prayer should be more specific & that God gives *what is asked for* & *does not substitute something else*." The proof was in scripture. God "has said, in the person of Christ, if children ask for an egg, will the parents give a scorpion, &c. This whole passage seems to imply, that God will actually grant what is asked for, always presuming the request to be reasonable."[56] That was the trick, of course.

In the summer of 1831 Schoolcraft went west to address disputes between the Ojibwes and Dakotas about their new boundaries. Jane, the children, and Ogeewyahnoquotokwa's daughter Charlotte, who'd lived with the Schoolcrafts from the beginning of their marriage and was about twelve years old, went again as far as Green Bay, then mother and children returned home to weep for his absence, as Jane wrote afterward.[57] The bulk of the few letters Schoolcraft wrote during his trip were accounts of geology. Every expedition to the West was an opportunity to scout future resources, and he seems to have been writing his account of them into his letters so that he'd have a copy on his return to make into a newspaper article or include in his report. He had quite a lot to say to Jane about copper. His secretary, a printer from Detroit named Melancthon Woolsey, did the same but for literary purposes; he wrote Jane pious reflections on the landscape that he later published in the *Southern Literary Messenger*.[58]

Schoolcraft had some advice while he was away. "We are all in the hands of an ever present, overruling God, who can neither deceive us, or be deceived himself, who requires the adoration of a pure heart & who will reward his followers most surely & abundantly," he observed. He worried about the children's future. "Johnston is willful & Janée is carried away by the indulgence of girlish sport" (they were at the time aged about two and four.) "Let us bring up our little ones in his nurture & fear, that when called away ourselves, we may at least say we had performed our duty to them," he wrote. "Try to restrain both, & you will earn another garland to adorn the brow of a wife, & to augment the love of a husband."[59] He warned her not to be inhospitable during his absence, and to look after herself. "*Cleanliness, exercise, & digestible* food in *modest* quantity are the *best* preservatives of health," he wrote. He wondered if she was "*after the manner of married women*" and asked for a sign if she knew.[60] She ignored his comments on Johnston, brushed off the same on Janée, and was coy on the possibility of being pregnant.[61]

Her letters featuring the children weeping in his absence had become a regular feature of their correspondence, but she was no longer afraid that he would leave her. She was angry that he abandoned his responsibilities as a husband and father for months at a time and irritated at his relentless effort to put her in her place. "A man may be seen too often as well as too seldom for his own good," she remarked in a letter to him while he was at Detroit, to which he departed immediately after returning from the West, adding, "but pardon me my dear Husband, I know I have *no right* to speak." She needed him to address "the disgraceful situation of our only domestick." This wasn't Harriet, who had moved into the village with her husband and baby; Sophia had run off with Henri Leveque, so it was a third woman in a "disgraceful situation," almost certainly sexual in nature. The Sault's residents likely found it gratifying that the most moral man in the village was persistently afflicted with flagrant women. "Our enemies scorn at us, & the *thoughtless* ridicule," Jane wrote.[62]

As this tension between them became a fixed part in their relationship, between 1831 and 1833, evangelicalism flooded into the Sault in the form of several white missionaries but also an important Methodist Ojibwe preacher, Shawundais or John Sunday, who brought with him a number of Ojibwe exhorters. Among the white missionaries this led to periods of intense competition for souls. During the two years of revivals and spiritual upset, neither Jane nor anyone else in the family seems to have been doing much if any writing, absorbed as they were in their spiritual struggles. The Ojibwe Methodists had been in the region since the summer of 1830, when they appeared at the annual distribution of presents at Penetanguishene, and on the strength of Shawundais's preaching they were invited to Sault Ste. Marie in the summer of 1831, then returned the following summer of 1832. Shingwaukonse was at Penetanguishene in 1830, as was Ozhaawshkodewikwe and probably Ogeewyahnoquotokwa, as were most of the people from both the US and Canadian Sault. Jane, her sisters, and their mother supported the Methodists when they were in the village and supported their followers when the Methodists had to return to their own communities. While Shingwaukonse never converted under the Methodists, Ozhaawshkodewikwe did, as did Ogeewyahnoquotokwa and Eliza Johnston.

The first missionary to the Sault had arrived earlier, in the spring of 1828, to take charge of the mission and school promised in the 1826 treaty. Abel Bingham, a Baptist, was a tall, gaunt man who'd lost a piece of his skull at the

Battle of Plattsburg.⁶³ He'd just been thrown off the Tonawonda Seneca reservation after several years of concerted effort by tribal leaders, including the famous orator Red Jacket, to rid themselves of him.⁶⁴ Unlike many missionaries of the time, he had no interest in learning Ojibwemowin; after he contracted with Charlotte to translate his sermons without Schoolcraft's permission, Schoolcraft regarded the offer an attack on his own authority and forbade it.⁶⁵ Afterward he made it a point to undermine Bingham whenever the opportunity arose, but because Bingham was as convinced of his moral rectitude as Schoolcraft was of his, they generally remained at a stalemate.

In September 1831 the Society for Converting and Civilizing the Indians and Propagating the Gospel among Destitute Settlers in Upper Canada (more concisely known as the Toronto Society) sent an Anglican missionary, James Cameron. Cameron was the son of an Ojibwe-Odawa woman named Okgwajibut and John Dougald Cameron, a fur trader at Sault Ste. Marie, Red River, and Rainy Lake.⁶⁶ He was in place for only a short period when in January 1832 a boy at his school whom he'd reprimanded ran away, afraid of being beaten, and froze to death trying to return to his parents.⁶⁷

Cameron had a profound crisis of faith. He became a Baptist a few months later, joined Bingham, and served Ojibwe communities at Tacquamenon and later Bay Mills, west of the Sault, until financial support for his mission was withdrawn in 1859, after Bingham's retirement.⁶⁸ In 1835 he caused a great scandal when he married according to Ojibwe practice a daughter of Shingabawossin; a year after his first wife died, he married again in the same manner.⁶⁹ In 1842, he petitioned the American Baptist Foreign Mission Society for better missionaries than Bingham and his wife Hannah. The Ojibwe Baptists needed a missionary who would "bide his tongue and [be] given to hospitality," with a wife who was "free from pride, not apt to make reflections upon her fellow creature," and who "[possesses] a tender heart towards the poor and sick, always willing to bear and lighten their burden."⁷⁰ The Baptist Board kept the Binghams in place until they retired to Grand Rapids in 1855.

The American Board of Commissioners for Foreign Missions sent William Boutwell to the Sault to study the language with Edwin James before going to western Lake Superior in the summer of 1832.⁷¹ Finally, in November 1831, at Schoolcraft's request the Presbyterian American Home Missionary Society sent Jeremiah Porter, a recent graduate of Princeton Theological Seminary. Schoolcraft's plan was that Porter would take Bingham's place as the spiritual leader of the white population at the Sault, however much Porter himself resisted the idea of competition among coreligionists, even if Bingham was a Baptist.

Porter kept a detailed journal of his experiences at the Sault. He was twenty-six years old, from Western Massachusetts, and distantly related to Jonathan

Edwards.[72] He admitted to being a snob. He was impressed by the Schoolcrafts not only for their piety but for their good taste, their fine living, and, it couldn't be denied, their romance. "The hall thro' which I passed showed the taste & the employment of the man," Porter wrote in his diary after his arrival at Elmwood.

> On one side stood two cases of minerals beautifully arranged showing the taste of the accomplished mineralogist. Upon the top & around these were Indian curiosities. The gourd, the pot, the rattle Satan's powerful engine. Skins with the fur, & birds of various plumage & size adorned the other walls. The latter showing his employment as an Indian Agent. Or his attachment to his wife whose mother was the daughter of a famous Indian Chief. The parlor & dinner table were a la mode New York. Mrs. S. received me very kindly & little Jane the daughter a light eyed light haired girl appeared like a lady.[73]

His sister had asked whether he was living in a log house. "I am occupying a better room than almost any one in my native town, in a house equal, if not superior to any one in Detroit," he wrote; "carpeted & papered & furnished my room is fit for a minister of state." Occasionally he noted the food he was served, as if he couldn't believe it himself. Over two days in January 1832, he sat down to, for meat, roast turkey, roast goose, roast ducks, roast beef, legs of ham, caribou steaks, broiled fowls, and broiled fish; as an accompaniment potatoes, beets, carrots, turnips, mangos, cranberry sauce; for dessert, mince pies, apple pie, tart, "*quince puffs*," apples, cheese, jellies, "*ice cream*." And no ardent spirits of course. "All this is in the best style of cooking," he wrote, and like McKenney before him he opined that "the city of Washington could not have furnished a more sumptuous dinner," although, he noted, the capital city grandees would not have had the opportunity of dining on venison steak.

It was a civilized world to which he was introduced, where most people, including in the Schoolcraft household, spoke Ojibwemowin. Sitting at the tea table one day, Porter counted "nine persons, four gentlemen & five ladies, all professing christians . . . under my ministry, six, all the ladies & one gentleman, of mixed blood & speaking the Indian language." "It was a pleasant, happy social circle, intelligent & refined."[74] Schoolcraft made himself felt. He'd captured and tamed a crane that "runs about the door like the fowls & follows its feeders like a doe," Porter wrote. "It usurps authority over the dogs, hens & children, all of which run from his threatening beak."[75]

Given the nature of his work, Porter quickly became an intimate of the extended Johnston family. Jane spoke freely to him about her childhood and family, and also of "her doubts of her own piety; the consciousness of the withdrawal of God's countenance; her willingness to forgive her enemies, and her desire to fall on their necks." The objects were Maria Schoolcraft Hulbert, from whom Jane had been estranged, and John Agnew, a customs agent, with whom she had had no contact for even longer.[76] Porter suggested that she "call & forgive Mrs. H & beg to be forgiven," and to invite Agnew to visit, which she did. The next day, Porter went with Jane to Maria Hulbert's, where "I saw her hang in silence on her neck," he wrote; "I trust the breach is forever healed."[77]

Wassidjeewunoqua died in December 1831. Porter cataloged the racial makeup of the mourners at her funeral, including "her husband a half Indian tall & of fine proportions his brother & four sisters, genteel & of fine appearance, Mr. Schoolcraft, the husband of one of the sisters, Indian agent at this place, a man of well cultivated mind of fine taste & refined manners & feelings, his children quite white, with these the mother & sisters of the deceased & the mother of Mr. J. pure Indians."

> The pallbearers were respectable white citizens; following these were many white citizens male & female, three clergy men, including myself, the officers of the fort with their rich regimentals were mingling with the lowest Frenchmen hardly distinguishable from the Indians, from their peculiar dress & physiognomy, & scattered thick amidst us all the pure Indian of every size & both sexes & in every variety of fantastic dress accompanying the substantial blanket thrown around them & bound with a girdle about the waist. Some of these were of fine proportions & elastic step, while many were decrepit with age & abuse from their demon whiskey. Yet in this motley collection there was nothing of impropriety, all walked seriously up thro' the path dug in the snow of about three feet, to the place of the dead & then stood silent while the coffin descended to its narrow house, except that the Indian mother could not suppress her emotions & sobbed aloud. As the lady was let down the bugle of the Fort sounded & peal of joyful note & the divine beat pleasantly. It seemed at the moment to me like the song of triumph, rising for one who is ascending to the abodes of bliss where there is no more death, for all who knew her agree that she gave evidence of a change of heart.[78]

The idea that one "gave evidence of a change of heart" on one's deathbed was an evangelical refrain—there had to be some peaceful look, some few words breathed at the very end to indicate acceptance of evangelical precepts. The pomp of Wassidjeewunoqua's funeral likely had to do with the status of the family that she had married into more so than any Christian piety on her or her family's part. In the spring of 1832, after a reorganization of the Indian Department, George went down to Mackinac as subagent with his children, put them to school at the mission there, and went to church. "Lord of might I give myself up to thee, do thou with me as seemeth good in thy sight," he wrote to Porter. "Teach us and realize in concert the prayers of the Saints, and be answered gloriously, 'Open your mouth wide and I will fill it.'"[79]

Porter also made a surprising discovery during his time at the Sault. "I had several times heard Mrs. Schoolcraft speak of a black girl Harriet who had lived with her for whom she felt much, as now married & who could read well & write," he wrote one day in February 1832. "This was a matter of astonishment here where one in twenty of the white French proprietors cannot read.... The word of her being able to read was: 'She came from Massachusetts.'" She'd attended his meetings, although he hadn't thought to visit her until his interest had been piqued by Jane's friendship with her, as well as her literacy. "I found her a fine looking woman, having an uncommonly intelligent, pleasing face for a black," he wrote; and there was something familiar about her. She had lived in Pittsfield, Jane told him, and when he questioned Harriet further she said that she had been brought up by Widow Williams. This was Porter's grandmother. In fact, Porter remembered playing with Harriet when they were both children. "To meet with her in this far corner of the world," Porter exclaimed to his journal; "could it be possible? I had as much expected to see one from the dead." He couldn't forget his business despite the surprise. Though she read her Bible and said her prayers, "she had no piety," Porter concluded. "I told her that if my coming here would be the means of her salvation I would be amply rewarded."[80] But despite several visits over the next weeks and Harriet's willingness to listen and pray with him, he didn't feel he was making progress.[81] Harriet was thinking of other things. Later that spring, just when the rivers were passable, Jane arrived at Harriet's house for dinner only to find that she and her husband, along with two other men—"making all our black population," Porter wrote—were gone. They had "absconded" south by canoe.[82]

Shawundais was from a Mississauga Ojibwe band on the Bay of Quinte on the north shore of Lake Ontario. He encountered Methodist missionaries from the United States who had made their first inroads into Canada in the late eighteenth century, following American loyalist settlers. By the early nineteenth century the Methodists considered themselves successful among the Indigenous bands and by the late 1820s thought that expansion into Anishinaabe territory in the Lake Superior region was the next step.[83] Though white Methodist ministers were the ostensible leaders of these missions, the Ojibwe preachers had the most effect. These included David Sawyer, who taught school at Matchedash Bay; Thomas M'Gee and John Thomas from Credit

River near the town of York; John Paul; and a man who is always identified as "P. Paul" from Grape Island, among others.⁸⁴

Kahkewaquonaby, or Peter Jones, the Ojibwe minister who initially converted Shawundais, wrote about the first time Shawundais preached in the Lake Superior region, at Penetanguishene in the summer of 1830. Shawundais spoke about "things... [that] will never spoil," unlike the British presents they received, Kahkewaquonaby wrote for the *Christian Advocate*, the denomination's newspaper. He spoke about "the wickedness of worshipping other spirits" and "the necessity of being made new creatures to enable us to keep all the words of the good Spirit." Shawundais spoke to his hearers "of the change and ruin of all things." "The Indians appeared to feel a great deal," Kahkewaquonaby wrote, "dropped their heads, and were much alarmed."

> In class meeting afterwards seven found peace, and were very happy in the Lord, and others called out for mercy. At sun two hours high we met for prayer meeting, and exhorted them before we commenced. We then invited the mourners to come forward to be prayed for. All arose, and came and knelt down, but did not seem to get hold of faith. We then arose and sung a hymn, and again knelt down. The Lord then poured out his Spirit upon them, and they began to shake, and to tremble, and to call on the Lord Jesus for mercy. Some were so exercised that they held on upon the logs which we prepared for the seats, to prevent themselves from falling down on the ground. The whole number that experienced religion this day was twenty-three. They prayed, and cried for mercy, and praised God, and were exercised in the way as the white people and the Indians at the older stations—proof that the work was the same as they had never seen any of these things before.⁸⁵

As Shawundais preached, across the bay "many of the wild Indians were drinking and dancing" and "strove to get our hearers to join with them," Kahkewaquonaby wrote, "[yelping] and [whooping] at us like the wicked white men at camp meeting."⁸⁶ This was a not-uncommmon scene. One of Shawundais's later exhorters, Kahgegahgabowh (or George Copway), described in his autobiography how, in 1835 at L'Ance, the friends of a recently converted mide man named Spear Maker "sent word to all, that they could excel us in worshiping the Great Spirit" while holding the Midewiwin ceremonies. As the Methodists held meetings on one side of a bay, the traditionalists were on the other, singing and beating drums. The standoff lasted a week.⁸⁷

At the end of the council Assiginack asked Shawundais to speak to the assembled people because most of them had refused to listen to the preaching. Like the sisters Magdelaine LaFramboise and Thérèse Schindler, Assiginack was from L'Arbre Croche on the northwest coast of Michigan, where Catholic missionaries had long been established, and like them he became a devout Catholic. He followed the British outpost to Georgian Bay, but many other Odawa people had begun migrating there as well, mainly to Manitoulin Island, as the Americans encroached on them; the migration eastward would continue over the next several years. Why were they "so backward in becoming Christians," Shawundais asked, "while their brethren encamped on the point were getting so happy in worshipping the Great Spirit?" Shingwaukonse told Shawundais and the others that he would think over what he and his followers had said and consult with the people at home about it. Others were more immediately convinced, at least by Shawundais's account. Once his hearers returned to their camps, Shawundais said, "they laid aside their feathers, cut their hair, and washed the paint from their faces."[88]

The Methodists' first trip to the Sault was brief, in the late summer of 1831. They stayed long enough for Bingham to inform them that he had a $1,000-a-year stipend from the US government to run his mission and for Schoolcraft to offer the Methodists land on Sugar Island in the St. Mary's River in hopes that they would stay and challenge Bingham's authority.[89] The Methodists returned in the summer of 1832, in time for Midewiwin ceremonies. This time Shawundais's men preceded him, including George Henry of Munceytown, River Thames, James Young, and David Lawyer from River Credit. Shawundais, who was at the Methodists' General Assembly in Philadelphia, would come north at the end of the summer. They arrived just as Schoolcraft was preparing to go on another expedition to the West, this one to the headwaters of the Mississippi River to scout out the situation of the local inhabitants. He took William Boutwell along to assess the susceptibility of the Ojibwes to Christianity and George as interpreter.[90]

Porter described the people who were beginning to gather for fishing and the Midewiwin ceremonies, the field for the Methodists' endeavors. Some were "noble looking" men, "six feet & some inches high ... with fine proportions broad chests & muscular arms." One of these men, from Lake Superior, prayed. "The Ojibwe language as it came from his mouth in prayer speaking rapidly seemed like the rolling of mighty waters," he wrote; "Maria who interpreted it thought it a delightful christian prayer." Anna Maria translated back Porter's message about "the place of salvation the fall of man in Adam, his restoration by Christ, the necessity of repentance, the final judgement, the future condition of the righteous & the wicked." She then translated the man's response for Porter (this was either from her directly or his memory of what she said):

> I heard you speak yesterday & it gave me pleasure to see you rise one after the other, & speak of the end of the world. This much you said is

A New Creation   147

what I used to hear my old fathers tell when I was a boy. I received what you said into my heart. I believe it: but I was told I must receive this without thinking about it.... I do not like to be urged to take your religion without [my young men] here. I must now be good. I would ... think & then tell my young men to come down & hear these things too. They are good.

Porter wasn't unaware of how his demands were perceived, supposing that "he did not like it that I urged upon him so closely the necessity of immediate repentance." He thought he may have been "injudicious" with the man but reasoned that "if we ask wicked men how we must preach they will tell us to give them only smooth things."[91]

Jane and Charlotte met with Sunday's hearers at their mother's house, translating Bible passages, praying, and singing hymns. "'Why is it,' said Charlotte, 'that singing is so much better in Indian than in English?'" Porter wrote after attending services one day; "This she uttered with her usual enthusiasm, & added, 'there is no doubt but that I am an Indian.'"[92] The Methodists were closer to the family than Porter was. He returned to Elmwood one day to hear "the voice of loud prayer" from Eliza's room—she'd been ill with an inflammation of the lungs. "It was Sunday pouring out his soul before the Lord for her who seemed so nearly home. A half dozen christian Indians were kneeling with him, beside the mother & sisters. After the prayer, Eliza spoke easily & for some time to the Indians in their language. This was a cheering scene. Which are the savages these praying red men, or the gentleman officers who spent the Sabbath in idle dissipation. Which will rise up in judgement to condemn?"[93]

Despite the Johnston family's close association with the Methodists, Ozhaawshkodewikwe became a member of the Presbyterian Church. It was a political decision—the Presbyterians, in the shape of Schoolcraft, had power in the village. Similarly, while Shingwaukonse never converted, he ultimately allied himself with the Anglicans.[94] When the Methodist exhorters left the village about a month after having arrived (most of the people had gone to Penetanguishene for the British distribution of presents), they took special leave of the Johnston family. Porter was again upstairs in the house when they came to take their leave of him. They reported sixty-one people in their last class, with about forty who "gave evidence of a change of heart" and the rest in a "hopeful state"; they'd accomplished much in a short period of time. Then they went downstairs to pray with the family. From his window Porter could see the preachers at the wharf in front of the house with the family and others. "About twenty Indians were kneeling.... Their prayer seemed most fervent," he wrote; "my heart exulted as I looked upon that interesting group,

I thought angels looked on with joy." Then they shook hands all around "& stepped into their light bark canoe, in which perhaps they are to make a voyage of 400 miles. They sailed easily down our beautiful river, under a perfect sky."[95]

Schoolcraft returned from the West in the summer of 1832 and went almost immediately down to Detroit. There was one exchange with Jane on this trip, during which he also escorted Maria to begin a journey to Massachusetts to attend a school suggested by Porter and his family, mainly to separate her from James Schoolcraft. Jane said or did something that earned a rebuke two weeks later. "Whatever *others* may do, 'do thou not consent to aught that has the semblence of evil,'" he wrote; "especially cultivate that holy & deep feeling of sacred love for your fellow mortals, which is called 'charity' in our version of the bible." "Strive to acquire a true idea of what this love is," he continued; "Paul had admirably described it. But many attach a false idea to his meaning from the restricted notions conveyed by the word charity, as if alms-giving & doing good for the mere sake of the record of doing good could answer the high & holy requisites of that holy love which 'knows no evil' &c. Think well of all who shew any indications of amendment. It is a common & vulgar fault to think ill & speak bitterly of others."[96] Jane apologized. "Excuse all you see amiss," she wrote, twice.[97]

A few weeks later, she was ill and being cared for at home by Douglass Houghton, a physician and geologist who'd gone with Schoolcraft on his last expedition. "My strength is gone & I am gradually sinking into nonentity, joyless & cheerless," she wrote in October; "my days upon the earth would pass, the rest of my probationary state were it not for the hope set before me in the precious promises of the Lord Almighty who doeth all things well. I trust I feel resigned & can say 'not my will but thine be done.'"[98] She'd visited Mrs. Bingham and thought there was more Christian feeling in the village that summer than before, although, she wrote, "I am disposed to feel that every body else is *doing* & *feeling* better than myself in all things. I trust a more enlarged spirit of charity is gradually taking possession of me, which if steadfastly pursued will be cause of much happiness to myself & of joy to you no doubt, as you have been a faithful one to me on that subject."[99] It's difficult to say whether she was being sincere or sarcastic at this moment.

Late in the fall Shawundais went to L'Ance for the winter at John Holiday's request, and Cameron's replacement arrived.[100] William McMurray's parents had emigrated from County Armagh to York when he was only a year old, in 1811; Sault Ste. Marie was his first assignment. Porter found him both "pleasant" and "attached to the evangelical clergy" of his church; he stayed at Elmwood with Porter and the family and opened his school. Porter also noted that McMurray was almost immediately becoming attached to Charlotte.

She was of great interest to the missionaries who passed through the Sault, all of them in the 1830s young men in search of suitable wives, not excepting Porter himself. John Hulbert remarked to Porter that the Methodists would be happy to have Charlotte connected with their mission, and that Brother Boutwell might be especially enthused to have her aid.[101] Each of the three exhorters wrote hymns in Ojibwemowin in Charlotte's new commonplace book (James Young signed himself "an Indian"), dedicated to "Miss O-ge-ne-bug-o-qua, Pow we ting."[102]

On New Year's Eve McMurray proposed.[103] On the day that Charlotte's engagement was announced, Jane told Porter that Charlotte Wabose "thinks she gave her heart to Christ while you were speaking this afternoon." "When she first came home I asked her what kind of meeting they had had," Porter recorded Jane saying. "She was silent for a moment & then came & taking me by the hand said: 'My sister I believe God has been good to my soul today.' She related how her heart melted in hearing the invitations, how it swelled & warmed with love, &c. And this is so different from her she is so retiring as usually to say nothing. I think she is a Xian & I am so happy that she submitted while you were speaking. You are her spiritual father.'" Porter took some solace in this, but he knew Jane was likely trying to make him feel better.[104] Later that winter McMurray preached at Mrs. Johnston's sugar bush, Charlotte interpreted, and a "Methodist Indian" exhorted and prayed. "I don't know when I have enjoyed a meeting so much," Charlotte said.[105]

PART II

Story of Manahbosho

Translated by William Johnston, Leech Lake, Winter 1833–1834[1]

The accounts that have been handed down from Father to son among the Chippewas of this remarkable personage called (as above named) by them, is vague, they have lost certain portions, which embrace his infancy and that of his more advanced age. That which I shall relate comprises that period of his life from the time he attained his twentieth year; till the first year of his leading a peaceful life on the southwestern head of the Great Lake. At this period it appears he was living with his Grand Mother and at this early age he was noted for his sagacity, cunning, perseverance and tricks he played on others; he could assume any shape he pleased, he frequently conversed with animals Fowls reptiles & Fishes. The energies of his mind was much superior to any who lived before or since his time. He is still considered to this day as having been a superior being or Moneto.

At this time he was frequently sent out by his grandmother to watch on the skirts of the plain, on the borders of which they lived. One evening he had climbed a tree to have a better view, when he heard the owl making its customary noise, he descended in haste from the tree, and arrived almost breathless at the lodge. "Noco, *Noco*" he cried, "I have heard a Moneto." But she only laughed, and asked him what noise it made; he said it made such: Coo coo co hoo. She told him he was young and foolish, and what he heard was only a bird; from which that bird derives its name.

He went back and continued his watch. While there he thought to himself, it is curious that I am so foolish, and that my grandmother knows so much, and that I have no father or mother. I have never heard a word about them, I must ask and find out. He went home and sat down in perfect silence, and appeared dejected. At last his grandmother asked: "Manahbosho, what is the matter with you." He answered: "I wish you would tell me if I have any parents or not, have I no relations living." She knew that he was wicked and revengeful and dreaded to tell him of his parentage. But he insisted on it. "Yes," she said, "you have a father and three brothers living. Your Mother is dead, she was taken without the consent of her parents, by your father the West. Your brothers the North East and South are older than you, and your father has given them great power with the winds, which bear their names. But you are the youngest, and I have nursed you from your infancy; for your mother died some time after your birth, and by ill treatment received from your father."

He appeared to be rejoiced to hear that his father was living; but he had already thought in his heart to try and kill him. He said he should leave in the morning to go and visit him; she told him it was a long distance to the place where Ningaubeeun lived, but that would not stop him for he had now attained manhood. He was remarkably powerful and had a giant's height. He started on his journey, and took only a short time to accomplish it, for every step he took covered a large surface of ground; he arrived at his father's who was very happy to see him, he also appeared rejoiced to see him. They spent several days in social conversation with each other. At last one evening in the course of conversation, he asked his father, what he was afraid of here on earth. He was told nothing here below. "But is there not some thing you dread here, tell me, what it is." At last his father told him: "Yes there is the black stone found in such a place; that is the only thing I am afraid of, for if it should hit me on any part of my body it would injure me very much."

He told his son this in confidence, but he had found this out for another purpose. His father now asked him in return. They were very formal one to another, knowing each other's power, though the son's was limited, yet he feared him on account of his strength. He answered nothing, in the mean time deciding not to tell, but only to name some trifling cause of his fear. He was asked again he said "Nothing." But the West said, "There must be something you are afraid of." "Well I will tell you," says Manahbosho, before he would name it, he pretended to dread it very much. "Well" says he "It is, it is, oh, oh, oh, I am afraid to name it." The West insisted he said as before, "It is, it is, oh, oh, oh. I cannot name it I am seized with such dread. The West said don't be afraid. He commenced again, "Oh, it is, it is, oh, oh, oh, my it is the bull rush."

He pretended to be fatigued from the exertion he made to name it. He was only acting a deceitful part. Some time after he observed "I will get some of the black rock." The West told [him] "Do not do so." He still said he would. "Well" says the West, "I will also get the rush." Manahbohsho cried out, "Don't, oh, oh, don't name it." But this was only to deceive the old man the more. He started and got a large rock of it, and brought it home; the West also took care to bring the dreaded rush. In the course of their conversation he asked his father, if he was the cause of his mother's death, he was told, "Yes." He then took hold of the rock and struck him.

Thence commenced one of the most noted single combats ever recorded. It continued for days, fragments of the rock can be seen to this day at the head of Lake Superior, which broke off in pieces from Manahbosho's repeated blows. Still he suffered severely from the blows of his father with his rock. At last the West was driven to the brink of this world. When he cried: "Stop my Son; you know it is impossible to kill me; desist and I will also portion you out, with as much power as your brothers, only that the four winds are occupied, but you can go and do a great deal of good to the people of this earth, which is infested with all kinds of large animals Serpents &c and who made great havoc in destroying the inhabitants. Go and do good you have the power now to do so, and your fame, with the grateful acknowledgements of the beings of this earth, will last forever. And after you have finished your work, I will have a place provided for you with us."

Manahbosho returned to his lodge and he was confined a long time from the wounds he received; but his grandmother was noted for her skill in roots, from which he soon recovered. She told him how his Grand Father was killed by Megisogwon, who lived on the opposite side of the Great Lake. "When he was alive I was never without fish oil to put on my head, and now my hair is fast falling [out] for the want of it. " "Well," says he, "Noco get cedar bark and make me a line, while I make a canoe." When all was ready he started for the middle of the Lake to fish. He put his line in the lake, saying, "Me she nah ma gwai (the name of a great fish) take hold of my bait." He kept saying this for some time; at last the King of the fishes said "Manahbosho troubles me—Here Trout take hold of his line." The Trout did so; he then commenced drawing up his line, which was very heavy, so that his canoe nearly stood perpendicular, but he kept crying out, "Wha se he," "Wha se he" till he could see the trout. As soon as he saw him he spoke to him: "Why did you take hold of my hook for? Esa, Esa, you ugly fish." The trout got so ashamed that he had to let go.

He put his line in the water again, saying, "King of the fishes take hold of my line." But the King of the fishes told a monstrous Sunfish to take hold of it, for Manahbosho was tiring him with his incessant calls. He again drew up his line with difficulty, saying as before "Wha se he. Wha se he" while his canoe was turning like a top. When he saw the Sunfish he cried out "Esa, Esa you odious fish, why did you dirty my hook by taking it in your mouth; let go I say, let go." The Sunfish did so, and he told the Kind of fishes, what Manahbosho said. Just at that moment his bait came near the King; and hearing him crying out, "Me she nah ma gwai! Me she nah ma gwai! Take hold of my hook." At last the fish did so, and allowed himself to be drawn up to the surface, and where with one mouthful he took Manahbosho and his canoe down.

Who when he came to himself found that he was in the fish's belly, and also his canoe. He now turned his thoughts as to the way in which to make his escape. Looking in his canoe he saw his war club, with which he immediately struck the heart of the fish; he felt a sudden motion as if he was going with great velocity. The fish observed to the others "I am sick at stomach, for having swallowed this dirty fellow Manahbosho." Just at this moment he received another severe blow on the heart. Manahbosho thought if I am thrown up in the middle of the lake I will perish, so I must prevent it. He drew his canoe and placed it across the fish's throat; for just as he had finished, the fish commenced vomiting, but to no effect. At the same time he saw a squirrel who had accompanied him unperceived till that moment. As he took an active part in placing the canoe in the situation they had, for which action he named him, saying the future boys shall always call you Ajidau-moo.

By repeated blows he succeeded in killing the Fish. Some time after he knew by the motion that he was beating against the shore. He waited a day longer to see what would happen, when the first thing that struck his eyes was daylight. And he could see the heads of the gulls who came looking in by the opening they had made. "Oh," cried Manahbosho, "My younger brothers, make the opening larger so that I can get out." They told each other that their brother Manahbosho was in the inside of the Fish. They immediately set about and in a short time liberated him. After he got out he told his brothers for the future you shall always be called *Kaaske* for your kindness to me. The place where the fish was driven ashore happened to be near his lodge; he went up and told his grandmother to go and prepare as much oil as she wanted, the remainder he should keep for himself.

Some time after this, he commenced making preparations for a war excursion against the Moneto who lived on the opposite side of the Great Lake and who had killed his grandfather, whose abode was defended by first by firey Serpents, who breathed fire, so that no one could pass them. The second obstacle was a large body of gum so soft, that whatever attempted to pass through it had to remain stuck to it. He continued making bows and arrows without number; but he had no heads for his arrows. At last his *Noco* told him that an old man who lived some distance could make them. He sent her to go and get some; she soon returned with her blanket[2] full, still he had not enough, he sent her again, she again returned with the same quantity, but he thought to himself I must find out the way for making these heads. "Noco" he said, "whilst I take my drum & rattle, & sing my war songs, you go and try to get me some larger heads for my arrows, for those you brought me are all of the same size. Go and see if the old man cannot make some a little larger." She started, he followed her at some distance and found out the process; he also saw the old man's daughter, she was very beautiful.

He got home first, commenced singing as if nothing had happened. When the old woman came near she heard his drum & rattle with no idea that he had followed her; she gave him the arrowheads. One evening the old woman said, "My son, you ought to fast before you go to war, as your brothers frequently do, and see if you will be successful or not." He said he had no objection, & he fasted several days. He would go a certain distance, or as far as his *Noco*'s voice could reach. At last he thought to himself I must find out why my Noco, is so anxious for me to fast. Next evening he went out a short distance. His Noco cried out a little further off, but he got nearer to the lodge, and cried out in a low voice so as to make it appear that he was far. His *Noco* cried out, "that is far enough." He had got so near, that he could see all that passed in the lodge. He had not long been where he was, when someone in the shape of a bear entered. He had very long hair; they commenced talking about him and appeared quite familiar. At that period they lived to a very old age, so his *Noco* was not over her meridian. He listened to their conversation for some time. At last he thought to himself, I must play him a trick. He got some fire and the Bear had his back turned towards him, he set his hair on fire. When he felt the flame he jumped out, but that only increased it, he was seen running all in a blaze. Manahbosho ran to his customary place of fasting; and commenced crying out "Noco Noco is it time for me to come home." "Yes" she said. [When] he came she told him what had taken place. He appeared to be very much surprised, although he had played the trick himself, after having fasted and sung his war songs, from which the Indians of the present day received the custom.

He got in his canoe fully prepared for war; he also had a plentiful supply of fish oil. He travelled night and day, at last he arrived in sight of the firey Serpents. He stopped to view them and he saw that they were some distance apart, and that only the flame which issued from them reached across. He commenced talking to them but they told him, "We know you Manabosho you cannot pass." He then thought of some means by which he could. He hit on this mode: he got his canoe as near as possible; when he was ready, he cried out, "What is that behind you?" The serpents without thinking turned their heads, and he passed them with one sweep of his paddle in safety. "Well," said he, "how do you like my exploit?" He took his Bow & arrows and shot them, which he found to be easy work, for the serpents were stationary and they could not move over a certain space in which their Prince had placed them.

He went on in his canoe till he came to the soft gum. He then took the oil and rubbed it on his canoe, and pushed into it. The oil softened so, that he could pass with ease, but he had to rub it on frequently. Just as his oil failed he extricated himself from the gum. He was the first who had succeeded in passing through it; and for which exploit the gum disappeared from the Great Lake. He now came in view of land, and on which he debarked in safety. He could see the lodge of the Moneto, situated on a hill. He commenced arranging himself for the fight; he then waited for the dawn of day to commence his attack. He started with yells & shouts, crying out, "Surround him, surround him; run up, run up; attack him" &c. Although alone he made this noise so that the Moneto might think he had a party of warriors with him. He advanced crying out, "It was you who killed my Grandfather," and with that shot his arrows. The combat lasted all day. Manahbosho's arrows had no effect, for his opponent was clothed or made of wampum; and he was now reduced only to three arrows. And it was only by exerting extraordinary agility that he could escape the blows, which the Moneto kept making at him.

At that moment a large woodpecker flew past, and lit on a tree.[3] "Manahbosho," he cried, "shoot at the lock of hair he wears on the crown of his head." He shot one arrow so as only to draw blood from that part, for he was a dead shot. The Moneto made one or two unsteady steps; but he recovered. "Manahbosho," he said, "Why don't you shoot at my body, and not at my head?" He was answered "You speak nonsense, nonsense!" and with it he received a second arrow, which went deeper. He fell on his knees; but again recovered. But the third arrow stuck deep, and he fell a lifeless corpse. Manahbosho took his scalp as a trophy, and he called the woodpecker to come and receive his payment for the information he had given. He took the blood of the Moneto, and rubbed it on the woodpecker's head, and which can be seen to this day, the feathers on his head are perfectly red; and which Indians use [to] ornament their pipes of ceremony &c.

After this he returned home, singing and beating his drum; his songs denoted victory. Which when his Noco heard it, she came to the shore, and welcomed him with songs & dancing &c. He did not like to remain inactive. He went out a fishing again and caught a very large fish and he got so much fat from him that it formed a little lake; he therefore invited all [the animals] and fowls to come and eat. Those who came first, such as the Deer Bear & others who are generally fat at certain seasons, all those swam in the fat, and which they have to this day. Others came too late such as the Hare Marten Partridge and others & which have no fat even to this day. He then told them to shut their eyes; they did so; he then commenced wringing off the heads of the fowls that was nearest him. When a small duck (the diver) opened one eye, and saw Manahbosho killing the duck, he gave a shout, "Harken Manahbosho is killing us." He made for the Lake and just as he [was] getting into the water Manahbosho kicked him, which happened to be near his tail, the force of which flattened his rump and so straightened his legs backwards, that when he now gets on land he could not walk, also the feathers of his tail fell out, and in the meantime all the others started, and left him to himself.

After this he starts to travel. One evening he was weary and hungry and as he was walking along the shore of the great Lake he saw an old Wolf with six young ones comes towards him. The old wolf as soon as he saw him told his children "Keep out of the way of Manahbosho, for I know it is him we see yonder." The young wolves were obeying. When Manahbosho cried out, "My grand children where are you going, stop and I will go with you." He appeared rejoiced to see the old Wolf; asked him where he was going; he was told they were looking out for a place, where they could find [the] most game and to pass the winter. He said he should like to go with them and he asked the old wolf, "Brother," he said, "are you willing that you should turn me into a wolf?" He was told they had no objections, but commenced immediately. He found himself a wolf in size with the others. "But" he cried out, "oh make me a little larger." They did so. "A little longer," he asked. They said, "Let us humour him," so they made him a little larger. "Well," said he; "that will do. He looked at his tail; "oh" cried he, "do make my tail a little longer and more bushy." They did so.

Then they started; after they had got in the woods some distance, they fell in with the tracks of a Moose. The young ones went after them. Manahbosho and the old wolf followed at their leisure. "Well" said the Wolf, "Who do you think is the farthest of the Boys, can you tell by the jumps they take?" "Why," he replied, "that one that takes such long jumps he is the farthest to be sure. "Ha, ha, you are mistaken," said the old Wolf. "He makes a good start, but he will be the first to tire out. This one who appears to be behind will be the one to kill the game. "They then came to the place where the Boys had started in chase; one had dropt his small bundle. "Take that Manahbosho," said the old Wolf. "Esa," he replied, "what will I do with a dirty dog skin?" The Wolf took it up; it was a beautiful robe. "Oh, I will now carry it," said Manahbosho. "Oh no," replied the old Wolf. They then came to a place where the moose had lain down; and they saw that the young wolves had started after them. "Why," said the old Wolf, "this moose is poor. I know by his tracks, for I always can tell if they are fat or not." They next came to a place where one of the wolves had bit at the moose and had broken one of his teeth on a tree. "Manahbosho," said the Wolf, "One of your grand children has shot at the game, take the arrow there it is." "No," he replied, "What will I do with a dirty dog tooth." The old Wolf took it and behold it was a beautiful arrow.

They then came up to the others. Manahbosho was very hungry. They had killed a very fat moose, but alas, he saw nothing but the bones picked quite clean; he thought to himself, just as I expected dirty greedy fellows. However he sat down without saying a word. At last the old Wolf spoke to one of the young ones, saying "Give some of the meat to your grandfather." One obeyed and came near to Manahbosho and opened his mouth as if he was going to vomit. He jumped up, saying, "You dirty dog you have eaten so much, that now you want to come and vomit before my face! Go away you dog, go and vomit some other place." He abused them very harshly. The Wolf went a little on one side and behold a heap of fresh meat with the fat lay there all ready prepared. He then put on a smiling face. "Why said he, how good the meat is," at the same time tasting it. "Yes," replied the Wolf. "It is always so with us, we get the best always."

They then commenced finding their winter quarters, while others of their number went in search of game; and they now had a large supply on hand.

One day the young wolves being away as usual, the old one amused himself in cracking the large bones of a moose. "Manabohsho," says he, "cover your head with the robe, and do not look at me while I am at these bones, for a piece may fly into your eye." He did as he was told, but he looked through a hole that was in the robe, to see what the other was about. Just at that moment the wolf was cracking a bone, when a piece flew and hit him in the eye. He cried out "Why do you strike me for you old dog?" The Wolf said "You must have been looking at me." "No, no, why should I want to look at you." "No, Manahbosho," said the Wolf, "you must have been looking, or you would not have got hurt." "No, no, I wasn't," he cried again. I will repay you for this thought Manahbosho. So next day he said to the Wolf, "Cover your head, and do not look at me for fear a piece may fly in your eye." The Wolf done so. He then took the leg bone of a moose. He looked first to see if the Wolf was well covered. He then hit him a blow will his might. The Wolf jumped up and fell again from the effect of the blow. "Why" said he, "Do you strike me so for?" "No" he replied; "You have been looking at me." "No" said the Wolf. "But" says Manahbosho, "You would not have been struck with it, if you had not been looking." He thought to himself I have well paid you back for the blow I received.

He went out one day and killed a fat moose; he was very hungry. He sat down to eat. "Well," said he, "I do not know where to commence. At the head? No, people will laugh and say he eat him backwards." He went to the side. "No, "said he, "they will say I eat him sideways." He then went to the hind quarter. "No," said he, "they will say I eat him forwards. I will commence here, say what they will." He took a delicate piece from the rump, and he was just ready to put it in his mouth, when a tree close by made that creaking, when rubbing against each other by the violence of the wind. He took the meat out of his mouth; he looked up. "Why I cannot eat when I hear such a harsh noise. Stop, stop," he said. He was putting it in his mouth again when the same noise was repeated; he took it out again, saying, "I cannot eat with such a noise." He left the meat although very hungry, without tasting it to go and put a stop to the noise. He climbed the tree, and was pulling at it when his arm got caught in it so that he could not extricate himself.

While there he saw a pack of wolves coming towards him. He cried out, "Go that way, go that way. What would you come and get here." The wolves said "Manabosho must have some thing there, or he would not tell us to go away." "I begin to know him," said an old wolf, "and all his tricks. Let us go and see." They came and found the moose with whom they soon made way. Manabosho looked on, to see them eat till they were satisfied and they left him only the bare bones. The next heavy blast of wind opened the trees and liberated him. He went home thinking to himself, see the effects of meddling with frivolous things when I had certain good in my possession. Next day the old wolf told him, "I am going to leave you, but I will leave you one of the young men to hunt for you." The wolves departed; he appeared very sorrowful for a short time. The wolf that was with him was a good hunter and he never was without food. One day he spoke to his grandson, as he called him, saying "I had a dream last night and it does not portend good, it is of that large lake, that is in that direction. You must never cross it, even if the ice should appear good, or if you should come to it at night weary or tired you must make the circuit of it.

Spring commenced the snow was melting fast, when one evening the wolf weary with the chase, came to this lake, and he disliked to go so far as to make a circuit of it. He thought there is no harm to try, the ice appeared good. He started but he had not got half way, when he fell in and he was immediately seized by serpents who knew it was Manahbosho's grandson. Night came, no son, the second and third night also but he did not appear. He was very sorry. "Well," said he, "he must have disobeyed me, he has lost his life in that lake I told him of. Well I must mourn for him." So he took coal and blacked his face. "Now," said he, " I wonder how I must do it. I will cry so 'Oh my grandson, Oh my grandson.'" He burst out alaughing. "No No, that wont do either. I will try so: 'Oh, my heart, Oh my heart.' Ha ha, that won't do either. I will try this: 'Oh, my grandson's obequoge,[4] Oh, my grandson's obequoge." This satisfied him, and he remained till his days of mourning was over. "Now," said he, "I will go in search of him."

He started, at last he came to the lake. He there raised the same cries as pleased him, for his grandson. He sat down near the small brook that emptied itself into the Lake. And he there repeated his cries. At last a bird called Ke-ske, mun e see (King Fisher) came near to him. The bird asked "What are you doing here?" He replied, "Nothing. But can you tell me if any one lives in this lake, and what brings you here." The Bird replied, "Yes the Prince of Serpents lives here; and I am watching to see if the obequoge of Manahbosho's grandson will not drift ashore, for he was killed by the serpents last spring. But are you not Manahbosho himself?" "No how do you think he would get to this place. But tell me do the serpents ever appear, when and where tell me all about them." "Do you see that beautiful white sandy beach?" "Yes; it is there that they bask in the sun. Before appearing the lake will be perfectly calm not even a ripple will appear; after midday you will see them." "Thank you I am Manahbosho himself. I have come in search, come near till I put a medal round your neck." The Bird came near. He got a white medal, it can be seen to this day, for he has a white spot on his breast. After giving the medal he wanted to wring the birds head off but he escaped, and the feathers of his head were only ruffled backwards, which caused the tuft of feathers on his head which is seen to this day. He had found out all he wished and then wanted to kill him.

He started and placed himself near the sandy beach, first turning himself into a large oak stump. He was not long there, before he saw the lake perfectly calm. A few minutes after he saw hundreds of monstrous Serpents crawling on the beach to bask. One was beautifully white, which was the prince; the other was red and yellow. The Prince spoke. "I never saw that black stump there before; it may be Manahbosho. There is no knowing, but what he may be somewhere about here." One of the large serpents immediately went and twisted himself round it very hard, the greatest pressure happened to be on his throat. He was just ready to cry out when the serpent let go. Eight of them went in turn and done alike and they always let go, as he was ready to cry out. They said it cannot be him, he is too great a coward for that. They then laid in a circle about their Prince; it was a long time before they fell asleep. Then Manahbosho took his bow and arrows and stepped over the serpents, til he came to the prince, who he shot on the left side. He gave a sau-sau-quan and was off on full speed.

The sound of the snakes was horrible; they cried "Manahbosho has killed our prince, go in chase of him." He ran over hill and valley for the interior part of the country. But he could hear that something was approaching him fast; he made for the highest mountain, climbed the highest pine tree. When dreadful to behold the whole was overflowed; it had already reached the foot of the pine tree. It rose fast, it now reached his chin. He cried out to the tree, "Grandfather stretch yourself." The tree did so, again he cried, he was obeyed. Again he said, the tree replied, "This is the last time, I cannot get any higher." The water then reached to his chin. But the water just happened to stop there. He then saw a loon. "Come here," he said, "dive down and fetch up some earth, so that I can make a new earth." He dove down but he came up a lifeless loon. He then saw a Muskrat. "Dive" said he, "and if you succeed, you will live either on land or water, just as you shall please, or I will give you beautiful little lakes with rushes to live in." He dove down, but he floated up senseless. He took him and breathed in his nose, and he came to life again. "Try again" he said. He did so; he came up senseless again. But he had a little earth in one [of] his paws, from which and the carcass of the Loon he created a new Earth, as large as the former, with all living animals fowls & fishes.

He was walking on the new earth, when he heard someone singing. He went to the place, where he found an old woman crying & singing. "Noco," said he, "what is the matter?" "Matter?" said she; "where have you been not to have heard how Manahbosho shot my son, the Prince of Serpents, and how the earth was overflowed, but he created this; so I brought my son here, that he may kill the inhabitants as we did in the one before. But I am afraid you are Manahbosho himself." "Ha! ha! ha! how can it be; has not the old earth, and all that was on it perished? Impossible, impossible. But Noco what do you do with all that cedar cord on your back?" "Why" said she; "I am fixing a snare for Manahbosho, if he should be on this earth and in the meantime looking for herbs to heal my son, it is only myself that can do him any good when I sing "Manabohsho a ne we quack, cond dau mau wah, ne we quack, cond dau mau wah." He found out all he wished from her. He then killed her, took off her skin, and put it on himself, took the cedar cord on his back, and limped away singing her songs. He also walked like an old woman. He was met by one who told him, "Make haste the prince is worse." At the lodge he took notice that they had his grandson's hide to hang over the door. "Oh dogs," he said, and passed on. He sat down by the door and commenced sobbing like an old woman.

One observed, "Why don't you attend the sick and not sit there making such a noise?" He took up a poker and laid it on them, mimicking the old woman, "Dogs that you are, why do you laugh at me, you know very well that I am so sorry, that I am nearly out of my head." With that he approached the Prince singing the song of the old woman without any suspicion. He saw that his arrow had gone in about one half. He pretended to extract it, but he only pushed it farther in, which soon put an end to the Prince's life. Just then making a movement he burst the old woman's hide. He made for the door, the serpents followed him crying out, "Manahbosho has come" and quite killed him. He ran over the plain and when he got to the mountains he saw a badger. "Brother" said he, "make a hole quick, for the Serpents are after me." The badger obeyed; they both went in and he threw all the earth back so that it filled up the way they came while underground. Manahbosho said "Pho, Pho; how you do stink." "What do you say?" inquired the badger. "Nothing," he replied, "Only that you are blinding with the dirt you throw back."

The serpents came to the opening, and they decided to watch. "We will starve him out," they said, so they remained there watching. Manahbosho told the badger to make an opening to the other side of the mountain from which he would go and hunt & bring the meat in. They then lived together for some time when one day the badger came in his way. He killed him and threw him out, saying I don't like you to be getting in my way so often. After living there alone some time he thought he would go out. He did so and he made the circuit of the mountain and came to the corpse of the Prince, who had been deserted by the Serpents to watch Manahbosho coming out. He set to work and skinned him. He then put on his skin [and] took his war club, in which were great virtues. He started for the place where he first went in the ground [and] still found the Serpents watching. When they saw their Prince as they thought, fear & dread took hold of them. Some fled, the remainder Manahbosho killed. Those who fled went opposite to the direction the sun passed the earth or they went probably south.

Chapter 6

Leech Lake

In the summer of 1833 William went to Leech Lake, home of the so-called Pillager band, with the intention of writing for Jane, who was at Mackinac and unhappy. Cass had given Schoolcraft the choice of continuing at the Sault or moving to Mackinac, and he chose the latter, it being better connected to the outside world and farther away from Jane's family, most importantly her mother. He prepared the agent's house for Jane and the children's arrival in May, then left for Detroit.

William had grown restless after Ozhawshkodewikwe sold her business to the American Fur Company (AFC), reducing him to a clerk in the company's employ. He was twenty years old, his father was gone, he was at loose ends, and the French balls and general debauchery on offer in the village proved too much for him. The family seems to have confronted him about this behavior. "Many think that I have no esteem or respect for my Friends or relations," he wrote later to George, "but they are deceived, if only they knew my inward thoughts they would acquit me of that charge."[1] He left in July 1833 with a party of fifty-five men, women, and children. He wrote Jane long letters detailing his preparations and the trip out, and he continued to write for as long as someone was available to carry the mail east as the weather got colder. "It is unnecessary to hide any thing from you," he wrote to her. Even if what he had to say didn't "instruct," it would show that though he was "wandering through Lakes, rivers, and forests that you are not forgotten; and may the conviction of this cause on your mind a glimmering of a pleasurable kind."[2] Over the winter he kept writing, producing two narratives about village life and the practice of hunting, likely several stories, and an almost-complete version of the Manabozho story cycle with which he returned to Sault Ste. Marie in the early summer of 1834.

His correspondence began with an account of the financial traps laid for traders and for Indigenous people, circling around two themes, that the trade was formerly more humane (in their father's time, before the advent of the American Fur Company) and that the misery in which people found themselves was apt to lead to their indulging in "excesses."[3] He wrote about the picturesque scenery and people as his father before him had written. He studied the Indigenous men he met, especially the men from Leech Lake, who were said to be the most warlike and unchanged by Europeans of the

Ojibwe bands.[4] "There was something manly about them," he wrote on first meeting a group traveling west with AFC traders, "and they showed such an independency of character, which I had never seen before in the Indians, which was very pleasing." Other Indigenous people showed them "great respect."[5] When William broached the idea of coming to Leech Lake as an opposition trader, they said the AFC would try to prevent it, but he persisted. "I . . . brought up to their minds, the injuries and wrongs they had always received from their [AFC] hands," he wrote to Jane. "I saw that the language I used to the Lake Indians would not suit their manners. I altered my tone, and gave it direction, to the spot where I thought it would take effect." "'Well,' said I, 'is it possible that you who have the name of Pillagers, and whom I have often heard spoken of as a brave band should be commanded by a few foolish traders; You are free, you are men, and it is only women that are ordered about. Why not do as you please, do not listen to their talk, for they are men of bad tongues.' I only tried to embitter their feelings against the opposition; and I saw that it took effect; for their eyes beamed with pleasure.'"[6]

He seems to have had his brother-in-law on his mind as he wrote to Jane, and the people at Leech Lake would have known to whom William was related. Schoolcraft had visited them the previous summer, during which he angered the leader Eshkibagikoonzh (known as "Guelle Plat" or "Flat Mouth" in English [his name refers to a kind of duck]), who gave "an impassioned impromptu speech" about the United States honoring its agreements, pointing out that if it didn't, the Pillagers would have to make agreements with the British instead. Rather than following protocol and responding, Schoolcraft left abruptly, angering everyone.[7] When William left for Leech Lake, Schoolcraft was completing *Narrative of an Expedition through the Upper Mississippi to Itaska Lake* (New York: 1834), his account of that trip and the one preceding, in the summer of 1831. By Schoolcraft's account, the Pillagers were the picture of recalcitrant savagery. Like all Indians, they lived "a life of want and vicissitude," lurching back and forth "between action and inanity, in the mind," he wrote. He thought it would be easy to convert them to Christianity, because "their institutions, moral and political, are so fragile as to be ready to tumble on the application of the slightest power."[8] The actual people at Leech Lake remained largely uninterested in Christianity.

William described songs sung by men and women in camp to Jane, analyzing them as he and Jane must have done at home. The singing "breathed through" an encampment on the St. Louis River "like a spell," he wrote, so that "it gradually filled the valley, and the surrounding hills prolonged the notes till they died away in the distance." "The sounds came from clear, full, and manly voices, and it was such as to stir up, and animate Indians to warlike deeds. The songs appeared to be only in couplets, the first part was sung by one or two and it would gradually increase till the next chorus rose to a full swelling sound, and again die away in the chorus." This was entirely different from the Lake Shore Indians, and there was "something of the martial in it.... I could see from their glancing eyes, and quick step, that their feeling of manliness was roused. Even their yells was entirely different, from those to which I had been accustomed to hear."[9] He translated a few of the songs.

> Nau me ug wau nin, kee chee daug,
> Ing kau be see daug, mon e to; o -
> Chorus   Yah au whee yah, ah - Yah. (repeated three times)

"The words convey this idea in English: 'When I cause them to dance, the Braves'; 'He will listen to me the Great Spirit.' In singing the Indians dwell long on the last notes, especially on those of the chorus; they gradually rise to the highest pitch, and as gradually soften down again."[10] Women often sang accompaniment to the war songs, "the notes of which pierce through the bass of the men; which is in addition, and the clear shrill notes can be distinctly heard. And what makes it more striking is, that the notes they use, are most commonly nasal; which is not the case, when singing other songs; although we will allow some exception to the last remark."[11]

Despite William's enthusiasm most of the people at Leech Lake continued to trade with the AFC. Those who would trade with him were in different ways outsiders working for their own benefit. William studied them as well.[12] One of these was an old and celebrated warrior named Big Cloud, who was about seventy at the time and had lost one eye but "was still straight and very active," William wrote to Jane. "Even now, I am told, no one dares to face, or contradict what he says."[13] Big Cloud offered his friendship and protection to William. "He said he liked me, he considered me as one of the band; and his age and inclination would not allow him he said of going out with the Band to hunt the Deer; but that he would remain, and make himself useful to me." "I will . . . be your soldier," Big Cloud said, "whoever speaks ill of you or touches you 'He speaks of me, he touches me.'" William accepted his offer. "He shook hands with me in a friendly manner and I told him that his wants in the Tobacco line should be satisfied throughout the winter."[14] What William didn't tell Jane was that Big Cloud was an especially disruptive man in the community, who gained power by cultivating non-AFC traders like William, offering alliance, aid, and gossip. He also prostituted his two wives to traders as a means of increasing that power. Big Cloud was feared in the community and his wives reviled, but he'd made himself powerful enough so that no one could stop him.[15]

William would have known this, eventually, and he may have told Jane. In his writing, however, Big Cloud became representative of old and respected warriors, which was probably the way Big Cloud wished to see himself. William described for his sister an Ojibwe world away from white settlements, where the fur trade had a negligible impact on the community's ability to continue in traditional practices and live in an orderly—and he and Jane would have said civilized—way, all of this contrary to what Schoolcraft would write in his forthcoming book. "The most perfect sincerity & cheerfulness, appears to prevail among the Indians while inland; and their intercourse is marked with the broadest principles of charity & neighbourly feeling," William wrote in "Notes on the Manner in Which the Chippewas Spend Their Time, while on Their Wintering Grounds." "The restraint & ever watchful suspicion which they evince at the Post, or in other situations exposed to the scrutiny and cupidity of white men, is thrown aside, and gives way to ease, sociability, and pleasantry."[16] They were free because they were free from white men. William devoted much of the second narrative, "Manners and Customs of the Leech Lake Indians," to describing the protocols of hunting, beginning with the elder who stood in the center of the village calling the men to assemble and giving instructions to the different parties, calling the women to prepare for the day, and "making a short speech to the Great Spirit, for the blessing of the approaching day; and that the hunters may be successful in procuring a sufficiency of foods for the old infirm, the women and children."[17] He described what the men wore and their expertise in tracking animals, but he was especially interested in the social relations of hunting.

Hunters felt "esteem and respect" for their chief, who kept reserves of ammunition and tobacco for those who needed it, and those men who did need it felt compelled to provide the chief meat in return. This was not a sign of subordination, William pointed out, but rather that they regarded the supplies as gifts that must be reciprocated. When one man shot an animal that another had been stalking or had wounded, the men divided the meat equally and the shooter claimed the hide. If a hunter was lazy, his successful companion could say "I have Pity, I make you the deer a present," and then "[walk] off without saying anything more satisfied within himself at what he has done, in showing pity." If a hunter was unsuccessful, his companion would only say "I lend him to you," after which he could expect the favor returned at a future hunt. Elderly men who killed an animal would sit and "smoke over the corpse saying that his children are hungry and that is the cause why he has killed it, and hopes that the spirit of the deer will not be angry" before cutting the animal up, putting the meat in the hide, and using the skinned legs as a collar to carry the meat home. They wasted no part of the animal because they "[dreaded] the supposed spirits." After a hunt there was a feast that "may be compared to the White peoples social dinner parties."

Domestic life was "kind and sociable." "As friends and relations," the people at Leech Lake "[inquired] into each other's concerns with as much interest as if it was their own," and gave each other presents of "meat, sugar, corn, or fruit, or any other dainties they may have." Anything of note was discussed by all, including "the least trifle [that] passed among the women and children." They cooked and got wood for their poor relations, sent their children to assist the infirm, "if blind they lead them by the hand, if they have two blankets they are sure to give to those who are in need." If the parents were "industrious," the children would be "likewise kind and affectionate," and everyone happy. The mother took "all the pains in her power to relieve their little wants, if sick she passes sleepless nights watching over it. Nothing she can invent or think of is wanting for her child, with the least noise of the child she is up and imprinting kisses on his cheeks." The father of the family in the privacy of the lodge told stories and instructed the children, and "laughs with his wife at their little tricks and remarks, telling each what they think [they] will be in future life."

In October Big Cloud invited William to go duck hunting, and William took the opportunity to again describe him in detail for Jane, this time in his hunting gear. He wore a long coat to the knee, pinned at the neck with a wooden fastener, close-fitting leather leggings, moccasins "just to suit the foot," garters trimmed with a fisher's tail, and "one war Eagle's feather [that] waved gracefully over his head." He carried his gun, powder horn and shot bag, tomahawk, and "scalper." "He feels young when he is thus set off, and I never saw a better looking Indian, tall and straight, his step quick and light, his eye showing within a Soul of independence and void of fear."[18] Later, Big Cloud invited him to travel to Cass Lake along with Yellow Hair.[19] (The Ojibwe name for the lake is Gaa-miskwaawaakokaag; it was called Lac du Cedre Rouge by French traders and Upper Red Cedar Lake before the Americans renamed it for Cass after his 1820 expedition to the area.) They crossed the lake on ice three or four inches thick, chasing the fish below as they walked, the ice so clear that they could see weeds and pebbles on the bottom.[20]

The two old warriors reminisced:

> The small lakes being numerous, and the land high and dry, and the woods very open, gave a beautiful appearance to the country, and we traveled on slowly; I listening to the stories of my wild companions who were warriors and who were telling of former days, when dark deeds of strife and blood took place on the borders. My questions to find out further of what I heard them state, they willingly answered them. And

their conversation was very lively, for they knew that there was no cause of suspicion, and my being with them gave no restraint to their conversation. The Yellow Hair told of war parties that he had taken part in, and of the bloody scenes he had witnessed, and the hardships they endured on the plains when in search of the Sioux, their shooting and tomahawking each other, and scalping the prostrate foe while yet living, the howls and cries of women and children as the lodges and prairie grass was set on fire. The Big Cloud considered himself the bravest warrior in the band, and he was; and now and then he would say "Kagate" to the other's story.[21]

William was likely not reporting on everything he saw or knew about life at Leech Lake. It wasn't a paradise of freedom from Americans, who made themselves felt in the trade, in Schoolcraft and his expeditions, in the missionaries scouting converts. Yet it seems that both he and Jane needed to believe that such a place existed. Since he could assume that Schoolcraft read everything he wrote to Jane, he was writing to Schoolcraft as well. He was writing, once again, about the humanity and civility of Ojibwe people, even taking into account reminiscing old warriors. It didn't change anything that Schoolcraft wrote, but it must have had some effect, if only because the more the family wrote about the civility of Ojibwe people, the stronger Schoolcraft's convictions about the threat of savages to Americans became.

William wrote to George about his travels with Big Cloud, and about visiting Boutwell for Sunday services or for hymn-singing with some of his men, including a fiddle-playing Irish ex-physician named Dr. Bell and Nishki, who was a Methodist. They usually made up the majority of Boutwell's hearers. He'd "spent many pleasant hours" with Boutwell, he wrote to George, "whose company has been a profit to me."[22] He also told George that his mind was "more relieved and my hopes for the future are not entirely darkened" at Leech Lake. He had "a few good books and being almost alone for the greater part of the time, gives me time to read and meditate." "You know I hate writing," he added incongruously; "I wrote this letter with a crow quill and you must therefore excuse all errors."[23]

Schoolcraft had gone from Detroit to Washington and New York in the summer of 1833, returning to Detroit in early fall to oversee the printing of *Narrative of an Expedition* there while Jane went to the Sault for Charlotte's wedding. "I was pleased to learn that you managed to live so well & contentedly in your *widowed* state, & since you have *so* kindly extended my furlough to the 1st of Oct I have consented to stay a few days longer," she wrote. Sault

Ste. Marie was much better than Mackinac. The ladies of the fort were kind and church was certainly better. She remarked on McMurray's extravagant purchases for his and Charlotte's new home and expressed no anxiety about her health; she was again pregnant, or thought she was (she wasn't).[24] In Detroit, Schoolcraft read a long poem on his usual themes to the Algic Society (founded by himself and dedicated to the amelioration of the Indian race). When he was asked for a copy for publication, "my answer was this," he wrote to Jane: "'I have considered the request contained in your note of this day. My compliance with it, results from feelings of sympathy for a noble but persecuted race, under which it was delivered.' So you see, I am in for it." He wasn't saying anything in the poem that would offend the sensibilities of the great men of Detroit in 1833, and *The Man of Bronze; or Portraitures of Indian Character* (Detroit, 1834) was no different than anything else he'd written on the topic.[25] He was trying to reassure Jane that he had the best interests of her relatives at heart.

After returning to Mackinac that fall he began systematically collecting information, more than likely with William on his mind. He spoke to Madame LaFramboise about the fur trade and her recollections of the Bonga family, Ojibwe fur traders descended from an enslaved man set free by a British officer before Britain vacated the island for the first time in 1796, as well as of the first American trader at Chicago, Pierre du Sable, a Black man whom she said was quite respectable—an achievement for any fur trader. He became interested in abandoned settlements on Round Island, a small island across the harbor from Mackinac, repeatedly asking Wauchusco and other men about the settlements' history. There were two, an ancient one marked by an eroded bank revealing bones as from a burial mound, and another that existed within the memory of the old men, probably from about the time the British moved their fort from the mainland to Mackinac Island in the 1760s.[26]

Around this time Jane wrote down her cousin Ogeewyahnoquotokwa's vision, along with some of her Mide songs. The narrative tells the story of her receiving the power to heal and to divine the future, but it also tells the story of the murder of her first husband as a result of the damage done to the community by the fur trade. (Ogeewyahnoquotokwa also drew a pictographic representation of her vision that Schoolcraft published in the Indian history in the 1850s, the original of which has been lost.) She would not likely have given this information until after her conversion to Christianity in the summer of 1832, and probably relatively soon after.

While Schoolcraft's inquiries might seem to be the origin of anything the family wrote down, in light of his habits the existence of this account is odd for a number of reasons. Schoolcraft was fearful of Ojibwe spirituality. In the Indian history he wrote about coming upon Wauchusco in 1822 and seeking

Island of Mackinac, Lake Huron, drawing by Anna Brownell Jameson, *Voyage to America Portfolio* (1837). Baldwin Collection of Canadiana, Special Collections and Rare Books, Toronto Public Library, Toronto, Ontario, Canada.

to mock him by requesting a shaking tent ceremony. Wauchusco invited Schoolcraft and his companion into the dark, "oppressively warm" lodge, then "began his incantations; beating accurate time on a little drum. When one staff of his chant had been finished, he stopped, waited a little, and then began another. The keys of these chants were varied—now high, now low, now mutteringly." Soon the "diablerie of the scene" overcame the two men, and they bolted from the lodge before the ceremony came to its conclusion.[27] It was all "demonology" to him, and though he interrogated Wauchusco about his spiritual practices, the only narrative he asked for was that of his conversion to Christianity. Schoolcraft knew Ogeewyahnoquotokwa from the time he arrived at the Sault, and considering that her daughter was part of the Schoolcraft family from the time of their marriage and had been a member of the Johnston household for a year before that, he had to have known quite a bit about her. But in an essay written in the summer and fall of 1834, he insisted that "females are excluded from participation in the priesthood, or jugglership," and that there is "not an instance of their having assumed this function is known to have occurred in the history of America."[28] (French writers used the term "jongleur," an archaic term for troubadour or minstrel, to describe Indigenous healers; British and American writers Anglicized that as "juggler.") His vehement and unequivocal denial points to Jane's account

Leech Lake 171

having been written before then—as if it bothered him, which anything having to do with Ojibwe spirituality did. He didn't publish Jane's translation of Ogeewyahnoquotokwa's narrative until after Jane died, and when he did, he couched the entire narrative in an account of Ogeewyahnoquotokwa's life as an exemplary Christian.

It's not difficult to see why Schoolcraft would suppress Ogeewyahnoquotokwa's narrative for so long. Jane's translation isn't pious, or sentimental, or romantic; she doesn't vilify her cousin for her spirituality. Christianity doesn't figure in the narrative at all. At the time of the events she related Ogeewyahnoquotokwa lived with her widowed mother, two older sisters, and younger brother at Shagwaamikong. "When I was a girl," the narrative begins, "of about twelve or thirteen years of age, my mother told me to look out for something that would happen to me. Accordingly, one morning early, in the middle of winter, I found an unusual sign, and ran off as far from the lodge as I could, and remained there until my mother came and found me out."[29] Her mother told her to build a lodge out of spruce branches, to keep busy by chopping wood and twisting basswood bark into twine, and to take no food or water, not even melted snow.

When her mother returned after two days, she brought not food but more instructions. "Who . . . will take care of us poor women?" she asked—all of her older sons and daughters were gone. She told her daughter to blacken her face and "fast really, that the Master of Life may have pity on you and me, and on us all." She would return in another two days. "He will help you, if you are determined to do what is right, and tell me whether you are favored or not, by the true Great Spirit." "If your visions are not good, reject them," she added.[30] In an account published by William in 1860, Wauchusco was also encouraged by family members to complete the fast when he appeared reluctant to do so. In his case, it was his grandmother and uncle who "urged him to comply with the ancient custom of their people, which was to fast, and wait for the manifestations of Gitchey-monedo,—whether he would grant him a guardian spirit or not, to guide and direct him through life." The ritual was a test and not everyone was successful, William noted; Wauchusco was warned that many young men had given in to their hunger and had failed to gain the spirits' attention.[31]

Ogeewyahnoquotokwa's mother returned in two days to give her a little melted snow to drink. "She again told me to get and follow a good vision; a vision that might not only do us good, but also benefit mankind, if I could."[32] She then left her daughter for another two days, returning with a little dried trout that Ogeewyahnoquotokwa couldn't eat because she was so sensitive "to all sounds, and my increased power of scent, produced by fasting." She could smell her mother before she arrived and the trout repulsed her. So her mother left off preparing it and "again encouraged me to persevere, and try to become a comfort to her in her old age and bereaved state."[33]

That night she had the first of two visions.

The night of the sixth day I fancied a voice called to me, and said, "Poor child! I pity your condition; come, you are invited this way"; and I thought the voice proceeded from a certain distance from my lodge. I obeyed the summons, and going to the spot from which the voice came, found a thin shining path, like a silver cord, which I followed. It led straight forward, and, it seemed, upward. After going a short distance, I stood still, and saw on my right hand the new moon, with a flame rising from the top like a candle, which threw around a broad light. On the left appeared the sun, near the point of its setting. I went on, and I beheld on my right the face of Kau-ge-gay-be-qua, or the everlasting standing woman, who told me her name, and said to me, "I give you my name, and you may give it to another. I also give you that which I have, life everlasting. I give you long life on the earth, and skill in saving life in others. Go, you are called on high."

I went on, and saw a man standing, with a large circular body, and rays from his head, like horns. He said, "Fear not; my name is Monido Winineeɡs, or the Little Man-spirit. I give this name to your first son. It is my life. Go to the place you are called to visit." I followed the path till I could see that it led up to an opening in the sky, when I heard a voice, and standing still, saw the figure of a man standing near the path, whose head was surrounded with a brilliant halo, and his breast was covered with squares. He said to me, "Look at me; my name is O-Shaw-wau-e-geeghick, or the Bright Blue Sky. I am the veil that covers the opening into the sky. Stand and listen to me. Do not be afraid. I am going to endow you with gifts of life, and put you in array that you may withstand and endure."

Immediately I saw myself circled with bright points, which rested against me like needles, but gave me no pain, and they fell at my feet. This was repeated several times, and at each time they fell to the ground. He said, "Wait, and do not fear, till I have said and done all I am about to do." I then felt different instruments, first like awls, and then like nails, stuck into my flesh, but neither did they give me pain, but, like the needles, fell at my feet as often as they appeared. He then said, "That is good," meaning my trial by these points; "you will see length of days. Advance a little farther," said he. I did so, and stood at the commencement of the opening. "You have arrived," said he, "at the limit you cannot pass. I give you my name; you can give it to another. Now return! Look around you. There is a conveyance for you. Do not be afraid to get on its back, and when you get to your lodge, you must take that which sustains the human body." I turned, and saw a kind of fish swimming in the air, and getting up on it as directed, was carried back with celerity, my hair floating behind me in the air.[34]

The surviving draft of the narrative appears to be an initial rough draft—the vision itself is out of place, and details are left out, for example, that of her hair floating behind her in the air. That was not Jane's invention, because a female figure on a fish with hair floating behind appears in the pictographic rendering. It's likely, then, that she wrote a rough draft, listening to Ogeewyahnoquotokwa tell the story and transcribing as she went, then produced a fair copy to give to Schoolcraft, who then, as was his habit, copied it.[35]

This narrative would not have been entirely unfamiliar to Schoolcraft, because Cass had gathered information on what may be earlier practices of Ojibwe people in which Everlasting Standing Woman figures. Cass gave his account (an example of the kind of information he likely destroyed) once again to Henry Whiting, who published it in the notes to his second epic star-crossed and doomed Indian lovers poem, *Sannillac* (Boston 1831). There Cass writes that an "eternal fire" was located west of Keweenaw Bay, where a hereditary chief called the Mutchekewis lived.[36] The Mutchekewis could engage in neither war nor hunting and was supported by a Muskinewa or provider, who solicited contributions for his living from the people when he needed them. The eternal fire was located in his village, near his lodge, and it was guarded by two men and two women, the spouses of whom supported them by doing the necessary domestic work and hunting. When one of the guardians died, the Mutchekewis selected a new wife or husband, so that the guardianship would never be broken. Those guardians who neglected their duties would be put to death, Cass writes, "without delay and without mercy."[37]

Once every eight years, the entire Ojibwe tribe assembled at the eternal fire for a ceremony. "The fire was called kaugageeshkoote, or the everlasting fire," Cass writes. "The principal male attendant was Kaugegee Keeghik, or the everlasting sun, and his assistant Kanawaudunkshkoote, or the fire keeper. The principal female was called Kaugagee Gaubeewekwa, or the everlasting standing woman, and her assistant Kabagaubewekwa, or the woman who stands all the time."[38] Since it appears that no scholar has ever written about the practice that Cass described, how Ogeewyahnoquotokwa's account relates to it is unknown.

When Ogeewyahnoquotokwa tried to chop wood after her first vision, she "fell back on the snow from exhaustion, and lay some time" before she could get up and go back to her lodge. As she lay there, the vision repeated itself, although she adds details that weren't transcribed in full: "I again saw the vision, and each person who had before spoken to me, and heard the promises of different kinds made to me, and the songs," she told Jane. "I went the same path which I had pursued before, and met with the same reception."[39] Her mother returned on the seventh day with boiled corn and asked her to fast three days longer. She had another vision, one that figured in her life as a healer.

> After the seventh day of my fast, while I was lying in my lodge, I saw a dark round object descending from the sky, like a round stone, and enter my lodge. As it came near I saw that it had small feet and hands like a human body. It spoke to me, and said, "I give you the gift of seeing into futurity, that you may use it for the benefit of yourself and the Indians—your relations and tribes-people." It then departed, but as it went away it assumed wings, and looked to me like the red-headed woodpecker in flight.[40]

Her mother retrieved her on the tenth day and took her home to make a feast in her honor. There were many guests. "I was told to eat sparingly, and to take nothing too hearty or substantial; but this was unnecessary, for my abstinence had made my senses so acute, that all animal food had a gross and disagreeable odor."[41]

Either Jane or Ogeewyahnoquotokwa wished to continue the narrative beyond the visions, first with an account of how Ogeewyahnoquotokwa used her powers. One winter night some time after she received her powers, the leader of her band came to her mother's lodge after she herself was asleep and requested that Ogeewyahnoquotokwa perform the shaking tent ceremony because the hunting was bad and the people were beginning to suffer. Her mother spoke to her about it, and then gave her consent to the chief. Ogeewyahnoquotokwa gave instructions for building the lodge.

> When it was finished, and tightly wound with skins, the entire population of the encampment assembled around it, and I went in taking only a small drum. I immediately knelt down, and holding my head near the ground in a position, as near as may be, prostrate, began beating my drum, and reciting my songs or incantations. The lodge commenced shaking violently, by supernatural means. I knew this by the compressed current of the air above, and the noise of motion. This being regarded by me and all without as proof of the presence of the spirits I consulted, I ceased beating and singing, and lay still, waiting for questions, in the position I had at first assumed.
>
> The first question put to me was in relation to the game, and where it was to be found. The response was given by the orbicular spirit, who had

appeared to me. He said, "How short-sighted you are! If you will go in a *west* direction you will find game in abundance." Next day the camp was broken up, and they all moved westward, the hunters, as usual, going far ahead. They had not proceeded far beyond the bounds of their former hunting circle when they came upon tracks of a moose, and that day they killed a female, and a young moose nearly full-grown. They pitched their encampment anew, and had abundance of animal food in the new position.[42]

Wauchusco told William about a similar initiation into his responsibilities, during a war expedition. When the party was running low on provisions and unsure of where the enemy was, Wauchusco said the chief "urged me incessantly, until I consented." As those outside the lodge waited for an answer, Wauchusco had a vision. "My soul embraced a large extent of country, which I had never before seen—every object plainly before me—our enemies were in their villages, unsuspicious of danger; their movements and acts I could plainly see; and mentally or spiritually, I could hear their conversation. Game abounded in another direction."[43]

The second additional story that Ogeewyahnoquotokwa wished to tell was that of the murder of her husband Strong Sky and its aftermath. Strong Sky was a good hunter; they had two children, a boy and a girl, and were happy. In the spring of 1822, they camped at the portage at Bow-e-ting, where her husband got into a fight with a "half-Frenchman named Gaultier." Jane's narrative is straightforward and harrowing.

> He had gone out, at a late hour in the evening, to visit the tent of Gaultier. Having been urged by one of the trader's men to take liquor that evening, and it being already late, I desired him not to go, but to defer his visit till the next day; and, after he had left the lodge, I felt a sudden presentiment of evil, and I went after him, and renewed my efforts in vain. He told me to return, and as I had two children in the lodge, the youngest of whom, a boy, was still in his cradle, and then ill, I sat up with him late, and waited and waited, till a later hour, and then fell asleep from exhaustion. I slept very sound. The first I knew was a violent shaking from a girl, a niece of Gaultier's, who told me my husband and Gaultier were all the time quarrelling. I arose, and went up the stream to Gaultier's camp-fire; it was nearly out, and I tried to make it blaze. I looked into his tent, but all was dark, and not a soul there. They had suddenly fled, although I did not, at the moment, know the cause. I tried to make a light to find my husband, but could find nothing dry, for it had rained very hard the day before. After being out a while my vision

became clearer, and turning toward the river side, I saw a dark object lying near the shore, on a grassy opening. I was attracted by something glistening, which turned out to be his ear-rings. I thought he was asleep, and in stooping to awake him I slipped, and fell on my knees. I had slipped in his blood on the grass, and putting my hand on his face, found him dead.[44]

She gathered her children and ran to her mother's lodge about a mile away. Her mother had already heard. "I reminded her that it was an act of Providence, to which we must submit," Ogeewyahnoquotokwa said. But her mother was crying for them because "I was left, as she had been years before, with nobody to provide for us." "In the morning the Indian agent came with soldiers from the fort to see what had happened," Ogeewyahnoquotokwa said, "but the murderer and all his bloody gang of relatives had fled."[45]

Schoolcraft found Strong Sky lying on the grass, stabbed in the torso and thighs. Gaultier and his brother Kogans were accused; Connasawaga of Grand Island witnessed the events. He had a coffin made so that Strong Sky could be buried at the burying ground adjacent to Fort Brady, a description of which he wrote in his journal for 22 July 1822. "Many persons collected to see the internment," he wrote. "The corpse was dressed in the best clothes of the deceased, with his warrior's cap & feathers; & wrapped round with a new blanket. Before the lid of the coffin was put down, Kakake his brother, raised the cap & pulled from the head a lock of hair, which he carefully wrapped in a piece of birch bark. After the coffin was let down, two poles were laid over the grave transversely; across which the sorrowing brother led the widow. He then led her back over the same poles. We were told that this ceremony signified protection."[46] Schoolcraft rewrote this episode in two separate pieces included in the *Literary Voyager*.

Jane took down about a dozen of Ogeewyahnoquotokwa's songs, for both the shaking tent ceremony and the Midewiwin, but there is no explanation of what they meant in context. Jane's draft manuscript survives only as notes for most of them.[47] Ogeewyahnoquotokwa was more powerful than even Wauchusco, Schoolcraft wrote in 1851, "of a good natural intellect, great shrewdness of observation, and some powers of induction and forecast"—unlike, according to him, the people with whom she lived.[48] It's plausible that after Ogeewyahnoquotokwa's conversion Schoolcraft solicited an account of her secret knowledge but then found that what she and Jane had produced was unsuited to his needs. If she had given an account of her conversion, he surely would have published it at the first opportunity, as he did with Wauchusco's narrative. He could have sought an account of her conversion to

Christianity that she was disinclined to give. Whatever happened, he kept this narrative hidden for as long as his finances allowed.

While William was away the family was upended for several weeks in the winter of 1834 by James and Anna Maria's developing romance, which no one in the family wanted, least of all her mother. To advance their cause the pair told Jane and Schoolcraft that they had Ozhaawshkodewikwe's permission to marry, which they didn't. When the family at the Sault found out what they'd done, Anna Maria and James lied, telling the Schoolcrafts that Ozhaawshkodewikwe had beaten Anna Maria with fire tongs. McMurray wrote letters for his mother-in-law. "I am . . . requested to say, that . . . if Maria proceeds, and does as she says, her Mamma will disown her as her child and entirely hide her face from her." James wrote indignant letters to the McMurrays defending his virtue (he accused the McMurrays and Eliza of saying that he treated Anna Maria as his "kept mistress") and chatty letters to Jane full of church news, protesting his innocence. No one was fooled, but no one could stop them, either. They would eventually be married in November 1834. Conveniently it was not a time when the Schoolcrafts could attend.[49]

Schoolcraft was gone for most of the summer of 1834, and Jane was ill again, in both mind and body. Her mother came down in June, when Schoolcraft was away, and in September with Maria when he was away again. McMurray visited in September on his way to Toronto on church business, only a month after his and Charlotte's first child, a boy named William, died at birth. They had brought the baby across the river for his grandmother to see him. McMurray thought that Maria was "a little humbled" by the scene, and she spoke to Charlotte for the first time since the drama of late winter.[50] George wrote several letters to Schoolcraft that summer mentioning the children and how they missed him, but wrote nothing about Jane, which might indicate that she wrote letters that haven't survived.[51] "You must try and keep your mind easy," McMurray wrote after returning to Sault Ste. Marie, "and trust that Mr. S will soon be restored to you."[52] Through George, she requested morphine and camphor.[53]

George was informed in July 1834 that the Michigan Superintendency of Indian Affairs, which included agencies from Indiana to Minnesota, was reorganizing. Subagents were terminated at Indiana, Chicago, Mackinac, Sault Ste. Marie, and Detroit—that would include George and Audrain, subagents at Mackinac and the Sault, respectively. Furthermore, no subagent could be compensated at the same time for being an interpreter—exactly George's position at that time. Only one interpreter (at $300 per year) was allowed at each agency (the agent's salary was $1,500 annually). Both gunsmiths and blacksmiths were terminated, although the rule would not go into effect for another year. George wrote in protest to Cass, who replied that Congress had passed the law and it was out of his hands, although he was not unsympathetic and volunteered to serve as a reference. Schoolcraft put George in the blacksmith position for the time being.[54]

William would have returned from Leech Lake in the late spring or early summer of 1834, and it can be assumed that Schoolcraft read what William had written as soon as he could get his hands on it. William's version of the Manabozho story cycle is only the second account of any detail and the longest to have been written down; most of the other fifty versions are brief outlines.[55] William didn't write down who told him the story, or why, or how he wrote it down. The fact that Schoolcraft made no mention of the Manabozho story cycle in any of his writing, published or not, until after William returned from Leech Lake suggests that the Johnstons either didn't know what it was or ,if they did, weren't allowed to write it down or possibly even speak of it. Other than the story published as "Papuckewis" (likely written by William) in *Literary Muzzeneigun* and "The Storm Fool" in *Algic Researches*, there are no surviving stories featuring Manabozho among those the Johnstons collected from their own circle of friends at Sault Ste. Marie, and only two others in which Manabozho is a secondary figure, both of which William also wrote down, one Saginaw Ojibwe and the other Odawa, told by Wauchusco.

Anishinaabe people were long in the habit of telling outsiders about Manabozho, but they'd only told portions of stories or made reference to his continued presence in the characteristics of animals, geographic features, or their own practices.[56] McKenney produced the first written account of the narrative in his book. He was told part of the story by the father of the girl—actually young woman—who'd never seen a spoon, but he was dissatisfied with it. "They knew nothing beyond the time Nanibojou made the earth," McKenney wrote. "I asked [O-she-we-gwun] where Nanibojou is now? He answered, 'somewhere towards the rising sun.' What is he like?—Is he a man in his appearance, or what does he resemble? He answered, 'He is like a man.' Was he ever married? 'Yes—but he has had no wife of late.' I then asked him who made Nanibojou? He said he was a twin, and was born of a woman who had never had a husband; and who, on giving Nanibojou and his twin brother life, vanished, and had never been seen since, *nor has Nanibojou's brother.*"[57] O-she-we-gwun was probably tired of McKenney's questions. His daughter had had a spell put on her by a man she refused to marry, and he likely had other things on his mind.[58]

Scholars have identified the main parts of the Manabozho cycle of stories: his mother is impregnated by the sun or the West Wind, then dies giving birth; he steals fire, giving it to humans; he leaves home and encounters other beings; he hunts with wolves; his wolf companion is killed by underwater spirits; he seeks revenge against the underwater spirits, wounding the principal one; he kills a healer, a toad-woman, and disguised in her skin kills the principal underwater spirit; he survives a flood the underwater spirits unleash and transforms the world for human beings.[59] In William's version the flood precedes killing the underwater spirit, which may have been a way on his part or the teller's to make the story available to outsiders. Closer to publication in *Algic Researches*, someone provided Schoolcraft with the additional information that Manabozho's grandmother was the daughter of the moon, who was tricked by a rival into getting on a grapevine swing and subsequently fell through the sky to the earth, after which she gave birth to a daughter who, once grown, was impregnated by the West Wind, and Manabozho was the result.[60]

The ethnologist Daniel Garrison Brinton, who corresponded with Schoolcraft as a young man in the 1850s, understood what Schoolcraft himself recognized, even if he could only articulate it in the layers of quasi-scholarly apparatus and turgid revisions. People "the world over" told stories about "such a personage" as Manabozho, Brinton wrote in 1868, "some such august character, who taught them what they knew, the tillage of the soil, the properties of plants, the art of picture writing, the secrets of magic; who founded their institutions and established their religions, who governed them long with glory abroad and peace at home; and finally, did not die, but like Frederick Barbarossa, Charlemagne, King Arthur, and all great heroes, vanished mysteriously, and still lives somewhere, ready at the right moment to return to his beloved people and lead them to victory and happiness."[61] Jane and William, and then Schoolcraft after them, would have immediately recognized the type of narrative William received. While Anishinaabe people wouldn't likely have found the category useful and Indigenous oral narratives do not reduce to the written forms of Western literature, for Jane, William, and Schoolcraft (albeit for different reasons), the Manabozho story cycle was recognizable as an epic, the founding narrative of a people. Savages, of course, could not be capable of such a thing. William had returned from Leech Lake with proof of a narrative tradition that brought Anishinaabe people into world history, a place they weren't supposed to be.

After William returned with "Story of Manahbosho" and likely after Jane wrote down Ogeewyahnoquotokwa's story, Schoolcraft wrote an essay in the summer and fall of 1834 for the Presbyterian *Literary and Theological Review* incorporating his new research. Ostensibly a review of the constitution of the Algic Society, which was probably written by himself ("We approve" of it, he wrote), and the Gospel of John as translated into Ojibwemowin by Peter Jones, the essay shows that although Schoolcraft concluded that the spirits were undoubtedly real and undoubtedly evil, the stories (about the spirits) were still compelling and even beautiful, as was the language itself. The discrepancy between the two main points in the essay is so distinct that it seems to mark more plainly than usual Jane's involvement in his writing. She was his principal "informant" on these topics; George wasn't in the habit of providing Schoolcraft with anything until the later 1830s, when he felt it was necessary to keep Schoolcraft's favor; William was in Sault Ste Marie.

He began the essay with Wauchusco's conversion narrative, more than likely written by Jane, who would often spend time with Wauchusco in the agency kitchen at Mackinac.[62] Wauchusco had been "the great juggler of his tribe," Schoolcraft writes, and was now a Christian. "What were his own conceptions of the power and arts he practised? How did these things appear to his mind, after a lapse of several years, during which his opinions and feelings had undergone changes, in many respects so striking?" Wauchusco told him, Schoolcraft says, that "he attributed all his ability in the deceptive arts, to the agency, of the Evil Spirit; and he spoke of it, with the same settled tone that he had manifested in reciting other points in his personal experience. He believed, that he had followed a lying spirit, whose object it was to deceive the Indians, and make them miserable."[63] This is not how Wauchusco described his relationship with the spirits; Wauchusco was as plain about the power of the spirits and his relationship with them as was Ogeewyahnoquotokwa in her narrative. He has nothing to say about evil spirits. The substance of his narrative will be discussed in more detail in chapter 9; for the moment, the point is that when Schoolcraft started asking about the spirits' role in Anishinaabe life, he knew because he was told that they were real, not primitive delusions or fantasies. If they were real, they could be nothing other than evil, the devil's work. He maintained this conviction for the rest of his life.

The Ojibwes were "spirit-ridden," he wrote, and even enslaved by them "as effectually as the hooks of iron, which pierce a whirling Hindoo's flesh." The spirits made him a better writer. "Whatever is wonderful or past comprehension, to their minds, is referred to the agency of a spirit. . . . A watch is a spirit. A piece of blue cloth, cast and blistered steel, a compass, a jewel, an insect, &c. are respectively a spirit. Thunder consists of so many distinct spirits. The Aurora Borealis is a body of dancing spirits." He railed against what he'd been told. "Every department of the universe" is "filled with invisible spirits," and they "hold . . . nearly the same relation to matter, that the soul does to the body. They believe not only that every man, but also *that every animal has a soul.*"

> And, as might be expected, under this belief, *they make no distinction between instinct and reason.* Every animal is supposed to be endowed with a reasoning faculty. The movements of birds, and other animals, are deemed to be the result, not of mere instinctive animal powers, implanted and limited by the Creator, without inherent power to exceed or enlarge them, but of a process of ratiocination. They go a step farther, and believe that animals, particularly birds, can look into, and are familiar with the vast operations of the world of spiritual life. Hence the great respect they pay to birds, as agents of omen, and also to some animals, whose souls they expect to encounter in another life. Nay, it is the settled belief among the northern Indians, that animals will fare better in another world, in the precise ratio that their lives and enjoyments have been curtailed in this.[64]

He was both amazed and incredulous. When Indians killed an animal in the hunt, they "had been known to ask the pardon of an animal which he had just killed."[65] He was thinking of William's accounts of hunting at Leech Lake. The spirits' materiality disturbed him. The afterlife was "clogged with sensual accidents": "The human soul hungers, and it must have food deposited upon the grave. It suffers, and the body must be wrapped about with clothes. It is in darkness, and a light must be kindled at the head of a grave. It wanders through plains and across streams, subject to the providences of this life, in quest of its place of enjoyment; and when it reaches it, it finds every species of sensual trial, which render it, not indeed a heaven of rest, but another world, very much like this."[66] Worse than this, there was no judgment in this afterlife. There was no savior, no Holy Ghost. "Darker and more chilling views it would be impossible to present."[67]

He asked Jane about the stories. The West Wind, Kabeun, impregnated "a maid, who incautiously exposed herself in bathing" and produced his sons, the East, North, and South, the subjects of "many most extravagant tales, of forest and domestic adventure." Manabozho, the fourth son of the West Wind the maid, was "a sort of terrene Jove, who could perform all things, but lived on earth, and excelled particularly in feats of strength and manual dexterity." "Kwasind is a sort of Samson, who threw a large mass of rock, such as the Cyclops cast at Mentor. Weeng is the god of sleep, who is represented to have numerous small emissaries at his service.... Pauguk is death, in his symbolic attitude. He is armed with a bow and arrows."[68] "The evening star... was formerly a woman," he continued, on another track. "An ambitious boy became one of the planets. Three brothers, traveling in a canoe, were translated into a group of stars. The fox, lynx, hare, robin, eagle, and numerous other species, retain places in Indian astronomy. The mouse obtained celestial elevation by creeping up the rainbow, which makes a flossy mass of bright threads, and by the power of gnawing, relieved a captive in the sky. It is a coincidence, which we note, that *Ursa Major*, is called by them, the bear."[69] There were giants, fairies, mermen, and ghosts.

Many of these details are not to be found in the stories written by members of the Johnston family, indicating that there may have been other stories—perhaps many other stories—written down and now lost. It seems that Schoolcraft asked Jane not only about the stories but the manner in which they were told. In storytelling "there is an equanimity of tone, and careless, easy vein of narration, or dialogue, in which the power of memory is most strikingly brought out. The very voice and words of the supposed speaker are exactly depicted; and the deepest interest, or merriment, are excited."[70] Schoolcraft had as much that was positive to say about the complexity of Ojibwemowin in this essay as did Heckewelder and Du Ponceau themselves on the Delaware language, surprisingly, considering his allegiance to Cass.[71] "All that relates to light and shade, to colour and quality, to purity or impurity, to fluid or solid, to matter or spirit, seems to be woven into the texture of the language with silken threads," he enthused, "light and sound, taste and feeling, hearing and smelling."[72]

Some of the stories "did admit of poetic uses."[73] Even if many of them featured the transformation of men and women into animals and other forms, such transformations were often "as accurately adapted for the purposes of amusement or instruction, as if Ovid himself had been consulted in their composition."[74] Schoolcraft couldn't reconcile the spirits, which were an implicit threat to Christian civilization, with the stories about the spirits, which through the tutelage of Jane and other members of the family he found remarkable and even enticing. He blustered about necromancy but he couldn't shake the beauty in the stories themselves, in their language, and even in their practice, once it had been explained to him.

He sent the essay off to be published, because he knew what Jane was saying was true.

In October several Indigenous men who needed to be licensed to trade visited Schoolcraft, but he couldn't speak to them without an interpreter. George was not to be found, however; Schoolcraft sent first the children and then Jane looking for him, but both returned with no information. George was with a

Captain Chehachiff of the Russian Imperial Guards, another of the many travelers who stopped at Mackinac in those years; they must have been talking about Indians, because George later copied out a speech that had been given to him when he left La Pointe in 1828. After he was done with Captain Chehachiff, George went to the blacksmith shop to make a bedstead for Janée's doll.

After dinner he joined the captain at the agency, at which point Schoolcraft burst out of the office "and accosted me in pretty severe & angry language and said he wished to see me in the office," George wrote in a statement describing the altercation. Schoolcraft made his accusations. In his defense, George said, "The Capt. had called on me, and I could not leave my room, and I remarked that I was always present and did not make it a practice to absent myself." Schoolcraft told him to sweep the office floor and go to the post office for letters, which were the duties of the interpreter. He complained that George didn't keep the office open long enough. That was his duty, too. "I told him if he thought that I had not performed my duty, then he was at liberty to engage one who would."[75]

George quit. Schoolcraft's "remarks this day were pointed, peevish, and beyond endurance," wrote George; his "harsh course & tyranny, blended with a disposition bordering on bearishness," was "not at all compatible for me to bear." He wrote a farewell letter to Jane thanking her for the kindness she had shown to his children, especially his oldest, Louisa, and put his trust in God, who "alone . . . has in tender love and compassion . . . so miraculously drawn me back from destruction and from the depths of everlasting woe. . . . Had I served my Lord & Master as zealously & faithfully as I have served this cold world, God's pleasure would have been visibly manifested to me at this time in plenitude of mercies."[76] He wrote to Cass as well—"for I have looked to the North & South, to East and West, and find none to whom I could address myself but to you." Cass counseled George to make up with his brother-in-law, since "you and I both know his worth and I further know that you have no better friend than he."[77] George was determined, however. He borrowed a hundred dollars from a friend to help his family make it through the winter and left for the Sault.[78]

George's situation undoubtedly caused Jane anguish. Some indication of her state of mind at about that time can be found in a letter to her from Grenville Sproat, a teacher at a missionary school at St. Ignace, across Mackinac harbor on the mainland. He had only recently graduated from Brown University, but the previous year he established the first school in the new city of Chicago.[79] After a year there he decided to become a missionary to the Indians instead and spent the winter of 1834–35 teaching school at St. Ignace before moving on to La Pointe. Sproat addressed Jane as "Mother" and effused on the scene of "these poor children" who were his charges. "Many are the tears that have run down these cheeks for them, and many more may follow ere they shall be brought into the fold of God." Despite his youth, he had some special advice for Jane. "Ill prepared, by nature for the storms and tempests of time, where, O! where shall the soul find refuge but in the bosom of its God!" he wrote. "You and I have *special* need to keep near the cross of Jesus. Let us live with him, and 'be crucified with him.' ... O! is not this all—to lose our own voice in this to say continually, 'not my will, but thine, O God, be done!'"[80]

William wrote to Schoolcraft after George had returned to the Sault before setting off for parts unknown. "Knowing that it is almost impossible for us [George and himself] to support ourselfs [sic]," he wondered also about the "prospect of a young man toward the west of the Mississippi, for I have a great desire to see that part of the country."[81] Schoolcraft replied within three days—as soon as he could have received the letter—offering him the interpreter job at Mackinac. He was on the island by February of 1835.[82]

In May Schoolcraft wrote unsolicited to Washington Irving, offering him "such facts or material, as I possess or could with but little effort, obtain" if Irving might be interested in writing something like "a series of Indian biographies or biographical sketches" that were unburdened by the "heaviness" of current books on the topic.[83] Irving was probably the most famous American writer of the moment. He was well known for his picturesque depictions of Indians and had just published *A Tour on the Prairies*, an account of his excursion to the territory west of Arkansas where the United States had been deporting Indigenous people from the Southeast. In his letter Schoolcraft observed that while most writing about Indians tended to history or manners and customs, what was wanted was real knowledge about "their mode of thinking & reasoning, their mode of communicating oral instruction, and their domestic manners," as well as "their strongly masked mythological lore & opinion." "The Indian is not, characteristically, a reflective being," Schoolcraft explained. "He acts mostly from impulses; and his character will be apt to be spoiled by attempting to show it up in a chain of meritorious ratiocination, such as usually accompanies the acts of well-educated white men." (Everyone knew Indians weren't capable of abstract thought.) He felt "induced" to suggest that perhaps Irving himself might write those biographies or "imaginative tales of a race of men who have exhibited no equivocal proofs of being warriors, counsellors, orators, martyrs or heroes."[84] This was Schoolcraft's first attempt to get a grip on his problem with the spirits and the stories told about them. He needed a writer more talented than he was to corral them in writing.

He was probably familiar with Irving's recent comments (or, those of Irving's alter ego, Diedrich Knickerbocker) on American literature. On Irving's return to the United States in 1832 after seventeen years in England and Spain, American critics had disagreed vehemently about just how American and thus worthy of praise Irving was.[85] The ongoing commentary on himself perhaps motivated Irving to either collaborate on or lend his pseudonym to a manifesto on the future of American literature published in a new periodical, *The Knickerbocker; or New York Monthly Magazine,* in June 1833.[86] The author of the piece, "A Conversation," was likely the *Knickerbocker*'s editor, Charles Fenno Hoffman, a member of an old and politically connected family in New York City. He was a young lawyer-turned-newspaper-writer-and-editor, most recently at the *New York American,* which he left in 1833 to found the *Knickerbocker,* its title an homage to Irving. He was also the younger half-brother of Irving's long-deceased fiancée, Matilda Hoffman; Irving had studied law with their father as a young man. Considering the current literary conversation around himself and that Hoffman was a friend, it seems fairly certain that Diedrich Knickerbocker spoke for Irving himself in this manifesto.

The editor stipulated that American literature ought to be the expression of "the mind of this land." "What signifies it that our dominions stretch from the rising to the setting sun—what availeth all the lavish magnificence which nature has displayed in this her favourite region, if no Mind of our own, arises to give life to the deep sublimities of thought, which tremble into existence at their contemplation? It is not unnumbered trophies that give splendour to a nation—no extent of empire, nor grandeur of achievement can confer the inestimable glory of intellectual greatness.... No ... eternal Fame, is to be found only in the native—the impregnated genius of the land." To which Diedrich Knickerbocker replied, some paragraphs later, "If you want to see the semina from which a national literature will spring, stand up and look around you." After an upswelling of sublime imagery on the part of the editor, Diedrich Knickerbocker added that a "National Literature" would arise "not from the exotic feeling and the transplanted associations of the settler or his descendant" but "it must rise from, and grow up with the soil with which it may be connected." That is, "it must be indigenous."

The land wasn't theirs, and they felt it. Of the people whose land it was, Diedrich Knickerbocker observed that Indians could have had a literature "corresponding in grandeur, in sublimity, in beauty with their magnificent land," if only they had become "conscious lords" of it "and developed into power and utility all its limitless resources." To put it crudely, a literature worthy of the name would not appear until the population was fully enmeshed in capitalist resource exploitation. "Then we may look for that truest poetry," continued Diedrich Knickerbocker, "that poetry of feeling—then we may expect that loftiest eloquence, whose images and energy spring only from the heart." The logic in back of this declaration was not remarkable. Indians couldn't have a literature because they weren't civilized, and they weren't civilized because they supposedly didn't engage in commercial agriculture, which everyone knew from the late eighteenth century forward, even if the subject of Indians and literature was an obscure one. While the Americans could extract an identity from the land as they did its resources, the Indians who refused to engage in the right kind of labor on the land had limited themselves to "the wild poetry of their eloquence, and the touching simplicity of their superstitions."

Schoolcraft likely read the manifesto—he later contributed to the *Knickerbocker* and had certainly absorbed similar ideas that were circulating at that time. Indians were regarded as fit matter for American literature and symbolic of the land from the beginning of the republic, as long as the right story was being told. Schoolcraft was offering Irving the first detailed account of the mythology of the Indians, untouched by European influence. This could certainly be seen as a conduit to the "mind of this land." He also wanted to give that material to someone who was not tied down by a dedication to science like himself; that person had to be free to invent, to tell the stories as they should have been told.

He may also have got wind that Irving was writing a history of John Jacob Astor's Oregon fur trading outpost Astoria at Astor's request using Astor's own records.[87] He perhaps thought he could make a similar arrangement. By the time Irving received Schoolcraft's letter, he and his nephew Pierre, his research assistant, had moved into Astor's grand columned estate overlooking Hell Gate in the East River to write the book.[88] Irving responded to Schoolcraft immediately. "I have but just received your letter of the 5th inst. and lose not a moment in expressing how interesting and acceptable I find its purport," he wrote at the end of May. "The little I have seen of our Indian tribes has awakened an earnest curiosity to know more concerning them, and, if possible, to embody some of their fast fading characteristics, and traditions in our popular literature."[89] While Irving may have been curious about Indians, he was also thinking of money to be made at a time when he was feeling some anxiety about coming up with new subject matter.[90] By midsummer, when he bought an old farmhouse on the Hudson River that needed extensive renovation, he was especially keen to increase his income.[91] "I know no one to whom I could look with more confidence in this respect than to yourself and I assure you I should receive as high and unexpected favors any communications of the kind you suggest; that would aid me in furnishing biographies, tales or sketches illustrative of Indian life, Indian character, and mythology and superstitions," Irving wrote. Send anything, he added, and do make sure to send it by the Post Office rather than by private means, money being "no object with me," just to be safe.[92]

Schoolcraft responded just as quickly as Irving. He was about to leave for Detroit for a month. He needed to have copies made, at Detroit and at Mackinac. He'd then send everything together, "the papers relating to biographies; to mythology & tales; to superstitious societies; & to domestic manners & traits, that you may judge of the character & scope of these things in convenience." For the moment, he gave a list of important chiefs to tide Irving over.[93] He eventually sent a marked-up draft of his own anecdotes of Shingabawossin and several other chiefs, at least one of which was taken from an account George wrote several years previous, and "Story of a Young Lady who had subsisted for nine years in a Cave," which he'd heard and written down years before while exploring for lead in Missouri. He included no Anishinaabe stories. This haphazard collection—it's held today by the New-York Historical Society—isn't the kind of thing a person would send America's most celebrated writer, especially if one were hoping to collaborate in some way. It's careless. Irving didn't respond until months later. He thanked Schoolcraft for the "very interesting documents of Indian history" and promised "in the case I may make of it," he would do his best to meet Schoolcraft's expectations.[94] That was the end of their correspondence on the matter.

Schoolcraft evidently changed his mind about what he might do with the material he had. By September 1835 he was at work on the first version of *Algic Researches*, which probably combined William's stories from Leech Lake with the stories from *Literary Voyager* and the earlier stories from the postwar anthology. "He is making a collection of moral tales of the Chippewas," wrote Chandler Robbins Gilman in his book *Life on the Lakes: Being Tales and Sketches Collected during a Trip to the Pictured Rocks of Lake Superior* (1836). Gilman, a New York City physician, and Martin Hoffman, the uncle of Charles Fenno, were both of them inspired by Irving to take a trip to the West and Gilman to write about it.[95] Jane gave Gilman "Origin of the Robin" and "Forsaken Brother" to copy and include in his book, which he got into print right away. He assured his readers that "Origin of the Robin" was "taken down by Mrs. S. verbatim, from the lips of an old Chippewa woman. Mrs. S tells me that she has since been assured by very many of the oldest and most intelligent of the tribe that the story . . . has been current in the tribe from their earliest recollections."[96]

O Mr. C!

Jane Johnston Schoolcraft, Mackinac, to William Hull Clarke, Chicago, ca. 1835

In answer to questions as to the condition of the Indian women, she said, that it was better than that of the white woman, taking into consideration the differences between the races. That is to say, although on account of many inevitable causes, the Indian woman is subjected to many hardships of a physical nature, yet her position, compared to that of man, is higher and freer than that of the white woman.

O Mr. C! why will they look upon one side? they either exalt the Red Man into a demi-god, or degrade him into a beast. They say he compels his wife to do all the drudgery, while he does nothing but hunt and amuse himself; forgetting that upon his activity and powers of endurance as a hunter depends the support of his family;[1] that this is labor of the most fatiguing kind, and that it is absolutely necessary that he should keep his frame unbent by burdens and unworn by toil, that he may be able to obtain the means of subsistence.[2]

I have witnessed scenes of conjugal and parental love in the Indian's wigwam from which I have often, often thought the educated white man, proud of his superior civilization, might learn an useful lesson. When he returns from hunting, worn out with fatigue, having tasted nothing since dawn, his wife, if she is a good wife, will take off his moccasons and replace them with dry ones, and will prepare his game for their repast, while his children will climb upon him, and he will caress them with all the tenderness of a woman; and in the evening the Indian wigwam is the scene of the purest domestic pleasures. The father will relate for the amusement of the wife, and for the instruction of the children, all the events of the day's hunt, while they will treasure up every word that falls, and thus learn the theory of the art, whose practice is to be the occupation of their lives.[3]

I have seen among them instances of refined delicacy of feeling, and traits of kindness of heart diffusing itself through the action and manners, which I have in vain sought in highly civilized communities. I have heard speeches which, had they been made by the sages of antiquity, would have been handed down to us with a world's applause; and I have asked myself, where is the intrinsic difference between the soul of this red man in his blanket, and that of him who is surrounded by all the accidents of education, civilization and manners; are not those noble sentiments—the feeling of the good, the great and the beautiful—intuitive?[4]

Chapter 7

Treaty of Washington

George corresponded with Jeremiah Porter after Porter left for Chicago as well as with William Boutwell, who wrote from Leech Lake, but religion couldn't keep him from unease.[1] He exchanged letters with a cousin, also named George Johnston, who worked in the Inspector General's Office of the London Customs House. They were about the same age; Cousin George had worked twenty years in Customs, first in Dublin and then in London, and he had known John Johnston. (Interestingly, the two cousins have nearly identical handwriting.) To him George lamented his struggle to find the means of making a decent living. His cousin responded with the kind of pious optimism that must have sounded like his father. "It grieves me extremely to hear your affairs or prospects at present appear rather gloomy," Cousin George wrote in April 1834. "Don't be cast down, energy, patience & perseverance in an honest man are powerful auxiliaries in his progress through life." George had brought up the family's losses in the War of 1812, about which Cousin George had to observe that "your Dear Father from notions of patriotism did not serve either himself or his family." "Don't be offended by my freedom," he added. London George was as voluble as Sault George was decorous. He remarked on the political conflict and "agricultural distress" ongoing in Britain at the moment; he was undecided on the corn laws himself. He wondered if it was better to emigrate, as his brothers Hugh and Samuel had, although he'd not heard from them since they arrived in Tennessee some years previously. On family news, the Rt. Honble. Wm. Saurin, their cousin the bishop of Dromore, "has dropped his correspondence with me, his politicks not being with the present ministry he has nothing in his power."[2]

His father's remaining a British subject was not the best idea, George had to agree. "My dear departed Father's patriotism, has truly been the ruin of himself and family. . . . I entertain very little hope of ever recovering a single shilling from the British government." Nevertheless, "the goodness of heart you manifest in relation to my welfare is cheering to me, and will tend to brace the relaxed nerve anew to perseverance and honest industry."[3] It was not only his decision to remain a British subject in American territory that made his family's fortunes more difficult; it was also, in George's case, that pious optimism of his father's, his belief that if an honorable man behaved honorably, all would be right in the world. It was Hugh Blair's prescription for upright masculinity, and it would never work in the United States for a man branded as "half-breed"—no matter how well-spoken, polite, and educated he might be.

This situation is revealed in the disposition of the "Irish money," as the family called it, which commenced when Uncle Henry Kearney wrote to George in August 1834 that his wife Jane, John Johnston's sister, had died, and that there was a legacy left to his wife by an aunt that was now to go to the Johnston Estate. It was about 500 pounds "in late Irish currency" (this seems to have been the projected source for Johnston's promised dowry of $10,000 on Jane's marriage to Schoolcraft). The bishop of Dromore was in possession of the money, but he was then on his deathbed; and a Mr. Neale claimed to have been owed some of it.[4] George wrote at least three different versions of his response to Kearney, two of which he copied into a large folio letterbook he started keeping at about this time. Judging by Kearney's near-histrionic response to Schoolcraft, the third version (of which there is no copy) related his conflicts with Schoolcraft and expressed a desire to see Reverend Kearney in Dublin himself, as soon as he could. "I think that I am called to this and I consider it a duty I owe to my family and to myself," George wrote in his earlier letter.[5]

Kearney was "much troubled" by George's letter, he wrote to Schoolcraft. "From the moment I read his letter, I could not but ask, Is this pride—is it precipitance—is it willfulness & improvidence of disposition—is he 'unstable as water" &c?" It was quite disturbing. "If he could not serve under the guidance & guardianship of the one who by his talents & conduct had earned his confidence & respect—who was so closely allied to him . . . to whom God had given grace to take Christ for his master, & make a [confidence] of his ways, & according to his own profession of religion, was in the highest sense, a brother—where can he hope to find a congenial element?" George's duty, as an Indian, was to subordinate himself to Schoolcraft, who, in his Christian benevolence, had only George's best interests at heart. It was Kearney's own position as well. Additionally, the mother of John Johnston's child had made herself known to the family (it's not clear when or where), and Kearney was "willing to let Mrs. Moore's [the mother of John Johnston's child] right in the matter rest altogether with Mrs. Johnston." He sent along two copies of an essay by "Dr. Humphrey of Amherst College on the proper observance of the sabbath," as well as the eulogies of two dead divines that he advised Schoolcraft to forward to McMurray after perusing the documents himself.[6]

Schoolcraft informed Kearney about George's calumnies by return mail. "I am aware of the grief and trouble by the immense expenditure of property by George in the absence of his father," Kearney wrote in return, evidently referring to George's abandonment of Montreal when he was nineteen, "for I have it recorded in language of sorrow and disappointment from the dear departed friend himself." George was improvident, as a "half-breed" would always prove to be. Schoolcraft felt so sympatico with Kearney that he offered him the position of minister at Mackinac in light of the closure of William Ferry's mission, but Kearney had to decline.[7] He noted that Mr. Neale determined that the estate owed him money; Reverend Kearney was looking into it.[8]

That spring George headed to Upper Canada, where he visited Maj. James Winnet, a former commander at Drummond who'd been appointed resident superintendent at Six Nations of the Grand River reserve.[9] He and George had "an hours conversation . . . upon private matters, which were satisfactory to me" at Brantford, after which he traveled by stage and steamboat to Toronto, where he secured a room at the Commercial Hotel and "hunted up" McMurray's brothers Thomas and Samuel, who owned a shop.[10] He visited Parliament, the garrison, and the government house and was introduced to Col. James Givins, chief superintendent of Indian affairs.[11] Givins was as old as John Johnston would have been (they possibly knew one another), having served in the British military during both the revolution and the War of 1812, then afterward in the British Indian Department. He had learned to speak Ojibwemowin while stationed at Detroit early in his career and supported Peter Jones and the Methodist settlement at Mississauga as an official in the Indian Department after the war.[12] George doesn't say what any of these meetings were about, although over a lifetime of such peregrinations he was usually working on some means of improving his situation.

He returned to the Sault from Penetanguishine in late May, when James Schoolcraft spied him getting off the steamboat, and began spinning a tale calculated to inflame his brother and increase his own standing in his brother's eyes. He wrote to Schoolcraft that George arrived "in a high state of intoxication . . . and the effects of which he has not yet recovered. He spoke very *large*—talks of recovering *his* war losses, and *his* this and *his* that—and *my* so and so." But, he added, "I think after a while he will find himself 'himself' again, and all will go along quietly."[13] Since James Schoolcraft was in the habit of lying about other people's behavior in order to benefit himself, his account of George may or may not have been true, or may have been only partly true. He and his brother cut George down because George was the eldest son and thus a potential brake on whatever plans they might have in relation to the family finances. James even opined that George's legitimacy was in question, since his parents didn't marry in the eyes of the United States until circumstances made it necessary in 1822.[14] Of course, if George was illegitimate, so were all the other Johnston siblings, including James's wife. Eventually he made the connection.

On his arrival George found a letter appointing him interpreter for a commission setting a boundary between the Dakotas and Ojibwes with instructions to leave immediately, and another from William, who after Leech

Lake was using his Ojibwe name, Meingun [ma'iingan], signing himself "Wm. Wolf." "You have some *kind friend* at the Sault, who has stated all your concerns ... even to the lowest words, such as that you would *kick* Mr. Schoolcraft burn him, going to England your accounts &c." "Keep your mouth closed," wrote William; "I never heard you say you would kick; so you told some pretended friend of yours, who has told or written here."[15]

George set off with his two boys for Fort Snelling, at the confluence of the Minnesota and Mississippi Rivers, and known to George and other fur traders as St. Peters for the trading post that preceded the American fort. It took over a month, traveling first to La Pointe, then inland and eventually down the Chippewa River, then up the Mississippi. He spoke to the chiefs at La Pointe about the boundary commission and sent wampum messages to Lac Courtoreille, Lac du Flambeau, and Red Cedar River.[16] His boys fished, and he met various people along the way—an Ojibwe Methodist family who gave the travelers fish, venison, and cranberries, a husband and wife who had killed two deer and gave one, then, after another "disagreeable" day paddling through mosquitoes and rain, five men in a lodge at the mouth of the Antawah River who shared "an abundant supply of venison."[17] When he arrived at Fort Snelling, George dined with Major Bliss and took tea with Major Taliaferro, the agent, who had been his devoted nemesis when George was subagent at La Pointe.[18] He was introduced to "Mr. Catline," the painter, who wished to paint the portraits of three of the men who came down with him.[19] He left his sons with the local missionary and set out, with a small group of Ojibwe men, to catch up with the surveying party.[20]

George was as civilized as a frontiersman could be. Like his father he read James Fenimore Cooper (again one wonders what he thought about those books and *Blackwood's Edinburgh Magazine*.[21] In the reminisces of white "pioneers" at the end of the century, he appears as a dignified man—the implication was, maybe too dignified.[22] He would mainly make his living as an interpreter or a guide for various expeditions in the region for the rest of his life, one of the few jobs left for mixed-race men. He seems to have enjoyed it. He was freed of the turmoil of trying to make a living among white settlers and was recognized for what he knew. He had time to think. "The weather was very cool & bracing" when he and his men broke camp on 3 July 1835, he wrote in his diary, but when they stopped to eat,

> the wind sprung up from the south, and the weather became extremely sultry, so much so that the breeze we inhaled was like a hot vapour. This indicated a prelude to a thunder storm, and which we experienced in all its awful grandeur. I had wished within my own mind to witness such a scene in an open & extensive prairie, this scene I realized. I got out of my canoe, ascended a hill from the margin of the river, and on reaching its

summit beheld such a solemn grandeur that I cannot easily forget. I stood leaning on a tree, the only shelter I had during the storm, the rain pouring down in sheets and this lasted for about an hour and a half. Although thoroughly drenched, I proceeded on my route, killed this day six ducks. Encamped upon one of the greatest bends I have observed since I left the falls of St. Anthony.[23]

Two weeks later his party caught up with the soldiers, who'd switched their horses and carts along the way for pack mules because of the dense undergrowth. They came upon first a dead mule and then a dead horse on their approach to the Americans' camp. George had persuaded a reluctant Ojibwe man to guide them all to Otter Tail Lake, and he tried to get Major Bean to let the man lead the way, but the major refused, despite the fact that the Americans had no idea where they were. George's guide "became disgusted and reluctant to answer questions, and said that he would not go beyond the setting sun with us, which was verified."[24] Later George visited this man and the men who were with him at an encampment near Otter Tail Lake, and "found them playing the platter game, one of whom seemed successful having a small tin kettle near him containing the fruits of his winnings. Leaden balls. They presented me with dried venison, and they all came to our camp." Major Bean appeared and, seemingly having understood his previous mistake, presented the men with flour, pork, and tobacco.[25]

George related his "voyaging" for the boundary line in which he didn't have much faith when he wrote to Kearney in November 1835, from Upper Canada, looking for an answer to his letters. He had remained a few days at the Sault when he returned from the boundary line expedition in October, but then set out for Upper Canada to hunt geese before heading to Toronto to buy goods for a store he planned to run on St. Josephs Island nearby the Sault in the St. Mary's River.[26] His plan to work with Andrew Mitchell, son of Elizabeth and David Mitchell, "had not worked out as expected" however. "His habits have been such that there would not be any safety in transacting business with him," wrote George.[27] Kearney was by that time corresponding about serious financial matters with Schoolcraft only; so fearful was he that George might turn up unexpectedly that he felt compelled to keep some of the money owed to the family in reserve.[28] In this and in other ways Reverend Kearney successfully whittled down the Irish money to almost nothing before it was finally distributed years hence, after Jane Schoolcraft's death.

The white men in the family sought other sources of income. McMurray pursued a reimbursement for war losses from the British government, but in the end the family could only claim 145 pounds, out of which Mr. Norton, their agent in Toronto, took his sizable attorney's fees.[29] In the summer of 1835 Schoolcraft hatched a plan to present a claim for the War of 1812 losses to Congress himself, that winter, in Washington.

He had other, bigger plans in motion. For the previous several years the Little Traverse band of Odawas at L'Arbre Croche, on the northwestern Lower Peninsula, had been trying to get a hearing in Washington about a plan they had to sell marginal land to the United States to settle their debts to the traders and thus to protect their hold on the rest of their land, in expectation of incoming whites. But the government had been uninterested in buying land that settlers wouldn't likely populate immediately, as there was still much land to be settled in the previously ceded territories of southern and southwestern Michigan. Schoolcraft had brushed off the Odawas in the summer of 1834, and Elbert Herring, then commissioner of Indian Affairs, refused to pay for their travel to Washington to see Jackson and Cass themselves.[30] By June 1835, though, Schoolcraft changed his mind; he wrote to his superiors that the Little Traverse Odawas wanted to sell Drummond Island and opined that now was the time for a treaty, as many Odawas, including Assigninack, fearful that the United States might start deporting people to the West, were emigrating to Manitoulin Island in Georgian Bay. He pointedly included the Upper Peninsula Ojibwes in that assessment. Herring excluded the Upper Peninsula Ojibwes from his instructions, however, giving Schoolcraft permission to canvass local Indigenous leaders about ceding Drummond Island and lands north of Grand River on the Lower Peninsula only.[31]

This was the beginning of the movement toward the 1836 Treaty of Washington, through which the Odawas at L'Arbre Croche and the Ojibwes of the eastern Upper Peninsula sold their land to the United States, and fur traders claiming to be owed money by the tribes would be paid out of the proceeds of the sale. Despite repeated declarations to the contrary, Schoolcraft was as interested in the financial outcome of the treaty as any of the fur traders, if not more so. The Johnston Estate, along with Ozhaawshkodewikwe separately after her husband's death and before she sold the business to the American Fur Company, claimed tens of thousands of dollars in unpaid debt accumulated between 1815 and 1831. Schoolcraft was only entitled to Jane's portion of the estate, but as agent and, later, sole commissioner for the US government, he had the upper hand in getting the terms most favorable to himself, and future events will show that as "guardian" of the family, he exercised complete authority over all of the family's money. His personal interest in a treaty involved more than payment for outstanding debts. While he reassured prospective missionaries and Jane herself that expulsion was unlikely because the land was unsuitable for intensive agriculture, which was true, he knew because he'd been writing about it since coming west that the land contained resources, including fish, timber, and minerals, waiting for exploitation. His own books were taken as guides by speculators advocating for a treaty, and he would later attempt to profit from that exploitation himself.[32] The Irish money and the evanescent war losses reimbursement paled in comparison with the potential fur trade money and the opening of Anishinaabe land to exploitation.

That summer Schoolcraft went down to Detroit and then on to Green Bay to buy Menominee land that had been ceded a few years earlier for himself and James.[33] Jane went to the Sault to visit her mother. She seems to have been ill for the entire spring and summer of 1835. "While a thousand sad & pleasing recollections rush upon my mind as I find myself once more in reality under the roof of my beloved & ever-lamented Father's hospitable Mansion—here where I first drew my breath—where I first claimed the names—the endearing & responsible names of Wife & Mother & where I found myself *Childless & fatherless*," she wrote, somewhat dramatically. The children were healthy, although Charlotte Wabose was disappointed that her mother had left for Penetanguishene before they arrived. "Pray write to me & inform me how you wish me to act in regard to the manner of my going home should my life be continued until then," she added.[34]

When Jane returned to Mackinac, there were visitors. If white settlers weren't necessarily forthcoming in the region, travelers certainly were, particularly the kind who wrote books about their experiences. In the summer of 1835 those visitors included George William Featherstonhaugh, a British immigrant who'd been given the task of producing a geological survey of the Louisiana Purchase for the US government in 1834. By July 1835 he was in the midst of a long trip across Michigan and Wisconsin and down the Mississippi.[35] He'd known Schoolcraft, but not Jane, whom he thought "a very pious, respectable young woman," when he met her. He understood Jane to have been educated in England. He found Jane's sister, "also a half-breed" and probably Anna Maria, "quite an agreeable person." Despite the family's "temperance and strict piety," Featherstonhaugh thought they were "very cheerful and communicative" as Jane and Anna Maria performed their usual roles of informing visiting white people about their relatives.[36] He thought Mackinac as charming as other white visitors did. "Nothing can be more pleasing than its appearance from the lake: the beautiful bay, with the neat little town at the edge of the water; the respectable-looking fort, rising above the town on an escarpment of rocks; and the conspicuous remains of the old French fort, at a greater distance inland. All these pleasing features were accompanied by another, that always has great attractions for me, an encampment of Indian wigwams," he writes. "Mrs. Schoolcraft's very comfortable house makes a conspicuous figure, being well situated at the foot of the hill, with a good garden in front, and the fort, of a dazzling white, rising behind it a little to the west."[37] Schoolcraft drove him around the island to see the sights, the same sights as today—the Arched Rock, Skull Cave, the Sugarloaf (a rock), and Fort Holmes, previously known as Fort George.

He also took Featherstonhaugh to Round Island, where they visited the settlements about which Schoolcraft had interrogated Wauchusco and other old men. There were still enclosures of cedar and birch bark on the graves of the more recent village, but the ancient one was marked only by burial mounds.[38] They decided to go grave-robbing. "For my portion of this body-snatching entertainment I selected a very antique-looking mound, standing on a steep bank immediately above the lake," Featherstonhaugh writes,

> the bank had already partly crumbled away into the water, so that my excavations were partly made by my hands. Having, with a little assistance, sufficiently opened the mound, we proceeded to plunder it, and I obtained for my share a noble skull with a remarkably fine set of teeth, without any marks of a pipe among them. This I destined for some learned craniologist; but if I had sufficiently counted the cost of all this desecration before I had engaged in it, it would have been more prudent; for in my anxiety to secure a number of Indian relics, that some of the party presented me out of their spoils, I put them into my pockets, and the skull into my pocket-handkerchief; on reaching my lodgings, however, and disencumbering my pockets hastily, to go to a dinner, which was to conclude the day, I found my hands and my clothes so infected with charnel-house nastiness, that I could not endure myself; so, throwing off all my clothes, and sending them immediately to be washed, I spent more than half an hour scrubbing my hands in vain to purify them: the horrid stench was in my nostrils all the evening; everything smelt of the dissection-room; and I must say that I never was more uncomfortable in my life. As to my bones and relics, I had them all put, on my return to my lodgings, in to a bag, and sent them to one of the party, who seemed to value them very highly; for if I had packed them up to take along with me, I should have passed for a resurrection-man wherever I went.[39]

Featherstonhaugh still stank of death the next day when he woke up, so he took brushes, soap, and a bottle of cologne to the lake to try scrubbing it out. He returned to his hotel (probably Madame LaFramboise's) to eat breakfast, after which, he wrote, "[I] determined to give myself an airing alone on the summit of the island."[40]

"If a party of Frenchmen had landed on the English coast, and amused themselves by opening the graves in the churchyard, whilst the villagers were engaged in their harvest-fields, their conduct would not have been more absurd and irrational than ours," he wrote.[41] Schoolcraft wrote in his memoirs, perfunctorily, that he'd gone to Round Island with Featherstonhaugh and Lieutenant Mather: "examined the ancient ossuaries and the scenery on that island."[42] It was Schoolcraft who took the skull and "curiosities" from Featherstonhaugh, and the Schoolcrafts' house to which he went to dinner, still in his mind reeking. It was Schoolcraft from whom he wanted to escape afterward, trying to understand, as he went alone to the remains of Fort George at the summit of the island to air himself out, why he'd done what he did.

He and Schoolcraft took the steamer to Sault Ste. Marie; Featherstonhaugh like all the other travel writers lamented having to leave "the lofty island" behind, and he was charmed anew by the "numerous groups of Indians standing near their lodges to view the departure of the steamer, which moved on in gallant style with four Kentish bugles playing a lively air."[43] He then traveled west, observing near Prairie du Chien pictographs featuring two men with a scalped captive, "a horse [that] was extremely well done, and an Indian dog still better," painted onto a blazed tree.[44] At the Mississippi he and his party came upon sandstone cliffs full of pictographs, with George Catlin's extravagant signature among them. By mid-September he met George Johnston, who was on his way home from the boundary survey. "He was an intelligent person, and gave me a great deal of information about the Indian country as high up as Otter Tail lake," Featherstonhaugh wrote, "which I returned in news about his friends at Michilimackinac."[45]

Soon after Featherstonhaugh's departure Chandler Robbins Gilman and Martin Hoffman appeared; they were on their way to the Sault and then the Pictured Rocks, a stretch of cliffs about a hundred miles west of the Sault, a third of the way along the coast to La Pointe, after which they returned to the Sault and Mackinac, then made their way by steamboat to Chicago. They visited the usual sites and perambulated the beach, poking their heads uninvited into lodges. "I stooped at the entrance to gain a view of the interior," Gilman writes. "A small fire was burning in the centre . . . around the fire lay four or five Indians wrapped in their blankets, and apparently half asleep; a Squaw stood in the centre cooking some corn in a small kettle; a half-naked boy and a quite naked infant completed the family group." They repeated this invasion, of another family, the next day.

"There is an *atmosphere* of vulgarity about him," Charles Fenno Hoffman once remarked to his brother of Gilman, "a *malaria* of conceit."[46] Gilman and Hoffman twice paused on their way to the Pictured Rocks to steal things from gravehouses they encountered, one of them a child's. That grave was at Grand Sable Dunes, some miles east of the Pictured Rocks. Gilman broke into it and took "a rude image made of white cedar, about four or five inches long," while

Hoffman contented himself with a "little mallet made of a bit of ivy, or some other vine."⁴⁷ "We could, I suppose, have been very sentimental on the subject of this little image of the savage boy, and the toy with which he in infancy had been amused, and which now his sorrowing parents had deposited in his grave, in the hope that, according to their simple creed, that which had been in this life a source of pleasure would contribute to the happiness of their child in the far-off spirit land to which he had been untimely removed," Gilman writes. "Instead, however, of sentimentalizing over these relics, we concluded to *steal them*; so the Major [Hoffman] pocketed the mallet, and I the image, and replacing the shingles to conceal our larceny from any chance passer-by, we went on our way rejoicing."⁴⁸

It was an enjoyable and enlightening trip as far as Gilman was concerned. Besides being given "Forsaken Brother" and "Origin of the Robin" to copy over for his book, someone—probably Schoolcraft—told him enough of the Johnston family history for him to use parts of it to write "The Fate of Wintemoyah: The Legend of Robinson's Folley," which he incorporated into his book as an authentic Indian narrative. This featured an Indian maiden (Wintemoyah) whose father (Peezhicki or "Le Boeuf") objects to her marrying a white man—"his noble mien, his glittering arms, his brilliant scarlet dress" (he was British)—and so kills them both by jumping off a cliff (it was his idea, not hers).⁴⁹ The actual Pizhiki or Buffalo was well known to the Johnstons, a brother or nephew of Waabojiig and a leader at Shagwaamikong into the 1850s.

Jane's job was to reflect well on Schoolcraft during these visits, and she did, judging by the commentary on her in the books produced by these and other writers. But one wonders what it was like to have to sit and listen to men like Chandler Robbins Gilman opine on the Indians and express his glee at what he had stolen from them. Another visitor to Mackinac who seems to have passed through at that time provided perhaps some relief. William Hull Clarke was the namesake of his grandfather Gen. William Hull, who'd distinguished himself during the revolution but more infamously surrendered Detroit in 1812 without a fight, for which he was court-martialed and came close to being executed. General Hull had been a friend of John Johnston's; he greeted Jane and her father when they landed at Detroit on their return from Ireland in 1810. In 1835 William Clarke would have been on his way to Chicago with his brother Samuel to set up in business as druggists.⁵⁰ There's no record of his visit—they would have traveled by steamboat from Detroit to Chicago around the Michigan peninsula, as the roads at the time were bad to nonexistent and Mackinac was a stopping place—but Jane did write him a letter that he kept close all his life. He showed it to two writers who then published parts of it separately. It's one of only two letters extant that Jane wrote that were not in Schoolcraft's possession, and it exists only because it was published.⁵¹

While his grandfather's terror of Indians in large part led to his downfall, Clarke had an interest in them, and he asked Jane what "the condition of women" was like in Indigenous communities. It was "higher and freer than that of the white woman," she said. This led to an anguished denunciation of the lies whites, including her own husband, told about Indigenous men and women. "O Mr. C!" she wrote; "they either exalt the Red Man into a demigod, or degrade him into a beast.[52] . . . I have witnessed scenes of conjugal and parental love in the Indian's wigwam from which I have often, often thought the educated white man, proud of his superior civilization, might learn an useful lesson."[53] Clarke must have been one of the few white people to whom she could say these things—and whom she could expect to be receptive. "I have seen among them instances of refined delicacy of feeling, and traits of kindness of heart diffusing itself through the action and manners, which I have in vain sought in highly civilized communities," she continued. "I have heard speeches which, had they been made by the sages of antiquity, would have been handed down to use with a world's applause; and I have asked myself, where is the intrinsic difference between the soul of this red man in his blanket, and that of him who is surrounded by all the accidents of education, civilization and manners; are not those noble sentiments—the feeling of the good, the great and the beautiful—intuitive?"[54]

The consensus among historians is that Schoolcraft used every means at his disposal to push through the Treaty of 1836 and especially to draw the Upper Peninsula Ojibwes into it because he stood to gain personally. The communities involved in the treaty included the Grand Traverse and Little Traverse Odawa bands on the northwest coast of Michigan's Lower Peninsula (collectively, L'Arbre Croche); the Grand River Odawas on the southwest coast; and Ojibwe villages and bands on both the northwest coast of the Lower Peninsula and the eastern Upper Peninsula. By 1835, most of those who eventually negotiated the treaty wanted the same things: a permanent land base, cleared debts, hunting and fishing rights on any ceded land unoccupied by whites, money or land for relatives not living in traditional communities, and government services like schools and blacksmith shops.[55] Among and between communities, opinions differed on how to achieve those goals.

When the Little Traverse Odawas previously presented their plan to the US government and got a negative response, the two other Odawa communities, Grand Traverse and Grand River, became alarmed and met in council, where they agreed to not sell any more land. In September 1835 the Little Traverse Odawas decided to go to Washington to try to push for their initial plan; on learning of this, the Grand River Odawas sent a delegation to protect their own interests and to head off any land cessions that their relatives might try to make.⁵⁶ The Little Traverse delegation also wanted to prevent Schoolcraft from convincing the government that anyone wanted a major land cession treaty. He had been agitating for the Upper Peninsula Ojibwes to make a treaty for months by then, although getting a sense for what the Upper Peninsula Ojibwes actually wanted at that time is difficult if not impossible because, Schoolcraft having control of information that came to the government, the record represents only the positions of those who supported land cessions.⁵⁷ At least a faction supported that plan, and possibly only a faction.

Though there are no personal or official documents related to Schoolcraft's August trip to the Sault, it's possible, maybe even probable, that his trip had to do with treaty-related maneuvering.⁵⁸ One point of leverage was blacksmith shops. In 1834, in the same budget-cutting directive that cost George Johnston his job as subagent at Mackinac, the government began phasing out its blacksmith shops at the Indian agencies. These shops were important for the repair of guns, fishhooks, farming equipment, and other goods, and shutting them down was likely intended to add to the pressure on the Ojibwes to cede land.⁵⁹ Schoolcraft's activities demonstrate how that angle worked. In September, he told Major Cobb at Fort Brady to tell the Ojibwes that if they considered ceding territory (this after he was told by his superiors that the government wasn't interested in the Upper Peninsula), provision for a blacksmith at Sault Ste. Marie for their use could be made part of a treaty. In November he wrote to Cobb again, just before he left for Detroit and then Washington, telling him that if the Ojibwes wanted to sell, "I think it important to have a good understanding with them that they should have a shop at St. Mary's."⁶⁰ Schoolcraft wrote William Johnston, who acted as his agent throughout the fall and winter of 1835–36, on the same day, 7 November, asking him to find out whether the chiefs were willing to sell. William spoke to his uncle, Waishkey, another man at Sault Ste. Marie, Shawono, and Ocunogeeged at Sugar Island. Their answer (in the case of Waishkey and Shawono, "on behalf of their young men") was that "they were willing to cede their lands to the United States on reasonable terms, the terms to be left to the discretion of the Agent appointed by government; with this provision, they, to have a full right to hunt, on the ceded lands, as long as they were unoccupied, and to make such reservations as they should think proper."⁶¹

The Johnstons were poor. James reported that Ozhaawshkodewikwe and the family "have not a pound of provisions for the winter" in October, adding—shameless as ever—that John McDouall was "a perfect drawback upon the resources of the family," associating with the lowest company and berating his mother when she rebuked him for it.⁶² (This again may have been true, may have been partly true, or may just have been an outright lie made up to manipulate his brother.) George had left his children with his mother while he'd gone to Upper Canada, looking for prospects. Eliza made moccasins and possibly quilled boxes and mokuks for sale in the local store.[63] William was dependent on Schoolcraft for employment, although in this fall and winter he was seriously entertaining the notion of going as a missionary to the western Ojibwes, in the spring, with a soon to be discharged sergeant from the fort.

By the time Schoolcraft left for Washington in November, the only financial expectation that anyone in the Johnston family seems to have had was that the Little Traverse Odawas would go through with their plan and that there would be a chance of some benefit to themselves. Ozhaawshkodewikwe instructed James to write Schoolcraft that "when the Drummond Island Indians [the marginal land the Little Traverse band wanted to sell included Drummond Island] come to treat for the sale of the island, to tell the chiefs that she is of the same totem as that band and that 'she hopes they will remember her in their council.'"[64] Later in the fall Ozhaawshkodewikwe had McMurray write to Schoolcraft "that as she relied upon the money from Toronto, she does not now know what to do, being disappointed."[65] This reminder would likely have had to do with Schoolcraft's plan to submit a memorial to Congress about the war losses.

Schoolcraft doesn't appear then to have told the Johnstons what he told his brother. At the end of October James remarked, with studied casualness, "by the bye if you hold a treaty with the savages next spring perhaps it will not be out of your power to provide for my furnishing a few thousand dollars worth of goods." These were goods that would be distributed as part of the treaty. "Perhaps you may effect this and if you do let me hear in time to make any disposition."[66] He was more pointed—and more confident of a significant treaty being convened—a few weeks later. Cass, he wrote, "*could not do less* than give me the furnishing of the goods of the *treaty*—should one be *held*, and *goods furnished*.... At all events I hope you will try to let me have the furnishing of the goods, so far as you may have it in your power to contribute." "If goods are furnished Gov Cass must (or should) give me a chance": James was in the habit of demanding "assistance" from those he thought should offer it. But he was only a small shopkeeper at the Sault, pessimistic about his prospects there and frustrated because he didn't have the means to move south, to Grand River, where he thought he could gain a better foothold. (The contract ultimately went to the American Fur Company.)

Schoolcraft took his leave with a great flourish of patriarchal dedication to his wife and children. He wrote his will and commended himself to the Almighty. Before leaving, he'd written two sketches featuring Wawanosh for the *Knickerbocker* (they were published in November and December 1835, just as he arrived in New York) in which Wawanosh travels to the East Coast and marvels at the achievements of the "grave, moral, and philosophical" Americans. It was supposed to be witty, but in context it reads like a pep talk for himself.[67] His objectives, as far as Jane knew, were to present a memorial to Congress petitioning for reimbursement of war losses to the Johnston Estate; to lobby for the territorial governorship of Wisconsin in light of impending Michigan statehood in January 1837; and to see about getting the first iteration of the collection of stories published. But he was primarily tailing the Odawas, and he had a plan. His correspondence with Jane shows him in high spirits, inspired by his mission. "If I could put my heart into this letter, and send it to you, I would do so," he wrote after a stormy passage to Detroit. He was leaving for New York immediately, but sending mittens for the children and a black fur cape, a black velvet bonnet, and face powder for her by way of the General Harrison.[68] Ozhaawshkodewikwe had requested that Jane spend the winter at the Sault. "Mrs. Johnston's particular request to Mr. S is to know if he has made up his mind to spend the winter in Washington," McMurray wrote for her. "If so she requests of him leave for Mrs. S to come over and spend the winter with her, that she may attend to her closely, in case of sickness." Schoolcraft refused her mother's request and accepted the idea of Eliza staying at Mackinac for the winter instead, but weather prevented Eliza from coming down, and Jane spent the winter with the children, who along with Charlotte Wabose almost as soon as Schoolcraft left came down with whooping cough.[69]

As he collected letters in support of his bid for the territorial governorship in New York and Philadelphia, Schoolcraft reveled in the nobility of his cause. "I will do all I consistently can, to secure the permanent worldly condition of my wife, children, & friends," he wrote to Jane, "and when I can feel a reasonable assurance that this is done, I shall be satisfied. My present journey is for your sakes."[70] He detailed his progress toward the capital city in several letters, as was his habit, "with such notices of passing things, great & small, as interest me, and will therefore interest you." In New York City, he dined with Dr. Gilman, whose book would soon be published, and met Charles Fenno Hoffman, who recently published *A Winter in the West* (1835), which detailed a trip he took to southern Michigan, Prairie du Chien, and Chicago inspired by Irving and Schoolcraft, whom he quoted liberally.[71] While he was in New York, Schoolcraft secured an agreement with Harper and Brothers to publish the stories and revised versions of his previous travel books.[72] He got Ramsay Crooks to dig up documents showing the prices of goods claimed in the memorial, sent away to Montreal for invoices from the period. "I hope divine wisdom will direct me, in all my ways, and it is my consistent endeavor to find out the path of duty, *Daily*, & to conform my will to the Almighty's," he wrote, confident that his virtue would guarantee success. "Poor worm! to think my self of sufficient importance to be noticed by the Almighty, yet such is the wonderful system revealed in Christ." He prayed constantly.[73]

From Philadelphia he reported on his movements, four hours from Amboy to Camden by railroad, then from Camden to Philadelphia in an open boat through ice floes on the Delaware River. He reported on the gentility of Gen. Robert Patterson, whom he'd met when Patterson passed through Mackinac the previous summer and who would write a letter of reference for him. "Here is frank Irish friendship," Schoolcraft observed, "and proves in relation to our attention to him & his, last summer, that 'we should not be neglectful to entertain strangers.'"[74] From Washington, on 26 December, he wrote how kindly Cass had received him, and how important he was, "the President's righthand man." On Christmas Day Cass got Schoolcraft an invitation to the president's reception, and he was finally introduced to the great man himself. The next day Schoolcraft gave gifts to Emily Donelson, Jackson's wife's niece and by that time the former White House hostess: an "Indian card rack," moccasins cut by Jane and sewn by Eliza, and mokuks of sugar and a quillwork box made by Ozhaawshkodewikwe. Jackson's son wrote a note of thanks, which Schoolcraft copied into his letter. The high import of these encounters brought Schoolcraft to a crescendo of feeling. "Now my dearest, these would be worthless trifles & wholly uninteresting to any one but *you*.... You will appreciate *my* motives," he wrote.

> We live for each other, and the slightest thing that excites interest in one, *should* & *ought* & *does*, I am persuaded, excite a corresponding interest in the other. My object, while here is, as you know, to improve my opportunity to pave the way for you & the children, so that, if called from the scene of action first, you may not be left to an unfeeling world, in a state of dependency.... Pray for me. Pray that I may have *grace & wisdom* imparted to me, in *equal* measures, & that I may keep down *self* & continually exalt Christ, in my *thoughts, words & affections*.[75]

He didn't tell her until three days later (he wrote this letter over several days) that Cass had told him to convene a treaty council with the Odawas and Ojibwes, in Washington, that winter. That was what he was thinking about in his paean to himself as heroic provider. Cass was at that moment waiting for a treaty expelling the Cherokees from land claimed by the state of Georgia, the Treaty of New Echota, which would be signed on 29 December 1835 and soon become known generally as a fraud, as Jackson's agent, Rev. John Schermerhorn, arranged for a faction of the Cherokees to sign away their land. It would be debated in Congress during the winter and spring, at the same time as the Ojibwe and Odawa Treaty of Washington was negotiated, and pass the Senate by only one vote.⁷⁶ Cass was indeed the president's right-hand man, and Schoolcraft was the same for Cass, who made Schoolcraft the sole negotiator with the Ojibwes and Odawas on the part of the federal government.

"How different from any thing I expected! Had notice been given before I left home, how easily could I have arranged a deputation," he exclaimed, for Jane's benefit. He gave instructions for William to "find suitable men" to come to Washington—no Catholics, however, as there would be enough of them from L'Arbre Croche. "I am anxious that the Chippewas should be well represented, in order that they may obtain their just rights," he wrote, the benefit to himself more than likely at the back of his mind and probably the front. There was much to guard against. The Odawas were claiming Ojibwe land north of the straits of Mackinac "by *right of conquest!!*" Jane should not fear that he was neglecting the state of his soul during these exciting times, however. "I never have been more attentive to my closet duties or realized the necessity & benefit of them more. Do thou the same.... Let us trust in God, & we have nothing to fear." He had some closing remarks of advice. "Exert your feeble strength to superintend the household, cheer up all with your influence & right sentiments—encourage William [to] govern the children, & pray for me."⁷⁷ Then he went to a New Year's Eve ball at Cass's house with 800 other guests, where he spent the evening with the postmaster general discussing the mails.

He received no word from the family until late January, and by then the children and Charlotte Wabose had been ill for weeks with whooping cough. They'd not yet received his late December letter about the treaty. Jane bore up well, according to William, who seems to have been trying to describe events in as congenial a light as possible. Though Jane complained of doing household work during the day and caring for the children, including Charlotte, at night, "I think that it is beneficial to her health & she also enjoys better spirits," he wrote.⁷⁸ The next day Jane finished her own letter with some annoyance. "3 sick children lying in my room to attend to all at the same time has indeed been a sore trial & in addition to all this do my own cooking & house work & go whole days & nights without *rest of any kind* & not take off my clothes all that time, will I am afraid, go near to kill me, & were it not from a sense of imperative duty I could not now go on scribbling, but the Express is to start off in an hour or two & I must send this just as it is."⁷⁹ Things would have been different if she and the children had spent the winter with her mother. She didn't write again until mid-February.

While waiting for his treaties Cass gave an oration at the Capitol to the American Historical Society, in which he ruminated on the crusades, Washington Irving, Herodotus, the Declaration of Independence, the French Revolution, the Golden Fleece, and Hernando de Soto. He declared Indians the

Roman ruins of America, and he taunted the Cherokees: "Where are the nomadic tribes who said You shall go no further!"[80] The Johnston Estate's chances with Congress sank to nothing by early January 1836, when a committee aide wrote to Schoolcraft that it was immaterial whether the Johnstons were legally married, or Mrs. Johnston was the estate's representative, or whether John Johnston was in Schoolcraft's opinion naturalized. The committee especially did not need the form letters that Schoolcraft had helpfully written up to be sent to his supporters Cass, Lucius Lyon (a land speculator in Detroit), or John Hulbert (Schoolcraft's brother-in-law) on behalf of the committee: those "are returned herewith." The committee remembered Lieutenant Holmes; they only wanted to know whether the goods were meant for Indians hostile to the United States (they were); whether the goods were carried through British territory (they were); and whether Johnston did anything to restrain the Indians against the Americans (he did not).[81]

The treaty preparations advanced. William reported in January about suspicions among the chiefs about each other's motives in relation to the still hypothetical treaty.[82] It wasn't until mid-February that William and Jane received Schoolcraft's letters from late December announcing that a treaty would be convened, immediately, and that Schoolcraft wanted William to find the right people to attend as soon as possible. "Your letters have acted like an electrick shock, on all the inhabitants of the place, and all are busy in talking of their claims, by losses, and through ties of blood," William wrote. He meant the other families of fur traders anticipating a payout. Schoolcraft had sent a legally meaningless document Cass titled a "Power of Sale" that he wanted signed by as many of the chiefs as William and Capt. John Clitz, then at Fort Brady, could secure before the delegations came to Washington.[83] William enlisted Aunce, Shaw wa wa, and Big Sail to get Odawa signatures, but many would not sign, especially the L'Arbre Croche Catholics, who encouraged farming and ran a successful school. The bands on the north shore of Lake Michigan supported the idea, however. William warned Schoolcraft to talk to the chiefs separately, because when they were together they feared one another's motives. They all stipulated that they would only sign a treaty "if they could procure land for their children either by grant or purchase from the government, after they have transferred it."[84]

At Mackinac, William wrote to James on Schoolcraft's direction, to collect representatives, including Waishkey and his son.[85] He also produced a document attesting to Ozhaawshkodewikwe's claims, over the local chiefs' signatures, for a $20,000 debt from 1814 to 1831. "Twenty thousand dollars would barely cover it," he added, because many people who owed both him and his father money were living on the Michigan peninsula. "I mention this to you, to let you know the feelings of their chiefs, to allow us something, for they promised me that [they] would speak in my favour of claims that were brought forward in Washington and I feel happy to think that you will let no opportunity pass unnoticed, which could advance our interests."[86]

William asked for Schoolcraft's advice on his spiritual welfare. "My obligations to you will be lasting in my heart, for your fatherly and friendly care and advice to me, which has opened my eyes to see the folly of the past, and for pointing and directing me to Christ." Nothing could prevent him from going west as a missionary but the care of Ozhaawshkodewikwe and the payment of old debts. Considering his behavior toward his brother-in-law before and after this moment, it's difficult to know how serious this request was. William still thought that the "great anxiety and fatigue" that Jane had been experiencing that winter were somehow beneficial to her. Her health "was better, compared to what it was last winter," he wrote. "She now complains of weakness, which is caused by her exerting herself too much, and allowing trifles to have too much weight with her, as respects servants, which she will inform you of."[87] He'd only received one story since Schoolcraft left, but it was "long and contains a great deal of interesting matter." Schoolcraft had evidently given instructions to collect more stories, despite his plan to publish *Algic* Researches that winter. William was copying over his Leech Lake writings for Jane, too, at her request. "I feel happy to think they are of so much interest to her."[88]

The prospect of moving west when Schoolcraft became territorial governor of Wisconsin occupied Jane. "Are you prepared to give up our residence at Mackinac, for the inconvenience, of a new settlement, bad roads, &c., &c," he'd written, uncharacteristically asking her opinion. His plans for his future success again made him romantic. "Tou meines Frau [*sic*]," he wrote.[89] She responded as affectionately. "You ask me to make up my mind to leave Mackinac, & to choose between a brilliant & a solid scene of future abode?" she answered. "With you and the dear Children, I feel it is immaterial where I spend my last days. But since you are kind enough to consult my feelings & wishes, I prefer the solid *natural* life you describe in the wilds of central Michigan, to all the brilliant scenes that South America can display or afford, & shall be ready to accompany *your dear self* and Children to a log cabin or palace, as it may happen, whenever you give the word to move."[90] "Central Michigan" would be present-day Wisconsin, after Michigan statehood. "Solid" is an odd word in this circumstance—hard, dense, stable, substantial—although coupled with "natural," Jane's meaning might be easier to understand. William had written from Leech Lake for her specifically; she'd had him copy over his writings so that she could keep them safe. What would have been more "natural" about the West than Leech Lake as William described it? So it seems that Jane eagerly anticipated going west, where the Ojibwes were more free from white encroachment, and as William told it, spoke a purer language, lived a purer life. They were "solid" even. That was what she cared about; of the treaty at this time, in mid-February, and later, she said nothing, as important as it was to Schoolcraft.

She complained of an "obstruction" which caused her "constant pain" and also seems to have at least briefly made her think that she was pregnant, but she was not. "Pray that I may have an humble submissive spirit, great grace is necessary to bear constant pain with calm resignation, & not only that, but disappointed hopes require great faith & trust in the goodness & mercy of our all wise Creator, who ordereth all things for the *best good* of his poor frail creatures."[91] She continued to write over several days. Janée, aged eight and a half, wrote her first letter to her father: "My dear Pa' I am sorry this letter is not better written it is the first I have ever written in my own hand." Jane copied a brief letter she'd sent to Trowbridge for Schoolcraft's perusal. Anticipating leaving Mackinac for the West, she thought a servant, with whom Schoolcraft had been planning to return, wouldn't be necessary, as "our stay on the island will be so short."[92]

In Washington, the negotiators, interested parties, and hangers-on began to gather. They included John Holiday, who'd gone blind, whom Schoolcraft picked as his interpreter; his daughter Mary, who looked after him; and his murderous son William, who had no particular role to play. Lucius Lyon, the Detroit land speculator, appeared. Ramsay Crooks fretted over the negotiations from his office in New York City, worried that his traders would receive short shrift, as both Mary and Schoolcraft kept him informed while he tended to fur sales in Liverpool and Leipzig and kept track of his fisheries in Michigan.[93] Rix Robinson, a trader who had taken over Madame LaFramboise's post at Grand River on her retirement, arrived with six additional men to those who had arrived previously, along with Robert Stuart, the AFC's former agent at Mackinac; John Drew, a Mackinac trader, escorted three chiefs from the island.[94] The night before the treaty, Schoolcraft escorted everyone, including all twenty-three council participants, to the White House to meet Jackson.[95] Mary Holiday wrote Crooks all about it.[96]

All the participants stayed at Brown's Indian Queen Hotel, Washington's most popular, especially for Indigenous delegations. Its sign was a "lurid" portrait of Pocahontas. They met at the Masonic Hall nearby, and the public came and went as it pleased. "Harold," a writer for the *New-Yorker*, was on the scene. The Indians "go filing across your path at almost all points" in the city, he wrote, "heroes enveloped in a blanket-coat as fairly as a modern lady is in a blanket-shawl—and there in the simple garments of Nature's furnishing, without any attention to a north-wester, the *spitting* of snow, or the absolute fright which they occasion of young girls and 'society in general.'" They wore medals around their necks, and John Holiday told him all it took to get such a medal was a "little cleverness." At the hotel, the men roamed the hallways wearing "frock-coats of blue cloth and blankets, girded with a crimson belt.... Often have I passed them ... with their thighs displaying their natural bronze, and the linen about their waists waving in the wind."[97] The Indians watched back. One night in his hotel room, Harold observed his door handle turning slowly, and then "a dark face was cautiously thrust into the room, and silently withdrawn, after the eye had passed about sufficient to satisfy the individual."[98]

Schoolcraft's control of the Ojibwe delegation from the Upper Peninsula was crucial to his pushing the treaty through. The Odawas, not surprisingly, hated him.[99] Everyone involved knew that if the Lower Peninsula Odawas and Ojibwes hesitated or rejected the sale of land, the Upper Peninsula Ojibwes, already vetted by Schoolcraft, would step in and sell the land whether or not they were its recognized owners.[100] In the hall, the Ojibwes and Odawas faced each other in rows of chairs with a map of Michigan Territory in between. Schoolcraft and Holiday sat at the head of the room. The government wanted all the land north of Grand River and on the Upper Peninsula as far west as the Chocolay River, near present-day Marquette. Schoolcraft offered money for debts and agricultural assistance, and the bands would determine the locations of reservations on the ceded territory. He announced that "personal reservations" for individuals or "white friends" would not be permitted. They would be "granted the 'usual' temporary right to reside upon and hunt on the ceded lands 'till they are wanted," he said, offering up some faux Indian talk about having "kind feelings" for each in conclusion.[101]

"I found myself in an atmosphere of strong tobacco smoke," Harold of the *New-Yorker* wrote, and "through the fumes, away in the extremity of the chamber, were seated, on benches and on the floor, Chiefs of all ages, dress, bearing, and intelligence." The spectators included a group of schoolboys and miscellaneous passers-by. Harold was much impressed with Augustin Hamelin, one of the speakers.[102] Hamelin, the son of a fur trader and the daughter of an important chief at L'Arbre Croche, had been educated by Catholics there and in Detroit, and chosen with his brother to study for the priesthood in Rome. But then his brother died under mysterious circumstances, and Augustin, disgusted by the prejudice he experienced in Rome and determined to help his people, returned home. Hamelin wore "the dress of an English gentleman," and he spoke English "with full facility," wrote Harold.

First "an old warrior" spoke, replying to the government agents "with emphasis and gesture." Then a younger man

> addressed the table with great rapidity, animation, and power. He had painted his face, to give effect to his appearance. It was wonderful to see

the ease with which he answered every question, and presented his own case; and, as his language was interpreted, he was not only bold but beautiful in his words, and truly poetical in his ideas. I know not that there was an instant's hesitation; and when the speaker passed from language to the pen, with which to trace lines upon the plan that lay before the Council, he used it with the adroitness and familiarity of an old engineer.

They passed around a pipe, and Harold noted half a keg of tobacco sitting in a corner. The language again got to Harold. "A half-breed then addressed the assembly, with great fluency and decision. I never before listened to Indian language, spoken by intelligent Indian Chiefs; and I can truly say that I was surprised at the melody and richness of its intonations. It was full, free, spirited, harmonious, and, I question not, far more musical to those to whom it is the mother tongue than the English can ever be made to be."

After several days the negotiations ended. The chiefs stood and shook hands with the government men at the table and left. "The whole exhibition was as good as could have been had by a pilgrimage to the forest," wrote Harold, "and I shall not soon forget the aboriginal character of the scene, when I recall the beaded dress—the fancy hood—the scarlet belt—the pipe—and the hawk's feather."[103] The councilors deliberated for three days back at the Indian Queen, fending off traders trying to influence how the debts would be paid—if at Washington, the rushed terms could benefit themselves and their sloppy bookkeeping, as well as their efforts to be reimbursed for the alcohol they'd sold illegally in Indian country. A commission determining payments that summer would make their lives more difficult. Eventually the tribal leaders agreed to the treaty with "sizable reservations" set aside. Schoolcraft suggested two of 100,000 acres each, determined by the chiefs after their return home; the Odawa negotiators succeeded in getting more than double that acreage, with an additional 50,000 acres on Little Traverse Bay. A commission that summer, at Mackinac, would determine the payment of debts. The treaty was signed on 28 March, Schoolcraft's birthday.[104]

He wrote to Jane immediately. "All that could be wished in the way of schools, missions, agricultural, mechanics, &c., &c., is granted," he wrote. "Much money will be annually distributed, their debts paid, their half-breed relatives provided for, every man, woman, & child of them, & large presents given out." The annuities meant people would be using that money at James's store; the "half-breed relatives" included his wife and in-laws. "Rejoice with me," he wrote. "The day of their prosperity has . . . finally reached them, in their lowest state of poverty, when their game is almost gone, and the country is shorn of all of its advantages for the hunter state.[105] He had saved them from their impending doom.

The treaty was signed and waiting for ratification for weeks while the Senate debated the Treaty of New Echota. Schoolcraft thought he'd go to New York to see about his books, but Cass put him to work making more treaties, with the Saginaw and the St. Clair bands of Ojibwes. "Events deeply important to me, to you & the children depend on my . . . visit to the seat of government," he wrote to Jane, anticipating her disapproval of his being away so long. Waishkey received $500 in the treaty, and his sons $100 each; a commission that summer would pay "all the just debts of the Indians." He would not be on the commission himself, he wrote, "from the delicacy of deciding on the claims of my relatives." But he had triumphed. "Justice will now be done to your mother, and something be obtained for each of the children." The "Ots & Chips" would receive $30,000 annually for twenty years, "and about a million dollars in pledges to various useful or benevolent projects for their benefit."[106] The letter reads as if he is justifying himself.

In mid-April he received the previous month's letters from Mackinac. The children were better, William wrote, but "Jane now feels the effects of exerting herself. She has been obliged to keep her bed, some portion of each day, for some time back, still her anxiety and feelings causes her to overcome it, and we see her up and attending to household duties, but she has often to return to her bed again from weakness." Charlotte was "rapidly declining": whooping cough had given way to consumption. The doctor thought she had three months to live.[107] She was still "in the land of the living," Jane wrote, but just barely:

> O! for grace & wisdom to improve that time to my poor souls good & to the benefit of all within my influence day after day I drag out a wretched miserable existence toiling against wind & tide, as it were in the discharge of my domestic duties; which are indeed in their nature (at least some of them) a sore trial to my faith & patience & to mind & body—without the aid of my natural, Earthly Protector—in a situation & circumstances which would be difficult & painful to bear even were I blessed with your cheering smile of approbation & encouragement & support—debilitated & worn down as I am—wanting all the nameless, kind attentions, so necessary to the comfort of a weak nervous Invalid.

She was nursing Charlotte Wabose through her last illness. "To see daily the near approach of Death, to hear her incessant coughing & groaning is wearing on my own already shattered health & spirits, more than unthinking people suppose, & indeed more than I can tell. O! that you were at home, my own dear Husband!" She only wished that Charlotte would live long enough to be sent home, to her "ungrateful Mother & relations" so that they "might have the mournful satisfaction of closing her eyes—that she might, with her own breath tell her *unjust* Mother, what I have undergone & done for her good, temporally & spiritually—I should feel thankful & content—indeed nothing has been left undone for C's recovery, & that is a consolation to me." Jane's exhaustion and anxiety made her cruel in the moment.[108]

To this Schoolcraft had some pious things to say about Charlotte's fate, and he then gave Jane some incongruous advice. "You must look into the papers, like our American ladies, & glean the outlines of domestic & foreign news." Jane was an Indian who didn't know how to behave; it was on his mind. He congratulated her on having made seventeen candles from the cow. It was "feather in your cap," he wrote. "You shall have a new dress by it."[109] Two weeks later he wrote to tell her that, besides the annuities, several people at the Sault would receive payments of a hundred dollars (for what he doesn't say), including one for Ogeewyahnoquotokwa. "These little things will enable you to say something agreeable to them, which is my object in adverting to them." He had news for her as well. He was now "supervisor of all the Indians within the lake region," and they would spend all or part of the summer at either Mackinac or the Sault. His campaign for the territorial governorship had been as successful as that for getting the war losses paid. Don't tell anyone about it, he said, "owing to the envy & ill will of those who may be fretted at my rise." It wasn't much of an improvement on his previous status, and it was clear that the principal responsibility of the job would be to continue making treaties. They would spend the winter in Detroit but still needed servants for the summer. He thought Charlotte "if she recovers" should be sent back to her mother. "I will endeavour to get a black, married or single, or a foreigner, as we shall probably have company during the summer, and cannot possibly get along without them."[110] His new status required the right kind of servants to advertise the fact.

He had thought he would at some point go to New York to oversee the printing of "my tales," but circumstances prevented it.[111] In early May he was still waiting for the Senate to ratify the Ojibwe and Odawa treaty. There were "some modifications," he wrote, proposed by the committee, that the Senate would likely accept. He did not say what these were, but they were very important. The Senate unilaterally tossed out the provisions for permanent reservations, making them expire at the end of five years, after which everyone would be deported. "The Chiefs will be convened at Mackinac to accede to their modifications," Schoolcraft wrote, "the Secretary of War [that is, Cass] has committed, from the outset, the whole matter to me, and its execution requires my attention, until the final vote is passed by the Senate for its acceptance." He'd been saying for years that no one would be removed, and now not only would the people be removed; he would be removing them himself. Jane and the chiefs would find out about this later. He could not come home just yet.[112]

On 10 May, Jane received Schoolcraft's brief note of early April saying that he would have to stay longer with a burst of anger. Charlotte Wabose had died, on 12 April, and though Jane was able to "get about the house" again, still "the incessant trials I experience daily to keep up *housekeeping* with none but thoughtless, *disobedient* Louisa to assist me, is wearing out my little remaining strength." This was not George's daughter but Louisa Piquette, who was likely related to the mother of Lewis's children Janette Piquette (Sangemanqua). As she did when she was angry, Jane mocked Schoolcraft's need to have authority over her. "If I thought it could possibly meet your sanction, I would this moment break up *housekeeping*—shut up house & go to my Mother for a while, to seek that necessary repose & relief, which should I soon not get, I shall be 'where the wicked cease from troubling, & the weary are at rest.'" She hadn't received any letters, if he'd sent them, but brief and unsatisfying reports. Even so, she wrote, "I shall continue to do my *duty* by *writing* as in all other ways, as far as I am able, as I find in all your last *hasty* letters, an accusation against me for not writing. I am sure I did not want the one additional trial of hearing that you did not receive my letters, or that you would for one moment believe that I have neglected one single opportunity to address you." She wrote by every express. He didn't.

She asked for "a good quantity of Laudanum."[113] She was still angry a few days later when she wrote again, having heard from Hulbert that Schoolcraft probably wouldn't return until June. When Hulbert called on Schoolcraft in Washington, he was out on a "party of pleasure in the country." "It is worse than Widowhood to be so often, & so long left alone," she wrote. "Frequent & long absences of the *Head* of the family is, I think, very injurious in more ways than one." Janée had written another letter, she wrote, without her knowledge, all by herself, with no encouragement from her mother. Across the top she wrote, "I feel sorry when I see my / poor Mother weap so often." "We were very sorry that you did not come in the first vessel," she continued in the body.

> My Mother is very low and often wishes you were back. I have written to Grand Ma' and I thought I would write to you. Poor Charlotte is dead, she died happy. I think she is now very happy in heaven. Though my Mother is hardly able to go about, she still, will take care of us and the house, because there is no one else to do so. I am very sorry that I did not receive an answer to my first letter. My Mother has written very often to you and we feel disappointed when so many vessels come in and bring no letter from you. Johnston and myself go to school everyday. It is only two weeks since I have commenced going. I study reading, writing, spelling, and geography.[114]

Jane seems to have stood over her little daughter, dictating.

Schoolcraft didn't receive these letters until he returned to Mackinac in June. Even without their influence, he kept justifying himself in his letters from Washington. "My *long seclusion* had placed me in a disadvantageous position, & that without this *active step on my part* I was likely to be left *unnoticed & forgotten*," he wrote, referring back to his supposed original purpose in spending the winter at the capital. He did it for her, and their children's "future competence," and with that in mind, he knew that she could not disagree. Cass had been made minister to France, effective that fall, and he wanted to show his gratitude for Cass's kindness "by preparing a box of Indian curiosities for him to take to that country. And if it is in your power to begin making arrangements for any articles, before my return, I trust you will do so. I propose to get some fine cloth and have a full female Chippewa dress made, & finely garnished. Small mocucks of sugar would be a capital article." He hadn't forgotten William. "If the treaty is ratified ... I shall have a place for him, which will give him a good living, without the necessity of his going inland as a subordinated missionary. He may exert himself beneficially for his people, without going into the interior."[115] The closer Schoolcraft got to finalizing the treaty, the more he thought of his wife and her family as Indians.

The treaty was ratified on 20 May. A small article by "a Lady-Tourist," dated 9 May, appeared in the *Southern Rose* of Charleston, South Carolina, telling of an Indian who appeared at her lodgings in Washington to see an officer who was also staying there. He was a Chippewa chief from Michigan, she wrote, "dressed in a rich and becoming costume, with broad silver belts around his arms and wrists, large glittering silver earrings, and scarlet trimmings." He'd gone to England with six of his tribe, but three of the party, including his wife and nephew, had died in London, where they were buried. "He came to Washington to negotiate about the lands of his tribe," the Lady-Tourist wrote, and "some of our party asked is he going to remove westward." "'Cut off head first,' was his reply, and he laughed so long and loud that it was painful to hear him."[116]

Paup-Puk-Keewiss

Saginaw, Translated by William Johnston,
Winter 1836–1837, Michilimackinac

A man of large stature, and great activity of mind and body, found himself standing alone on a prairie. He thought to himself, "How came I here? Are there no beings on this earth like myself? I must travel and see. I must walk till I find the abodes of men."[1] So soon as his mind was made up, he set out, he knew not where, in search of habitations. No obstacles could divert him from his purpose. Neither prairies, rivers, woods, nor storms had the effect to daunt his courage or turn him back. After travelling a long time he came to a wood, in which he saw decayed stumps of trees, as if they had been cut in ancient times, but no other traces of men. Pursuing his journey, he found more recent marks of the same kind; and after this, he came to fresh traces of human beings; first their footsteps, and then the wood they had cut, lying in heaps. Continuing on, he emerged towards dusk from the forest, and beheld at a distance a large village of high lodges, standing on rising ground. He said to himself, "I will arrive there on a run." Off he started with all his speed; on coming to the first large lodge, he jumped over it. Those within saw something pass over the opening, and then heard a thump on the ground.

"What is that?" they all said.

One came out to see, and invited him in. He found himself in company with an old chief and several men, who were seated in the lodge. Meat was set before him, after which the chief asked him where he was going and what his name was. He answered, that he was in search of adventures, and his name was Paup-Puk-Keewiss. A stare followed.

"Paup-Puk-Keewiss!"[2] said one to another, and a general titter went round.

He was not easy in his new position; the village was too small to give him full scope of his powers, and after a short stay he made up his mind to go farther, taking with him a young man who had formed a strong attachment for him, and might serve him as his mesh-in-au-wa.[3] They set out together, and when his companion was fatigued with walking, he would show him a few tricks, such as leaping over trees, and turning round on one leg till he made the dust fly, by which he was mightily pleased, although it sometimes happened that the character of these tricks frightened him.

One day they came to a very large village, where they were well received. After staying in it some time, they were informed of a number of manitoes who lived at a distance, and who made it a practice to kill all who came to their lodge. Attempts had been made to extirpate them, but the war-parties who went out for this purpose were always unsuccessful. Paup-Puk-Keewiss determined to visit them, although he was advised not to do so. The chief warned him of the danger of the visit; but finding him resolved,

"Well," said he, "if you will go, being my guest, I will send twenty warriors to serve you."

He thanked him for the offer. Twenty young men were ready at the instant, and they went forward, and in due time descried the lodge of the manitoes. He placed his friend and the warriors near enough to see all that passed, while he went alone to the lodge. As he entered he saw five horrid looking manitoes in the act of eating. It was the father and his four sons. They looked hideous; their eyes were swimming low in their heads, as if half starved. They offered him something to eat, which he refused.

"What have you come for?" said the old one.

"Nothing," Paup-Puk-Keewiss answered.

They all stared at him.

"Do you not wish to wrestle?" they all asked.

"Yes," he replied.

A hideous smile came over their faces.

"*You* go," they said to the eldest brother.

They got ready, and were soon clinched in each other's arms for a deadly throw. He knew their object—his death—his *flesh* was all they wanted, but he was prepared for them.

"Haw! haw!" they cried, and soon the dust and dry leaves flew about as if driven by a strong wind.

The manito was strong, but Paup-Puk-Keewiss soon found that he could master him; and, giving him a trip, he threw him with a giant's force head foremost on a stone, and he fell like a puffed thing.

The brothers stepped up in quick succession, but he put a number of tricks in force, and soon the whole four lay bleeding on the ground. The old manito got frightened and ran for his life. Paup-Puk-Keewiss pursued him for sport; sometimes he was before him, sometimes flying over his head. He would now give him a kick, then a push or a trip, til he was almost exhausted. Meantime his friend and the warriors cried out, "Ha! ha! a! ha! ha! a! Paup-Puk-Keewiss is driving him before him." The manito only turned his head now and then to look back; at last, Paup-Puk-Keewiss gave him a kick on his back, and broke his back bone; down he fell, and the blood gushing out of his mouth prevented him from saying a word. The warriors piled all the bodies together in the lodge, and then took fire and burned them. They all looked with deep interest at the quantity of human bones scattered around.

Paup-Puk-Keewiss then took three arrows, and, after having performed a ceremony to the Great Spirit, he shot one into the air, crying, with a loud voice,

"*You* who are lying down, rise up, or you will be hit!" The bones all moved to one place. He shot a second arrow, repeating the same words, when each bone drew towards its fellow-bone; the third arrow brought forth to life the whole multitude of people who had been killed by the manitoes. Paup-Puk-Keewiss then led them to the chief of the village who had proved his friend, and gave them up to him. Soon after the chief came with his counsellors.

"Who is more worthy," said he, "to rule than you? *You* alone can defend them."

Paup-Puk-Keewiss thanked him, and told him he was in search of more adventures. The chief insisted. Paup-Puk-Keewiss told him to confer the chieftainship on his friend, who, he said, would remain while he went on his travels. He told them that he would, some time or other, come back and see them.

"Ho! ho! ho!" they all cried, "come back again and see us," insisting on it. He promised them he would, then set out alone.

After travelling some time he came to a large lake; on looking about he discovered a very large otter on the island. He thought to himself, "His skin will make me a fine pouch," and immediately drew up, at long shots, and drove an arrow into his side. He waded into the lake, and with some difficulty dragged him ashore. He took out the entrails, and even then the carcass was so heavy that it was as much as he could do to drag it up a hill overlooking the lake. As soon as he got him up into the sunshine, where it was warm, he skinned him, and threw the carcass some distance, thinking the war-eagle would come, and he should have a chance to get his skin and feathers as head ornaments. He soon heard a rushing noise in the air, but could see nothing; by-and-by, a large eagle dropped, as if from the air, on the otter's carcass. He drew his bow, and the arrow passed through under both his wings. The bird made a convulsive flight upward with such force, that the heavy carcass (which was nearly as big as a moose) was borne up several feet. Fortunately, both claws were fastened deeply into the meat, the weight of which soon brought the bird down. He skinned him, crowned his head with the trophy, and next day was on his way, on the lookout for something new.

After walking a while he came to a lake, which flooded the trees on its banks; he found it was only a lake made by beavers. He took his station on the elevated dam, where the stream escaped, to see whether any of the beavers would show themselves. He soon saw the head of one peeping out of the water to see who disturbed them.

"My friend," said Paup-Puk-Keewiss, "could you not turn me into a beaver like yourself?" for he thought, if he could become a beaver, he would see and know how these animals lived.

"I do not know," replied the beaver; "I will go and ask the others."

Soon all the beavers showed their heads above the water, and looked to see if he was armed; but he had left his bow and arrows in a hollow tree at a short distance. When they were satisfied, they all came near.

"Can you not, with all your united power," said he, "turn me into a beaver! I wish to live among you."

"Yes," answered their chief; "lay down"; and he soon found himself changed into one of them.

"You must make me *large*," said he; *larger* than any of you."

"Yes, yes!" said they. "By-and-by, when we get into the lodge, it shall be done."

In they all dove into the lake; and, in passing large heaps of limbs and logs at the bottom, he asked the use of them; they answered, "It is for our winter's provisions." When they all got into the lodge, their number was about one hundred. The lodge was large and warm.

"Now we will make you large," said they. "Will *that* do?" exerting their power.

"Yes," he answered, for he found he was ten times the size of the largest.

"You need not go out," said they. "We will bring your food into the lodge, and you will be our chief."

"Very well," Paup-Puk-Keewiss answered. He thought, I will stay here and grow fat at their expense. But, soon after, one ran into the lodge out of breath, saying, "We are visited by Indians." All huddled together in great fear.[4] The water began to lower for the hunters had broken up the dam, and soon they were on the roof of the beaver lodge breaking it open; out jumped all the beavers into the water and all escaped; Paup-Puk-Keewis tried to follow, Alas! they had made him so large that he could not creep out of the hole that the others did, he tried to call them back, but to no effect—he worked himself so much in trying to escape, that he looked like a bladder—. He could not turn himself back into a man, although he heard and understood all that the hunters said. One of them put his head in at the top of the lodge.

"*Ty-au! Tut Ty-au!*" he cried; "Me shau-mik—King of the Beavers is in. They all got at him and they knocked his head as soft as his brains—still he was not dead, he thought as well as ever he did, although he was a beaver. They took him home, seven or eight of them carrying him with poles. He thought to himself, "What will become of me? My ghost or shadow will not die." After they got home, they invited each other to a feast, and the women took him out into the snow to skin him, but his flesh got cold and his *Jee-bi* went off.

For he found himself near a prairie, standing, having again been turned into the shape of a man; after walking a short distance he saw a herd of elk feeding—He thought to himself, this would be a pleasant life; to run about and feed on the prairies; He asked them if they could not turn him into their shape.

"Yes," they answered after a while. "Get on your hands and feet," they said. And he soon found himself turning into an elk.

"Make me large," he said. "I want big horns, big feet, I wish to be very large."

"Yes, yes," they said to him. "Are you big enough?" they asked.

"Yes," he answered, for he saw that he was very large. They spent a good time in grazing and running. And being rather cold one day they went into a thick wood for shelter, they had not been long there, before some elks who were behind passed the others like a wind laying the woods flat—He ran with the others.

"Keep out on the plains," they said.

But he found it was too late, as they had gone in the thick woods some way. Soon Paup-Puk-Keewis smelt the hunters they were following his trail; they had left all the others & followed him; soon as they saw his hoof prints which by their size made them follow him; he jumped and ran and although he tore down saplings it only retarded his progress. Soon he felt an arrow pierce his body; he jumped over trees, but before he fairly touched the ground, the arrows clattered on his side and one entered his heart; soon after he fell to the ground and then he heard the whoop of joy sounded by the hunters. They all came up about sixty of them; they had invited each other for the hunt, for one the day before had seen the large prints of his hoofs. They looked on him with astonishment and with their hands up to their mouths *Ty-au!* they said. After skinning him, and his flesh getting cold—His *Jee-bi* took its flight from the carcass—and he again soon found himself in the shape of a man, with a bow and arrows.

But his wish for adventure was not as yet cooled, for on coming to a large lake with a sandy beach, he saw a flock of brant; he spoke to them, and asked them if they would turn him into a Brant.

"Yes," they replied.

"But I want to be very large," he said.

"Very well," they answered; and he soon found himself a large brant all the others in a circle gazing at him.

"You must fly as leader," they said.

"No," Paup-Puk-Keewis answered, "I will fly behind."

"Very well," they said. "One thing more we have to say to you that is in flying you must not look down, for something may happen to you.

"Well it is so," Paup-Puk-Keewis replied—& soon the flock rose up into the air for they were bound north, and they flew very fast; he behind. One day while going with a strong wind and fast as their wings could flap, for the wind took them like something passing through it—they happened to be passing over a large village of Indians, who raised a great shout on seeing the flock, but more on Paup-Puk-Keewis's account, for his wings were broader that two large *aupukwa*.[5] They made such a noise that he forgot what was told him about looking down, for they were then going like arrows—for soon as he brought his neck in and stretched it down to look at them crying out—His tail was caught with the wind and over & over he was blown. He tried to right himself but to no effect; down, down he went making more turns than he wished for, from a height of five or six miles—The first thing he knew was, that he was jammed into a large hollow tree; to get back or crawl out was out of the question. There he remained till his brant life was ended by starvation. His *Jee-bi* again left the carcass & he found himself in the shape of a human being once more.

While he was traveling he came to a lodge, in it he found two old men with heads white from age. They treated him very well & [he] told them he was going back to his village to see his friend & people. They said that they would aid him all in their power and pointed out the direction he should go to reach the village—He left them and after walking all day he came to a lodge very much like the first, with two old men—but they never told him of his mistake, but pretended to be strangers. After walking the third time, and coming back to the same place, he found them out in their tricks, for he had cut a notch on the door post.

"Who are you," he said to them, "to treat me so?" and he gave one a kick and one a slap which killed them, and the rocks will ever bear testimony of their blood which he shed. He then burnt their lodge down and freed the earth from two pretending white headed manitoes.

He then went on his journey not knowing exactly where to go, at last he came to a big lake, he got on the highest hills to try & see the opposite side, but he could not. He then commenced and made a canoe in which he took a sail out into the lake; on looking into the water which was very clear, before he got to the abrupt depth, he saw the bottom covered dark with fishes; he then thought he would return to his village & bring his people to live near this lake. He went on & towards evening he came to a large island where he encamped and eat the fish he had speared.

Next day he returned to the main land; and in wandering along the shore, he met a more powerful manito, by name Meanaubosho [Manabozho]. He thought best after playing him a trick to keep out of his way. He again thought of going to his village & he turned himself into a partridge and took his flight towards it; in a short time he got there, and all welcomed with feasting & songs. He told them of the lake he had found of the immense numbers of fish in it, & told them to go and live there, as it would be easier for them to live. They all said they would, and he began to move them by short encampments towards the lake. After he got them there and they began to catch plenty of fish a messenger came for him in the shape of a Bear, who said that their King wished to see him immediately at his village. Paup-Puk-Keewis was soon ready; and the messenger told him to get on his back which he did, and off they started on a run. Towards evening they went up a high mountain and in a cave lived the King of the Bears—who invited him in, he was very large. And some time after he said, he had sent for him, on hearing that he was the Chief who was moving a large party towards his hunting grounds.

"You must know that you have no right here," he said. "And I wish you would leave with your party, or else the strongest will by force take possession of it."

"Very well," replied Paup-Puk-Keewis, "so be it." He did not wish to do any thing to him for fear of his village, he saw the Bear King was mustering his war party. He then told him he would go, although it was night. The Bear King replied it made no difference with them, for one of his young men would take him home; without saying any thing more, He got on his back and rode home; when he got at the village he told his young men to kill the Bear and make a feast for he knew that the Bear spies would soon take the news to their Chief.

Next morning Paup-Puk-Keewis got all his young warriors ready for a fight with the bears. The day after the bear war party came in sight making a tremendous noise. The Bear Chief advanced and said, that he did not wish to shed the blood of the young warriors; but that if [Paup-Puk-Keewis] consented they should have a race and the conqueror should kill the other, and his young men should be slaves to the others. Paup-Puk-Keewis agreed and they ran before all the warriors. Paup-Puk-Keewis however let him and came in first; he only now and then showed him how fast he would run; by forming eddies and whirlwinds with the sand as he jumped and turned about him. Paup-Puk-Keewis then as the Bear Chief came up drove an arrow through him, and a mighty one fell. Paup-Puk-Keewis told his young men to take all those blackfish (meaning the bears) and tie them so many at the door of each lodge, and that they should for the future serve as servants.

Paup-Puk-Keewis after seeing that all was quiet in the village and prosperous and his desire for adventures returning, he took a kind leave of his friends and people and started off on his travels. After wandering a long time he came to the lodge of Manabozho, who was not at home, so he thought he would play him a trick, he turned every thing in his lodge upside down; and killed the chickens of Manabozho, among the number was a raven, who he tied by the neck, being the meanest of birds, and hung him up in the lodge, he could not have insulted him more than by so doing. He then went on and came to a very high point of rocks which lay out into the lake and from the top he could see the country back as far as the eye could reach. While he was sitting there Manabozho's feathered chickens flew round and past him, in great numbers so out of spite he shot them, every arrow hit, for they flew so very thick, he killed a great many whom he threw down the rocks. At last one cried out, "Paup-Puk-Keewis is killing us. Go and tell our father." And off flew a great many—soon he saw Manabozho on the plain below making towards him; he ran down on the opposite side. Manabozho cried out from the hill,

"The Earth is not so very large, but what I can get up to you." Off Paup-Puk-Keewis started for life for he knew [Manabozho] was powerful and he after him. He ran over hills and prairies still he could see Manabozho at a distance following hard after him. Paup-Puk-Keewis stopped and climbed a large pine tree and stripped it of all its green foliage and threw them to the winds; he came down and ran for he saw Manabozho quite near when he came to the pine tree.

"Manabozho," said the tree of pine, "Will you give me my life again? Paup-Puk-Keewis has killed me."

"Yes," Manabozho replied, and it took him some time to gather together the green foliage of the pine tree, before he again started in pursuit. He done the same to the hemlock and various other trees; and Manabozho would always stop and restore what Paup-Puk-Keewis had displaced, by which he got in advance; Manabozho however persevered, and [Paup-Puk-Keewis] again saw him nearing him. Paup-Puk-Keewis happened to see an elk, he asked him to take him on his back, which the elk did, and for some time made considerable progress, but still Manabozho was in sight. Paup-Puk-Keewis dismounted and coming to a large sandstone rock he broke it in pieces and scattered the grains. Manabozho was so near that he had to run, who when he came to the rock, "Haye! Nemosho," said the rocks foundation, "Paup-Puk-Keewis has spoiled me, will you not restore me to life?" Yes; replied Manabozho and he formed the rock like its previous shape. He advanced rapidly and in a short time was almost in reach of Paup-Puk-Keewis; he stretched his arm to catch him—Paup-Puk-Keewis dodges, he was missed. Trees were broke, leaves & sand was carried off by the whirls and turns they made; again and again Manabozho's hand was put out to catch him, but by dodging and turning worried and troubled him. They raised such a dust and their turning formed such eddies and whirlwinds of the air, that Paup-Puk-Keewis was glad to creep in to a hollow tree, which had been blown down, he turned into a snake and crept out at the roots of the tree. Well that he did; for at the moment he had got out, Manabozho (Ogebaugomon) struck it with his power and it was in fragments. Paup-Puk-Keewis was again in human shape—again Manabozho pressed him hard. At a distance he saw a very high bluff, jutting out into the lake, he ran for the foot of the precipice which was very high and abrupt. When he got near it the manito of the place opened his door and told him to come in. The moment they had shut the door, Manabozho knocked.

"Open it," he cried.

The manito was afraid of him but he said, "since I have sheltered you, sooner than open the door, I would rather die with you," he said to Paup-Puk-Keewis.

"Open it," Manabozho cried again.

They kept silent. [Manabozho] however made no attempt to open it by force. "Very well," he said; "I give you only till night to live." The manito trembled, for he knew he would be shut up under the earth.

Night came, the clouds hung low and black and from them every now and then the forked lightening would flash; the black clouds advanced slowly, and still, and behind them was the rumbling noise of the coming thunderers, when they came near the precipice the thunderers made a noise, the lightening flashed, the solid rocks shakes totters, falls, and crushes the human bodies of Paup-Puk-Keewis and the manito.

It was only then that Paup-Puk-Keewis found that he was really dead, he had been killed in different animal shapes, but now his body in human shape was crushed. Manabozho came and took their spirits or Jee-bi-ug.

"You," said he to Paup-Puk-Keewis, "Shall not again be permitted to live on the earth. I will give you," he said, "to Paup-Puk-Keewis the shape of the war eagle and you will be the chief of all fowls, and your duty shall be to watch over their destinies."[6]

Chapter 8

Mercenary and Stupid White Man

They spent the winter of 1836–37 in Detroit, leaving William at Mackinac as acting subagent and keeper of the Indian Dormitory, which was to house visiting Indigenous people and was as yet unbuilt.[1] Jane had been ill over the summer, again; perhaps that was why an Ojibwe girl was with them, as a servant. In succession that summer Ozhaawshkodewikwe, Charlotte, and Eliza had come down to Mackinac.[2] Charlotte brought her new baby, her first surviving child. "I hear by sister Owen that your health is very miserable," Grenville Sproat wrote to Jane from La Pointe, where he had joined the mission there as a teacher. "O to die as the good man dies!" he expostulated; "the smile that lights on his brow is not of earthly radiance. No, it is the peace of God that passeth all understanding, and it descends on him as he goes down through the dark valley.... O may such an exit be yours, my sister."[3] He went on like this at some length.

Four thousand people attended the July council where the new terms for the treaty were accepted, and at least as many were present in September for the settlement of debt claims and the distribution of goods and cash payments. Tribal leaders acceded to the five-year limit on reservations and the provision for deportation to the Southwest, that is, west of Arkansas, after the expiration of five years. Schoolcraft continued to maintain that the ceded land would not be wanted by whites for settlement for the foreseeable future, insinuating that the five-year term was only hypothetical. The Ojibwe and Odawa bands at L'Arbre Croche had long planned to use whatever money they secured to purchase their own land back so as to have a permanent land base safe from settlers whenever they arrived.[4] The Upper Peninsula Ojibwes still counted on whites not getting too close.

The late arrival of $150,000 worth of goods, supplied by the American Fur Company, delayed the distribution. When tribal leaders protested that that was too much, that $10,000 in goods was more appropriate and the rest could be retained for future distribution or given as cash payments, the Americans brushed them off.[5] Andrew Blackbird, an Odawa attendee, wrote later that he thought Schoolcraft and other officials had skimmed some of those goods for themselves.[6]

The total claimed by all traders was $438,383.58; $220,954.57 was allowed. While Schoolcraft pointedly recused himself from involvement with any of the family's claims (including those of his brother-in-law John Hulburt), his biographer Richard Bremer observes that the extended Johnston-Schoolcraft family "faired somewhat better than average" in comparison to other traders. They claimed a total of $107,877.55 and were allowed $56,885.61. This included $2,287.42 to James Schoolcraft; $10,521.54 to William Johnston, covering the period after his father's death to 1833; $7,820 to Ozhaawshkodewikwe for the period after John Johnston's death until she sold the business to the AFC in 1831; $300 to George (of a $450 claim); and, finally, $32,463.72 to the Johnston Estate (of a $69,000 claim).[7] In comparison, Rix Robinson received almost all of his $24,000 claim, and an additional $20,000 in cash allotted to his Odawa children and extended Odawa family. But the AFC trader Robert Stuart received only $17,000 of a $32,000 claim. He did better than the independent Mackinac traders Edward Biddle and John Drew, however, who claimed $87,000 and received $17,000.[8] Like the Odawas, these (and other) traders felt wronged by Schoolcraft and would remember it.

Of the $32,476.32 allowed the Johnston Estate, Schoolcraft divided $6,739.40 of it among Jane, Charlotte, and Anna Maria as marriage portions. Of the $7,820 allowed Ozhaawshkodewikwe, he gave himself $6,976.92 of it because, he said, John Johnston had promised to pay Schoolcraft the value of his Irish inheritance as well as the legacy left to Jane by her great aunt as an additional marriage portion. It's unclear how he arrived at any of these numbers, but the Johnstons accepted his accounting. Schoolcraft then took $25,000 of Ozhaawshkodewikwe's money—the balance of the Johnston Estate—to invest, mainly in Detroit real estate. These actions sent James Schoolcraft into a letter-writing frenzy in the fall and winter of 1836 and 1837, and only after several weeks of harsh words and astonished remonstrations did James acquiesce to his brother's will. When the other members of the family, including McMurray, handed over their money to Schoolcraft to invest that fall, he had about $44,000 at his disposal.[9]

Into this moment of regional and family upheaval, between the treaty council and the payments, a mustachioed and saber-scarred Scotsman who styled himself General John Dickson appeared at the Sault seeking recruits for a mixed-race army to liberate Santa Fe and invade California. It turned out that General Dickson was a friend of Cousin George in London, who wrote to Sault George in September that General Dickson was "the red man's friend, listen to what he will say to you," although this letter would have reached the Sault some months after Dickson had cleared out. The general was "on his way to California with a small band of determined hearts, who join him in the emancipation of the suffering tribe of Indians," wrote London George, as if he wished to join the expedition himself.[10]

Dickson had surfaced in New York and Washington at the end of 1835, apparently well educated and well financed, seeking recruits for his "Army of the Liberator" to join the Texians in their fight for independence. When recruits were not forthcoming, he went to Montreal and renamed his expedition "The Indian Liberating Army," this time seeking the mixed-race sons of Hudson's Bay factors for his new scheme to invade California and establish a new state with himself at the head. He had about sixty men, including some white adventurers, when they left Buffalo in a chartered schooner in August 1836. By then Dickson had a new plan to establish an independent Indian state, which kept getting bigger the more he described it, so that it eventually stretched from Rupert's Land to California and Texas. He'd written a manifesto and declared himself Montezuma II.[11]

George was at the time at loose ends, again, and drinking, so much so that the post physician had hired a discharged soldier to watch him.[12] Dickson wrote to him about a 400-man Chippewa Cavalry that he envisioned, to be "filled up to the arm with swords and holster pistols—the pistols to have a flange on the side to fit into a belt. Also a rifle with rings and a belt to fasten behind the back. And if possible to get bayonets to fit to the rifle." The Chippewa Cavalry was to rendezvous with the rest of the army at the Hudson's Bay Company Red River Colony, in advance of the coming winter. Regrettably, he wouldn't be able to pay for this operation until next June or July.[13] On the same day Dickson wrote this letter to George, he also wrote two letters of introduction to US Army officials in Washington, D.C. "To no one am I more indebted for information about the country through which I have to pass," he wrote to one about George, and to the other he praised George as a "perfect gentleman and scholar."[14] George may have been thinking of going to Washington for some reason, but there are only these letters and some sarcastic remarks about Dickson in another by James Schoolcraft. Dickson was just another of the strange white men pursuing fantasies who regularly turned up in the forest.[15] During his first winter at La Pointe, John Johnston discovered an Italian count taking measurements to determine whether the earth was flatter at the poles than at the equator. He told Johnston he'd climbed Mont Blanc and ascended over Paris in a balloon (he did—and George Washington refused to meet him because he was a monarchist).[16] Dickson had to hire a crew to get his remaining six warriors from Sault Ste. Marie to Red River, and soon after that he entirely disappeared from history.[17]

The Schoolcrafts boarded at the American Hotel along with a boy named Lafayette Bunnell, who worked for a druggist and as an old man left an account. In between errands, some of which may have included deliveries to Jane, Lafayette attached himself to the "Chippewa Indian maid" living with the Schoolcrafts. "She seemed lonely and pleased with my notice," he wrote, "and she was a nice, modest, attentive girl, too." He ran with French and Ojibwe boys in Detroit and fancied himself highly accomplished in Indian ways, including the language. His new friend corrected him. He spoke "French Chippewa," she told him, while she herself spoke "real old Chippewa." Lafayette also remembered Schoolcraft working on his "manuscripts."[18] There were a lot of them that season and in the one following. After his inability to see the book of stories to publication in the spring of 1836, Schoolcraft sought to expand the collection and put out a call for material. Charlotte wrote two stories, William started collecting in earnest, and Schoolcraft and likely Jane solicited others to write. It doesn't seem that Jane herself was writing, or writing much, in this period, but she was likely editing the stories that were sent on to Detroit that winter, as when they can be compared to a manuscript by one of the family, their published versions clarify points of the narrative and lack the excess verbiage of which Schoolcraft was fond.

She remained ill over the winter in Detroit, and her family tried to find ways to comfort her. William sent more copies of his Leech Lake papers. He sent gossip as well. Hiram Campbell married Yarrow's daughter against the priest's wishes, Mrs. Gansy has had a baby, the AFC house is to be turned into a hotel—adding, "All my Indian visitors always ask about you, for they find no one in the kitchen, with a soothing hand to feed them."[19] In March her mother wrote to her (Charlotte translated and McMurray transcribed), anxious for her return to Mackinac, where they would at least be closer than they were then. She was diplomatic; she knew Schoolcraft would read the letter. "I have a request to make, which I trust may be in your power to perform, that is, to come and spend the summer, or some portion of it, with me, which I think might be for your health," she wrote.[20] She accompanied this request with praise for her son-in-law, thanking him for being "kind enough to attend to my little requests and say to him, that I again send him my thanks for his protection & assistance of the Fatherless & Widow; may God reward him for it. He has done *much, much* more than even my own Sons for me, for which I can never repay him."[21] George "has just recovered from insanity brought on by intemperance," she reported. "May God show him his folly and wickedness, and restore him to his favour," McMurray wrote for his mother-in-law.[22]

Schoolcraft went about his duties. He finalized treaties with the Saginaws and smaller Ojibwe bands at Swan Creek and Black River.[23] Sometimes individuals or different groups of Indigenous people stopped in the office, and Schoolcraft dispensed the necessary aid. He got reports from them about settlers occupying their hunting grounds and sugar bushes.[24] Visiting Wyandots from River Huron complained of settlers making mill-dams and flooding tribal lands.[25] The War Office had heard from a Dr. Warren of Boston, who was "desirous of procuring specimens from the different tribes, and from the mounds in the different sections of the country." "I gather," remarked Schoolcraft in his journal, "that he wishes to procure a few complete skeletons, and a number of crania, and that it will be desirable to have as much as possible of the history of each head."[26]

In December 1836 Jane's writing was noticed in the *American Monthly Magazine*—the writer was probably Charles Fenno Hoffman, who was still editor—in a review of John Smith's *The Fairy Book* (1836), a collection of French and English fairy tales put out by Schoolcraft's publisher Harper & Brothers. Smith's book would have been improved, Hoffman wrote, if instead of the familiar European fairy tales he published "some *American fables*, of which our aborigenes have furnished us with not a few." There were not even a few Indigenous stories published at that time, and most of those that were published were written by Jane; possibly Hoffman had heard about Trowbridge's collections for Cass, but those were likely already sitting in the desk drawer where Trowbridge would find them fifty years later. Hoffman was particularly thinking of Jane's stories as just published in Chandler Robbins Gilman's book. "In beauty of moral and felicity of conception," he wrote, "we venture to say, that nothing, in the whole range of similar compositions surpasses the exquisite story of the Robin as translated from the Chippewa by Mrs. Schoolcraft.... The evils of misplaced ambition and the reward of that tenderness as shown in the loss of the bereaved father, and the happy transformation of the obedient son, is the most poetic sermon that ever was preached."[27]

It was exactly how she would have wanted the story to be read, to reveal its moral intelligence in a beautiful design, signifying to her that Anishinaabe people were fully conscious human beings, not savages. Neither Charlotte nor William followed her example in the stories they began sending to Detroit. While William remained fond of romance and adventure, Charlotte seems to have chosen the stories she solicited for their cultural significance; neither of them injected a conventional Western moral into their versions. Neither Jane nor Schoolcraft substantially revised or rewrote the stories for publication, however. If Jane edited them, she didn't feel compelled to bring them more into line with her own approach. Schoolcraft's efforts to control the meaning of the stories in publication remained outside of the text—footnotes, endnotes, forewords, afterwords.

That winter William reported to Schoolcraft that food was scarce and people were coming into the agency desperate, from Grand Traverse, Beaver Island, and elsewhere. Their corn crops had failed, and those who'd held on to money to buy land had to use it to buy food. "Large parties are coming in almost every day," he wrote in February 1837, "and all the provisions in the

Fort will have to be issued, only retaining a sufficiency to feed the most indigent, their situation is imperative and knowing as circumstances are now, that you would feed them I will have to issue from the flour cellar, but not more than 5 or 8 barrels at most."[28] Wauchusco had sold his corn and needed provisions as well.[29] Incoming visitors to the agency boarded along with William at the empty mission house.

He worried about the investments Schoolcraft had made for him in Detroit, hoping Schoolcraft could sell some of his property so that he would have the cash. He thought of buying the mission farm, but Schoolcraft didn't respond to his requests.[30] The reason for that concern is clear in a letter he wrote to Jane on the same day as the letter he wrote to Schoolcraft—he was courting Susan Davenport, daughter of Ambrose Davenport, a fur trader, and his Ojibwe wife, also named Susan.[31] He wrote to Jane, casually: "Dear Jane as for the Young Ladies I cannot say much in their favour. Nancy Dousman is old, although reusable—Mary Ann wants intelligence, she is not fond of books. Susan Davenport is good looking, very lively and considerable good sense; disposition below par and there is also Miss Clitz who inherits too much pride. Take them as a whole, I believe Susan Davenport the most preferable."[32] He and Susan would be married in July of that year. He'd given up his plan of becoming a missionary then. He was also writing stories. He was carrying the mail to Saginaw that winter. He sent a Saginaw story to Detroit in March, writing that it was "the only correct one I procured from them, although they told me one or two more I could not in any way make any thing out of them." The stories showed a French influence, "which made them uninteresting and [they] contained very few Indian ideas."[33] A few weeks later, on his return to the office at Mackinac, he wrote to say that he'd "procured several interesting stories" since last writing and that he'd get as many as he could.[34]

There are three identifiable Saginaw stories in the Johnston archives, two that Schoolcraft published with damning commentary and one that he declined to even identify as Saginaw. Schoolcraft had a problem with the Saginaws. In commentary appended to the story published as "The Weendigoes" (discussed in chapter 4 for its version of the rolling head legend), Schoolcraft wrote that the Saginaws were impure, the "Seminoles of the North"; they were all refugees from other Ojibwe bands. There were no preachers, schools, or teachers among them and never had been. There were no Christians, and there was "not one individual of unmixed blood in the tribe, who can read." They were cruel, deceitful, intemperate; they had "a blind adherence to their idolatrous customs and superstitions." Their language was vulgar, their stories had "less originality, less morality, and less adherence to the ancient manners and customs of the original stock than any other of the traditionary fictions yet examined," he insisted; "most of their lore is of murders and thefts . . . or vicious adventures of some sort."[35] Schoolcraft's other writing doesn't give any clues as to why he found the Saginaws such an abomination in comparison to other bands; one wonders, given the violence of his feelings, whether some embarrassment or personal slight was involved. None of this stopped him from publishing their stories.

In "The Weendigoes," perhaps it was the Maujeekequawis's determined pursuit of the depressed younger brother at the end of the story (that he didn't publish, as that part of the story duplicated Jane's version) that dismayed Schoolcraft, or the beginning of the story (that he did publish) where a Windigo eats the mother and throws her lodge to the winds and the brothers acquire two Thunderbirds and a Meshegenebigo (Mishiginebig), the horned serpent, for pets. The three Saginaw stories (there are no other identifying characteristics, such as the names of tellers) taken together show William's approach to traditional narratives in contrast to Jane's. He wanted a story full of "vicious adventures"—the more the better—not morals that outsiders could readily discern.

In the second Saginaw story, titled by William "Mudjee Monedo and the Genius of Benevolence," a manitou lays waste to a village by challenging foolish men to a race that they will lose because he has the capacity to change himself into any animal known for its speed. At the conclusion of the race the manitou slits their throats; despite the bloody knife at which the race starts and the bleached bones of defeated competitors surrounding the manitou's lodge at the end, the men keep volunteering to race because the manitou "hurts their feelings" by calling them cowards. Then a stranger appears, who marries the daughter of a family down to its last son. The stranger challenges the manitou to a race, transforms himself into a partridge to defeat the manitou, and when the manitou asks for mercy, the stranger cuts his throat. Afterward the manitou, his wife, and their child are revealed to be giant Meshegenebigoes. The stranger cuts the heads off the wife and child and burns the bodies. He then returns the bleached bones of the dead competitors to human form by shooting arrows into the sky three times while shouting "Arise!" The stranger stays with the people for a time to "direct and teach you all I can, and show you how to live happily" before "[disappearing] towards the West." "It is from his taking the partridge's form, that no tribes have the partridge for their totem," William writes.

The story takes place in a kind of golden age, "long ere the white man had set foot on the Indian country." At that time "the unlimited prairies were covered with all kinds of animals necessary for food; the trees were alive with various feathered birds, who cheered all with their innocent melody, they were tame, for man had not made them shy by his cruelty."[36] The romance between the stranger and the daughter of the family echoes Willliam's treatment of

Morning Star and Waving Plume in "Traits of Personal Attachment among the Ojibways." She was "[a] rare forest gem," William writes, "tall and graceful." "Her limbs and figure were complete in their formation, her colour was light, tinged with dark red, rather a high forehead, soft black eyes, and teeth white as snow, and her long black hair was neatly parted from the crown of her head, and when it was parted a line of vermilion more plainly showed, her hair was fastened just above the shoulders with an ornamented string, and the remainder was allowed to hang loosely in long wreathing curls, down her back, a circular spot of vermilion on each cheek gave an additional glow; her brow was also encircled with wild roses and evergreens; all her dress was very neat and plain." William doesn't give the stranger's appearance quite as much attention, but still he is the picture of a warrior. He "had every thing prepossessing, a tall straight and manly figure; his dress was such as warriors wore, his leggings and hunting accoutrements were splendidly ornamented, and the war eagles feathers gracefully wave over his head"; he spoke to her in her own language. When he came to meet her mother, "his ornaments [jingled] at every step he took."

Like Jane, William incorporated psychological detail in his stories, only in his case it wasn't edited out for publication. Before the stranger's arrival, the mother worries about her son and grieves her husband. "She felt sorrow even unto death," William writes, "but it was only on account of her children, that she still wished to enjoy a few more bitter days, so that she might see how they would commence life"—knowing of course that the manitou would inevitably challenge her son. Indeed the manitou did challenge her son so that he could race both the stranger and the young man at the same time. Taking the boy up on a hill with a view of the lake around which they would race, the stranger pointed to the bloody knife that hung on a post where the race started and "in a despising way asked the young man if he would run . . . and said also, 'When men run with me they generally make a bet, and expect to keep it.'" This has the predictable effect on the young man. He "was cut to the quick; he said he was a man, and would run although the distance was great; he also saw the knife stained with blood, and numerous bones whitening the ground, and he expected no mercy if he was beaten." But like all the other competitors he thought he could win, kill the manitou, and save his people, so he accepted.

The story features extravagant transformation. During the race the manito first turned into a fox and "soon passed the stranger, and then went leisurely on." The stranger "exerted his magic powers which were aerial, and he assumed the shape of a partridge and soon passed the manito" himself, turning back into a human once he passed. The manito became a wolf; the stranger allowed him to pass, became a partridge again and flew ahead, saying to the manito as he passed, "My friend this is the extent of your speed," at which the manito "began to have his forebodings." He "took the forms of almost all of the animals that were noted for speed," including a reindeer and buffalo. The stranger passed him one last time in the form of a partridge, saying as he passed, "My Friend is this your only speed?" The manito begged the stranger to stop—"for . . . he knew that he would be beaten and wished to beg for his life"—but the stranger only laughed and said, "I will speak to you at the starting post." Taking up his knife, the stranger faced the manito, who "came with fear, cowardice marked on his face," William writes. "'My friend, spare my life, give me to live,' he asked in a low tone, and moved off as if he was going to run away. 'As you have done to others, so I will do to you,' was the answer; and his bleeding head rolled down the sloping hill; the spectator's ideas and feelings of the past were such that they fell on him with one accord and cut him up, into numberless pieces."

The people take the stranger to the manito's lodge, where behind a partition they find "human bones, skulls, pieces of human flesh here and there" and "two dead bodies cut open and hanging up to dry over poles placed purposely [sic] for that object." Worse—"who can imagine the horror," writes William—were "two monstrous black snakes in girth large as pine trees, coiled up, one on each side of the lodge; it appears one was the wife of the manito, the other was their young." These were "Meshegenebigoes or devils," as was it was then clear the manito himself. The Meshegenebigoes were trapped, however, because "the opening from which they had made their exit to this world from the depths below was closed." The stranger—"the magic blade [glimmering]" in his hand—chopped off their heads. He and the people then gathered up the Meshegenebigoes and lit their lodge on fire, the smoke from which formed into "fiery serpents" as it "curled up in the air."

William's story is equal parts romance and adventure. That the stranger stays to teach the people "how to live happily" for a time might be taken for a conventional ending. But it's only temporary, and on a "cloudless" day the stranger ascends into the sky, leaving his wife behind, who weeps and tears her hair. "You are all weak and foolish beings," he says to the assembled as he ascends, "soon as I am gone you will forget me, and my counsel, soon I see that your condition will again be miserable; you are to be pitied, your natures are weak."

William liked the stories too much to rein them in; he didn't hide the fluidity of human, animal, and spirit in Anishinaabe thought. This is even more pronounced in the third Saginaw story, "Paup-Puk-Keewiss." Schoolcraft identified the story only as "Algic," possibly because he didn't want to give the Saginaws any more credit. It's about the adventures of Paup-Puk-Keewis (Pukawiss) and his eventual fate at the hands of his younger brother

Manabozho.[37] The story begins as many of the Johnston stories do, with a lone person who decides to seek out others. "A man of large stature, and great activity of mind and body, found himself standing alone on a prairie," William writes; "he thought to himself, "How came I here? Are there no beings on this earth like myself? I must travel and see. I must walk till I find the abodes of men.'" This was Manabozho's older brother Paup-Puk-Kewiss, who over the course of the story has an itch for "adventures," wrestles evil spirits, and seemingly on a whim decides to become one animal after another, just to see what it would be like. Each time he does, he dies because of his own desire to be made bigger than all the other beavers, elk, or brant. Each time, he wakes to find himself turned back into a man, after which he goes off on more adventures.

Finally he provokes Manabozho into chasing him, a pursuit in which trees and rocks plead with Manabozho to restore them after Paup-Puk-Kewiss has knocked them down. "Great chief," says a pine tree "stripped ... of all its green foliage, will you give me my life again? Paup-Puk-Kewiss has killed me." Manabozho gathers up all the leaves and fixes the tree, then continues after Paup-Puk-Kewiss. Manabozho traps Paup-Puk-Kewiss in the lodge of a "local manito," and William concludes the story with one of the set pieces of which he was fond. "Night came. The clouds hung low and black, and every moment the forked lightning would flash from them," he writes. "The black clouds advanced slowly, and threw their dark shadows afar, and behind there was heard the rumbling noise of the coming thunder.... The thunders broke, the lightning flashed, the ground shook, and the solid rocks split, tottered, and fell. And under their ruins were crushed the mortal bodies of Paup-Puk-Keewiss and the manito." This time Paup-Puk-Keewiss really died, along with the fearful spirit. Manabozho "took their Jee-bi-ug or spirits," telling Paup-Puk-Keewis that he "'shall not be again permitted to live on the earth. I will give you the shape of the war-eagle, and you will be the chief of all fowls, and your duty shall be to watch over their destinies.'"[38]

With their romance, adventure, and psychological drama, William's stories would seem to have been at least somewhat recognizable to a white readership. Charlotte's stories make no use of Western conventions, however, which may be why Schoolcraft gave them fairy-tale titles—"The Enchanted Moccasins" and "The Magic Bundle"—that have little to do with the main action of either story. Both were told by a man named Little Salt, who lived at Michipicoten, on the north shore of Lake Superior. He seems to have been an Ojibwe man named in records as Chigenaus, who is described as one of the "principal men" living on the north shore of Lake Superior in the Robinson-Superior Treaty of 1850 between Britain and the Ojibwe bands in the region.[39]

Charlotte requested him to tell those stories in particular, waiting until he was able to come to the Sault to be recorded. They are (at least in part) about the use of medicine and the relation of human beings to the animals that they hunt. They also appear to be Cree stories. Schoolcraft identified the stories as "Maskego," which he used for "Maskegon," or today, Swampy Cree people, who lived in northern Manitoba and Ontario, along the shores of Hudson and James Bays. As usual, Charlotte dictated to McMurray. "I have written the story as near to the language in which Charlotte reported it as possible," McMurray wrote when transmitting one of the stories to Schoolcraft, "leaving you the task to clothe it out, as may suit those which you have already collected."[40] The published versions of both stories show editing and some additional language for clarity, likely indicating that it was Jane who worked on the stories that winter in Detroit rather than Schoolcraft.

In "The Enchanted Moccasins," a figure called Onwee Bahmondung or the Boy Who Carries the Ball on His Back (in publication this is explained as "from an idea of his having supernatural powers" and the ball itself is a warclub) lives with his sister away from others. When he comes of age, he wishes to go to a large village to find himself a wife; he asks his sister to make moccasins for his journey. On this journey he first encounters an old woman who says to him, "My poor Grandchild I suppose you are one of those, who are seeking for that distant village from where no person has ever yet returned and unless your Guardian is more successful than the guardians of your predecessors, you will have a similar fate. Be careful to provide yourself with the oshebahgahnun, without which you cannot succeed."[41] A note in the published version clarifies oshebahgahnun as bones used in the medicine dance that "can penetrate and go through any substance."[42] The old woman tells him to go to a lodge suspended in a tree at the center of the village, where the chief's two daughters live.

At the village, every time he tries to reach the lodge, the tree springs up a little so that it is always out of reach. He calls on his guardian spirit and turns into a squirrel, then uses the oshebahgahnun to slow down the tree's progress. Finally, with the tree at the "arch of heaven," he finds the chief's two daughters and kills them for what they had done to all the suitors who preceded him. On the ground afterward he's pursued by the two sisters' brother, Mudjikewis, who vows revenge. Onwee Bahmondung transforms himself into a dead moose and uses the moccasins to dupe Mudjikewis, then shoots what the published version identifies as magic arrows at him. Finally he transforms himself into an old man with two daughters of his own and invites Mudjikewis to eat. The published version provides more detail on the end of the story. Mudjikewis "ate so heartily as to produce drowsiness, and soon fell into a profound sleep. Onwee Bahmondung watched his opportunity, and, as soon as he found [Mudjikewis's] slumbers sound, resumed his youthful form. He then drew the magic ball from his back, which turned out to be a heavy war-club, with one blow of which he put an end to his pursuer, and thus vindicated his title as the Wearer of the Ball."[43]

The story appears to be about (at least in part) the necessity of using spiritual power—as were many of the Johnston stories. The moccasins that Onwee Bahmondung tells to go to the ends of the earth while he is disguised as a moose carcass are not the main focus of the story. Nor is the "Magic Bundle" of the second story Charlotte solicited from Little Salt, a more complex story than the first. A poor man who "[wanders] about from place to place forlorn, without relatives, and almost helpless," wraps his medicine bundle in a blanket and hangs it in a tree, then goes off to hunt.[44] When he returns, he finds a lodge in which a beautiful woman sits with his blanket beside her. He'd shot a deer, but when the woman tries to bring it in, she breaks both her legs. "The man looked at her with astonishment and then said within himself, 'I thought I was blessed, but I now find my mistake. Gweengweeshee [night-hawk] I will leave my game with you that you may feast on it,'" Charlotte writes.[45] The next day he puts his bundle in a tree and goes off hunting as before. He returns with a deer and again sees a beautiful woman in the lodge, sitting with his blanket by her side. The woman brings the deer inside, where he "beheld her eating all of the fat of the deer; he exclaimed 'I thought I was blessed but I find that I am mistaken,' and continued, 'poor Wabizhas [Marten] (addressing the woman) feast on the game that I have brought.'"

Again he puts his bundle back up in a tree and goes off hunting, returning with another deer and finding another lodge with another beautiful woman sitting inside by herself, this time with his medicine bundle by her side. She collects the deer and cooks dinner for the hunter. He says to himself, "Now I am certainly blessed." This routine continues for four days, but the hunter never sees the woman eat and when he asks her about it she says, "I have food of my own which I eat." On the fourth day the hunter leaves a poplar branch that he had been using as a cane by the door of the lodge. He soon hears the woman laughing and saying to herself, "This is very acceptable which he has brought." The hunter goes outside and is astonished to see her "eating the bark of the Poplar cane he had just brought with him, after the manner of the Beaver." Which she is, and "ever afterwards on returning from his hunt, he always brought with him a small bough of the Poplar or else the Red Willow. When she would exclaim 'Oh! this is very acceptable: This is a change;

for one gets tired eating Whitefish always (meaning the Poplar), but the bark is a pleasant change,' meaning the Red Willow."

The hunter is pleased with his wife—"by her industry she made him splendid bags"—and in the spring "they found themselves blessed with two children, one of them resembling the Father and the other the Mother." One day the hunter gives the son who resembles himself a bow and arrows and tells him to "shoot at the little Beavers, when they are beginning to swim about the rivers." This makes his mother "highly displeased," so much so that she abandons the lodge in the middle of the night, builds a dam in a nearby river, and lives with her children in a lodge "after the manner of the Beavers." The distraught hunter eventually finds his wife and children, and throwing himself on their lodge says "Here I will lie until I die."[46] (The published version gives his declaration in Ojibwemowin: "Shingisshenaun tshee neeboyaun.")[47] The mother lets their children visit but will not let them touch their father, and then, to continue tormenting him, says she will take them away.

Despairing and almost starved, the hunter sees a different young woman approach, telling him to eat the raspberries in a makak that she offers him. His wife sees this and berates the young woman: "Why do you wish to show any kindness to that animal, who has but two legs, you will soon regret of it," and she mocks her, saying, "Look at her, she has a long nose, she is just like a Bear." That is true; the young woman is a bear, and in return for being abused she breaks the Beaver's dam, letting the water drain out and nearly killing the Beaver. "Follow me, I will be kind to you," she says to the hunter. "Follow me closely for you must now take courage for there are three persons who are desirous of marrying me. Be you confident of yourself, follow me closely and just as we approach the lodge, put your feet in the print of mine, for I have eight sisters, who will do their utmost to divert your attention and leave the way I have gone. Look neither to the right nor to the left, but enter the lodge just as I do, and take your seat where I do."

The hunter does as he was told and enters the lodge where eight sisters "unanimously addressed him 'O Ogidahkumigo [a note in *Algic Resources* translates this as "a man that lives on the surface of the earth, as contradistinguished from beings living under ground"] has lost his way,' and then wished him to take his seat with one of them, desiring to draw him from their Sister." The hunter sits down and then "a great rush of water, as a river came through the center of the lodge, which also brought in its course a large stone and left it before the man." Then, in succession, a white bear, a yellow bear, and a black bear come into the lodge, each biting and scratching at the stone, saying, "This is the manner in which I would handle Ogidahkumigo if I was jealous."[48] The hunter "took up his bow and arrow, shot at the stone, and said "This is the way I would treat Odanamekumigo ["he who lives in the city under ground"] if I was jealous.'" The Bears turned around "with their eyes fixed on him, and thus left the lodge, which highly delighted the woman, to think that her husband had vanquished the Bears," Charlotte writes.

One of the old Bears announces that they should gather acorns for the winter. As they leave, he says to his daughter, "Tell Ogidahkumigo to go to the place where your Sisters have gone to gather and let him select one, so that he may have some food for himself for the Winter but be sure and tell him to be very careful, when he is taking her skin from her, that he does not cut the flesh." The hunter selects a sister-in-law, but "when he was taking the skin from her, although careful, he cut her a little upon one of her arms; when she jumped up and ran home." Ogidahkumigo returns home and finds the sister-in-law with a bandaged arm.

The woman tells her husband during the winter that the time had arrived when she must give herself up to be killed by the Ogidahkumigoes. Soon after that a hunter finds them, and the woman tells her husband, "Move aside for I am giving myself up." Odigahkumigo—the first hunter, the husband of the Bear—reveals himself to the hunter who killed his wife, telling him "what he must hereafter do when he killed Bears, that he must not cut them when he was taking the skin from them, nor hang up the feet with its flesh, when drying it, but he must take the head and feet, and decorate them handsomely and place Tobacco on the head for they were very fond of it, for on the fourth day they come to life again."

Charlotte wanted these two stories. It was the year after the treaty, and the stories Little Salt agreed to tell were about important aspects of Indigenous life—the power of medicine and the nature of the relations they had with the animals they hunted. It may represent the "theory" of hunting that Jane mentioned in her letter to William Hull Clarke. Though there are few if any comments on individual stories in the response to *Algic Researches*, this story would seem to have baffled a contemporary white audience, with its wives who are beavers and bears, its mysterious river and stone, the very idea of consulting with the animals one hunts for food. Charlotte either didn't recognize or didn't care about what white people could be expected to think. She was the most pious and placid of the sisters, who after her marriage was responsible for most of the interpretation, teaching, and occasionally writing that went on at McMurray's mission. This was so much the case that Thomas Anderson, the British Indian Department official, recommended that she be paid for her work.[49] McMurray never had much success at missionizing; unlike James Cameron, he appears to have disdained Indigenous people. When Charlotte took her new baby to Mackinac during the council and payments in the summer of 1836, McMurray wrote to her from the Sault that the local Indians were playing ball "like little children." The Ojibwes on the Canadian

Charlotte McMurray Johnston, ca. 1860. Box 1, Johnston Family Papers 1822–1936, Bentley Historical Library, University of Michigan, Ann Arbor.

side of the St. Mary's River were engaged in a two-days-long game against their relatives on the US side. He would soon put a stop to it, McMurry wrote. "This might lead to worse, and the best and only way is to 'nip sin in the bud.'"[50] Why Charlotte wanted these particular stories she kept to herself.

———

Visitors came and went to Sault Ste. Marie and especially Mackinac, and most of them wanted someone to explain the locals into whose lodges they poked their heads. One of them after another in their inevitable books credits Jane, Charlotte, Anna Maria, and occasionally George for information. To judge by her letter to William Hull Clarke, Jane was fairly bursting to tell the truth about Anishinaabe people to anyone she thought might understand. After ten years of dead Indian maidens, constant allusion to the inevitability of her relatives' demise, and a treaty by which they would be expelled from their land, that person was not her husband. When in the summer of 1837 the English writer and critic Anna Brownell Jameson came to visit the Schoolcrafts on an expedition to gather information about the lives of Indian women, Jane took advantage of the opportunity. She told Mrs. Jameson what she wouldn't have told her husband or what he would not have found relevant; she took Mrs. Jameson to visit Ozhaawshkodewikwe, who told her story as well. She gave Mrs. Jameson stories to copy and publish, and although Gilman had published two of them, "Forsaken Brother" and "Origin of the Robin," she also gave Mrs. Jameson "Mishosha," which was probably the most ambitious story she'd written so far. She had hopes for Mrs. Jameson.

Jameson had met the McMurrays when they were in Toronto with their toddler son William, anticipating McMurray's ordination by the bishop, but they discovered the bishop wasn't in town.[51] McMurray took the opportunity to show off Charlotte, whom he thought the picture of Indian civilization and good for the missionary cause. They attended a ball held by Sir Francis and Lady Bond Head, he the lieutenant governor of Canada about whom McMurray and other clergymen had high expectations for government support of missions since his arrival earlier that year. Word about them—about Charlotte—got around, which they discovered when they were called upon, unexpectedly, by Anna Jameson, celebrated authoress. Mrs. Jameson had heard about Charlotte from an acquaintance and soon repaired to the McMurrays' hotel for a visit. She had an interest in Indians, especially Indian women, she told them; she was going to write another book.

Anna Jameson was a former governess, the daughter of an unsuccessful Irish miniaturist in London, when she married Robert Sympson Jameson, a distant relative of Coleridge, in 1825, after a four-year engagement. A trip to the continent had provided the material for her first book, *Diary of an Ennyuee* (1826), a fictional account of her experiences that ends with the narrator's heartbroken death. The book's popularity launched her career. She wanted to travel and write, but her new husband wasn't interested. When he accepted a government position in Dominica in 1829, Anna remained in England, publishing *Memoirs of the Loves of the Poets* in 1829; *Memoirs of Celebrated Female Sovereigns* in 1831; *Characteristics of Women* (on Shakespeare's heroines) in 1832; and *The Beauties of the Court of King Charles the Second* in 1833. She favored biographical sketches of historical and literary women emphasizing romance and matrimony, accompanied by, her biographer Clara Thomas writes, "anecdotes of historical interest and a measure of innocuous and vapid criticism." She enthused; she reacted to her subjects "personally and violently."[52]

Robert Jameson was made attorney general of Upper Canada in 1833, and by 1836, when he was in line for an appointment as the vice chancellor for the province, he requested that Anna come to Toronto to assure his superiors that he was a dependable family man. She went, in October 1836, because even with

Anna Jameson by David Octavius Hill and Robert Adamson (salted paper print, ca. 1844). Art Institute of Chicago, Chicago, Illinois.

her success as a writer she needed money from her husband to help support her elderly parents and four sisters. Robert Jameson was also entitled to take whatever money she earned by her writing.[53] According to Thomas, he wasn't demanding by the standards of the time, nor was he violent; he just seems to have been too boring for his wife to contemplate a life with him.[54] Before she returned to England at the end of 1837, Jameson had secured a separation agreement from him.

Mrs. Jameson was unprepared for Charlotte's "grace and . . . perfection of form"; she was so unlike "the specimens of Indian squaws and half-caste women I had met with," she wrote in that book about her travels, *Winter Studies and Summer Rambles in Canada* (1838). It was written in the epistolary style, to an unnamed recipient and completed in New York City, where she waited for her separation agreement to arrive, freeing her to go home. "Her features are distinctly Indian," wrote Mrs. Jameson, "but softened and refined, and their expression at once bright and kindly. Her dark eyes have a sort of fawn-like shyness in their glance, but her manner, though timid, was quite free from embarrassment or restraint." She found that Charlotte spoke English very well, although with a slight, seemingly German accent. "In two minutes I was seated by her—my hand kindly folded in hers—and we were talking over the possibility of my plans." As Mrs. Jameson spoke to Charlotte about "her own fated race," Charlotte encouraged her to visit Mackinac to talk to Jane and Schoolcraft.[55] McMurray wrote to Schoolcraft, thrilled by this encounter. He thought Mrs. Jameson's sudden appearance "Providential," as a book such as she planned would bring Indians to "the notice of the people at home and may eventually benefit them much." "She is one of the finest writers of the day," he added.[56]

She arrived at Mackinac at the end of July. Like everyone else, she was struck by the scenery and the savages, who were gathering for the first distribution of annuities after the previous year's treaty. She didn't know that she was expected when she arrived at Mackinac early in the morning on the steamboat, so she put up at a boardinghouse kept by "a very fat half-caste Indian woman, who spoke Indian, bad French, and worse English." This was Madame Laframboise. Anna Jameson thought addressing such a woman as "Madame" a bit much as she departed to get a closer look at the Indians in their lodges. "Even while I looked the inmates were beginning to bestir themselves and dusky figures were seen emerging into sight from their picturesque dormitories," she wrote. They "stood gazing" on the white tourists "with folded arms, or were busy about their canoes, of which some hundreds lay along the beach."[57] Mrs. Jameson got out her sketchbook.

Jane had a room prepared for her even though she'd been unable to leave her own room for several days. When Jane finally appeared, Mrs. Jameson was "charmed":

> She received me with true lady-like simplicity. The damp, tremulous hand, the soft, plaintive voice, the touching expression of her countenance, told too painfully of resigned and habitual suffering. Mrs. Schoolcraft's features are more decidedly Indian than those of her sister. . . . Her accent is slightly foreign—her choice of language pure and remarkably elegant. In the course of an hour's talk, all of my sympathies were enlisted in her behalf, and I thought I perceived that she, on her part, was inclined to return these benignant feelings. I promised myself to repay her hospitality by all the attention and gratitude in my power. I am here a lonely stranger, thrown upon her sufferance, but she is good, gentle, and in very delicate health, and there are a thousand quiet ways in which woman may be kind and useful to her sister woman. . . . We shall soon be the best friends in the world![58]

Mrs. Jameson cultivated extravagant emotions as a matter of course. She was fond of the picturesque—the island was picturesque, Jane was picturesque,

The beach at Mackinac, drawing by Anna Brownell Jameson, *Voyage to America Portfolio* (1837). Baldwin Collection of Canadiana, Special Collections and Rare Books, Toronto Public Library, Toronto, Ontario, Canada.

her mother when Mrs. Jameson eventually met her was picturesque. She developed a fixation on Jane, who was at first bemused, then irritated, then angry. Mrs. Jameson was so sympathetic, so enthusiastic, she might have been able to help. But it became clear to both Jane and Charlotte even before the publication of her book that Mrs. Jameson wasn't capable of understanding what they were telling her, however much they tried to explain.

She wanted to hear about Indian women, and Jane told her about the young woman who dreamed she married the sun and so lived the rest of her life "with a place for her husband." She told Mrs. Jameson that the Ojibwes and Odawas were neither celibate nor profligate before marriage, that women determined the best course for their children, and that widows were beholden to their in-laws only for two years after their husband's death, after which they were free to marry again. She told her about the woman warrior at Mackinac. Mrs. Jameson took notes. "While in conversation with her, new ideas of the Indian character suggest themselves; new sources of information are opened to me, such as are granted to few, and such as I gratefully appreciate." Jane was proud of her Indianness, Mrs. Jameson noted, and "takes an enthusiastic and enlightened interest" in her relatives' welfare. But "there is a melancholy and pity in her voice, when speaking of them, as if she did indeed consider them a doomed race."[59] Mrs. Jameson was trying to maintain her equilibrium.

Jane told Mrs. Jameson that girls as well as boys would fast for a guardian spirit—Mrs. Jameson didn't understand, though, or she didn't want to, as she described the experience as merely a fever dream.[60] She told Mrs. Jameson about the man who "suckled his surviving infant" after his wife died (her mother knew him, and he "retained something of the full feminine form" afterward).[61] She told Mrs. Jameson about a man hunting with his family who'd performed a Caesarian on his wife and saved both her and the baby, all of them still living at the Sault.[62]

She told Mrs. Jameson about storytellers. "Like the Arabians, they have among them story-tellers by profession, persons who go about from lodge to lodge amusing the inmates with traditional tales, histories of the wars or exploits of their ancestors, or inventions of their own, which are sometimes in the form of allegories or parables, and are either intended to teach some moral lesson, or are extravagant inventions, having no other aim or purpose to excite wonder or amazement," she wrote. This is what Jane told Schoolcraft, "The story-tellers are estimated according to their eloquence and powers of invention," Mrs. Jameson continued, and she noted that some people were "story-tellers by profession," while others, like Ozhaawshkodewikwe, were just good at it. Jane told her about "an Indian living at Sault Ste. Marie, who in this manner amuses and instructs his family almost every night before they go to rest."[63]

Jane, the children, and Mrs. Jameson traveled to the Sault to visit Ozhaawshkodewikwe in a bateau captained by a young man who sang Ojibwe hymns to keep awake. Mrs. Jameson became even more enamored of Jane, whom she watched "bending over her sleeping children, and waving off the mosquitoes, singing all the time a low, melancholy Indian song; while the northern lights were streaming and dancing in the sky, and the fitful moaning of the wind, the gathering clouds, and chilly atmosphere foretold a change in the weather."[64] At Sault Ste. Marie Ozhaawshkodewikwe didn't disappoint. She was "a woman of pure Indian blood, of a race celebrated in these regions as warriors and chiefs from generation to generation, who had never resided within the pale of what we call civilized life, whose habits and manners were those of a genuine Indian squaw, and whose talents and domestic virtues commanded the highest respect."[65] As was her custom, Ozhaawshkodewikwe set out a great spread for her visitor, who, echoing McKenney and Porter, judged it "the best dressed and best served dinner I had seen since I left Toronto, and presided at her table, and did the honours of her house with unembarrassed, unaffected propriety."[66]

Voyage with Mrs. Schoolcraft, drawing by Anna Brownell Jameson, *Voyage to America Portfolio* (1837). Baldwin Collection of Canadiana, Special Collections and Rare Books, Toronto Public Library, Toronto, Ontario, Canada.

In their first meeting, Ozhaawshkodewikwe saw that Mrs. Jameson was ill and "laid me down on a couch, and began to rub my feet, soothing and caressing me." She called Mrs. Jameson "Nindannis, daughter, and I called her Neengai, mother," thinking to herself "how different from my own fair mother . . . as I looked up gratefully in her dark Indian face."[67] After dinner Mrs. Jameson along with Jane visited Waishkey and his family in their lodge, which she pronounced comfortable and even elegant, "according to the Indian notions of both."[68] They told her the family history and showed her the oil portrait of John Johnston, painted before he left Ireland, whom she had heard from Canadian friends was "a very clever, lively, and eccentric man, and a little of the *bon vivant.*"[69] George told Mrs. Jameson, who no doubt asked, about Indian practices in war—he also pointed out that although Indians were always accused of being merciless savages, they didn't compare at all to Europeans on the point. His description of shooting the rapids were so enticing that Mrs. Jameson had to do it herself.

"They told me I was the first European female who ever performed it, and assuredly I shall not be the last."[70] The trip was about three-quarters of a mile and took about seven minutes to complete. Ozhaawshkodewikwe embraced her "several times," Mrs. Jameson writes, and "I was declared duly initiated, and adopted in to the family by the name of Wah,sah,ge,wah,noqua." Her new family had been calling her O,daw,gaungee, *the fair changing moon,* or rather,

Wayish-ky's Lodge, July 31, 1837, drawing by Anna Brownell Jameson, *Voyage to America Portfolio* (1837). Baldwin Collection of Canadiana, Special Collections, Toronto Public Library, Toronto, Ontario, Canada.

the fair moon which changes her place" on account of her "complexion and . . . traveling propensities." Her new name, she wrote, "signifies *the bright foam*, or more properly, which the feminine adjunct *qua*, *the woman of the bright foam*; and by this name I am henceforth to be known among the Chippewas."[71]

Everybody loved Mrs. Jameson, according to Mrs. Jameson, and her leave-taking was suitably emotional. She was going with the McMurrays to Penetanguishene for the annual distribution of presents there. At dawn, Ozhaawshkodewikwe and Jane, each in her own canoe, paddled across to say goodbye, with gifts. She and Mrs. Jameson "exchanged a long farewell embrace," and she "got into her little canoe . . . and handling her paddle with singular grace and dexterity, shot over the blue water, without venturing once to look back! I leaned over the side of our boat, and strained my eyes to catch a last glimpse of the white spray of the rapids, and her little canoe skimming over the expanse between, like a black dot; and this was the last I saw of my dear good Chippewa mama!"[72] She'd been with the family for about two days.

After Mrs. Jameson left, Jane wrote to Schoolcraft that it was a good thing she decided to go along with Mrs. Jameson because "I found she did not know how to get along *at all, at all*." She "cried heartily when she parted with M'a &

myself & children, she is indeed a Woman in a Thousand. George came down with her the Rapids in fine style & spirits & she insisted on being captured and named in *Indian*. . . . We named her W*a*s*a*wgewonoqu*a*, with which she was mightily pleased." Schoolcraft had written a few days previous to tell her to come home "as early as possible," but Jane stayed four or five days "with swelled feet & limbs." "By constant fermentations of vinegar & brandy they are in a better condition at present, tho' I am still unable to walk any distance. They alarmed me at first, exceedingly, for they were as thick round my ancle as my thighs usually are, yet I called *not* for the Doctor."[73]

Mrs. Jameson went on to Penetanguishene, along with Charlotte and McMurray, their little son and nurse Angelique, Waishkey's sixteen-year-old daughter—a great beauty, according to Mrs. Jameson. Angelique held a parasol while Mrs. Jameson sketched. From Manitoulin Island in Georgian Bay to Penetanguishene on the eastern shore, Louie Solomon, Charlotte's halfsister Marguerite's youngest son, then about sixteen years old, served as one of the boatmen. He'd been born at Drummond in 1821, and it's possible he was named for his uncle Lewis. Louie well remembered Mrs. Jameson when he was interviewed as an old man by one of the many gentleman historians who proliferated at the end of the century. His additional job was to be "a sort of protector" to Mrs. Jameson. He slept in her tent, separated by a sheet, but had to crawl in after she'd gone to sleep without waking her up. Louie's job was not as onerous as that of his friend Neddy McDonald, who carried Mrs. Jameson to shore on his back, a job he didn't appreciate.

Louie remembered Mrs. Jameson as kind and considerate, and she listened to him sing voyageurs' songs. There was one unfortunate incident. The party stopped at Skull Island, the site of a burial pit carved into solid rock, the result of seventeenth-century conflicts between the Anishinaabeg and Haudenosaunees. Midewiwin ceremonies were conducted there.[74] According to another man on the trip, Jean Baptiste Sylvestre, Mrs. Jameson wanted a skull, so Thomas Leduc climbed down into the pit and got one. When she put it near Jean Baptiste's feet in his canoe, he told her to take it away. She brought it into her own canoe with Louie Solomon, who remembered more than one skull. He "persuaded" her to throw them away, "as I did not fancy their company." Mrs. Jameson had no hard feelings, though; when they shook hands when parting, Louie found "four five dollar gold pieces in my hand."[75]

Jane returned to Mackinac in mid-August, with a crew of Odawa boatmen managed by herself, as George needed to take care of his children. "Nothing would give me greater pleasure than to accompany Jane and her dear little ones," George wrote to him, but Jane seemed "to place that confidence in her own management, and my own conviction of the steadiness of the crew . . . that nothing now remains but to place implicit reliance upon divine providence for their safe and speedy arrival."[76] They both knew Schoolcraft would be incensed.[77] Soon after her arrival, she received a letter from Mrs. Jameson, then in Toronto. "If I were to begin by expressing all the pain it gave me to part from you I should not know when or where to end," she wrote. "As long as I live the impression of your kindness, of your character altogether, remains to me, your image will often come back to me and I dare to hope that you will not forget me quite." She hoped Jane would write to her, despite her responsibilities. Her trip to Manitoulin and Penetanguishene had been a success. The scenery was "extraordinary" and "the wildest" she'd ever beheld. "I recall it as a dream." She needed more information about Indian women, though. After her return to Toronto she haunted the lodges there. She regretted not spending more time with Ozhaawshkodewikwe; she'd written to Charlotte asking more questions about women. She offered some initial thoughts. "I remark generally that the propinquity of the white man is destruction to the red man," she observed to Jane. "And the farther the Indians are removed from us, the better for them." She felt quite intimate with Jane. "In their own woods they are a noble race. Brought near to us, a degraded and stupid race. We are destroying them off the face of the earth," opined Mrs. Jameson. "May God forgive us our tyranny, our avarice, our ignorance—for it is very terrible to think of."[78] She would write again, she promised, before leaving in mid-September for Boston and New York.

But before she left Canada for good, Mrs. Jameson went back to Mackinac in August, apparently still looking for more information.[79] She wrote to Jane from Detroit at the end of the month, having returned to the city on the steamboat, wondering why Jane hadn't seen her off. "I lingered a few moments hoping to receive a 'parting kiss' until the sound of the second bell aroused me from my meditations and I then felt that you were perhaps too ill to see me." Her tone is much less familiar in this second letter. "It would have been extremely gratifying could we have spent more moments in sweet 'converse' but I must forbear and endeavour deeply to impress on 'Henry's tables' the few short, but interesting conversations we were permitted to enjoy." (Henry's tables were Mrs. Jameson's notebooks of choice.) Her mother and sisters enjoyed her description of the "Fairy Isle" of Mackinac, and she vowed not to open the makak of sugar Jane had given them until the first wedding in the family.

Mrs. Jameson was chagrined by the neglect. "It is asking too much to claim a reply to this and my last, but I should really enjoy a letter from you," she wrote. She seems to have spoken to Jane on her second trip about a plan she'd hatched for Jane's daughter Janée and George's daughter Louisa to attend a school her mother and sisters kept in England. "My Mother begs me to say that should you conclude upon committing your little Jane to our care you may be assured we shall receive her with *motherly* and *sisterly* affection. She will probably be our youngest Pupil and as such will of course be entitled to some *extra indulgences*. To your Niece every attention shall be paid which her melancholy situation claims." (A badly healed knee injury that had permanently disabled Louisa.) Mrs. Jameson needed them to decide. "Should they commence at an early period it will be more advantageous as our classes will be formed in a few days." She really would like an Indian Story from George.[80]

Mrs. Jameson wrote to Charlotte as well at this time to tell her that she'd begun the "little book which will be finished and printed in London this winter." "Tell me therefore any thing and every thing relative to the morals and manners of your people." By way of reassurance, she let Charlotte know that "when you tell me any thing *confidential*—put a cross before & after & it shall remain *sacred*—you will see in all my other books how scrupulous & conscientious [I am] on the subject of personal confidence."[81]

It's quite likely that Mrs. Jameson's first letter distressed Jane (along with the mysterious second episode at Mackinac) because she had Schoolcraft answer it, and he didn't write to Mrs. Jameson until November when he was in Detroit while Jane and the children spent the winter at Mackinac. "You will perceive that I have attempted what I deem no more than a just defence of the Indian female character," he wrote to Jane, enclosing a copy of the letter. Although the note implies that he composed the letter himself, the bulk of the letter's contents aren't entirely congruent with Schoolcraft in either feeling or style. It seems very likely, especially given the subject of the letter, that Jane drafted a response to Mrs. Jameson but had Schoolcraft revise what she'd written to produce a suitable reply. (It's also not clear whether he actually sent the letter as copied or at all.) Perhaps she didn't think Anna Jameson would listen to her but would her husband; Charlotte had McMurray answer a letter from Mrs. Jameson as well. The first part of the letter expresses disgust with the dehumanizing representation of Indigenous women:

> We feel a deep interest in the success of your forthcoming work on Indian female character, and at the same time, a high and confident expectation that it will dissipate many of the popular errors on this subject. With many, the Indian female is regarded merely as a domestic animal, who chops wood and draws water for her husband. The common observer has been satisfied with some passing external observations on the hardships of her condition, without inquiring whether there be any domestic felicity to repay her for her devotion to her husband and

children under these adverse circumstances—and without the means, and in too many cases, without the inclination to inquire into the truth or falsehood of existing prejudice or ignorance. That the aboriginal woman of America has a *heart*—that she has strong and deep *attachments*—has principles of *fidelity*, and an exalted conception of *her kindred and race*, which furnishes a constant theme of domestic reference and contemplative satisfaction, is, however, true. She follows her husband amid snows and tempests—she ministers to him in all his afflictions, which are neither small nor few. She nourishes his children provides them with garments by her own industry, and makes it her study, day and night, to exhibit to her lord, every attainable comfort. To spread a table, in the wilderness, is no slight task, as the Omnipotent himself has declared, but to spread it, under [these] circumstances of misery surrounding the Indian wife & mother, is certainly one of the highest efforts of female heroism and affection.[82]

Thus far, the letter is not beyond Schoolcraft's capacity, as it can be read to emphasize the submission of Indigenous women to men. But then the letter expresses some ideas unlike himself in the extreme:

Does the mercenary and stupid white man, who has just sense enough to buy and sell a pack of Beaver skins or a barrel of fish—who look on the Indian lodge and the Indian canoe, as the natural appendages of an animal, a little higher in order, than the shell fish, does he pronounce that ardent and daring help mate of her husband, without high *sentiments*—without strong *affections*? It is a gross and unjustifiable error! When the Indian mother hears her child's cry, think you not that her bosom yearns for it. When she sees her family group without a morsel to eat, think you not she feels. Or when the blast of a polar winter enters her fragile tenement, think you not, she shivers. What is the courage, the sentiment, the devotion, the domestic worth of a Christina, a Catherine, or an Elizabeth to this. I will not so far sink the modest, careful, virtuous, affectionate hunter's wife, for in the forest and remote from European attainments and vices, as to compare her, *in the primary point of female exaltation & honor*, to the Zenobias and Cleopatras, who shine on the pages of ancient history—like spangles of tinsel on a rotten sepulchre.

This was a pointed reference to Mrs. Jameson's *Characteristics of Women* (1831), and while especially after Jane's death Schoolcraft was in the habit of sentimentalizing Indigenous women as mothers and wives, denouncing a white man, any white man, as "mercenary and stupid" was quite beyond him.

It doesn't seem likely that he would have been a close reader of Mrs. Jameson's books on women, either, as his reading tended to scientific works and books by travelers like himself. The writer of this passage, wherever it originated, was very, very angry at what Mrs. Jameson had to say about Indigenous people, women in particular.

What the Schoolcrafts had to say had little or no effect on Mrs. Jameson, who was writing away in New York City, waiting for her husband's formal release before returning to London. Jane must have let Mrs. Jameson copy her letter to William Hull Clarke, because in her book Mrs. Jameson echoes the language of the letter quite closely. "A hunter goes out at dawn, knowing that, if he returns empty, his wife and little ones must *starve*," writes Mrs. Jameson.

> He comes home at sunset, spent from fatigue, and unable even to speak. His wife takes off his moccasins, places before him what food she has, or, if latterly the chase has failed, probably no food at all, or only a little parched wild-rice. She then examines his hunting-pouch, and in it she finds claws, or beak, or tongue of the game, or other indications by which she knows what it is, and where to find it. She then goes for it, and drags it home. When he is refreshed, the hunter caresses his wife and children, relates the events of the chase, smokes his pipe, and goes to sleep—to begin the same life on the following day.[83]

But Mrs. Jameson drew entirely different conclusions than what Jane intended. While Indian women weren't entirely "the absolute slave, drudge and nonentity" that they were commonly held to be, they were coarse and not at all picturesque. They were even violent. The Indian woman "is despotic in her lodge, and everything it contains is hers; even of the game her husband kills, she has the uncontrolled disposal," Mrs. Jameson writes. "If her husband does not please her, she scolds and even cuffs him; and it is in the highest degree unmanly to answer or strike her."[84] Indian women were unfeminine, then, an assessment William Robertson had made in the eighteenth century. The male travelers who preceded Mrs. Jameson were right. While Indian men were "the noblest and bravest of their kind," they thought their women were "of no account," and they were therefore "despised and oppressed." When hunting was all important, women naturally "sink" in comparison and become "a dependent drudge."[85] The best thing that you could say was that Indian women held their "true natural position relative to the state of men and the state of society."[86] This wasn't quite as awful as being an absolute drudge. An Indian woman "was sure of protection; sure of maintenance, at least while the man has it; sure of kind treatment; sure that she will never have her children taken away from her but by death; sees none better than herself, and has no conception of a superior destiny."[87]

Six Indians Visit to the Sun and Moon

Told by Wauchusco, Translated by William Johnston, Michilimackinac, ca. 1838[1]

One day five young men and a boy who was about ten years of age went out a shooting, with their bows and arrows. They had left there with the appearance of daylight and they had reached the woods, and were on a rising eminence, before the Sun rose. While they were all standing there, suddenly the Sun burst forth in all its glory of a summer's day. And it appeared to them to be only a short distance. "How very near it is," they all said. "It cannot be very far," said the eldest, "so if any of you will accompany me, we will see if we cannot reach it." "I will go; I will go"; burst from all their lips. Even the boy, he said he would go also. They told him that he was too young. But he replied, "If I do not go with you, I will mention all you intend to do to all your parents." They all then said to him, you shall go with us, so be quiet.

They then arranged it among themselves to beg from their parents as many pairs of Mockesins as they could and also new clothing of leather & they pitched on a spot, where they should conceal all their articles till they were ready to start. When they had fully decided on the course they would pursue for the future, they went home, and a long interval passed before each one could get all in readiness. And they kept it a profound secret, even to the boy. And they frequently met at their appointed rendezvous to consult. At last every thing was in readiness and they decided on a certain day for their departure. The Boy the morning they were to start shed tears for a new pair of leather leggings; he got them at last by saying, "Don't you see how my companions are drest?" This course they all had pursued, stirring up the envy and pride of their relations by pointing to the dresses of their comrades.

That morning they all pretended to start in different directions to hunt and they said they would see who would bring home the most game. They all soon met at their rendezvous where they had hidden their articles, also stone axes, knives & kettles for their journey, and as many arrows as they had time to make. They then took each something on their backs and started. They traveled day after day, through a thick wilderness but the sun was always at the same distance. "We must," said they, "travel towards Waubbononge; and we will get to him sometime or other." None was discouraged although winter overtook them; they made a lodge and hunted till they got as much dried meat as they all could carry and continued. This they done for several winters in succession, no one ever being dissatisfied or discouraged.

One day they came to a river whose waters ran towards Waubbononge. They followed it down day after day. One day while walking they came to a rising ground from whence they could see something white or clear, through the trees. Next morning they came suddenly in view, with an immense body of water; no land could be seen, as far as the eye could reach. One or two of them laid down on the beach to drink. As soon as they got the water in their mouths, they spit it out and said with surprise "Shewetaugonaubo! Salt Water." While looking on the water, again suddenly the Sun arose as if from the deep and went on its steady course through the heavens, enlivening the then wild and beautiful scenery of the east with its animating beams. They thought best to encamp and to consult whether they ought to go on or not. They said, we see that the Sun, is still on the opposite side of this great water. They all however said, "Let us continue on, we will walk round it, and follow the shore."

Next morning they started and they took the northerly shore to go around, but they made only a short distance and they came to a large river. They again encamped. While sitting before their fire they asked each other if any of them had ever dreamt of water or of walking on it. After a long silence the eldest said he had and soon after they laid down to sleep. Next morning the eldest said, "We have done wrong in having come north, for last night my spirit appeared to me and told me to go south and that but a short distance from where we left yesterday, we would see a river with high banks and by looking off of which we should see an Island and that Island will approach the main land. And he said we should all get on it. He told me to cast my eyes towards the waters and I done so. And I saw all as he said. Day after tomorrow is the time he said we must go south from hence for I believe, it will happen just as he told me, in my dream."

They then retraced their footsteps and towards evening they reached the river that the elder had dreamt of. It had high banks and behind which they encamped and there patiently waited for the expected fulfillment of the elder one's dream. The day after tomorrow arrived and they all said, "We will see if that will be seen, midday is the promised time." They were in great anxiety; two had been on the look out since the rising of the sun. They suddenly cried out: "There it is, there it is." They all rushed to the spot and they did behold something like an Island advancing steadily towards the shore. It had now approached so near that they could see that something was moving on it in various directions. They said, "It is a Moneto let us be off into the woods." "No, No," cried the eldest, "let us stay and watch." It now became stationary and the height of the imaginary Island disappeared and they now saw only three trees as they thought, resembling trees on a pinery that had been burnt. The wind also had been off the lake, but now it had died away into a perfect calm. They now saw something leaving the Island and coming towards the mouth of the river and throwing and flexing its wings on the water, like a loon when he attempts to fly in calm weather. It approached and entered the river. They were for running away but the eldest dissuaded them. "Let us hide in this hollow," he said, "and we will see what it can be." They done so; it was near the river.

Soon they heard someone creeping and they soon heard several trees fall; when suddenly and unexpectedly a person came up to where they were. He stood still looking at them with utter amazement. So did they. They were perfectly surprised; he had something on his head and he had his ax in his hand. After looking at them some time he advanced and extended his hand towards them. The eldest took it and they shook hands. He then spoke, but they could not understand each other. He then cried out for his comrades. They soon came and they examined the dresses & very minutely of the new found beings. They again tried to converse. They then motioned to the Naubequan and to the Naubequanance, wishing them to embark.[2] The travelers consulted but a short time and the eldest motioned that they would go. They then went into the little Boat, which they found to be loaded with wood, and they all embarked.

When they reached the side of the supposed Island how surprised were they to see a number of people on it & who all came to the side and looked at them with open mouths. One spoke out, above the others, and they were motioned to get on board. The one who spoke appeared to be the leader. He looked and examined them and took them down into the cabin and set things before them to eat and he treated them very kindly. When they came on deck again, all the sails were spread and they were fast losing sight of land. In the course of the night and the following day they were sick at stomach, but they soon got over it. When they had been out at sea ten days, they were sorry. And as they could not converse with those who had hats on, the following night the elder dreamt, that his spirit appeared to him and who told him not to be discouraged and that he would open his ears so that he could understand all what the people with hats said to them. "I will not permit you to understand much," said the Spirit; "only sufficient, so that you can ask for your wants. And also sufficient to know what they say to you." He told all to his friends, and they were satisfied and encouraged.

When they had been out about thirty days the leader told them and motioned to them to change their dress of leather for such as they had on (or if they did not his master would be displeased) (it was here that the eldest first understood a few words of what was said to them) (which was *La que notte* and from one word to another soon was capable of understanding and of being understood). One day they cried out, "Land." And soon after they heard a sound like thunder and soon after another peal, as they thought of thunder. When they had got over their fear they were shown the pieces of cannon, which made such a noise. Soon after they saw a vessel smaller than their own sailing out of Bay and came towards them. She had flags on her masts and when she came near she fired a shot and the large vessel also hoisted her flags. And a boat came along side and the leader told them that he had six strangers on board and that such had never been seen before and told them to go and tell their master or King. The small vessel ran into the Bay (and soon after they heard peal on peal of cannon fired off). And it was some time before the large [ship] got near the City; it was then dark, but they could see people standing and horses & carts & wagons.

Soon after they were taken on shore and placed in a covered wagon and driven off. At last they stopped, and they were taken into a large splendid room. They then were told that the great chief wished to see them. They were shown into a very large room filled with men and women, all the room was Show-neau-cau-da.[3] The Chief then asked them their business, where they were from and where they were going. He tried to dissuade them, telling them what trials and difficulties they would have to undergo and that so many days march from his country was a bad Spirit or Moneto who foretold and foresaw all who entered into his country. "And it will be impossible," he said, "my children for you ever to arrive at the object you are in search of." The eldest spoke, "Nosa" he said, and they could see the Chief blushed in being called father. He continued on speaking that he might get over his shame. "We have come so far on our way and we will continue on. We will do so for we think our lives are of no value, for we have given them up for this object. *Nosa*, do not then prevent us from going on our way." The Chief said he appointed next day to speak to them again and he dismissed them with valuable presents and he had provided for them every thing they needed or wished for. Next day came & they were again summoned to appear before the King. He again tried to dissuade them; he said he would send them back to their country again in one of his ships. But all he said had no effect. "Well," said he, "since you will go, I will furnish all your needs for your journey." He had every thing provided for them and he told them three days before they reached the bad Spirit he had spoken of they would hear his Sheshegwon.[4] He told them to be wise for that he felt he should never see them again.

They left and traveled some time through villages but they soon left them behind and forest and plains commenced. They found every thing they saw—trees, animals, birds—entirely different from what they had been accustomed to see on the other side of the great waters. They traveled and traveled till they wore out all the clothing that had been given them and they had to take to their leather clothing again. The three days the chief spoke of meant three years, for it was only at the end of the third that they could hear the noise of the spirit Sheshegwon. The sounds appeared to be near but still they continued on day after day for a long time. Still the sound appeared to be at the same distance. Suddenly they came to a plain that was very extensive. They could only see the blue ridges rising above the horizon of the opposite mountains. They pushed on, for they thought they would get there before dark, but they were soon overtaken by it. And they were now on a stony part of the plain that was covered by about a foots' depth of water. They were weary and fatigued. Some of them said, "Let us lie down." "No, No," said the others, "Let us push on." They did so & soon they stood on firm ground. But it was as much as they could do to stand.

They however made preparations to encamp and they had got their fire lit and they had eaten and then they commencing conversing about the sound of the Sheshegwon, that they had not heard it for some time. When suddenly the rattle commenced, it sounded as if it was subterranean & it shook the ground. It sounded as if it was only a few yards from them. They tied up their bundles and went towards the spot. They soon came to a very extensive building and it was all illuminated. As soon as they got to the door there came out rather an elderly man, who said, "How do you do, my grandsons; walk in; walk in; I am glad to see you. I knew when you started and the object of your journey and I saw you encamping. Sit down and tell me the news of the country you left for I feel interested in it." They told him all about it and even presented him with a piece of Tobacco. He then told them of their future journey and that they would accomplish their object. "I don't say all of you," he said; "you have got over the three fourths of your way. And I will tell you how you will do, when you get to the edge of the earth. Soon after you leave this you will hear a deafening sound; it is the sky descending on the edge but it keeps moving up and down. You will watch and when it moves up, you will see a vacant space between it and the earth. You must not be afraid; a chasm of awful depth is there which separates the unknown from this earth and a veil of darkness conceals it. Fear not, you must leap through it, and if you succeed you will find yourselves on a beautiful plain and in a soft and mild light emitted by the moon." They thanked him for his advice.

"I have told you the way," he said; "now tell me again of the country you left, for I committed dreadful ravages there. Does not the country show marks of it and do not the inhabitants tell of me to their children? I came out this place to mourn over my bad actions and to try by my present course of life to relieve my mind of the load that is on it." They told him that their fathers spoke often of Manahbosho. "I will now tell you; I am he"; and they looked at him with astonishment and fear. "Do you see this pointed house," he said; pointing to one that resembled a sugar loaf. "You now each can speak out your wishes and desires and you will be answered from that house." Speak; ask what you each want and it shall be granted." One of them who was vain asked with some presumption that he might live for ever and never be in want. He was answered you wish shall be granted. The second and he also received the same answer as the first. The third asked to live longer than common people and to be always successful in his war excursions and not ever to lose one of his young men. He was told: your wishes are granted. The fourth made the same request and he received the same reply. The fifth made a humble request asking to live as long as men generally do and that he might be successful in hunting so that he might provide for his parents and relations. The sixth made the same request and it was granted in pleasing tones from the pointed house.

After this they got ready to start. They were told by Manahbosho that they had been there upwards of a year and they were just ready to start, when Manahbosho said, "Stop. You two who asked for eternal life, your wishes will be granted immediately." He spoke and one was turned into a stone called Shingaubawossin to remain till the end of time. The other also into a red cedar tree and it stood near the sugar loaf temple. "Now," said he to the rest, "you can go." They left him in fear, saying we are fortunate to escape so, for the King told us he was wicked and that we would not probably escape from him.

Soon after leaving they heard the sound of the beating sky they continued on, bent on accomplishing their object. After a long interval, they had got near and the sound was stunning to their senses, for when the sky came down its pressure would force gusts of wind from the opening so strong that it was with difficulty that they could keep their feet, and he, the Sun, passed but a short distance over their heads. They however approached boldly and they had to wait some time before they could exert energy sufficient to leap through the darkness that covered the passage to the other world. The sky would come down with violence but it would rise slowly and gradually. The two who had made the humble requests stood near the edge and they one after another with great exertion leapt through and succeeded in gaining a firm footing. The remaining two were fearful and undecided. The others spoke to them through the darkness, saying, "Leap, leap; the sky is on its way down." Those two looked up and saw it descending, but fear paralyzed their effort and they made but a feeble attempt. They only could reach with their hands the opposite side. The sky at the same moment struck the earth with a terrible and deafening sound & they were forced into that dreadful black chasm.

The other two found themselves in a beautiful country. The light was mild & pleasant and they could see the moon approaching, as if it was coming from behind a hill. They advanced and an old woman spoke to them, who appears mild & white, but she looked rather old, and she spoke to them in a very kind manner. They knew from this that she was the moon. She asked them several questions and she told them that she knew of their coming and was happy to see them, and she told them, that they were half way to her brother's and that from the earth, to her, was half the distance. "I will have leisure, I will go and conduct you to my brother's by and by for he is now absent, on his daily course," she said. "You will succeed in your object and you will return in safety to your country and friends with the good wishes, I am sure, of my brother." While there she treated them to every thing they needed. And soon after she said, "My brother is now rising from below and we will soon see his light, as he comes over that distant edge. Come," she said, "I will lead you up." They started, and in some way or other ascended directly up, something like ascending steps.

They then came to an immense plain declining towards the direction, that he, the Sun, was approaching. When he came near, she, the moon, spoke: "I have brought you these persons that we knew were coming." And with that she disappeared. He the Sun motioned with his hand for them to follow him, which they did. They found it difficult as the way was ascending and rather steep at first. That was from the edge of the earth till they got half way between that and midday. When there, He, the Sun stopped and sat down to rest. "What, my children, has brought you here? I could not speak to you before. I could not stop any place but at this, for this is my first resting place; then at the center, which is at midday then half way from that to the western edge. Tell me all, what first induced you to perform this journey, what has happened to you on the way, tell me all."

They done so; they said their main object was to see him and that they had lost four of their friends and they wished to know if they could return to the earth, and tell their relatives and friends, all that they had seen and asked him to grant their former wishes. "Yes, certainly," he said, "yours shall be granted, and you shall return in safety. But your companions were vain and presumptuous in their demands. They were Gau ge bau de sewog.[5] That was the cause of their losing their lives; they aspired to what only Monetos could enjoy. But you two, as I said, you will return and you will be as happy as a hunter's life can make you and you shall never be in want of any thing as long as you will be permitted to live and you will have the satisfaction of telling the mortals below of your journey and also of me."

"Follow me; follow me," he said, commencing his course again. The ascent was now gradual and they soon came to a level plain; they traveled some time and he sat down again to rest, which was at midday. "You see if it is level," he said; "at this place but a short distance from this, my way descends gradually to my last resting place; and from there, there is a steep descent. But that is not it. You wish to return, your wishes are granted, come here quick," he said, and placed them on something and they commenced descending. "I grant all your wishes," said the Sun and started from his resting place. But they kept descending as if they were let down by ropes.

In the meantime these young men's parents dreamt that their sons were returning and that they would soon see them. They placed the utmost confidence in their visions and they left their lodges early in the morning for a certain, and very remote forest, for it was there they expected to meet them. They were not long there before they saw them coming, for they had descended a short distance from there. The young men knew it was their fathers. They met; and happy was that meeting. They told all about their journey, all that had befallen them. And they now showed their gratitude to the different Monetos for their preservation by feasting and offering gifts to them, for their safe arrival among their parents and relations.

It is hardly necessary to remark, that Indians speaking of the Sun consider it as animate and the same in regard to the Moon, which they consider as feminine. They take this idea from its mild and pleasant rays and its appearance being so much below the effulgent glory of the Sun. Or in the same light that a woman is held by the Indians of the Upper Mississippi; when compared to a Brave Warrior (Gitchy dau) one who has led a war party, taken a scalp or a prisoner, all of which feats shine so much above the more gentle qualities of the woman in their estimation. And which answers the idea of the Sun & Moon.

Chapter 9

Wauchusco and the Spirits

Before Schoolcraft left for Detroit in the fall of 1837, he and Jane exchanged watches and watch chains, symbolizing, he wrote to her later, "the golden chain of matrimony" that bound them forever despite their being apart so often.[1] He also, by his own account, held a council in September with the Ojibwes and Odawas where he presented additional claims for payment by the Johnston Estate, James Schoolcraft, William McMurray, and George Johnston. According to himself, later, those claims were accepted. There is no other record of this council, however. What is verifiable is that several traders and the Johnston Estate presented additional debt claims totaling $106,000 to Commissioner of Indian Affairs Carey A. Harris in October 1837. Schoolcraft recommended that $40,000 of the amount be paid, including the claims made by the estate and members of the family. Harris determined immediately that the Johnston claims were beyond the scope of the treaty and thus not allowed, but he referred all of the claims to John W. Edmonds, who had been a treaty commissioner in the summer of 1836. In March 1838, Edmonds filed a report with Harris, agreeing that Schoolcraft was right to disallow claims by the fur traders Edward Biddle and John Drew, Rix Robinson, and Samuel Abbott, but rather than refuse Schoolcraft's claims outright, he deferred them until a general council of the Ojibwes and Odawas could be assembled. This would seem to indicate that the September 1837 council either didn't happen or wasn't valid for some reason. Schoolcraft claimed $8,200.36 for the Johnston Estate and $1,585.36 for James Schoolcraft. The $8,200.36 was Schoolcraft's account of the losses suffered when Lieutenant Holmes looted and burned the Johnston warehouses and home in 1814. Like the stories, any debt the Johnstons could potentially claim Schoolcraft regarded as his own and he wanted that money.[2]

By the end of 1838 he needed it. Historians describe the Panic of 1837 as mainly the effect of too much cotton. Because cotton was such a large part of the US economy, and speculation, in cotton and in land, was rampant in the period leading up to the panic, the entire US economy (despite a brief recovery in 1838) was sunk into a depression that lasted until the early 1840s. Indigenous land was at the heart of this speculation. As Jackson made treaties with Indigenous nations across the South (Cherokee, Choctaw, Chickasaw, Creek, Seminole), millions of acres were opened up to plantation agriculture.

Cotton planters bought land and supplies, including human beings, on credit, against the coming harvest; they sold their cotton in Britain and France to textile manufacturers who bought cotton on credit against the profits they would make from the finished product. Enslaved people and the land they worked were so productive that by 1834 the price of cotton began declining and by 1836 there was so much cotton on hand in Britain that the Bank of England began denying loans to the textile manufacturers there. They were buying no new cotton then, in Britain or in France, and when the Americans received the news, by March 1837, "arrays of interlinked debtors and creditors began to cascade down," writes historian Edward Baptist.[3]

As a result of treaty-making, the federal government had millions of acres of land to sell not just in the South but in the Old Northwest, so much so that in 1836, profits from the sale of Indigenous land were the federal government's largest source of income.[4] Politics obliged the government to sell the land quickly, and credit was readily available because Jackson shut down the Bank of the United States, leading to a proliferation of local banks happy to lend money with little or no regulation. As Schoolcraft was finishing up with the Treaty of Washington in the summer of 1836, public land was being sold at the rate of five million dollars' worth a month.[5] To slow down speculation and against his advisers' wishes, Jackson decreed that beginning in August 1836 the sale of public land would have to be paid for in gold or silver. As a result, land sales declined and banks began charging fees for using gold and silver, driving up the cost of everything.[6]

A frenzy for land had overtaken Michigan Territory in the 1830s—in 1836, more Indigenous land was sold to settlers in Michigan than had been sold in the entire United States in 1833.[7] Schoolcraft participated in that frenzy when he traveled to Green Bay to buy Menominee land in the summer of 1835. The boom made all land more valuable; between 1830 and 1836, the value of all real estate in the United States rose 150 percent.[8] Investors believed that the value of land could only go up and behaved accordingly. Baptist writes that Americans fell into a kind of "disaster myopia" in the 1830s—nobody believed that anything bad could happen until it inevitably did.[9]

Just before disaster struck, Schoolcraft invested all of the family's money in Detroit real estate. He also took out loans to buy even more. In the winter of 1836–37 he bought lots in Detroit worth $21,000, then put much of his own and the rest of the family's money, along with that of other investors who included C. C. Trowbridge and Henry Whiting, into two former farms that consisted of undeveloped land fronting the Detroit River and extending back into what would become the center of the city. (These were "ribbon farms," a narrow strip extending back from the river bank, following French practice.) One of these, the Cass Front, had been bought by Lewis Cass in 1816.

Schoolcraft thought he had bought shares in Cass's concern, but he'd only bought a right to a share of the profit should the land be sold, and he was still obligated to pay Cass interest on the principal of the loan through which he purchased his share of the scheme as well as taxes on the land.[10]

Everyone in the family had made plans based on the idea that the income from the real estate would be available to them. Requests to Schoolcraft for disbursements from the expected real estate income came from William, George, Eliza, and their mother after 1837.[11] James Schoolcraft, who'd left the Sault for Detroit with Anna Maria in the summer of 1837 on account of what he described as his "colic," bought a farm near Detroit and had a house built, only to lose it in 1838.[12] George had sent his two sons, John George and Henry William, to Detroit to attend a school run by Washington Alswon Bacon. The boys boarded with Mr. Bacon, who reported them to be good scholars and good boys who helped around the house. "I like my school very well," wrote Henry William; "we study arithmetic, Geography, read, write, spell, and *write composition*." They went to church with Schoolcraft when he was in the city— he had a pew, while Mr. Bacon didn't—and their uncle James even gave them a dollar to buy ice skates.[13] All seemed well for a time, until the money to pay Mr. Bacon came due and there was nothing forthcoming. Mr. Bacon's pleas for payment changed from "Friend Johnston" to "Mr. Johnston Sir" by the summer of 1838. He was in the same position as everyone else, he wrote to George; his money was tied up in land, but land had no value and his creditors had to be paid. He had competitors in the school business, namely, at the university, and he wondered whether he could continue at all.[14] Then he became ill in the summer and had to close the school temporarily anyway, and the boys went home to the Sault.[15]

The winter rounds of letter-writing commenced. William passed the news along to George that winter that Audrain had died at Fort Gibson in Indian Territory. After being dismissed from Sault Ste. Marie when the department budget was cut, he'd gone to Fort Gibson to teach Choctaw children, paid for out of the tribe's annuities, but was dismissed for being a drunk. Poor Mrs. Audrain had to send her four children to live with different officers and was pregnant with a fifth; later she'd return to the Sault for the birth.[16] William wondered whether George might want to keep a store with him at Mackinac.[17] McMurray wrote to both Jane and Schoolcraft to tell them he was giving up the missionary business. "I think my services would be more beneficial amongst the whites," he wrote to the Schoolcrafts. "The Indians have of late given themselves over to drink, which is very discouraging, particularly when one is endeavouring to do all in their power for them: not only so, but the non-performance of the promises made to them by the Government had made them dissatisfied, so that there is little pleasure in remaining and little good to be expected if one did so."[18] He and Charlotte would leave in the spring.[19] He didn't mention how Charlotte felt about the plan.

McMurray relayed messages to Jane from Ozhaawshkodewikwe, who'd spent most of September with her daughter. When she returned to the Sault, she sent down a friend of hers, O-ge-she-au-bon-o-qua (Angelique Pelletier), to look after Jane over the winter.[20] This was likely Ozhaawshkodewikwe's way of getting around Schoolcraft's desire to keep Jane away from her and shows the level of concern she had for Jane's health.[21] "Mamma sends her compliments to Mrs. Peltier [sic] and feels happy that she is remaining with you, and she desires you to say to her, that she wishes her to take good care of you, and that she places as much confidence in her doing so, as if she were herself present," McMurray wrote for Ozhaawshkodewikwe early in January.[22] When Jane wrote to her mother later that month about her illnesses and anxieties, Ozhaawshkodewikwe again replied through McMurray. "Mamma desires me to say to you for her, that she was delighted to hear from you and that you are still able to write; no less delighted to hear from all her absent children that they were in tolerable health, and that those who were laid in a bed of sickness were fast recovering.... She desires you to take courage and not to despair at the departure of Mr. S this winter: God will take care of him and return him to you as heretofore.... She feels pleased that you have Mrs. Peleteir [sic] ... and feels that she will assist you as much as in her power."[23] Mrs. Pelletier was likely skilled in the "Indian medicine" that Ozhaawshkodewikwe regularly administered to Jane.

In mid-January Jane wrote Schoolcraft about what she described as heart palpitations and an "Obstruction," again, for which she needed medication.[24] She asked Schoolcraft to get her digitalis—he tried to get Zina Pitcher's opinion of it (Pitcher had left the army and set up as a physician in Detroit), but Pitcher was never home.[25] She wrote to McMurray for laudanum—he, too, had difficulty finding a physician and didn't have much laudanum on hand himself. He sent the small bottle that he did have, some opium, and a recipe: to the two ounces of opium he sent, add one quart of "the strongest high wines or whiskey," let stand fourteen days and then filter with common brown paper. If necessary, however, "it may ... be used the second day."[26]

Adding to Jane's physical and mental distress, her household was disordered. William and Susan were expecting their first child in the spring, and he was not as attentive as he usually was. Louisa Piquette had become "*impudent & assuming*" in Schoolcraft's absence "& slams the door in my face whilst speaking to her, & does as she pleases."[27] (Louisa was sixteen at the time and the Schoolcrafts had some responsibility for her, as Schoolcraft reassured Jane that he would bring a couple back with him in the spring to work in the house and they could find another place for Louisa at Mackinac.)[28] Schoolcraft sent his unemployed nephew Francis Shearman to Mackinac for the winter to teach the children because the mission school had closed, but Francis was soon in the habit of wandering the village at all hours, staying out until late at night and leaving the children unattended during the day. In November Jane reported that the children told her Francis declared himself "sick of the place & had a great mind to return to Detroit."[29] He didn't.

Francis was assigned the patriarch's task of reading scripture at the Presbyterian church on Sunday, which William reported he did with good attendance, but Jane had heard he'd attempted lording it over others in town, "both in public & *private*," and when she questioned him about it, he said that he had been doing perfectly fine in Detroit and had only come to Mackinac because Schoolcraft made him and that his mother had warned him not to do it. He spent most of his daytime hours with the old trader Edward Biddle, who "*fascinated* him," Jane wrote, "& when I send the children in the office to write or cipher or spell, he sends them out, saying 'you disturb me, I have other business.'" His own father had warned them, she reminded Schoolcraft, when he'd told them both that Francis "*can gamble the truth when it suits his convenience.*"[30] As he did when James made a nuisance of himself, Schoolcraft downplayed Jane's complaints. It was only a "partial" neglect of the children, and Francis's distractedness was probably attributable to the literary journal for which he was engaged in collecting material—and so entirely understandable.[31]

Schoolcraft spent his time in Detroit drawing up additional treaties and finalizing others—this and the administration of annuities and other payments were virtually all his job entailed after 1836. He did find the time to propose a system of Indian names for the counties, towns, and villages of the new state of Michigan and to publish *Iosco, or the Vale of Norma*, a long poem about his childhood home in Albany, with Indians. As he was a regent of the new University of Michigan and president of the Michigan Historical Society, he had duties associated with those endeavors, too. While he was out and about he attended a series of ten lectures on phrenology given by Joshua Toulmin Smith, a young Englishman, along with Zina Pitcher and the other "men of education & strong mental powers" of the town, according to Mrs. Toulmin Smith in the diary she wrote with her husband.[32] They were honeymooning in America, collecting skulls and giving lectures.

Pitcher had developed an interest in skull collecting and associated activities by the time he returned to Michigan. While he was stationed at Fort Gibson the craniologist Samuel George Morton wrote from Philadelphia asking for his aid in procuring specimens. Pitcher shipped Morton a whole skeleton and a number of skulls—he seems to have had these on hand when Morton inquired. These skulls belonged to an Osage man named Buffalo Tail, a unknown Shawnee person (Pitcher had acquired the skull in his travels), and an unnamed pregnant Delaware woman who died in a village near the fort. The skeleton was a Creek man named Bill Fifer, who fought for the United States in the Creek War and over whose deathbed Pitcher presided.[33] After his grave-robbing expeditions, Schoolcraft's interest in phrenology had been sharpened. He was so impressed with Toulmin Smith, he gave him the skull of Etowigezhik, a Saginaw man who'd been killed at the trader and interpreter Henry Conner's farm some years previous.[34] He also had this skull on hand, in his office.

"I have had numerous requests from your friends, from time to time, to tell you things, such as births, marriages, &c," Schoolcraft remarked to Jane, "but now that I wish to recall them I can scarcely recollect a fact." Instead he rebuked her for her disinterest in an ongoing revolt in Upper Canada that had found much support in the United States. "I would have you possess acquaintance with the general political occurrences of *the age*, and particularly of *our own country*," he wrote; "I deprecate the *study* of politics by ladies, but . . . There is a great difference between making political events a *study*, and having a general *acquaintance* with them." "Every mother should know her rights, & be able to tell her children theirs," he continued. "That country is *freest*, and the state of society the most *refined & exalted* where female intellect is cultivated, and all its powers matured & brought out, by varied instruction, and a vigorous habit of correct thought." He'd sent a copy of *Mothers Magazine* by the last express on exactly this topic.[35]

At Mackinac, Francis copied over the stories Jane and William were writing to send on to Detroit, including "Mon-daw-min; or, the Origin of Indian Corn."[36] He thought the story "a good one," he wrote to Schoolcraft, but it was "too much anglicised. It strikes me, that the manatoo must have been instructed perilously in the English notions to some extent, little though it may have been—or perhaps the idea originates with me, on account of the verbal construction." Francis much preferred William's "very fine stories"—William had read them to him—that he would soon be sending.[37] Francis irritated Jane, and it seems that the story did, too. "I hope it will please you better than it did him," Jane wrote to Schoolcraft about the story. "I was almost tempted to throw it into the fire after I read it to him & copy the remark he made but I send it to *you*, as it is, he has been accustomed to write out some of the storys William collected so full of majic &c that he imagines there is no such sentiments among the Indian tribes."[38]

William's best stories, the "very fine" ones most full of "majic," were told by Wauchusco, who had died in September 1837. Schoolcraft described him as a small man, not more than five foot four, and "of very light make." His "expression of cunning and knowingness" gave him his name, which translated as "muskrat." People thought that "he resembled the muskrat, just rising from the water, after a dive."[39] He wore a blue broadcloth coat with yellow metal buttons, dark trousers, a vest, hat, and moccasins. In old age he used a cane.[40] At the time of Wauchusco's death in September 1837, he was living in a house built for him on Round Island, the site of Featherstonhaugh and Schoolcraft's grave-robbing expedition two summers previous.[41] Schoolcraft writes in his memoirs that he sent over the interpreter to bury Wauchusco, and if this is true, that was William, with whom Wauchusco was close.[42] He was more than seventy years old, having been a young boy around the time the more recent village was abandoned in the 1760s.[43]

Every time Schoolcraft mentioned Wauchusco in any of his books, he insisted that Wauchusco repudiated the spirits as satanic and threw them off entirely on professing Christianity. Schoolcraft never quoted Wauchusco directly. Wauchusco "attributed all his ability in the deceptive arts, to the agency of the Evil Spirit," Schoolcraft wrote. "He believed, that he had followed a lying spirit, whose object was to deceive the Indians, and make them miserable. . . . This is the theory drawn from his replies."[44] Jane probably wrote down Wauchusco's story after the family moved to Mackinac; it has mainly to do with overcoming the power that alcohol had over him. His account begins with his wife's having had "*four* long talks" with him on God, sin, and the Bible prior to his conversion. He came to understand what she was talking about, and although he was wary that the missionaries had sent her to convert him, still he felt unsatisfied with "my old way of life." His wife paid special attention to his drinking, "which I was very fond of."[45]

> The first time that I felt I was a sinner, and that I was in danger of being punished for sin, by God, is clearly in my mind. I was then on an island, making sugar, with my wife. I was in a conflict of mind, and hardly knew what I was about. I walked around the kettles, and did not know what I walked for. I felt sometimes, like a person wishing to cry, but I thought it would be unmanly to cry. For the space of two weeks, I felt in this alarmed and unhappy mood. It seemed to me sometimes, as if I *must* die. My heart and my bones felt as if they would burst and fall asunder. My wife asked me if I was sick, and said I looked pale. I was in an agony of body and mind, especially during *one* week. It seemed,

during this time, as if an Evil Spirit haunted me. When I went out to gather sap, I felt conscious that this Spirit went with me. It appeared to animate my own shadow.

My strength was failing under this conflict. One night, after I had been busy all day, my mind was in great distress. This shadowy influence seemed to me, to persuade me to go to sleep. I was tired, and I wished to rest, but I could not sleep. I began to pray. I kneeled down and prayed to God. I continued to pray, through the night. I then lay down, and went to sleep. Here I date my peace. In the morning my wife awoke me, telling me it was late. When I awoke I felt placid and easy in mind. My distressing fullness had also left me. I asked my wife what day it was. She told me it was the Sabbath (in the Indian, prayer-day). I replied, how I wish I could go to church at the Mission. Formerly, I used to avoid it, and shunned those who wished to speak to me of praying to God, but now my heart longs to go there. This feeling did not leave me.[46]

It was "as if an Evil Spirit" was goading him, Wauchusco says, not "the" Evil Spirit as Schoolcraft told it. When Wauchusco went to the mission, "my first feeling when I landed, was Pity for my drunken brethren," and he and the other Indigenous converts prayed "that they might also be brought to . . . find peace through God's Son."[47] This recalls the "power-control belief system" Mary Black Rogers described. Individuals sought to be "in control" of themselves, Black Rogers wrote, or "*not to be controlled* by [their] environment—'environment' including other people as well as other natural beings or forces that could affect one's outcomes and render one helpless."[48] Alcohol had power over Wauchusco, and he found that a relationship with evangelical Christian belief allowed him to right the balance, to regain control over his body and his environment. His conversion itself, usually a moment of high drama in these kinds of narratives, occurred when he was asleep.

Despite being a Christian in good standing for the last ten years of his life, Wauchusco never repudiated in the power of the spirits. This can be known because in the 1850s William wrote a now-lost history of Mackinac Island, an excerpt from which he gave in 1860 to W. P. Strickland, a minister who wrote an early book catering to the vacationing white people who would soon displace the fisheries as the fisheries had displaced the fur trade in the island's economy. He writes that he visited Wauchusco "a few days previous to his death." They lit their pipes, and William said to him, "Ne-me-sho-miss, (my grandfather), you are now very old and feeble; you cannot expect to live many days; now, tell me the truth, who was it that moved your chees-a-kee lodge when you practiced your spiritual art." Wauchusco paused, William writes, and then answered, "Nosis, as you are in part of my nation, I will tell you the truth. I know that I will die soon. He had fasted for ten days, he told William, and "while my body was feeble from long fasting, my soul increased in its powers."

> It appeared to embrace a vast extent of space, and the country within this space, was brought plainly before my vision with its misty forms and beings—I speak of my spiritual vision. It was, while I was thus lying in a trance, my soul wandering in space, that animals, some of frightful size and form, serpents of monstrous size, and birds of different varieties and plumage, appeared to me and addressed me in human language, proposing to act as my guardian spirits. While my mind embraced these various moving forms, a superior intelligence in the form of a man, surrounded by a wild, brilliant light, influenced my soul to select one of the bird-spirits, resembling the kite in look and form, to be the emblem of my guardian spirit, upon whose aid I was to call in time of need, and that he would be always prepared to render me assistance whenever my body and soul should be prepared to receive manifestations.[49]

This narrative was published after Schoolcraft had ceased publishing himself but was well known for his multivolume Indian history, which stood as an official government account. He continued to invoke Wauchusco's confession of satanic influence in that series. William wanted to make sure that Wauchusco's account of his powers and refutation of what Schoolcraft had to say about them made it into print.

Wauchusco described how he was called upon to use his powers to divine the future in the fall of 1815. When the winter's shipment of goods was a month overdue and the window for travel on Lake Huron was fast closing, the new US agent at Fort Mackinac called on Wauchusco to perform the shaking tent ceremony to find out what was going on. Whether or not the agent was serious about this request, Wauchusco fasted and prepared a lodge constructed of saplings covered with skins, drawn tight to form a pyramid shape, the saplings a particular number and each a different kind of wood. Then, covered in cloth and bound up tightly, he was placed in the lodge.[50] Both Indigenous people and whites surrounded the lodge. "I had no sooner commenced shaking my rattle and chanting when the spirits arrived," he said.

> The rustling noise they made through the air, was heard, and the sound of their voices was audible to all. The spirits directed my mind toward the southern end of Lake Huron—it lay before me with its bays and islands; the atmosphere looked hazy, resembling our Indian Summer; my vision terminated a little below the mouth of St. Clair River—there lay

the vessel, disabled! The sailors were busy repairing the spars and sails. My soul knew that they would be ready in two days, and that in seven days she would reach this Island, (Mackinaw,) by the south channel [at that time an unusual route,][51] and I so revealed it to the inquirers. On the day I mentioned the schooner hove in sight, by the south channel.

The captain of the ship confirmed Wauchusco's vision.

"This is the truth," Wauchusco told William: "I possessed a power, or a power possessed me, which I cannot explain or fully describe to you. I never attempted to move the lodge by my own physical powers—I held communion with supernatural beings or souls, who acted upon my soul or mind, revealing to me the knowledge which I have related to you."[52] "I could enumerate many instances in which this power has been exhibited among our Indians," William added. Healers like Wauchusco "had the power of influencing the mind of an Indian at a distance for good or evil, even to the deprivation of life among them: so also in cases of rivalship, as hunters or warriors. This influence was even extended to things material, while in the hands of those influenced. The soul or mind—perhaps nervous system of the individual, being powerfully acted upon by a spiritual battery, greater than the one possessed more or less by all human beings."[53] Given Schoolcraft's interest in Wauchusco it seems likely that he either read this account, if it was written at the time William spoke to Wauchusco, or he was familiar with what Wauchusco had to say.

Wauchusco gave William at least four and as many as seven of the stories in the collection. The story William titled "Shagwonabee" and that Schoolcraft published as "Wassamo, or The Fire Plume," features Wauchusco's favored structure, a story within a story, and a prominent place given to women, which was not the case with most of the other stories that William wrote down, as well as a trip to (and return from) a celestial world. In this story, two cousins go out fishing, and while one sleeps, the other finds two beautiful women in the forest laughing, at which he falls down senseless. He wakes up in the sky world to Old Spirit Man, who is the spirit of the Grand Sable Dunes on Lake Superior, telling him that he wants Shagwonabee to marry his elder daughter, despite the fact that she'd been promised to "the spirit who rules all Islands, that are out in the lakes" and was "guardian of waterfalls, rapids, rivers, &c."[54] After the marriage, because the people below had not been making proper offerings at the sand banks, Old Spirit Man sends his daughter and son-in-law down to get tobacco. When Shagwonabee and his wife return having accomplished their mission, Old Spirit Man consults with the other spirits and they agree to make Shagwonabee a spirit as well, then they send him and his wife down for one last visit. At the end of that visit, William describes the people sitting on the banks waiting for them to finally leave for the sky world. "The day was mild, the sky was clear of clouds, not a breath of wind to disturb the blue surface of the water," William writes. "Not a whisper was heard. Shagwonabee and his wife waded out, into the water waving their hands. His parents, relations, all, one and all raised their voices and wept aloud. They looked; but Shagwonabee and his wife had disappeared forever."[55]

In an afterword Schoolcraft wrote that this story "opens a chapter in Indian demonology," but he had no further analysis to offer. He felt compelled to note that "Chusco" (Schoolcraft always called him this) possessed authentic knowledge, having "acquired notoriety and power . . . from the successful display of these arts," but that he was still a Christian who, again, "continued to affirm to the last, that his power as a Jossakeed, or juggler, was derived from a *direct energy* communicated by the Great Evil Spirit."[56] Schoolcraft's persistent need to say that Wauchusco repudiated the spirits is like his denial that women ever became healers when he was well acquainted with Ogeewyahnokwotokwa. He believed that the spirits were real because he'd been told and possibly had even been a witness to them himself, but as in his lifelong rewriting of Jane he kept telling the story the way he needed it to be. The stories demonstrated that Indigenous spirituality was evil, an unequivocal and active rejection of Christianity, therefore Wauchusco must actively repudiate the spirits. He also characterized the stories as "Oriental," which was another way of saying the same thing in that, in his version of the lost tribes story, Indigenous people rejected proto-Christianity when they became "lost." Another of Wauchusco's stories, written by William as "Story of Meshsegenebigo" and published as "Iamo, or the Undying Head," required two pages of Schoolcraft's insisting that it demonstrated that Anishinaabe people definitely originated in biblical times. This story involved a sister and a brother (later they're identified as Meshegenebigoes) living "in a sequested spot, towards the north." The brother tells the sister that she must live separately when she menstruates and keep her implements always in order so that they don't get contaminated, then goes off hunting. The sister of course violates the rule, and as a consequence, the brother's body begins to rot; he commands her to cut off his head to save it, and she does. She hangs the head in a tree, where it tells the sister what to do.

Then things happen: there are ten brothers who sneak away from their wives to embark on a war party in which they fight an all-powerful Bear and steal his magnificent wampum belt, and a chase ensues. The head tells his sister about the approaching brothers and the Bear from which they are trying to escape, gives her instructions on how to defeat the Bear that include tossing himself (the head) into the air, and welcomes the war party to live with them for a time. Then another party of "unknown Indians" attacks and kills the ten brothers and steals the head, after showing it "all kinds of indignity" (later the head cries at his suffering). The sister infiltrates the enemies' lodge to locate her brother, resurrects the war party, and goes off to find wives for all the brothers, then sends the wives to rescue the head (one by one they untie it from where it was hung over a fire to dry out), after which the sister brings her brother back to life. At the end of the story the brothers are changed to spirits and "were assigned different stations in the invisible world.... They were commanded as they would have it in their power to do good to the inhabitants of the earth and to forget their sufferings in procuring the wampum, but to give them [humans] all things with a liberal hand.... The Spirits ... amidst their songs and shouts took their flight, to their respective abodes on high. And Meshegenebigo with this Sister Meshegenebigoquay descended into the depths below."[57]

Forty years later, no less an Indian hater than Mark Twain singled out "The Undying Head" as a remarkable example of "Indian imagination," so remarkable that he incorporated the whole story as an appendix to *Life on the Mississippi*.[58] Surprisingly Schoolcraft doesn't bring up evil spirits in his afterword to the story, offering only that the wampum belt worn by the bear must be a symbol for the Savior and that the Hebrews also separated women during menstruation, both of which points proved that Indigenous people originated in the Middle East in biblical times and emigrated across the Berring land bridge to North America. For such a complex and strange story, it wasn't much to say.

Wauchusco told stories about Anishinaabe experience that pointedly obtruded into American time, including a long historical account of a warrior who became "part of a moneto." Titled by William "Saugemau," this account was published in part and much reduced by Schoolcraft as "The Charmed Arrow." It appears to be set in the wake of the Great Peace of Montreal of 1701, in which the French attempted a grand alliance with the tribes of the east and the Great Lakes region in order to protect the fur trade. Participants included the Anishinaabeg and the Haudenosaunee, who had long been in the habit of making incursions into the Lake Superior region, as well as Mesquakie, Sauk, Mascouten, Kickapoos, and numerous other tribes.[59] The treaty had the opposite effect of what was intended.[60] As the French turned their attention to enforcing the peace in the east, they neglected the west, the result of which was an increasing number of conflicts among Indigenous nations of the Great Lakes region.[61] Saugemau appears to be "Sakima," a figure in archival records who puzzles historians to this day.[62] Sakima was a warrior at Michilimackinac of mixed Odawa and Potawatomi descent who enters European records as a leader of the Anishinaabe, Miami, and Illinois against

Mesquakie, Sauk, Kickapoo, and Mascouten people in 1710–11, a conflict that stretched from Green Bay to Detroit and in which thousands were killed.[63] The Odawas seem to have been fearful of Mesquakie power, and hence the conflict, historian Michael Witgen writes, but still he notes that even that kind of conflict would have called for Anishinaabe civil leaders to resist open warfare. They did not, he writes; "instead, there seemed to be a uniformly aggressive determination to destroy the Mesquakie by use of force."[64] Wauchusco's narrative recounts Saugemau's early years as a warrior, his rise as a leader, his theft of a magic lance, and his relationship with Kaubenau, a similiarly "part moneto" Ojibwe leader, culminating in Kaubenau's defeat of Saugemau and the Odawas allying themselves to the Ojibwes. The story narrates Saugeumau's ruthless exploits, tricking his enemies by pretending to be weak, single-handedly slaughtering dozens at a time, taking revenge on any who dared to mock him. It was the kind of story William particularly liked. Saugemau may have seemed like a savage, but his exploits showed that he was powerful and unimpeded by Europeans and their claims.

This was characteristic of Wauchusco's story "Six Indians Visit to the Sun and the Moon," in which Indigenous people exist in historic time, travel across the ocean to England and then to the celestial world, and Europeans, including the King of England, are incidental. Manabozho inhabits his own territory at the edge of the world, where he reflects on what he considers his bad acts and tests the youths on their relationship to the spirits. Only two of the six youths return from the celestial world, having leaped across the place where the earth and sky meet and seen the sun and moon, and offer a feast and gifts to "the different monetos for their preservation ... [and] for their safe arrival among their parents and relations." On the one hand, it's an adventure story with a recognizable theme: don't make the mistake of "[aspiring] to what only monetos could enjoy." On the other hand, Wauchusco and William seem to be very consciously brushing aside the tropes of savages cowed by European (and American) civilization and technological advances while representing a finely imagined celestial world. The connection that many American readers made to *The Arabian Nights* becomes more clear. There doesn't seem to be any European or American writing of the period or before that is even loosely analogous to Wauchusco and William's depiction. It's another world, beautiful and strange.

The savage told Americans that Indigenous people had absolutely nothing in their heads but blood and vengeance. They needed to believe it. The stories were "the unadulterated offspring of untutored minds of savages," wrote Henry Whiting in a review of *Algic Researches* for the *North American Review* that was more than likely arranged by Schoolcraft and expressing his views. They were "disjoined, extravagant, and repulsive."[65] Schoolcraft appends another account of Wauchusco's conversion and his supposed renunciation of "idolatry" to "Six Indians." He suggests that it might "remind the reader of South American history, of the alleged descent of Manco Capac and the Children of the Sun," but, and this was unusual for Schoolcraft to admit, he didn't really know whether that was relevant.[66] The story was entirely beyond him.

When Schoolcraft returned in April, he dismissed William from the Indian Department because William was operating a store on the side against department regulations. Doing so would seem to have been counterproductive. William wrote so many stories, and he had big plans. But William's sprawling narratives of war and the supernatural were too much for Schoolcraft, judging from the effort he put into containing their excesses when he published them. Considering that he'd been soliciting both Francis Shearman and George for stories that winter, and Jane was always available, perhaps Schoolcraft thought he'd have plenty of material without William. Written just before he left for the West in May 1838, George's stories, it turned out, were just as fantastic but not as carefully structured as William's, incorporating as they did Nabunway's commentary on the contemporary state of affairs at Sault Ste. Marie. Schoolcraft published them later, in the 1840s, and did not include them in his subsequent revision of *Algic Researches* in 1856. Francis never really came up with anything publishable himself. Schoolcraft gave James the job as Keeper of the Indian Dormitory, which included an apartment in the new dormitory building for his family, as well as an office for Schoolcraft. After his dismissal, William went to New York City and bought supplies for the store, and out of pique or desperation he signed George's name to the invoice for the goods. George didn't know about this until the creditors came looking for him.[67]

All the family had hoped that the government would deem the supplemental claims made that past September valid, but after Edmonds decided that there would have to be another council, the claims go unmentioned in the family correspondence.[68] McMurray and Charlotte, along with their two boys, went down to Detroit that summer, McMurray hoping to see the bishop to find out where they would be sent—eventually, this turned out to be Dundas, a small town south of Toronto in Upper Canada.[69] He sent a flurry of letters dispensing spiritual advice and worrying about the family finances. He relayed news of Mrs. Jameson as well. She'd written him before leaving New York that winter, he told Jane, wondering about Jane's health in light of Schoolcraft's last letter, from the previous November. "I feel really anxious about her," Mrs. Jameson had written; "I had a letter from her husband, which has rather increased my anxiety; and I will write to her certainly." (This raises the possibility that the letter Schoolcraft sent to Mrs. Jameson was not the same as the copy he showed to Jane or that Mrs. Jameson was being willfully ignorant of the subject matter of the letter.) She wondered also about mentioning names of the family in her book but then dismissed her own momentary concerns. "What need of discretion," expostulated Mrs. Jameson to McMurray, "when all I saw inspired feelings of good will, and the most animated pleasure."[70]

Early that summer, at Mackinac, just as George was about to leave for the Southwest as interpreter for a party of Ojibwes and Odawas looking at land pending expulsion, London George appeared in the flesh. "Prepare yourself for a shock or two," he'd previously written to George from Mr. Richard's Boarding House on Water Street in New York City. He'd decided to act on his fascination for thrilling scenes of the West after his retirement from the Customs House. Unfortunately he had been immediately robbed of his portmanteau on arriving in New York. "This if I may use the expression has completely floored me, in fact I don't know what I should have done had not one of my fellow passengers advanced me a small sum for temporary relief," he wrote, but, he added, "I will not say that I am forlorn in a foreign land when I have a beloved kinsman to apply to . . . & assist me out of my present distress."[71] It doesn't seem likely that George or any of the Johnstons could help him replace the sixty pounds in cash, the gold watch, new clothes, four elegant scotch shawls, and various "nick nacks" he had lost, but they could shelter him at least. After he landed at Mackinac and George went on his way, London George headed to the Sault, where he made himself at home for a long enough time that some were wondering whether he would ever leave.

Ozhaawshkodewikwe was not well herself but invited him to stay, apologizing that she had not much more than fish to offer; Eliza remained "very silent" despite her cousin's gallantries. London George made himself useful working in the garden, hoeing peas, planting cabbage, and tending to potatoes; his new clothes left him appearing "as decent as other folks," so he seemed to fit right in.[72] He and George's daughter Louisa boarded with Mrs. Cadotte—this was Sangemanqua, the mother of Lewis Johnston's daughters. Mrs. Cadotte almost threw them out, however, when she didn't receive a barrel of flour as promised, but the flour was produced, everyone was reconciled, and George was quite cozy. He kept his cousin apprised of the goings on with his sons and the health and welfare of his daughter, keeping track of the medicine she required for her injured leg. America turned out to be more pastoral than thrilling. "We got a load of hay which I put in the stable, the weather has been uncommonly fine not a shower since you left but fine heavy dews at night," he wrote in September. "Heaven has been propitious in sending so fine a season on my first arrival in this wilderness, it demands unbounded praise to the Almighty, this, I trust . . . endowed by grace not to forget."[73]

George wasn't present for most of his cousin's visit, intentionally or not. Schoolcraft had made his brother James "superintendent and conductor" of the party; what his duties were or what he did George doesn't mention in his diary of the trip. They traveled by steamboat to Chicago, then eventually to West Port, near the Kansas River, stopping along the way to get a look at the new Illinois Penitentiary in Alton and bury a planter who died on board at St. Charles. The Kansas River was a "beautiful stream," George remarked, and the Shawnees were "living in a beautiful wooded country and land good, their fields are splendid, they grow corn in abundance, and wheat & other vegetables, raise plenty of horses and cattle. They have a large council house."[74] The temperature in July was above 100 degrees, however. The previous summer, an expedition of Swan Creek and Black River Saginaw Ojibwes made the same trip, although many other Ojibwe and Odawa people were crossing over into Canada rather than face deportation.[75] George records the second party having "accepted the land shown to them . . . unanimously, and with expressions of thanks."[76] In the end the economic depression had slowed settlement so much that the commissioner of Indian affairs, Hartley Crawford, let the people stay where they were, and not one of George's group went to Indian Territory.[77]

George made the return trip to Chicago, then continued up to La Pointe to investigate the possibility of benefiting from the 1837 treaty at St. Peters between the United States and Ojibwes of western Lake Superior. He told the assembled men "that I need not remind them that my ancestor owned the lands around us, and that he had fought and bled and won from his enemies the lands now sold to the Govt." He wished his children to be recognized on the "half breed" list for grants of land associated with the 1837 treaty, which they were, over the objections of the subagent at La Pointe. George noted down in his diary Governor Dodge's barely contained glee in getting the land (between the Mississippi in north-central present-day Minnesota, the St. Croix River, and western Lake Superior) as cheaply as he did because the Ojibwe negotiators left it to him to value it properly.[78]

Jane was unable to get out of bed in early summer. Schoolcraft was back in Detroit, getting treaties finalized at Grand Rapids and Saginaw. McMurray prayed to God to give her strength but reminded her that she must submit to His will. "There is but one door by which we must all depart from this transitory scene, and that is death, and our chief desire should be to leave this probationary state in the manner God expects; or else awful, beyond description will be our condition hereafter." Jane wrote on the envelope of this letter, "Jesus! / Thou must save & thou alone; / In my hand no pole I bring, / Simply to thy cross cling."[79] This is a reference to Numbers 21:8–9, where the Israelites in the wilderness begin to doubt Moses and God sends poisonous serpents to torment them, after which they realize their sin and confess to Moses, seeking mercy. Moses prays and God instructs him to put a bronze serpent on a pole so that the Israelites may look at it and be healed, signifying that they should do as God commands regardless of whether or not it seemed logical (healing yourself by looking at a snake) and that they had been sinners (for which God sent snakes to plague them). God sent this illness to her, and Jane didn't know why or what to do.

Schoolcraft was at home for only a short time before he left for Washington to finish up that season's work. Jane was still in bed in the middle of July, reporting constant thunderstorms "with excessive thunder & lightening, which no doubt has had a material effect upon my poor weak frame, [and] it has kept this lonely house so damp that everything is mouldy."[80] She wished a music box that played sacred music, and if not, "Hail, Columbia."[81] "You know now what an effect music has upon me. It almost has the same effect as it had upon Saul of old."[82] "There are a great many letters for you," she added, a few days later.[83] From Washington Schoolcraft advised her to "take the carriage & horse. Try moderate daily *exercise*, which will produce *appetite* & of course *strength*. This depends, however, upon two points 1. *moderation*. 2. *continence*." He had a plan. "You must prepare yourself to go with me to see the Pictured Rocks, with the children. It will be worth all the springs & fashionable places in the World."[84] It must have seemed like the thing to say to one's wife, if she were an American lady.

A new missionary, a young Princeton graduate like Jeremiah Porter, had appeared on the island, his post still to be determined. Peter Dougherty found Jane "very feeble" but "pleasant and an unusually intelligent woman." She insisted that he stay at the agent's house while he was on the island, showed him the *Voyager*, and had the children escort him to the sights when she didn't feel up to it herself. "She is a woman of a highly cultivated mind," Dougherty wrote in his journal. "Has read extensively english litrature [sic]." Dougherty managed to scare up some gossip during his brief time on the island. Reverend Ferry, the recently departed missionary, was better at business than preaching he heard, and he'd been accused by Catholics and some of the children of improprieties with girls at the mission school. Schoolcraft defended Ferry, but many believed the children and wouldn't hear his preaching any longer. Then Ferry confessed that "he had laid himself open to the enemy." The children were telling the truth.[85] He left the island just in time.

William and Jane alternately took tea with Dougherty and told him about the people in the vicinity and where they lived. Jane told him about "the Juglers medicine sack" and how the children fast for a vision "to invoke a guardian spirit or to learn their future destiny in life." William advised him on suitable locations for the mission and told him that he didn't think the people would be deported because "the chiefs have money laid aside and design to purchase their lands as soon as they come in the market."[86] The Ojibwes were more "energetic, active and . . . military," he learned, while the Odawas were "mild and peaceable [and] are the agracultural population." Jane said something to him that she must often have said to inquirers about Anishinaabe people and Anishinaabemowin. "There is said to be a kind of learned aristocracy which speake the language more purely & perfetly," Dougherty wrote. "They have a kind of court and common dialect."[87] Dougherty noticed Janée sitting outside on the step doing quillwork.[88]

Back in Detroit Schoolcraft received another letter from Toulmin Smith, reminding him that he'd said that Mackinac "abounded" in skulls for the taking. Toulmin Smith wondered, since he and his wife were now moving on to New York City (a possible job at the new university in Ann Arbor had fallen through), whether Schoolcraft could without "much trouble . . . procure several [of] these—whether chiefs or otherwise & if of more races or tribes than one so much the better." He was especially keen to get hold of "*female* [2] Indian skulls" for comparison. Smith had decided he'd discovered the "moral direction group" of the brain contemplating the few skulls he apparently had (and carted around with him). But he needed more. "A box of these skulls addressed to me 'care of Bell & Co' New York, New York' will immediately reach me," he wrote; "perhaps I might be favored with a line informing me of its dispatch."[89] Schoolcraft filed the letter under "phrenology," but he doesn't seem to have answered it, probably because he was cultivating a more important man. That past winter he'd heard—probably from Zina Pitcher and about the time they were both attending Toulmin Smith's phrenology lectures— about Samuel George Morton. In May Schoolcraft invited Morton to Mackinac to see the annuity payments in late summer, where, he wrote, "the opportunity for observing [the Indians'] mental and physical characteristics will be favourable," and more so because the Ojibwes and Odawas who attended "constitute the best characterological type of the great *Algic* family of North America."[90] This was probably the same thing he told Toulmin Smith. Schoolcraft also wanted a copy of the plates from Morton's book *Crania Americana: Or, a Comparative View of the Skulls of Various Aboriginal Nations in North and South America* (Philadelphia, 1839).[91] Morton sent the plates in June, hinting about needing "some crania of the Northern tribes" before publishing, but in the end illness prevented him from making the trip.[92]

The lithographs had been much praised in the press. The pictures were drawn with "fidelity and elegance, and of the natural size, one head being placed on each plate," wrote the *American Journal of Science and Arts*.[93] They are "as accurate as they are beautiful," said the *American Medical Intelligencer*, putting in a plug for Morton himself, who "would feel obliged if those gentlemen who possess Indian skulls would permit him to inspect them; by so doing they would be rendering an essential service to science."[94] Morton included Buffalo Tail, the pregnant Delaware woman, and Bill Fifer. Schoolcraft provided him an Ojibwe skull, perhaps from Round Island. The plates are indeed beautiful and finely detailed; the skulls float in space, most of them complete with mandible, at least one of them with what looks like a bullet hole. The job of a government official like Schoolcraft was to alienate Indigenous people from their land; for a scientist like Morton (or Schoolcraft), their job was to turn those alienated bodies and minds into data to be manipulated and re-presented to a white audience as definitive knowledge about Indians' inherent inferiority, thus demonstrating that they had no real claim on the land in the first place. Morton's idea was to fill an empty skull with birdshot to measure its volume. Schoolcraft didn't get the plates until he returned to Mackinac, where the package was waiting for him in the mail that had piled up, which Jane was in the habit of opening in his absence.

They went to the Pictured Rocks in August—Schoolcraft, Jane, the children, her niece Julia as nursemaid, seven boatmen, and Placidus Ord, the son of the subagent at Sault Ste. Marie. The purpose of the trip was to account for Ojibwe "improvements" in the ceded territory, so that the people could be compensated when they were deported. Considering that Placidus Ord was on the trip to keep accounts and being a young man was inexperienced in that part of the world, it's highly likely that Jane's job on this trip was to translate. That Schoolcraft's accounts for this period show $300 per annum paid to the obstreperous Louisa Piquette as interpreter make it highly likely that he was pocketing that money and Jane herself was regularly serving as agency translator.[95] Their boat had a mast and sails, with an awning in the center. Schoolcraft remembered it fondly in his memoirs. "Magazines, a spy-glass, &c., &c., served to while away the time, and a well-furnished mess-basket served to make us quite easy in that department."[96] Jane and Julia were available to cook.

There were eight bands living on the ceded territory, about 569 people, Schoolcraft wrote in his memoirs. They reported to him that their numbers were fewer than at the time of French and British presence, mainly because the game was almost hunted out. Schoolcraft noted the "large old fields, not now in cultivation" at Portagunisee, on the straits of St. Mary's, and at Grand Island that proved their contention. He found 125 and a half acres currently in cultivation by individuals, a hundred acres by bands collectively, 1,459 acres of old fields, 3,162 acres of village sites, twenty-seven fixed dwellings, and nineteen apple trees. "In proportion as they had little, they set a high value on it, and insisted on showing everything, and they gave me a good deal of information. The whole sum appraised to individuals was $3,428.25; and to collective bands, $11,173.50."[97]

Schoolcraft memorialized the trip in another way, in two sketches that were published in the *Knickerbocker* in September of 1839 and September of 1840. The first installment is dated Grand Island, 1838, and it discusses the Ojibwe improvements in light of how white people would use them. He also noted that this was where "Kabina" had lived, the "renowned warrior, priest, and necromancer." Kabina was probably a real person, he wrote, but the rest of the story was "daemonology."[98] The second of Schoolcraft's installments was dated Castle-island, 14 August.[99] Schoolcraft described visiting the island with his children, noting that, according to his Indian guides, no white man before him had ever visited it before. He had much to say that was picturesque and returned to the harbor at Grand Island for more reflections on the potential of the land for its fisheries and pineries and mineral extraction. The party continued on to the Pictured Rocks.

A partial draft of this sketch remains, and it tracks the published version but for its excision of Jane. Schoolcraft describes the danger of trying to get on the island, as the only landing place was a kind of dyke in the rock where there was a way to climb up and onto the land. If the wind shifted, however, "it would have driven the waves off the wide lake into this dyke, and rendered the wreck of the boat inevitable." He and the two children, aged eight and ten, presumably along with Jane, clambered up with the aid of the boatmen. There was nothing but water and sky all around, and low mountains on the shore in the distance. "On looking down into the water, at the foot of the cliffs, we could perceive the vast rugged marshes of reed through the transperant medium," he wrote, "horrid chasms appeared in the rock, on the northeast side of the island, which are [said] to have encountered the worst might of the lake tempests."[100] And here in his draft, he inserts a poem by Jane, "a free translation of some lines in the Ojibwa language" that she handed him—when, he doesn't say.

> Here in my native inland sea,
> From pain and sickness would I flee
> And from its shores & islands bright
> Gather a store of sweet delight.
> Lone island of the saltless sea!
> How wide, how sweet, how fresh & free
> Now all transporting is the view

Of rocks & skies & waters blue
United, as a song's sweet strains
To tell, here nature only reigns.
Ah nature! here forever may
Far from the haunts of men away
From here, there are no sordid fears,
No crimes, no misery, no tears
No pride of wealth, the heart to fill,
No laws to treat my people ill.

They were her people he was working to dispossess, and worse, he made her participate in it. She wrote the poem first in Ojibwemowin, for herself, then gave him a copy in English that he could read—or he insisted on taking it. Schoolcraft copied it over as was his habit—then, as was also his habit, he realized what she was writing about and discarded the poem, as it appears nowhere else in the surviving papers, nor in the published essay, where it was replaced by a great deal of straining after aesthetic effect in a description of a cave. "We were sorry to learn that the trip in Lake Superior was not as beneficial to Mrs. S's health as we could have wished," McMurray wrote to Schoolcraft from Detroit afterward. The family was about to leave to spend the winter at New York City, where Schoolcraft would see about publishing *Algic Researches* and they would put the children to school. "However we are in hopes that a visit to, and sojourn in the Atlantic states will add much to it."[101]

Mukakee Mindemoea; or, The Toad-Woman

Translated by Jane Johnston Schoolcraft[1]

Great good luck once happened to a young woman who was living all alone in the woods, with nobody near her but her little dog, for, to her surprise, she found fresh meat every morning at her door. She felt very anxious to know who it was that supplied her, and watching one morning, very early, she saw a handsome young man deposit the meat. After his being seen by her, he became her husband, and she had a son by him. One day not long after this, the man did not return at evening, as usual, from hunting. She waited till late at night, but all in vain. Next day she swung her baby to sleep in its tikenágun, or cradle, and then said to her dog: "Take care of your brother whilst I am gone, and when he cries, halloo for me." The cradle was made of the finest wampum, and all its bandages and decorations were of the same costly material. After a short time the woman heard the cry of her faithful dog, and running home as fast as she could, she found her child gone and the dog too. But on looking round, she saw pieces of the wampum of her child's cradle bit off by the dog, who strove to retain the child and prevent his being carried off by an old woman called Mukakee Mindemoea, or the Toad-Woman. The mother followed at full speed, and occasionally came to lodges inhabited by old women, who told her at what time the thief had passed; they also gave her shoes, that she might follow on. There were a number of these old women, who seemed as if they were all prophetesses. Each of them would say to her, that when she arrived in pursuit of her stolen child at the next lodge, she must set the toes of the moccasins they had loaned her pointing homewards, and they would return of themselves. She would get others from her entertainers farther on, who would also give her directions how to proceed to recover her son. She thus followed in the pursuit, from valley to valley, and stream to stream, for months and years; when she came, at length, to the lodge of the last of the friendly old Nocoes, or grandmothers, as they were called, who gave her final instructions how to proceed. She told her she was near the place where her son was, and directed her to build a lodge of shingoob, or cedar boughs, near the old Toad-Woman's lodge, and to make a little bark dish and squeeze her milk into it. "Then," she said, "your first child (meaning the dog) will come and find you out." She did accordingly, and in a short time she heard her son, now grown, going out to hunt, with his dog, calling out to him, "Monedo Pewaubik (that is, Steel or Spirit Iron), Twee! Twee!" She then set ready the dish and filled it with her milk. The dog soon scented it and came into the lodge; she placed it before him. "See my child," said she, addressing him, "the food you used to have from me, your mother." The dog went and told his young master that he had found his *real* mother; and informed him that the old woman, whom he *called* his mother, was not his mother, that she had stolen him when an infant in his cradle, and that he had himself followed her in hopes of getting him back. The young man and his dog then went on their hunting excursion, and brought back a great quantity of meat of all kinds. He said to his pretended mother, as he laid it down, "Send some to the stranger that has arrived lately." The old hag answered, "No! why should I send to her—the Sheegowish."[2] He insisted; and she at last consented to take something, throwing it in at the door, with the remark, "My son gives you, or feeds you this." But it was of such an offensive nature, that she threw it immediately out after her.

After this the young man paid the stranger a visit, at her lodge of cedar boughs, and partook of her dish of milk. She then told him she was his real mother, and that he had been stolen away from her by the detestable Toad-Woman, who was a witch. He was not quite convinced. She said to him, "Feign yourself sick, when you go home, and when the Toad-Woman asks what ails you, say that you want to see your cradle; for your cradle was of wampum, and your faithful brother, the dog, bit a piece off to try and detain you, which I picked up, as I followed in your track. They are real wampum, white and blue, shining and beautiful." She then showed him the pieces. He went home and did this as his real mother bid him. "Mother," said he, "why am I so different in my looks for the rest of your children?" "Oh," said she, "it was a very bright clear blue sky when you were born; that is the reason." When the Toad-Woman saw he was ill, she asked what she could do for him. He said nothing would do him good, but the sight of his cradle. She ran immediately and got a cedar cradle, but he said "That is not my cradle." She went and got one of her own children's cradles (for she had four,) but he turned his head and said, "That is not mine." She then produced the real cradle, and he saw it was the same, in substance, with the pieces the other had shown him; and he was convinced, for he could even see the marks of the dog's teeth upon it.

He soon got well, and went out hunting, and killed a fat bear. He and his dog-brother then stripped a tall pine of all its branches, and stuck the carcass on the top, taking the usual sign of his having killed an animal—the tongue. He told the Toad-Woman where he had left it, saying "It is very far, even to the end of the earth." She answered, "It is not so far but I can get it," so off she set. As soon as she was gone, the young man and his dog killed the Toad-Woman's children, and staked them on each side of the door, with a piece of fat in their mouths, and then went to his real mother and hastened her departure with them. The Toad-Woman spent a long time in finding the bear, and had much ado in climbing the tree to get down the carcass. As she got near home, she saw the children looking out, apparently, with the fat in their mouths, and was angry at them, saying, "Why do you destroy the pomatum of your brother." But her fury was great indeed, when she saw they were killed and impaled. She ran after the fugitives as fast as she could, and was near overtaking them, when the young man said, "We are pressed hard, but let this stay her progress," throwing his fire steel behind him, which caused the Toad-Woman to slip and fall repeatedly. But still she pursued and gained on them, when he threw behind him his flint, which again retarded her, for it made her slip and stumble, so that her knees were bleeding; but she continued to follow on, and was gaining ground, when the young man said, "Let the Oshau shaw go min un (snake berry) spring up to detain her," and immediately these berries spread the scarlet all over the part for a long distance, which she could not avoid stooping down to pick and eat. Still she went on, and was again advancing on them, when the young man at last, said to the dog, "Brother, chew her into mummy, for she plagues us." So the dog, turning round, seized her and tore her to pieces, and they escaped.

Chapter 10

At the Depot

As soon as they arrived in New York in late November 1838, after a month in Detroit and some weeks in Buffalo where Janée recovered from scarlet fever, Schoolcraft wrote to Anna Jameson for help in getting *Algic Researches* published at London. In his letter he did what he usually did with respect to who actually wrote the stories—he didn't quite lie, but obscured the truth. "I propose publishing the result of my observations on the mental characteristics of the various tribes of this continent," he wrote. "It is proposed to open the way by a couple of volumes of 'Indian Tales, mythologic and allegoric' collected from oral tradition during a residence of twenty years in the territory, eighteen of which, have been in the character of a public agent of the govt.—a fact I mention, merely to indicate that my opportunities for obtaining information on the subject have been good." He wanted Mrs. Jameson to "edit" the book for publication at London. He was offering her the stories as he had done Washington Irving, only these were the stories as published in *Algic Researches* for her to revise and presumably make appropriate for popular consumption.

He hadn't received a timely reply, so he wrote to Washington Irving to inquire about his London publisher, but eventually Mrs. Jameson's response reached him. She gave him her publisher's terms and dismissed his idea that she would edit anything. She encouraged the publication of the stories, though, noting that she'd "published in my little journal one or two [stories] which Mrs. Schoolcraft gave me & they have excited very general interest."[1] Mrs. Jameson knew who was doing the writing. She offered some literary advice. "The more exactly you can in translation adhere to the *style* of the language of the Indian nation instead of emulating a fine or correct English style—the more *characteristic* in all respects—the more original, the more interesting your work will be."[2] Whatever Indians were saying, it couldn't be conveyed in correct English style because they were Indians and Indian languages couldn't possibly have an equivalent in correct English style. What that Indian language might be when translated into English she didn't say. The retired politician and diplomat Albert Gallatin had offered similar advice when Schoolcraft had seen him earlier that winter, warning Schoolcraft to "take care that, in publishing your Indian legends, you do not subject yourself to the imputations made against Macpherson."[3] Gallatin had taken up the study of Indian languages. The suspicion raised against the Ossian poems were that they were too strangely literary to be real, and therefore that Macpherson had to have made them all up.

Both Jameson and Gallatin were reminding Schoolcraft of the impossibility, if you knew what a savage was, of Indians having a literature—of using language for moral and aesthetic effect.[4] An "Indian" way of writing in English would have to preserve their notions of the difference and inferiority of Indigenous people and neither of them could articulate what that might actually look like. Schoolcraft knew that the stories were both told and written by Indian people, so the idea that these Indian people were not demonstrating a sufficiently Indian way of writing in English didn't make sense to him. The problem for him was what was in the stories, what they were about—spirits, transformation—not how they were written. After abandoning his initial idea to have Irving rewrite them, his solution in *Algic Researches* was to surround them with his own commentary, in two introductory essays, multiple forewords and afterwords, and numerous footnotes. But as has been noted, in all that commentary Schoolcraft could only say again and again that the stories were evidence of Indians' demonology, of evil spirits, and even he knew that wasn't especially explanatory let alone convincing, especially when at least some people could perceive the stories' charms. By the time he arrived in New York with the revised collection, after having received stories from the Saginaws, Little Sault, and Wauchusco, he was back to where he started.

Mrs. Jameson's friend, Catharine Maria Sedgwick, also a working writer, met the Schoolcrafts not long after Jameson's book had been published in late 1838. "They . . . are anticipating great success for the tales you have handled," she wrote to Mrs. Jameson, but "they seem not to have thought of the difference between an artists & a common light." Sedgwick had made a great splash in American literature ten years previously with the frontier romance *Hope Leslie*, a novel that featured a heroic Pequot woman suffering from unrequited love for a Puritan that caused her father to accidentally chop off her arm at the conclusion of which the Indians accepted their fate (that is, death) and graciously left the country to settlers. The "common light" required such things because white people needed to be told their own story, a story about who they were and why they were in North America. That the Schoolcrafts were hopeful about the reception of the stories speaks to Schoolcraft's faith in his burgeoning scientific fame despite his anxieties, and Jane's faith in the power of the stories to do what she wanted them to do.

Sedgwick had come to visit the Schoolcrafts in the wake of notice being taken of Jane's role in Mrs. Jameson's book. A review in the *Albion*, a long-running "journal of news, politics, and literature" in New York, noted Mrs. Jameson's reliance on Jane, "a lady of Indian blood, the daughter of a chief, who was not only the greatest warrior of his tribe, but also the greatest poet and story-teller." It found the "curious specimens of the Red-Indian romances exceedingly interesting" and "a curious addenda to our history."[5] Sedgwick came to see the romantic Mrs. Schoolcraft for herself. "Her sweet voice reminded me of yours," she wrote to Mrs. Jameson, "at least so far as it indicated refinement of feelings & *civilization*." "When I spoke of you she said 'Oh how I love that woman—I cannot express how much I love her. If I could see her again & lay my head on her lap as I did when she was at my house!' Her eyes absolutely glowed while she spoke of you. She was mourning like Rachel for her children whom she has put to boarding schools & for the first time in her life goes back to her home with a heavy heart."[6]

They had taken the children to their new boarding schools before going to Washington for a month, first Johnston at the Edgehill School in Princeton, New Jersey, and then Janée at the Misses Gould's school in Philadelphia. In Philadelphia they spent a few days with Gen. Robert Patterson and his family, giving Schoolcraft time—one wonders if Jane was present for this—to visit with Dr. Morton and his skulls. In Washington Schoolcraft, who is the only record of this trip, enjoyed himself basking in his perceived importance and socializing in what must have been his usual manner while in the city. They stayed at a boarding house run by "my excellent friends, the Miss Polks." Schoolcraft spoke to President Van Buren, Secretary of War Joel Poinsett, and James Kirke Paulding, the secretary of the navy (as well as late defender of slavery [*View of Slavery in the United States*, 1836], friend of Washington Irving, and author of a successful Broadway play about Davy Crockett). Jane met Mrs. Paulding. Schoolcraft took himself, and possibly Jane, to the New Year's reception at the White House, which caused him years later to reflect on how the crowd evinced a "general loyalty . . . to the constitution and government, and supreme law of the land."[7] Jane attended a "general and crowded party" thrown by Gen. Alexander Macomb, who at the time was the commanding general of the army. Macomb had known Jane and her father since that time long ago when John Johnston had protected the Americans whom he'd recently fought from being massacred by the Ojibwes at Bow-e-ting.[8]

Schoolcraft got two things in Washington that meant very much to him: permission to use government Indian education money to pay for the publication of a dictionary and grammar of the "Indian languages"—this would be a dictionary and grammar of Ojibwemowin—and permission to take a leave of absence to visit Europe.[9] He thought his fame was assured in Europe, where men of science could not but be supportive, as all the leading intellectuals were in the United States. Indeed, the celebrated historian of the United States George Bancroft wrote to Schoolcraft in February, telling him it was his "duty" to "[press] forward" in his work. "I have never met any one who combined so much philosophy with so exact personal knowledge," Brancroft wrote. He did not doubt Schoolcraft's success. "Go on: persevere: build a monument to yourself & to the unhappy Algonquin race." That was exactly what Schoolcraft wanted to hear.[10]

New York was supposed to improve Jane's health, which it seemed to do; she enjoyed New York society, she wrote to Charlotte, who worried about their mother and was unhappy in Dundas, a place that seemed "quite out of the world."[11] Schoolcraft insisted that Jane see Chandler Robbins Gilman in his professional capacity, an appointment she put off for as long as she could.[12] In a letter to Schoolcraft, Gilman refers to "deleterious matters" she was in the habit of taking, which seem to have been laudanum and digitalis.

Laudanum was commonly prescribed for coughing, diarrhea, and pain, and digitalis as a sedative.[13] The dangers of laudanum especially were well known. Newspaper accounts of suicide by laudanum as a consequence of broken romances or business failures were a common feature of every newspaper in the period.[14] But it had its allure. Although Thomas De Quincey's *Confessions of an Opium-Eater* (1821) detailed the negative effects of laudanum, he was criticized at the time for making its "pleasures" much too attractive. (We know now of numerous writers who regularly took laudanum, including Elizabeth Barrett Browning, Walter Scott, and Harriet Martineau.)[15] Gilman congratulated Jane on her own efforts to stop relying on the medicines and prescribed the infusion of wild cherry bark in lime water—wild cherry bark was prescribed for gastrointestinal complaints but also for "nervous excitability" or "chronic hysteric complaints."[16]

To everyone's shock and amusement, London George's wife called on Jane at their boardinghouse in lower Manhattan, bringing along his child.[17] She was looking for her husband, or financial support, or both. (One effect of the notoriety given the Johnstons in McKenney's and Jameson's books was that two mothers of John Johnston's children born out of wedlock were also able to locate the family.) Schoolcraft attended lectures at the Stuyvesant Institute, visited Ramsay Crooks at his counting-house in Ann Street, and cultivated his friendship with Charles Fenno Hoffman, whose sister Julia was at the time busy copying Charles's *Wild Scenes in the Forest and Prairie*, a second book derived from his western tour, for publication at London.[18] There's a very good chance that he and possibly Jane called on George Catlin, who had recently finished a run at Faneuil Hall in Boston and was preparing for another that spring in Philadelphia. Schoolcraft had written an endorsement for his first catalog attesting to the verisimilitude of his portraits and their revelation of Indian character. His exhibitions included a room full of portraits filling the walls top to bottom, lectures by himself, dances by Indigenous performers, Indian curiosities, a stray scalp. They were always popular; even visiting Indian delegations came to see.[19] Some of the portraits were people Jane knew, as Catlin had spent time recently at Sault Ste. Marie, in 1836, while on his way to Fort Snelling. He was off to Philadelphia by the end of March, however, and after that, to Europe for several decades as it turned out, when it became clear that the government wouldn't buy his pictures for the benefit of the nation.[20]

Jane visited the wife of William Leete Stone, a newspaper editor and writer who'd just recently produced a biography of Joseph Brant or Thayendanegea, a Mohawk political and military leader during the revolutionary period. Mrs. Stone had sent Jane a copy of the book and thought so much of Jane's simple thank-you note that she kept it and had it bound with one of Schoolcraft's epic poems about Indians and the West, published a few years later. "The life of Thayendanegea will be perused with new zest, as the gift of the wife of the Author of this valuable contribution to the biography of Native chiefs," Jane wrote, as if Schoolcraft were watching over her shoulder. Stone was the kind of man he'd want to cultivate. "I hope the Algic race will hereafter share in your sympathies, & I beg leave to offer you a copy of my Husband's 'Indian Tales and Legends' gathered from their oral traditions which will be published in the present month." The publisher would send a copy. "My Son is still suffering from cold & probably the effects of indigestion, but I trust he will be restored to his usual health in a day or two," she writes. "My Daughter has returned to her school at Philadelphia this morning."[21]

The children were always on her mind; she hadn't wanted to put them in boarding schools, as that meant that she would only see them at the end of summer, and only for a month. "You can hardly conceive how great an ordeal it was to part with my poor children as they never were absent from them more than a few days since their birth," she wrote to Mrs. General Patterson. That a draft of this letter survives in Schoolcraft's papers probably means that he supervised its writing. "I have indeed been at times a sad picture of forlornness, but I know it is for their good & I strive to feel reconciled." She worried about Johnston especially, who was so small and alone among "40 other boys utter strangers to him." Janée was among friends and "in the best of schools for a girl of her age." She would occupy herself, she wrote, "by assisting Mr. S [writing] a dictionary & grammar & my native Algic tales of the

Jane Susan Ann Schoolcraft, artist unknown (ca. 1837). Chippewa County Historical Society, Sault Ste. Marie, Michigan.

Ojibway nation." If her husband went to England as planned, "I think I should prefer remaining near my dear little ones whilst he is gone."[22]

In his memoirs Schoolcraft includes a poem dated 18 March 1839 that Jane wrote on leaving the children at school. As was usually the case with Jane's poems, he printed his own "free translation" but in this case he also printed the Ojibwemowin that Jane had to have handed him, perhaps to establish his scientific bona fides. In his revision, Schoolcraft has Jane asking, "What are cities to me, / Oh! land of my mother, compared unto thee?"

> One feeling more strongly still binds me to thee,
> There roved my forefathers, in liberty free—
> There shook they the war lance, and sported the plume,
> Ere Europe had cast o'er this country a gloom;
> Nor thought they that kingdoms more happy could be,
> White lords of a land so resplendent and free.

John Johnston Schoolcraft, artist unknown (ca. 1837). Chippewa County Historical Society, Sault Ste. Marie, Michigan.

The poem is a recitation of the savage story. He also has Jane dutifully acquiescing to his desires, as in the letter to Mrs. General Patterson. In the poem Jane says she must surrender her children because "it is learning that calls them," and "duty commands me / and duty must sway."

Schoolcraft could assume that no one among his readers would be able to translate the Ojibwemowin. Luckily Dennis Jones, Heidi Stark, and James Vukelich translated the poem for a collection of Jane Schoolcraft's writings published by Robert Dale Parker in 2005. In their translation Jane laments having to leave behind "My little daughter / My little son" to return to "My land / Far in the west."

> That is the way that I am, my being
> My land
>
> My land
> To my home I shall return
> I begin to make my way home
> Ahh but I am sad[23]

That Schoolcraft forced her to leave her children behind in the East was cruel, as if he was trying to destroy her.

When they returned to the West, Schoolcraft went to Detroit to wait for instructions from Washington and Jane went to Mackinac. He'd given her permission that she could, finally, spend the winter with her mother at Sault Ste. Marie; he even paid for a new roof for Ozhaawshkodewikwe's house. But he also insisted that she set up house at Mackinac for the summer so that he and the children could be together before they went their separate ways in the fall. Then he became angry about the expense. She was angry back at him. "You have my thanks for ordering my *paternal home* to be made *fit to live in*, & you have anticipated my wishes in *your* desire to *me* to pass the winter there. I do not wish to *recriminate*, when I say, that worlds, I would not pass such a winter again as the past. [She's talking about the winter of 1837–38 at Mackinac.] *My feelings*, as well as your own, have suffered, & God alone can be the *right Judge*."[24] She did have some recriminations, though. Mrs. Flemming and her "*unborn* Babe" had died after three days' sickness and would be buried the next day. "What makes her death more melancholy, is, that her *affectionate* husband was away, having gone to the Grand Traverse. Mrs. Flemming visited me on Saturday & appeared quite well, & on Monday we heard she was ill, Anna & I went to see her, & I had a pleasant conversation with her, and the next morning she was a corpse at 4 o'clock. Mr. Flemming arrived last night, having been sent for, to take a last look of his poor Wife."[25]

On the same day that Jane wrote this letter, Schoolcraft was in Detroit writing a stilted letter of his own, dismissing her playfulness in an earlier letter. "If you will look at the 'margin' of your heart and that 'Rock' upon which all human hopes of salvation are built, you would, it is believed, employ your chamber meditations with more profit, and a more salutary influence upon your own life & opinions, than by a continuance of these silly marginal inuendoes."[26] He worried about money. He had inquired of Trowbridge whether he could sell some of his property to him, willing to take half its value. But Trowbridge didn't have any money to spend—an ongoing effect of the economic depression.[27] Jane caught this when he wrote.

> You mentioned something about your pecuniary affairs which I had known before, & as you say 'you have no higher duties, than to support & educate your children,' & as I suppose you draw all your motives from scripture, I agree with you, & if any *privation* on *my part* can further the object, I am perfectly willing to bear all things, & I can safely say that I love my children as much as you do, & their education is of far greater consequence than a large Estate—which I know from *sad experience* &

your intended visit to Europe will require *large funds*. May God in mercy bless every project is all I can—or wish to say.[28]

She couldn't resist including another of scene of maternal anguish. She went "every day into Anna's Parlour & *look* & *talk* at the pictures of the dear children [their portraits had been painted in Detroit the previous winter], & I sometimes water with my tears the two plants of geranium which Janée & Johnston told me to call by their names."[29] And she added a postscript: "*James* talks of sending Anna Maria to St. Mary's, & of boarding out, I feel sometimes like a fish out of water *no home*—no, *nothing*—Alas! Alas!—yet I thank God for peace of mind, mellowed with sadness, which softens the heart & draws it *inwards*, '*I feel all alone*' as H. Kirk White said, & yet *I am not alone* for God is nigh."[30]

It was what she said about the children that set him off. He insisted, again, that it was imperative that they be educated in the East. "Without education, children grow up, like the beasts that perish," he wrote. "And hard as the separation is, it is a duty we owe to them & to our selves. I am satisfied that I think *more* of my children, than I should if they were simply *of annointed blood*. And my hopes of their success in life are especially based, on the mixture of Anglo-Saxon blood, which they derive from their father, with the *eastern mind*, as strongly exemplified in the *Algic* race. Without the *former*, the result is, a want of *foresight*, and *firmness*—to traits that man *cannot* espouse and excell in the stern duties of human life."[31] He thought more of their children than she did because her Indian blood put them in grave danger of failure in civilized life. It must have been becoming clear to her that Schoolcraft thought it imperative that she and the children be separated as much as possible in order to save them from her Indian blood.

It must also have been clear that he was telling her about herself in the arrangement and contents of *Algic Researches*. He was also telling her about herself in the arrangement and contents of *Algic Researches*. He included his Wawanosh story, subtitled "A Chippewa Tale" in the first volume—the story of the humble young suitor who goes on a war party to prove himself to Chief Wawanosh so that he can marry the chief's daughter. But he dies, then she dies, unable to go on without him. The second volume concludes with his "The Vine and Oak," from *Literary Voyager*, in which the oak advises the vine that her wish to "grow *independently*" was "unnatural."[32] The third story of his own that Schoolcraft included in *Algic Researches*, also in the second volume, speaks to another attachment of Jane's of which he disapproved. He never let up. The third story of his own that Schoolcraft included in *Algic Researches*, in the second volume, speaks to another attachment of which Schoolcraft disapproved. In "Leelinau"—Jane's pen name signifying her Ojibwe identity in *Literary Voyager*—the title character, a "pensive" Indian maiden, spends all her time with fairies in a Sacred Grove, a "fearful spot" full of "Puk Wudj Ininees, or the little wild men of the woods, and Mishen Imominakog, or turtle-spirits, two classes of minor spirits or fairies who love romantic scenes."[33] When her parents inform Leelinau that they've chosen her a husband, she runs away to the Sacred Grove and communes with a pine tree, who addresses her. Think of me as "thine own dear lover," says the tree, "with bright green nodding plume," as in "Corn Story." "Fly from man, that bloody race," he says, offering her shelter. "Come, and on the mountain free / Rove a fairy bright with me."[34] Leelinau returns home, dresses herself for the wedding, then announces to her mother that she's going to the Sacred Grove. "'Adieu! Adieu!'" Leelinau cries as she leaves.[35] When she doesn't return for days and search parties find no trace of her, the truth becomes clear. One night spearfishers see a female figure near Spirit Grove, but when they land their canoe, she runs away, and "they recognised, in the shape and dress, as she ascended the bank, the lost daughter, and they saw the green plumes of her lover waving over his forehead, as he glided lightly through the forest of young pines."[36]

Schoolcraft's "Indian" writing directed at Jane is generally transparent: she needed to submit to his authority. This story is different. Their marriage began with Jane worrying that he would abandon her, as white men in that part of the world generally did Indigenous women, but she had to have understood soon enough that he depended on her knowledge in multiple ways, even if she had to pretend that he didn't. He wouldn't abandon her, no matter how much time he spent in Detroit and Washington. She told him everything he asked. He eventually learned that the world of spirits that Anishinaabe people inhabited was real. The stories they told weren't fantasy; they had meaning that he couldn't in the least understand. He could only see demons. "Leelinau" not only associates Jane with Anishinaabe spirituality; it suggests that she was more at home there than with him.

Most of the reviewers of *Algic Researches* had some difficulty in reconciling themselves to what they saw on the page. The stories were "very simple romances" yet at the same time "very peculiar," said the *Ladies Companion*, "told, we should imagine, much as they are related among the Indians themselves, that is, an unadorned, literal translation is given."[37] What that last seems to have meant is that the stories weren't modified appropriately for American readers. The *Boston Weekly Magazine* judged the stories "unique" and compared them, again, to *The Arabian Nights*, but noted that while "the Arabian legends bestow upon the brute the intelligence and dignity of human reason, the Indian transformation degrades the man to the level of the appetites and propensities of the beast," thus countering whatever might have been attractive in the stories with a reminder of their savagery.[38]

Schoolcraft arranged for a few supportive reviews. Francis Shearman, by then married and embarked on a career as an educator, remained an enthusiast for the stories, writing in the Detroit-based *Journal of Education* that "no proof is now wanting, of [Indians'] ability and even skilfulness in the creation of fictious legends." They did remind him of the *"Arabian Knights"* [sic], however, and he was careful to reiterate that one should of course read them for the "manners and customs" they revealed.[39] Schoolcraft's friend Henry Whiting (to whom he dedicated *Algic Researches*), writing at length for the *North American Review*, agreed, pointing out as well that the stories had "an intrinsic merit," one "a child could discover." Even the "most cursory reader" could find in them "invention . . . wildness, occasional sublimity, severity of satire, high moralizing, and instruction."[40]

Whiting took pains to establish the stories' authenticity and Schoolcraft's authority. Schoolcraft had broken through the Indians' "close reserve" and established "paternal relations" with the Indians, leading to "circumstances of intimacy."[41] Inevitably this led Whiting to Jane, for whom he provided a more embellished than usual origin story, now that she was a public figure. She was educated in Europe, overseen by "several ladies of rank" for patrons, "who took delight in watching the effect of cultivation on an exotic from so remote a region."[42] Once married to Schoolcraft, she "was a most zealous and efficient coadjutor of her husband in his researches and observations." That facilitation was as far as Jane's contribution went, according to Whiting. It was Schoolcraft who saw that the "'oral traditions" were important, it was he who started collecting them, and it was only he who could interpret them.[43]

Several months before Whiting's review was published, in July, a review appeared in the *Corsair*, a New York literary magazine, written by someone who seems to have been familiar with the Schoolcrafts, Jane in particular. "The tales and legends were in the first instance taken down by actual oral tradition from the lips of the Indians," writes the *Corsair*. "They were then rendered into English for Mr. Schoolcraft's use by several accomplished persons, the most of whom deriving their origin from Indian parents upon one side." These writers "were thoroughly familiar with the genius of the language which they translated." There's no mention of Schoolcraft's expertise here, although the writer congratulated Schoolcraft on not embellishing the stories, as the editors of the Ossian poems and *The Arabian Nights* had done to their detriment. Schoolcraft published them with their "blemishes" intact, indicating that the "rendering" was written down. Those blemishes attested to the stories' authenticity, the writer observed, without detracting from the "rich vein of poetry pervading the majority of them."[44] It seems that someone knowledgeable—perhaps Jane herself, socializing with new friends—talked to the writer of this review about who actually wrote the stories that Schoolcraft claimed as his own.

The children arrived at the beginning of August and stayed on the island about a month; Jane wrote only a few complacent letters about the state of the island and her social life while Schoolcraft was still away.[45] He discovered that Washington disapproved of his habit of spending the winter in Detroit, and he was told to remain at his post in the North, so Jane abandoned her plan of staying with her mother. He seems to have traveled as much as he could that summer and through the next winter. He accounted for Ojibwe improvements on the Upper Peninsula and inspected the mission at Grand Traverse, without Jane, in July 1839.[46] He was back in Detroit in August, then back again in November, and went back again to Grand Traverse in December.

Through the publication of *Algic Researches*, Jane modeled her stories on established forms and downplayed supernatural elements to write for Schoolcraft and Cass. "Corn Story" is the culmination of that approach. It's an origin story; it can be read as both a quaint allegory and an endorsement of agriculture over hunting, as Schoolcraft read it; and it has no loose ends. She chose the stories with her audience in mind—white readers generally but Schoolcraft in particular and in the earliest days Cass. After Jane's death Schoolcraft published three stories that show her taking an almost entirely different approach to her writing, all three of which appeared in the 1840s in *Oneota*, Schoolcraft's short-lived monthly periodical. Of the three stories two can be directly related to Jane. The first, "The Little Spirit, or Boy-Man" was subtitled by Schoolcraft "An Odjibwa Fairy Tale," and it gives Mrs. H. R. Schoolcraft as the author; for the second, "Wa-wa-be-zo-win: or The Swing on the Lake Shore," a draft exists in Jane's hand. The third, "Mukakee Mindemoea; or, The Toad-Woman," is similar to the other two in that, unlike Jane's previous stories, it doesn't follow an established form, it depicts gruesome violence, and it centers female characters. Based on what can be known at present, no one else in the family could have written it.

In "The Little Spirit, or Boy-Man," a girl lives in a cave with her brother, who "never grew larger as he advanced in years." He asks his sister to make a ball for him and then goes off to play with it on a frozen lake, in the course of which he steals fish from a man who calls his own brothers to take vengeance on the boy. The brothers converge on the door of the boy-man's lodge and get it open a crack—but then the boy-man shoots them in the eye with an arrow, one after another, after which he chops the brothers into pieces, saying "henceforth let no man be larger than you are now."[47]

This is more violent than Jane allowed in previous stories, and earlier in her career it would have been a good place to conclude, but there was more to say. The next spring, the boy-man tells his sister to make him a new bow and arrows, which she does because he "never did anything himself of a nature that required manual labor." Despite his sister's admonitions he shoots an arrow into the lake and then goes out into the deep water "so as to attract the attention of his sister." When she comes to the shore, her brother says, "*You*, of the *red fins*, come and swallow me":

> Immediately that monstrous fish came and swallowed him; and seeing his sister standing on the shore in despair he hallooed out to her, "Me-zush-ke-zin-ance." She wondered what he meant, but on reflection she thought it must be an old mockisin. She accordingly tied the old mockisin to a string and fastened it to a tree. The fish said to the Boy-man, under water, "What is that floating?" The Boy-man, said to the fish "Go, take hold of it, swallow it as fast as you can." The fish started towards the old shoe and swallowed it. The Boy-man laughed in himself, but said nothing, till the fish was fairly caught. He then took hold of the line and began to pull himself and fish to shore. The Sister, who was watching, was surprised to see so large a fish, and hauling it ashore she took her knife and commenced cutting it open. When she heard her brother's voice inside of the fish, saying, "Make haste and release me from this nasty place," his sister was in such haste that she almost hit his head with her knife but succeeded in making an opening large enough for her Brother to get out. When he was fairly out, he told his sister to cut up the fish and dry it as it would last a long time for their sustenance, and said to her, never, never more to doubt his ability in any way. So ends the Story.[48]

"So ends the story" was a common way to conclude in Anishinaabe stories collected from oral informants later in the nineteenth century; this is the only time Jane used the phrase (assuming this was not Schoolcraft's addition). Having set aside Western form for this story, Jane seems to be trying to bring the actual teller of the story closer to the printed text.

After Jane's death Schoolcraft no longer had anyone to supply him with stories, so in *Oneota* he published everything he had on hand; he still hid how much he depended on her by only sometimes attributing stories to her (or indeed to anyone else who'd written for him). "Wa-wa-be-zo-win, or The

Swing" he'd particularly not want to be associated with Jane, featuring as it does a murderous grandmother and Mishipeshu, the underwater panther, in this story a tiger. In the story an old widow lives with her daughter, son-in-law, their baby, and their foster son. The old woman grows jealous of her daughter because her son-in-law brings home delicacies for his wife like bear's kidney, which she would then fry up crisp "so as to make a sound in eating it." One day the widow asks her daughter to leave the baby in the care of her foster son and come out and swing with her, so they go to the lake shore and make a swing, from a tree on a high rock. The old woman "undressed, & only fastened a piece of leather round her loins, & commenced swinging, but only for a short time, when she stopped & told her daughter to do the same," Jane writes. The daughter undresses, ties the leather on and starts swinging—then "the old woman cut the cords & let her daughter fall in the lake." The daughter "found herself taken hold of by a tiger whose tail twisted round her body & drew her to the bottom," where she "found a fine lodge & all things ready for her reception as a bride & she became the wife of the water tiger." This is Mishipeshu, the spirit who has power over the underwater world.

The old woman disguises herself in her daughter's clothes and goes home, where she tries unsuccessfully to give the crying baby her breast. The foster son knows that the old woman was disguised and asks her where his mother is. Still swinging, the old woman says, and when the foster son says that he will look for her, the old woman tells him not to, asking him, "What should you go for?" Just then the husband returns and gives a "coveted morsel to his supposed wife," which she eats up while trying to keep the hungry baby still. The husband, who sees that his mother-in-law is missing, asks why the child cries, but the old woman "[averted] her face" and says she doesn't know. After this the husband stays home from hunting to care for his baby son, who doesn't stop crying. When the old woman leaves to gather firewood, the foster son tells his father what happened. At this the man "painted himself black & placed his spear upside down in the ground requesting the great spirit to give lightening, thunder & rain, in hopes the body of his wife might rise from the water." He sends his foster son with the baby to the shore to play while he fasts to prepare himself. The children go to the lake and are throwing pebbles into the water when they see a gull come from the center of the lake to the shore. When it gets to the shore "it [assumed] the human shape & when the boy looked again he recognized his sister as he had always called her with a belt of leather round her loins & in addition a belt of white nettle which was the tail of her tiger-water-husband which streaked away out to the depths of the lake."

She tells the foster son to bring the baby whenever he cries to the shore so she can nurse him. The boy takes the baby home and tells the husband, so when the child cries again, the husband this time goes along to the shore with them. He hides himself in trees at first. The gull appears, with "a long shining belt," and transforms into his wife, who begins to nurse her baby. Her husband breaks the chain that binds his wife with his spear. The family goes home, and "when they went into the lodge the old woman looked up & then her head sunk immediately & jumping up [she] flew out of the lodge, having on her daughter's clothes & was never heard of more."[49]

The only previous story that Jane wrote down that can be compared to these three later ones is "Moowis," but while that story has a female protagonist, Schoolcraft read it to demonstrate the dangers of coquetry and likely took it from her before she was finished writing it. American readers might recognize the mother in "Wa-wa-be-zo-win" as a witch who gets her comeuppance, but the underwater tiger is a figure both human (he takes a bride) and animal (but he is an underwater tiger) at the same time, with no explanation given. (The only change Schoolcraft made to the manuscript was to substitute the more modest "waist" for "loins.") "Mukakee Mindemoea" is about a mother of both a boy and a spirit dog, whose baby is stolen by Toad-Woman, a figure Vecsey gives as the grandmother of the underwater spirits.[50]

The mother runs off after Toad-Woman and her son, encountering along the way old women in lodges "who seemed as if they were all prophetesses." The story is about a conflict between two women and is populated by women. These old grandmothers help her as she follows the Toad-Woman "from valley to valley, and stream to stream, for months and years." After she finds and convinces her son (with the aid of the dog) that she is his real mother by having him drink her breast milk from a bark dish and identifying his cradle, her son and the dog destroy Toad-Woman. First they bait her with a bear they've impaled on a pine tree while they kill both of her real children, "[staking] them on each side of the door, with a piece of fat in their mouths." When she chases after them, they distract her with obstacles, but she gains on them. "Brother, chew her into mummy," says the stolen son finally to his dog, "for she plagues us." The story ends, "So the dog, turning round, seized her and tore her to pieces, and they escaped."[51]

These are not "pretty" stories. The three stories could conceivably have been written at any time, but given the fact that violence didn't prevent Schoolcraft from publishing any other stories and the fact that whenever the stories were too much for him, all he had to do was call them demonic and add footnotes or afterwords, it seems likely that Jane wrote these stories after the publication of *Algic Researches*. She was likely influenced by Charlotte and William in her writing, although neither Charlotte nor William wrote stories that can be as strongly identified with women. At the time of her exchange with Schoolcraft on "Corn Story," Jane seems to have been losing interest in writing the kinds of stories that interested him; she seems only to have wanted him to stop bothering her about it. These late stories about women and plainly supernatural figures are without the signposts of conventional form, morality, or theme to make them more acceptable to white readers. Jane doesn't seem to want to reach that audience any longer. She seems to have been writing for herself, or someone who could understand the stories as they were told.

William had seen Schoolcraft in Detroit, despite their rift—"he appears very well"—in the summer of 1839, probably about the family's property but there was nothing to do about it. "No business of any consequence going on," he wrote to George.[52] They could only hold on and hope for better times. That summer Schoolcraft had new jobs for George and John at Grand Traverse, an Odawa village. White settlement had slowed down considerably, and the expectation in government was that people wouldn't be deported until whites wanted their land. Schoolcraft's offer to George came with a requirement. George had formed an attachment with a white woman named Mary Rice, a Baptist missionary who had been working in the Bingham household for several years. Schoolcraft offered George the job of mechanic at $600 a year, and to Mary, who did not speak Ojibwemowin, he offered the job of interpreter at $300 a year provided they get married. This meant that George acted as both mechanic and interpreter. It appears that either or both of them had been hesitating on marriage, but they did get married in June 1839.[53] Schoolcraft made John government farmer.

Soon after this moment of his ascendance, Schoolcraft's arrogance and high-handedness caught up with him, and in about eighteen months he was dismissed from the Indian service. It began with William's anger at Schoolcraft's having dismissed him as interpreter for running a store but also at Schoolcraft's having published his stories in *Algic Researches* without attribution or payment. He told this, inexplicably, to James Schoolcraft, who then informed Schoolcraft not only that William was planning on getting him dismissed from government and thrown out of his church but that Schoolcraft would be made to "pay over part of the proceeds arising from the sale of the 'Algic Researches'—that man Johnston claiming authorship!"[54]

It wasn't just William who had had enough of Schoolcraft. The traders were still angry at having been cut off from treaty money, and the Odawas were angry at how the money had been distributed, too. William and Augustin Hamelin got themselves appointed agents of the Odawas to travel to Washington to argue for disbursement of more treaty money, mainly so that they could buy their land back. Before leaving for Washington, William signed an affidavit attesting to Schoolcraft's having taken for his own use or even sold food, supplies, and other goods meant for distribution to Indigenous people, as well as having prepared false vouchers for reimbursement and pocketing the money. Edward Biddle gave an affidavit charging Schoolcraft with refusing to let Indigenous people stay in the dormitory as well as his rampant nepotism. At the time James Schoolcraft was keeper of the dormitory; John Hulbert was the subagent at Saginaw; Schoolcraft's brother Abraham, James Schoolcraft, and George Johnston had all been paid to accompany expeditions to the Indian territory; George, his wife Mary, and John were all newly employed at Grand Traverse; and there was another girl, this time working in James and Anna Maria's household, who was paid $300 per annum as interpreter (which likely meant that Anna Maria was working as interpreter).[55]

T. Hartley Crawford, the commissioner of Indian affairs, appointed Samuel Abbott and John R. Williams of Detroit to investigate, neither of whom was sympathetic to Schoolcraft, Abbott because he was a disgruntled fur trader and Williams because he was a Catholic angry at Schoolcraft's bigotry toward his faith. They met first at Mackinac, and Jane was made to answer Interrogatories in May of 1840.

> 5. Has it been customary for the Indian women, children, orphans, & the Indian poor generally to apply for relief at the kitchen of the agency, indeed of the office, during the time (till 1838) that they were both under the same roof?

It has and I have often interpreted & often wept for them (given—

> 6. Has relief been granted in such cases, by cold victuals, clothes, medicines, or other articles?

Always & many a dose of medicine I have, without clothes, & when things would make them comfortable.

> 7. Has not the number of private applications for relief of the Indians been bothersome?

Extremely so, but have never sent them away.

> 8. Could any little present of game &c. brought by the Indians from the forest, on such occasions, be refused without giving offense?

No—it could not without giving offense.

9. Did the agent frequently observe, that he wished the Indians would never bring him presents, but sell every thing they had to the traders?

He did very often.

There were questions about linen sheeting supplies in 1835 and 1836, and whether they were "Indian goods ... diverted from their rightful purposes"; she was asked about how Charlotte Wabose was paid, and whether Louisa Piquette's treaty money was used for her education—ask the missionary, said Jane, since that was where she lived prior to her recent marriage. Were potatoes grown on the agency lot given to the Indians? "They were—& often delivered by myself when no other person was present, whose duty it was"; private and public property were kept strictly apart, Jane said. Lastly:

19. Do you deem the lists of charges made by Mr. Johnston numbers from 1 to 28, veracious?

I do not.[56]

After an initial investigation at Mackinac, the commission moved to Detroit in June. Schoolcraft followed, then went on to Washington to defend himself. He left instructions for Jane to keep a diary, and she diligently reported on it in her letters. (It hasn't survived.) When Schoolcraft faced adversity, and this was the most adversity he'd ever faced, she devoted herself to being obedient. He expected spiritual ruminations from her, and possibly information on his enemies' movements. Her diary would be "a *faithful tell-tale*, when you come to examine it, & will be better than many a *living witness*," she wrote. "*Your* bible is now my bosom & private companion morning & evening. I consult it *first* and *last*, every day, for reproof, for correction, for instruction & guidance & I feel it is the best & kindest of friends." She promised not to burden her letters with town gossip, saving "the *minutia* of every day ... for your satisfaction when you come home."[57] She tried to stick to the plan, "faithfully recording everything" in her journal "that takes place within my own observation & noting down every visit and visitor I receive." She even expressed fear "especially at nights" about "Indians" on the island, defaulting to that old habit meant to show Schoolcraft she needed his protection.

As was usually the case, complaints, or what Schoolcraft would perceive as complaints, began to appear. Schoolcraft had taken Janée to Washington, but not Johnston, who'd done something to anger his father. This bothered Jane and led her to suggest that they ought to "get a worthy, intelligent man" to teach the children "*at home*."[58] In July she started to get anxious that the children—"my only, earthly treasure"—wouldn't be home until mid-August, and there were the usual dramas of household management to relate.[59] "I regret to perceive a spirit of dissatisfaction & petty fault finding," Schoolcraft replied, ignoring her concerns about the children. Janée, aged twelve, had acquitted herself well in the city, leaving "a very favourable impression with all who have become acquainted with her," including "the President, the Secretary of the Treasury, Navy, Patent Office, &c."[60]

Abbott and Williams upheld most of William's charges and recommended Schoolcraft's dismissal. They kept their report until they were sure that Congress had adjourned for the summer, probably to keep Schoolcraft from lobbying the relevant politicians. They also didn't forward the additional letters and statements that Schoolcraft had gathered, including the material submitted in defense of George and other employees.[61] Hartley Crawford turned out to be not as harsh as his investigators, though, and according to Schoolcraft, he read over the material he did receive and concluded that while many of the charges laid against Schoolcraft, including those made by William, were true, they weren't of a sufficient magnitude to dismiss Schoolcraft. "Although some things are found which are censurable and must be amended," Crawford wrote in his final judgment, "there is nothing sordid or corrupt proved, or which wounds the character of the Superintendent materially or affects his honor or principles."[62] He also found that while there was no substance to the complaints about the other employees, the department couldn't support such nepotism, and therefore all the agent's family members were dismissed—except Schoolcraft's two white male relatives, James and Hulbert, who remained in place.[63]

Schoolcraft's reprieve was short-lived; the animosity he stoked wherever he went remained. The Whigs swept the November 1840 elections, during which Schoolcraft had signed a letter inviting the Democratic vice-presidential candidate to visit Michigan. In late March, Crawford signed an order providing for the dismissal of any federal employee engaging in partisan activity.[64] By mid-April 1841, Schoolcraft was on his way to Washington yet again to defend himself to Crawford and the secretary of war, but to little effect. He was returning home, in late April, when Jane opened a letter announcing that the ex-AFC trader Robert Stuart was to take Schoolcraft's place. Schoolcraft had been investigating schools for the children in Albany when he learned his fate.[65]

In all this, Jane played a passive role, continuing to write encouraging letters from Detroit, where the family, including the children, lived in the winter of 1840–41, a choice made in part because Schoolcraft couldn't afford the children's education in the East. She played an important but occluded role in Schoolcraft's final interaction with the government. In February 1841, before leaving office, Crawford had disbursed $20,000 to the Michigan Superintendency in order to pay outstanding debt claims before the change in administrations. In April, just before he left in his last desperate effort to defend himself in Washington, Schoolcraft began making moves to finally take the $8,200 he believed he was owed for Lieutenant Holmes's raid on the Johnston storehouses and homestead in 1814. He enlisted Jane in the subterfuge. She signed a printed form in her mother's name as administratrix of the Johnston Estate on 10 April 1841 for $1,172.41, an eighth share of the total claim. She evidently received the money at that time, in coin.[66] Jane did not have permission to sign for her mother, however, as Ozhaawshkodewikwe averred in a deposition taken after Jane's death.[67] Surely Jane would have known that. The fact that she signed as her mother for an eighth share, which would have been her own share had this been a legal transaction, suggests that the receipt was Schoolcraft's means of duping his wife as to what exactly he was doing.

What seems to have been the case was that Schoolcraft had the $8,200 in hand and was spending it as soon as he got hold of it. His biographer Richard Bremer writes that Schoolcraft more than likely thought he'd make the theft a "*fait accompli*" and be excused if and when he was caught.[68] Over almost twenty years, none of his other financial irregularities had brought him down, and subsequent events show that he had an elaborate and righteous explanation at the ready, as he always did. He paid a $4,000 debt on the Cass Front. He also, in addition to the $8,200, paid James his separate $1,500 claim—no doubt guaranteeing his silence, because no one else in the family would know what Schoolcraft had done for some time. He did not, however, give James Anna Maria's share of the $8,200 claim, which caused a certain amount of fireworks later on.

With James shut up for the moment and the rest of the family living apart from one another, or in the case of William, not speaking, it would not seem to have been difficult to hide what was going on. It's difficult to believe that Jane would have willingly or knowingly taken money not from her mother, who knew nothing about the claim, but from the Ojibwes and Odawas, whose money it was. There's nothing in her history that would allow her to steal from her relatives—but her response to this situation is entirely unknown. She returned to Mackinac in May 1841 to sell the contents of their house while having to fend off Robert Stuart, who wanted to move his family into the agency house immediately.[69] She was still there in July when she wrote to Schoolcraft wanting to know about prices to be put on the furniture. He'd just received notice from the US Treasury that he owed the government $16,532.24, half of which had actually been distributed to claimants and could be cleared up, but the other half of which was the money Schoolcraft had taken for himself and for James.[70] In August, the family left for New York City.

There's a surviving letter in the Schoolcraft papers from a very gracious man by the name of Butler who lived near Washington Square thanking Jane for having sent him a "note and articles." He'd not been able to call on her. "I am bound to acknowledge that from whomsoever descended you have the ascendency in the act and power of pleasing over me who has the pleasure in subscribing himself."[71] This was Benjamin Franklin Butler, Andrew Jackson's attorney general from 1833 to 1838. The US Army had named its North Carolina headquarters for him; the camp housed thousands of Cherokees—prisoners—who would be marched next to Tennessee and then further on, past Arkansas.[72] Schoolcraft must have known him through Cass. He shared his law practice with his brother Charles, who'd got rich buying up Potawatomi land at the site of Chicago, and then in railroads. They were great philanthropists, founders between themselves of New York University and Union Theological Seminary. There's a good chance that the "notes and articles" Jane sent were an effort to educate the man, as that was a family habit.

They came to New York because a literary career was Schoolcraft's only way of making a living. Before leaving Detroit, he issued a prospectus for the "Algic Magazine and Annals of Indian Affairs," although it didn't come to fruition. Instead he lectured at the Broadway Tabernacle on "Indian Character, Traits, &c." He maintained his professional ties, helping to found the American Ethnological Society with Albert Gallatin, at the New-York Historical Society that fall. He and Jane—probably mainly Jane—worked away on his dictionary and grammar. He spent "nearly a thousand dollars" of the stolen Ojibwe and Odawa money furnishing rooms in a townhouse at 224 Nineteenth Street "from carpets to crockery," Bremer writes.[73] He put the children to school at Albany.

He sought other ways to make money, engaging in yet more financial speculation, buying tax title leases in New York in partnership with another man. This arrangement ended in mutual recriminations and the loss of more than $2,000 when the leases were ruled invalid in state court.[74] He began planning his trip to Europe, to begin the next spring. He'd spend the next summer lecturing there and seeing about the publication of his works. Like the dictionary and grammar, the European trip was a sign of his intellectual fame that he especially needed at that moment. He was an explorer, a scientist, and the Europeans would surely be interested. He'd already been made an honorary member of their learned societies. He'd received an invitation to a soiree from Sir Roderick Murchison of the Royal Geographic Society, although sadly he would not arrive in London in time to attend.[75] Over the course of several months, he gathered by his own count about fifty letters of introduction.

Charlotte hadn't heard what happened until September, and she wrote Jane that she should have confidence that "as long as [Schoolcraft] has his health and can hold his pen, he will be able to make you all comfortable and happy as long as you all shall need the comforts of this changeable world." She also wondered if Schoolcraft "might try and get some of the Irish property, as I am quite poor [Negedemahgis]."[76] Anna Maria wrote with news of her as-yet unnamed infant son—he was "very fat, he is getting quite interesting, he jumps & dances whenever John plays on his flute, and he puts out his little hands when he is spoken to"—and envied Jane's new life in the city, where "the change and bustle, would just suit me."[77] It seems to have suited Jane as well, as she had written to Charlotte about "old friends" from the West who came to visit, as well as, as Charlotte put it (Jane's letter to her doesn't exist), "those "Relatives from whom you may at least receive some sympathy."[78] It's not clear who those relatives might have been, or if they were Anishinaabe. A variety of people they knew from the West were familiar with the city, usually for business reasons. Ramsay Crooks lived in the city with his large family, and there were those with whom her father and brothers did business. The only, scant, record of the Schoolcrafts' time in New York, from September 1841 to April 1842, shows them socializing with the literary set. Charles Fenno Hoffman, who'd become good friends with Schoolcraft, provided the introductions.

They arrived in New York when Indians were very much in vogue among the poets and story-writers, many of whom knew or were eager to know the Schoolcrafts, especially Jane, after her appearance in Mrs. Jameson's latest work. They filled the pages of a constantly shifting array of polite literary periodicals—*New World: A Weekly Family Journal of Popular Literature, Science, Art and News*; *Brother Jonathan, a Weekly Compendium of Belles Lettres and the Fine Arts*; *Arcturus, a Journal of Books and Opinion*; *Godey's Lady's Book, and Ladies' American Magazine.* Everyone was writing about Indians. The expulsion of the Cherokees and other southeastern nations had occurred only a few years previously amid much political controversy, and the Seminole War—the second of three—was ongoing, with dispatches relating carnage in the swamps of Florida a regular feature of their newspapers. Catlin had only recently departed for Europe, and his exhibition rooms stacked ceiling-high with portraits of wild Indian savages from the West had given everyone a good picture of whom and what they were dealing with. These writers did their job, cranking out one poem after another, yet more stories. Indians were the perfect subject matter for an American writer. All the critics said so.

One old friend of Jane's in New York was Anna G. Snelling, who kept the Schoolcrafts apprised on the progress toward publication of her novel *Kabaosa; Or, The Warriors of the West*, a fictionalized account of her father-in-law Josiah Snelling's experiences in the War of 1812, featuring Indians. Henry and Anna Snelling were newly married when they arrived in Detroit in 1836, and during their relatively short time in the city they acquired a print shop and founded three different periodicals: the *Michigan Agriculturalist*; *Eglantine* (a literary periodical), renamed *The Mirror of the Lakes*; and a newspaper called *The Spirit of '76*.[79] Anna had initially written her novel as a poem, and her husband was publishing it himself, in installments, counting on the popularity of the theme.[80] He was librarian at the New York Lyceum, and she was the sister of George Palmer Putnam, who as part of the concern Wiley and Putnam published books by Cooper, Irving, and Bryant. Anna and Henry were planning a periodical called "The Columbian," she wrote to Schoolcraft, wondering if he would contribute. They wouldn't be able to pay at the beginning, but the Snellings had gathered a respectable group of writers, some who were willing to let their names be printed and some who couldn't, as they wrote for competitors.

While novels about Indians had long been popular—in January 1842 the literary periodicals reported that Cooper's *The Deerslayer* was being readied for the press—around the time the Schoolcrafts were in New York, quite a few writers were trying their hands at Indian epics, long poetic works that sought to say something grand about America, usually with footnotes. Schoolcraft himself had been writing them for years by then. Hoffman's first book of poems, *The Vigil of Faith and Other Poems* (1842), began with a thirty-one-page, forty-seven-canto title poem in which an "idler" living along the Hudson River tells the story of Indian friends ("grown children of the wild / When in their native forest walk, / Confiding, simple as a child") competing for the love of "Bright Nulkah" with tragic (for Nulkah, who takes two cantos to die) consequences.[81] (His previous book had been a novel in the manner of Walter Scott about the border wars of the eighteenth century, featuring in a subordinate role an Indian maiden named Spreading Dew.)[82] While Jane was in New York, Lydia Huntly Sigourney, a well-regarded poet, published *Pocahontas, and Other Poems* (1841), the title poem of which describes the domestication through Christianity of the titular "forest-child"—and then her death, the moment of which takes four cantos to relate.[83] Seba Smith, a former newspaper editor in Bangor who'd made his name writing satirical pro-Jackson essays during the Jackson administration, contributed *Powhatan*, a 150-page "metrical romance" dedicated to "the young people of the United States." At the end of the poem Powhatan is literally the last man standing, on the realization of which he "took his war-club for a staff, / and his footsteps westward turn'd, / Where the ruddy sunset burn'd."[84]

Hoffman circulated through what seems to have been a constant stream of social engagements with his fellow writers and critics, carrying on a flirtatious correspondence about ladies who didn't interest him with the married poet Emma Embury.[85] He was in between editing jobs, working in the Customs House and writing poetry. His friend Rufus Griswold, a fellow critic who'd abruptly abandoned both his job at Horace Greeley's *New York Tri-*

bune and his wife and two daughters for Philadelphia and a job with the *Daily Standard*, consulted with Hoffman on Griswold's new project, an anthology called *Poets and Poetry of America* (1842)—it was meant to summarize both the accomplishments and promise of American literature. Griswold was a determined literary nationalist who prided himself on his superior taste. He included forty-five of Hoffman's poems in the collection, more than anyone else, including Henry Wadsworth Longfellow and William Cullen Bryant. He included only three by his fellow Philadelphia critic Edgar Allan Poe. Poe was then editor of *Graham's Magazine* in the city and had published such stories as "Murders in the Rue Morgue" and "The Fall of the House of Usher" in addition to his poetry. It was the beginning of a contentious relationship between the two men.

When Jane arrived in New York, her new friend Catharine Maria Sedgwick, who was acclaimed to the point of being beloved, had just published *Letters from Abroad to Kindred at Home* (1841), about her travels in Europe. William Leete Stone had recently published *The Life of Red Jacket* (1840)—also well received, and if the family was in town (Colonel Stone had been appointed envoy to the Hague by President Harrison but recalled by President Tyler) during the Schoolcrafts' stay, there is a very good chance that Jane visited again with Mrs. Stone, Susana Wayland, the daughter of a Baptist minister who was president of Brown University. While Washington Irving had removed himself to his renovated house in the Hudson Valley (Sunnyside was so famous itself that the *Dollar* magazine advertised engravings of it, suitable for framing), he still frequented the city and possibly saw the Schoolcrafts before leaving for Spain—President Tyler had appointed him consul that winter.

Irving was in town long enough to be the chief participant in the event of the season, the visit of Charles Dickens and his wife, which necessitated two balls, one very large dinner, and multiple smaller receptions over a few days in February. Martin Hoffman, Charles Fenno's uncle and Dr. Gilman's traveling companion, was one of the organizers of the "Boz Ball," held on Valentine's Day.[86] Three thousand people attended, and they ate 50,000 oysters and 10,000 sandwiches. The ball included tableaux vivant showing scenes from Dickens's novels in between quadrilles, waltzes, a "Spanish Dance," and a gallopade in the Park Theatre, amid "festoons of flowers, garlands, draperies, and trophies emblematical of the different states of the Union," as a writer for the *Albion* described it.[87]

All the leading lights went to the balls (Dickens was exhausted and waved off the second), so Schoolcraft would probably have wanted to be there, too, despite his piety. Hoffman had been ill and missed them himself, but he met with Dickens later, writer to writer, privately. "The City has been half crazy

Elizabeth Oakes Smith by John Wesley Paradise (ca. 1845). National Gallery of Art, Washington, D.C.

about Boz he was the all engrossing topic while he was in town poor man," Julia Hoffman wrote to her brother George. "He must have been a good deal bored I should think he was sought after and written to by all sorts of people." This included the "fashionable" Mrs. Jones, who gave him a "splendid party at which Mrs. Jack Downing stuck to him like a leech and whenever he would break from her she followed him and seized upon him again."[88] "Mrs. Jack Downing" was Mrs. Seba Smith—Jack Downing was Seba Smith's dated satirical alter-ego—who is better known today as the poet and early women's rights campaigner Elizabeth Oakes Smith. Elizabeth Oakes Smith was a friend of Hoffman, as well as of Rufus Griswold, and she attached herself to Jane Schoolcraft as she did to Charles Dickens.

Mrs. E. O. Smith was a force in the manner of Anna Jameson, a clever woman making a living from her writing and asserting herself in literary society. She'd published innumerable poems, stories, and commentaries since arriving in New York with her husband and four sons after the failure of his newspaper during the depression. Worse, his writing fell out of favor, too

(*Powhatan* did nothing to revive it), and so she became the primary breadwinner for the family. Like everyone else, Mrs. Smith had dabbled in Indian stories before encountering Jane, but her principal work at the time was her well-received seven-part poem "The Sinless Child" (it did not involve Indians), which appeared in the *Southern Literary Messenger* in January and February 1842. Her collected poems, under the same title and with an introduction by Griswold, would appear later that year.[89] It was the height of her career in poetry.[90] After the Civil War, disgraced by slave-trading sons and in voluntary exile near Morehead, North Carolina, she began writing reminiscences about her antebellum literary heyday for *Beadle's Monthly*, *Appleton's Journal*, and a variety of periodicals concerned with physical and mental hygiene.[91] For twenty-five years before her death in 1893, she remembered N. P. Willis, William Cullen Bryant, Charles Fenno Hoffman, Frances Sargent Osgood, Edgar Allan Poe, John Neal (his mother was her childhood teacher in Bangor, she noted, more than once), and especially Margaret Fuller, on whose faults (she didn't mingle, couldn't converse, didn't know how to dress) Mrs. Smith never missed an opportunity to elaborate, at length.

One of the earliest of her reminiscences was of Jane Schoolcraft. She either forgot or made up the biography. She had Jane's mother as a "Mohawk Queen" and Jane herself being educated in France along with a sister. According to Mrs. Smith, Jane and her imaginary sister had olive complexions, with straight "purple black" hair. Jane "was rather above the ordinary height, straight and slender, with a graceful, easy motion, and like her people, with very small feet and hands. Her mouth was flexible, or a good width, and very soft and sweet in expression, and with white even teeth when she smiled, was a most attractive feature." Indians, Mrs. Smith observed, had very soft mouths, as was attested by Fitz-Green Halleck in his poem on Red Jacket. She could not possibly describe Mrs. Schoolcraft's eyes. "They were deep-set, of a dark gray, deepening in emotion to black, the lid large and clear," she wrote, "but there was, when at rest, a look of intense sadness, and when she broke the silence after this expression her voice was a musical sight, something like an echo dying out, which was very touching." "I have noticed this cadence in more than one Indian," Mrs. Smith added, "but never in the negro, whatever his status."[92]

Mrs. Smith described an evening with the Schoolcrafts and others, including Dr. Peter Wilson, a Cayuga physician and lecturer who lived at the Cattaraugus Seneca reservation.[93] All of her guests, she wrote, "talked with animation, but I observed the Doctor seemed ill at ease in our ordinary drawing-room chairs, his bulky figure quite protruding over them, and testing their strength fearfully." Another guest suggested cigars, which were broken out, although Mrs. Smith provided the doctor a pipe, "which I begged him to consider a calumet." Dr. Wilson "settled his head down into his collar, much as Horace Greeley used to do preparatory to a sleep in church, and began to pour out volumes of smoke." The party took turns reciting poems. Then Mrs. Smith asked for a "war whoop," having heard Catlin, who was "lithe and springing as a leopard," do it himself. Dr. Wilson "threw back his shoulders, sprang forward, and beginning low, rose to a fearful yell—so deep that it made me think of a lion's roar—so intense that the windows rattled." "These Indians are apt to go back to their original wildness," Mrs. E. O. Smith wrote knowledgably, "and I could not but suspect, that a few repetitions of the war-whoop might suggest to him the propriety of taking our scalps."[94]

Despite the heavily embroidered biography (Jane was a little over five feet tall, for one thing), this would seem to have been the kind of evening Jane Schoolcraft spent in New York, reciting poetry or stories with a lively company of other writers. That winter she'd also met Lord Morpeth, the Earl of Carlisle, "a British nobleman of great public and private worth," according to the *Albion*, who spent a year traveling in the United States after losing a parliamentary election. He'd been chief secretary of Ireland before that and was feted in New York almost as elaborately as Dickens would soon be (although it involved a full-length portrait of Queen Victoria and a marble bust of Chief Justice John Marshall instead of tableaux vivant). The Hoffman family seems to have been the connection, again, as Ogden Hoffman, Charles Fenno's older half-brother, the current US attorney for the Southern District of New York, was one of the principal celebrants at Morpeth's banquet. Jane must have impressed Lord Morpeth at some later social occasion at which ladies were present. According to Mrs. Smith, Jane had invited Morpeth to visit Michigan, and she of course wanted Mrs. Smith to go along with them.[95]

> "Go with us," [Jane] said, "and you shall be paddled down the Sault Ste. Marie, in the handsomest canoe, by the handsomest Indian of the West"; and again she reiterated, "You have an Indian soul, all that an Indian exults in would speak to your mind, you should go to the sources of the Mississippi, which my husband was the first to discover, and we would talk over those rare old mythologies, so little known and appreciated by white people. You will delight to hear the language of the Indian spoken in the midst of waterfalls and mountains; listen"; she raised her eyes with wonderful pathos, and solemn depth of intonation, uttered what caused cold chills to run down my back and my breath to stop with awe.
>
> "What was it?" I whispered.
>
> "Our Lord's Prayer in Algonquin."

"How inspired she looked!" wrote Mrs. Smith, wondering whether civilized women could ever learn to be as "thoroughly true and earnest."

If any of this passage is true, Jane was teasing Mrs. Smith. "Mrs. Schoolcraft delighted to recite the legends of her people, and would playfully, sometimes when her listener was fully absorbed, go off into Algonquin, which had a most musical sound," Mrs. Smith continued. "She was, unquestionably, nearly, if not quite, the author of the *Algic Researches*."[96] Jane was a woman who had mocked her husband's fixation on dead Indian maidens years since, who was well aware that whites' feelings of sympathy for Indians had nothing to do with actual understanding. She had Mrs. Jameson's example; she pointed it out to William Hull Clarke. And when she had sufficiently charmed her listeners with stories, Jane spoke Ojibwemowin. What would she have been saying? Mrs. Smith would never know.

But Jane talked about her writing, and Mrs. Smith would remember that for the rest of her life. Given Schoolcraft's public stance on the writing of *Algic Researches*, someone had to have informed Mrs. Smith that Jane was "nearly, if not quite" the author of the book, and that someone was probably Jane herself. Perhaps she said this at a party, in a drawing room, while they told stories and traded poems, and Dr. Wilson smoked his calumet. In the spring Mrs. Smith sent Jane some writing, and Jane sent a letter back acknowledging the gift, a fragmentary draft of which remains, in Schoolcraft's papers. He certainly read the letter, as Mrs. Smith was an important woman with important friends in the literary circle Schoolcraft wanted to join. "*Thou*, who has the *same* feelings, with *me, a poor child of the forrest* [sic]—I address not in pompous style or strains; but in the true language of the heart," Jane wrote, knowing full well how white peoples construed poor children of the forest and with a certain amount of pomp nonetheless. "I have heard of your devotion to your dear children & Husband—notwithstanding the attention you have given to the highest designs of *mind*, after the beauties of creation, &, to sing its praises, as well as of other subjects, which tend to elevate, & soften the mind of us poor mortals, & I feel a desire to thank you for setting an example to *our* sex that *both* can be accomplished, without detriment to either duties & my wish *is* to copy your example in *both* if I possibly can." This is a remarkable statement at the time, that women could be both writers and mothers while devoted to "the highest designs of mind." She sought to follow that example herself: did she have plans to write, for herself, or, possibly, did Schoolcraft, who was reading this letter, think that she could contribute to the family's upkeep like so many other women writers of the period, by writing pretty stories? Either way, Jane in her "child of the forest" guise denied any difference between herself and Mrs. Smith. "With the aid of *Our God*," she concluded, both she and Mrs. Smith could show "that neither Language, or Nation, can possibly have a different set of Morals to be governed by—but these which the *Great Creator, himself* has ordained. The fulfilling of which, is the great end of our being."[97]

Jane was in Dundas, where she was to stay with Charlotte for the duration of Schoolcraft's European trip, when she received Mrs. Smith's response, a poem praising her "primitive simplicity and truthfulness of character."[98] Like other Americans, other westerners, Mrs. Smith needed her savages, and there was only so much contrary to the idea that she could manage.

Before they left the city, Schoolcraft tried to clear up his financial dealings with the Johnston Estate in what looks very much like attempting to cover for the money he would have owed them from the money he took. McMurray was suspicious; and he and Schoolcraft exchanged testy letters, in the course of which Schoolcraft demanded payment from the other Johnston heirs for sums he said they owed him. He had Janée write out the most involved letter, suggesting that Jane didn't know what was going on or wanted no part of it.[99] Then he withdrew the receipt he'd left in Michigan for Jane's ostensible share of the money and substituted another form, also signed by Jane for her mother, for the whole amount, plus some.[100] They put their belongings in storage in the third story of 224 West Nineteenth Street, including "a quantity of household furniture, useful & ornamental, together with books, pictures, mineralogical specimens & other articles."[101] Then they took a schooner from the West Side docks, up the Hudson to Albany, changed at the depot for a train to Buffalo, then took a steamboat at Buffalo to St. Catherines, where McMurray came for them in a carriage. Afterward Schoolcraft wrote his daughter that Jane was tired and had had a cold but was no worse than she'd been that winter in the city, and neither of them thought anything of it. They said their goodbyes in the morning, and Schoolcraft returned to the city to set out on his expedition.[102]

She died several weeks later, at the end of May. McMurray wrote to say that he and Charlotte very much regretted that Jane had lost consciousness when Charlotte was out of the room. Jane had asked Charlotte to go downstairs for something, and she went, because Jane seemed better and even to be recovering. When Charlotte returned, McMurray wrote, Jane "was not dead, but she was too far clutched in death's embrace to know her or to utter a word." Charlotte insisted on laying Jane out, and "when she was to be removed to the house appointed for all living, we went to her room alone and after taking a final look, and pressing her cold lips, we covered her once lovely and cheerful face, with the unsightly shroud, and thus hid for ever from our eye, all that was earthly of our beloved Sister."[103]

Schoolcraft didn't notice that Jane's carpetbag was missing until they had arrived in Dundas. It held all of her papers. It had disappeared at the Albany depot, and Schoolcraft scolded Jane in the last letter that she received from him for being careless about it. Inside the carpetbag was likely all of the writing that currently doesn't exist: her correspondence, the diaries Schoolcraft made her keep, poems in Ojibwemowin and English, stories that Schoolcraft hadn't got hold of yet, and the dictionary and grammar. Presumably she would have wanted to keep all of that close, particularly the last, because that dictionary and grammar were Schoolcraft's means of establishing himself as the foremost Indian expert in the country, the one who had knowledge that no one else had, which was even more important when he was no longer employed by the government. He may not have realized what exactly was in the carpetbag until long afterward. The dictionary and grammar especially could have been left in the city with everything else. But they weren't, and Schoolcraft never published anything new in the way of philological analysis after Jane's death. The only material on Ojibwemowin in his papers dates from the 1820s and Cass's questionnaire. How the carpetbag was lost is a mystery.

It's true that there is no eyewitness account, no newspaper report of a small woman in a black dress heaving a carpetbag into the Hudson River on a cool spring day. Whatever happened most likely happened inside the depot. Some nefarious fellow could have scooped up the bag when her back was turned, just as Cousin George had suffered in New York City. But it would have been easy to kick it under a bench, or put it too close to someone else's bags. Everything in the carpetbag was irreplaceable—to Schoolcraft, not to her. She could remember the stories and poems and had no use for the diaries he'd insisted she write. It certainly wasn't she who needed that dictionary and grammar. He stole from her relatives; he involved her in the scheme. He kept her children from her, he said, to protect them from her malign Indian influence. After all that he had done in the past and promised to do in the future, it would have been easy enough to drop the bag and walk away from it. She didn't have to say anything at all.

PART III

A Narrative of Wabwindigo

Told by Shingabawossin, Translated by George Johnston, Sault Ste. Marie, 10 June 1845[1]

When he had attained the middle age, an old woman of his tribe, a Roman Catholic by profession, taught him to read, and in the course of one fall, one winter & spring he had mastered a little book and could read it fluently. He also became perfect master of the Roman Catholic ritual and forms of prayer, and in the course of time had collected a considerable little library of religious books which he kept in his trunk, and in fine had abandoned the professed religion of his forefathers, and adopted the Roman Catholic religion in full faith.

After this period, he was suddenly taken sick and died. His coffin was made, and he was laid in it, and those who were watching the corpse, on occasional examination found a heaving or pulsation in the chest, and the arms became pliant, finally the head. Wabwindigo rose and sat up as if awakening from a deep sleep, and addressing himself to his friends narrated to them what had occurred to him during the time he imagined he slept for it did not appear to him that he had been sick and died, but he spoke like one awakening from a deep sleep.

He said that he saw an Indian ladder before him and on looking up, the top reached an opening in the sky, and he was fully impressed with the belief that it was the way which the priest so often spoke of to reach heaven. He immediately resolved to ascend it, and when he had reached a great way up he looked down and beheld the diminutive appearance of the earth with its yet visible verdure, and he still ascended, until he reached the opening in the sky. It appeared to him like a narrow door, and a man stood there and enquired of him what he wanted. He replied that this was the way that was pointed out to him to obtain happiness and everlasting life. He was told by this person, who appeared to be a guard, that he was mistaken, and that it was not the way for the Indians.

Wabwindigo insisted, saying that it was the way he was taught to seek. Stepping higher to get in, he saw two more men running towards him from within the door, and they enquired him what he wanted, and he answered as he had already done. They told him that this was not the way for the Indians; "that it was the way for white men only." After this reply they shoved him backwards and he became senseless, and was unconscious of the height from whence he had fallen, and on falling to the ground, he awoke. He then desired his friends to fetch his trunk and to open it.

The priest came in at this time and Wabwindigo addressing himself to him said, "I found the way to happiness, which you have taught me to seek, that was not intended for the Indians." "Yes! my son, it is," replied the priest, "but God does not yet require you." "I know it is not," replied Wabwindigo emphatically, and taking the books from his trunk, threw them into the fire in the presence of the priest, one volume after another until they had burnt the whole, resolving never more to follow the white man's religion, and from that moment relinquished it, and again adopted his forefathers'.

He was restored to health and he would drink ardent spirits from time to time, as the Indians generally do, and attained extreme old age and dying in reality after having walked over life's way.

Epilogue

The government sent William and George another questionnaire in late 1847.[1] With the help of his new wife, an aging southern belle named Mary Howard, Schoolcraft had secured a commission to write—something, it wasn't clear what at that point, but following Cass's familiar model he would collect the information necessary. Both William and George had been in periodic contact with Schoolcraft since 1842. While George sent occasional notes on pictographs or the language, William wrote to him whenever it seemed like the Ojibwes and Odawas wished to settle their affairs at Washington, providing as far as William was concerned an opening for the family to make claims for payment of debts.[2] Nothing ever happened, and William's plans eventually fizzled out.

The letter and its accompanying questions came over Commissioner of Indian Affairs William Medill's signature, so William may not yet have known about Schoolcraft's involvement. He could only answer questions 347 and 348 in the circular, he wrote, not having the time to devote to any more of them despite his having collected substantial "manuscript & notes" over the years. He congratulated the government for seeking out information so that white people would judge Indians "cordially," so that "their preconceptions, will be changed by authenticated truths." "The time is not far distant when information from the Indian himself will have passed away & no permanent traces will be left by him, to guide others in their researches for the promotion of knowledge respecting him," William observed, and then he reminded the commissioner of how that situation came to be. "What has become of the Red Man; what was his history, manners, & customs," he asked. "The answer will be, this great and glorious Republic had them under their guardianship, its treatment of them that obliterated all traces of their being once inhabitants of this portion of our continent." If Medill truly wanted to pursue the matter, he added, the most authentic information was to be found at the headwaters of the Mississippi, where William had spent that winter years before. A "competent interpreter" was of paramount importance in such endeavors, and, though he himself had suffered through the "mis-statements of a former Supt of Ind Affairs," he was particularly suited to such a task in view of his previous position as an interpreter at Mackinac and his status as a "half-breed," as the US government classified people like him.[3]

William Johnston, carte de visite (ca. 1850). Chippewa County Historical Society, Sault Ste. Marie, Michigan.

William then reflected on the failure of white writers to convey anything of value about Indigenous life. They were such a failure that "I cannot now particularize," he wrote. "I have read the oldest & latest authors, who refer to this portion of the country & its inhabitants. The incidents of travel, description of scenery & the features of the country are nearly correct, but when they refer to the Indian, apart from their own external observations of them, they are in most cases void of truth." He'd certainly have read McKenney, Gilman, and Jameson; there were also Calvin Colton, Frederick Maryatt, Harriet Martineau, and by the time he was writing, Margaret Fuller.[4] The only "correct information" could be had "from those, who are familiar with the Indians, who by their conduct towards them, have lulled all suspicions the Indians have . . . towards whites." Unfortunately, and he was probably thinking of Schoolcraft, "the latest works published on the Indian Character, are based on some correct information, but the authors have erroneously upon the limited information gone on, & built a fabric of their own, giving out to the public, their own opinions & constructions & called them Indian manners & customs."

"I have noticed travelers from our states & foreigners writing the incidents of their travels in the Indian country, apparently as well acquainted with their characters, customs &c. (in their own views) as the Indians were themselves," he continued. "How did they obtain their information, they are utterly ignorant of their language *in fact* know not an Indian Word correctly; they have seen small bands of them in traveling along, they believed they have obtained all the knowledge they need & *they set down as facts* their opinion of the Indian's thoughts, his mental capacities &c. and have them published as facts." These travelers "[procured] their information" from "the voyager & half-breeds who have paddled them along the shores of Lakes; who are actually more brutalized in mental feeling than the Indians." (Here William seems to refer to people of French and Anishinaabe ancestry and Catholic faith, reflecting in part his father's anti-Catholicism.) While there may be exceptions to this rule, "it is a noted fact, that the traders & voyagers when they see an individual with pen or pencil in hand, writing or sketching & asking questions for information, that they are on the alert & the word passed among them to hoax him." And in addition to that, "many errors spring from the incompetency of the Govt. Interpreters, who are looked to for correct information, & also other individuals."[5]

William was squeezing words onto the bottom of the page, and there the letter ended, unless Schoolcraft in a fit of pique got rid of the rest of it. He kept the vocabulary William wrote out, however.

William Leete Stone received the news of Jane's death with "unfeigned sorrow," he wrote in his newspaper, the New York *Spectator and Commercial Advertiser*. "Mrs. Schoolcraft was a half-blood Ojibbeway, and rather darker than is usual with half-bloods," he wrote. "But she was highly educated—possessed great sweetness of manner and conversation—and was one of the most interesting ladies it has been our happiness to know."[6] A writer for the *Weekly Messenger*, a missionary paper in Chambersburg, Pennsylvania, shared Stone's sorrow, even if he didn't know Jane personally. He recommended Mrs. Jameson's book for her account of both Jane and Charlotte, where readers might "make the acquaintance for themselves with the charming specimens of Indian character there introduced."[7]

Schoolcraft didn't cut short his trip after Jane's death. He gave a lecture on the water levels in the Great Lakes in London, left his cards around town, then departed for the continent, where he was edified in Germany and appalled in France.[8] No one was interested in publishing his books. He'd written to Jane in a letter that arrived after her death that it was too expensive for the children to go to Dundas for the summer, but they ended up going there after all, where they were unexpectedly visited by Eliza Cameron, the daughter of another of John Johnston's illegitimate children, who seems to have had ulterior motives. "I suppose you know how Mother found her out in New York so I will not mention any thing about it," Johnston wrote to George.[9] (Later Miss Cameron became a housekeeper for Schoolcraft, moving with the family from one boardinghouse to the next until his remarriage.)[10]

From Europe, Schoolcraft had his one rich relative, his cousin John Laurence Schoolcraft, an Albany banker married to William Seward's daughter, arrange for a headstone to be placed on Jane's grave at McMurray's church. He sent the inscription to his cousin. "Carefully educated, and of polished manners and education, she was early fitted to adorn society: yet of retiring and modest deportment," he wrote. "Early imbued with the principles of true piety, she patiently submitted to the illness, which, for several years, marked her decline, and was inspirited, through seasons of bodily & mental depression, with the lively hope of a blessed immortality."[11] He'd arranged for a chest tomb, and it must have been impressive in the new cemetery, but with the inscription on its flat top the words would sooner fade away. He never paid for it.[12]

In London he wrote an account of Jane's life for Mrs. Jameson that was mainly about her father and that doesn't appear to have been completed.[13] In a different draft letter to Jameson, Schoolcraft told the plain truth about Jane. She "was my constant standard of reference" in his researches, he wrote. "In all questions calling for it, she ascertained, & brought to the task the aid & [knowledge] of her mother, & other members of the family." It was Jane, he admitted, to which "we owe, the first notice of the existence of traditionary oral imaginative tales & allegories among her people. She had heard these stories from her childhood—some of the simpler of them, she traced to her memory. The long winter evenings in that latitude are favorite times of the activity of this nature, to pass away the time in amusements & plays, and in narrating the tales of wonder, adventure, superstition, or instruction."[14] This letter is a fragment of a draft, and there is no telling whether or not it represents anything Jameson received. That he told the truth about Jane makes that unlikely, however, given his habits.

He tried to write an appropriate account of her mother for Janée while he was in Europe. Jane "had not the advantages of a mother (in the refined sense of the term) to bring her up," he told his daughter. "Her education & manners were, in great measure, formed by *her father*, and that she had many & peculiar trials to encounter on coming into the broad & mixed circle of society." She had "refinement," proper manners, and a "purity & delicacy in language, & correctness of sentiment" that "few females, in any rank or station, possess." He'd written poems to Jane that Janée should read, "if *all* were not in the ill fated carpet bag." (As there are numerous poems Schoolcraft wrote to Jane extant, she does not seem to have kept them with her.) Jane was a good mother and a good housekeeper. "Her taste in literature, was chaste," he wrote. "She wrote many pretty pieces, which I have carefully traduced."[15]

In April 1843, the US government arrested Schoolcraft for fraud; the bond was $20,000, but he was released because he had neither money nor assets.[16] In advance of an October trial the district attorney George Bates deposed Eliza, William, John McDouall, and Ozhaawshkodewikwe at Sault Ste. Marie. Despite being listed for it, Anna Maria wasn't deposed. Each member of the family reported the same thing, that they had not received any money after 1836. Ozhaawshkodewikwe also testified that, as the clerk Samuel Ashmun (then justice of the peace) rendered it, she had never given Schoolcraft "any proper voucher or writing signed by her as the administratrix of the estate of the late John Johnston authorizing him ... to present a claim for monies due from the Indians to the estate of the late John Johnston under the treaty made between the United States & the Ottoways & Chippewas in March 1836."[17] William interpreted for both Ozhaawshkodewikwe and Eliza, who signed with a mark like her mother.

"I have never failed to apprize Mrs. J. of the progress made, from time to time, in the collection and security of the old Indian debt matters," Schoolcraft sputtered in a letter to his lawyer. William was "bitter and reckless," and he'd duped his mother, who knew nothing of business.[18] James opined that the only way out was to give him the money and say that he had been holding it for his mother-in-law since 1841.[19] The problem with this plan was that Schoolcraft didn't have any money, and less than a month before the trial, he still didn't know what he would do. He was saved, however, when only Anna Maria made the trip down to Detroit and he and his lawyer successfully argued for a postponement to the next court session, to June when travel would be easier. By then Schoolcraft had his plan. He would give William, George, and Eliza the New York City tax title leases in which he had invested, telling them that they could exchange the leases for the value of their share of the $8,200. Presumably they would then testify favorably for him. When he gave the Johnstons the leases, he knew that they were worthless.[20]

Ozhaawshkodewikwe died at the Sault in November 1843. Bingham had preached at her fishing lodge a few weeks earlier. "Mrs Johnston related some of the religious impressions she had some years ago, which lead her to hope she was a christian," he noted in his diary. Someone was interpreting for her, because Bingham never made any effort to learn the language. She "spoke of God's kindness, & faithfulness in providing for all her wants since she had been a widow, & even since she had been settled in the world."²¹ James, who'd finally been dismissed from government and had moved Anna Maria and their two children back to the Sault, wrote to George on the day she died, of "suffocation," in Anna Maria's arms. "The only absent one she expressed a wish to see, *was yourself*," James wrote to George. "She said she would like to have talked to you before she left the world. Her only pain on going was, she said, that Ev and Howard would come, as they are in the house every morning, to see Grandma, and Grandma would be gone."²²

Eliza, George, and William went down to Detroit to testify in June 1844, but Anna Maria did not. She was ill, Schoolcraft wrote in a motion to postpone the trial a second time. "*Mrs. Ann Schoolcraft . . . is a most material and important* witness," he told the court. She was the only person still living who could testify that Mrs. Johnston gave her daughter Jane Johnston Schoolcraft permission to sign for her and that Mrs. Johnston knew about the disbursement to the Johnston Estate. But Anna Maria had become ill before the opening of navigation and remained ill, as Deputy US Marshall Howard discovered when he appeared at her house, presumably with a subpoena. "You are aware that I have been ill for some time and am still unable to sit up," Anna Maria wrote to Schoolcraft on 12 June, "but I am in hopes that in two or three weeks I shall get about."²³ While it's possible that Anna Maria had been pregnant and lost her baby (to say a woman was "sick" or "ill" was a common way to refer to pregnancy and any of its complications at the time) or did have some illness, considering that there is no discussion in any of the family papers, including by her loquacious husband, about what it was from which Anna Maria may have suffered at so important a moment in the disposition of the family's finances, one wonders whether her mother had something to say to Anna Maria before she died.²⁴

The trial proceeded without her. Under questioning Eliza, George, and William stretched the truth as far as they could. All of them testified that Ozhaawshkodewikwe was in the habit of asking whichever of her children was closest to hand to sign documents for her—although they couldn't positively say what had happened in April 1841 when Jane signed the voucher, as their mother was not at Mackinac then. They were vague and deflected on Ozhaawshkodewikwe's knowledge of the supposed 1837 allowance, and were caught out when Bates, the district attorney, read back their depositions. William testified that his mother was at Mackinac in September 1837 when the phantom council supposedly approved Schoolcraft's claims, and that she had spoken of those claims to him and indicated that Jane had permission to sign documents for her. But, he stipulated, "this conversation was always in the Chippewa language and the word used was one which meant *papers generally* [*mazina'igan*] and there is no word in the language which means particular kinds of papers and when they intend to designate a specific paper they have to describe it by other means."

He testified that after 1837 his mother spoke to him about the claim a few times when she visited Mackinac mainly because she was concerned that Schoolcraft would deny William his share, going so far as to request through Jane a meeting with Schoolcraft to make her apprehension clear to him. Finally, William maintained that after her deposition was taken in October 1843, Ozhaawshkodewikwe told him that "she was sorry she had signed them [the deposition papers] because on reflection she had authorized Mrs. Jane S. to sign papers for the allowance." Under Bates's questioning William admitted that a "reconciliation" had occurred between himself and Schoolcraft since he had arrived in Detroit that month. "Mr. S. did not speak of his evidence or make any offer to pay him money," wrote the clerk. "But he [William] has recd his share of the $8200 since he came here from Schft. This payment was made by a Deed of some property being the same offered him a year or two since by Mr. Schoolcraft." William testified that George had received the same.[25]

Schoolcraft was ordered to pay the judgment, wiping him out financially.[26] In the end George and Eliza were unable to lie to the degree necessary and William, who made more of an effort, was betrayed by his lifelong habit of telling the truth when it came to his own actions, which he considered entirely righteous. It seems quite possible that Schoolcraft expected Anna Maria to lie and she got out of the situation in the only way that a lady could, by becoming so ill she couldn't be deposed or testify. She fully recovered, with no effects that anyone had anything to say about.

A month after the trial, Eliza asked George to write to Schoolcraft. "Your brother James received a letter from Mr. McMurray again inviting Eliza to go down and live with them in Dundas, but poor Eliza cannot make up her mind to do so," George wrote. "James says that he will not advance her anything more, and Eliza has requested me to write to you, begging that you may soon dispose of her claim in New York. I have also made her an offer to come & live with us, but she feels determined to have her own way."[27] That same month, William wrote to Schoolcraft asking for him to sell the leases so that he could pay off old debts. "For two years I have done very little of anything," he wrote.[28] There was no work to be had. All of them soon learned the truth of their situation.[29]

In New York Schoolcraft began publishing *Oneota*, a haphazard periodical anthology of whatever he had on hand, including Ojibwe and Odawa stories he hadn't yet published, excerpts from his published travels, scraps of information like a list of Indigenous property in Michigan from 1837, Jane's heavily rewritten poems, and more of Wawanosh, who'd become his occasional alter ego. He published eight numbers of the series over 1844 and 1845, then collected them into books published in 1845, 1847, and 1848 under different titles, presumably so that readers would think they were getting different books. Johnston returned to school for the time being, but Janée stayed with Schoolcraft in New York. She copied her father's letters and manuscripts when his paralysis struck, as it did more frequently the older he got, and when he was away from home she became the correspondent that he wished her mother to have been, prattling on about boardinghouse gossip in a way that didn't irritate him.[30]

He gained a new lease on life in the summer of 1846, when he became attached to Mary Howard and James Schoolcraft was murdered, shot in the back right out of his slippers in a field behind his house. When newspaper reports confused him and his brother, obituaries for himself began to circulate, and he cut them out of the papers and kept them, even duplicates, as if to remind himself that time was short but he was still alive. "God spared my life . . . while he took my brother's," he wrote to Mary Howard.[31]

At first everyone blamed the murder on John Tanner, the celebrated "white captive" whose 1830 account of his life was written in Sault Ste. Marie by Edwin James.[32] He'd been making a variety of threats against Schoolcraft and everyone else for years; when his house burned down and he disappeared at the time of the murder, the villagers all pretended to think that he had done it and to be afraid that he was lurking in the woods nearby.[33] They were actually afraid of the soldiers in the garrison, however, as many of them knew—and shortly, no doubt, all of them did—that the murderer was Lt. Bryant Tilden, and the cause was a conflict over a woman.[34] What the exact nature of the conflict was no one would say, but it was enough to involve the entire garrison in the coverup. As soon as James hit the ground, wanted posters naming Tanner as the culprit appeared, their ink dry; the soldiers took the lead in searching for and not finding him. Luckily for everyone involved, the soldiers were soon to ship out to the war in Mexico. George pieced together these facts several years after it happened, interviewing witnesses and writing periodic reports on his discoveries for Schoolcraft, who preferred to stick to the original story for obvious reasons. Tanner was reported by George's informants to have been seen in northern Wisconsin and at Red River, hunting with one of his sons. He may have cooperated in Tilden's plan.[35] He was old at the time of the murder, alienated from most of his children (to whom he was physically and possibly sexually abusive), and reduced to the village bogeyman.[36]

Anna Maria was about six months pregnant and in Detroit when it happened. James had insisted that she go, with their two small children, to consult Zina Pitcher about her health. George and John were in the west of Lake Superior; Eliza was the only one of the family present to stand over James's

Anna Maria Johnston, carte de visite (ca. 1850). Chippewa County Historical Society, Sault Ste. Marie, Michigan.

coffin.[37] When her daughter Minnie was about a year old, in October 1847, Anna Maria determined to conclude James's business herself, traveling to Detroit and New York City for the purpose. Charlotte wouldn't let her go alone to New York, McMurray reported to Schoolcraft, "which was a formidable undertaking you know for her."[38] The two sisters (and Minnie) visited Johnston while on their trip to the East. Anna Maria and her children lived with Charlotte in Dundas for a few years, then she married an Episcopalian minister named Oliver Taylor and moved to Pontiac, where she died in 1852.[39]

Schoolcraft, his new wife, and Janée decamped from New York to Washington in 1847, leaving behind Johnston, who'd had to leave his apprenticeship to a grocer and become a copyist to support himself after his father abandoned him for his new life in the capital. Mary Howard had plans for Schoolcraft and for her place in society. Soon she sold some of her slaves, and Schoolcraft bought a townhouse on F Street, three blocks from the White House.[40]

Writers continued to remember Jane after her death, and some of them had opinions. In *Summer on the Lakes in 1843* (1844), Margaret Fuller went out of her way to cut Jane. Fuller had traveled west to Chicago with her friend Sarah Freeman Clarke, sister of William Hull Clarke, and their mother, to visit William and Samuel. According to some scholars, Fuller and William Clarke had developed a doomed romance on his previous visits home to Boston, or at least a serious flirtation, one that affected them both for some time. "He knows his path as a man, and follows it with the gay spirit of a boy," she wrote in her notebook; "we do not see such people at the East."[41] She appears to have modeled her trip and the narrative that resulted in part on Mrs. Jameson's; after visiting Chicago, she and Sarah Clarke took a steamboat to witness the annuity payments at Mackinac and Fuller traveled by herself to Sault Ste. Marie, where Indians took her down the rapids in a canoe.

Like Anna Jameson, Fuller included critical remarks on the relevant works on her subject in her book; echoing Jameson's comments to Schoolcraft himself, Fuller found the stories in *Algic Researches* inauthentic because of their literary qualities. They should show "the Spartan brevity and sinewy grasp of Indian speech," she wrote, and not "the flimsy graces . . . of annuals and souvenirs."[42] The stories written out by Mrs. Jameson in her book Fuller found sentimental but at least not offensive. They showed that while a "mine of poesy" was lost in Mrs. Schoolcraft's death, it was only Anna Jameson who "would have known how to coin a series of medals for the history of this ancient people."[43] Fuller thought that she was writing about Jameson's writing, but she was in fact writing about Jane's—Mrs. Jameson copied Jane's versions of the stories for inclusion in her book, making few if any changes.[44]

By way of contrast to Schoolcraft's deficiencies, Fuller included a story titled "Muckwa, or The Bear" that she copied from William Clarke's own Indian researches.[45] It's a much-reduced version of the story Little Salt told to Charlotte and Schoolcraft published in *Algic Researches* as "Iena, or The Magic Bundle." It doesn't especially exhibit Spartan brevity—it's just less complicated, because Clarke was either taking down dictation or remembering what he'd been told.[46] Elsewhere in her book Fuller included her own poem featuring Indian chiefs capable of no more than an "earnest yaw" when confronted by the glories of civilized Boston, and she recommended as well Chandler Robbins Gilman's *Life on the Lakes*, for the charming story "The Fate of Wintemoyah: The Legend of Robinson's Folley."[47] This was the story of the Indian maiden who wants to marry a British officer, but after informing her father of her intention, he kills both her and himself by jumping off a cliff. No one on Mackinac knew about the story when she asked, but still she believed it to be a "genuine legend."[48]

Fuller admired Mackinac as other travelers did, visited the usual sights, and reported herself mingling with Indigenous women at their lodges on the lakeshore. Rather than taking out her sketchbook, she communicated with the women through signs, which they perfectly understood, according to herself. What she communicated she didn't say. "I liked very much to walk or sit among them," Fuller wrote. "They are almost invariably coarse and ugly, with the exception of their eyes, with a peculiarly awkward gait, and forms bent by burdens. This gait, so different from the steady and noble step of the men, marks the inferior position they occupy."[49] Here she quoted Jane's letter to William Clarke on the subject of Ojibwe women and men. Clarke let her copy it. She was unimpressed. Hunting wasn't an art, and the idea that it could have a theory was absurd, for one thing. She much preferred the account given by Anne MacVicar Grant, a Scottish woman who lived in New York among the Mohawks as a child in the 1750s. Indigenous women were drudges, Mrs. Grant wrote in *Memoirs of an American Lady* (1808), "carrying burdens too heavy to be borne, and other slavish employments considered beneath the dignity of man." "Wherever man is a mere hunter, woman is a mere slave," observed Mrs. Grant.[50] Fuller thought Mrs. Grant's account was "much nearer the truth than Mrs. Schoolcraft's, because, though her opportunities for observation did not bring her so close she looked more at both sides to find the truth."[51]

After the publication of Fuller's book, those who knew Jane spoke up in her defense. William Gilmore Simms, defender of slavery, editor, and writer most recently of the story collection *The Wigwam and the Cabin* (1845), wrote an article favorably comparing Indian literature and art to those of the Norsemen and Greeks, noting that Schoolcraft owed his prominence in the study of such works to Jane, "an Indian woman of great intelligence and beauty," who permitted Schoolcraft "to see her people, if we may so phrase it, without disguise."[52] Simms was an acquaintance of Schoolcraft's who'd met Jane in Washington.[53] Elizabeth Oakes Smith, in the midst of a story modeled on those in *Algic Researches* ("Na-wi-qua. A Metowac Legend.") written for the Christmas gift book *American Wild Flowers and Their Native Haunts* (1845), "[recalled] with melancholy pleasure, since the object is no more, a brief acquaintance with one, descended from the royalty of nature, a woman whose original graces of mind, and literary acquirements, might well have qualified her to present the characteristics of her people in a just light before the public." Mrs. Smith was perhaps trying to send a message to her sometime friend Margaret.[54] "The accomplished Mrs. Jameson makes honorable mention of one, who never failed to awaken the sympathy and respect for all who approached her; and none, who have ever listened to her simple and earnest recital of the traditions of the red man will fail of a sad tribute to her memory. Through her we beheld the aboriginal in his own domain. Her stories had life and soul, quaintness and humor, and a directness of detail akin to that of *The Arabian Nights*."[55] Smith knew Jane as a writer; when Fuller attacked the quality of the stories in *Algic Researches*, she attacked Jane.

It was Schoolcraft's friend Rufus Griswold who took the fight directly to Fuller in the pages of *Prose Writers of America* (1846), another of his canon-making exercises. In his entry on Schoolcraft, Griswold commended him for supplying American writers with the proper material to transform into literary works on properly American themes, writers like Charles Fenno Hoffman, Henry Wadsworth Longfellow, Mrs. Elizabeth Oakes Smith, and James Russell Lowell. The source of Schoolcraft's knowledge was the European-educated Mrs. Schoolcraft, "an accomplished and highly interesting woman." Schoolcraft's writings were important because of "the knowledge possessed by his wife and her family," Griswold wrote.[56]

While he had qualified praise for Fuller's style, he devoted a fair amount of space in his entry on her to attacking Fuller's comments on Jane. Of Fuller's observation that the stories in *Algic Researches* ought to have been translated in the "Spartan brevity and sinewy grasp of Indian speech" and not the "flimsy graces common to the style of annuals and souvenirs," Griswold wrote, "Nothing can be more ridiculous." "The phraseology of the tales has of course been 'set aside' in translating them into a language radically different, but the antique simplicity of the originals has been well preserved as the genius of the English tongue permitted." He was thinking of Jane's writing specifically.

> The wife of the amiable and learned author who is thus assailed, herself of the aboriginal race, and distinguished for whatever is peculiar in their character, wrote down and translated many of these myths and traditions, and it is amusing to see even part of her work ranked on the score of fidelity below the few stories written out by Mrs. Jameson, who, however excellent as a critic of art, was here quite out of her depth—almost as ignorant as Miss Fuller herself, who when this was composed had been about one week west of Buffalo, and had seen perhaps a dozen vagabond Indians across the streets of Detroit and Chicago.[57]

Like Fuller, Griswold assumed that Jameson's copies were Jameson's own versions when they were in fact Jane's, but the point remained: Fuller was wrong about Jane and her writing, which included, as far as he understood it, *Algic Researches* generally. Horace Greeley, Fuller's editor at the *New York Tribune*, thought Griswold had been unfair to Fuller (she had by then gone to Italy as a correspondent). Griswold admitted to the publisher James Fields that what he had to say about Fuller and Mrs. Schoolcraft "was very badly written though all true."[58]

In the wake of this controversy, Schoolcraft tried a number of times to write about Jane's poetry and song translations. He may have been trying to define Jane publicly at a moment when his reemergence as a government expert was reminding the public that he had had an Indian wife—and for many of them, still had. (Mary Howard reconciled herself to this situation by styling herself "the Indian Queen" in her correspondence.)[59] There is a manuscript titled "Dawn of Literary Composition by Educated Natives of the Aboriginal Tribes" that appears to have been prepared for the Indian history in the late 1840s or early 1850s; a long letter to the editor of *Putnam's Monthly* dated 28 January 1853; and a manuscript collection of his and Jane's poems, titled "Original Poetry by Mr. and Mrs. H. R. Schoolcraft."[60] In each instance, Schoolcraft did what he always did, revising both Jane and her poems into something that suited him better than what was. "Her heart sympathized deeply with her woodland people whom she viewed as pursuing false objects, through false hopes," he explained in "Dawn of Literary Composition." Jane knew as did he that the stories were demonology. "The fires of truth that flashed upon her own mind had . . . burned out the picturesque tapestry that adorned the temple of her native mythology, and left its frame standing as a collapsed wreck at which she gazed, often with pensive and melancholy thoughts." When Christianity revealed the truth, she couldn't be anything other than pensive and melancholy. He had it inscribed on her tomb. But in keeping with his habit of conceding the truth, if only because he couldn't keep his story straight, he added that despite "all she had witnessed in Ireland and England" (of "civilization," as an eight-year-old, although he was fudging that point as usual in this essay), "she clung with a strong attachment, to the landscape and history of her mother's side of her heritage—her picturesque and wild relations."[61] For all of the mental effort he put into rewriting Jane over the course of his life some small part of himself, perhaps the part that knew he didn't really know what he was talking about and wasn't much of a writer anyway, kept him from completing the task.

He was beside himself with the publication of *Hiawatha*, however. As soon as he could, he published *The Myth of Hiawatha* (1856), a revised version of *Algic Researches*, and dedicated it to Longfellow. When Longfellow acknowledged the honor, Schoolcraft wrote back to praise him for having "solved the problem" to which Schoolcraft had dedicated his life. From the beginning, he knew that the stories were "a new element for our literature," but one that would take skill—skill that he himself didn't have—to absorb. "To render an

Indian tale successful, Indian manners & sentiments & opinions must be accurately copied. Above all, the Indian mythology & superstitions, as shewn in their rites & ceremonies, must be observed," he wrote. "Without inventing new incidents, you have generalized fragmentary legends, & invested them with a vitality of description & a poetic garb, which we have no reasons to expect from such barren, & disjointed materials. . . . You have rendered justice to my assiduity in the labour of collecting legends, to which I attached some importance, but which the public has agreed to neglect."[62]

Longfellow had begun writing his poem in June 1854. He was forty-seven years old and worried that his job as professor of modern languages at Harvard was preventing him from writing, and worse, time was running out because no one wrote good poetry after fifty.[63] He documented his progress on the poem in his diary, working diligently through the summer. In September, he retired from Harvard. "I am now free!" he wrote. He kept working through the fall, winter, and next spring, reading Schoolcraft, Heckewelder, Tanner, Gilman, Jameson, McKenney. "'Hiawatha' occupies and delights me," he wrote in October 1854. "Have I no misgivings about it?—Yes—sometimes. Then the theme seizes me, and hurries me away, and they vanish."[64] He made a glossary of Indigenous words for reference. For material, he mainly used *Algic Researches*, as Schoolcraft must have perceived immediately.

In the first canto, he used "Iamo; Or the Undying Head" from *Algic Researches*, the story that William had taken down from Wauchusco and titled "Story of Meshegenebigo"; William's "Story of Manabozho"; an Ojibwe story Schoolcraft published in 1845 titled "Shingebiss"; and an Ojibwe story that Schoolcraft wrote down from dictation and published in *Algic Researches* as "Shawondasee." He took the third and fourth cantos from "Story of Manabozho"; in the fifth, in addition to characters from "Story of Manabozho," Longfellow used Jane's story "Mon-daw-min; or The Origin of Indian Corn." In the sixth canto, he used an Ojibwe story titled "Kwasind, or The Fearfully Strong Man" from *Algic Researches*; in canto eight he used "Story of Manabozho"; in canto nine he used "Story of Manabozho" and "Moose and Woodpecker," also written by William at or after he was at Leech Lake. Longfellow took canto eleven from "Paup-Puk-Keewiss," the Saginaw story written by William, and "Iagoo," another of the stories dictated to Schoolcraft that he included in *Algic Researches*. In canto twelve, he used two stories from *Algic Researches* whose writers are as yet unidentified, "The Red Swan" ("from the Algic") and "Osseo; or, The Son of the Evening Star. An Algonquin Tale," as well as a song written by Charlotte that Schoolcraft wrote down in the 1830s and included in the Indian history. He used the "The Traditionary Story of Mash qua shay guong, or the Red Head," told by Nabunway to George at Sault Ste. Marie in 1838, as well as "The White Stone Canoe," an

Odawa story that William probably wrote down, both of them published by Schoolcraft in the 1840s, in canto fifteen. In canto sixteen he returned to William's "Paup-Puk-Keewiss" and used his story "Ogeeg Annung or The Fisher" from *Algic Researches* as well as some material on the game of bowls that George wrote and Schoolcraft published in the Indian history. In canto seventeen Longfellow returned to "Paup-Puk-Keewiss" as well as what was probably William's early story first published in *Literary Voyager* and then in *Algic Researches* as "La Poudre or the Storm Fool." In canto eighteen, he returned to "Kwasind," and in canto nineteen he used Jane's story "The Two Ghosts" and John Johnston's story "Gitche Gauzinee." He again used William's "Moose and Woodpecker," as well as Schoolcraft's transcribed narrative "Pauguk," in canto nineteen. Finally, in canto twenty Longfellow used Jane's version of her mother's story "Peboan and Seegwun," also from *Algic Researches*.

Longfellow ate the stories right up. He thought the same things about Indians that his Indian epic-writing contemporaries did, but he was a more skillful poet, enough to fit the stories and their characters into a conventional savage story. In Longfellow's version Manabozho/Hiawatha fights his father, Mudjekewiss, who deserted his mother, Wenonah (she died), then goes on adventures, during which he meets and falls in love with the arrow-maker's daughter Minnehaha, who is Dakota, then Minnehaha dies, after which Hiawatha greets the incoming whites ("Let us welcome, then, the strangers, / Hail them as our friends and brothers") while simultaneously slipping into a prophetic depression:

> I beheld our nations scattered,
> All forgetful of my counsels,
> Weakened, warring with each other,
> Saw the remnants of our people
> Sweeping westward, wild and woeful,
> Like the cloud-rack of a tempest,
> Like the withered leaves of Autumn![65]

The same story, every time. The poem's thumping meter opened it to parody, the first one of which appeared within a few days of publication. Famously, an early critic accused Longfellow of plagiarizing the *Kalevala*, a Finnish epic, and numerous other writers piled on. (Poe had accused Longfellow of plagiarism in different circumstances years before.) He was congratulated by some for giving primitive Indian stories the gloss of literature and attacked by others for doing the same.[66] Longfellow dismissed the controversies. "Critics may assail me as they please," he wrote in his diary. He was making good money on his poem. Almost all the first run of 5,000 copies was bought up on publication; Ticknor & Fields put out another 5,000 copies before a month was out, and the poem's popularity only grew afterward. Several months after publication, Longfellow betook himself to McKay's shipyard to witness the launch of the *Minnehaha*, the figurehead of which was a likeness of Mrs. Julia Barrow, who gave dramatic recitations of the poem at the Roxbury Theatre. "This lady is reaping gold dollars, as well as golden opinions, by her illustrations from this poem," observed the theater reviewer for the *Spirit of the Times*.[67]

While *Algic Researches* may have disappeared from public consciousness in the wake of *Hiawatha* if it ever spent any time there, Elizabeth Oakes Smith continued to remember Jane and her book. In 1858, she published another of her "Indian" stories in *Emerson & Putnam's* ("Puck-wud-jees") with another digression. "Limited as were the North American Indians in the appliances of civilization, they had, nevertheless, embodied a mythology at once delicate and fanciful, and in many points vying with the Greek in its fineness and beauty," wrote Mrs. Smith. "The Indians, as we have more than once heard Mrs. Schoolcraft affirm . . . delighted in story-telling, and she has left behind her vast quantities of this material, which should be given to the world. Of Indian blood, she was proud of her people and fond of relating their legends. Her husband, Mr. Henry R. Schoolcraft, many years ago published a collection of these under the name of *Algic Researches*, which were without doubt taken from the lips of his wife, who was a woman of much intellect, of a vivid fancy, and highly educated."[68] Smith seems to be purposefully obfuscating who wrote the stories in *Algic Researches* and whether anything unpublished remained. The "vast quantities" of material could have been written by Jane, and Schoolcraft published but didn't write them— or maybe Mrs. Smith knew something about that lost carpet bag. She seems to have been motivated to speak up in no small part by the idea of a woman writer not getting credit for what she had produced. This was not the last time she would write about Jane. Despite the fleeting nature of their relationship, Mrs. Smith defended Jane in her peculiar way across decades.

In accord with Everlasting Standing Woman's prophesy and despite her trials, Ogeewyahnoquotokwa did live a long life. James Cameron crossed paths with her in the forest one day in the summer of 1865, her hair "white as a snowball." She was still "very active," Cameron reported to Abel Bingham; "very few women can do more work than she can." Unfortunately, however, she was also still a "thorough stiff Methodist, in addition to her good qualities."[69]

At Sault Ste. Marie, Eliza did have her own way: she stayed in the Johnston homestead almost to the end of her life, only moving in with John McDouall and his family when she was too infirm to live alone, in spite of numerous efforts on the part of the white men in the family to place her in someone else's household. She died aged eighty-two.[70] Schoolcraft's daughter Janée found Eliza "quite an oddity" when she saw her at Dundas in 1849. Eliza had brought John Johnston's oil portrait with her on her trip for Janée to see once more; she was homesick even though she was only visiting. There was no place like the Sault, Eliza said; there "I am monarch of all I survey." She spoke English when she thought it necessary.[71] In separate reminiscences written in the early 1900s, the grown daughters of John McDouall and Abel Bingham, old ladies themselves at the time, fondly remembered Eliza and her house, for the rose garden at the front, how Eliza threw open all of the windows in summer so that the house smelled of the lilac and sweet-briar under its windows. Eliza sang hymns, made cakes, and let them dress up in her old gowns. She told them stories. Molly Johnston demanded to be told "over and over again of the parties they used to have, when the rooms would be filled with guests, what their names were, and where they came from."[72]

George led a somewhat less peripatetic life after marrying Mary Rice, but he was still dependent on whatever he could get for a living, and they often struggled. He and Mary soon had four children: Benjamin Howard, James Laurence, Samuel Abbott, and Eliza Jane.[73] He continued to write, occasionally, in his notebooks. In June of 1845, he remembered a story told by Shingabawossin years before, about a Christian Indian who dies and on approaching the gates of heaven is refused entry by the white men in charge, who tell him that only white men went to heaven. Wabwindigo, the protagonist, comes back to life, then summons the priest to witness him burning the religious books he'd collected, one by one. Having thrown off Christianity, Wabwindigo "would drink ardent spirits from time to time, as the Indians generally do, and attained old age and dying in reality after having walked over life's way."[74] This was a popular story in the region and had been for years. Edwin James included it in Tanner's *Narrative* in 1830, and Johann Kohl recorded it at Shagwaamikong in 1860.[75] A missionary named Sarah Tuttle complained about the story in 1839. An Indigenous man "who had given some evidence of being a very serious inquirer if not a Christian" told the missionary Sherman Hall, the missionary at Fond du Lac, that

> the chiefs reported a case of a *praying Indian*, who died far away to the north. He had prayed a long time. On his death he went to heaven, but was refused, on the ground that no *praying Indians* were admitted there. He then went to the place where the [Indian] people go; but was there told that he had been a *praying Indian*, and had forsaken the customs of his fathers, and they would not receive him, and ordered him away. After

George Johnston and son Samuel Abbott (ca. 1850). Chippewa County Historical Society, Sault Ste. Marie, Michigan.

these repulses, he came back again to this world, and assumed the body he had before inhabited.

As a consequence the Indians were "afraid to have any thing said to them on religious subjects," Tuttle wrote, much to her frustration.[76]

Occasionally George would send things to Schoolcraft that struck him as significant. He was at La Pointe at annuity payments in 1847 with a Major Burk and stuck on a steamboat because all the boardinghouses on the island were full. Major Burk opined, George related to Schoolcraft, "that the Indian songs contained no words of expression, but simply a monotonous sound, of We yah we, yay, & continually repeated."[77] This wasn't true. "I told him that in all Indian songs it required a keen ear to detect the words of the song and its variations, and that all their songs, more or less yielding poetry, rhime [sic] & sentiment, but that a veil was thrown over the words, which required a quick ear, and thorough knowledge of the language to detect the meaning."[78] Still thinking of Major Burk, sometime afterward when he was on an "exploring expedition through the head waters of the Montreal, Chippewa, Wisconsin, Manominie & Ontonagan rivers," George wrote down a song sung by Penayshee, a young man who acted as messenger for the Lac Vieux Desert chiefs.

Mary Rice Johnston and daughter Eliza Jane (ca. 1850). Chippewa County Historical Society, Sault Ste. Marie, Michigan.

While they waited together in a tent for the rain to stop, Penayshee sang a song that George transcribed "while amusing myself writing in my note book."[79]

He provided Schoolcraft with a transcription along with a prose translation. "The composition appears to commence with delicacy and deference," George writes.

> He commences his song by saying that I will walk into his or her house, the next line expresses that he will walk into his or her house during the course of the night, in the third line he addresses himself direct to his love, and intimates that he will in the course of the winter walk in or enter her home, playing as it were with time and her feelings, by intimating in the first place the mean time of entering her home; and then prolonging the time to winter, finally he becomes more decisive and boldly affirms that he will enter her house during the course of the night.[80]

As was his habit, Schoolcraft versified George's English translation (and changed the Ojibwe transcription somewhat), then published it without attribution.[81]

Sometimes things just occurred to George. One January day in 1850 he was reading the *Iliad*, probably given his tastes Alexander Pope's translation. He thought how familiar it was.

> Through the first to the tenth book, I find that the belief, habits & customs of the Greeks spoken of, in those days correspond with those of the Chippeway's, for instance. The Greeks addressed inferior deities & acknowledged a supreme being. This is precisely what the Chippewas do and acknowledge. The Greeks have tutelar gods; and so have the Chippewas. The Greeks believed in a race of men divine. So do the Chippewas. The Greeks had their godlike men; and so have the Chippewas. The Greeks had their signs in birds ominous of good or evil, so have the Chippewas. The Greeks had their seer's, so have the Chippewas. The Greeks believed in dreams so do the Chippewas. The Greeks sacrificed, and poured libations on the ground, and so the Chippewas also. The Greeks believed in the God of thunder, the god of war, the God of the winds, & the god of the main so also the Chippewas believe. The Greeks sucked the blood from wounds, and so the Chippewas likewise. The Greeks recited their deeds in war, so the Chippewas also. The Greeks had their belief in shades and realms below, and so have the Chippewas. I do not know of any thing that has struck me with more force than this coincidence, portraying a similitude of trait, I may say in character and belief.[82]

He sent this off to Schoolcraft, but it made no impression.

By the late 1850s the Sault had a new canal and business opportunities were expanding. The village was becoming a boomtown. William Cullen Bryant, poet and newspaper editor, had visited in the summer of 1846 and recorded how the copper explorers and fisheries entrepreneurs were already displacing the Indigenous habitants in the vicinity.[83] Smart young people were unafraid to mock Bingham's Sunday services, and Hannah Bingham had more than once been ejected from a home where someone was dying for being too complacent about the inevitable.[84] Bingham retired in 1855 with little fanfare (of his farewell sermon Hannah observed, "If Mr. B had given some Indian narrative I should have been rather more gratified") and moved his family to Grand Rapids.[85] George had long been critical of the Binghams. In "the language of the Indians," he had written to Schoolcraft, "missionaries are living among Indians, to make money out of the Indians."[86] George and his family moved into the vacated mission, where he ran a boardinghouse for travelers and businessmen. He wrote the names and addresses of his guests on the flyleaves of his old letterbook, Baltimore, New York, Toronto, Providence. Among them, in faint pencil, there is a translation:

Burial Song
The birds of the air, the birds of the air,
They term me the black soaring bird
The black soaring eagle they term me,
         We, yah, we, yay[87]

It's as if he heard or remembered it while he was standing over his book one day, released from other concerns for the moment. By then two of the Methodist exhorters who'd come to the Sault in the 1830s and written poems in Charlotte's commonplace book had gone on to become writers. George Copway published his autobiography in 1847, a short-lived newspaper in 1850, and an account of his travels in Europe in 1851. George Henry or Maungwudaus, Peter Jones's half-brother, left mission work to form a dance troupe, publishing an account of his own travels in Europe in 1854. William Whipple Warren, great nephew of Jean-Baptiste Cadotte, wrote a history of the Ojibwes from their origins to the present before he died in 1853. Francis Assiginack, the Odawa leader's son, graduated from Upper Canada College and published several articles on Anishinaabe culture and history in 1858. Peter Jones's wife would arrange for the posthumous publication of her husband's *Life and Journals* (1860) and *History of the Ojebway Indians* (1861).[88]

At Mackinac William was writing his history of that place, but he needed money to get it published. Although by his own account he'd spent part of the 1840s "dissipated," by 1850 he'd begun to fill a number of jobs (lawyer, school teacher, justice of the peace, county commissioner) at Mackinac as its economy turned to fisheries and tourism.[89] He wrote to Johnston after the publication of *Hiawatha*, not knowing that Johnston, who had been working in Washington for his father, had been unable to endure his stepmother (she was in the habit of exclaiming over the horror of having Indian stepchildren) and left town.[90] Schoolcraft got the letter. "Dear Nephew, You will probably be surprised to receive a letter from me," William wrote. Since Schoolcraft was no longer in the habit of answering William's letters, he wanted Johnston to talk to his father for him. "I have been engaged for the last two years in preparing a small work.... Travellers & Visitors to this place have urged me to the task and which I have now nearly completed, it contains a history of the Conquest of the Island & County in its vicinity by the Ottawas & Chippewas, its early settlement by the French &c. up to this period, with various other miscellaneous matters, embellished with a plat of the island, with various wood cuts illustrating points of interest on the Island & likenesses of Indian Women & Indians." He needed to pay for its publication, "which I can only do at New York." Unfortunately, though he made enough money to provide his family "a decent support," he had nothing to spare and he thought

Schoolcraft ought to help him publish his book, considering how he had profited from the family in the past. "Ever since the investment of your father, of our all, in Detroit real estate, my means have been limited and my little ones (only Eight) has prevented me from changing location from fear of sickness &c." He needed $200, "payable next June at ten per cent. All I can now give you is the Word & honour of an Ojibway of its payment." "I aided your father without recompense, in translating the traditions &c in the Algic Researches & now embraced in Hiawatha," he added.[91] Schoolcraft, of course, never responded. William gave excerpts of this "small work" to that Presbyterian minister, including Wauchusco's account of his powers, but the rest of the book is (as yet) lost.

A few years later, in the summer of 1861 just after the start of the war, another white man who wished to know about Indians made his appearance at Mackinac. He spoke to William, then the town clerk, over several days. This was Henry David Thoreau, and he and his young friend Horace Mann Jr. were on their way home after a brief trip to Minnesota, where they collected botanical specimens, visited Minnehaha Falls, and were disappointed at not seeing buffaloes.[92] In company with a German band, they had taken a steamboat to annuity payments at Lower Sioux Agency, during which the Dakota chief Little Crow appeared to Thoreau to be "dissatisfied."[93] (Little Crow would soon become a leader in the Dakota War of 1862; he was killed by a settler in 1863.) At Mackinac they saw the sights and collected more specimens. As he tramped the island, Thoreau might have remembered his friend Margaret Fuller, for whose body he had searched the beaches of Fire Island ten years previous.

Thoreau had been a student of Indians for years. He kept multiple notebooks on the topic, excerpting the relevant authors, compiling his thoughts. He considered Schoolcraft the leading authority on Indians in America.[94] There are only his cryptic notes for his encounter with William, whom he described as "born by half breeds and French"—he didn't know to whom he was speaking, although one imagines Schoolcraft's name came up at some point.[95] They sat by the fire at the Mackinac House hotel, another former mission house, because Thoreau was weak from the tuberculosis that would kill him within the year. In his writing Thoreau reduced Indigenous people to the trails on which he traveled the forests; he had no interest in their stories, and even less in their actual lives.[96] Instead, he pored over the white writers on Indians. He wanted to subsume himself in Nature and it was white writers on Indians who would help him get there. Those white writers told how Indians walked through the woods undetected, how they were satisfied with almost nothing. He wanted that Indian inside himself, the primitive, essential man.[97]

What would William have thought of that white man by the fire, wishing to know how the mails were carried in winter and how big a Mackinaw boat was? It was all he could think to ask someone like William, as much as he could imagine.

Acknowledgments

I'm grateful to librarians for their aid in doing the research for this book at the Detroit Public Library, Detroit, Michigan; the Bayliss Public Library, Sault Ste. Marie, Michigan; the Bentley Historical Library, Anne Arbor, Michigan; the Clarke Historical Library, Central Michigan University, Mt. Pleasant, Michigan; the New-York Historical Society, New York, New York; the George Peabody Library, Johns Hopkins University, Baltimore, Maryland; and the Library of Congress, Washington, D.C.

In Sault Ste. Marie, Susan James and Mary M. June of the Chippewa County Historical Society tracked down pictures of the extended Johnston family. Dr. Barbara Bair at the Library of Congress explained the history and provenance of the very confusing Schoolcraft Papers. A. LaVonne Brown Ruoff, emerita Professor of English at the University of Illinois–Chicago, encouraged this project a long time ago, and Mark Simpson-Vos, editor of this book, has supported it over more years than I want to think about. Finally, I'm grateful to the three anonymous readers for the work they put into reading not the most refined narrative, especially the first time around, during a pandemic and its many unforeseeable effects.

Notes

Abbreviations

AMJS	Anna Maria Johnston Schoolcraft
AR	*Algic Researches*
CJM	Charlotte Johnston McMurray
GJ	George Johnston
HRS	Henry Rowe Schoolcraft
HRS LC	Henry Rowe Schoolcraft Papers, Library of Congress, Washington, DC
JJS	Jane Johnston Schoolcraft
JP	Jeremiah Porter
JSAS	Jane Susan Ann Schoolcraft [Howard]
MHC	Michigan Historical Collections
NARA	National Archives and Records Administration
WJ	William Johnston
WM	William McMurray

The Weendigoes

1. William titled this story in manuscript "Saganaw's Story." It reads, "Once there lived in a sequestered spot, a man and his wife; and who were blest with a son. As it is customary for Indians to hunt all day, in order to procure food for their families. It was at a time when this man was absent in the chase. That his wife in going out of the lodge, looked towards the lake, near which the lodge was situated, and strange to tell she beheld a very large man approaching walking on the lake; he had already advanced so near that flight was useless. She thought to herself, what shall I say to him that will please. As he came near she at last, ran in and took her boy, who was three or four years old, by the hand and led him out. Speaking very loud she said; My son see your Grandfather; she said this in a pitying tone of voice; saying also My Son, your Grandfather will have pity on us. The large man advanced and said in a sneering way, Yes my son! Have you anything to eat?, fortunately the lodge was filled with meat of various kinds, the woman to please him handed him some meat that was cooked, he pushed it away in a dissatisfied manner, and took the raw carcass of a deer which the hunter had brought home, which he greedily eat up, sucking the bones and drinking the blood." It was more than likely edited for publication by Jane Schoolcraft. It appears in the two-volume manuscript *Muzziniegun, Comprising Notes on Indian History, Languages, and Mythology*, reel 65, HRS LC.

Prologue

1. HRS to JJS, 2 December 1837, reel 27, HRS LC.
2. JJS, "Corn Story (Or the Origin of Corn)," in Parker, *Sound the Stars Make*, 185–87. There is a small but growing body of scholarship on Jane Johnston Schoolcraft, most of it focused on her poetry. Parins, "Jane Johnston Schoolcraft" (1997), and Ruoff, "Early Native American Woman Auhors" (1998), first brought her to scholarly attention. Parker, in *Sound the Stars Make*, published an edition of her writings in 2007. See also Wisecup, *Assembled for Use*. On contemporary Anishinaabe literature, see Spry, *Our War Paint*; Noodin, *Bawaajimo* and Henry, Noodin, and Stirrup, *Enduring Critical Poses*. On Anishinaabe Studies generally, see Doerfler, Sinclair, and Stark, *Centering Anishinaabeg Studies* and Simpson, *Dancing on Our Turtle's Back* and *Short History of the Blockade*. On Ojibwe language studies, see Treuer, *Living Our Language* and *Language Warrior's Manifesto*.
3. JJS to HRS, 15 January 1838, reel 8, HRS LC.
4. HRS to JJS, 9 February 1838, reel 28, HRS LC.
5. Bremer, *Indian Agent*, 57.
6. Porter, Journal 4 11 May 1832. Chicago Historical Society.
7. HRS, "Notes for a Memoir," 95–96 and "Memoir of John Johnston," 58–61; John Askin Jr. to Charles Askin, 8 January 1811, Askin, *John Askin Papers*, 2:669.
8. JJ to Lewis Cass, 22 January 1822, NARA M1, roll 10; Jameson, *Winter Studies*, 2:153–54.
9. Jameson, *Winter Studies*, 2:244–45.
10. JJS, "Vision of Catherine Wabose," in HRS, *Historical and Statistical*, 1:388–401.
11. Knight and Chute, "In the Shadow," 91.
12. McNally, *Honoring Elders*, 240–41.
13. Porter, Journal 4, 12 March 1832.
14. HRS to LC, 25 October 1822, reel 3, HRS LC. In the letter, Schoolcraft tells Cass that it was thought that the language suffered when in proximity to the fur trade. Jane is the only one who could have made him aware of this, and her source would have been her mother, with whom she consulted on Schoolcraft's many queries.
15. Macpherson, "Dissertation," xix–xx.
16. HRS, "Memoir of John Johnston," 77.
17. Johnston, "Autobiographical Letters," 331–32.
18. Bigsby, *Shoe and Canoe*, 128.
19. HRS, "Memoir of John Johnston," 64.
20. Schoolcraft mentions a "manuscript collection of traditional songs" and a collection of "tales . . . taken from the oral relations of the Chippewa" some years previous to the time of his writing, to which he declined to "make any material alterations in the language adopted" in order to preserve authenticity. Schoolcraft, *Travels*, 426–27, 409. In a note to the translations included there he writes, "We are indebted for this fragment, and for the preservation of the two succeeding specimens of Indian poetry, to the polite attainments and literary taste of Miss Jane Johnston, of Johnston Hall, Sault Ste. Marie" (426). Schoolcraft used "Miss Jane Johnston" to refer to Jane and what she wrote before their marriage.
21. Nichols, "Ojibwa Oral Literature," 843, 842.
22. HRS, "Preliminary Observations," *AR* 1:52–53.
23. In "Preliminary Observations," Schoolcraft both claimed that he wrote the stories himself and hedged on what he said. "It was found that they possessed a story-telling fac-

ulty, and I wrote down from their narration a number of these fictitious tales," he writes at first. Later he refers to "those who have aided me in the collection and translation of these materials" (*AR* 1:38, 43).

24. HRS, "Preliminary Observations," *AR* 1:42, 41.

25. HRS, "Preliminary Observations," *AR* 1:42.

26. HRS, "Preliminary Observations," *AR* 1:42.

27. HRS, "General Considerations," *AR* 1:12.

28. HRS, "Preliminary Observations," *AR* 1:42.

29. HRS, "General Considerations," *AR* 1:27.

30. As with so many of Schoolcraft's ideas, this was a variation of something Cass had to say, in *Discourse Pronounced at the Capitol of the United States*.

31. HRS to JJS, 26 January 1838, reel 28, HRS LC.

32. See, for example, Armour, *North American Indian Fairy Tales* and Larned, *American Indian Fairy Tales*.

33. In using "expel" rather than "remove," I'm following Saunt in his book *Unworthy Republic* (xi–xix). "Remove" had a benign connotation in the nineteenth century, which is probably why it was used in the way it was. The term commonly appeared in newspaper notices informing the public that a business had "removed" from one address to another, for example. On Ojibwe resistance to expulsion, see Witgen, *Seeing Red*. On Ojibwe history in the nineteenth century, including efforts to dispossess Ojibwe bands of the land they retained, in addition to Witgen, see Kugel, *To Be the Main Leaders*; Meyer, *White Earth Tragedy*; and Treuer, *Assassination*.

34. Round, *Removable Type*, 150–52. The text of Cusick's book is edited by Paul Royster and available at https://digitalcommons.unl.edu/libraryscience/24, accessed 20 August 2021. Jane and Schoolcraft visited Niagara Falls in the summer of 1830; Schoolcraft subsequently wrote about Cusick's book in the Indian history.

35. JJS, "Wa Wa Be Zo Win, or The Swing," reel 58, HRS LC.

36. WJM to HRS, 5 September 1836, reel 24–25, HRS LC.

37. See, for example, Smith, *Decolonizing Methodologies* and Battiste and Henderson, *Protecting Indigenous Knowledge*.

38. Brinton, *Lenape and Their Legends*, 145n2.

39. David Witkin to Luke Lea, 30 May 1851, reel 40, HRS LC. George Johnston also sent Schoolcraft information, GJ to HRS, 25 August 1851, 20 November 1851, reel 40, HRS LC; HRS to GJ, 17 September 1851, George Johnston Papers, Detroit Public Library, Burton Historical Collection. Schoolcraft's discussion of pictographs appears in the first volume of *Historical and Statistical Information*, 333–430.

40. Vecsey in *Traditional Ojibwa Religion* lists the "primary" written accounts of the Manabozho story cycle at 87–88.

41. For example, Blackfeet scholar Roslyn E. LaPier in her book *Invisible Reality* writes that in the late nineteenth century, elders willingly talked to white anthropologists in order to control information that they wanted to pass on to future Blackfeet people (xxv).

42. See Clements, "Schoolcraft as Textmaker." The presumption seems to have been that the form of late nineteenth- and early twentieth-century anthropological accounts of Indigenous stories, pared down and linguistically unembellished, coupled with the avowedly scientific objectives of anthropologists, establishes an authentic account.

43. Early collections of Ojibwe stories include those by William Jones (collected in the early 1900s, published in 1917 and 1919) and Paul Radin and A. B. Reagan (collected in the early 1910s, written by Ojibwe writers Edwin Maness and Andrew Maness, and published in 1928). See Teuton, "Indigenous Orality and Oral Literatures" for a discussion of the complexity of traditional knowledge and an argument for reframing discussions of "oral literature" generally.

44. HRS, "General Considerations," *AR* 1:18–20.

45. Patel and Moore, *History of the World*, 51.

46. LaPier, *Invisible Reality*, 25.

47. Vance, "Ovid and the Nineteenth Century," 216; Schacker-Mill, "Otherness and Otherworldliness," 165–67.

48. The story is characteristic of settler colonial societies generally. See Wolfe, "Settler Colonialism."

49. Pearce, *Savagism and Civilization*, 82–83.

50. Parkinson, *Thirteen Clocks*, 2.

51. Declaration of Independence, www.archives.gov/founding-docs/declaration-transcript, accessed 3 June 2021. In *Notes on the State of Virginia*, Thomas Jefferson complained that squeamishness on the part of southern slavers and their northern partners forced him to excise his denunciation of the king's instigation of slave revolts from the final draft of the document (47).

52. Patel and Moore, *History of the World*, 190–92.

53. Wood, *Origin of Capitalism*, 96–97, 106–8, 152–55.

54. Wood, *Origin of Capitalism*, 108, 115, 156.

55. HRS, "General Considerations," *AR* 1:18–19.

56. Wood, *Origin of Capitalism*, 109–15.

57. Armitage, "John Locke."

58. Locke, *Two Treatises of Government*, 288.

59. Locke, *Two Treatises of Government*, 302.

60. Tully, "Rediscovering America," 146–46.

61. Banner, *How the Indians Lost*, 20, 43, 29.

62. Banner, *How the Indians Lost*, 102–5.

63. Kakel, *Post-Exceptionalist Perspective*, 36.

64. Knox, "Report of Henry Knox," 53.

65. Mehta in *Liberalism and Empire* writes that lunatics, idiots, and children are "explicitly and unambiguously excluded from the consensual politics of the *Second Treatise*" (59).

66. Sheehan, *Seeds of Extinction*, 165–66.

67. Thomas Jefferson to William Henry Harrison, 27 February 1803, and Thomas Jefferson to Benjamin Hawkins, 18 February 1803, in Jefferson, *Political Writings*, 525, 521–23; Banner, *How the Indians Lost*, 162–70; Robertson, *Conquest by Law*, 99–100.

68. Ostler, *Surviving Genocide*, 4.

69. Brackenridge, "Thoughts on Indian Treaties," *Gazette Publications*, 104–7.

70. He made the argument in 1777 in the *United States Magazine* and in 1779 in the *Pittsburgh Gazette*; he mentioned it in *Indian Atrocities* (a captivity narrative) in 1782, then printed it again in a collection called *Gazette Publications* in 1806 (102–3). Brackenridge was the founder of the *United States Magazine* in Philadelphia and the *Pittsburgh Gazette*;

he also founded a school that became the University of Pittsburgh. He's better known today as the writer of a satirical anti-Irish novel, *Modern Chivalry* (1792–1815).

71. Brackenridge, *Law Miscellanies*, 121.
72. Brackenridge, *Law Miscellanies*, 123.
73. Brackenridge, *Law Miscellanies*, 124.
74. Brackenridge, *Law Miscellanies*, 125.
75. In the nineteenth century *Johnson v. McIntosh*'s revised doctrine of discovery was used to deny Indigenous land rights in Canada, Australia, and New Zealand (Watson, "Impact," 508–9). Today it is recognized as the foundation of US property law (Robertson, *Conquest by Law*, x).
76. Deloria, *Playing Indian*, 191.
77. HRS to Cass, 25 October 1822, reel 2, HRS LC.
78. Borrows, "Heroes," 819.
79. Johnston, *Manitous*, 221–22.
80. Borrows, "Heroes," 836–37.

Chapter 1

1. JJ to GJ, 8 August 1814, George Johnston Papers, Detroit Public Library, Burton Historical Collection. He and Jane arrived with their party at Mackinac about 23 July, the day the Americans arrived at the Sault; Andrew Holmes to George Croghan, 27 July 1814, "Expedition against Michilimackinac," 246. Holmes writes that he (unknowingly) passed Johnston on his way up the St. Mary's.
2. Hannay, *History*, 302; Lt. Daniel Turner to Captain Arthur Sinclair, 28 July 1814, "Expedition against Michilimackinac," 246.
3. Hannay, *History*, 303; Lucas, *Canadian War of 1812*, 125. John Johnston put the number of Indigenous warriors at "50 or 60." JJ to GJ, 8 August 1814, George Johnston Papers, Burton. McDouall had previously sent an expedition of 150 local militia and 500 Indigenous warriors to take Prairie du Chien from the Americans, which they did in July 1814. Hannay, *History*, 300–301.
4. Hannay, *History*, 303.
5. JJ to Lewis Cass, 22 January 1822, NARA M1, roll 10.
6. Robert McDouall to George Prevost, 14 August 1814, Colonial Office Records, 593.
7. John Askin Jr. to John Askin Sr., 19 July 1812, MHC 32 (1903): 482.
8. Robert McDouall to George Prevost, 14 August 1814, Colonial Office Records, 591; Arthur Sinclair to William Jones [Secretary of the Navy], 9 August 1814, "Public Papers," *Niles Weekly Register* vol. 7, no. 182 (25 February 1815): 129.
9. JJ to GJ, 8 August 1814, George Johnston Papers, Burton.
10. O'Brien, *Names of Places*, 31. Ambrose Davenport, a US-allied fur trader and the future father-in-law of William Johnston, "urged Major Holmes to take off his uniform and put on a common suit, or the Indians would certainly make a mark of him. Holmes replied that his uniform was made to wear and that he intended to wear it, adding that if it was his day to fall, he was willing. He was among the first to fall in battle" (31).
11. Robert McDouall to George Prevost, 14 August 1814, Colonial Office Records, 591–93; George Croghan to William Jones [Secretary of the Navy], 9 August 1814, "Expedition

against Michilimackinac," 246–49; N. H. Moore, "Return of the killed, wounded, and missing" of 4 August, gives one major and twelve privates killed; two captains, one lieutenant, six sergeants, three corporals, one musician, and twenty-eight privates wounded ("Expedition against Michilimackinac," 250); Arthur Sinclair to William Jones, 3 September 1814, "Expedition against Michilimackinac," 256–59; Arthur Sinclair to William Jones, 28 October 1814, "Expedition against Michilimackinac," 259–60; JJ to GJ, 8 August 1814, George Johnston Papers, Burton; Andrew Bulgur, a British army officer on the island, gives an account of the men taken captive from the American ships (*Autobiographical Sketch*, 13–14). Wood, *Historic Mackinac*, 313–14 gives an account of the potential killers of Holmes and the disposition of his body afterward.

12. Jameson, *Winter Studies*, 2:153–54.

13. Schoolcraft, whose habitual editing of Jane's life lasted until his own death, twice asserted that Jane and her father were on a "visit" to Mackinac when the island was attacked (and thus were innocent bystanders). These are in "Memoir of John Johnston," written after Johnston's death in 1828 for publication by the Michigan Historical Society, and "Notes for a Memoir of Mrs. Henry Rowe Schoolcraft," an unfinished response to Anna Jameson's request after Jane's death for "some sketches of Mrs. S" to show "the applicability of [education] and [Christianity] to the native Indian family" (95). In both instances he appears to have been concealing both John Johnston's allegiance to the British Crown (particularly when the family was petitioning the US government for reimbursement of their losses at the Sault) and Jane's unladylike and equally un-American activities. His story is highly unlikely, since it was widely understood in the summer of 1814 that Mackinac was the Americans' principal target in the region after their recapture of Detroit in September 1813. Food and supplies on the island were scarce as well in the summer of 1814 and had been since the previous winter. By mid-July McDouall's Indigenous informants were warning of an American attack in the next month; he and it might be expected others on the island were fearful of a potential American blockade over the winter. Robert McDouall to George Prevost, 20 July 1814, Colonial Office Records, 588–89.

14. Schoolcraft, "Memoir of John Johnston," 76.

15. JJS, "Stanzas," in Parker, *Sound the Stars Make*, 155.

16. HRS, "Memoir of John Johnston," 60.

17. Johnston, "Autobiographical Letters," 331–32.

18. Examples of embroidery and quillwork done by members of the Johnston family can be seen at the River of History Museum in Sault Ste. Marie, Michigan. Jane also taught her daughter Janée to do quillwork (Dougherty, Diary, 14 July 1838, Dougherty Papers, Bentley. ("Little Jane gave me three mocacks full of sugar and worked outside with porcupine quills." Janée was ten years old at the time.)

19. Greig, *Beau Monde*, 19–26.

20. Johnston, "Autobiographical Letters," 340.

21. Klein, "Politeness," 875.

22. HRS, "Memoir of John Johnston," 63.

23. Nardin, "Hannah More"; Scheuermann, "Hannah More."

24. More, *Christian Morals*, 27.

25. More, *Christian Morals*, 37.

26. More, *Christian Morals*, 33–34.

27. More, *Christian Morals*, 33–34.
28. More, *Christian Morals*, 56.
29. Johnston, *Manitous*, 221–22.
30. HRS, "Dawn of Literary Composition," in Parker, *Sound the Stars Make*, 244.
31. JJS, "Stanzas," 145.
32. More, *Christian Morals*, 32.
33. Nelson, *Orders of the Dreamed*, 88.
34. Nelson, *Orders of the Dreamed*, 88.
35. Nelson, *Orders of the Dreamed*, 89.
36. Nelson, *Orders of the Dreamed*, 91–92.
37. Nelson, *Orders of the Dreamed*, 91–92.
38. Black, "Ojibwa Power Belief System," 145; McNally, *Honoring Elders*, 48–51.
39. Katz, *Beth El Story*, 13–22; Armour, "William Solomon"; Osborne, "Migration of Voyageurs," 123–66. Although his wife had their children baptized Catholic, Ezekiel kept his own faith, and in 1768 he founded the first synagogue in Montreal (a structure for which was built on land donated by the family of the fur trader David David several years later). William Solomon was about twenty years older than Marguerite, who was his second wife. They were married shortly before the war and went on to have ten children. There's some evidence that Marguerite practiced Judaism, or so one of the many traveling boundary surveyors of the late teens and early twenties thought. In *Unfortified Boundary*, Delafield wrote that "she is of the Jewish faith and a very clever and kind woman. She gives me a plate of Seneca grass handsomely braided by an Indian, and a little Indian mat to add to my stock of curiosities" (318–21). She seems to have had the Johnston habit of politeness to those who inquired after the lives of Indians.
40. JJ to JJS, n.d. 1817, in HRS, "Memoir," 76.
41. JJS to JJ, 14 July 1818, reel 1, HRS LC.
42. JJ to GJ, 30 October 1818 and 12 November 1819, George Johnston Papers, Burton.
43. JJ to GJ, 26 March 1816, George Johnston Papers, Burton.
44. McKenney, *Sketches*, 186.
45. GJ, "Reminiscences," 605–7.
46. JJ to GJ, 13 November 1815, George Johnston Papers, Burton.
47. JJ to GJ, 26 March 1816, George Johnston Papers, Burton; Robert McDouall to Secretary Foster, 8 March 1816, *Copies of Papers*, 440.
48. Neill, "History," 449.
49. Knight and Chute, "In the Shadow," 87.
50. David Mitchell to Robert McDouall, 26 March 1816, *Copies of Papers*, 448; 4 May 1816, *Copies of Papers*, 451. McDouall was warned to stop Mitchell's "unauthorized expenses" further up the chain of command (De Watteville to Foster, 18 April 1816, *Copies of Papers*, 450). At least eleven men died of the disease. Douglass, *Uppermost Canada*, 92–93.
51. Robert McDouall to [??], 19 June 1816, *Copies of Papers*, 469.
52. "Indian Council Speeches," 29 June 1816, *Copies of Papers*, 484.
53. Robert McDouall, "Farewell Address," 30 June 1816, *Copies of Papers*, 486–87.
54. JJ to GJ, 16 October 1816, George Johnston Papers, Burton. At about that time at Sault Ste. Marie, Ozhaawshkodewikwe gave birth to their last child, to whom they gave the English name John McDouall. Though he was promoted to colonel in July 1830 and major-

general in November 1841, McDouall never saw active duty again. He returned to his birthplace, Stranraer, Scotland, where he became an adherent of the Free Church of Scotland and died there in 1848. Allen, "Robert McDouall."

55. GJ, Memorandum Book, George Johnston Papers 1792–1944, Bayliss Public Library. Entries in the journal extend into the 1850s.

56. Pope, "Eloisa to Abelard," in *Whole Poetical Works*, 336.

57. Shenstone, *Poetical Works*, 1:15–18.

58. Shakespeare, *Titus Andronicus*, 218.

59. Shakespeare, *Titus Andronicus*, 218.

60. Johnson, *Johnson on Shakespeare*, 166. "All the editors and criticks agree with Mr. Theobald in supposing this play spurious. I see no reason for differing from them; for the colour of the stile is wholly different from that of the other plays, and there is an attempt at regular versification, and artificial closes, not always inelegant, yet seldom pleasing. The barbarity of the spectacles, and the general massacre which are here exhibited, can scarcely be conceived tolerable to any audience; yet we are told by *Johnson* [sic], that they were not only borne, but praised. That Shakespeare wrote any part, those Theobald declares it *incontestable*, I see no reason for believing" (166).

61. Noble, "'And Make Two Pasties,'" 690.

62. Pearson, "'That Bloody Mind,'" 39.

63. Shakespeare, *Titus Andronicus*, 232.

64. It was how he got around at the time.

65. Bigsby, *Shoe and Canoe*, 2:148.

66. Armour, "David and Elizabeth."

67. Hannay, *History*, 302.

68. Kane, *Wanderings of an Artist*, 11–12; Rowe, "Anderson Record, from 1699–1896," 134.

69. King, *Balancing Two Worlds*; Leighton, "Jean-Baptiste Assiginack."

70. *New Manual of Devotions* (1708); Richard Allestree, *The Whole Duty of Man* (1659); Vicesimus Knox, *Elegant Extracts; Or, Useful and Entertaining Passages in Prose, Selected for the Improvement of Young Persons; being similar in Design to Elegant Extracts in Poetry* (1797).

71. Blair, "On the Importance of Order in Conduct," in *Works of Hugh Blair*, 1:282–83.

72. Blair, "On the Importance," 286; 289; 291; 292.

73. Blair, "On the Importance," 292.

74. JJ to GJ, 15 June 1817, George Johnston Papers, Burton.

75. JJ to GJ, 15 January 1817, George Johnston Papers, Burton.

76. Schenck, "Lewis Saurin Johnston," 25–26; Lt. Col. Maule to Secretary Addison, 31 May 1817, *Copies of Papers*, 581.

77. GJ, "Reminiscences," 607–8. George misremembered the date as July 1816 rather than 1818.

78. Alexander Macomb to John C. Calhoun, 7 September 1818, in Carter, *Territorial Papers*, 10:781.

79. The collection of songs was written in both Ojibwemowin and English; it seems to have been the first time that any North American Indigenous songs had been transcribed in the language. French Jesuits in the seventeenth and eighteenth centuries studied Indigenous languages and produced wordlists, dictionaries, and grammars, but they didn't transcribe examples of oral traditions. Leahey, "'Comment peut un muet prescher l'évangile?,'" 108.

80. HRS, *Travels*, 426–27, 409.

81. For example, in his various publications he was in the habit of giving Jane as a source under her maiden name, her married name, her Ojibwe name, a nickname or pseudonym, or, most often, not at all in such a way as to make it seem that he had more sources than he did. Similarly, for Anishinaabe stories he sometimes used Algic (his neologism), sometimes Algonquin, sometimes Chippewa, and sometimes Saginaw in cases that were all stories supplied by members of the Johnston family, again making it seem that he had a wider range of information than he in fact had.

82. Benedict, "Paradox of the Anthology," 235.

83. Benedict, "Paradox of the Anthology," 232. Benedict defines the anthology as "a book of no less than three distinct works of literary art, each registered and read independently of others, yet all understood by readers as part of the anthology as a whole."

84. Sleeper-Smith, "'Unpleasant Transaction'"; Broadside, 9 September 1815, *Copies of Papers*, 253; William Henry Puthuff to Ensign George Mitchell, 9 September 1815, *Copies of Papers*, 253; Robert McDouall to Talbot Chambers, 2 October 1815, *Copies of Papers*, 307.

85. Syba, "After Design," 615.

86. Syba, "After Design," 616.

87. Robertson, *History of America*, 89.

88. Robertson, *History of America*, 89, 93.

89. For examples, see De Puy, *Bibliography*.

90. For an example of a noble Indian speech, see Jefferson, *Notes*, 124; an early historical account that uses treaties is Colden, *History* (1727/1747); see, for example, 107–8. Warburton in *Divine Legation* provides an example of the thinking on metaphor at 174–75. See also Adair, *History*, 11 and Blair, "Origin and Process of Language," in *Essays on Rhetoric*, 47.

91. Densmore, *Chippewa Music* 2, 13.

92. This is Schoolcraft's account in the manuscript "Dawn of Literary Composition by Educated Natives of the Aboriginal Tribes," which is entirely about Jane's poetry and was written in 1851, possibly for inclusion in the Indian history. Parker, *Sound the Stars Make*, 241–55.

93. Robertson, *History of America*, 103.

94. HRS wrote a version of "Peboan and Seegwun: An Allegory of the Seasons" in a journal entry for 1 April 1823, and he wrote that he heard "Origin of the Robin" on 14 April 1823 (*Personal Memoirs* 164, 165). The stories were published in 1827, in a manuscript literary magazine Schoolcraft produced at the Sault (chapter 4).

95. Schoolcraft, *Schoolcraft's Ojibwe Lodge Stories*, 3–4.

96. Fletcher, "Myths," 103.

97. Fletcher, "Myths," 112–13.

98. Schoolcraft, *Schoolcraft's Ojibwe Lodge Stories*, 37.

99. Schoolcraft, *Schoolcraft's Ojibwe Lodge Stories*, 38.

100. Schoolcraft, *Schoolcraft's Ojibwe Lodge Stories*, 38.

101. Witgen, *Infinity of Nations*, 52. See also Black Rogers, "Ojibwa Power Belief System."

102. McKenney, *Sketches of a Tour*, 189–90. It was reprinted a number of times in the 1830s. Samuel Colman incorporated the poem into his play, *Pontiac: or The Siege of Detroit* in 1835 (Boston: Samuel Colman 1835), 31, and George Turner reprinted it in *Traits of Indian Character*, vol. 1 (Philadelphia: Key & Biddle, 1836), 75–76, with a heading stating, "The following is a translation of an Indian Song, sung in a Council of the Chippewas, at Sault

de St. Marie, at the outlet of Lake Superior." It was also printed with correct attribution in *Waldie's Octavo Library [Philadelphia]* ("Furnishing the Best Popular Literature"), vol. 3, no. 10, 7 March 1837, n.p.

103. McNally, *Honoring Elders*, 44–45.
104. HRS, *Travels*, 425–26.
105. McNally, *Honoring Elders*, 49.
106. Grenby, "Tame Fairies," 10.
107. JJS, "Index," HRS LC, reel 56.
108. HRS, *Travels*, 413.
109. For example, see the opening of William Apess's "Indian's Looking-glass for the White Man," (1833).
110. HRS, *Travels*, 412–13.
111. HRS, *Travels*, 414.
112. HRS, *Travels*, 414.
113. HRS, *Travels*, 414–15.
114. HRS, *Travels*, 415.
115. HRS, *Travels*, 416, 415.
116. HRS, *Travels*, 416.
117. HRS, *Travels*, 417.
118. HRS, *Travels*, 418.
119. HRS, *Travels*, 419–20.
120. HRS, *Travels*, 420.
121. Lewis Cass to GJ, 27 October 1818, Office of Indian Affairs Records of the Michigan Superintendency of Indian Affairs 1814–1851, Letters Sent by the Superintendent 1818–1823, National Archives, Washington, DC.
122. JJ to GJ, 12 January 1819, George Johnston Papers, Burton.
123. JJ to GJ, 27 February 1819, George Johnston Papers, Burton.
124. Ruckman, "Ramsay Crooks," 22.
125. Ramsay Crooks to GJ, 16 December 1818, George Johnston Papers, Burton.
126. Ramsay Crooks to JJ, 11 January 1819, George Johnston Papers, Burton. "Food of the camelia" means decomposed wood and leaves.
127. Treaty with the Chippewas, 5 August 1826, in Peters, *United States Statutes*, 7:294; Weaver, *Descendants of John Johnston*, 5.
128. Ramsay Crooks to JJ, 11 January 1819, George Johnston Papers, Burton.
129. JJ to GJ, 12 November 1819, George Johnston Papers, Burton.
130. HRS, "Memoir of John Johnston," 79. Lewis visited the Sault in the fall of 1819, during which time he submitted a memorial for compensation for his war wounds and imprisonment with his father acting as his attorney, although it was eventually rejected. Schenck, "Lewis Saurin Johnston," 25–26; Lt. Col. Maule to Secretary Addison, 31 May 1817, *Copies of Papers*, 581; JJ to GJ, 12 November 1819, George Johnston Papers, Burton.
131. Lewis Cass to John C. Calhoun, 8 October 1819, in Carter, *Territorial Papers*, 10:868–70.
132. Bremer, *Indian Agent*, 31–32.
133. Extract of a letter from John C. Calhoun to Lewis Cass, 5 April 1820, in Dickens and Forney, *American State Papers*, 5:47–56.

134. Bremer, *Indian Agent*, 32–35.
135. GJ, "Reminiscences," 609.
136. GJ, "Reminiscences," 609–10; Witgen, *Infinity of Nations*, 341.
137. HRS, *Narrative Journal*, 138.
138. Witgen, *Infinity of Nations*, 342.
139. HRS, *Summary Narrative*, 80–81.
140. HRS, Private Journal of Indian Affairs, 1822–1836, 16 July 1822, reel 2, HRS LC.
141. GJ, "Reminiscences," 610.
142. GJ, "Reminiscences," 610–11.
143. Witgen, *Infinity of Nations*, 342.
144. Lewis Cass to John C. Calhoun, 17 June 1820, in Carter, *Territorial Papers*, 11:36.
145. JJS, "[Pensive Lines]," in Parker, *Sound the Stars Make*, 114–15.

Chapter 2

1. HRS, 26 July 1822, Private Journal of Indian Affairs, reel 2, HRS LC.
2. HRS, 10 July 1822, 1 August 1822, Private Journal of Indian Affairs, reel 2, HRS LC.
3. HRS, 24 September 1822, Private Journal of Indian Affairs, reel 2, HRS LC. Odabit later became a Methodist missionary.
4. HRS, 27 September 1822, Private Journal of Indian Affairs, reel 2, HRS LC.
5. Cass, *Inquiries*.
6. Lewis Cass to HRS, 26 September 1822, reel 3, HRS LC.
7. HRS, *Personal Memoirs*, 125.
8. HRS to Lewis Cass, 25 October 1822, reel 2, HRS LC.
9. HRS to JJS, 24 October 1822, reel 2, HRS LC.
10. HRS to JJS, 22 January 1823, reel 16, HRS LC.
11. HRS, "To a Young Lady, on Receipt of a Pensive Note," "Metrical Rambles," reel 56, HRS LC.
12. JJS, "An answer, to a remonstrance," in Parker, *Sound the Stars Make*, 144.
13. Bremer, *Indian Agent*, 8.
14. HRS, "Reminiscences," reel 19, HRS LC.
15. Bremer, *Indian Agent*, 23, 50.
16. Langford, "Uses of Eighteenth-Century Politeness" and Klein, "Politeness."
17. Bremer, *Indian Agent*, 51.
18. HRS, *Personal Memoirs*, 191.
19. Robert Laird, "Extracts from the Journal of Mr. Laird, Continued," *New York Religious Chronicle*, 10 April 1824, 26.
20. HRS, "Reminiscences," reel 19, HRS LC.
21. HRS, "An Indian Lament at St. Mary's Falls, near the outlet of Lake Superior, on the prospects of the Chippewa Nation," reel 56, HRS LC.
22. JJS, "Invocation to My Maternal Grandfather," in Parker, *Sound the Stars Make*, 100–101.
23. McDowell, "Therese Schindler of Mackinac," 131–32; on Indigenous women in the fur trade, see Van Kirk, *Many Tender Ties* and Brown, *Strangers in Blood*.
24. Armour, "David and Elizabeth," 20.

25. According to a young government clerk stuck on the island that winter, Pierce had become infatuated with the "dashing half breed French and Indian girl," who was "quite dark"—although that was tempered by her convent education and "polished" manners. Irwin, "Government Factor's Journal," 75. Josette had a son and a daughter but died in childbirth, with her baby, in 1821.

26. Baird, "Reminiscences," 40–41. This was a broadcloth skirt with ribbon and beadwork, broadcloth leggings with the same, leather moccasins with more beadwork, a red or blue blanket worn like a Spanish mantel, and a loose-fitting silk blouse, with layers of beaded necklaces and silver broaches. Elizabeth Baird misremembered or suppressed the date of the wedding. Baird has it at summer 1817 and has Madame Laframboise, Mrs. Schindler, and Mrs. Mitchell attending the ceremony at the fort with the officers.

27. Widder, *Battle for the Soul*, 21–22. Hester Crooks married the American Board of Commissioners for Foreign Missions missionary William Boutwell. Hester, Mary, and Nancy all attended the Presbyterian mission school at Mackinac.

28. Porter, Journal 7, 25 August 1832. [Miss Nancy Holiday to marry Lt. Jamieson of Fort Brady.] On 29 August 1832 they were married by Porter. He wrote, "The parents to Miss H. were present. Her mother, a pure Indian, seems inquiring the way of life. She does not speak English, but her daughter & several of the ladies speak Indian so she could converse very well. Her father was delighted with the marriage. He little expected that his daughter would do so well, as to marry a man of such mind, such standing, such ability to provide, & such piety. The last he speaks of with much satisfaction, tho' he is far from impiety himself." Mary Holiday married Dr. Holt in 1840; Jane cattily remarked to Schoolcraft that she'd given her age as twenty-five when her true age was thirty-one (JJS to HRS, 8 June 1840, reel 31, HRS LC).

29. JJS, Fragment, reel 56, HRS LC.

30. Bremer, *Indian Agent*, 97.

31. Lewis Cass to John C. Calhoun, 29 October 1821, in Cass, *Letter from the Secretary of War*, 113–14.

32. Gilman, *Henry Hastings Sibley*, 16–17.

33. Lewis Cass to John C. Calhoun, 6 April 1821, in Carter, *Territorial Papers*, 11:116–17.

34. Lewis Cass to the Acting Secretary of War [name?], 20 July 1815, in Carter, *Territorial Papers*, 10:581. He reiterated his suggestion that the United States employ interpreter-spies in a letter to Calhoun on 8 October 1819 (Carter, *Territorial Papers*, 10:869).

35. Cass, *Inquiries*, 12–20.

36. Andresen, *Linguistics in America*, 22–24. Benjamin Smith Barton, a naturalist influenced by European works, compiled a comparative wordlist of American Indian languages in his *New Views of the Origin of the Tribes and Nations of America* (1797).

37. Andresen, *Linguistics in America*, 52.

38. Cass, *Inquiries*, 58.

39. Cass, *Inquiries*, 24–25.

40. Forell, "Moravian Missions"; Harper, "Looking the Other Way."

41. Heckewelder, *Account*, 125.

42. Heckewelder, *Account*, 92.

43. Heckewelder, *Account*, 103.

44. Heckewelder, *Account*, 222.

45. Heckewelder, *Account*, 250.
46. Heckewelder, *Account*, 148, 149.
47. Heckewelder, *Account*, 133.
48. Heckewelder, *Account*, 88.
49. Heckewelder, *Account*, 203.
50. Heckewelder, *Account*, 244.
51. Heckewelder, *Account*, 247–48.
52. Heckewelder, *Account*, 277.
53. Heckewelder, *Account*, 278.
54. Heckewelder, *Account*, 319–20.
55. Du Ponceau, "Corresponding Secretary's Report," xxiii.
56. Du Ponceau, "Corresponding Secretary's Report," xxvi–xxvii.
57. Heckewelder and Du Ponceau, "Correspondence," 384–85.
58. Heckewelder and Du Ponceau, "Correspondence," 393.
59. Heckewelder and Du Ponceau, "Correspondence," 406.
60. Heckewelder and Du Ponceau, "Correspondence," 407–8.
61. Heckewelder and Du Ponceau, "Correspondence," 407–8.
62. Heckewelder and Du Ponceau, "Correspondence," 416.
63. Heckewelder and Du Ponceau, "Correspondence," 416–17.
64. Heckewelder and Du Ponceau, "Correspondence," 415.
65. Heckewelder and Du Ponceau, "Correspondence," 417.
66. Heckewelder and Du Ponceau, "Correspondence," 417.
67. Heckewelder and Du Ponceau, "Correspondence," 418.
68. Pickering, Review of *Account*, 169.
69. Pickering, Review of *Account*, 170.
70. Pickering, Review of *Account*, 179.
71. Pickering, Review of *Report*, 188.
72. Pickering, Review of *Discourse*, 112.
73. Andresen, *Linguistics in America*, 73.
74. Pickering, Review of *Discourse*, 14.
75. Andresen, *Linguistics in America*, 108–9. Heckewelder died in 1823.
76. Pickering, Review of *Discourse*, 114.
77. McKean, "Fieldwork Legacy," 448.

78. McLane and Slatkin, "British Romantic Homer," 692; Korsin, "Reconfiguring the Past," 247–48.

79. O'Halloran, "Irish Re-Creations," 83, 86. An 1805 review established that while Macpherson's works were based on authentic Irish and Scottish oral traditions and manuscript materials, he had made extensive modifications to them, including changing names and the sequence of episodes, leaving out characters and episodes, and adding his own invented material. Porter, "'Bring Me the Head,'" 399.

80. Blair, "Critical Dissertation," 314–15, 316, 317.

81. It appears in Barton, *Memoir*, 15–16.

82. See, for example, "Esquimaux," *Knickerbocker* 1.1 (January 1833): 56; Edward Allan Talbot, *Five Years' Residence in the Canadas* (London, 1824): 181–84; "Oneyo and Marano: An Indian Tale," *New-York Mirror* 1.13 (25 October 1823): 98; "Eldred Wilis, an Indian Tale,"

Souvenir 1.10 (5 September 1827): 74; "Namoya: A Fragment of an Indian Tale," *Bouquet: Flowers of Polite Literature* 3.2 (6 July 1833): 1; Benjamin Smith Barton, "On the Supposed Fascinating Power of the Rattle-snake," *A Journal of Natural Philosophy, Chemistry, and the Arts*, edited by William Nicholson (London: Printed for the Author, 1806), 300–305.

83. Campbell, "Biographical Sketch," 13.

84. Lewis Cass to HRS, 29 May 1823, reel 2, HRS LC.

85. Lewis Cass to HRS, 20 April 1824, reel 2, HRS LC.

86. JJS, "Scrutiny of the Power of the Indian Language to Express Abstract Ideas, of Preserving precision in the use of pronouns. Translation of Selected Sentences into the Chippewa, with the original variations. By Mrs. H. R. Schoolcraft," reel 65, HRS LC.

87. On the history of the case, see Robertson, *Conquest by Law*.

88. Johnson and Graham's Lessee v. McIntosh, 8 Wheaton 543; in Brightly, *Reports of Cases*, 573.

89. *Johnson and Graham's Lessee v. McIntosh* 583.

90. *Johnson and Graham's Lessee v. McIntosh*, 583.

91. *Johnson and Graham's Lessee v. McIntosh*, 590.

92. *Johnson and Graham's Lessee v. McIntosh*, 590–91.

93. Cass makes this explicit in his 1830 *North American Review* article. Harvey, "'Must Not Their Languages,'" 521.

94. WJ in Strickland, *Old Mackinaw*, 27; HRS, *Historical and Statistical*, 1:389.

95. Cass in Whiting, *Ontwa*, 113–14.

96. Lewis Cass to John C. Calhoun, 15 May 1823, in Carter, *Territorial Papers*, 11:262.

97. Schorer, *Indian Tales*, xi.

98. Campbell, "Biographical Sketch," 20.

99. Campbell, "Biographical Sketch," 26–27.

100. C. C. Trowbridge to Lyman Draper, 14 March 1874, in Schorer, "Indian Tales of C. C. Trowbridge: Toadstool Man," 140.

101. Schorer, "Indian Tales of C. C. Trowbridge: The Gambler," 229–35.

102. Schorer, "Indian Tales of C. C. Trowbridge: The Red Head," 86–95.

103. Schorer, "Indian Tales of C. C. Trowbridge: The Star Woman," 21.

104. Schorer, "Indian Tales of C. C. Trowbridge: Toadstool Man," 144.

Chapter 3

1. GJ, "Secret History of the Lac du Flambeau War Party Who Killed Finley & His Men, on Lake Pepin in 1824," reel 65, HRS LC and "Names of the Men Composing a War Party in 1824," reel 65, HRS LC. Also Bremer, *Indian Agent*, 62.

2. Warren, in his *History of the Ojibway Nation* (1885) has a somewhat different account of this episode at 389 ff. He may have heard this version through his father Lyman Warren, a trader at La Pointe.

3. Witgen, *Infinity of Nations*, 350–51; Schoolcraft, *Personal Memoirs* 198–99 ("scalp-coffin").

4. Schoolcraft thought the army was a threat to civil liberties, and all his life he was aggressive toward any man whom he believed to be impinging on his authority. The officers found Schoolcraft's moralizing hypocritical and his association with the family of a man

who had fought them only ten years before disgusting. When Maj. Enos Cutler succeeded Lt. Col. William Lawrence in the summer of 1823, the feud continued and began to center on Schoolcraft's desire for a fine house; in order, Schoolcraft wrote to Cass and Calhoun, to impress the Indians with the power of the United States. Bremer, *Indian Agent*, 82–88.

5. Lewis Cass to HRS, 30 May 1824, reel 2, HRS LC.
6. McKenney, *Sketches*, 113–14, 122.
7. Lewis Cass to HRS, 5 December 1824, reel 2, HRS LC.
8. Schacker-Mill, "Otherness and Otherworldliness," 168.
9. Warner, *Stranger Magic*, esp. 20–26; Baird, "Circulating Things," 80–83.
10. Warner, *Stranger Magic*, 15.
11. Warner, *Stranger Magic*, 21; also Baird, "Circulating Things," 84.
12. Lewis Cass to HRS, 5 December 1824, reel 2, HRS LC.
13. HRS to JJS, 13 July 1825, reel 3, HRS LC.
14. Lewis Cass to HRS, 13 March 1823, reel 2, HRS LC.
15. Lewis Cass to HRS, 19 October 1823, reel 2, HRS LC.
16. "Western Missionary Society," *Religious Miscellany, Containing Information Relative to the Church of Christ*, 9 April 1824, 184.
17. Schoolcraft, *Personal Memoirs*, 207–8.
18. Schoolcraft, *Personal Memoirs*, 204–5; "Zoology," *Atlantic Magazine*, 1 December 1824, 162.
19. Samuel Conant to HRS, 19 July 1825, reel 3, HRS LC.
20. HRS to JJS, 27 July 1825, reel 3, HRS LC.
21. Lewis Cass to HRS, 7 February 1825, reel 3, HRS LC; Lewis Cass to HRS, 17 December 1824, reel 3, HRS LC.
22. HRS to JJS, 15 January 1825, reel 3, HRS LC.
23. HRS to JJS, 15 January 1825, reel 3, HRS LC.
24. Van Kirk, *Many Tender Ties*, 28–52.
25. This idea took the central concern of the German school of philology, that the study of grammar would reveal the geographic distribution of languages over time and extended it to historical events, Indians themselves being unable to narrate their own history. Schoolcraft, *Travels*, 294, 380.
26. Schoolcraft, *Travels*, 421. The historical (Joshua) Wawanosh was an Ojibwe chief, a veteran of the War of 1812 who converted to Christianity in the 1830s and settled at Sarnia Reserve in southwest Ontario, opposite Port Huron, Michigan (Schmaltz, 136–37). The reserve is now Aamjiwnaang First Nation.
27. Schoolcraft, *Travels*, 424.
28. Schoolcraft, *Travels*, 424–25.
29. Schoolcraft, *Travels*, 425.
30. HRS to JJS, 17 August 1825, reel 3, HRS LC.
31. Review of *Travels in the Central Portions of the Mississippi Valley*, *New York Review and Atheneum Magazine* 1 (July 1825): 104.
32. Lewis Johnston to JJS, 13 February 1825, reel 3, HRS LC.
33. Campbell, "Biographical Sketch," 24.
34. Lewis Cass to HRS, 6 May 1825, reel 3, HRS LC.

35. "Message from the President of the United States" (27 January 1825), in Littlefield and Parins, *Encyclopedia of American Indian Removal*, 2:5–6.

36. "Gitche Iauba and Followers Talk Addressed to Their Great Father," reel 65, HRS LC; John Holiday to Captain N. S. Clarke, 3 February 1825, reel 65, HRS LC.

37. Schoolcraft, *Personal Memoirs*, 210.

38. JJS to HRS, 2 July 1825, reel 3, HRS LC.

39. Bremer, *Indian Agent*, 84–85. Schoolcraft comments on the murderers and their trial in a letter that appears to have been written for publication in the newspaper and that he included in volume 2 of *Literary Muzzeniegun* under the title "Identity of Manners &c between the Modern and Ancient Indian," reel 65, HRS LC. He writes, "It is sufficiently evident, on the enquiries that have already been made, that several of the war party, did not participate in the atrocious act, but when they found the murderers intent on their foul deed, withdrew to a distance, & even used their influence to prevent the attack. Of their number, who acted thus magnanimously, was Kewaynokwut, the leader, who is now at the Sault with several of his band, and will attend the council at Prairie du Chien."

40. HRS to JJS, 30 June 1825, reel 3, HRS LC.

41. JJS to HRS, 2 July 1825, reel 3, HRS LC.

42. HRS to JJS, 13 July 1825, reel 3, HRS LC.

43. HRS to JJS, 27 July 1825, reel 3, HRS LC.

44. HRS, Journal 1825, AMS 1031/24, Rosenbach.

45. HRS to JJS, 17 August 1825, reel 3, HRS LC.

46. HRS, Journal 1825, 27.

47. HRS, Journal 1825, 28.

48. HRS, Journal 1825, 38–39.

49. HRS, Journal 1825, 50–51.

50. JJS, ["A Mother's Lament for the Absence of a Child"], reel 44, HRS LC.

51. JJ to GJ, 14 January 1826, George Johnston Papers, Detroit Public Library, Burton Historical Collection.

52. Samuel Conant to JJS and HRS, 29 November 1825, reel 3, HRS LC.

53. GJ, "Statement," 2 November 1825, George Johnston Papers, Burton.

54. Pierre Duvernay's Ojibwe wife, Minedemoeyah, is listed for a grant of land in the 1826 Treaty of Fond du Lac.

55. GJ, 16 March 1826, Memorandum Book, George Johnston Papers, Bayliss Public Library.

56. GJ, 17 March 1826, Memorandum Book, George Johnston Papers, Bayliss.

57. GJ, 17 April 1826, Memorandum Book, George Johnston Papers, Bayliss.

58. GJ, 17 March 1826, Memorandum Book, George Johnston Papers, Bayliss.

59. GJ, 18 March 1826, Memorandum Book, George Johnston Papers, Bayliss.

60. HRS to GJ, 14 January 1826, George Johnston Papers, Burton.

61. HRS to John Holiday, 14 January 1826, George Johnston Papers, Burton.

62. HRS, "Speech to Gitche Iauba," 14 January 1826, George Johnston Papers, Burton.

63. GJ to HRS, [15 January 1826], George Johnston Papers, Burton.

64. GJ, "Copy of Speech Delivered to the Chiefs, Principal Men & Young Warriors, of Lac du Flambeau and Its Vicinity Convened in Public Council by George Johnston & by Order of Henry R. Schoolcraft Esqr. U.S. Indian Agent, This 15th April 1826," reel 65, HRS LC.

65. GJ, 17 April 1826, Memorandum Book, George Johnston Papers, Bayliss.

66. GJ, 3 June 1826, Memorandum Book, George Johnston Papers, Bayliss.

67. James Barbour, Letter from the Secretary of War to the Chairman of the Committee on Indian Affairs, Accomplished by a Bill for the Preservation and Civilization of the Indian Tribes within the United States (3 February 1826), in Littlefield and Parins, *Encyclopedia of American Indian Removal*, 2:7.

68. The full titles are John Dunn Hunter, *Manners and Customs of Several Indian Tribes, Located West of the Mississippi, Including Some Account of the Soil, Climate, and Vegetable Productions; and the Indian Materia Medica; to Which Is Prefixed the History of the Author's Life, during a Residence of Several Years among Them* (Philadelphia, 1823) and John Halkett, *Historical Notes, respecting the Indians of North America, with Remarks on the Attempts Made to Convert and Civilise Them* (London, 1825).

69. Cass, Review of *Manners and Customs*, 53.

70. Cass, Review of *Manners and Customs*, 56.

71. Cass, Review of *Manners and Customs*, 60.

72. Cass, Review of *Manners and Customs*, 63. He was referencing Keating, *Narrative of an Expedition*, 164.

73. Cass, Review of *Manners and Customs*, 78.

74. Cass, Review of *Manners and Customs*, 67.

75. Cass, Review of *Manners and Customs*, 68.

76. "Preservation of the Indians," *Niles' Weekly Register*, 10 June 1826, 273.

77. The full title is *Sketches of a Tour to the Lakes, of the Character and Customs of the Chippeway Indians, and of Incidents Connected with the Treaty of Fond du Lac* (Baltimore, 1827).

78. McKenney, *Sketches*, 69. Samuel Kirkland was a missionary to the Oneidas and the Tuscaroras who lived with them.

79. McKenney, *Sketches*, 69–70.

80. Barbour, "Letter from the Secretary of War," 7–8.

81. Barbour, "Letter from the Secretary of War," 9.

82. McKenney, *Sketches*, 73–74, 165–67, 239.

83. Barbour, "Letter from the Secretary of War," 10.

84. McKenney, *Sketches*, 73–74, 165–67, 259, 267.

85. McKenney, *Sketches*, 329.

86. McKenney, *Sketches*, 330.

87. McKenney, *Sketches*, 330.

88. McKenney, *Sketches*, 458.

89. Krause, "Testing a Tradition," 624–26. The boulder now resides in the Smithsonian Institution National Museum of Natural History in Washington, DC, where officials have resisted repatriating it since the 1990s. See Redix, "'Our Hope and Our Protection.'"

90. Pomedli, *Living with Animals*, 184–87, 235–38.

91. McKenney, *Sketches*, 459, 464.

92. McKenney, *Sketches*, 459.

93. McKenney and Hall, *Indian Tribes*, 1:158. Schoolcraft also wrote that the land grants were Shingabawossin's idea in *Literary Voyager* 2 (December 1826), in Mason, *Schoolcraft's Ojibwa Lodge Stories*, 30–31. See also Bremer, *Indian Agent*, 69.

94. McKenney, *Sketches*, 459.

95. McKenney, *Sketches*, 478.

96. McKenney, *Sketches*, 350.

97. McKenney, *Sketches*, 192.

98. McKenney, *Sketches*, 184–85.

99. McKenney, *Sketches*, 184.

100. McKenney, *Sketches*, 201.

101. McKenney, *Sketches*, 201.

102. McKenney, *Sketches*, 382.

103. McKenney, *Sketches*, 382.

104. McKenney, *Sketches*, 368.

105. McKenney, *Sketches*, 370.

106. McKenney, *Sketches*, 185–86.

107. McKenney, *Sketches*, 186. Parker in *Sound the Stars Make* identifies nine versions of the song, including versions likely rewritten by Schoolcraft (201–4). Jane's manuscript copy is in reel 56, HRS LC.

108. McKenney, *Sketches*, 188.

109. Peters, "Indian-Grave Robbing," 57–58.

110. "Dr. Gall's System of Craniology," *Literary Magazine and American Register* 3.19 (April 1805): 261.

111. Caldwell, *Elements of Phrenology*, 3–4.

112. Riegel, "Introduction of Phrenology," 73–38; Parssinen, "Popular Science and Society," 1–20.

113. Peters, "Indian-Grave Robbing," 52.

114. Peters, "Indian-Grave Robbing," 55.

115. Peters, "Indian-Grave Robbing," 58–59.

116. Peters, "Indian-Grave Robbing," 72–73. Peters suspected that Zina Pitcher may have been involved in the grave robbing in 1826, especially considering that within several years he would be sending Indian skulls to Samuel George Morton, the Philadelphia craniologist, and it would be entirely within Schoolcraft's habits to take advantage of an opportunity to do damage to an enemy and lie to protect a friend.

117. HRS to GJ, 20 May 1826, George Johnston Papers, Burton.

118. Lewis Cass to HRS, 21 August 1826, George Johnston Papers, Burton. HRS to GJ, 28 August 1826, George Johnston Papers, Burton.

119. "Speech Addressed to the Indian Agent at Sault Ste. Marie on the 8th of September 1826. Shingauba W'Ossin (Spirit Stone)," reel 65, HRS LC.

120. The Ojibwe words in parentheses were probably in George's original translation.

121. Witgen, *Infinity of Nations*, 5. See also Black, "Ojibwa Power Belief System," 141–51 and Miller, *Ogimaag*, 21–25.

122. Peters, "Indian Grave-Robbing," 59–60, 60n18.

123. Lyman Foot started working as an assistant to the scientist Benjamin Silliman when he was twelve years old (and of "unfortunate parentage"); eventually he received a medical degree from Yale, and on the recommendation of Silliman and others to their former student and current Secretary of War John Calhoun, Foot became a surgeon in the US Army. After Sault Ste. Marie, he served in the Seminole and Black Hawk Wars. He died of dysentery during the Mexican War. Fisher, *Life of Benjamin Silliman*, 1:209–99.

124. Warren, *History of the Ojibway Nation*, 393.

Chapter 4

1. Kinietz, "Schoolcraft's Manuscript Magazines," 154; Mason, Introduction to *Schoolcraft's Ojibwa Lodge Stories*, xix, 167n9.
2. "The Forsaken Brother" and "Mishosha" were published in *Literary Voyager*. The third part is "Origin of the Whitefish," which Schoolcraft published in *Narrative of an Expedition through the Upper Mississippi to Itasca Lake* (1834), his account of expeditions undertaken in 1831 and 1832. It's likely that Jane wrote that story in the 1820s and it first appeared in one of the missing numbers of the *Voyager*.
3. Granzberg, "Rolling Head Legend," 3. The disembodied head or skull menacingly rolling along is a motif in Indigenous stories across North America, appearing in Arapaho, Caddo, Maidu, Pawnee, and numerous other traditions. See Berens, *Memories, Myths, and Dreams*, 164–70 for an Ojibwe version told in 1933.
4. WJ, "Saganaw's Story," reel 78, HRS LC. The story was published as "The Weendigoes."
5. GJ, "Mash-kwa-sha-kong," 139–45.
6. Vecsey, *Traditional Ojibwa Religion*, 74–75; Johnston, *Manitous*, 120–23.
7. Grenby, "Tame Fairies."
8. Black, "Ojibwa Power Belief System," 145.
9. Black, "Ojibwa Power Belief System," 143.
10. Black, "Ojibwa Power Belief System," 143.
11. McNally, *Honoring Elders*, 48.
12. HRS, *Narrative of an Expedition*, 147.
13. HRS, *Narrative of an Expedition*, 148.
14. HRS, *Narrative of an Expedition*, 148–49.
15. HRS, *Narrative of an Expedition*, 149.
16. Mason, *Schoolcraft's Ojibwe Lodge Stories*, 94.
17. Mason, *Schoolcraft's Ojibwe Lodge Stories*, 94.
18. Mason, *Schoolcraft's Ojibwe Lodge Stories*, 94–95.
19. Mason, *Schoolcraft's Ojibwe Lodge Stories*, 95.
20. Mason, *Schoolcraft's Ojibwe Lodge Stories*, 95.
21. Mason, *Schoolcraft's Ojibwe Lodge Stories*, 95.
22. Mason, *Schoolcraft's Ojibwe Lodge Stories*, 95.
23. Mason, *Schoolcraft's Ojibwe Lodge Stories*, 95–96.
24. Mason, *Schoolcraft's Ojibwe Lodge Stories*, 96.
25. Mason, *Schoolcraft's Ojibwe Lodge Stories*, 96.
26. Mason, *Schoolcraft's Ojibwe Lodge Stories*, 64.
27. Mason, *Schoolcraft's Ojibwe Lodge Stories*, 64.
28. Mason, *Schoolcraft's Ojibwe Lodge Stories*, 64–65.
29. Mason, *Schoolcraft's Ojibwe Lodge Stories*, 65.
30. Mason, *Schoolcraft's Ojibwe Lodge Stories*, 65–66.
31. JJS, "Mishosha," in Parker, *Sound the Stars Make*, 172.
32. JJS, "Mishosha," 173.
33. JJS, "Mishosha," 173.
34. JJS, "Mishosha," 173.
35. JJS, "Mishosha," 173.

36. JJS, "Mishosha," 173.
37. JJS, "Mishosha," 173.
38. JJS, "Mishosha," 175.
39. JJS, "Mishosha," 175.
40. JJS, "Mishosha," 175.
41. Johnston, *Manitous*, 19.
42. WJ, "Saganaw's Story" ["The Weendigoes"], reel 78, HRS LC.
43. Johnston, *Manitous*, 30.
44. Johnston, *Manitous*, 32.
45. Mason, *Schoolcraft's Ojibwe Lodge Stories*, 118.
46. Mason, *Schoolcraft's Ojibwe Lodge Stories*, 118–19.
47. A note says that *muckumick* means "take it away."
48. Schenck, *Voice of the Crane*, 77.
49. Mason, *Schoolcraft's Ojibwe Lodge Stories*, 16.
50. Mason, *Schoolcraft's Ojibwe Lodge Stories*, 36–37.
51. Mason, *Schoolcraft's Ojibwe Lodge Stories*, 88.
52. Mason, *Schoolcraft's Ojibwe Lodge Stories*, 33,
53. Mason, *Schoolcraft's Ojibwe Lodge Stories*, 12.
54. Mason, Schoolcraft's Ojibwe Lodge Stories, 19–20.
55. Mason, *Schoolcraft's Ojibwe Lodge Stories*, 21.
56. Mason, *Schoolcraft's Ojibwe Lodge Stories*, 104.
57. Mason, *Schoolcraft's Ojibwe Lodge Stories*, 97.
58. The word for excrement in Ojibwemowin is *moo*.
59. HRS, "Moowis"; HRS, "Moowis, or, The Man Made Up of Rags and Dirt," *Oneota*, 381–84. Henry Wadsworth Longfellow included the Moowis story, as well as a reference to Jane Schoolcraft, in his poem *Evangeline: A Tale of Acadie* (Boston, 1847).
60. Mason, *Schoolcraft's Ojibwe Lodge Stories*, 56.
61. Mason, *Schoolcraft's Ojibwe Lodge Stories*, 56.
62. Mason, *Schoolcraft's Ojibwe Lodge Stories*, 56.
63. Mason, *Schoolcraft's Ojibwe Lodge Stories*, 56–57.
64. Mason, *Schoolcraft's Ojibwe Lodge Stories*, 57.
65. Mason, *Schoolcraft's Ojibwe Lodge Stories*, 57.
66. Mason, *Schoolcraft's Ojibwe Lodge Stories*, 57.
67. Cass asserts this point in his 1826 Review of *Manners and Customs of Several Indian Tribes*.
68. Mason, *Schoolcraft's Ojibwe Lodge Stories* 32.
69. Mason, *Schoolcraft's Ojibwe Lodge Stories*, 32.
70. Mason, *Schoolcraft's Ojibwe Lodge Stories*, 32.
71. Mason, *Schoolcraft's Ojibwe Lodge Stories*, 63.
72. Mason, *Schoolcraft's Ojibwe Lodge Stories*, 102.
73. Mason, *Schoolcraft's Ojibwe Lodge Stories*, 108.
74. Mason, *Schoolcraft's Ojibwe Lodge Stories*, 108.
75. Mason, *Schoolcraft's Ojibwe Lodge Stories*, 109–10.
76. Jefferson, *Notes*, 178.
77. Mason, *Schoolcraft's Ojibwe Lodge Stories*, 110–11.

78. Mason, *Schoolcraft's Ojibwe Lodge Stories*, 111.

79. If Schoolcraft was responding to a published article, it's not clear which one it was or if it appeared in one of the lost issues.

80. Mason, *Schoolcraft's Ojibwe Lodge Stories*, 48.

81. In relation to the substance of what William had to say, there is an analog in the writing of John Dunn Hunter, whose *Memoirs of a Captivity among the Indians of North America* (London, 1824) was the ostensible subject of Cass's recent *North American Review* diatribe. Hunter was a white man taken captive as a child by the Kickapoos who lived with them and other tribes until he was nineteen or twenty. According to Hunter, white people who'd been kidnapped were happy with the tribes and seldom left, and he maintained that the Indians "display . . . as great energy of mental powers, and capability of accommodating it to particular exigencies, as any other people have." Hunter, *Memoirs of a Captivity*, 14, 199.

82. Mason, *Schoolcraft's Ojibwa Lodge Stories*, 78.

83. Mason, *Schoolcraft's Ojibwe Lodge Stories*, 79.

84. Mason, *Schoolcraft's Ojibwe Lodge Stories*, 79.

85. Mason, *Schoolcraft's Ojibwe Lodge Stories*, 79–80.

86. Mason, *Schoolcraft's Ojibwe Lodge Stories*, 80.

87. Mason, *Schoolcraft's Ojibwe Lodge Stories*, 81.

88. Mason, *Schoolcraft's Ojibwe Lodge Stories*, 81.

89. Mason, *Schoolcraft's Ojibwe Lodge Stories*, 122.

90. Mason, *Schoolcraft's Ojibwe Lodge Stories*, 123.

91. Mason, *Schoolcraft's Ojibwe Lodge Stories*, 124.

92. Mason, *Schoolcraft's Ojibwe Lodge Stories*, 124.

93. Mason, *Schoolcraft's Ojibwe Lodge Stories*, 124.

Chapter 5

1. JJS to GJ, 26 March 1827, Steere Special Collection, George Johnston Papers 1792–1944, Bayliss Public Library.

2. Mason, *Schoolcraft's Ojibwe Lodge Stories*, 146.

3. "Extract of a letter, dated March 22nd 1827," Mason, *Schoolcraft's Ojibwe Lodge Stories*, 150.

4. Samuel Conant to HRS and JJS, 29 May 1827, reel 4, HRS LC.

5. Daly, *When Slavery Was Called Freedom*, 10–29.

6. Daly, *When Slavery Was Called Freedom*, 28.

7. Carwardine, *Evangelicals and Politics*, xv.

8. Daly, *When Slavery Was Called Freedom*, 19.

9. HRS to JJS, 3 July 1827, reel 4, HRS LC.

10. JJS to HRS, 11 July 1827, reel 4, HRS LC.

11. HRS to JJS, 20 July 1827, reel 4, HRS LC.

12. HRS to JJS, 24 July 1827, reel 4, HRS LC. Anderson had captured Prairie du Chien from the Americans in the War of 1812; he remained in the British Indian Department for the rest of his career, moving to Penetanguishene in late 1828, after Drummond Island was transferred to US jurisdiction.

13. Thomas L. McKenney to Lewis Cass, 7 March 1827, NARA, M1, reel 20. "As to the estimate of Mr. Schoolcraft I have to state that in *no case* can he be allowed more than two thousand dollars for the agency house,—this is the maximum; and any thing beyond this must be paid for out of his own resources. I do not understand the item in Mr. Schoolcraft's estimate for French interpreter and Chippewa interpreter, if these are intended to apply to Michaels Island—nor for the French interpreter *any* where. I . . . have earnestly to request that the strictest economy be observed, and that each item be disbursed, in such a way as to be accounted for in all the agencies of your Superintendency with reference to a very unsparing responsibility, in the settlement of the accounts there."

14. Money, "'Elmwood' The Schoolcraft House."

15. JJS, Diary, 28 April 1828, reel 48, HRS LC. The diary is in two parts in Schoolcraft's papers: 28 April to 11 May 1828 is on reel 4; 12 May to 3 June 1828 is on reel 48.

16. A "makak" is a basket or box, especially of birch bark.

17. George Boyd, a Marylander who married a sister of Mrs. John Quincy Adams, had six surviving sons: John Quincy Adams Boyd died of yellow fever at Norfolk while serving in the navy; Joshua Johnson Boyd, a fur trader, was murdered "by an Indian" in Wisconsin in 1832; Thomas Alexander Brooks Boyd was Indian agent at Prairie du Chien and died of cholera; Robert Dundass Boyd was clerk of the Circuit Court at La Pointe and was "shot and killed there about 1850"; William Henry Crawford Boyd served in the Civil War; and James Madison Boyd became his father's interpreter at Green Bay, the post to which George Boyd transferred in 1832. Tanner, "Sketch of George and James M. Boyd," 268–69. Whistler was US Army commandant at Fort Mackinac in 1823 and 1833, having other assignments in between. Baily might be a brother of Joseph Bailly, a fur trader who was the father of Eleanor Bailly; Joseph was at Mackinac until 1822, when he and his family moved to their trading post in Indiana (Baird, "Reminiscences of Early Days," 43).

18. Widder, *Battle for the Soul*, 127–43. Mary and Nancy were twelve and nine, respectively, when they started school in 1824; William attended only the 1825–26 term. Mary left in 1829 and Nancy in 1831.

19. JJS, Diary, 1 June 1828, reel 48, HRS LC.

20. JJS, Diary, 1 June 1828, reel 48, HRS LC.

21. HRS to JJS, 23 May 1828, reel 4, HRS LC.

22. HRS to JJS, 15 June 1828, reel 4, HRS LC.

23. HRS to JJS, 15 June 1828, reel 4, HRS LC.

24. JJ to HRS, 14 August 1828, reel 4, HRS LC.

25. HRS to Henry Kearney, 30 September 1828, reel 4, HRS LC.

26. JP, 11 May 1832, Journal 5, Jeremiah Porter Journals 1831–1848, Chicago Historical Society.

27. JS to HRS, 3 September 1829, reel 4, HRS LC.

28. HRS, "Lines to My Pen," 3 October 1830, reel 56, HRS LC.

29. HRS to Jared Sparks, 13 October 1829, reel 5, HRS LC.

30. Muster and Descriptive Roll of Veteran Volunteers, 11 May 1864, NARA.

31. Osborn and Osborn, *Schoolcraft-Longfellow-Hiawatha*, 527.

32. HRS, "Discourse," 51–109, 88, 87.

33. HRS, *Indian Melodies*.

34. The poem, "High heav'd my breast," survived in Jane's hand among Schoolcraft's papers but is unfinished. "High heav'd my breast," in Parker, *Sound the Stars Make*, 213–14. HRS, "Why heaves my breast with troubled sighs," in *Indian Melodies*, 29–30.

35. HRS, *Indian Melodies*, 37.

36. Colton, *Tour*, 1:82.

37. Colton, *Tour*, 1:82.

38. Colton, *Tour*, 1:87.

39. HRS to JJS, 22–24 November 1830, reel 5, HRS LC.

40. JJS to HRS, 6 December 1830, reel 5, HRS LC.

41. JJS to HRS, 22 November 1830, reel 20, HRS LC.

42. JJS to HRS, 27 November 1830, reel 5, HRS LC.

43. JJS to HRS, 19 November 1830, reel 5, HRS LC.

44. HRS to JJS, 24 November 1830, reel 5, HRS LC.

45. Burton, Stocking, and Miller, *City of Detroit*, 2:240, 1351–52.

46. "Irwin v. Wells," in Houck, *Reports of Cases*, 22–24.

47. JJS to HRS, 27 November 1830, reel 5, HRS LC.

48. JJS to HRS, 6 December 1830, reel 5, HRS LC.

49. Chippewa County Marriage Record, Chippewa County, MI.

50. JJS to HRS, 6 January 1831, reel 5, HRS LC.

51. HRS to JJS, 22 December 1830, reel 5, HRS LC.

52. AMJS to JLS, 5 January 1831, reel 5, HRS LC.

53. JJS to HRS, 6 March 1831, reel 5, HRS LC.

54. JJS to HRS, 7 March 1831, 20 March 1831, reel 5, HRS LC.

55. HRS to JJS, 22 December 1830, reel 5, HRS LC.

56. HRS to JJS, 8 March 1831, reel 5, HRS LC. The verse is Luke chapter 11, verses 11–13: "If a son shall ask bread of any of you that is a father, will he give him a stone? or if he ask a fish, will he for a fish give him a serpent? Or if he shall ask an egg, will he offer him a scorpion? If ye then, being evil, know how to give good gifts to your children: how much more shall your heavenly Father give the Holy Spirit to them that ask him?"

57. JJS to HRS, 27 June 1831, reel 5, HRS LC.

58. Melancthon Woolsey to JJS, 17 July 1831, reel 5, HRS LC.

59. HRS to JJS, 3 July 1831, reel 5, HRS LC.

60. HRS to JJS, 10 July 1831, reel 5, HRS LC.

61. JJS to HRS, 29 July 1831, reel 5, HRS LC.

62. JJS to HRS, 22 November 1831, reel 5, HRS LC.

63. Charles E. Hulbert, "Reminiscences of Rev. Abel Bingham," box 1, folder 1–2, Abel Bingham Papers, Clarke Historical Library.

64. Bingham tells the story of his struggle to remain at Tonawanda, and his efforts to convince Red Jacket to become a Christian, in his diaries from 1822 to 1827. See especially entries for 9 April 1822; 27 January 1823, Abel Bingham Papers, box 1, folder 1–4, Clarke.

65. Abel Bingham, 29 February 1829, Journal 1828–1832, Abel Bingham Papers, Clarke.

66. Hele, "James D. Cameron," 140–41.

67. JP, 30 January 1832, 13 February 1832, Journal 3, Chicago.

68. JP, 6 March 1832, 7 March 1832, Journal 4, Chicago.

69. Abel Bingham, 4 June 1835, Journal 1, box 1, folder 1–7, Clarke; Hele, "James D. Cameron," 144–45.

70. Hele, "James D. Cameron," 152.

71. JP, 29, 30 November 1831, Journal 2, Chicago.

72. Otis, *First Presbyterian Church*, 228.

73. JP, 26 November 1831, Journal 2, Chicago.

74. JP, 14 May 1832, Journal 5, Chicago.

75. JP, 14 May 1832, Journal 5, Chicago.

76. John Agnew is listed as a customs inspector at Sault Ste. Marie in 1833 in Weaver, *Register of Officers and Agents*, 56.

77. JP, 7–8 December 1832, Journal 2, Chicago.

78. JP, 24 December 1831, Journal 2, Chicago.

79. GJ to JP, 19 November 1832, Johnston Letterbook, Bentley Historical Library.

80. JP 10 February 1832, Journal 3, Chicago

81. JP, 28 March 1832, Journal 4, Chicago.

82. JP, 11 May 1832, Journal 5, Chicago

83. Smith, *Mississauga Portraits*, 221–30.

84. "Missionary Intelligence," *Christian Advocate* 4, no. 23 (5 February 1830): 89.

85. "John Sunday," *Christian Advocate* 4, no. 52 (27 August 1830): 205.

86. "John Sunday," *Christian Advocate* 4, no. 52 (27 August 1830): 205.

87. Copway, *Life, History, and Travels*, 73.

88. "John Sunday," 205.

89. *Christian Advocate*, 6.14 (2 December 1831): 54.

90. Bremer, *Indian Agent*, 131.

91. JP, 29 May 1832, Journal 5, Chicago.

92. CJM, Commonplace Book, River of History Museum, Sault Ste. Marie, Michigan.

93. JP, 10 September 1832, Journal 7, Chicago.

94. JP, 11 May 1832, Journal 5, Chicago; Chute, *Legacy of Shingwaukonse*, 42–44.

95. JP, 10 July 1832, Journal 6, Chicago.

96. HRS to JJS, 7 September 1832, reel 5, HRS LC.

97. JJS to HRS, 18 September 1832, reel 5, HRS LC.

98. JJS to HRS, 9 October 1832, reel 5, HRS LC.

99. JJS to HRS, 12 October 1832, reel 5, HRS LC.

100. JP, 16 November 1832, Journal 8, Chicago.

101. JP, 18 June 1832, 25 June 1832, Journal 6, Chicago. After a year spent with the Ojibwes at Fond du Lac, Boutwell married Hester Crooks, Ramsay Crooks's Odawa daughter and a graduate of the Presbyterian mission school at Mackinac.

102. CJM, Commonplace Book, River of History Museum.

103. JP, 31 December 1832, Journal 9, Chicago.

104. JP, 2 January 1833, Journal 9, Chicago.

105. JP, 2 April 1833, Journal 11, Chicago.

Story of Manahbosho

1. WJ, "Story of Manahbosho," reel 65, HRS LC.

2. Comaus [?] [William's note.]

3. Mama [William's note; the contemporary spelling is "meme" (pileated woodpecker).]

4. This may be related to *opikwad*, meaning "gut," or *obiwai*, having fur (of an animal), from Baraga, *Dictionary of the Ojibway Language*, 312, 332.

Chapter 6

1. WJ to GJ, 14 January 1834, George Johnston Papers, Detroit Public Library, Burton Historical Collection.

2. WJ, "Letters on the Fur Trade," 133–34.

3. WJ, "Letters on the Fur Trade," 135–36.

4. Nicolas Perrot wrote that the Pillagers got their name after they robbed the first white trader who came to them of his goods (HRS, *Narrative of an Expedition*, 81).

5. HRS, *Narrative of an Expedition*, 155–56.

6. HRS, *Narrative of an Expedition*, 156–57.

7. Miller, *Ogimaag*, 78–79.

8. HRS, *Narrative of an Expedition*, 68.

9. WJ, "Letters on the Fur Trade," 161.

10. WJ, "Letters on the Fur Trade," 161.

11. WJ, "Letters on the Fur Trade," 162.

12. One of these appears to have been a man that Schoolcraft met, Flat Mouth's "companion and pipe-lighter, Maji Gabowi, a very tall, gaunt, and savage looking warrior, who appears to be made up, body and mind, of sensualities." Schoolcraft identified him as "the murderer of Gov. Semple" at the Red River settlement in Canada (*Narrative of an Expedition*, 103). According to Miller in *Ogimaag*, this man was actually Flat Mouth's miishinoo or ambassador or secretary (71, 276). His name is rendered today "Majigaabaw." "A miishinoo apprenticed himself to an ogimaa, gechi midewid, or gichi-anishinaabe, forging a lifelong relationship between the two through a fictive kinship bond akin to adoption but with a different set of responsibilities that focused more on instruction and training.... When a hereditary ogimaa took on a miishinoo, this individual served as his oshkaabewis [lieutenant, assistant, or pipe bearer] and in some cases as his giigidowinini, or speaker, as well," Miller writes (84).

13. WJ, "Letters on the Fur Trade," 181; William Boutwell, 16 October 1833, Diary, William T. Boutwell Papers 1832–1881, Minnesota Historical Society, St. Paul, Minnesota.

14. WJ, "Letters on the Fur Trade," 190.

15. William Boutwell, 7 May 1835; 16 October 1833; 24 June 1836, Diary, Minnesota; Kugel, *To Be the Main Leaders*, chapter 1. Big Cloud's two wives were sisters, Boutwell wrote in his diary, and were paid in "strouds, scarlet red worsted, beads, gartering, &c. this is the way the old man clothes his women." On 7 May 1835, Big Cloud's "old woman," who was pregnant, had been caused to miscarry by a Frenchman "visiting" her the previous night. Any babies born, Big Cloud and this wife killed. "He has no children by either of the women he now keeps, tho' she (his older wife) has two. One of these is by Mr. [William] Aitkin the other by an Indian. She had one last spring by the clerks here, (George Bonga, a colored man, whose mother is an Indian woman,) which she killed herself, as a woman who was present when it was born, told my wife. This is the only instance among the Indians, that I know of, where a man keeps women for the use of Frenchmen, designedly. While the old woman was sick, the old man, (I am told) said: 'if she dies, I will kill the one

who has caused her death.' Such is the character of this old man." Boutwell, 7 May 1835, Diary, Minnesota.

16. WJ, "Notes on the Manner in Which the Chippewas Spend Their Time, While on Their Wintering Grounds," reel 65, HRS LC.

17. "Manners and Customs of the Leech Lake Indians," reel 65, HRS LC.

18. WJ, "Letters on the Fur Trade," 191.

19. Schoolcraft mentions a guide called Oza Windib or Yellow Head in *Narrative of an Expedition*. He was the leader of a band living at Cass Lake (32–34).

20. WJ, "Letters on the Fur Trade," 206.

21. WJ, "Letters on the Fur Trade," 206-7.

22. WJ to GJ, 14 January 1834, George Johnston Papers, Burton.

23. WJ to GJ, 14 January 1834, George Johnston Papers, Burton.

24. JJS to HRS, 22 September 1833, reel 6, HRS LC.

25. HRS to JJS, 16 October 1833, reel 6, HRS LC.

26. HRS, *Personal Memoirs*, 449–50, 476–77, 478–79.

27. HRS, *Information* 4:491.

28. HRS, "Mythology, Superstition and Languages," 104.

29. JJS, "Vision of Catherine Wabose," in HRS, *Information*, 1:391.

30. JJS, "Vision of Catherine Wabose," 392.

31. Strickland, *Old Mackinaw*, 24–25.

32. JJS, "Vision of Catherine Wabose," 392.

33. JJS, "Vision of Catherine Wabose," 393.

34. JJS, "Vision of Catherine Wabose," 392–93.

35. JJS, "Indian maiden's story of fast and vision, undated," reel 66, HRS LC; HRS, "Confessions of Catherine Ogee Wyan Akwut Okwa," in *Oneota*, 430–35; HRS, *Information*, 1:390–401. "Visions & Medicine Songs of Oge wy ahn ak wut o quay alias Catherine Wabose," reel 56, HRS LC. A partial copy of the narrative exists in Jane's hand; when Schoolcraft published it, first in 1845 in his serial *Oneota*, then in 1851 in the Indian history, he made only minor editorial changes, giving Jane as the author and setting it off in quotation marks. The songs are in the hand of both Jane and Henry Schoolcraft and only a fragment of her translation of the songs exists. The manuscript pictographic representation of the vision does not survive.

36. Cass defines a Mutchekewis as a hereditary leader; Basil Johnston describes a "Maudjee-Kawiss" as "first son" in *Manitous* (17).

37. Cass in Whiting, *Sannillac*, 140–41.

38. Whiting, *Sannillac*, 141.

39. JJS, "Vision of Catherine Wabose," 393.

40. JJS, "Vision of Catherine Wabose," 393–94.

41. JJS, "Vision of Catherine Wabose," 393.

42. JJS, "Vision of Catherine Wabose," 394.

43. Strickland, *Old Mackinaw*, 26–28.

44. JJS, "Vision of Catherine Wabose," 395.

45. JJS, "Vision of Catherin Wabose," 395.

46. HRS, 22 July 1822, *Private Journal of Indian Affairs at Sault Ste Marie and Michilimackinac*, reel 2, HRS LC.

47. "Visions & Medicine Songs of Oge wy ahn ak wut o quay alias Catherine Wabose," reel 56, HRS LC. The manuscript is in the hand of both Jane and Henry Schoolcraft.

48. JJS, "Vision of Catherine Wabose," 391. As a result of Schoolcraft's publications, Catherine Wabose became somewhat well known; by the end of the century, Scottish aristocrats were writing epic poems about her; see Carnegie, *Meda Maiden*.

49. JLS to CJM, n.d., copy in reel 21, HRS LC; JLS to JJS, 8 February 1834, reel 22, HRS LC; WM to HRS, 4 March 1834, reel 6, HRS LC; JJS to CJM, 4 March 1834, reel 6, HRS LC.

50. WM to JJS, 23 August 1834, reel 22, HRS LC.

51. GJ to HRS, 18 July 1834, reel 6, HRS LC.

52. WM to JJS, 6 September 1834, reel 22, HRS LC.

53. GJ to HRS, 6 September 1834, reel 7, HRS LC.

54. Stevens T. Mason to GJ, 11 July 1834, and Lewis Cass to GK, 15 September 1834, George Johnston Papers, Burton.

55. Vecsey has a list of the published versions in *Traditional Ojibwa Religion*, 87-88.

56. Schoolcraft notes this habit in his introduction to "Manabozho," *AR*, 1:142n, as does the later German traveler Johann Georg Kohl in his *Kitchi-Gami*, 415-16.

57. McKenney, *Sketches*, 304.

58. McKenney, *Sketches*, 302.

59. Nichols, "Ojibwa Oral Literature," 842.

60. HRS, "Manabozho," *AR*, 1:135-36.

61. Brinton, *Myths*, 160.

62. HRS, *Personal Memoirs*, 450. In the 1840s Schoolcraft wrote that he received the Wauchusco's account "through an interpreter" in "Mythology, Superstitions, and Religion of the Algonquins," *Indian in His Wigwam* (rpt. *Oneota*), 207.

63. HRS, "Mythology, Superstitions and Languages," 103.

64. HRS, "Mythology, Supersitions and Languages," 103.

65. HRS, "Mythology, Superstitions and Languages," 105.

66. HRS, "Mythology, Superstitions and Languages," 106.

67. HRS, "Mythology, Superstitions, and Languages," 106-7.

68. HRS, "Mythology, Superstitions, and Languages," 107.

69. HRS, "Mythology, Superstitions, and Languages," 109.

70. HRS, "Mythology, Superstitions, and Languages," 109.

71. In *Narrative of an Expedition*, Schoolcraft offered the theory that the complexity of Ojibwemowin demonstrated that the Ojibwes had formerly been "in a more advanced and cultivated state," which observation allowed him to digress on the Ojibwes' degeneration from some unspecified earlier moment in time (97-98).

72. HRS, *Narrative of an Expedition*, 112.

73. HRS, *Narrative of an Expedition*, 107, 109.

74. HRS, *Narrative of an Expedition*, 108.

75. GJ, "Statement of Particulars. Account at the Office of Indian Agency," 4 October 1834, George Johnston Papers, Burton and GJ to Captain Chethechiff, 6 October 1834, George Johnston Letterbook, Bentley Historical Library.

76. GJ to JJS, n.d. October 1834, George Johnston Letterbook, Bentley.

77. GJ to LC, 6 October 1834, George Johnston Letterbook, Bentley.

78. GJ to Rouissan, 4 November 1834, George Johnston Papers, Burton.

79. Clark, *Public Schools of Chicago*, 11.

80. Grenville Sproat to JJS, 23 October 1834, reel 22, HRS LC.

81. WJ to HRS, 17 November 1834, reel 7, HRS LC.

82. "Family Temperance Pledge," 13 February 1835, signed by Schoolcraft, Jane, Janée, Johnston, Charlotte Wabose, Louise Piquette, Christian and Mary Wachter, Grenville T. Sproat, and William Johnston, reel 23, HRS LC.

83. HRS to Washington Irving, 6 May 1835, reel 23, HRS LC.

84. At the time, two recently published books titled *Indian Biography* (one by Samuel Gardner Drake and the other by Benjamin Bussey Thatcher) recounted the lives of famous chiefs and their battles from colonization through the War of 1812. Thatcher, *Indian Biography* and Drake, *Indian Biography*. Both books began as biographical dictionaries of figures taken from early records; Drake revised his second edition (1833) into a narrative history centered on New England.

85. "Washington Irving, Esq.," *Atkinson's Saturday Evening Post*, 4 May 1833, 3; "American Literature," *Boston Literary Magazine*, December 1832, 381–83; "Adulation," *North American Magazine*, November 1833, 66.

86. "A Conversation," *Knickerbocker*, June 1833, 1.

87. Burstein, *Original Knickerbocker*, 160. Irving also became "better acquainted" with Astor when they were both in Paris in the early 1820s.

88. Washington Irving to Pierre Munro, 26 September 1835, in Irving, *Life and Letters*, 279. Astor's estate stretched from East Ninety-Fourth Street to East 128th Street, from the East River to Lexington Avenue, encompassing much of the present Upper East Side and East Harlem neighborhoods. His actual house was at East Eighty-Sixth to East Eighty-Seventh Street at East End Avenue.

89. Washington Irving to HRS, 25 May 1835, reel 23, HRS LC.

90. Washington Irving to Peter Irving, 8 January 1835, in Irving, *Life and Letters*, 270.

91. Washington Irving to Peter Irving, 8 July 1835, in Irving, *Life and Letters*, 276–77.

92. Washington Irving to HRS, 25 May 1835, reel 23, HRS LC.

93. HRS to Washington Irving, 15 June 1835, reel 23, HRS LC.

94. Washington Irving to HRS, 5 October 1835, reel 23, HRS LC.

95. Hoffman, *Genealogy*, 200–204.

96. Gilman, *Life on the Lakes*, 1:159.

O Mr. C!

1. Hathaway, *League of the Iroquois*, 304n22.
2. Fuller, *Summer on the Lakes*, 175.
3. Fuller, *Summer on the Lakes*, 175–76.
4. Hathaway, *League of the Iroquois*, 307n30.

Chapter 7

1. William Boutwell to GJ, 27 December 1833, George Johnston Papers, Detroit Public Library, Burton Historical Collection.
2. George Johnston [London] to GJ, 24 April 1834, George Johnston Papers, Burton.
3. GJ to George Johnston [London], 24 June 1834, George Johnston Papers, Burton.

4. Henry Kearney to GJ, 12 August 1834, George Johnston Papers, Burton. Kearney had corresponded with John Johnston; Henry Schoolcraft had written him when Johnston died. There were some financial dealings after Johnston's death, and George wrote a brief letter stating that his parents' marriage had been legitimate, but there was nothing more until his aunt Jane died. GJ to Henry Kearney, 20 March 1831, George Johnston Papers, Burton.

5. GJ to Henry Kearney, 17 December 1834, George Johnston Papers, Burton.

6. Henry Kearney to HRS, 6 March 1835, reel 23, HRS LC. There is no other information about Mrs. Moore or her child in the Schoolcraft papers.

7. Ferry closed the mission school in the spring of 1834 and moved with his family to Grand Haven, Michigan, where he became quite successful in business, in timber, banking, and shipping (Bremer, *Indian Agent*, 152).

8. Henry Kearney to HRS, 7 August 1835, reel 23, HRS LC.

9. J. Keating to Colonel Darling, 14 June 1822, in Canadian Archives, Military Posts, 306.

10. GJ, Diary, 9 April and 1 May 1835, George Johnston Papers, Burton.

11. GJ, Diary, 1 May 1835, George Johnston Papers, Burton.

12. Leslie, "Givins, James."

13. JLS to HRS, 27 May 1835, reel 23, HRS LC.

14. JLS to HRS, 21 May 1835, reel 23, HRS LC.

15. WJ to GJ, 19 May 1835, George Johnston Papers, Burton.

16. GJ, Diary, 12 June 1835, George Johnston Papers, Burton.

17. GJ, Diary, 18 June, 24 June 1835, George Johnston Papers, Burton.

18. Their relationship was complicated by Taliaferro's pronounced distress when jurisdiction for Ojibwes was transferred from his own to Schoolcraft's agency in the later 1820s, leading to Schoolcraft installing George as subagent at La Pointe in 1828. Taliaferro complained about the situation in his diaries; he also wrote to Schoolcraft alleging that the local Indigenous people didn't like George (some people continued to go to Fort Snelling on government business) and furthermore that he was a drunk. He wrote Schoolcraft a letter making these charges in 1829. Schoolcraft forwarded the charges to George for explanation (no written reply exists). Taliaferro also challenged Schoolcraft, whom he hated for (again) having jurisdiction of the Ojibwes, to a duel. Schoolcraft didn't reply. Lavender, *Fist in the Wilderness*, 376; HRS to GJ, 3 November 1829, George Johnston Papers, Burton. George writes in his diary for 1828–29 about being undermined by fur traders during his time at La Pointe (Burton).

19. GJ, Diary, 28 June, 30 June, 1835, George Johnston Papers, Burton.

20. GJ, Diary, 29 June 1835, George Johnston Papers, Burton.

21. Receipts in George's papers show him purchasing Milton's *Paradise Lost* and *Paradise Regained* in 1822 and in 1829; James Fenimore Cooper's *The Spy* (1821); *The Pioneers* (1823) (the first Leatherstocking book); *The Pilot* (1824); and *The Red Rover* (1828). Receipt 26 July 1822 and Receipt from James L. Schoolcraft 1831, George Johnston Papers, Burton.

22. Gilbert, "Memories of the 'Soo,'" 631–32.

23. GJ, Diary, 3 July 1835, George Johnston Papers, Burton.

24. GJ, Diary, 17 July 1835, George Johnston Papers, Burton.

25. GJ, Diary, 24 July 1835, George Johnston Papers, Burton.

26. JLS to HRS, 7 December 1835, reel 23, HRS LC; WM to HRS, 9 March 1836, reel 24–25, HRS LC.

27. GJ to Henry Kearney, 15 November 1835, George Johnston Papers, Burton.

28. Henry Kearney to HRS, 31 August 1836, reel 24–25, HRS LC.

29. WM to HRS, 21 May 1835, reel 23; WM to HRS, 8 September 1835, reel 23; JLS to HRS, 12 October 1835, reel 23, HRS LC.

30. Cleland, *Faith in Paper*, 59.

31. Karamanski, *Blackbird's Song*, 70n109.

32. Cleland, *Faith in Paper*, 56.

33. Oberly, *Nation of Statesmen*, 54. This cession precipitated a land rush between 1835 and 1838 and an ensuing influx of squatters. In 1835, about 100,000 acres were sold; the next year, double the amount. (While he was there, he bought a fawn to put in his garden for picturesque effect. When it was grown, it roamed freely, jumped six-foot-high fences, and had, according to Schoolcraft in his memoirs, a "remarkable" habit of attacking ladies by sneaking up on them from behind and "in the gentlest manner possible" putting its feet on the victim's shoulders. It must have been the only deer on the island. Predictably the deer ate whatever was in the garden, was banished from it, then had its leg broken by someone who caught it eating something else it shouldn't have, and after the fawn had three years of freedom, Schoolcraft had it shot. HRS, *Personal Memoirs* 521.

34. JJS to HRS, 5 July 1835, reel 23, HRS LC.

35. Berkeley and Berkeley, *George William Featherstonhaugh*, 114, 153.

36. Featherstonhaugh, *Canoe Voyage*, 1:138.

37. Featherstonhaugh, *Canoe Voyage*, 1:139.

38. HRS, *Personal Memoirs*, 476–77.

39. Featherstonhaugh, *Canoe Voyage*, 1:142–43.

40. Featherstonhaugh, *Canoe Voyage*, 1:143.

41. Featherstonhaugh, *Canoe Voyage*, 1:142.

42. HRS, *Personal Memoirs*, 519.

43. Featherstonhaugh, *Canoe Voyage*, 1:149.

44. Featherstonhaugh, *Canoe Voyage*, 1:228.

45. Featherstonhaugh, *Canoe Voyage*, 1:154–55.

46. Charles Fenno Hoffman to George Hoffman, 1 January 1830, box 4, Fenno-Hoffman Family Papers, Clement Library.

47. Gilman, *Life on the Lakes*, 2:19.

48. Gilman, *Life on the Lakes*, 2:20.

49. Gilman, *Life on the Lakes*, 1:128, 129, 157.

50. Fisher, *Fisher Genealogy*, 321–22.

51. The two books are Fuller, *Summer on the Lakes*, and Hathaway, *League of the Iroquois*. Clarke showed both writers (see below on his relationship with Fuller) the letter and they copied it down, Fuller in 1843 when she visited Clarke in Chicago, and Hathaway sometime before 1871, when Clarke's house burned down in the Chicago Fire (Ebert, "Early History," 263–64; Chesbrough, "William Hull Clarke," 118–19; Bolster, *James Freeman Clarke*, 292–93). The second letter is from Jane to Mrs. William L. Stone, and is tipped into a copy of Schoolcraft's *The Rise of the West: Or a Prospect of the Mississippi Valley, a Poem* (New York: William Applegate, 1841) in the New York Public Library.

52. Hathaway, *League of the Iroquois*, 304n22.

53. Fuller, *Summer on the Lakes*, 175–76.

54. Hathaway, *League of the Iroquois*, 307n30.

55. Cleland, *Faith in Paper*, 61–62.
56. Fletcher, *Eagle Returns*, 18.
57. Cleland, *Faith in Paper*, 59.
58. Cleland, *Faith in Paper*, 60.
59. Fletcher, *Eagle Returns*, 20.
60. Cleland, *Faith in Paper*, 60
61. Cleland, *Faith in Paper*, 61.
62. JLS to HRS, 12 October 1835, reel 23, HRS LC.
63. AMJS to JS, 30 September 1835, reel 23, HRS LC.
64. JLS to HRS, 17 September 1835, reel 23, HRS LC.
65. WM to HRS, 10 October 1835, reel 23, HRS LC.
66. JLS to HRS, 23 October 1835, reel 23, HRS LC.
67. HRS, "Travels of an Indian Prince."
68. HRS to JJS, 16 November 1835, reel 23, HRS LC.
69. WM to HRS, 8 September 1836, reel 23, HRS LC; JJS to HRS, 24 November 1836, reel 7, HRS LC.
70. HRS to JJS, 7 December 1835, reel 23, HRS LC.
71. Hoffman, *Genealogy*, 204–6.
72. HRS to JJS, 19 December 1835, HRS LC.
73. HRS to JJS, 12 December 1835, reel 23, HRS LC.
74. HRS to JJS, 19 December 1835, reel 23, HRS LC.
75. HRS to JJS, 26–31 December 1835, reel 23, HRS LC.
76. Martin, "Treaty of New Echota (1835)," in Littlefield and Parins, *Encyclopedia of American Indian Removal*, 245–46.
77. HRS to JJS, 26–31 December 1835, reel 7, HRS LC.
78. WJ to HRS, 12 December 1835, reel 23, HRS LC.
79. JJS to HRS, 24 November, 13 December 1835, reel 23, HRS LC.
80. Cass, *Discourse*, 30, 43.
81. E. Whiting to HRS, 13 January 1836, reel 24–25, HRS LC.
82. WJ to HRS, 15 January 1836, reel 24–25, HRS LC.
83. Cleland, *Faith in Paper*, 62. Captain Clitz died as the commander at Mackinac in November 1836 (Andreas, *History of the Upper Peninsula*, 357).
84. WJ to HRS, 16 February 1836, reel 7, HRS LC.
85. WJ to HRS, 16 February 1836, reel 24, HRS LC.
86. WJ to HRS, 18 February 1836, reel 24; 20 February 1836, reel 7, HRS LC.
87. WJ to HRS, 15 January 1836, reel 24, HRS LC.
88. WJ to HRS, 16 February 1836, reel 24, HRS LC.
89. HRS to JJS, 15 January 1836, reel 24, HRS LC.
90. JJS to HRS, 13 February 1836, reel 7, HRS LC.
91. JJS to HRS, 19 February 1836, reel 7, HRS LC.
92. JJS to HRS, 18 February 1836, reel 7, HRS LC.
93. Cleland, *Faith in Paper*, 62.
94. Mary Holiday to Ramsay Crooks, 11 March 1836, no. 1366, Nute, *Calendar of the American Fur Company's Papers*, 157.
95. Fletcher, *Eagle Returns*, 21–22.

96. Mary Holiday to Ramsay Crooks, 17 March 1836, no. 1385, AFC Papers, roll 23, 159–60.
97. "Harold," *New-Yorker*, 16 March 1836, 9.
98. "Harold," *New-Yorker*, 16 March 1836, 9; Karamanski, *Blackbird's Song*, 80–81.
99. Karamanski, *Blackbird's Song*, 78.
100. Fletcher, *Eagle Returns*, 21.
101. Karamanski, *Blackbird's Song*, 80.
102. Karamanski, *Blackbird's Song*, 71–72.
103. "Harold," *New-Yorker*, 2 April 1836, 25 (dated 23 March 1836).
104. Karamanski, *Blackbird's Song*, 81–86.
105. HRS to JJS, 28 March 1836, reel 24, HRS LC.
106. HRS to JJS, 10 April 1836, reel 24, HRS LC.
107. WJ to HRS, 14 March 1836, reel 24, HRS LC.
108. JJS to HRS, 15 March 1836, reel 7, HRS LC.
109. HRS to JJS, 14 April 1836, reel 24, HRS LC.
110. HRS to JJS, 24 April 1836, reel 24, HRS LC.
111. HRS to JJS, 4 April 1836, 8 May 1836, reel 24–25, HRS LC.
112. HRS to JJS, 8 May 1836, reel 24, HRS LC.
113. JJS to HRS, 10 May 1836, reel 7, HRS LC.
114. JJS to HRS, 13 May 1836, reel 7, HRS LC.
115. HRS to JJS, 16 May 1836, reel 24, HRS LC.
116. "Notes of a Northern Excursion. By a Lady-Tourist," *Southern Rose*, 28 May 1836, 156 (dated 9 May 1836).

Paup-Puk-Keewiss

1. WJ, "Paup-Puk-Keewiss," *AR* 1:200–208.
2. "This word appears to be derived from the same root as *Paup-puk-ke-nay*, a grasshopper, the inflection *iss* making it personal. The Indian idea is that of harum scarum. He is regarded as a foil to Manabozho, with whom he is frequently brought in contact in aboriginal story craft." *AR* 1:201n.
3. "This is an official who bears the pipe for the ruling chief, and in an inferior dignity in councils." *AR* 1:201n.
4. William Johnston's manuscript begins after this point.
5. "Mats." *AR* 1:211n.
6. The story is mislabeled as "Baush'kwudosh or Animal with the Hair Blown off His Skin," reel 58, HRS LC. It was published as "Paup-Puk-Keewiss" in *AR* 1:200–220. The first page of the LC manuscript is numbered "5" and the first few lines may not be William's handwriting.

Chapter 8

1. Today the Indian Dormitory is the Richard and Jane Manoogian Mackinac Art Museum.
2. They must also have been interested in the outcome of the treaty settlement—although Charlotte at one point hesitated, telling Jane, "I have been told here, I need not mention

the manner, that I was to be included at the Treaty, for what reason I do not know.... Let me know whether there is any foundation for such, which I hope is not the case." CJM to JJS, 13 June 1836, reel 25, HRS LC.

3. Grenville Sproat to JJS, 7 August 1836, reel 25, HRS LC.
4. Karamanski, *Blackbird's Song*, 88–89.
5. Karamanski, *Blackbird's Song*, 90.
6. Karamanski, *Blackbird's Song*, 90.
7. Bremer, *Indian Agent*, 173.
8. Bremer, *Indian Agent*, 173–74.
9. Bremer, *Indian Agent*, 174.
10. George Johnston [London] to GJ, 4 September 1836, George Johnston Papers, Detroit Public Library, Burton Historical Collection.
11. McLeod, "Diary of Martin McLeod," 351–52. Some documents related to Dickson are published in Nute, "Documents": 173–81.
12. Susan Johnston to JJS, 14 March 1837, reel 26, HRS LC.
13. General James Dickson to GJ, 6 September 1836, George Johnston Papers, Burton.
14. General James Dickson to Major [James H.] Hook, 6 September 1836; General James Dickson to General [Oakley], 6 September 1836, George Johnston Papers, Burton.
15. Jacobus del Gracia [James L. Schoolcraft] to GJ, 7 October 1836, George Johnston Papers, Burton.
16. Johnston, "Autobiographical Letters," 341; Smith, "Count Andreani," 34–40.
17. Nute, "Documents."
18. Bunnell, *Winona and Its Environs*, 170–71; Farmer, *History of Detroit*, 480–82. Bunnell later went west in the gold rush and participated in the genocide of Indigenous people in the Mariposa War, an experience he described in *Discovery of the Yosemite and the Indian War of 1851 Which Led to That Event* (1892).
19. WJ to JJS, 15 March 1837, reel 26, HRS LC.
20. Susan Johnston to JJS, 14 March 1837, reel 26, HRS LC.
21. Susan Johnston to JJS, 14 March 1837, reel 26, HRS LC.
22. Susan Johnston to JJS, 14 March 1837, reel 26, HRS LC.
23. HRS, *Personal Memoirs*, 558, 553. The Saginaws were to leave in the spring for the headwaters of the Osage River.
24. HRS, *Personal Memoirs*, 552.
25. HRS, *Personal Memoirs*, 555.
26. HRS, *Personal Memoirs*, 559.
27. "The Fairy Book," *American Monthly Magazine* 8 (December 1836): 622.
28. WM to HRS, 14 February 1837, reel 26, HRS LC; also 13 February 1837, reel 26, 15 March 1837, reel 26, HRS LC.
29. WM to HRS, 15 March 1837, reel 26, HRS LC.
30. WJ to HRS, 15 March 1837, reel 26; 3 April 1837, reel 26, HRS LC.
31. In the intended grants of land to Indigenous relatives in the Treaty of La Pointe (1826), she is listed as Susan Davenport, wife of Ambrose Davenport, and granddaughter of Misquabunoqua.
32. WJ to JJS, 15 March 1837, reel 26, HRS LC.
33. WJ to HRS, 15 March 1837, reel 26, HRS LC.
34. WJ to HRS, 3 April 1837, reel 26, HRS LC.

35. "The Weendigoes," *AR* 1:117–18.

36. WJ, "Mudjee Monedo and the Genius of Benevolence," reel 58, HRS LC.

37. The story is in William's hand except for the first four pages.

38. [WJ], "Paup-Puk-Keewiss," *AR* 1:219–20.

39. WM to HRS, 5 September 1836, reel 24–25, HRS LC. He seems also to have signed two treaties with the British government. McMurray's handwriting is often difficult to decipher; he gives an Ojibwe name for Little Salt as (what looks like) "Chinetahgause." There is signatory to the Robinson-Superior Treaty of 1850 (Canada) named "Chigenaus," so Little Salt may be that person. Government of Canada/Gouvernement du Canada, Treaty Texts—Ojibewa Indians of Lake Superior, Copy of the Robinson Treaty Made in the Year 1850 with the Ojibewa Indians of Lake Superior Conveying Certain Lands to the Crown. http://central.bac-lac.gc.ca/.redirect?app=fonandcol&id=3963984&lang=eng. Chigenaus's name also appears on the Manitoulin Island Treaty of 1836, dated 9 August 1836, according to Bellfy in "Cross-Border Treaty Signers," 28.

40. WM to HRS, 5 September 1836, reel 24–25, HRS LC.

41. CJM, "The Enchanted Moccasins," in WM to HRS, 5 September 1836, reel 24–25, HRS LC.

42. CJM, "The Enchanted Moccasins," *AR* 1:227n.

43. CJM, "Enchanted Moccasins," *AR* 1:232.

44. A Sweet Grass Cree version of this story is "The Bear-Woman," told by Coming-Day in Bloomfield, *Sacred Stories of the Sweet Grass Cree*, 57–61.

45. McMurray has something like "Queanguashe."

46. This is translated into Ojibwemowin in the published version (a sign of Jane's involvement): "Shingisshenaun tshee neeboyaun" ("The Magic Bundle," *AR* 1:185).

47. "The Magic Bundle," *AR* 1:185n.

48. Charlotte has Ojibwemowin: "magequawahming" for "jealous" [McMurray's handwriting is not entirely legible]. "Jealous" is from "The Magic Bundle," *AR* 1:187.

49. Captain T. G. Anderson to Captain G. Philpotts, 18 July 1835, Strachan Papers, Archives of Ontario, in Knight, "Study in Failure," n70. Anderson writes that Charlotte was the principal translator at McMurray's mission. "Tho' Mr. McMurray has exerted himself with great and manifest success, he could not have affected so much, had he not the benefit of Mrs. McMurray's perfect knowledge of the Indian character, and her incessant labours as interpreter. Knowing this to be the case, I have, without his knowledge, taken it upon myself to recommend her getting the salary as an act of common justice."

50. WM to CJM, 21 June 1836, reel 24–25, HRS LC.

51. This was William Strachan McMurray, born September 1835; their other children were John Henry, born January 1838; James Saurin, born May 1840; and Charlotte Elizabeth Jane, born July 1843.

52. Thomas, *Love and Work Enough*, 49.

53. Thomas, *Love and Work Enough*, 102–5.

54. Thomas, *Love and Work Enough*, 113–14.

55. Jameson, *Winter Studies*, 1:241–42.

56. WM to HRS, 15 June 1837, reel 26, HRS LC. WM to HRS, 16 June 1837, reel 25, HRS LC.

57. Jameson, *Winter Studies*, 2:119.

58. Jameson, *Winter Studies*, 2:126–27.
59. Jameson, *Winter Studies*, 2:148.
60. Jameson, *Winter Studies*, 2:178.
61. Jameson, *Winter Studies*, 2:148.
62. Jameson, *Winter Studies*, 2:209.
63. Jameson, *Winter Studies*, 2:159–60.
64. Jameson, *Winter Studies*, 2:214–15.
65. Jameson, *Winter Studies*, 2:224.
66. Jameson, *Winter Studies*, 2:225.
67. Jameson, *Winter Studies*, 2:225.
68. Jameson, *Winter Studies*, 2:226.
69. Jameson, *Winter Studies*, 2:245.
70. Jameson, *Winter Studies*, 2:234–35.
71. Jameson, *Winter Studies*, 2:234–35.
72. Jameson, *Winter Studies*, 2:265.
73. JJS to HRS, 5 August 1837, reel 26; HRS to JJS, 3 August 1837, reel 26, HRS LC.
74. Schmaltz, *Ojibwa of Southern Ontario*, 23–24.
75. Osborne, "Migration of Voyageurs," 136.
76. GJ to HRS, 14 August 1837, reel 27, HRS LC.
77. GJ to HRS, 14 August 1837, reel 27, HRS LC.
78. Anna Jameson to JJS, 20 August 1837, reel 27, HRS LC.
79. WM to JJS, 28 September 1837, reel 27, HRS LC. McMurray was disappointed that Mrs. Jameson hadn't reimbursed him for money he'd given her while at the Sault, WM to JJ Schoolcraft, 28 September 1837, reel 27, HRS LC.
80. Anna Jameson to JJS, 31 August 1837, reel 27, HRS LC.
81. Anna Jameson to CJM, 26 August 1837, Henry Sproatt Collection, Thomas Fisher Rare Book Library, University of Toronto, quoted in Johnston, *Anna Jameson*, 118.
82. HRS to Anna Jameson, 18 November 1837, reel 27, HRS LC.
83. Jameson, *Winter Studies*, 2:303.
84. Jameson, *Winter Studies*, 2:152.
85. Jameson, *Winter Studies*, 2:303.
86. Jameson, *Winter Studies*, 2:302.
87. Jameson, *Winter Studies*, 2:303.

Six Indians Visit to the Sun and Moon

1. WJ, "Six Indians Visit to the Sun and the Moon," reel 65, HRS LC. Published as "Iosco, or A Visit to the Sun and Moon," in *AR* 2.
2. Ship and boat. These terms exhibit the simple and diminutive forms of the name for ship or vessel. It is also the term for a woman's needlework, and was perhaps transferred in allusion to a ship's ropes. HRS, *AR* 2:46n.
3. "Massive silver," HRS, *AR* 2:48n.
4. "A rattle," HRS, *AR* 2:49n.
5. "This is a verbal form, plural number, of the transitive adjective—foolish." HRS, *AR* 2:57n.

Chapter 9

1. HRS to JJS, 22 January 1838, reel 28, HRS LC.
2. Bremer, *Indian Agent*, 262–64; 221–24.
3. Baptist, *Half Has Never Been Told*, chap. 8.
4. Roberts, "'Ungovernable Anarchy,'" 200.
5. Roberts, "'Ungovernable Anarchy,'" 197.
6. Baptist, *Half Has Never Been Told*, chap. 8.
7. Roberts, *America's First Great Depression*, 53.
8. Roberts, "'Ungovernable Anarchy,'" 197.
9. Baptist, *Half Has Never Been Told*, chap. 8.
10. Bremer, *Indian Agent*, 220–21.
11. WJ to HRS, 26 May 1837, reel 26; WM to JJS, 3 March 1838, reel 29, HRS LC.
12. JLS to HRS, 11 August 1837, reel 27 HRS LC.
13. Henry William Johnston to GJ in W. A. Bacon to GJ, 9 February 1838, George Johnston Papers, Detroit Public Library, Burton Historical Collection.
14. W. A. Bacon to GJ, 18 June 1838, George Johnston Papers, Burton.
15. W. A. Bacon to GJ, 10 March 1838; 16 April 1838; 18 June 1838; 22 June 1838; 10 December 1838, George Johnston Papers, Burton.
16. HRS to JJS, 25 November 1837, reel 27, HRS LC. Payments under the Treaty of 1830, for schools in the nation, Report of the Secretary of the Interior, 28 February 1855, 33d Cong., 2d Sess., Ex. Doc. No. 64. WM to JS, 13 June 1838, reel 29, HRS LC: "Mrs. Audrain arrived here a few days ago; and has since her arrival been confined; she is in a most pitiable and destitute situation; her second son is at the point of death from an injury received on their way from the South to Detroit, since which he has never seen a well day; he cannot [illeg./seal] and indeed it would be a blessing to them both should he be taken away."
17. WM to GJ, 16 January 1838, George Johnston Papers, Burton.
18. WM to HRS, 27 September 1837, reel 27, HRS LC.
19. WM to JJS, 18 November 1837, reel 27, HRS LC.
20. Mrs. Johnston was at the Sault between 28 August and 27 September. McMurray to HRS, 28 August 1837, reel 27; McMurray to HRS, 27 September 1837, reel 27, HRS LC.
21. A contract exists for O-ge-she-au-bon-o-qua to receive $3 per month through 1 June 1838. If she left before then or did anything leading to her being dismissed, like drinking, she would forfeit all of her pay. A receipt on the back has her paid on 28 April 1838, on Schoolcraft's return to Mackinac, $15 for five months' work, with her daughter paid an additional $3. Agreement with O-ge-she-au-bon-o-qua, reel 27. Written by HRS, witnessed by Francis Shearman and William Johnston.
22. WM to JJS, 8 January 1838, reel 28, HRS LC.
23. WM to JJS, 21 January 1838, reel 28, HRS LC.
24. JJS to HRS, 15 January 1838, reel 8, HRS LC.
25. HRS to JJS, 22 January 1838, reel 28, HRS LC.
26. WM to JJS, 31 January 1838, reel 28; WM to JJS, 21 January 1838, reel 28, HRS LC.
27. JJS to HRS, 20 November 1837, reel 27, HRS LC.
28. HRS to JJS, 3 March 1838, reel 29, HRS LC. The 1836 Ottawa and Chippewa Census lists a Louisa Piquette, who was fourteen years old. A note says that she is half Chippewa and that her father is a drunkard and her mother dead. The relation of Janette to Louisa is

unclear. She was still working for the family in the following winter of 1837–38. 1836 Census of Ottawa and Chippewa Half Breeds, www.mainlymichigan.com/nativedata/1836OttChipCensus/1836OttChippPaging.aspx, 14 May 2023.

29. JJS to HRS, 20 November 1837, reel 27, HRS LC.
30. WJ to HRS, 24 December 1837, reel 27; JJS to HRS, 31 January 1838, reel 16, HRS LC.
31. HRS to JJS, 3 March 1838, reel 29, HRS LC.
32. Smith, *Journal in America*, 22–23; 28–29.
33. Zina Pitcher to S. G. Morton, 11 Sepember 1832; 16 December 1832; 4 March 1834, Series I Correspondence, Samuel George Morton Papers, American Philosophical Society.
34. HRS, *Personal Memoirs*, 594. Conner was a trader at Saginaw and interpreter at treaties; he interpreted for Schoolcraft in Detroit occasionally and is listed as an informant in *Algic Researches*. Cleland, *Rites of Conquest*, 179, 213, 217.
35. HRS to JJS, 22 January 1838, reel 28, HRS LC.
36. HRS to JJS, 2 December 1837, reel 27, HRS LC.
37. Francis Shearman to HRS, 15 January 1838, reel 8, HRS LC.
38. JJS to HRS, 15 January 1838, reel 8, HRS LC.
39. HRS, *Personal Memoirs*, 449–50, 572. Entries for 12 October 1833 and 1 October 1837.
40. HRS, *Personal Memoirs*, 449–50. Entry for 12 October 1833.
41. HRS, *Personal Memoirs*, 476–77. Entry for 1 May 1834.
42. HRS, *Personal Memoirs*, 573. Entry for 1 October 1837.
43. Strickland, *Old Mackinaw*, 24. Wauchusco told William that he was eight or ten years old at the time of the 1763 massacre of the British at Fort Michilimackinac on the mainland.
44. HRS, "Mythology," 100, 101.
45. HRS, "Mythology," 98.
46. HRS, "Mythology," 97–99.
47. HRS, "Mythology," 99.
48. Black, "Ojibwa Power Belief System," 143.
49. WJ in Strickland, *Old Mackinaw*, 25–26.
50. WJ in Strickland, *Old Mackinaw*, 27; HRS, *Historical and Statistical Information*, 1:389.
51. WJ's note.
52. WJ in Strickland, *Old Mackinaw*, 28–29.
53. WJ in Strickland, *Old Mackinaw*, 29.
54. WJ, "Shagwonabee," reel 65, HRS LC.
55. WJ, "Shagwonabee," reel 65, HRS LC.
56. HRS, "Wassamo," *AR* 2:151.
57. WJ, "Story of Meshegenebigo," reel 65, HRS LC.
58. "'The Undying Head' is rather a long tale," Twain wrote, "but it makes up in weird conceits, fairy-tale prodigies, variety of incident and energy of movement, for what it lacks in brevity" (Twain, *Life on the Mississippi*, 484). Twain satirized the kind of faux Indian story that Schoolcraft himself was in the habit of making up before presenting both William's "The Undying Head" and Jane's "Peboan and Seegwun" as "genuine" poetry.
59. HRS, "Iamo," *AR* 1:120–21.
60. Witgen, *Infinity of Nations*, 279.
61. Witgen, *Infinity of Nations*, 275.

62. Witgen, *Infinity of Nations*, 276–77.

63. Nabunway, whose stories George wrote down in the spring of 1838, translated *saugemau* as "evil."

64. Witgen, *Infinity of Nations*, 294; McDonnell, *Masters of Empire*, 83.

65. Witgen, *Infinity of Nations*, 295.

66. Whiting, Review of *Algic Researches*, 360.

67. HRS, "Iosco: A Visit to the Sun and Moon" [WJ], *AR* 2:59–60.

68. GJ to HRS, 19 September 1840, reel 31, HRS LC.

69. Edmonds filed his report with Commissioner Harris on 17 March 1838 (Bremer, *Indian Agent*, 224).

70. WM to HRS, 13 August 1838, reel 29, HRS LC.

71. WM to JJS, 27 April 1838, reel 29, HRS LC.

72. George Johnston [London] to GJ, n.d., George Johnston Papers, Burton.

73. George Johnston [London] to GJ, 24 June 1838, George Johnston Papers, Burton.

74. George Johnston [London] to GJ, 10 September 1838, George Johnston Papers, Burton. There's nothing more in the family papers about London George, so it's not clear when he finally left the Sault and there is no indication what happened afterward.

75. GJ, Journal, 13 July, 18 July 1838, Western Americana Collection, Beinecke Library, J643, Johnston, George, S-116.

76. Bremer, *Indian Agent*, 195. The Saginaws eventually removed to the Southwest in 1839, but it was a disaster; promised provisions didn't exist; there was no game; the prairie had just burned; and the people were starving. Eventually most who survived made their way back to Michigan (195).

77. GJ, Journal, 24 July 1838, Western Americana Collection, Beinecke, J643 Johnston, George, S-116.

78. Bremer, *Indian Agent*, 195.

79. GJ, Journal September 1838–September 1840, entries for 29 September 1838, 2 October 1838, 9 October 1838, George Johnston Papers, Burton.

80. WM to JJS, 13 June 1838, reel 29, HRS LC.

81. JJS to HRS, 11 July 1838, reel 29, HRS LC.

82. JJS to HRS, 7 July 1838, reel 29, HRS LC.

83. JJS to HRS, 7 July 1838, reel 29, HRS LC.

84. JJS to HRS, 11 July 1838, reel 29, HRS LC.

85. HRS to JJS, 7 July 1838, reel 29, HRS LC.

86. Dougherty, Diary, 6 July 1838, Peter Dougherty Papers, Bentley Historical Library.

87. Dougherty, Diary, 12 July 1838, Peter Dougherty Papers, Bentley.

88. Dougherty, Diary, 16 July 1838, Peter Dougherty Papers, Bentley.

89. Dougherty, Diary, 14 July 1838, Peter Dougherty Papers, Bentley. Dougherty eventually went to the Odawa village at Grand Traverse, where George, his wife, and John McDouall were employed as mechanic, interpreter, and farmer. George noted an accusation of rape against Dougherty in his diary in the summer of 1840. Esquaquonabay, the chief, had been told by someone else that when Dougherty asked another man why he'd quit coming to church, on being pressed on it, the man said that "some years ago young men had come in their midst as teachers, and had not acted right with their women, that a similar course had now been pursued that one of their women had been taken forcibly by Mr. D. Mr. D. replied that he had not taken her forcibly, but it was a mutual act on either of them from affection

one towards another" (25 May 1840). About a month later, Mrs. McGulpin told George that "an Indian Keweydin was at [Mackinac], that he was asked why he did not go to the Traverse for his wife he replied that Mr. Dougherty kept her, & on that account would not return to her" (25 June 1840). Dougherty spoke to Esquaquonabay "respecting reports" on himself, telling him "that they had better throw away such stuff. The chief replied, if I had it in my hands, I would do so, but it is in the mouth of every old woman" (4 August 1840, Journal September 1838–September 1840, George Johnston Papers, Burton). Dougherty left at the end of summer for the East and several months later returned to Grand Traverse with a wife who, George wrote to Jane, " is a poor weak little woman, she is not able to knit her own stockings and is little capable of teaching others in household affairs. Every time an Indian goes into their house she sweeps the dirt or snow off, and the Indians feel rather diffident, and say they have never seen white people act so." GJ to JS, 2 February 1841, reel 32, HRS LC.

90. Joshua Toulmin Smith to HRS, 14 August 1838, reel 29, HRS LC.

91. HRS to Samuel George Morton, 5 May 1838, Samuel George Morton Papers, American Philosophical Society.

92. HRS to Samuel George Morton, 5 May 1838, Samuel George Morton Papers, American Philosophical Society.

93. Samuel George Morton to HRS, 4 June 1838, reel 8, HRS LC.

94. *American Journal of Science and Arts* 34.1 (July 1838): 183.

95. *American Medical Intelligencer* 1.22 (15 February 1838): 400.

96. Bremer, *Indian Agent*, 200–201.

97. HRS, *Personal Memoirs*, 600–601; Bremer, *Indian Agent*, 182–83.

98. HRS, *Personal Memoirs*, 602. Later in August he noted a statement published by the Indian Bureau, "showing, 1. That upwards of fifty treaties have been concluded with various tribes since Jan. 1, 1830, for their removal to the west, in accordance with the organic act of May 28th, 1830. 2. That by these treaties 109,879,937 acres of land have been acquired. 3. That the probable value of this land in the United States is $137,349,946. 4. That the total cost of these cessions, including the various expenses of carrying the treaties into effect, is $70,059,505" (605–6).

99. HRS, "Sketches of a Trip to Lake Superior," 254.

100. This island is today called Granite Island and is due north of Little Presque Isle in Lake Superior. The Ojibwe name is Na-Be-Quon, meaning ship or vessel. Parker, *Sound the Stars Make*, 92.

101. HRS, "Castle Island," reel 50, HRS LC.

102. WM to HRS, 12 September 1838, reel 29, HRS LC.

Mukakee Mindemoea

1. JJS, "Mukakee Mindemoea; or, The Toad-Woman," in *Oneota*, 79–81.

2. *Sheegowiss*, a widow, and *mowigh*, something nasty (note in *Oneota*).

Chapter 10

1. HRS to Anna Jameson, 3 December 1838, reel 8, HR LC; Washington Irving to HRS, 24 February 1839, reel 9, HRS LC; HRS to Thomas Aspinwall, 8 March 1839, reel 29, HRS LC.

2. Anna Jameson to HRS, 9 January 1838, reel 8, HRS LC.

3. HRS, *Personal Memoirs*, 625.

4. Henry Whiting, in his review of *Algic Researches* for the *North American Review*, writes that Schoolcraft "at first, feeling some distrust whether the Tales would be acceptable or popular in their present shape, thought of submitting them to some polished pen, which like the pencil in respect to many of the Indian portraits that have been given to the public eye, would have detracted from their merit in proportion to the embellishment thrown over them. It is fortunate for the public, that he did not yield to this idea" (360).

5. Anna Jameson, "Visit to Mackinaw," *Albion* 1.4 (26 January 1839): 25. The *Albion* had earlier praised Mrs. Jameson's book in its review, but that review didn't mention Jane. "Mrs. Jameson's New Work," *Albion* 1.2 (12 January 1839): 12.

6. Catharine Maria Sedgwick to Anna Brownell Jameson, 24 March 1839, box 2, folder 3, Catharine Maria Sedgwick Papers, Massachusetts Historical Society.

7. HRS, *Personal Memoirs*, 626, 630.

8. HRS, *Personal Memoirs*, 10 January 1839, 631.

9. HRS, *Personal Memoirs*, 626–27; Bremer, *Indian Agent*, 404–5n23.

10. George Bancroft to HRS, 21 February 1839, HRS LC.

11. CJM to JJS, 25 February 1839, reel 29, HRS LC.

12. Chandler Robbins Gilman to HRS, 29 March 1839, reel 29, HRS LC.

13. Chandler Robbins Gilman to HRS, 4 April 1839, reel 9, HRS LC; Wood and Bache, *Dispensatory*, 281–84.

14. For example: "A man by the name of Gates, formerly a Baptist preacher, of Leyden, Mass., became deranged [after attending a protracted meeting] and terminated his life by taking laudanum" (*Evangelical Magazine and Gospel Advocate* 6.3 (17 January 1835): 23; "Miss Huldah Rich of this city, a nurse, who has heretofore borne a respectable character, and has been employed in some of the first families, committed suicide by taking a quantity of laudanum on Friday, 23rd ult.," *Zion's Herald* 5 (4 February 1835): 19; "A Mrs. Tryon, about 20 years of age, in Vandam street, New York, who had been married about six months, swallowed a shilling's worth of laudanum on Monday evening, and died on Tuesday morning. She had been deserted by her husband, and this is supposed to have prompted her to the fatal act." "Chapter of News," *Zion's Herald* 6.19, 75.

15. Hodgson, *Into the Arms of Morpheus*, 59–64.

16. Chandler Robbins Gilman to HRS, 4 April 1839, reel 9, HRS LC; Wood and Bache, *Dispensatory*, 577; Eberle, *Treatise on the Practice*, 111.

17. WJ to GJ, 25 January 1839, George Johnston Papers, Burton Historical Collection.

18. Julia Hoffman to George Hoffman, 15 January 1839, Fenno-Hoffman Family Papers, William L. Clements Library; Schoolcraft, *Personal Memoirs*, 645–46.

19. *Expositor*, 12 January 1839. A year previously he'd successfully monetized the death of the Seminole leader Osceola by leaving his exhibition in New York and rushing down to Osceola's prison cell the moment he heard the man was not long for this world. He got his portrait, Osceola died, and Catlin did quite well for himself in lithographs, incorporating an account of Osceola's nobility and eloquence into his lectures.

20. "Catlin's Indian Gallery," *Niles' National Register* (10 November 1838): 164.

21. JJS to Mrs. William Leete Stone, 4 April 1839. Bound into Henry R. Schoolcraft, *The Rise of the West: or, a Prospect of the Mississippi Valley, a Poem* (New York: William Apple-

gate, printer, No. 17 Ann Street, cor. Theatre Alley, 1841), Eames Collection, New York Public Library, New York, New York. This letter appears to be the only surviving letter written and sent by Jane Schoolcraft to someone outside of the family.

22. JJS to Mrs. General Patterson, 26 January 1839, HRS LC.

23. Parker, *Sound the Stars Make*, 142–43. Parker gives the Ojibwemowin at 141:

Nyau nin de nain dum
May kow e yaun in
Ain dah nuk ki yaun
Waus sa wa kom eg
Ain dah nuk ki yaun

Ne dau nis ainse e
Ne gwis is ainse e
Ishe nau gun ug wau
Waus sa wa kom eg

She gwau go sha ween
Ba sho waud e we
Nin zhe ka we yea
Ishe ez hau jau yaun
Ain dah nuk ke yaun

Ain dah nuk ke yaun
Nin zhe ke we yea
Ishe ke way aun e
Nyau ne gush kain dum

24. JJS to HRS, 25 May 1839, reel 32, HRS LC.
25. JJS to HRS, 25 May 1839, reel 32, HRS LC.
26. HRS to JJS, 25 May 1839, reel 29, HRS LC.
27. HRS to Charles Christopher Trowbridge, 22 May 1839, reel 29, HRS LC.
28. JJS to HRS, 26 May 1839, reel 32, HRS LC.
29. HRS to JJS, 11 February 1837, reel 26, HRS LC. The portraits are now owned by the Bayliss Memorial Library, Sault Ste. Marie, Michigan.
30. JJS to HRS, 26 May 1839, reel 32, HRS LC.
31. HRS to JJS, 27 May 1839, reel 9, HRS LC.
32. HRS, "Vine and Oak," *AR* 2:244.
33. HRS, "Leelinau," *AR* 2:78.
34. HRS, "Leelinau," *AR* 2:83.
35. HRS, "Leelinau," *AR* 2:83.
36. HRS, "Leelinau," *AR* 2:84.
37. "Algic Researches," *Ladies Companion* (September 1839): 248.
38. "Algic Researches," *Boston Weekly Magazine* 1.47 (27 July 1839): 375. A year later, the *Christian Review* of Boston said what the other reviewers couldn't quite say, dismissing the stories as immoral and blasphemous. "If we find a man in any strait, instead of human exertions used to overcome it, we find him changed into bird, beast, or fish, as the case may be, or possessing magic pipes, in a manner at once coarse and vulgar, often intensely dis-

gusting," said the *Christian Review*. "The legends of Manabozho exhibit the grossest absurdity and contariety of powers and means, and with no reference whatever, in most cases, to any moral justice." The only use to be made of such stories was for what they might reveal of "the Indian mind and character, and habits of action and thought." "Algic Researches," *Christian Review* 5.19 (1 September 1840): 474.

39. "Algic Researches," *Journal of Education* 2.5 (1839): 40.

40. Whiting, Review of *Algic Researches*.

41. Whiting, Review of *Algic Researches*, 357–58.

42. Whiting, Review of *Algic Researches*, 358.

43. Whiting, Review of *Algic Researches*, 359.

44. "Algic Researches," *Corsair: A Gazette of Literature, Art, Dramatic Criticism, Fashion, and Novelty* 1.19 (20 July 1839): 298.

45. HRS to GJ, 13 September 1839, George Johnston Papers, Burton.

46. Bremer, *Indian Agent*, 182–83.

47. Parker, *Sound the Stars Make*, 191.

48. Parker, *Sound the Stars Make*, 192.

49. "Wa-wa-be-zo-win, or The Swing," reel 46–47, HRS LC.

50. Vecsey, *Traditional Ojibwa Religion*, 96.

51. [JJS], "Mukakee Mindemoea," 81.

52. WJ to GJ, 17 May 1839, George Johnston Papers, Burton.

53. JLS to GJ, 6 July 1839, George Johnston Papers, Burton.

54. JLS to HRS, 13 June 1840, reel 31, HRS LC.

55. Bremer, *Indian Agent*, 199.

56. JJS, Interrogatories, 27 May 1840, reel 9, HRS LC.

57. JJS to HRS, 1 June 1840, reel 31, HRS LC.

58. JJS to HRS, 17 June 1840, reel 31, HRS LC.

59. JJS to HRS, 7 July 1840, reel 31, HRS LC.

60. HRS to JJS, 17 July 1840, 24 July 1840, reel 31, HRS LC. The secretary of the navy was James Kirke Paulding.

61. HRS to GJ, 31 August 1840, George Johnston Papers, Burton.

62. Bremer writes that William "fired off an indignant letter to Poinsett in which, among other things, he credited himself with persuading the Indians to accept the Senate modifications in the 1836 treaty" (*Indian Agent*, 205).

63. Bremer, *Indian Agent*, 204–5.

64. Bremer, *Indian Agent*, 207.

65. JJS to HRS, 14 April 1841, reel 32, HRS LC. Schoolcraft was en route to Washington in this letter. He was officially dismissed on 17 April 1841, and Jane opened the letter delivering the news at Detroit, on 29 April 1841. JJS to HRS, 29 April 1841, reel 32, HRS LC.

66. Bremer, *Indian Agent*, 265–66.

67. Depositions of Susan Johnston, John Johnston, William Johnston, and Maria Schoolcraft, 5 September 1843, Records of Districts, Record Group 21, U.S. Circuit Court, Eastern District of Michigan, Southern Division, Detroit, Law Case Files 1837–1922, Case 1386, U.S. v. Oliver Newberry, National Archives, Chicago, IL.

68. Bremer, *Indian Agent*, 261.

69. JJS to GJ, 26 June 1841, George Johnston Papers, Burton.

70. James had claimed $1,585.36 for losses in the Indian trade between 1825 and 1832 (Bremer, *Indian Agent*, 261).

71. B. Butler to JJS, 17 February 1842, reel 9, HRS LC.

72. "Fort Butler," North Carolina Trail of Tears Association, www.nctrailoftears.org/fort-butler.

73. Bremer, *Indian Agent*, 253.

74. Bremer, *Indian Agent*, 259–60.

75. Invitation to a President's Soiree from Sir Roderick Murchison, 16 Belgrave Square, London, 21 April 1842, reel 9, HRS LC.

76. CJM to JJS, 1 September 1841, reel 32, HRS LC.

77. AMJS to JJS, 15 November 1841, reel 32, HRS LC. Anna Maria and James Schoolcraft's children were Evelyn, born March 1839; Howard, born June 1841; and Mary Elizabeth Leontine, born October 1846.

78. CJM to JJS, 4 April 1842, reel 32, HRS LC.

79. Beasecker, "'With Extreme Diffidence,'" 1–2.

80. Review of *Kabaosa; Or the Warriors of the West*, by Anna L. Snelling, *Orion: A Monthly Magazine of Literature, Science & Art* (1 September 1842): 396.

81. Hoffman, *Vigil of Faith*, 14.

82. Barnes, *Charles Fenno Hoffman*, 127.

83. Sigourney, *Pocahontas, and Other Poems*.

84. Smith, *Powhatan*, 155.

85. Charles Fenno Hoffman to Emma Embury, 4 November 1842, 16 December 1842, box 1, Emma Embury Papers, New York Public Library.

86. Hoffman, *Genealogy of the Hoffman Family*, 204–6.

87. "Welcome to Charles Dickens: The Boz Ball," *Albion* 1.6 (5 February 1842): 62.

88. Julia Hoffman to George Hoffman, 3 March 1842, Fenno-Hoffman Papers, Clements Library.

89. "Editorial Remarks," *Southern Literary Messenger* 8.1 (January 1842): 86.

90. Richards, *Gender*, 157.

91. Mrs. Smith and her slave-trading son were remembered by Elizabeth Drew Stoddard, another antebellum writer. Mrs. Smith "was, as a true biographer ought to say, 'of aristocratic mien,' handsome, and one whose will never bent except from her own purpose. Appleton Oaksmith, handsome like his mother, made a stir in our war time. He ran slaves into places where he expected to be safe. It was said he scuttled one vessel with two hundred slaves, while he escaped on his consort ship. He was captured at Fire Island while waiting for a bark to be fitted out as a slaver, and was put in Fort Lafayette, Fort Warren and the Boston jail. His escape from that last made a furor. After the war Appleton was prominent in the South, and died there some years after. From there [Smith and her husband] moved to Patchogue. Mr. Smith died there in 1868, and Mrs. Oaksmith refused to go to his bedside, and when she was brought there for burial there was not a single mourner" ("Literary Folk as They Came and Went with Ourselves," *Saturday Evening Post* 172.2 (26 May 1900): 1126–27. Smith lived with her son Appleton near Beaufort, North Carolina, after the war until her death. William McCrillis Griswold, Rufus Griswold's son, reprints an unflattering obituary for Smith that appeared in the local Patchogue, Long Island, newspaper in *Passages from the Correspondence*, at 131–32.

92. E. O. Smith, "Mrs. Henry R. Schoolcraft," 2.

93. Dr. Wilson was an acquaintance of Hoffman's. Charles Fenno Hoffman to Daniel Embury, undated fragment, Emma Embury Papers, box 1, New York Public Library. "Doctor Wilson an educated Cattaraugus chief who brings me a personal letter of introduction from the west and who will show you documents that approve his claim to the interest and respect of men of letters like himself. His present objects I know will awaken in you the most stirring sympathy. I shall do all that I can to advance them on this side of the river and if you and Mr. Murphy will rouse the press of Brooklyn you can give him a public meeting there that would have the best result—I write in much haste with the printer's devil at my back, but if I had not begun an article I would cut the Gazette for to-day and go about to see what could be done for persecuted Americans in these days of freely feeding foreigners."

94. Smith, "Mrs. Henry R. Schoolcraft," 2.

95. George Howard, Lord Morpeth, after 1858 Earl of Carlisle (1802–1864), visited New York in November 1841. He was a Whig politician and had been chief secretary for Ireland for Prime Minister William Lamb, from 1835 to 1841. "Grand Banquet in Honor of Lord Morpeth," *Albion* 3.49 (4 December 1841): 424.

96. Smith, "Mrs. Henry R. Schoolcraft," 2.

97. JJS to Mrs. S. Smith, n.d. [April 1842], reel 8, HRS LC.

98. Mrs. S. Smith to JJS, 25 April 1842, reel 32, HRS LC.

99. WM to HRS, 22 March 1842, reel 32; HRS to WM, 4 April 1842; HRS to WM, 5 April 1842, reel 32, HRS LC.

100. Indian debt statement for Susan Johnston, Records of Districts, Record Group 21, U.S. Circuit Court, Eastern District of Michigan, Southern Division, Detroit, Law Case Files, 1837–1911, Case 1386, US v. Oliver Newberry.

101. Receipt for Storage, 30 April 1842, reel 32, HRS LC.

102. HRS to JSAS, 16 June 1842, reel 32 HRS LC.

103. WM to HRS, 22 July 1842, reel 32, HRS LC.

A Narrative of Wabwindigo

1. GJ, "A Narrative of Wabwindigo, Told by Shingabawossin," 10 June 1845, Legends file, George Johnston Papers, Detroit Public Library, Burton Historical Collection.

Epilogue

1. Dippie, *Catlin*, 174. Like Cass, Schoolcraft had a difficult time getting anyone to answer it at any length; most, like George and William, answered only a few questions.

2. WJ to HRS, 20 August 1844, reel 34; HRS to WJ, 6 September 1844, reel 34; WJ to HRS, 15 October 1846, reel 35; WJ to HRS, 29 May 1847, reel 36; WJ to HRS, 26 August 1847, reel 36, HRS LC.

3. See Witgen, *Seeing Red*, 321–22, for a discussion of the term "half-breed."

4. Colton, *Tour of the American Lakes* (1833); Martineau, *Society in America* (1837); Marryat, *Diary in America* (1839); and Fuller, *Summer on the Lakes* (1844).

5. WJ to William Medill, 15 January 1848, reel 37, HRS LC.

6. "Death of Mrs. Schoolcraft," *New York Spectator*, 9 June 1842.

7. "Death of Mrs. Schoolcraft," *Weekly Messenger*, 6 July 1842.

8. Bremer, *Indian Agent*, 257.

9. John Johnston Schoolcraft to GJ, 3 July 1842, George Johnston Papers, Detroit Public Library, Burton Historical Collection.

10. John Johnston had three identifiable illegitimate children: Marguerite Solomon, Mrs. Moore's child, and Mrs. Mary Cameron. Mrs. Moore and Mrs. Cameron both seem to have contacted the family as a result of their appearance in McKenney's and Anna Jameson's books. Henry Kearney mentions both of them in correspondence, which might signify that both Mrs. Moore and Mrs. Cameron emigrated from Ireland. Eliza Cameron likely contacted the family while they were in New York in 1841–42. While it doesn't seem that Jane Schoolcraft wanted to pursue a relationship with Mary and Eliza Cameron, after Jane's death, mother and daughter became good friends of Schoolcraft and the children, and Eliza seems to have acted as a housekeeper for Schoolcraft before his remarriage. Henry Kearney to HRS, 6 March 1835, reel 23; Henry Kearney to HRS, 5 May 1842, reel 9, HRS LC. In the midst of his court case with the US government, Schoolcraft tried to get each member of the family to contribute $25 for Mrs. Cameron's benefit. Mary Cameron was in poor health, Schoolcraft writes, and had been a widow for thirty years. Her son John J. had died in 1838, and her daughter Eliza had been ill as well. Beyond the fact that no one had any money to spare, McMurray objected on the grounds that it would be a tacit admission of Mrs. Cameron's legitimacy and would be a means of her making further claims on the estate. HRS to Heirs, 23 April 1844, reel 34, HRS LC.

11. Epitaph for JJS, reel 5, HRS LC.

12. WJM to HRS, 6 January 1843, 16 January 1843, reel 33, HRS LC. McMurray writes that the tombstone was "a very different sort of thing, from that which I had expected" after talking to John L. Schoolcraft in Albany. "Neither the quality of the stone, lettering, shape or finish pleased us, and yet I did all I could to make the most of it. But you must judge for yourself, when you see it." John L. Schoolcraft to HRS, 26 April 1843, reel 33, HRS LC; 1 October 1844, reel 34, HRS LC.

13. HRS, "Notes for Memoir of Mrs. H. R. Schoolcraft."

14. HRS to Anna Jameson, September 1842, reel 32, HRS LC.

15. HRS to JSAS, 16 June 1842, reel 32, HRS LC.

16. Bremer, *Indian Agent*, 262.

17. Depositions of Susan Johnston, John Johnston, William Johnston, and Maria [sic] Schoolcraft, Records of Districts, Record Group 21, U.S. Circuit Court, Eastern District of Michigan, Southern Division, Detroit, Law Case Files, 1837–1922, Case 1386, U.S. v. Newberry, National Archives, Chicago, IL.

18. HRS to Charles Stewart, 28 September 1843, reel 33, HRS LC.

19. JLS to HRS, 4 October 1843, reel 33, HRS LC.

20. Bremer, *Indian Agent*, 263, 266. Charlotte and McMurray had no idea what was going on until much later.

21. Abel Bingham, 29–30 October 1843, Journal 4, box 1, folder 1–9, Abel Bingham Papers, Clarke Historical Library.

22. JLS to GJ, 28 November 1843, George Johnston Papers, Burton.

23. Affidavits of H. R. Schoolcraft and T. Romeyn for Continuance, 25 June 1844, Records of Districts, Record Group 1, U.S. Circuit Court, Eastern District of Michigan, Southern Division, Detroit, Law Case Files, 1837–1922, Case 1386, U.S. v. Oliver Newberry, National Archives, Chicago, IL.

24. Anna Maria married James in November 1834; her first child was a stillbirth, and afterward her children were Evelyn, born March 1839; Howard, born in 1841; and Mary Elizabeth Leontine (Minnie), born October 1846. A year after James Schoolcraft's murder, Anna Maria wrote to Schoolcraft about selling his business to John Hulbert, their brother-in-law. She was also asking through Hulbert for some financial help to send her son Howard to school. The tone of the letter makes it appear that she wasn't optimistic about Schoolcraft helping her and that she had done something that caused Schoolcraft to cut her off in the past. "I have often regretted that I should have offended you in any way, and I am sure I have the same feelings of affection for you & yours that I had before I lost the only true friend I ever possessed," she writes. "Every day I feel [James's] loss more deeply, and would most willingly be at rest with him. My dear brother if you knew what I suffer in mind sometimes, you would perhaps feel some sympathy and still take an interest in one you once felt a kindness for." AMJS to HRS, 12 August 1847, reel 36, HRS LC.

25. Minutes of Evidence, June 1844, reel 9, HRS LC.

26. Bremer, *Indian Agent*, 267–68.

27. GJ to HRS, 30 August 1844, George Johnston Papers, Burton. Schoolcraft promised to have his lawyer arrange for the sale of the leases when it was necessary. WJ to HRS, 25 September 1844, reel 34, HRS LC.

28. WJ to HRS, 20 August 1844, reel 34, HRS LC.

29. Mary Rice Johnston to HRS, 20 October 1848, reel 38, HRS LC; HRS to Mary Johnston, 7 November 1848, George Johnston Papers, Bayliss Public Library.

30. For example, see JSAS to HRS, 18 May 1846, reel 35, HRS LC. She grew closer to her father when Charles Fenno Hoffman proposed to her in the summer of 1849. He'd been living with the Schoolcrafts and working for the government in Washington, DC, after having been hospitalized for a mental breakdown in New York. He seems not to have told friends about the impending marriage, however, and in any case he suffered another breakdown close to the proposed wedding day and was hospitalized at Mt. Hope Asylum in Baltimore in September 1849 and afterward at the Pennsylvania State Hospital in Harrisburg for the rest of his life. Janée eventually married Mary Howard's half-brother, Benjamin Screven Howard. They moved to Richmond during the war, where Howard was a clerk for the Confederate government; afterward he opened a book and stationery store. Janée maintained a correspondence with her stepmother in which she wrote sardonically about the free Blacks of Richmond, wondering as many Confederate sympathizers did how a righteous God could have let this happen to them. Jane Johnston Schoolcraft's daughter, who began life speaking Ojibwemowin to her grandmother and doing quillwork on the doorstep of the agency house at Mackinac, ended her life as an embittered Southern lady. CFH to Emma Embury, 10 May 1849, box 1, Emma Embury Papers, New York Public Library; MHS to George Hoffman, 30 September 1849, reel 12, HRS LC; JSAS to HRS, 9 November 1849, reel 39, HRS LC; MHS to Miss Cass, 26 February 1857, reel 43, HRS LC; Moses D. Hoge, "Mrs. Jane S. Howard. A Memorable History," in *Central Presbyterian*, n.d., Section 55, Mss1H6795a1678–1686, Hoge Family Papers, Virginia Historical Society.

31. Bremer, *Indian Agent*, 291.

32. *A Narrative of the Captivity and Adventures of John Tanner (U.S. Interpreter at the Saut de Ste. Marie): During Thirty Years Residence among the Indians in the Interior of North America* was published at both New York and London in 1830.

33. Tanner's life is summarized in Fierst, "Return to 'Civilization.'"

34. Chase Osborn in *Schoolcraft—Longfellow—Hiawatha* writes that Tilden and James "had quarreled at a party on the preceding Fourth of July over a young French girl. Tilden had threatened publicly to kill James. His words were recalled, when the body was found, but there was no evidence except the threat and the kind of bullet. Tanner as well as Tilden had borrowed an army rifle" (511). Osborn gives no source for this information. Tilden was a graduate of West Point and was promoted to first lieutenant in 1847, several months after James Schoolcraft's murder. During the war in Mexico, he was sentenced to be hung for burglary and murder (of someone else), but he was able to resign his commission in 1848. Afterward, he was a school principal in Boston and then an engineer working on railroads and coal mines in Massachusetts, New York, and Pennsylvania. He died in 1859, at age forty-two. Osborn and Osborn, *Schoolcraft—Longfellow—Hiawatha*, 511–12.

35. GJ to HRS, 8 November 1847, reel 37; 29 June 1848, reel 38; 9 September 1848, reel 38, HRS LC. In 1849, George met a young man from Green Bay named François Ladebanche, who'd been told by a clerk in that town that he'd seen Tanner among the Dakotas on the upper Mississippi. The clerk had gone to trade but didn't speak Dakota; one day, one of the Dakota men he was trading with asked another, "aged" man to translate. Tanner was dressed in "Sioux costume" and, writes George, "said that if he made himself known, no one could touch him as the Sioux had bound themselves to protect him with their lives." He told the clerk "that he had burnt his own house on the fourth day of July in the evening, and that on the sixth day of July at 4 oclock he had killed James Schoolcraft, and at the time he designed killing two other persons, the Rev. Mr. Bingham and the Rev. Mr. Brockway, and so long as those two persons were living he would not deliver himself up to Justice, for he entertained hopes of yet killing them, but should he hear of their death he would then deliver himself up to Justice." George was unable to get the name of the clerk from Green Bay to confirm the story. GJ to HRS, 26 July 1849, reel 39, HRS LC.

36. Gilbert, "Memories of the 'Soo.'" See Fierst, "Return to 'Civilization'" and Dowd, "Michigan Murder Mysteries." Gilman and Hoffman in *Life on the Lakes* came upon Tanner's daughter Mary when they were in the St. Mary's River on their return trip to Mackinac. Villagers at the Sault had sent Mary back to her mother by canoe, but the boatman's other passengers left when he was in the river, taking his firestarter with them. At the moment Gilman and Hoffman came upon him, he was unsure what to do. Gilman and Hoffman took Mary in and returned her to her mother at Mackinac. Hoffman at first sees Mary huddled by the fire. She was "the daughter of T_____, a white Indian, i.e. a white man who had adopted the habits, acquired all the vices, and escaped the slightest contamination from any of the virtues of the Savages," he writes. "He resides at the Saulte [sic], and has already, by his brutal cruelty, driven his wife, an Indian, and the one daughter, from him. This daughter, Mary, remained with him, subject to every description of ill-usage; till of late he had made attacks upon her in a manner too shocking to particularize. Some benevolent individuals had interfered, and persuaded Dick [the boatman] to give her a passage in his canoe" (Gilman, *Life on the Lakes*, 2:190).

37. JSAS to HRS, 16 July 1846, reel 35, HRS LC. In a letter in which he congratulated Anna Maria for "[adding] a nice light daughter to the family," Schoolcraft's brother-in-law John Hulbert reported to him that she had been bedridden for more than a month after the birth, "afflicted with various diseases & [suffering] much." John Hulbert to HRS, 7 October, 12 November 1846, reel 35, HRS LC. Anna Maria and her children at first moved into the

old homestead, but she and Eliza soon fell out, and she moved them all into the fort, where they remained through the birth of her daughter Minnie in October and into the next spring. She didn't return to the Johnston homestead until she and Eliza worked out an agreement to divide the house exactly in half between them in the summer of 1847. GJ to HRS, 3 August 1847, reel 36, HRS LC; WJM to HRS, 1 October 1846, reel 35, HRS LC.

38. WJM to HRS, 18 November 1847, reel 37, HRS LC. The two sisters visited Johnston while they were in New York. Johnston to HRS, 26 October 1847, reel 37, HRS LC.

39. The children, Howard, Evelyn, and Minnie, were sent to live with Schoolcraft relatives in Buffalo after their mother's death. The sisters married there, but their brother went west, to San Francisco, in the late 1850s. He wrote to Schoolcraft in 1863, looking for assistance after having been in California for five years. He'd "been sick most of the time," he wrote his uncle, "but have not let my sisters know it. I do not want them to worry about me." He'd been discharged from the cavalry regiment for which he'd signed up when his horse threw him and he was injured. At the time of writing, he couldn't do hard labor or "work at my trade." His trade must have had something to do with Indigenous people, because in August 1865 he was killed by Apaches in New Mexico Territory. According to his sisters, he'd married "a Mexican lady of wealth & position, and had intended coming with his bride to spend part of the winter" with them in Buffalo when he was killed. Howard Schoolcraft to HRS, 27 January 1863, reel 42, HRS LC; Charlotte McMurray Jr. to Mary Howard Schoolcraft, 3 December 1866, reel 43, HRS LC.

40. Bremer, *Indian Agent*, 307. See also John H. Howard to Sarah Howard, 14 February 1848, reel 37, HRS LC.

41. Sarah Margaret Fuller, "Brief Notes of a Journey to the West, by S. M. Fuller, June 1842," 18–19, Perry Clarke Collection, Massachusetts Historical Society quoted in Berg and Perry, "'Impulses of Human Nature,'" 43.

42. Fuller, *Summer on the Lakes*, 32.

43. Fuller, *Summer on the Lakes*, 201.

44. Parker, *Sound the Stars Make*, 163; 175–76; 180.

45. "Indian Legend (copied from Wm. Clarke's journal) Muckwa, or the Bear," b MS Am 1086A, box 1, folder A, Reading Journal J, Margaret Fuller Family Papers, Houghton Library, Harvard University.

46. Fuller, *Summer on the Lakes*, 203–5.

47. Fuller, *Summer on the Lakes*, 187, 207.

48. Fuller, *Summer on the Lakes*, 207.

49. Fuller, *Summer on the Lakes*, 175.

50. Fuller, *Summer on the Lakes*, 176–77.

51. Fuller, *Summer on the Lakes*, 178.

52. William Gilmore Simms, "Literature and Art among the Indians," *Southern and Western Magazine and Review* 1 (1845):153. In 1852, Simms published a review of a pamphlet Mary Howard Schoolcraft wrote defending slavery, but most of the review was taken up by a letter correcting the journal's previous misimpressions about the first Mrs. Schoolcraft. The vocabulary of the letter makes it a strong possibility that Mary Howard Schoolcraft wrote the letter herself. The first Mrs. Schoolcraft, writes the correspondent, was no "simple squaw." Rather, she was the daughter of an aristocratic father who lived in a capacious mansion in Sault Ste. Marie. He married an Indian princess but then sent his daughter to be educated in Ireland, "under the supervision of *his* family." There she stayed for several years,

returning to Michigan to marry Henry Schoolcraft. "True, she was a perfect mistress of the language of the redmen of her nation, but her English was not the less excellent in consequence." She felt "romantic pride" in her noble Indian ancestors, which was what caused her to perfect her knowledge of the language. "On the subject of taste, talent and Christian education, there can be no sort of question." The writer also takes care to supplant Ozhaawshkodewikwe in Jane's story by having Jane replace her mother at the family table once she returned from Europe, especially when there were guests, as Mrs. Johnston, says the writer, was embarrassed at her own deficiencies. Schoolcraft tells a similar story in "Dawn." Mary Howard Schoolcraft, like many of her slave-owning compatriots, was fond of construing everyone associated with herself as aristocrats.

53. Schoolcraft gave Simms as a personal reference to John Howard, the brother of Mary Howard Schoolcraft, when he asked permission to "open a correspondence" with Howard's sister (the two were already engaged by the time he asked). HRS to John Howard, 21 August 1846, reel 35, HRS LC.

54. Smith unleashed a lifetime's worth of resentment in an 1889 article for the *Phrenological Journal and Science of Health* titled simply "Margaret Fuller." Fuller "solemnly believed she was the greatest woman that was ever born," Smith wrote, and "that, give her a fair chance, she would effect a total revolution in the human race. Sappho, Hypatia, Cleopatra, were mere babies compared with what she felt was latent in her veins." Furthermore, Fuller was "devoid of grace and attractiveness," "naturally contentious," and her marriage "ill assorted and suspicious," although Mrs. Smith didn't want to judge. "Margaret no more stood alone than other women, except as her disagreeable methods drove people away from her. . . . In New York, Margaret, without beauty, always self-conscious, and without repartee, preferring a monologue, was apt to be given a wide berth."

55. Smith, "Na-wi-qua: A Metowac Legend," 193–94.

56. Griswold, *Prose Writers of America*, 299–300.

57. Griswold, *Prose Writers of America*, 537. The stories Jameson copied into *Winter Studies* differ only slightly from the *Literary Voyager* versions.

58. Rufus Griswold to James Fields, 7 March, 1847, in Griswold, *Passages from the Correspondence*, 224.

59. Mary Howard Schoolcraft to Mrs. Geig, 18 October 1855, reel 14, HRS LC.

60. HRS, "Dawn of Literary Composition by Educated Natives of the Aboriginal Tribes," in Parker, *Sound the Stars Make*, 241–55; HRS to Editor of Putnam's Monthly, 28 January 1853, reel 40, HRS LC; HRS, "Original Poetry by Mr. and Mrs. H. R. Schoolcraft," n.d., SC2299, Illinois State Library, Springfield, IL.

61. HRS, "Dawn of Literary Composition," in Parker, *Sound the Stars Make*, 243.

62. HRS to HWL, 16 June 1856, Henry Wadsworth Longfellow Papers, Houghton.

63. Henry Wadsworth Longfellow, 13 June 1850, Diary 1845–1853, Henry Wadsworth Longfellow Papers, Houghton.

64. Henry Wadsworth Longfellow, 9 October 1854, Diary 1853–1855, Henry Wadsworth Longfellow Papers, Houghton.

65. Longfellow, *Song of Hiawatha*, 153.

66. Margaret Fuller also famously criticized Longfellow, as a sentimentalist with "no style of his own." Capper, *Margaret Fuller*, 250.

67. Henry Wadsworth Longfellow, 14 March 1856, Diary 1856–1857, Henry Wadsworth Longfellow Papers, Houghton; "Letter from 'Acorn,'" *Spirit of the Times* 26.7 (29 March 1856):

73; "'Edg'd Tools,' and Theatricals in Boston," *Spirit of the Times* 26.10 (19 April 1856): 109. On the reception and criticism of *Hiawatha*, see Roylance, "Northmen and Native Americans"; on its performance history, see Gaul, "Discordant Notes."

68. E. O. Smith, "Puck-wud-jees," *Emerson's Magazine and Putnam's Monthly* 7.49 (July 1858): 97.

69. James Cameron to Abel Bingham, 9 July 1865, box 11, Abel Bingham Papers, Clarke. At the time, the Methodists and Baptists in the area had joined their churches on account of the smallness of their congregations.

70. John M. Johnston to John Gourno, 11 January 1882, John McDouall Johnston Papers, Bentley Historical Library. Eliza had contacted the Poor Master (Gourno) of the town because she was unhappy with her treatment in John's house, but it seems likely she was unhappy at having to leave her home at the end of her life. In more lucid times she'd begged John to take her in, he wrote to Gourno, "& not let her die among Catholics."

71. JSAS to HRS, 9 November 1849, reel 39, HRS LC.

72. Anna Maria [Molly] Johnston, "Recollection of One of the Old Houses of the Soo," [1910 or 1911], John McDouall Johnston Papers, Bentley; Mrs. Thomas O. Gilbert [Angie Bingham], "Memories of the 'Soo,'" 629–31. In "Memories of the 'Soo,'" Angie Bingham claimed to have spoken Ojibwemowin as a child and even interpreted (625). When she was about nineteen, her older brother Judson lamented her "Indian habits and feelings" to their mother Hannah. "She is the most backward of the family with regard to her personal appearance," he added, asking his mother to send Angie to Utica, New York, where he was living with his new wife, in order that she be properly "civilized." Judson Bingham to Hannah Bingham, 21 November 1852, Hannah Bingham Diary, box 2, Abel Bingham Papers, Bentley.

73. Of George's children, the two oldest, Henry William and John George, married and lived at Bay Mills, an Ojibwe community on Whitefish Bay. His older daughter Louisa died unmarried in September 1864. His three sons with Mary Rice all died in the Civil War. James Lawrence died of illness soon after arriving at Bladensburg, Maryland, in October 1861. Benjamin Saurin was promoted to sergeant but died in August 1862 at Second Bull Run. Benjamin appears in the records as Benjamin "Johnson"; James appears as "James K. Johnston" (his full name was James Lawrence Kearney Johnston). NARA M545, roll 21. A definitive record for Samuel Abbott Johnston couldn't be located. In the early 1860s, after both Mary and George had died, Eliza Jane was sent to her mother's relatives in Boston; she became a coat maker and tailoress, never married, and died in the 1920s. George Johnston to Angie Bingham, 29 September 1858, Abel Bingham Papers, box 10, Clarke. Benjamin Johnston to Aunt, 1 November 1858; Benjamin Johnston to Eliza Jane Johnston, 21 February 1859, George Johnston Papers, Burton; Blake and Mason, *Keene City Directory*, 103. George died in January 1861, having gone out into a storm and become disoriented; William died in November of 1863 at Mackinac. Charles W. Hatch to Abel Bingham, 2 March 1861, box 10, Abel Bingham Papers, Clarke. Charlotte died at Niagara-on-the-Lake, Ontario, to which she and McMurray had been transferred some years previous, in January 1878.

74. GJ, "A Narrative of Wabwindigo, told by Shingabawossin," 10 June 1845, Legends file, George Johnston Papers, Burton.

75. Vecsey, *Traditional Ojibwa Religion*, 69–70; Tanner, *Narrative of the Captivity*, 161–62; Kohl, *Kitchi-Gami*, 217, 277–78.

76. Tuttle, *Letters on the Mission*, 68. The text has "white" for "Indian" in brackets: from the sense of the sentence, this appears to be an error.

77. This was in the wake of the Treaty of La Pointe of 1842 (Witgen, *Seeing Red*, 352–53).

78. GJ to HRS, 22 November 1847, reel 37, HRS LC.

79. GJ to HRS, 22 November 1847, reel 37, HRS LC.

80. George's transcription of Penayshee's song is as follows:

We he heway, way yah way } refrain
We he heway, way yah way.   }

Ningah pindegay aindahyaig,

We he heway, way yah way.   }
We he heway, way yah way.   }

Nenemoshain aindahyaig.
Non dah de bik nin gah pinde gay.

We he heway, way yah way.   }
We he heway way yah way.   }

Nin e moshain nondah peboan,
Ningah pindegay.

We he heway, way yah way   }
We he heway, way yah way   }

Non dah te bik nin gah pindegay.

We he heway way yah way.   }
We he heway way yah way.   }

81. Penayshee's song is in Volume 5 of *Historical and Statistical Information*, among a collection of other translated songs, all of them given without attribution (559).

82. GJ to HRS, 5 January 1850, reel 39, HRS LC.

83. Bryant, "Early Northwest." He visited about a month after James Schoolcraft was murdered and remarked on Mrs. Schoolcraft's staying in the fort for her own safety (71–72).

84. Hannah Bingham Diary, 30 March 1855, box 3, folder 9, Abel Bingham Papers, Clarke.

85. Hannah Bingham, 7 October 1855, Diary, November 1854–August 1855, box 2, Abel Bingham Papers, Bentley.

86. GJ to HRS, 8 November 1847, reel 37, HRS LC.

87. George Johnston, Letterbook, flyleaf, Bentley.

88. Copway, *Life, History* and *Traditional History; Running Sketches of Men and Places in England, France, Germany, Belgium, and Scotland* (1851); Maungwudaus (George Henry), *An Account of the Chippewa Indians, Who Have Been Travelling among the Whites in the United States, England, Ireland, Scotland, France and Belgium* (1848); Peter Jones (Kahkewaquonaby), *Life and Journals* (1860) and *History of the Ojebway Indians* (1861). Warren completed his book *History of the Ojibway People, Based upon Traditions and Oral Statements* before his death in 1853, but it wasn't published until 1885, by the Minnesota Historical Society. Francis Assiginack's articles appeared in the *Canadian Journal* in 1858, including

"Legends and Traditions of the Odawah Indians," "Social and Warlike Customs of the Odahwah Indians," and "The Odahway Indian Language."

89. William is listed as a justice of the peace and inspector of elections in 1841, in *Documents Accompanying the Journal of the House of Representatives, of the State of Michigan, at the Annual Session of 1841*, vol. 2 (Detroit, MI: George Dawson, 1841), 10–22; as a lawyer in 1851 in Livingston, *Livingston's Law Register*, 91; as the only teacher on the island in 1856 in Sutherland, *State of Michigan Gazetteer*, 149; and as city clerk, county clerk, schoolteacher, and notary public in Hawes, *Hawes' Michigan State Gazetteer*, 234–35. This is assuming that these are all the same William Johnston.

90. By the later 1840s and into the 1850s Johnston worked off and on as a clerk (he wrote a large, looped script, like a child), sometimes in Washington in a job his father secured for him. Periodically he disappeared for days or months, and Schoolcraft would hear about him through acquaintances who reported being visited by a young man who said he was Schoolcraft's son, asking for money because of one unfortunate mishap or another. These acquaintances included Longfellow in Cambridge, just after the publication of *The Song of Hiawatha*, where Johnston may or may not have married the daughter of the landlord to whom he owed rent, and Anna Jameson in London. His aimless travels went on for years until Johnston enlisted in the New York Volunteers at the beginning of the Civil War. He fought in Northern Virginia and was wounded at Gettysburg; his letters to his father give detailed accounts of the ordinary miseries of a soldier's life. He seemed to have wanted to produce a true report of the war, but Schoolcraft's responses were always the same—Johnston must go to the commanding officer, tell him who he was, and get a commission. After being mustered out of active duty because of illness, Johnston ended the war a guard at the Elmira prison camp in New York, where he died several months after his father, in April 1865. HWL to HRS, 31 May 1856, in Longfellow, *Letters of Henry Wadsworth Longfellow*, 541; John Johnston Schoolcraft to HRS, 14 May 1852, reel 13, HRS LC.

Ramsay Crooks felt compelled to speak up for Johnston after one of his episodes. "Had you not made me the medium of communication with your son," he wrote to Schoolcraft, "I should not feel at liberty to express any opinion; but . . . I will say, that I believe Johnston is really an estimable young man, intelligent, respectable, industriously disposed, and willing to work if he has an opportunity . . . you ought to . . . get your son home until you can place him elsewhere to greater advantage. I fear you will not thank me for the advice, but I cannot help it; for your son has valuable qualities that are well worth preserving, and I think you do him injustice in your suspicion as to his deportment, while at the same time the course you are now pursuing is very likely to shake even the sound morality of your Boy who may be cited as a pattern to young men in general." Ramsay Crooks to HRS, 12 August 1848, reel 38, HRS LC.

91. WJ to HRS, 6 September 1856, reel 42, HRS LC.

92. Steensma, Roede, and Kyle, "Henry David Thoreau's Final Journey," e75–e76; Thoreau, *Thoreau's Minnesota Journey*, 26–27.

93. Henry David Thoreau to Franklin B. Sanborn, 25 June 1861, in Harding and Bode, *Correspondence*, 621.

94. Sayre, *Thoreau and the Indians*, 113, 120. On Thoreau's "Indian Notebooks," see Bellin, "In the Company."

95. Steensma, Roede, and Kyle, "Henry David Thoreau's Final Journey," e75–e76; Thoreau, *Thoreau's Minnesota Journey*, 26–27.

96. Sayre (55) writes that Thoreau didn't know about the Indigenous stories until the first half of 1851, when he took Schoolcraft's *Onéota; or Characteristics of the Red Race of America* (1844), a reprint of the several numbers of *Oneota*, out of the library and took notes on the story "Shingebiss" in one of his notebooks. Willsky-Ciollo, "Apostles of Wilderness," 584–88.

97. Willsky-Ciollo, "Apostles of Wilderness," 553, 581–82.

Bibliography

Manuscript Collections

Ann Arbor, MI
   Bentley Historical Library
      Abel Bingham Papers
      Peter Dougherty Papers
      George Johnston Letterbook
      John McDouall Johnston Papers
   William L. Clements Library, University of Michigan
      Fenno-Hoffman Family Papers
Boston, MA
   Massachusetts Historical Society
      Catharine Maria Sedgwick Papers
Cambridge, MA
   Houghton Library, Harvard University
      Margaret Fuller Family Papers
      Henry Wadsworth Longfellow Papers
Chicago, IL
   Chicago Historical Society
      Jeremiah Porter Journals, 1831–1848
Detroit, MI
   Detroit Public Library, Burton Historical Collection
      George Johnston Papers
Mt. Pleasant, MI
   Clarke Historical Library
      Abel Bingham Papers
New Haven, CT
   Yale University, Beinecke Library Western Americana Collection
      George Johnston Journal
New York, NY
   New-York Historical Society
      Henry Rowe Schoolcraft Papers
   New York Public Library
      Emma Embury Papers
Philadelphia, PA
   American Philosophical Society
      Samuel George Morton Papers

Historical Society of Pennsylvania
    Peter Stephen Du Ponceau Correspondence
Rosenbach Museum
    Henry Rowe Schoolcraft Journal, 1825, AMS 1031/24
Richmond, VA
   Virginia Historical Society
       Hoge Family Papers
Saint Paul, MN
   Minnesota Historical Society
       William T. Boutwell Papers, 1832–1881
Sault Ste. Marie, MI
   Bayliss Public Library
       Steere Special Collection, George Johnston Papers, 1792–1944
   River of History Museum
       Charlotte Johnston Commonplace Book
Springfield, IL
   Illinois State Library
       "Original Poetry by Mr. & Mrs. H. R. Schoolcraft"
Syracuse, NY
   Syracuse University Libraries
       Gerrit Smith Papers
Washington, DC
   Library of Congress
       Henry Rowe Schoolcraft Papers (HRS LC)
   National Archives and Records Administration (NARA)
       Index to Compiled Service Records of Volunteer Union Soldiers Who Served in Organizations from the State of Michigan (M545)
       Office of Indian Affairs Records of the Michigan Superintendency, 1814–1851 (M1), Letters Received by the Superintendent, 1819–1835 (rolls 10, 20)

Newspapers

Albion, a Journal of News, Politics and Literature (New York, NY)
American Journal of Science and Arts (New Haven, CT)
American Medical Intelligencer (Philadelphia, PA)
Atkinson's Saturday Evening Post (Philadelphia, PA)
Atlantic Magazine (New York, NY)
Boston Literary Magazine (Boston, MA)
Boston Masonic Mirror (Boston, MA)
Boston Weekly Magazine (Boston, MA)
Bouquet: Flowers of Polite Literature (Boston, MA)
Christian Advocate (New York, NY)
Christian Intelligencer and Eastern Chronicle (Portland, ME)
Christian Register (Boston, MA)
Christian Review (Boston, MA)
Corsair: A Gazette of Literature, Art, Dramatic Criticism, Fashion, and Novelty (New York, NY)
Emerson's Magazine and Putnam's Monthly (New York, NY)
Episcopal Watchman (Hartford, CT)
Evangelical Magazine and Gospel Advocate (Utica, NY)
Evening Star (Washington, DC)

Expositor (New York, NY)
Graham's Lady's and Gentleman's Magazine (Philadelphia, PA)
Hazards Register of Pennsylvania (Philadelphia, PA)
Journal of Belles Lettres (Philadelphia, PA)
Journal of Education (Detroit, MI)
Knickerbocker (New York, NY)
Ladies Companion (New York, NY)
Literary Magazine and American Register (Philadelphia, PA)
Museum of Foreign Literature, Science, and Art (Philadelphia, PA)
New World: A Weekly Family Journal of Popular Literature, Science, Art and News (New York, NY)
New York American (New York, NY)
New-York Mirror (New York, NY)
New York Religious Chronicle (New York, NY)
New-York Spectator (New York, NY)
New-Yorker (New York, NY)
Niles' Weekly Register (Baltimore, MD)
North American Magazine (Philadelphia, PA)
Orion: A Monthly Magazine of Literature, Science & Art (Penfield, NY)
Philadelphia Album and Ladies' Literary Portfolio (Philadelphia, PA)
Religious Intelligencer (New Haven, CT)
Religious Miscellany (Carlisle, PA)
Southern and Western Magazine and Review (Charleston, SC)
Southern Literary Messenger (Richmond, VA)
Southern Rose (Charleston, SC)
Souvenir (Philadelphia, PA)
Spirit of the Age and Journal of Humanity (Boston, MA)
Spirit of the Times (New York, NY)
United States Catholic Miscellany (Charleston, SC)
Waldie's Octavo Library (Philadelphia, PA)
Weekly Messenger (Chambersberg, PA)
Workingman's Advocate (New York, NY)
Zion's Herald (Boston, MA)

Books and Articles

Adair, James. *The History of the American Indians*. London: Edward and Charles Dilly, 1775.
Allen, Anne Beiser. "A Bridge between Cultures: Rosalie Laborde Dousman's Indian School." *Wisconsin Magazine of History* 94, no. 1 (Autumn 2010): 14–25.
Allestree, Richard. *The Whole Duty of Man, Laid Down in a Plain and Familiar Way for the Use of All, But Especially the Meanest Reader*. London: Printed for T. Garthwait, 1659.
Andreas, A. T. *History of the Upper Peninsula of Michigan*. Chicago: Western Historical Company, 1883.
Andresen, Julie Tetel. *Linguistics in America 1769–1924*. London: Routledge, 1990.
Armitage, David. "John Locke, Carolina, and the *Two Treatises of Government*." *Political Theory* 32, no. 5 (2004): 602–27.
Armour, David A. "David and Elizabeth: The Mitchell Family in the Straits of Mackinac." *Michigan History* 64, no. 4 (1980): 17–29.
———. "William Solomon." *Dictionary of Canadian Biography Online*. www.biographi.ca/009004-119.01-e.php?&id_nbr=4195&terms=de.
Armour, R. C. *North American Indian Fairy Tales: Folklore and Legends*. Philadelphia: Lippincott, 1905.
Arneil, Barbara. *John Locke and America: The Defence of English Colonialism*. New York: Oxford University Press, 1996.

Arthur, Elizabeth. "Dickson, James." *Dictionary of Canadian Biography*. www.biographi.ca/en/bio/dickson_james_7E.html.
Askin, John. Askin Papers. *Michigan Historical Collections* 25 (1903): 474–515.
———. *The John Askin Papers*. Vol. 2. Detroit, MI: Library Commission, 1931.
Assiginack, Francis. "Legends and Traditions of the Odahwah Indians." *Canadian Journal of Industry, Science and Art* 14 (March 1858): 115–25.
———. "The Odahwah Indian Language." *Canadian Journal of Industry, Science and Art* 18 (November 1858): 481–85.
———. "Remarks on the Paper Headed 'The Odahwah Indian Language,' Published in the *Canadian Journal* for November, 1858." *Canadian Journal of Industry, Science and Art* 26 (March 1860): 182–86.
Bacon, Leonard. *Sketch of Rev. David Bacon*. Boston: Congregational Publishing Society, 1876.
Baird, Elizabeth. "Reminiscences of Early Days on Mackinac Island." *Wisconsin Historical Society Collections* 14 (1898): 17–64.
———. "Reminiscences of Life in Territorial Wisconsin." *Wisconsin Historical Society Collections* 15 (1900): 205–63.
Baird, Ileana. "Circulating Things, Circulating Stereotypes: Representations of Arabia in Eighteenth-Century Imagination." In *All Things Arabia: Arabian Identity and Material Culture*, edited by Ileana Baird and Hülya Yagcioglu, 69–87. Leiden: Brill Academic Publishers, 2020.
Bancroft, Aaron. *Importance of Education*. Worcester, MA: Thomas & Sturtevant, 1806.
Bank, Rosemarie K. "Staging the 'Native': Making History in American Theatre Culture, 1828–1838." *Theatre Journal* 45, no. 5 (December 1993): 461–86.
Banner, Stuart. *How the Indians Lost Their Land: Law and Power on the Frontier*. Cambridge, MA: Harvard University Press, 2005.
Baptist, Edward. *The Half Has Never Been Told: Slavery and the Making of American Capitalism*. New York: Basic Books, 2014.
Baraga, Frederic. *A Dictionary of the Ojibway Language*. St. Paul: Minnesota Historical Society Press, 1992.
Barbour, James. "Letter from the Secretary of War to the Chairman of the Committee on Indian Affairs, Accompanied by a Bill for the Preservation and Civilization of the Indian Tribes within the United States (3 February 1826)." Vol. 2 of *Encyclopedia of American Indian Removal*, edited by Daniel F. Littlefield Jr. and James F. Parins, 7–9. Santa Barbara, CA: Greenwood, 2011.
Barnes, Homer Francis. *Charles Fenno Hoffman*. New York: Columbia University Press, 1930.
Barton, Benjamin Smith. *A Memoir Concerning the Supposed Fascinating Faculty of the Rattle-Snake, and Other American Serpents*. Philadelphia: The Author, 1796.
———. *New Views of the Origin of the Tribes and Nations of America*. Philadelphia: Printed for the Author, by John Bioren, 1797.
Battiste, Marie, and James Youngblood (Sa'ke'j) Henderson, eds. *Protecting Indigenous Knowledge and Heritage: A World Challenge*. Saskatoon, Saskatchewan: Purich, 2000.
Beasecker, Robert. "'With Extreme Diffidence': Anna L. Snelling's *Kabaosa* (1842): A Provisional Publishing History and Census." Paper 52. ScholarWorks@GVSU. http://scholarworks.gvsu.edu/library_sp/52.

Bellfy, Phil. "Cross-Border Treaty Signers: The Anishinaabeg of the Lake Huron Borderlands." In *Lines Drawn upon the Water: First Nations and the Great Lakes Borders and Borderland*, edited by Karl S. Hele, 21–42. Waterloo, Ontario: Wilfrid Laurier University Press, 2008.

Bellin, Joshua David. "In the Company of Savagists: Thoreau's Indian Books and Antebellum Ethnology." *The Concord Saunterer* 16 (2008): 1–32.

Benedict, Barbara M. "The Paradox of the Anthology: Collecting and Difference in Eighteenth-Century Britain." *New Literary History* 34, no. 2 (Spring 2003): 231–56.

Berens, William. "Rolling Head." In *Memories, Myths, and Dreams of an Ojibwe Leader*, edited by Jennifer S. H. Brown and Susan Elaine Gray, 164–70. Montreal: McGill-Queen's University Press, 2009.

Berg, Martha, and Alice de V. Perry, eds. "'The Impulses of Human Nature': Margaret Fuller's Journal from June through October 1844." *Proceedings of the Massachusetts Historical Society* 102 (1990): 38–126.

Berkeley, Edmund, and Dorothy Smith Berkeley. *George William Featherstonhaugh: The First U.S. Government Geologist*. Tuscaloosa: University of Alabama Press, 1988.

Bieder, Robert E. *Science Encounters the Indian 1820–1880: The Early Years of American Ethnology*. Norman: University of Oklahoma Press, 1986.

Bigsby, John Jeremiah. *The Shoe and Canoe, or Pictures of Travel in the Canadas*. 2 vols. London: Chapman and Hall, 1850.

Black, Mary B. "Ojibwa Power Belief System." In *The Anthropology of Power: Ethnographic Studies from Asia, Oceania, and the New World*, edited by Raymond D. Fogelson and Richard N. Adams, 141–51. New York: Academic Press, 1977.

Blackbird, Andrew J. *History of the Ottawa and Chippewa Indians of Michigan; A Grammar of Their Language, and Personal and Family History of the Author*. Ypsilanti, MI: Ypsilantian Job Printing House, 1887.

Blackstone, William. *Blackstone's Commentaries: With Notes of Reference to the Constitution and Laws, of the Federal Government of the United States; and of the Commonwealth of Virginia*. 5 vols. Edited by St. George Tucker. Philadelphia: William Young Birch and Abraham Small, 1803.

Blair, Hugh. "Critical Dissertation on the Poems of Ossian, the Son of Fingal." Vol. 2 of *The Works of Ossian* by James Macpherson, 313–443. London: T. Becket and P. A. Dehondt, 1765.

———. *Essays on Rhetoric: Abridged Chiefly from Dr. Blair's Lectures on that Science*. London: Crosby and Letterman, 1701.

———. *The Works of Hugh Blair*. 5 vols. London: Printed for T. Cadell and W. Davies, 1820.

Blake, Hiram, and Andrew R. Mason, eds. *Keene City Directory for the Years 1895–96*. Keene, NH: Sentinel Printing Company, 1895.

Bloomfield, Leonard. *Sacred Stories of the Sweet Grass Cree*. Ottawa: F. A. Aland, 1930.

Bolster, Arthur S., Jr. *James Freeman Clarke: Disciple to Advancing Truth*. Boston: Beacon, 1954.

Borrows, John. "Heroes, Tricksters, Monsters, and Caretakers: Indigenous Law and Legal Education." *McGill Law Journal* 61, no. 4 (2016): 795–846.

Boucherville, Thomas Vecheres de. *War on Detroit: Chronicles of Thomas Vecheres de Boucherville and the Capitulation by an Ohio Volunteer*. Chicago: Lakeside, 1940.

Bowen, Francis. Review of *Historical and Statistical Information Respecting the Indian Tribes of the United States*. North American Review 77, no. 160 (July 1853): 245–62.

Brackenridge, Hugh Henry. *Gazette Publications*. Carlisle [PA]: Printed by Alexander & Phillips, 1806.

———. *Indian Atrocities: Narratives of the Perils and Sufferings of Dr. Knight and John Slover*. Cincinnati, OH: U. P. James, 1867.

———. *Law Miscellanies: An Introduction to the Study of Law*. Philadelphia: P. Byrne, 1814.

———. *Modern Chivalry: Containing the Adventures of a Captain and Teague O'Regan, His Servant*. 2 vols. Pittsburgh: R. Patterson & Lambdin, 1819.

Bremer, Richard G. *Indian Agent and Wilderness Scholar: The Life of Henry Rowe Schoolcraft*. Mt. Pleasant: Clarke Historical Library, Central Michigan University, 1987.

Brightly, Frederick C. *Reports of Cases Argued and Adjudged in the Supreme Court of the United States, February Term 1823. By Henry Wheaton*. Vol. 21. New York: Banks Law Publishing Company, 1904.

Brinton, Daniel Garrison. *Aboriginal Authors and their Productions*. Philadelphia: D. G. Brinton, 1883.

———. *The Lenape and Their Legends; with the Complete Text and Symbols of the Walam Olum*. Philadelphia: D. G. Brinton, 1885.

———. *Myths of the New World: A Treatise on the Symbolism and Mythology of the Red Race of America*. New York: Leypoldt & Holt, 1868.

Brown, Jennifer S. H. *Strangers in Blood: Fur Trade Company Families in Indian Country*. Norman: University of Oklahoma Press, 1996.

Bruchac, Margaret M. *Savage Kin: Indigenous Informants and American Anthropologists*. Tucson: University of Arizona Press, 2018.

Bryant, William Cullen. "The Early Northwest." Vol. 2 of *Prose Writings of William Cullen Bryant*, edited by Parke Godwin, 51–82. New York: D. Appleton and Company, 1884.

Bulger, Andrew. *An Autobiographical Sketch of the Services of the Late Captain Andrew Bulger of the Royal Newfoundland Fencible Regiment*. Bangalore: Printed at the Regimental Press, 1865.

Bulgur, Alfred Edward. Bulgur Papers. Edited by Reuben Gold Thwaites. *Wisconsin Historical Collections* 13 (1895): 1–162.

Bunnell, Lafayette Houghton. *Discovery of the Yosemite and the Indian War of 1851 Which Led to That Event*. New York: Fleming H. Revell, 1892.

———. *Winona and Its Environs on the Mississippi in Ancient and Modern Days*. Winona, MN: Jones & Kroeger, Printers & Publishers, 1897.

Burns, Robert. *The Poems of Robert Burns*. Edinburgh: Oliver & Company, 1806.

Burstein, Andrew. *The Original Knickerbocker: The Life of Washington Irving*. New York: Basic Books, 2007.

Burton, Clarence Monroe, William Stocking, and Gordon K. Miller, eds. *The City of Detroit, Michigan, 1701–1922*. 5 vols. Detroit, MI: S. J. Clarke, 1922.

Caldwell, Charles. *Elements of Phrenology*. Lexington, KY: The Author, 1824.

Campbell, James V. "Biographical Sketch of Charles C. Trowbridge." *Michigan Historical Collections* (June 1883): 478–91.

Canadian Archives. *Military Posts 1790-1824*. *Michigan Historical Collections* 23 (1895): 252–328.

Capper, Charles. *Margaret Fuller: An American Romantic Life; the Public Years*. New York: Oxford University Press, 2007.
Carlson, Nathan D. "Reviving Witiko (Windigo): An Ethnohistory of 'Cannibal Monsters' in the Athabasca District of Northern Alberta, 1878–1910." *Ethnohistory* 56, no. 3 (Summer 2009): 355–94.
Carnegie, James. *The Meda Maiden, and Other Poems*. London: Macmillan, 1877.
Carter, Clarence Edwin, ed. *Territorial Papers of the United States. Michigan Territory 1805–1820*. Vols. 10–11. Washington, DC: US Government Printing Office, 1942.
Carwardine, Richard J. *Evangelicals and Politics in Antebellum America*. New Haven, CT: Yale University Press, 1993.
Cass, Lewis. *A Discourse Pronounced at the Capitol of the United States, in the Hall of Representatives, before the American Historical Society, January 30, 1836, by the Hon. Lewis Cass, President of the Society*. Washington, DC: P. Thompson, 1836.
———. *Inquiries, Respecting the History, Traditions, Languages, Manners, Customs, Religion &c. of the Indians, Living within the United States*. Detroit, MI: Sheldon & Reed, 1823.
———. *Letter from the Secretary of War, Transmitting Information in Relation to the Superintendency of Indian Affairs, in the Territory of Michigan During the Year 1820, and Part of the Year 1821*. February 11, 1822. Washington, DC: Gales & Seaton, 1822.
———. Review of *Documents and Proceedings Relating to the Formation of a Board in the City of New York, for the Emigration, Preservation, and Improvement of the Aborigines of America*. *North American Review* 30, no. 66 (January 1830): 62–124.
———. Review of *Indian Treaties, and Laws and Regulations Relating to Indian Affairs . . . compiled and published under Orders of the Department of War*. *North American Review* 24, no. 55 (April 1827): 365–442.
———. Review of *Manners and Customs of Several Indian Tribes . . .* by John D. Hunter (Philadelphia 1823) and *Historical Notes, Respecting the Indians of North America . . .* by John Halkett (London 1825). *North American Review* 22, no. 13 (January 1826): 53–119.
———. Review of *Travels in the Central Portions of the Mississippi Valley . . .* by Henry R. Schoolcraft . . . and *A Vindication of Rev. Mr. Heckewelder's History of the Indian Nations* by William Rawle. *North American Review* 26, no. 59 (April 1828): 357–402.
Chapman, Charles M., ed. "The Historic Johnston Family of the 'Soo.'" *Michigan Historical Collections* 32 (1903): 305–53.
Charlevoix, Pierre Francois Xavier de. *A Voyage to North-America: Undertaken by Command of the Present King of France*. 2 vols. Dublin: John Exshaw and James Potts, 1766.
Chesbrough, E. S. "William Hull Clarke." *Proceedings of the Western Society of Engineers* 4 (1879): 118–19.
Child, Brenda J. *Holding Our World Together: Ojibwe Women and the Survival of Community*. New York: Penguin, 2012.
Chute, Janet E. *The Legacy of Shingwaukonse: A Century of Native Leadership*. Toronto: University of Toronto Press, 1998.
Clark, Hannah Belle. *The Public Schools of Chicago, a Sociological Study*. Chicago: University of Chicago Press, 1897.
Cleland, Charles E. *Faith in Paper: The Ethnohistory and Litigation of Upper Great Lakes Indian Treaties*. Ann Arbor: University of Michigan Press, 2014.

———. *Rites of Conquest: The History and Culture of Michigan's Native Americans.* Ann Arbor, MI: University of Michigan Press, 1992.

Clements, William M. "Schoolcraft as Textmaker." *Journal of American Folklore* 103, no. 409 (April–June 1990): 177–92.

Colden, Cadwallader. *The History of the Five Indian Nations of Canada, which are dependent on the province of New-York in America, and are the barrier between the English and French in that part of the world.* London: John Whitson, 1750.

Colman, Samuel. *Pontiac: or The Siege of Detroit.* Boston: Samuel Colman, 1835.

Colonial Office Records. *Michigan Historical Collections* 25 (1895): 1–681.

Colton, Calvin. *Tour of the American Lakes and among The Indians of the North-West Territory in 1830.* 2 vols. London: Frederick Westley and A. H. Davis, 1830.

Copies of Papers on File in the Dominion Archives at Ottawa, Canada, Pertaining to the Relations with the British Government with the United States During and Subsequent to the Period of the War of 1812. Michigan Historical Collections 16 (1890).

Copway, George. *The Life, History, and Travels of Kah-ge-ga-gah-bowh, a Young Indian Chief of the Ojebwa Nation.* Philadelphia: Harmstead, 1847.

———. *Running Sketches of Men and Places, in England, France, Germany, Belgium, and Scotland.* New York: J.C. Riker, 1851.

———. *Traditional History and Characteristic Sketches of the Ojibway Nation.* London: Charles Gilpin, 1850.

Daly, John Patrick. *When Slavery Was Called Freedom: Evangelicalism, Proslavery, and the Causes of the Civil War.* Lexington: University Press of Kentucky, 2002.

Delafield, Joseph. *The Unfortified Boundary: A Diary of the First Survey of the Canadian Boundary Line from St. Regis to the Lake of the Woods.* New York: Privately printed, 1943.

Deloria, Philip. *Playing Indian.* New Haven, CT: Yale University Press, 1995.

Deloria, Vine, Jr. *The World We Used to Live In: Remembering the Powers of the Medicine Men.* Golden, CO: Fulcrum, 2006.

Denham, Dixon, et al. *Narrative of Travels and Discoveries in Northern and Central Africa . . . in the Years 1822, 1823, and 1824.* London: John Murray, 1826.

Denham, James M., and Keith L. Huneycutt. "Historic Notes and Documents: 'Everything Is Hubbub Here': Lt. James Willoughby Anderson's Second Seminole War, 1837–1842." *Florida Historical Quarterly* 82, no. 3 (Winter 2000): 313–59.

Densmore, Frances. *Chippewa Music.* Bureau of American Ethology Bulletin 45. Washington, DC: US Government Printing Office, 1910.

———. *Strength of the Earth: The Classic Guide to Ojibwe Uses of Native Plants.* St. Paul: Minnesota Historical Society Press, 2008.

De Puy, Henry F. *A Bibliography of English Colonial Treaties with the Indians.* New York: Lenox Club, 1917.

Dickens, Asbury, and John W. Forney, eds. *American State Papers: Documents of the Congress of the United States, in Relation to Public Lands.* Vol. 5. Washington, DC: Gales & Seaton, 1860.

Dippie, Brian. *Catlin and His Contemporaries: The Politics of Patronage.* Lincoln: University of Nebraska Press, 1990.

Documents Relating to Detroit and Vicinity, 1805–1813. Michigan Historical Collections 40 (1929).

Doerfler, Jill, Niigaanwewidam James Sinclair, and Heidi Kiiwetinepinesiik Stark. *Centering Anishinaabeg Studies: Understanding the World through Stories*. East Lansing: Michigan State University Press; Winnipeg: University of Manitoba Press, 2013.

Douglass, R. Alan. *Uppermost Canada: The Western District and the Detroit Frontier, 1800–1850*. Detroit, MI: Wayne State University Press, 2002.

Dowd, Gregory Evans. "Michigan Murder Mysteries: Death and Rumor in the Age of Indian Removal." In *Enduring Nations: Native Americans in the Midwest*, 124–59. Champaign-Urbana: University of Illinois Press, 2008.

Drake, Samuel Gardner. *Indian Biography: Containing The Lives of More than Two Hundred Indian Chiefs*. Boston: Josiah Drake, 1832.

Du Ponceau, Peter. "Corresponding Secretary's Report to the Committee, on the Languages of the American Indians." Vol. 1 of *Transactions of the Historical and Literary Committee of the American Philosophical Society*, xvii–xlvi. Philadelphia: Abraham Small, 1819.

Eastman, Carolyn. "The Indian Censures the White Man: 'Indian Eloquence' and American Reading Audiences in the Early Republic." *William and Mary Quarterly* 65, no. 3 (2008): 535–64.

Eberle, John. *A Treatise on the Practice of Medicine*. 2 vols. Philadelphia: John Grigg, 1831.

Ebert, Albert E. "Early History of the Drug Trade of Chicago, Compiled from the Records of the Chicago Veteran Druggists' Association." *Transactions of the Illinois State Historical Society* 8 (1903): 239–60.

Eldredge, Robert F. *The Past and Present of Macomb County, Michigan*. Chicago: S. J. Clarke, 1905.

Embury, Emma C. *American Wild Flowers in their Native Haunts*. New York: D. Appleton, 1845.

Evans, Daniel H., and David Mack Cooper. *In Memoriam. Funeral Obsequies on the Death of Rev. William Montague Ferry*. Detroit, MI: Tribune Job Printing, 1869.

"Expedition against Michilimackinac." Vol. 4 of *Historical Register of the United States*, edited by T. H. Palmer, 246–62. Philadelphia: Printed and published by G. Palmer, 1816.

Farmer, Silas. *History of Detroit and Michigan*. Detroit, MI: Silas Farmer, 1884.

Featherstonhaugh, G. W. *A Canoe Voyage up the Minnay Sotor*. 2 vols. London: Richard Bentley, 1847.

Fierst, John T. "Return to 'Civilization': John Tanner's Troubled Years at Sault Ste Marie." *Minnesota History* 50, no. 1 (Spring 1986): 23–36.

Fifty-Seventh Annual Report of the Superintendent of Public Instruction of the State of Michigan with Accompanying Documents for the Year 1893. East Lansing, MI: By Authority, 1894.

Fisher, George P. *Life of Benjamin Silliman*. 2 vols. New York: Scribner, 1866.

Fisher, Philip A. *The Fisher Genealogy: Record of the Descendants of Joshua, Anthony and Cornelius Fisher of Dedham, Massachusetts 1616–1640*. Everett, MA: Massachusetts Publishing Company, 1898.

Fletcher, Matthew L. M. *The Eagle Returns: The Legal History of the Grand Traverse Band of Ottawa and Chippewa Indians*. East Lansing: Michigan State University Press, 2012.

Fletcher, Robert. "Myths of the Robin Redbreast in Early English Poetry." *American Anthropologist* 2, no. 2 (April 1889): 97–118.

Force, Peter. *The National Calendar, and Annals of the United States.* Vol. 11. Washington City: Printed and published by Peter Force, 1833.

Forell, George Wolfgang. "Moravian Missions among the Delawares in Ohio during the Revolutionary War." *Transactions of the Moravian Historical Society* 23, no. 1 (1977): 41–60.

Fuller, Margaret. *Letters of Margaret Fuller.* Vol. 1. Edited by Robert N. Hudspeth. Ithaca, NY: Cornell University Press, 1983.

———. *Summer on the Lakes, in 1843.* Boston: Charles C. Little and James Brown, 1844.

Gaul, Theresa Strouth. "Discordant Notes: Longfellow's *Song of Hiawatha*, Community, Race, and Performance Politics." *Journal of American Culture* 27, no. 4 (December 2004): 406–14.

Gilbert, Mrs. Thomas O. "Memories of the 'Soo.'" *Michigan Historical Collections* 30 (1905): 623–33.

Gilman, Chandler Robbins. *Life on the Lakes: Being Tales and Sketches Collection during a Trip to the Pictured Rocks of Lake Superior.* 2 vols. New-York: George Dearborn, Publisher, 1836.

Gilman, Rhoda R. *Henry Hastings Sibley: Divided Heart.* St. Paul: Minnesota Historical Society Press, 2004.

Granzberg, Gary. "The Rolling Head Legend among Algonquians." *Anthropologica* 36, no. 1 (1994): 3–33.

Greig, Hannah. *The Beau Monde: Fashionable Society in Georgian London.* Oxford, UK: Oxford University Press, 2013.

Grenby, M. O. "Tame Fairies Make Good Teachers: The Popularity of Early British Fairy Tale." *The Lion and Unicorn* 30 (2006): 1–24.

Griswold, Rufus Wilmot. *Prose Writers of America, with a Survey of the Intellectual History, Conditions and Prospects of the County.* Philadelphia: Carey and Hart, 1849.

Griswold, William McCrillis, ed. *Passages from the Correspondence and Other Papers of Rufus W. Griswold.* Cambridge, MA: W. M. Griswold, 1898.

Hambleton, Elizabeth, and Elizabeth Warren Stoutamire. *The Johnston Family of Sault Ste. Marie.* Washington, DC: John Johnston Family Association, 1992.

Hannay, James. *History of the War of 1812.* Toronto: Morang, 1905.

Harding, Walter, and Carl Bode, eds. *The Correspondence of Henry David Thoreau.* Washington Square: New York University Press. 1958.

Harper, Rob. "Looking the Other Way: The Gnadenhutten Massacre and the Contextual Interpretation of Violence." *William and Mary Quarterly*, 3rd series, 64, no. 3 (July 2017): 621–44.

Harvey, Sean P. "'Must Not Their Languages Be Savage and Barbarous Like Them?': Philology, Indian Removal, and Race Science." *Journal of the Early Republic* 30, no. 4 (2010): 505–32.

Hathaway, Benjamin. *The League of the Iroquois, and Other Legends. From the Indian Muse.* Chicago: Donnelley, Gassette & Lloyd, Printer, 1881.

Haugen, Kristine Louise. "Ossian and the Invention of Textual History." *Journal of the History of Ideas* 59, no. 2 (April 1998): 309–27.

Hawes, George W. *Hawes' Michigan State Gazetteer and Business Directory for 1860.* Detroit, MI, 1859.

Heckewelder, John. *An Account of the History, Manners, and Customs, of the Indian*

Natives Who Once Inhabited Pennsylvania and the Neighbouring States. Philadelphia: Abraham Small, 1819.

Heckewelder, John, and Peter Du Ponceau. "Correspondence between Mr. Heckewelder and Mr. Duponceau, on the Languages of the American Indians." Vol. 1 of *Transactions . . . of the American Philosophical Society*, 351–450. Philadelphia: Abraham Small, 1819.

Hele, Karl. "James D. Cameron and the Baptist Mission at Bawating, 1831–1859." *Papers of the Thirty-Fifth Algonquin Conference.* Winnipeg: University of Manitoba, 2004, 137–61.

Henry, Alexander. *Travels and Adventures in the Years 1760–1776.* Chicago: R. R. Donnelley & Sons, 1921.

Henry, Gordon, Jr., Margaret Noodin, and David Stirrup, eds. *Enduring Critical Poses: The Legacy and Life of Anishinaabe Literature and Letters.* Albany: State University of New York Press, 2021.

Hodgson, Barbara. *Into the Arms of Morpheus: The Tragic History of Laudanum, Morphine, and Patent Medicines.* Buffalo, NY: Firefly Books, 2001.

Hoffman, Charles Fenno. *The Vigil of Faith and Other Poems.* New York: Harper & Brothers, 1845.

———. *A Winter in the West.* 2 vols. New York: Harper & Brothers, 1835.

Hoffman, Eugene A. *Genealogy of the Hoffman Family 1657–1899. Descendants of Martin Hoffman. With Biographical Notes.* New York: Dodd, Mead, 1899.

Homfray, Irving L. *Officers of the British Forces in Canada during the War of 1812–1815.* Ontario: Welland Tribune Print, 1908.

Houck, Louis, ed. *Reports of Cases Argued and Determined in the Supreme Court of the State of Missouri, from 1821 to 1827.* Vol. 1. Cape Girardeau, MO: The Author, 1870.

Howe, Frances R. *The Story of a French Homestead in the Old Northwest.* Columbus, OH: Press of Nitschke Bros., 1907.

Hunter, John Dunn. *Memoirs of a Captivity among the Indians of North America, from Childhood to the Age of Nineteen.* London: Longman, Hurst, Rees, Orme, Brown, and Green, 1824.

Irving, Pierre, ed. *Life and Letters of Washington Irving.* New York: G. P. Putnam, 1863.

Irving, Washington. *A Tour on the Prairies.* Philadelphia: Carey, Lea, and Blanchard, 1835.

Irwin, Matthew. "A Government Factor's Journal: Chicago from 1816 to 1822." In *The Development of Chicago 1674–1914: Shown in a Series of Contemporary Original Narratives*, edited by Milo Milton Quaife, 71–82. Chicago: Caxton Club, 1916.

James, Edwin. Review of *A Grammar of the Language of the Lenni Lenape or Delaware Indians, Translated for the American Philosophical Society, from the German Manuscript of the late Rev. David Zeisberger*, by Peter Stephen Duponceau. *American Quarterly Review* 3, no. 6 (June 1828): 391–422.

Jameson, Anna Brownell. *Winter Studies and Summer Rambles in Canada.* 2 vols. New York: Wiley and Putnam, 1839.

Jefferson, Thomas. *Notes on the State of Virginia with Related Documents.* Edited and introduction by David Waldstreicher. Boston: Bedford/St. Martin's, 2002.

———. *Political Writings.* Edited by Joyce Appleby and Terrence Ball. Cambridge: Cambridge University Press, 1999.

Johnson, Rebecca Carol, Richard Maxwell, and Katie Trumpener. "The Arabian Nights, Arab-European Literary Influence, and the Lineages of the Novel." *Modern Language Quarterly* 68, no. 2 (June 2007): 243–79.

Johnson, Samuel. *Johnson on Shakespeare*. Edited by Walter Raleigh. London: Henry Frowde, 1908.

Johnston, Basil. *The Manitous: The Spiritual World of the Ojibway*. St. Paul: Minnesota Historical Society Press, 2001.

———. *Ojibway Ceremonies*. Toronto: McClellan and Stewart, 1982.

Johnston, George. "Mash-kwa-sha-kong, or the Traditionary History of the Red Head and His Two Sons." In *Oneota; or Characteristics of the Red Race in America from Original Notes*, by Henry Rowe Schoolcraft, 139–45. New York: Wiley & Putnam, 1845.

———. "Reminiscences." *Michigan Historical Collections* 12 (1888): 605–11.

Johnston, John. "An Account of Lake Superior, 1792–1807." Vol. 2 of *Les Bourgeois de la Compagnie du Nord-Ouest*, edited by L. R. Masson, 145–74. Quebec: De L'Imprimerie Generale A. Cote et Cie, 1890.

———. "Autobiographical Letters." *Michigan Historical Collections* 32 (1902): 328–53.

Johnston, Judith. *Anna Jameson: Victorian, Feminist, Woman of Letters*. Brookfield, VT: Scholar Press, 1997.

Johnston, William. "Letters on the Fur Trade 1833." *Michigan Historical Collections* 37 (1910): 132–207.

Jones, Peter. *History of the Ojebway Indians; with Especial Reference to Their Conversion to Christianity*. London: A. W. Bennett, 1861.

———. *Life and Journals of Kah-ke-wa-quo-nā-by: (Rev. Peter Jones) Wesleyan Missionary*. Toronto: A. Green, 1860.

Jones, William. *Ojibwa Texts*, edited by Truman Michelson. Vol. 7, pt. 1, Publications of the American Ethnological Society, edited by Franz Boas. New York: E. G. Stechert, 1917.

———. *Ojibwa Texts*, edited by Truman Michelson. Vol. 7, pt. 2, Publications of the American Ethnological Society, edited by Franz Boas. New York: G. E. Stechert, 1919.

Kakel, Carroll P., III. *A Post-Exceptionalist Perspective on Early American History: American Wests, Global Wests, and Indian Wars*. New York: Palgrave Pivot, 2019.

Kane, Paul. *Wanderings of an Artist among the Indians of North America*. London: Longman, Brown, Green, Longmans, and Roberts, 1859.

Kappler, Charles, ed. *Indian Affairs: Laws and Treaties*. 2 vols. Washington, DC: US Government Printing Office, 1904.

Karamanski, Theodore J. *Blackbird's Song: Andrew J. Blackbird and the Odawa People*. East Lansing: Michigan State University Press, 2012.

Katz, Irving I. *The Beth El Story, with a History of the Jews in Michigan before 1850*. Detroit, MI: Wayne State University Press, 1955.

Keating, William H. *Narrative of an Expedition to the Source of the St. Peter's River*. London, 1825.

King, Cecil O. *Balancing Two Worlds: Jean-Baptiste Assiginack and the Odawa Nation, 1768–1866*. Saskatoon, Saskatchewan: Cecil O. King, 2013.

Kinietz, Vernon. "Schoolcraft's Manuscript Magazines." *Bibliographic Society of America* 35, no. 2 (Second Quarter, 1941): 151–54.

Klein, Lawrence E. "Politeness and the Interpretation of the British Eighteenth Century." *The Historical Journal* 45, no. 4 (2002): 869–98.

Knight, Alan. "A Study in Failure: The Anglican Mission at Sault Ste. Marie, Upper Canada, 1830–1841." *Journal of the Canadian Church Historical Society* 63 (2003): 133–224.

Knight, Alan, and Janet E. Chute. "In the Shadow of the Thumping Drum: The Sault Metis—The People In-Between." In *Lines Drawn upon the Water: First Nations and the Great Lakes Borders and Borderlands*, edited by Karl S. Hele, 85–114. Ontario: Wilfred Laurier University Press, 2008.

Knox, Henry. "Report of Henry Knox, Secretary of War, to the President of the United States, Relating to the Several Indian Tribes," 7 August 1789. In *American State Papers* I Class II Indian Affairs, 12–54. Washington, DC: Gales & Seaton, 1832.

Knox, Vicesimus. *Elegant Extracts: Or, Useful and Entertaining Passages in Prose, Selected for the Improvement of Young Persons*. London, 1797.

Kohl, Johann Georg. *Kitchi-Gami. Wanderings Round Lake Superior*. London: Chapman and Hall, 1860.

Korsin, Paul J. "Reconfiguring the Past: The Eighteenth Century Confronts Oral Culture." *Yearbook of English Studies* 28 (1998): 235–49.

Krause, David J. "Testing a Tradition: Douglass Houghton and the Native Copper of Lake Superior." *Isis* 80. no. 4 (December 1989): 622–39.

Kugel, Rebecca. *To Be the Main Leaders of Our People: A History of Minnesota Ojibwe Politics, 1825–1898*. East Lansing: Michigan State University Press, 1998.

Langford, Paul. "The Uses of Eighteenth-Century Politeness." *Transactions of the Royal Historical Society* 12 (2002): 311–31.

LaPier, Rosalyn R. *Invisible Reality: Storytellers, Storytakers, and the Supernatural World of the Blackfeet*. Lincoln: University of Nebraska Press, 2017.

Larned, William Trowbridge. *American Indian Fairy Tales*. New York: P. F. Volland, 1921.

Lavender, David. *Fist in the Wilderness*. Lincoln: University of Nebraska Press, 1998.

Laws of the Territory of Michigan. Vol. 3. Lansing: W. S. George, 1874.

Leahey, Margaret J. "'Comment peut un muet prescher l'évangile?': Jesuit Missionaries and the Native Languages of New France." *French Historical Studies* 19, no. 1 (Spring 1995): 105–31.

Leighton, Douglass. "Jean-Baptiste Assiginack." *Dictionary of Canadian Biography*. www.biographi.ca/en/bio/assiginack_jean_baptiste_9E.html.

Leslie, John F. "Givins, James." *Dictionary of Canadian Biography*. www.biographi.ca/en/bio/givins_james_7E.html.

Littlefield, Daniel F., Jr., and James W. Parins. *Encyclopedia of American Indian Removal*. 2 vols. Santa Barbara, CA: Greenwood, 2011.

Livingston, John. *Livingston's Law Register: Containing the Name, Post-Office, County, and State of Every Lawyer in the United States*. New York, 1851.

Locke, John. *Two Treatises of Government*. Edited by Peter Laslett. Cambridge: Cambridge University Press, 2000.

Longfellow, Henry Wadsworth. *Evangeline: A Tale of Acadie*. Boston: William D. Ticknor and Company, 1847.

———. Vol. 3 of *The Letters of Henry Wadsworth Longfellow*, edited by Andrew Hillen. Cambridge, MA: Belknap Press of Harvard University, 1968.

———. *The Song of Hiawatha*. Edited by Daniel Aaron. London: J. M. Dent, 1991.

Lucas, Charles Prestwood. *The Canadian War of 1812*. Oxford: Clarendon Press, 1906.

Lyons, Scott Richard. *X-Marks: Native Signatures of Assent*. Minneapolis: University of Minnesota Press, 2010.

Macpherson, James. "A Dissertation Concerning the Antiquity &c. of the Poems of Ossian the Son of Fingal." Vol. 2 of *The Works of Ossian* by James Macpherson, i–xxiv. London: T. Becket and P. A. Dehondt, 1765.

Marryat, Frederick. *A Diary in America, with Remarks on Its Institutions*. 3 vols. London: Longman, Orme, Brown, Green & Longmans, 1839.

Martineau, Harriet. *Society in America*. 2 vols. Paris: Baudry's European Library, 1837.

Mason, Philip P., ed. and introd. *Schoolcraft's Ojibwa Lodge Stories: Life on the Lake Superior Frontier*. East Lansing: Michigan State University Press, 1997.

Mathews, Cornelius. *The Indian Fairy Book: From the Original Legends*. New York: Mason Brothers, 1856.

Maungwudaus. *An Account of the Chippewa Indians, Who Have Been Travelling among the Whites, in the United States, England, Ireland, Scotland, France, and Belgium*. Boston: Published by the Author, 1848.

Mazzuchelli, Samuel. *Memoirs Historical and Edifying of a Missionary Apostolic*. Chicago: W. F. Hall Printing Company, 1914.

McDonnell, Michael A. *Masters of Empire: Great Lakes Indians and the Making of America*. New York: Hill and Wang, 2015.

McDowell, John E. "Therese Schindler of Mackinac: Upward Mobility in the Great Lakes Fur Trade." *Wisconsin Magazine of History* 61, no. 2 (Winter 1977–1978): 125–43.

McKean, Thomas A. "The Fieldwork Legacy of James Macpherson." *Journal of American Folklore* 114, no. 454 (Autumn 2001): 447–63.

McKenney, Thomas. *Documents and Proceedings Relating to the Formation and Progress of a Board in the City of New York, for the Emigration, Preservation, and Improvement of the Aborigines of America, July 22, 1829*. New York: Vanderpool & Cole, 1829.

———. *Sketches of a Tour to the Lakes, of the Character and Customs of the Chippeway Indians, and of Incidents Connected with the Treaty of Fond du Lac*. Baltimore: Fielding Lucas, 1827.

McKenney, Thomas, and James B. Hall. *Indian Tribes of North America*. 2 vols. Philadelphia: D. Rice, 1872.

McLane, Maureen N., and Laura M. Slatkin. "British Romantic Homer: Oral Tradition, 'Primitive Poetry,' and the Emergence of Comparative Poetics in Britain, 1760–1830." *ELH* 78, no. 3 (Fall 2011): 687–714.

McLeod, Martin. "The Diary of Martin McLeod." Edited by Grace Lee Nute. *Minnesota Historical Society Bulletin* 4 (1922): 351–52.

McNally, Michael. *Honoring Elders: Aging, Authority, and Ojibwe Religion*. New York: Columbia University Press, 2009.

Mehta, Uday Singh. *Liberalism and Empire: A Study in Nineteenth-Century British Liberal Thought*. Chicago: University of Chicago Press, 1999.

Meyer, Melissa. *The White Earth Tragedy: Ethnicity and Dispossession at a Minnesota Anishinaabe Reservation, 1889–1920*. Lincoln: University of Nebraska Press, 1994.

Miller, Cary. *Ogimaag: Anishinaabeg Leadership, 1760–1845*. Lincoln: University of Nebraska Press, 2010.

Momryk, Myron. "Ermatinger, Charles Oakes." *Dictionary of Canadian Biography*. www.biographi.ca/en/bio/ermatinger_charles_oakes_6E.html.

Money, Robert. "'Elmwood' The Schoolcraft House." Architectural Plans. September 2010.
More, Hannah. *Christian Morals*. New York: Eastburn, Kirk, 1813.
Nardin, Jane. "Hannah More and the Problem of Poverty." *Texas Studies in Literature and Language* 43, no. 3 (Fall 2001): 267–84.
Neider, Charles, ed. *The Complete Tales of Washington Irving*. Garden City, NY: Doubleday, 1975.
Neill, Edward D. "History of the Ojibways, and Their Connection with Fur Traders, Based upon Official and Other Records." *Collections of the Minnesota Historical Society* 5 (1897): 395–510.
Nelson, George. *The Orders of the Dreamed: George Nelson on Cree and Northern Ojibwa Religion and Myth, 1823*. Edited by Jennifer S. H. Brown and Robert Brightman. Winnipeg: University of Manitoba Press, 1988.
A New Manual of Devotions. London: Printed for F. C. and J. Rivington, et al., 1815.
Nichols, John. "Ojibwa Oral Literature." In *Encyclopedia of Literature in Canada*, edited by William H. New, 842–44. Toronto: University of Toronto Press, 2002.
Noble, Louise. "'And Make Two Pasties of Your Shameful Heads': Medicinal Cannibalism and Healing the Body Politic in 'Titus Andronicus.'" *ELH* 70, no. 3 (Fall 2003): 677–708.
Noodin, Margaret. *Bawaajimo: A Dialect of Dreams in Anishinaabe Language and Literature*. East Lansing: Michigan State University Press, 2014.
Nute, Grace Lee. "A Description of Northern Minnesota by a Fur Trader in 1807." *Minnesota History Bulletin* 5, no. 1 (February 1923): 28–39.
———. "Documents Relating to James Dickson's Expedition." *Mississippi Valley Historical Review* 10 (1923–1924): 173–81.
———, ed. *Calendar of the American Fur Company's Papers, Part I: 1831–1840*. Annual Report of the American Historical Association for the Year 1944. Vol. 2. Washington, DC: US Government Printing Office, 1945.
Oberly, James Warren. *A Nation of Statesmen: The Political Culture of the Stockbridge-Munsee Mohicans 1815–1972*. Norman: University of Oklahoma Press, 2005.
O'Brien, Frank. *Names of Places of Interest on Mackinac Island, Michigan*. Michigan Historical Commission Bulletin No. 5. Lansing, MI: Wynkoop, Hallenbeck, Crawford, 1916.
O'Halloran, Clare. "Irish Re-Creations of the Gaelic Past: The Challenge of Macpherson's Ossian." *Past & Present* 124 (August 1989): 69–95.
Osborn, Chase S., and Stellanova Osborn. *Schoolcraft—Longfellow—Hiawatha*. Lancaster, PA: Jaques Cattell, 1942.
Osborne, A. C. "The Migration of Voyageurs from Drummond Island to Penetanguishene in 1828." *Ontario Historical Society* 3 (1904): 123–66.
Ostler, Jeffrey. *Surviving Genocide: Native Nations and the United States from the American Revolution to Bleeding Kansas*. New Haven, CT: Yale University Press, 2019.
Otis, Philo Adams. *The First Presbyterian Church 1833–1913*. Chicago: Fleming H. Revell, 1913.
Parins, James W. "Jane Johnston Schoolcraft." In *Native American Writers of the United States*, edited by Kenneth M. Roemer, 274–75. Detroit, MI: Thomson Gale, 1997.
Parker, Robert Dale, ed. *The Sound the Stars Make Rushing through the Sky: The Writings of Jane Johnston Schoolcraft*. Philadelphia: University of Pennsylvania Press, 2007.

Parkinson, Robert G. *Thirteen Clocks: How Race United the Colonies and Made the Declaration of Independence*. Chapel Hill: University of North Carolina Press, 2021.

Parkman, Francis. "Indian Superstitions." *North American Review* 3, no. 212 (July 1866): 1–18.

Parssinen, T. M. "Popular Science and Society: The Phrenology Movement of Early Victorian Britain." *Journal of Social History* 8, no. 1 (Autumn 1974): 1–20.

Patel, Raj, and Jason W. Moore. *A History of the World in Seven Cheap Things*. Berkeley: University of California Press, 2017.

Pearce, Roy Harvey. *Savagism and Civilization: A Study of the Indian and the American Mind*. Berkeley: University of California Press, 1988.

Pearson, Meg. "'That Bloody Mind I Think They Learned of Me': Aaron as Tutor in *Titus Andronicus*." *Shakespeare* 6, no. 1 (April 2010): 34–51.

Peters, Bernard C. "Indian-Grave Robbing at Sault Ste. Marie." *Michigan Historical Review* 23, no. 2 (Fall 1997): 49–80.

———. "Wa-bish-kee-pen-as and the Chippewa Reverence for Copper." *Michigan Historical Review* 15, no. 2 (Fall 1989): 47–60.

Peters, Richard, ed. *United States Statutes at Large*. Vol. 7. Boston: Charles C. Little and James Brown, 1846.

Pickering, John. Review of *A Discourse on the Religion of the Indian Tribes of North America; Delivered before the New York Historical Society, December 20, 1819*, by Samuel Farmer Jarvis. *North American Review and Miscellaneous Journal* 11, no. 28 (July 1820): 103–13.

———. Review of *An Account of the History, Manners and Customs of the Indian Who Once Inhabited Pennsylvania and the Neighbouring States* by John Heckewelder. *North American Review and Miscellaneous Journal* 9, no. 24 (June 1819): 155–78.

———. Review of *Report of the Corresponding Secretary (Peter S. Duponceau, Esq.) to the Historical and Literary Committee of the American Philosophical Society, of His Progress in the Investigation of the General Character and Forms of the Languages of the Americans Indians* and *A Correspondence between the Rev. John Heckewelder, of Bethlehem, and Peter S. Duponceau, Esq., Corresponding Secretary of the Historical and Literary Committee of the American Philosophical Society, Respecting the Languages of the American Indians* (Philadelphia, 1819). *North American Review and Miscellaneous Journal* 9, no. 24 (June 1819): 179–87.

Pitezel, John. *Life of Rev. Peter Marksman: An Ojibwa Missionary*. Cincinnati, OH: Western Methodist Book Concern, 1910.

Pomedli, Michael. *Living with Animals: Ojibwe Spirit Powers*. Toronto: University of Toronto Press, 2014.

Pope, Alexander. *The Whole Poetical Works of Alexander Pope*. Edited by Samuel Johnson. London: Andrew Miller, 1800.

Porter, James. "'Bring Me the Head of James Macpherson': The Execution of Ossian and the Wellsprings of Folkloristic Discourse." *Journal of American Folklore* 114, no. 454 (Autumn 2001): 396–435.

Potkay, Adam. "Virtue and Manners in Macpherson's *Poems of Ossian*." *PMLA* 107, no. 1 (January 1992): 120–30.

Radin, Paul. *The Trickster: A Study in American Indian Mythology*. New York: Schocken Books, 1976.

Radin, Paul, and A. B. Reagan. "Ojibwa Myths and Tales: The Manabozho Cycle." *Journal of American Folklore* 41, no. 159 (January–March 1928): 61–146.

Redix, Eric M. "'Our Hope and Our Protection': Misko-biiwaabik (Copper) and Tribal Sovereignty in Michigan." *American Indian Quarterly* 41, no. 3 (Summer 2017): 224–49.

Reed, Charles Bert. *Masters of the Wilderness*. Chicago: University of Chicago Press, 1914.

Reed, John Bailey. *Mackinac, Formerly Michilimackinac; A History and Guide Book, with Maps*. Grand Rapids, MI: Tradesman, 1909.

Rena-Dozier, Emily. "Hannah More and the Invention of Narrative Authority." *ELH* 71, no. 1 (Spring 2004): 209–27.

Richards, Eliza. *Gender and the Poetics of Reception in Poe's Circle*. Cambridge: Cambridge University Press, 2004.

Richardson, John. *The War of 1812*. London: Musson Book Co., 1902.

Riegel, Robert E. "The Introduction of Phrenology to the United States." *American Historical Review* 39, no. 1 (October 1933): 73–78.

Roberts, Alasdair. *America's First Great Depression: Economic Crisis and Political Disorder After the Panic of 1837*. Ithaca, NY: Cornell University Press, 2012.

———. "'An Ungovernable Anarchy': The United States' Response to Depression and Default, 1837–1848." *Intereconomics/Review of European Economic Policy* 45, no. 4 (August 2010): 196–202.

Robertson, Lindsay G. *Conquest by Law: How the Discovery of America Dispossessed Indigenous People of Their Lands*. Oxford: Oxford University Press, 2005.

Robertson, William. *The History of America*. Vol. 2. London: A. Strahan, 1803.

Rockwell, Stephen J. *Indian Affairs and the Administrative State in the Nineteenth Century*. New York: Cambridge University Press, 2010.

Round, Philip H. *Removable Type: Histories of the Book in Indian Country, 1663–1880*. Chapel Hill: University of North Carolina Press, 2010.

Rowe, Mrs. S. "Anderson Record, from 1699–1896." *Ontario Historical Society Papers and Records* 6 (1905): 109–35.

Roylance, Patricia Jane. "Northmen and Native Americans: The Politics of Landscape in the Age of Longfellow." *New England Quarterly* 80, no. 3 (September 2007): 452–58.

Ruckman, J. Ward. "Ramsay Crooks and the Fur Trade of the Northwest." *Minnesota History* 7, no. 2 (March 1926): 18–31.

Ruoff, A. LaVonne Brown. "Early Native American Women Authors: Jane Johnston Schoolcraft, Sarah Winnemucca, S. Alice Callahan, E. Pauline Johnson, and Zitkala-Sa." In *Nineteenth-Century American Women Writers: A Critical Reader*, edited by Karen L. Kilcup, 81–111. Malden, MA: Blackwell, 1998.

Samson, George Whitefield. *Henry R. Schoolcraft*. Washington, DC: Chronicle Print, 1864.

Saunt, Claudio. *Unworthy Republic: The Dispossession of Native Americans and the Road to Indian Territory*. New York: W. W. Norton, 2020.

Sayre, Robert F. *Thoreau and the Indians*. Princeton, NJ: Princeton University Press, 1977.

Schacker-Mill, Jennifer. "Otherness and Otherworldliness: Edward W. Lane's Ethnographic Treatment of *The Arabian Nights*." *Journal of American Folklore* 113, no. 448 (Spring 2000): 164–84.

Schenck, Theresa. "Lewis Saurin Johnston (1793–1825)." In *The Johnston Family of Sault Ste. Marie*, edited by Elizabeth Hambleton and Elizabeth Warren Stoutamire, 25–30. Washington, DC: John Johnston Family Association, 1992.

———. *The Voice of the Crane Echoes Far: The Sociopolitical Organization of the Lake Superior Ojibwa, 1640–1855*. New York: Garland, 1997.

Scheuermann, Mona. "Hannah More and the English Poor." *Eighteenth-Century Life* 25, no. 2 (Spring 2001): 237–51.

Schmaltz, Peter S. *The Ojibwa of Southern Ontario*. Toronto: University of Toronto Press, 1991.

Schoolcraft, Henry Rowe. *Algic Researches*. 2 vols. New York: J. & J. Harper, 1839.

———. "A Discourse Delivered on the Anniversary of the Historical Society of Michigan, June 4, 1830." In *Historical and Scientific Sketches of Michigan, Comprising a Series of Discourses Delivered before the Historical Society of Michigan, and Other Interesting Papers Relative to the Territory*, 51–109. Detroit, MI: Stephen Wells and George L. Whitney, 1834.

———. *Indian Melodies*. New York: Elam Bliss, 1830.

———. *Information Respecting the History, Condition and Prospects of the Indian Tribes of the United States*. 6 vols. Philadelphia: Lippincott, Grambo & Company, 1853–57.

———. "Memoir of John Johnston." *Michigan Historical Collections* 36 (1908): 53–94.

———. "Moowis, or The Indian Coquette." *Columbian Lady's and Gentleman's Magazine, Embracing Literature in Every Department* 1 (February 1844): 90.

———. *Myth of Hiawatha, and Other Oral Legends, Mythologic and Allegoric, of the North American Indians*. Philadelphia: J. B. Lippincott, 1856.

———. "Mythology, Superstitions and Languages of the North American Indians." *Literary and Theological Review* 2, no. 5 (March 1835): 96–121.

———. *Narrative of an Expedition through the Upper Mississippi to Itasca Lake* (New York, 1834).

———. *Narrative Journal of Travels through the Northwestern Regions of the United States*. Albany, NY: E. & E. Hosford, 1821.

———. "Notes for a Memoir of Mrs. Henry Rowe Schoolcraft." *Michigan Historical Collections* 36 (1908): 95–100.

———. *Oneota; or Characteristics of the Red Race in America from Original Notes*. New York: Wiley & Putnam, 1845.

———. "Our Indian Policy: With a Map." *United States Magazine and Democratic Review* 14, no. 68 (February 1844): 169–84.

———. *Personal Memoirs of a Residence of Thirty Years with the Indian Tribes on the American Frontiers*. Philadelphia: Lippincott, Grambo, & Co., 1851.

———. Review of *La Decouverte des Sources du Mississippi* by J. C. Beltrami (New Orleans, 1824). *North American Review* 27, no. 60 (July 1828): 89–114.

———. Review of *Proceedings of the Fourteenth Annual Report of the Board of Managers of the Baptist Convention . . .* [and] *A Discourse on the Occasion of Forming the African Mission School Society*. *North American Review* 29, no. 63 (April 1829): 354–69.

———. *The Rise of the West: or, a Prospect of the Mississippi Valley, a Poem*. New York: William Applegate, 1841.

———. *Schoolcraft's Ojibwe Lodge Stories: Life on the Lake Superior Frontier*. Ed. and introd. by Philip P. Mason. East Lansing: Michigan State University Press, 1997.

---. "Sketches of a Trip to Lake Superior." *Knickerbocker* 14, no. 3 (September 1839): 254–56.

---. *Summary Narrative of an Exploratory Expedition to the Sources of the Mississippi River, in 1820.* Philadelphia: Lippincott, Grambo, and Company, 1855.

---. *Travels in the Central Portions of the Mississippi Valley.* New York: Collins and Hannay, 1825. 6

---. "Travels of an Indian Prince in the United States." *Knickerbocker* 6, no. 5 (November 1835): 425–30.

---. "Travels of an Indian Prince in the United States. *Knickerbocker* 6, no. 6 (December 1835): 503–8.

Schoolcraft, Jane Johnston. "Mukakee Mindemoea; or, The Toad-Woman." Part 2 of *Oneota, or The Race of America*, by Henry Rowe Schoolcraft, 79–81. New York: Burgess, Stringer, 1844.

---. "Vision of Catherine Wabose." Vol. 1 of *Historical and Statistical Information Respecting the History, Condition and Prospects of the Indian Tribes of the United States*, by Henry Rowe Schoolcraft, 388–401. Philadelphia: Lippincott, Grambo & Co., 1851.

Schorer, C. E. *Indian Tales of C. C. Trowbridge.* Brighton: Green Oak, 1986.

---. "Indian Tales of C. C. Trowbridge: The Gambler." *Midwest Folklore* 13, no. 4 (Winter 1963–64): 229–35.

---. "Indian Tales of C. C. Trowbridge: The Red Head." *Midwest Folklore* 10, no. 2 (Summer 1960): 86–95.

---. "Indians Tales of C. C. Trowbridge: The Star Woman." *Midwest Folklore* 12, no. 1 (Spring 1962): 20–24.

---. "Indian Tales of C. C. Trowbridge: The Toadstool Man." *Midwest Folklore* 9, no. 3 (Autumn 1959): 139–44.

Shakespeare, William. *Titus Andronicus.* Vol. 8 of *The Plays of William Shakespeare.* London: Printed for J. Nichols and Son, 1811.

Sheehan, Bernard. *Seeds of Extinction: Jeffersonian Philanthropy and the American Indian.* New York: W. W. Norton, 1774.

Shenstone, William. *The Poetical Works of William Shenstone.* Vol. 1. London: Joseph Wen, 1780.

Sigourney, Lydia H. *Pocahontas, and Other Poems.* New York: Harper & Brothers, 1841.

Simpson, Leanne Betasamosake. *Dancing on Our Turtle's Back: Stories of Nishinaabeg Re-Creation, Resurgence and a New Emergence.* Winnipeg: Arbeiter Ring, 2011.

---. *A Short History of the Blockade: Giant Beavers, Diplomacy, and Regeneration in Nishnaabewin.* Saskatoon: University of Alberta Press, 2021.

Skinner, Constance. *Adventurers of Oregon: A Chronicle of the Fur Trade.* New Haven, CT: Yale University Press, 1920.

Sleeper-Smith, Susan. *Indian Women and French Men: Rethinking Cultural Encounter in the Western Great Lakes.* Amherst: University of Massachusetts Press, 2001.

---. "'An Unpleasant Transaction on This Frontier': Challenging Female Autonomy and Authority at Michilimackinac." *Journal of the Early Republic* 35 (Fall 2005): 417–43.

Smith, Donald B. *Mississauga Portraits: Ojibwe Voices from Nineteenth-Century Canada.* Toronto: University of Toronto, 2013.

Smith, Elizabeth Oakes. "Margaret Fuller." *Phrenological Journal and Science of Health* 3, no. 87 (1889): 104.

———. "Mrs. Henry R. Schoolcraft." *Baldwin's Monthly* 8, no. 3 (March 1874): 2.
———. "Na-wi-qua. A Metowac Legend." In *American Wild Flowers and Their Native Haunts*, edited by Emma Embury, 193–94. New York: D. Appleton, 1845.
Smith, G. Hubert. "Count Andreani: A Forgotten Traveler." *Minnesota History* 19, no. 1 (March 1938): 34–40.
Smith, Joshua Toulmin. *Journal in America, 1837–1838*. Edited by Floyd Benjamin Streeter. Metuchen, NJ: Printed for Charles F. Heartman, 1925.
Smith, Linda Tuhiwai. *Decolonizing Methodologies: Research and Indigenous Peoples.* London: Zed, 2004.
Smith, Seba. *Powhatan: A Metrical Romance in Seven Cantos.* New York: Harper & Brothers, 1841.
Spaulding, K. A. "A Note on Astoria: Irving's Use of the Robert Stuart Manuscript." *American Literature* 22, no. 2 (May 1950): 151–57.
Spry, Adam. *Our War Paint Is Writers' Ink: Anishinaabe Literary Transnationalism.* Albany: State University of New York Press, 2018.
Steensma, David P., Carole A. Roede, and Robert A. Kyle. "Henry David Thoreau's Final Journey: Minnesota." *Mayo Clinic Proceedings* 93, no. 7 (July 2018): e75–e76.
Stewart, W. Brian. *The Ermatingers: A 19th Century Ojibwa-Canadian Family.* Vancouver: University of British Columbia Press, 2007.
Storrow, Samuel A. "The North-West in 1817: A Contemporary Letter." *Wisconsin Historical Collections* 6 (1872): 154–87.
Strickland, W. P. *Old Mackinaw.* Philadelphia: James Challen, 1860.
Sutherland, James. *State of Michigan Gazetteer and Business Directory for 1856-7.* Detroit, MI, 1856.
Syba, Michelle. "After Design: Joseph Addison Discovers Beauties." *Studies in English Literature 1500–1900* 49, no. 3 (Summer 2009): 615–35.
Tanner, Herbert R. "Sketch of George and James M. Boyd." *Wisconsin Historical Collections* 12 (1892): 266–98.
Tanner, John. *A Narrative of the Captivity and Adventures of John Tanner.* Edited by Edwin James. Minneapolis, MN: Ross and Haines, 1956.
Taylor, Alan. *The Civil War of 1812: American Citizens, British Subjects, Irish Rebels, and Indian Allies.* New York: Knopf, 2010.
Teuton, Christopher. "Indigenous Orality and Oral Literatures." In *Oxford Handbook of Indigenous American Literature*, edited by James M. Cox and Daniel Heath Justice, 167–74. New York: Oxford University Press, 2014.
Thatcher, Benjamin Bussey. *Indian Biography: Or An Historical Account of Those Individuals Who Have Been Distinguished among the North American Natives as Orators, Warriors, Statesmen, and Other Remarkable Characters.* New York: J. & J. Harper, 1832.
Thomas, Clara. *Love and Work Enough: The Life of Anna Jameson.* Toronto: University of Toronto Press, 1967.
Thompson, Charles N. *Sons of the Wilderness: John and William Conner.* Indianapolis: Indiana Historical Society, 1937.
Thoreau, Henry David. *Thoreau's Minnesota Journey.* Edited by Walter Harding. Geneseo, NY: Thoreau Society, 1962.
Treuer, Anton. *The Assassination of Hole in the Day.* St. Paul, MN: Borealis Books, 2011.

———. *The Language Warrior's Manifesto: How to Keep Our Languages Alive No Matter the Odds*. St. Paul: Minnesota Historical Society Press, 2020.

———. *Living Our Language: Ojibwe Tales & Oral Histories: A Bilingual Anthology*. St. Paul: Minnesota Historical Society Press, 2001.

Tully, James. "Rediscovering America: The Two Treatises and Aboriginal Rights." In *An Approach to Political Philosophy: Locke in Contexts*, 137–78. London: Cambridge University Press, 1993.

Turner, George. *Traits of Indian Character; as Generally Applicable to the Aborigenes of North America*. 2 vols. Philadelphia: Key and Biddle, 1836.

Tuttle, Sarah. *Letters on the Mission to the Ojibwa Indians*. Boston: Massachusetts Sabbath School Society, 1839.

Twain, Mark. *Life on the Mississippi*. New York: Harper & Brothers, 1917.

Van Fleet, James Alvin. *Old and New Mackinac*. Cincinnati, OH: Western Methodist Book Concern, 1874.

Van Kirk, Sylvia. *Many Tender Ties: Women in Fur-Trade Society, 1670–1870*. Norman: University of Oklahoma Press, 1983.

Vance, Norman. "Ovid in the Nineteenth Century." *Ovid Renewed: Ovidian Influences on Literature and Art from the Middle Ages to the Twentieth Century*, edited by Charles Martindale, 215–32. New York: Cambridge University Press, 1988.

Vecsey, Christopher. *Traditional Ojibwa Religion and Its Historical Changes*. Philadelphia: American Philosophical Society, 1983.

Vennum, Thomas. "The Ojibwa Begging Dance." In *Music and Context: Essays for John M. Ward*, edited by Anne Dhu Shapiro, 54–78. Cambridge, MA: Harvard University Press, 1985.

Waddilove, W. J. D. *The Stewart Missions*. London: J. Hatchard, 1838.

Wallace, Anthony F. C. *Jefferson and the Indians: The Tragic Fate of the First Americans*. Cambridge, MA: Harvard University Press, 1999.

Walls, Laura Dassow. *Thoreau: A Life*. Chicago: University of Chicago Press, 2017.

Warburton, Warren. *Divine Legation of Moses Demonstrated in Nine Books*. Vol. 3. London: A Millar and R. Tonson, 1765.

Warner, Marina. *Fantastic Metamorphoses, Other Worlds: Ways of Telling the Self*. Oxford: Oxford University Press, 2002.

———. *Stranger Magic: Charmed States and the Arabian Nights*. Cambridge, MA: Harvard University Press, 2012.

Warren, William Whipple. *History of the Ojibway Nation*. Minnesota Historical Society Collections 5 (1885): 21–394.

Watson, Blake A. "The Impact of the American Doctrine of Discovery on Native Land Rights in Australia, Canada, and New Zealand." *Seattle University Law Review* 34, no. 2 (Winter 2011): 507–52.

Weaver, Margaret Curtiss. *The Descendants of John Johnston and Oshauguscodaywayquay of Sault Ste. Marie, Michigan*. N.p.: n.d.

Weaver, William. *Register of Officers and Agents, Civil, Military, and Naval, in the Service of the United States on the Thirtieth September, 1833*. Washington, DC: Francis Preston Blair, 1833.

Weygant, Charles H. *The Hull Family in America*. Pittsfield, MA: Hull Family Association, 1913.

Whiting, Henry. *Ontwa: The Son of the Forest*. New York: Wiley & Halsted, 1822.

———. Review of *Algic Researches* by Henry Rowe Schoolcraft. *North American Review* 49, no. 105 (October 1839): 354–72.

———. *Sannillac, A Poem. With Notes by Lewis Cass and Henry Rowe Schoolcraft, Esqs.* Boston: Carter, Hendee and Babcock, 1831.

Widder, Keith R. *Battle for the Soul: Métis Children Encounter Evangelical Protestants at Mackinaw Mission, 1823–1837.* East Lansing: Michigan State University Press, 1999.

Willsky-Ciollo, Lydia. "Apostles of Wilderness: American Indians and Thoreau's Theology of the World." *New England Quarterly* 91, no. 4 (December 2018): 551–91.

Wisecup, Kelly. *Assembled for Use: Indigenous Compilation and the Archives of Native American Literatures*. New Haven, CT: Yale University Press, 2021.

Witgen, Michael. *An Infinity of Nations: How the Native New World Shaped Early America*. Philadelphia: University of Pennsylvania Press, 2012.

———. *Seeing Red: Indigenous Land, American Expansion, and the Political Economy of Plunder in North America*. Chapel Hill: University of North Carolina Press, 2022.

Wolfe, Patrick. "Settler Colonialism and the Elimination of the Native." *Journal of Genocide Research* 8, no. 4 (December 2006): 387–409.

Wood, Edwin Orin. *Historic Mackinac*. New York: Macmillan, 1918.

Wood, Ellen Meiksins. *The Origin of Capitalism: A Longer View*. London: Verso, 2017.

Wood, George B. *A Biographical Memoir of Samuel George Morton*. Philadelphia: Printed by T. K. and P. G. Collins, 1853.

Wood, George Bacon, and Franklin Bache. *The Dispensatory of the United States of America*. Philadelphia: Grigg and Elliot, 1845.

Wood, William Charles Henry, ed. *Select British Documents of the Canadian War of 1812*. 3 vols. Toronto: Champlain Society, 1920.

Index

Abanokue, 59
Abbott, Samuel, 260, 300
Algic Researches: Charlotte's role in, 234–39; Henry Rowe Schoolcraft efforts to rewrite stories, 7–8, 113, 284–85, 331–34; Henry Rowe Schoolcraft efforts to use *Algic Researches* to criticize Jane Johnston Schoolcraft, 292–95; Henry Rowe Schoolcraft production of, 188, 273, 280; Henry Rowe Schoolcraft scholarly apparatus for stories, 6, 7, 109, 229, 285; Jane Johnston Schoolcraft role in, 6, 294–95, 295–96, 311, 328–30, 334; reviews of, 10–11, 272–73, 293–95, 386n40; scholarship on, 10; white readers, 10–12, 110, 234; William's role in, 185, 230, 299–300, 339–40
American Fur Company, 48, 164–66, 196, 203, 209, 225–26, 228, 302
Anderson, Thomas, 127, 129–30, 238
Apess, William, 9
Arabian Nights, The, 12, 77, 272, 293, 294, 330
Askin, John, Jr., 23–24
Assiginack, 37, 146–47, 339
Assiginack, Francis, 339
Astor, John Jacob, 48, 132, 187
Audrain, Francis, 129, 137–38, 178, 262
Audrain, Mrs., 138, 262
Aunce, 207
Awbota-ki-chick, 86

Bailly, Eleanor, 8, 366n17
Bancroft, George, 287
Barbour, James, 91–92
Bethune, Angus, 139
Biddle, Edward, 226, 260, 264, 300
Big Cloud, 166–69, 369n15
Big Sail, 207

Bigsby, Jeremiah, 36–37
bimaadiziwin, 29, 45, 48
Bingham, Abel, 141–42, 147, 149, 299, 323, 334–35, 338
Bingham, Hannah, 142, 338
Blackbird, Andrew, 225
Blair, Hugh, 5, 37, 68–69, 87, 191–92
Borrows, John, 19
Boudinot, Elias, 9
Boutwell, William, 142, 147, 150, 169, 191
Bowen, Joseph, 138–39, 145
Bow-e-ting, 3–4, 102–3, 176, 286
Brackenridge, Hugh Henry, 16–18
Bremer, Richard, 57, 58, 226, 303, 304
Brinton, Daniel Garrison, 10, 180
Brown, Catherine, 111–12
Bryant, William Cullen, 307, 309, 308
Bunnell, Lafayette, 227–28
Butler, Benjamin Franklin, 303–4

Cacabichin, 75, 86
Cadotte, Janette Piquette. *See* Sangemanqua
Cadotte, Jean-Baptiste Jr., 33, 37, 38, 94, 339
Calhoun, John C., 39, 49–51, 53, 58, 60–61, 72, 79
Cameron, Eliza, 322
Cameron, James, 142, 149, 238, 334
Cass, Lewis: C. C. Trowbridge, 72–73; "Chippewa murderers," 83, 93; George Johnston, 87, 96–97, 179, 184; government position, 75–76, 97, 100, 127, 164, 212, 215; Heckewelder and Du Ponceau, 62; Indigenous people, opinion of, 49, 60–61; Indigenous stories, fascination for, 56, 70, 76–77, 101; intellectual pretensions, 70, 101–2, 206–7; knowledge of Jane Johnston Schoolcraft's writing, 70; questionnaire, 55–56, 61–62; relationship

Cass (cont.)
  with Henry Rowe Schoolcraft, 112, 119, 206, 207, 213, 304; researches, 2, 6, 18, 70–71, 72–74, 76, 79, 89–91, 174; Sassaba, 51–52; Treaty of Fond du Lac (1826), 93–94; Treaty of Prairie du Chien, 82–83; Treaty of Sault Ste. Marie, (1820), 50–53; Treaty of Washington (1836), 8, 205–6; writing, 89–91, 132–33
Cherokee language, 67
Cherokee Nation, 117, 205–6, 207, 260–61, 304, 305
Chingachgook, 91
Clark, William, 82, 91
Clarke, Samuel, 200, 328
Clarke, Sarah Freeman, 328
Clarke, William Hull, 189, 200, 239, 251, 311, 328–29
Clitz, John, 207
Conant, Samuel, 78–79, 86, 125
Cooper, James Fenimore, 5, 91, 194, 306
Copway, George, 146, 339
Crawford, T. Hartley, 300
Crooks, Hester, 59
Crooks, Ramsay, 48–49, 59, 204, 287, 305
Cusick, David, 9, 10
Cutler, Enos, 82–83

Davenport, Ambrose, 230, 349n10
Davenport, Susan, 230
Declaration of Independence, 13, 18, 206
Delaware language, 62, 64–68
Deshome, Francis, 129, 139
Deshome, Mrs., 139
Dickens, Charles, 307–8
Dickson, John, 226–27
Dougherty, Peter, 276–77, 382–83n90
Draper, Lyman, 73
Drew, John, 209, 226, 260
Dubois, Louise. *See* Okimabinesikwe
Duck Wing, 89
Du Ponceau, Peter S., 62, 64–70, 90, 101, 116, 183
Du Sable, Pierre, 170
Duvernay, Pierre, 86–87

Embury, Emma, 306
Ermatinger, Charles Oakes, 128
Everlasting Standing Woman, 173–74, 334

Featherstonhaugh, George William, 197–99, 266
Ferry, William, 135, 193, 276
Foot, Lyman, 96–97, 100
Franklin, Benjamin, 15
Fuller, Margaret, 309, 320, 328–31

Galland, Antoine, 77
Gallatin, Albert, 284–85, 304
Gardiner, Harriet, 137–39, 141, 145
Gilman, Chandler Robbins, 188, 199–200, 204, 229, 240, 287, 307, 320, 328–29, 332
Gitche Gauzinee, 5, 43–44, 47, 95, 333
Gitche Iauba, 59–60, 88–89, 123
Givins, James, 193
Great Peace of Montreal (1701), 271
Greeley, Horace, 310, 330
Grimm Brothers, The, 73–74
Griswold, Rufus, 306, 308, 330–31

Hamelin, Augustin, 210–11, 300
Harris, Carey A., 260
Haudensaunee Confederacy, 8, 9, 41, 247, 271
Heckewelder, John, 62–70, 71, 90–91, 116, 183, 332
Henry, George. *See* Maungwudaus
Hoffman, Charles Fenno, 186–87, 199, 204, 229, 287, 305, 309, 330, 388n95, 390n30
Hoffman, Martin, 188, 199, 307
Hoffman, Ogden, 310
Holiday, John, 23, 32, 50, 59–60, 75, 88–89, 130, 149, 209–10
Holiday, Mary, 8, 209
Holiday, Nancy, 356n28
Holiday, William, 130–31, 209
Holmes, Andrew, 24, 198, 207, 260, 303
Houghton, Douglass, 149
Hulbert, John, 130, 150, 207, 214, 300, 302, 390n24, 391n37
Hulbert, Mary Schoolcraft, 82, 144
Hull, Gen. William, 200
Hunter, John Dunn, 89

Irving, Washington, 5, 185–88, 206, 265, 284–86, 307

Jackson, Andrew, 304
James, Edwin, 139, 142, 326, 335
Jameson, Anna Brownell: and Catherine Maria Sedgwick on Jane Johnston Schoolcraft, 285–86; Charlotte and William McMurray, 240, 247; Charlotte Johnston McMurray, 241; collecting information, 248–49; collecting skulls, 247; fixation on Jane Johnston Schoolcraft, 242–43, 248–49, 273–74; Henry Rowe Schoolcraft on Jane Johnston Schoolcraft to, 322; Henry Rowe Schoolcraft request to edit stories, 284–85; Indigenous people, 248, 251, 285; Indigenous storytelling, 244; Indigenous women, 242, 243–44; Jane Johnston Schoolcraft letter to, 249–51; Jane Johnston Schoolcraft relationship with, 239–40, 246–47, 311; Longfellow and, 332; Margaret Fuller on, 328–30; marriage and separation, 240–41; Ozhaawshkodewikwe, 245–46; plan to write about Indigenous women, 239–40; Rufus Griswold on, 330–31; visit to Sault Ste Marie, 24–25, 244–46
Jameson, Robert Sympson, 240–41
Jane Johnston Schoolcraft: *Algic Researches*, 1–2, 293–95; Anna Jameson, 239–40, 242–47, 248–51, 273–74, 328–31; Catherine Maria Sedgwick, 285–86, 307; charges against Henry Rowe Schoolcraft, 300–303; Charles Fenno Hoffman, 229; Charlotte Johnston McMurray, 31, 127, 128, 129, 132, 148, 169–70, 225, 287, 304, 305, 312; Charlotte Wabose, 140, 150, 197, 204, 206, 212–13; childhood and education, 4, 5–6, 26–29, 31, 127; children, 83–84, 85–86, 124, 130, 141, 214, 286, 288–92; death, 312, 321–23; description, 95, 197, 242, 309, 310–11; diaries, 128–31, 137, 301; Elmwood, 143; E. O. Smith, 308–12, 334; *Hiawatha*, 332–33; illness, 276; Ireland, 1809, 3; John Johnston, 23–24, 25–27, 29–31, 39–40, 115, 131–32; laudanum, 214, 263, 287; literary ambitions, 311; *Literary Voyager*, 101–9, 113–15, 121–23; Louisa Piquette, 263–64; Mackinac Island, 1814, 23–25; Margaret Fuller, 328–31; New York City, 1825, 78–81; 1839, 285–91; 1841–1842, 303–12; notoriety, 78, 95, 134–35, 294–95, 305–6; Ogeewyahnoquotokwa, 172–78, 212–13; Ozhaawshkodewikwe's care for, 178, 204, 225, 263; Ozhaawshkodewikwe's training of, 3, 28–29; Pictured Rocks, 1838, 278–80; poems: "An Answer, to a remonstrance on my being melancholy, by a Gentleman, who, *sometimes* had a *little pleasing* touch of melancholy himself," 57, "Invocation: To my Maternal Grandfather on hearing his descent from Chippewa ancestors misrepresented," 59, "Language Divine!" 27–28, "Lines written at Castle Island, Lake Superior," 279–80, "A mother's lament for the absence of a child," 85–86, "On leaving my children John and Jane at School, in the Atlantic States, and preparing to return to the interior," 289–91, "Pensive Hours," 53, "Sweet Willy," 124; post-war anthologies, 39–48; stories: "Origin of the Miscodeed, or, The Maid of Taquimenon," 121–23, "The Two Ghosts, or Hospitality Rewarded," 45–48, 101, 122, 333; tension in marriage, 1–2, 83–84, 111–13, 127, 130–31, 140–41, 180–83, 204, 213, 265, 291–93; translations: "Confessions of Catherine Ogee Wyan Akwut Okwa; or The Woman of the Blue-Robed Cloud, The Prophetess of Chegoimegon," 170–78, "Corn Story" ["Mon-daw-min; or The Origin of Indian Corn"], 1–2, 7, 293, 295, 299, 332, "Do not—do not weep for me," 41, "The Forsaken Brother," 103, 104–6, 188, 200, 240, "The Little Spirit, or Boy-Man," 295–96, "Mishosha, or The Magician and His Daughters," 103, 106–9, 240, "Moowis the Indian Coquette," 113–15, 122, "Mukakee Mindemoea; or, The Toad

Jane Johnston Schoolcraft (cont.)
Woman," 281–83, 298–99; "The O-jib-way Maid," 96, "The Origin of the Robin," 42–43, 101, 103, 122, 188, 200, 240; "Origin of the White-fish," 103–4, 106; "Peboan and Seegwun," 42–43, 56, 95, 101, 333; "Song for a Lover Killed in Battle," 44–45; "Wa-wa-be-zo-win; or The Swing," 295, 296–98; Treaty of Washington (1836), 208–9, 226; Waabojiig, 59; Washington, D.C., society, 286; William Hull Clarke, 189–90, 200–201, 251, 311

Jarvis, Samuel Farmer, 67–68
Jefferson, Thomas, 15, 24, 61
Johnson, Samuel, 5, 35–36, 69
Johnson v. McIntosh (1823), 17–18, 71–72
Johnston, Basil, 108–9
Johnston, Eliza: and American society, 31–32; Anna Maria, 391n37; Christianity, 31, 141, 148; court case (1843), 323–25; education, 5, 49; end of life, 394n70; finances, 203, 262, 325; James L. Schoolcraft, 178, 326–27; Jane Johnston Schoolcraft, 127–28, 204, 225; Johnston homestead, 334–35; Ojibwemowin, 129; Ozhaawshkodewikwe, 31–32; refusal to speak English, 31, 96, 274; traditional crafts, 203, 205;War of 1812, 31–32; writing, 70 Johnston, George, 23–25, 32–33, 34–39, 48–49, 50–53, 249, 262–63, 273; additional claims (1837), 260; court case (1843), 323–25; death of James Schoolcraft, 326; exploration, 194–95, 274–75; George Johnston (London, UK), 191–92, 274–75; government employment, 87–89, 178–79, 193–95, 302; John Dickson, 226–27; marriages and children, 144–45, 202–3, 262, 335, 394n73; relationship with Henry Rowe Schoolcraft, 192–95, 325–26; translations: "Burial Song," 339, "Narrative of Wabwindigo," 317–18, 335–36, "Penayshee's Song," 336–37, 395nn80–81, "Tsheetshegwyung's war song," 41, "The traditionary story of Mash qua shay guong, or the Red Head and his two sons, who became orphans," 332; writing, 5–6, 8, 39–43, 98, 335–339

Johnston, George (London, UK), 191–92, 226, 274–75, 287, 313
Johnston, Henry William, 87, 194, 262, 274, 394n73
Johnston, John: attitudes, 25–26, 58; children out of wedlock, 29, 192, 287, 322; concerns about Lewis Johnston, 38; death, 131–32; fascination for Indigenous narrative, 4–5; Gen. William Hull, 200; George Johnston, 48–49; influence on his children, 5–6, 25; knowledge of Ojibwemowin, 3, 115; La Pointe, 2, 227; literary interests, 5, 39, 43–44, 333; oil portrait, 245, 335; relations with Americans, 32–33, 55; relationship with Jane Johnston Schoolcraft, 3, 26–27, 134, 226; Robert McDouall, 33; Sangemanqua, 38; Thomas McKenney, 94–95; War of 1812, 23–24, 250n13
Johnston, John George, 87, 194, 262, 274, 394n73
Johnston, John McDouall, 4, 49, 202, 323, 335, 351n54, 394n70
Johnston, Lewis, 4, 25, 29, 33, 38, 82, 94, 247, 274
Johnston, Louisa, 49, 87, 184, 248–49, 274, 394n73
Johnston, Mary Rice, 299, 335, 337, 394n73
Johnston, Molly, 335
Johnston, Polly, 38
Johnston, Sophia, 76, 138, 141
Johnston, Susan. *See* Ozhaawshkodewikwe
Johnston, William, 4, 6, 8–9, 225, 228, 229–30, 262, 264, 265; charges against Henry Rowe Schoolcraft, 299–303; court case (1843, 324–26; *Hiawatha*, 339; at Leech Lake, 164–69; narrative accounts: "Letters on the Fur Trade in 1833," 164–66, "Manners and Customs of the Leech Lake Indians," 167–69, "Native Comity," 118–19, "Notes on the Manner in Which the Chippewas Spend Their Time, while on Their Wintering Grounds," 167, "Traits of Personal

Attachment among the Ojibways," 119–21, 232; relationship with Henry Rowe Schoolcraft, 118–21, 185, 208, 273, 319–21; Thoreau, Henry David, 340–41; translations: "Madjee Monedo and the Genius of Benevolence," 231–33, "The Moose and Woodpecker," 332, "Ogeeg, or the Fisher," 333, "Papuckewis," 109–10, 179, 333, "Paup-Puk-Keewis," 216–24, 233–34, 332–33, "Saganaw's Story" ["The Weendigoes"], xi, 108–9, 230–31, 345n1, "Saugemau," 271–72; "Shagwonabee," 269–70, "Six Indians Visit to the Sun and Moon," 252–59, 272–73, "Story of Manahbosho" ["Manabozho; or, The Great Incarnation of the North"], 6, 10, 153–63, 180–81, 332–33, "Story of Meshegenabigo" ["Iamo; or The Undying Head"], 270–71, 332, "The White Stone Canoe," 332–33; Treaty of Washington (1836), 206, 207–8; Wauchusco, 266–73; writing, 102–3, 108, 110, 116, 118–21, 164–69, 179–80, 228, 230–34, 319–21
Johnston Estate, 192, 196–97, 204, 207, 226, 260, 303, 312, 324
Jones, Peter. *See* Kahkewaquonaby

Kabaosa, 305
Kahgegahgabowh. *See* Copway, George
Kahkewaquonaby, 146, 181, 193, 339
Karahmannie, 33
Kawawbandebay, 75, 86–87
Kearney, Henry, 192–93, 195
Kewaynokwut, 75, 83, 86, 88
Knox, Henry, 15, 16

Laframboise, Josette, 24, 31, 59
Laframboise, Magdelaine, 24, 59, 146, 170, 198, 209, 242, 356n26
Laird, Robert McMurtrie, 58, 78
LaPier, Roslyn, 11, 347n41
Lawyer, David, 147
Le Clair, 38
L'Espagnol, 24
Leveque, Henri, 129, 138, 141
Little Corbeau, 33

Little Crow, 340
Little Frenchman. *See* Waymitiggoashance
Little Salt, 10, 234–39, 328
Locke, John, 13–15, 16, 71, 126
London Quarterly Review, 90
Longfellow, Henry Wadsworth, 8, 307, 330, 331–34, 364n59, 396n90
Lyon, Lucius, 207, 209

Macomb, Alexander, 38–39, 286
Macpherson, James, 4–5, 37, 68–69, 284–85
Ma Mongazida, 59, 121–22
Manabozho story cycle, 4, 6–7, 8, 10, 153–63, 164, 178–81, 347n40; Longfellow's use of in *Hiawatha*, 8, 332–34
Mananowe, 128
Mann, Horace Jr., 340
Marshall, John, 71, 310
Mathews, Cornelius, 8
Maungwudaus, 147, 339
McDonald, Neddy, 247
McDouall, Robert, 23–24, 32–33, 37, 38, 40, 50, 52
McKenney, Thomas, 31, 91–96, 127, 134, 143, 179, 244, 287, 320, 332
McMurray, Charlotte Johnston: Anna Jameson, 240, 241–42, 243, 272–73, 321; Anna Maria, 327; children, 178, 378n51; Christianity, 148; commonplace book, 5, 150, 339; death, 394n73; education, 5, 31, 49; Jane Johnston Schoolcraft, 127, 128, 129, 132, 225, 304–5, 312; Little Salt, 10, 328; marriage, 59, 149–50, 169, 170, 262–63, 378–79n49; Ojibwemowin, 95–96, 129, 142, 148; singing, 96, 148; travelers, 239; Treaty of Washington (1836), 226; writing, 6, 8, 10, 70, 228, 229, 234–39, 298–99, 332, 339
McMurray, William: additional claims (1837), 260; Anna Jameson, 240, 242, 246, 249, 273–74; death of Jane Johnston Schoolcraft, 312, 322; Eliza Johnston, 325; family, 149, 193; James Schoolcraft, 178; Jane Johnston Schoolcraft, 178, 263, 275, 280; Johnston Estate, 312; marriage, 150, 170, 327; mission, 149–50, 239, 262, 273;

McMurray (cont.)
  Ozhaawshkodewikwe, 178, 203, 228, 235, 263; Treaty of Washington (1836), 226, 260; war losses reimbursement, 195–96
Medill, William, 319
Mitchell, Andrew, 195
Mitchell, David, 33, 36, 59, 195
Mitchell, Elizabeth, 33, 40, 59
Monroe, James, 83, 89
Monsoketick, 86
Moozobodo, 88–89
More, Hannah, 3, 26–29, 37
Morpeth, Lord (George William Frederick Howard, Earl of Carlisle), 310
Morton, Samuel George, 264, 277

Naugichigomie, 98, 99–100
Nelson, George, 28–29

Occom, Samson, 9
Ocwaygan, 75, 87
Odabit, 54
Odyssey, The, 68
Ogeewyahnoquotokwa, 4, 54, 140, 141, 170–78, 180–81, 213, 268–69, 334
O-ge-she-au-bon-o-qua, 263
Okimabinesikwe, 29
Old Tabac pure, 86
Omuckackeence, 59–60
Ossian, 4–5, 68–69, 285, 294
Ovid, 12, 183
Ozhaawshkodewikwe: American Fur Company, 196; Anna Jameson, 240, 244–46, 248; Anna Maria, 178, 324; children, 4, 351n54; Christianity, 4, 111, 141, 148; court case (1843), 303, 323, 324–25; death, 323–24; debt claims, 203–4, 225–26; description, by McKenney, 94–95; family, 2, 4; finances, 202, 203, 291; George Johnston (London, UK), 274; Henry Rowe Schoolcraft keeping her from Jane Johnston Schoolcraft, 132, 204; Jane Johnston Schoolcraft, 3, 27–29, 204, 225, 263; Henry Rowe Schoolcraft misrepresentation of, 110–11, 392–93n52; hospitality, 38, 95; Johnston Estate, 226;

Lewis Cass, 52–53, 95, 100; Lewis Johnston, 82; marriage, 3–4; political authority, 52–53, 139, 98–99, 100; storyteller, 4, 42, 95, 244; Treaty of Fond du Lac (1826), 94; Treaty of Sault Ste. Marie (1820), 52–53; War of 1812, 23, 49; William, 208; William Henry, 124–25

Passing Cloud. *See* Kewaynokwut
Paulding, James Kirke, 286
Pelletier, Angelique. *See* O-ge-she-au-bon-o-qua
Penn, William, 91
Pickering, John, 66–70, 101
Pierce, Benjamin K., 59
Pierce, Franklin, 59
Pierce, John, 50
Piquette, Louisa, 214, 263–64, 278, 301, 380n28
Pitcher, Zina, 97, 124, 263, 264, 277, 326
Poe, Edgar Allan, 307, 309
Pope, Alexander, 5, 34, 49, 68, 81–82, 338
Porter, Jeremiah, 142–45, 147–50, 191
power-control belief system, 103, 267
Putnam, George Palmer, 306

Raimond, Louisa. *See* Wassidjeewunoqua
Robertson, William, 40, 41–42, 251
Robinson, Rix, 209, 226, 260
Robinson-Superior Treaty (1850), 235
Rogers, Mary Black, 29, 103, 267
rolling head legend, 102–3, 106, 108, 110, 230

Sagetoo, 75
Sakima, 271
Sangemanqua, 33, 38, 214, 274
Sassaba, 50–52, 54, 70
savage story: Anna Jameson, 245–47, 248–49, 251; Cass, 2, 89–91; capitalism, 11; Elizabeth Oakes Smith, 309–12; evangelicalism, 125–26; George Catlin, 305; George Johnston, 36, 40; Heckewelder's refutation of, 62–64; Henry Rowe Schoolcraft, 18, 55, 81, 116–18, 293; *Hiawatha*, 332–34; history of in North America and US, 13–18; Hugh Henry

Brackenridge, 16–18; Indian epics, 305–6; Jane Johnston Schoolcraft, 249–51; John Locke, 14–15; John Pickering, 66–68; *Johnson v. McIntosh*, 71–72; literature, 40–41, 68–70, 73–74, 101–2, 180, 229, 284–85; "Miscodeed," 122–23; Nature/Society split, 16–17; reviews of *Algic Researches*, 293; Thomas McKenney, 91–93; treaties, 15–16; US official, 16, 53; US politics and culture, 12–13, 18; Wauchusco, 272–73

Schindler, Thérèse, 59, 146

Schoolcraft, Abraham, 300

Schoolcraft, Anna Maria: childhood and education, 5, 49, 76, 128; children, 305, 387n79, 390n24; court case (1843), 323–25; death, 327; Eliza, 391n37; James L. Schoolcraft, 139–40, 178, 262, 292, 326–27, 391n37; Jane Johnston Schoolcraft, 129; Ojibwemowin, 147–48, 300; travelers, 197, 239; Treaty of Washington (1836), 226, 303

Schoolcraft, Henry Rowe: Anna Jameson, 249–51, 284–85, 321–22, 396n90; anxiety about Jane Johnston Schoolcraft's knowledge, 1–2, 80–81, 110–13, 123; Charles Fenno Hoffman, 204, 287–88, 305; children, 124–25, 133, 292, 322–33, 390n30, 396n90; conversion experience as critique of Jane Johnston Schoolcraft, 135–37; court case (1843), 323–26; dependence on Jane Johnston Schoolcraft's knowledge, 56–57, 180–83; emotional detachment, 170, 265; emotional manipulation, 131, 170, 205, 265, 292–93, 311; evangelical Christianity, 124–26, 135–38; finances, 225–26, 261–62, 304; government job, 299–302; grave-robbing, 96–100, 198–99, 264–65, 277–78; Henry Wadsworth Longfellow, 331–34; ideas about Indigenous people, 11–12, 18–19, 58–59, 75–76, 79, 115–18, 284–85; Indigenous spirituality, 170–72, 177–78, 181–83; Jane Johnston Schoolcraft diaries, 128, 130, 301, 313; relationship with Johnston family, 6–7, 58–59, 76–77, 101; rewriting Jane Johnston Schoolcraft's works, 133–34, 278–80, 289–93, 331; Rufus Griswold, 306–07, 330; steals from Anishinaabeg, 260, 273, 303, 304, 323, 325; Treaty of Washington (1836), 195–97, 201–15, 225–26; Washington Irving, 185–88, 284; Wauchusco, 181, 266, 269, 270

Schoolcraft, James Lawrence: additional claims (1837), 260, 303; arrives in Michigan, 82; buying Indigenous land, 197; children, 390n24, 392n39; court case (1843), 323–24; Eliza Johnston, 325, 326–27; finances, 262, 303; frustration of Jane Johnston Schoolcraft with, 140–41; government employment, 273, 274–75, 300, 302; lying, 178, 193, 202, 299; murder, 326–27, 391n35; Ozhaawshkodewikwe, 203, 207; potential murder charge, 137, 139; relationship with Anna Maria Johnston Schoolcraft, 149, 178, 292, 390n24; Treaty of Washington (1836), 203, 211, 226

Schoolcraft, Jane Susan Anne (Janée): Anna Jameson plans for, 248–49; Charles Fenno Hoffman, 390n30; childhood and education, 127, 286, 288; Eliza Johnston, 335; George Johnston, 184; Henry Rowe Schoolcraft, 140, 209, 301–2, 312, 327; Jane Johnston Schoolcraft, 129, 130, 141, 214, 292; marriage, 390n30; quillwork, 277, 350n18; scarlet fever, 284; white supremacist beliefs, 390n30

Schoolcraft, John Johnston: Anna Maria Johnston Schoolcraft, 327; birth and childhood, 132, 133, 134, 214; Charlotte Johnston McMurray, 327; Civil War, 396n90; education, 286, 326; George Johnston, 322; Henry Rowe Schoolcraft relationship with, 134, 140, 301–2, 396n90; Jane Johnston Schoolcraft on, 141, 288, 290–91, 292; New York city, 327; Ramsay Crooks on, 396n90; William Johnston, 339–40

Schoolcraft, John Laurence, 322

Schoolcraft, Mary Howard, 319, 326, 327–28, 331

Schoolcraft, William Henry, 60, 79–80, 83–85, 115, 124–27, 130

Sedgwick, Catharine Maria, 285–86, 307
Seward, William, 322
Shakespeare, William, 5, 34–37, 57, 240
Shaw, Tom, 4, 128–29
Sha wa wa, 207
Shawundais, 31–32, 141, 145–49
Shearman, Francis, 264–65, 273, 294
Shenstone, William, 34, 81–82
Shingabawossin, 50, 52, 55, 93–94, 97–100, 110–11, 142, 188, 317, 335
Sigourney, Lydia Huntly, 306
Simms, William Gilmore, 329
Skenandoah, 91
Smith, Elizabeth Oakes, 308–12, 329–30, 334
Smith, Seba, 306, 308
Snelling, Anna G., 305–6
Solomon, Ezekiel, 29, 351n39
Solomon, Louie, 247
Solomon, Marguerite Johnston, 29, 247, 351n39, 389n10
Solomon, William, 29, 37, 351n39
Songageezhig. *See* Strong Sky
songs: "Burial Song" (George Johnston), 339; "Do not—do not weep for me" (Jane Johnston Schoolcraft), 41; "The O-jibway Maid" (Jane Johnston Schoolcraft), 96; "Penayshee's Song" (George Johnston), 336–37, 395n80–81; "Song for a Lover Killed in Battle" (Jane Johnston Schoolcraft), 44–45; "Tsheetshegwyung's war song" (George Johnston), 41
Sproat, Grenville, 184–85, 225
Stone, Mrs. William Leete (Susana Wayland), 288, 307
Stone, William Leete, 288, 307, 321
stories: "Alark Oakwaa. The Star Woman" (C. C. Trowbridge), 73; "Corn Story" ["Mon-daw-min; or The Origin of Indian Corn"] (Jane Johnston Schoolcraft), 1–2, 7, 293, 295, 299, 332; "The Forsaken Brother" (Jane Johnston Schoolcraft), 103, 104–6, 188, 200, 240; "The Funeral Fire" (John Johnston), 44, 95; "Git-chee-gau-zinee, or the Trance" (John Johnston), 44, 47, 333; "Hotoo We Linnee. The Toadstool Man" (C. C. Trowbridge), 73; "Iagoo," 332; "An Indian Tale Related by . . . Little Salt," / "The Enchanted Moccasins" (Charlotte Johnston McMurray), 234–36; "Kwasind, or The Fearfully Strong Man," 332; "The Little Spirit, or Boy-Man" (Jane Johnston Schoolcraft), 295–96; "Madjee Monedo and the Genius of Benevolence" (William Johnston), 231–33; "Meskwaunkwaatar. The Red Head" (C. C. Trowbridge), 73; "Mishosha, or The Magician and His Daughters" (Jane Johnston Schoolcraft), 103, 106–9, 240; "The Moose and Woodpecker"(William Johnston), 332; "Moowis the Indian Coquette" (Jane Johnston Schoolcraft), 113–15, 122; "Mukakee Mindemoea; or, The Toad Woman" (Jane Johnston Schoolcraft), 281–83, 298–99; "Narrative of Wabwindigo," (George Johnston), 317–18, 335–36; "Ogeeg, or the Fisher" (William Johnston), 333; "The Origin of the Robin" (Jane Johnston Schoolcraft), 42–43, 101, 103, 122, 188, 200, 240; "Origin of the White-fish" (Jane Johnston Schoolcraft), 103–4, 106; "Osseo; or, The Son of the Evening Star," 332; "Papuckewis" / "La Poudre, or the Storm Fool" (William Johnston), 109–10, 179, 333; "Pauguk," 333; "Paup-Puk-Keewis" (William Johnston), 216–24, 233–34, 332–33; "Peboan and Seegwun" (Jane Johnston Schoolcraft), 42–43, 56, 95, 101, 333; "The Red Swan," 332; "Saganaw's Story" / "The Weendigoes" (William Johnston), xi, 108–9, 230–31, 345n1; "Saugemau" (William Johnston), 271–72; "Shagwonabee" (William Johnston), 269–70; "Shingebiss," 332; "Six Indians Visit to the Sun and Moon" (William Johnston), 252–59, 272–73; "Story of the Bear" / "Iena, or The Magic Bundle" (Charlotte Johnston McMurray), 234–35, 236–39, 328; "Story of Manahbosho" / "Manabozho; or, The Great Incarnation of the North" (William Johnston), 6, 10,

153–63, 180–81, 332–33; "Story of Meshegenabigo" / "Iamo; or The Undying Head" (William Johnston), 270–71, 332; "Tolewautee Wee Linnee. The Gambler—or Puauskeesekoowee. The Man without Eyes" (C. C. Trowbridge), 73; "The Traditionary Story of Mash qua shay guong, or the Red Head and His Two Sons, Who Became Orphans" (George Johnston), 332; "The Two Ghosts, or Hospitality Rewarded" (Jane Johnston Schoolcraft), 45–48, 101, 122, 333; "Wa-wa-be-zo-win: or The Swing" (Jane Johnston Schoolcraft), 295, 296–98; "The White Stone Canoe" (William Johnston), 332–33
Strong Sky, 54, 176–77
Stuart, Robert, 135, 209, 226, 302, 303
Sunday, John. *See* Shawundais
Sylvestre, Jean Baptiste, 247

Taliaferro, Lawrence, 194, 373n18
Tanner, John, 326
Thomas, Clara, 240
Thoreau, Henry David, 340–41
Tilden, Bryant, 326, 391n34
Titus Andronicus, 34–37
treaties, 14–16, 49, 50, 62, 70, 92, 111, 126, 239
Treaty of Butte des Morts (1827), 127
Treaty of Fond du Lac (1826), 91–94, 141–42
Treaty of Greenville (1795), 50, 52, 53
Treaty of New Echota (1835), 205, 212
Treaty of Prairie du Chien (1825), 82–83

Treaty of Saint Peters (1837), 275
Treaty of Sault Ste. Marie (1820), 98–99
Treaty of Washington (1836), 8–9, 195–97, 201–15, 225–26, 238, 242, 260–61, 300–301, 323
treaty speech, 40–41, 47, 210
Trowbridge, Charles Christopher (C. C.), 72–74, 76, 82, 104–5, 209, 229, 261–62, 291

Von Humboldt, Wilhelm, 68

Waabojiig, 2–4, 41–42, 43–44, 56, 59, 110, 121, 123, 200
Wabose, Catherine. *See* Ogeewyahnoquotokwa
Wabose, Charlotte, 140, 150, 197, 204, 206, 212–13, 214, 301
Waishkey, 4, 202, 207, 212, 245, 247
Washington, George, 15, 16, 227
Wassidjeewunoqua, 49, 94, 144
Wauchusco, 9–10, 170–72, 176–79, 181, 198, 230, 252, 266–73, 332, 340
Waymitiggoashance, 75
White Head, the. *See* Kawawbandebay
Whiting, Henry, 72, 133, 174, 261, 272–73, 294
Wilson, Peter, 309–10
Woolsey, Melancthon, 140

Yellow Dog , 24
Yellow Hair, 168–69
Young, James, 147

Zeisberger, David, 62, 64

www.ingramcontent.com/pod-product-compliance
Lightning Source LLC
Chambersburg PA
CBHW021847230426
43671CB00006B/294